Post Office Department Canada

List of Post Offices in Canada

Post Office Department Canada

List of Post Offices in Canada

ISBN/EAN: 9783742862518

Manufactured in Europe, USA, Canada, Australia, Japa

Cover: Foto ©ninafisch / pixelio.de

Manufactured and distributed by brebook publishing software
(www.brebook.com)

Post Office Department Canada

List of Post Offices in Canada

OF

POST OFFICES IN CANADA,

WITH THE

NAMES OF THE POSTMASTERS

ON

THE 1st JULY, 1873.

Printed by Order of the Postmaster General.

OTTAWA:
PRINTED BY I. B. TAYLOR, 29, 31 & 33 RIDEAU STREET.
1873.

TABLE OF CONTENTS.

(Memorandum.)

POST OFFICE DEPARTMENT,
1st July, 1873.

Should any Postmaster discover an error in the description of his Office, as set forth in this List, he will please notify the same to this Department without delay.

A List of Rates of Postage for Foreign Countries, &c., is appended to this List.

PRINCIPAL OFFICERS OF THE POST OFFICE DEPARTMENT.

—:o:—

HON. JOHN O'CONNOR,	*Postmaster General.*
WILLIAM HENRY GRIFFIN,	*Deputy Postmaster General.*
HORATIO ASPREY WICKSTEED,	*Accountant.*
WILLIAM WHITE,	*Secretary.*
PETER LeSUEUR,	*Superintendent, Money Order Branch.*
J. CUNNINGHAM STEWART,	*Superintendent, Savings' Bank Branch.*
JOHN ASHWORTH,	*Cashier.*
WILLIAM HENRY SMITHSON,	*Assistant Accountant*

—:o:—

INSPECTORS.

				STATION.
John Dewe, *Chief Inspector*				*Ottawa.*
Arthur Woodgate	in charge of	Nova Scotia	Division	*Halifax.*
John McMillan	„	New Brunswick	„	*St. John.*
W. G. Sheppard	„	Quebec	„	*Quebec.*
E. F. King	„	Montreal	„	*Montreal.*
Robt. W. Barker	„	Kingston	„	*Kingston.*
M. Sweetnam	„	Toronto	„	*Toronto.*
G. E Griffin	„	London	„	*London.*

LIST OF

POST OFFICES IN CANADA

On THE 1st JULY, 1873.

The Offices printed in Italics are authorized to Grant and Pay Money Orders.

*The Offices marked * are Savings' Bank Offices.*

The letters " W. O." following the name of a Post Office, signify " Way Office."

The capital letters on the right of the County column indicate the several Provinces of the Dominion.

NAME OF POST OFFICE.	TOWNSHIP OR PARISH.	ELECTORAL COUNTY OR DIVISION.		NAME OF POSTMASTER.
Abbott's Corners	St. Armand	Missisquoi	Q	Charles Hope
Abbotsford		Rouville	Q	O. Crossfield
Aberarder	Plympton	Lambton	O	D. McBean
Abercorn	Sutton	Brome	Q	Benjamin Seaton
Aberfoyle	Puslinch	Wellington, S. R.	O	S. Falconbridge
Abingdon	Caistor	Monck	O	Thomas Pearson
Acacia	Middleton	Norfolk, N. R.	O	R. P. Scidmore
Acadia Mines		Colchester	N S	Robert Forman
Acton	Esquesing	Halton	O	J. Matthews
Acton Vale	Acton	Bagot	Q	A. Quintin-dit Dubois
Adamsville	Farnham East	Brome	Q	George Adams
Adare	McGillivray	Middlesex, N. R.	O	Mrs. Agnes Lavett
Adderley	Inverness	Megantic	Q	John F. Taylor
Addington Forks, W. O		Antigonishe	N S	Norman Macdonald

NAME OF POST OFFICE.	TOWNSHIP OR PARISH.	ELECTORAL COUNTY OR DIVISION.	NAME OF POSTMASTER.
Addison	Elizabethtown	Brockville ....O	Coleman Lewis .....
Adelaide............	Adelaide	Middlesex, N. R. ....O	John S. Hoare......
Admaston	Admaston	Renfrew, S. R........ ..O	Miss Jane Patterson.
Adolphustown	Adolphustown	Lennox.................O	J. J. Watson ....
Advocate Harbor.....	....	Cumberland ....N S	Nathan B. Morris ..
Agincourt	Scarboro'...........	York, E. R.............O	John Milne.........
Ailsa Craig	East Williams	Middlesex, N. R........O	Shackleton Hay.....
Aird	Clarenceville........	Missisquoi.............Q	H. A. Hawley ......
Airlie	Mulmur	Simcoe, S. R.......... ..O	Richard Bradley ....
Albany.......	No. 27	Prince ....P E I	James Donelly......
Albert Bridge, W. O.	....	Cape Breton..........N S	Thomas Bourke ....
Albert Mines, W. O.	....	Albert ....N B	John L. Harris .....
Alberton	Ancaster	Wentworth S. R........O	Job Franklin ......
Alberton	No. 4	Prince ....P E I	R. M. Costin ....
**Albion*.............	Albion	Cardwell . ...O	George Evans.......
Albury	Ameliasburg........	Prince Edward...... ....O	James H. Peck .....
Aldboro'	Aldboro'............	Elgin, W. R............O	Samuel Kirkpatrick.
Aldershot	Flamboro', E	Wentworth, N. R.... . O	Alexander Brown ...
Alderville	Alnwick.............	Northumberland, W. R. O	James Curtis ....
Alexander's Point, W. O.	....	Gloucester.... .... ..N B	F. Alexander ....
**Alexandria*	Lochiel.....	Glengarry ....O	Duncan A. Macdonald ....
Alfred..............	Alfred..............	Prescott................O	John B. Lawlor.....
Algonquin..........	Augusta............	Granville, S. R ....O	W. L. McKenzie....
Allanburg	Thorold	Welland . ...O	John Rennie........
Allan Park	Bentinck	Grey, S. R. ....O	Chas. F. Goodeve...
Allan's Corners	Durham...........	Chateauguay ....Q	Thomas Bryson .....
Allan's Mills	Burgess N..........	Lanark, S. R...........O	William Allan ......
Allendale	Innisfil	Simcoe, S. R ....O	Andrew Miscampbell
Allenford	Amabel	Bruce, N. R............O	William Sharp .....
Allensville..........	Stephenson	Muskoka ....O	Allen McNicol......
Allisonville	Hallowell	Prince Edward..........O	Benjamin Titus.....
Alliston	Tecumseth..........	Simcoe, S. R...........O	George Fletcher.....
Alloa..............	Chinguacousy.......	Peel....... ....O	Mahlon Silverthorn.
Allumette Island....	Allumette Island....	Pontiac ....Q	John Lynch ....

NAME OF POST OFFICE.	TOWNSHIP OR PARISH.	ELECTORAL COUNTY OR DIVISION.	NAME OF POSTMASTER.
Alma..............	Peel...............	Wellington, C. R.......O	W. J. McElroy.....
Alma, late Salmon River, W. O......	....	Albert,..............N B	George Kiersted....
Alma, W. O........	....	Pictou...............N S	Janet Archibald....
Almira	Markham	York, E. R. .... O	John Bowman .....
**Almonte*...........	Ramsay	Lanark, N. R. ....O	James H. Wylie, jun.
Alport	Muskoka	Muskoka ....O	W. H. Taylor ......
Alton	Caledon	Cardwell ....O	Mrs. Agnes Meek...
Altona	Pickering	Ontario, S. R ....O	Joseph Monkhouse..
Alvanley	Derby..............	Grey, N. R............O	Christopher Tupling.
Alvinston	Brooke	Lambton ....O	J. W. Branan ......
Amberley	Ashfield...	Huron, N. R ....O	James Wilkie.......
Ambleside..........	Carrick	Bruce, S. R............O	Wm. Zinger........
Ameliasburg........	Ameliasburg........	Prince Edward .... O	wen Roblin ....
Amherst...........	....	Cumberland ....N S	Mrs. A. Chipman...
**Amherstburgh*......	Malden	Essex ....O	Ernest G. Park.....
Amherst Hill, W.O.	....	Cumberland .... NS	Daniel Pugsley .....
Amherst Point, W. O....	....	Cumberland ....N S	Jonathan Pipes.....
Amiens	Lobo	Middlesex, N. R........O	John McArthur ....
Ancaster...........	Ancaster..........	Wentworth, S. R ....O	Anna M. McKay...
Ancienne Lorette...	Ancienne Lorette...	Quebec.................Q	Louis Robitaille ....
Ancienne Lorette, (sub)...........	Ancienne Lorette...	Quebec.................Q	George Dufresne....
Anderson...........	Blanchard	Perth, S. R........... .O	Humphrey White ..
Anderson, W. O.....	....	Westmoreland........N B	Archibald Simpson..
Anderson's Corners .	Hinchinbrooke	Huntingdon ....Q	James Anderson....
Andover...........	....	Victoria..............N B	Wm. B. Beveridge..
Ange Gardien	Ange Gardien	Montmorency ....Q	Joseph Goulet ......
Angeline...........	Ange Gardien	Rouville ....Q	Onésime Boisvert...
Angers.............	Buckingham........	Ottawa. ....Q	L. Moncion ....
**Angus*...........	Essa	Simcoe, S. R...........O	J. R. Brown ....
Annagance	....	King's ....N B	Stanford Palmer....
Annapolis	... .	Annapolis ....N S	Thos. A. Gavaza....
Antigonishe	....	Antigonishe..........N S	H. P. Hill ....
AntigonisheHarbour W. O........ ..	....	Antigonishe..........N S	John Chisholm .....

NAME OF POST OFFICE.	TOWNSHIP OR PARISH.	ELECTORAL COUNTY OR DIVISION.	NAME OF POSTMASTER.
Antler Creek	....	Cariboo ....B C	....
Antrim	Fitzroy	Carleton ., ...O	John Wilson ......
Antrim, W. O.	....	Halifax.............N S	Samuel Kerr ......
Apohaqui........ .	....	King's ....N B	Thomas E. Smith...
Appin.............	Ekfrid	Middlesex, W. R ....O	Angus McKenzie ...
Appleby	Nelson	Halton ....O	James W. Cotter ...
Apple Grove	Stanstead	Stanstead ....Q	John G. Christie....
Apple River, W. O .	....	Cumberland .... N S	W. R. Elderkin ....
Appleton	Ramsay	Lanark, N. R...........O	Albert Teskey ......
Apsley	Anstruther	Peterborough, E. R .....O	Thomas Castlands ...
Apto.........	Flos	Simcoe, N. R. ....O	C. McLaughlin .....
ArchibaldSettlement W. O	....	Restigouche ....N B	R, Archibald ......
Arden.............	Kennebec	Addington ....O	Wm. B. Mills ......
Ardoch......... ...	Clarendon	Addington ....O	Bramwell Watkins..
Ardtrea	Orillia	Simcoe, N. R...... ....O	William Blair, sen..
Argyle..	Eldon	Victoria, N. R..........O	John McKay ......
Argyle, W. O......	....	Yarmouth ....N S	Mrs. S. Ryder.....
Arichat	....	Richmond ....N S	W. G. Ballam ......
Arisaig, W. O......	....	Antigonishe..........N S	Wm. Gillis ....
Arkell.........	Pushlinch	Wellington, S. R........O	Wm. Watson.......
**Arkona*...........	Warwick...........	Lambton ....O	Miss Louisa Schooley
Arkwright	Arran....	Bruce, N. R ....O	... .
Arlington	Adjala	Cardwell C	Thomas Kidd.......
Armadale	Scarboro'..........	York, E. R ....O	....
Armagh...........	St. Cajetan.........	Bellechasse .... Q	C. Roy............
Armand...........	Armand............	Temiscouata ....Q	Paschal Lebel ......
Armow............	Kincardine.........	Bruce, S. R... ....O	Alexander Gardner..
Armstrong's Brook, W. O...........	....	Restigouche ....N B	John C. Bent......
Armstrong's Corner, W. O...........	....	Queen's .... N B	George Mills ......
Arnott	Holland	Grey, N. R ....O	Wm. G. Murray....
**Arnprior*	McNabb	Renfrew, S. R ....O	Ezra A. Bates .....
Aroostook, W. O....	....	Victoria.............N B	Albert D. Olmstead.
Aros	Bexley	Victoria, N. R ....O	Charles McInnes ...

NAME OF POST OFFICE.	TOWNSHIP OR PARISH.	ELECTORAL COUNTY OR DIVISION.	NAME OF POSTMASTER.
Arthabaska Station.	Arthabaska	Arthabaska............Q	Louis Foisy ....
**Arthur*	Arthur	Wellington, N. R ....O	Mrs. Janet Small...
Arthurette, W. O...	....	Victoria.............N B	....
Arundel............	Arundel...........	Argenteuil ....Q	William Thomson ..
Arva	London	Middlesex, E. R ....O	W. B. Bernard .....
Ascot Corner	Ascot	Sherbrooke ....Q	Fred G. Stacey .....
Ashburn	Whitby	Ontario, S. R ....O	Edward Oliver......
Ashburnham	Otonabee..........	Peterborough, E. R .....O	Robt. D. Rodgers...
Ashcroft	....	Yale.....................B C	H. P. Cornwall.....
Ashdown	Humphrey	Muskoka ....O	James Ashdown ....
Ashgrove...........	Esquesing	Halton ....O	Robert Smyth ......
Ashley	Derby.....	Grey, N. R. ....O	George Follis ....
Ashton.............	Goulburn...........	Carleton ....O	John Sumner.......
Ashworth	Scott..........	Ontario, N. R...........O	John Mustard ......
Assametquagan.....	Assametquagan.....	Bonaventure............Q	Charles McCarron ..
Aston Station	Aston	Nicolet.................Q	Antoine Vachon....
Atha	Pickering	Ontario, S. R ....O	John M. Bell.......
Athelstan	Hinchinbrooke	Huntingdon ....Q	Joshua Breadner....
Athens	Scott...............	Ontario, N. R...........O	R. Bingham ....
Atherley	Mara	Ontario, N. R ....O	Arthur Reeve ......
Atherton	Windham	Norfolk, N. R ....O	G. C. Willson ......
Athlone.	Adjala	Cardwell ....O	John Kidd ....
Athol	Kenyon	Glengarry ....O	M. A. Fisher.......
Athol	....	Cumberland ....N S	F. A. Donkin ......
Attercliffe..........	Caistor	Monck .... .O	James Crawther ....
Aubigny	Ripon	Ottawa ....Q	P. G. Aubry ....
Aubrey	South Georgetown ..	Chateauguay ....Q	A. Lafleur..........
Auburn	Wawanosh	Huron, N.R ....O	Samuel Caldwell....
Audley.............	Pickering	Ontario, S. R ... .O	Daniel McBrady....
Aughrim	Brooke	Lambton ....O	J. McKeune........
Augustine Cove	No. 28..............	Prince ....P E I	Eliza McKenzie ....
Au Lac W. O	....	Westmoreland.... ...N B	Ira H. Patterson....
Aultsville	Osnabruck	Stormont ....O	I. R. Ault ....
**Aurora*...........	Whitchurch	York, N. R... ....O	Charles Doan.......
Avening............	Nottawasaga	Simcoe, N. R ....O	R. Morris ....

NAME OF POST OFFICE.	TOWNSHIP OR PARISH.	ELECTORAL COUNTY OR DIVISION.	NAME OF POSTMASTER.
Avignon	Matapedia	Bonaventure ... **Q**	Octave Martin
Avoca	Grenville	Argenteuil ... **Q**	John McCallum
Avon	Dorchester North	Middlesex, E. R ... **O**	G. C. Smith
Avonbank	Downie	Perth, S. R ... **O**	John McMillan
Avondale, W. O		Carleton ... **N B**	John E. McCready
Avondale, W. O		Pictou ... **N S**	Robert McDonald
Avonmore	Roxborough	Stormont ... **O**	E. N. Shaver
Avonport, W. O		King's ... **N S**	W. A. Reid
Avonport Station W. O		King's ... **N S**	W. F. Newcomb
Avonton	Downie	Perth, S. R ... **O**	A. Shields
Ayer's Flat	Hatley	Stanstead ... **Q**	C. Ayer
Aylesford		King's ... **N S**	T. R. Harris
**Aylmer (East)*	Hull	Ottawa ... **Q**	J. R. Woods
**Aylmer (West)*	Malahide	Elgin, E. R ... **O**	Philip Hodgkinson
Aylwin	Aylwin	Ottawa ... **Q**	J. Little
**Ayre*	Dumfries	Waterloo, S. R ... **O**	Robert Wylie
Ayton	Normanby	Grey, S. R ... **O**	Robert Smith
Baby's Point	Sombra	Bothwell ... **O**	Edward Keely
Back Bay, W. O		Charlotte ... **N B**	Joseph McGee
Back Lands, W. O		Antigonishe ... **N S**	William Doyle
Baddeck		Victoria ... **N S**	R. Elmsly
Baddeck Bay, W. O.		Victoria ... **N S**	C. McDonald
Baddeck Bridge, W. O		Victoria ... **N S**	Alex. McRae
Baden	Wilmot	Waterloo. S. R ... **O**	Jacob Beck

NAME OF POST OFFICE.	TOWNSHIP OR PARISH.	ELECTORAL COUNTY OR DIVISION.	NAME OF POSTMASTER.
Bagot	Bagot	Renfrew, S. R ....**O**	Patrick Kennedy
Bagotville	St. Alphonse	Chicoutimi ....**Q**	E. Levesque
Baie St. Paul	Baie St. Paul	Marquette ....**M**	Felix Chenier
Baie Verte		Westmoreland ....**N B**	John Carey
Baie Verte Road, W. O		Westmoreland ....**N B**	John Copp, jun.
Bailey's Brook, W.O.		Pictou ....**N S**	D. D. Macdonald
Bailieboro'	South Monaghan	Peterborough, W. R ....**O**	John D. Perrin
Baillargeon	St. Etienne de Lauzon	Lévis ....**Q**	Frs. Xavier Bilodeau
Baillie, W. O		Charlotte ....**N B**	W. S. Robinson.
Bairdsville, W. O		Carleton ....**N B**	Henry Baird
Bala	Medora	Muskoka ....**O**	Thomas Burgess
Balderson	Drummond	Lanark, S. R ....**O**	John W. Cowie
Ballantrae	Whitchurch	York, N. R ....**O**	Robert Hill
Ballantyne's Station	Pittsburgh	Frontenac ....**O**	John Hysop
Ballinafad	Erin	Wellington, S. R ....**O**	John S. Appelbe
Ballycroy	Adjala	Cardwell ....**O**	Peter Small
Ballyduff	Manvers	Durham, E. R ....**O**	J. C. Williamson
Ballymote	London	Middlesex, E. R ....**O**	T. W. Johnson
Balmoral	Rainham	Haldimand ....**O**	Geo. B. Lundy
Balsam	Pickering	Ontario, S. R ....**O**	Ira Palmer
Baltimore	Hamilton	Northumberland, W. R. .**O**	Thos. J. Milligan
Bamberg	Wellesley	Waterloo, N. R ....**O**	F. Walter
Banda	Mulmer	Simcoe, S. R ....**O**	John Cleminger
Bandon	Hullet	Huron, C. R ....**O**	James Allen
Bannockburn	Madoc	Hastings, N. R ....**O**	William H. Wilson
Barachois, W. O		Westmoreland ....**N B**	Thos. Gallang
Barachois de Malbay	Malbay	Gaspé ....**Q**	Thomas Tapp
Bardsville	Monck	Muskoka ....**O**	Charles Bard
Barkerville		Cariboo ....**B C**	John Bowron
Bark Lake	Jones	Renfrew, S. R ....**O**	
Barnaby River, W.O		Northumberland ....**N B**	Mrs. E. J. Dalton
Barnesville, W. O		King's ....**N B**	Thomas Worrell
Barnett	Nichol	Wellington, C. R ....**O**	James Elmslie
Barney's River, W. O		Pictou ....**N S**	Donald Nicolson

NAME OF POST OFFICE.	TOWNSHIP OR PARISH.	ELECTORAL COUNTY OR DIVISION.	NAME OF POSTMASTER.
Barnston	Barnston	Stanstead ... Q	Sam'l Goodhue
Barrett's Cross	No. 19	Prince ... P E I	William Glover
**Barrie*	Vespra	Simcoe, N. R ... O	Jas. Edwards
Barrington	Hemmingford	Huntingdon ... Q	Oliver Lyttle
Barrington		Shelburne ... N S	R. H. Crowell
Barrington Passage, W. O		Shelburne ... N S	Leonard Knowles
Barrio's Beach, W. O	Antigonishe	Antigonishe ... N S	Benj. Boudrot
Barronsfield, W. O.		Cumberland ... N S	William Baker
Bartibog, W. O.		Northumberland ... N B	Robert Wall
Bartonville	Barton	Wentworth, S. R ... O	W. J. Gage
Bass River, W. O.		King's ... N B	Robert Brown
Bass River, W. O.	Londonderry	Colchester ... N S	Mrs. A. Dickey
Basswood Ridge, W. O		Charlotte ... N B	Margaret Love
Batchewana	Fisher	Algoma ... O	W. J. Scott, jun
Bath	Ernestown	Lennox ... O	John Belfour
Bath		Carleton ... N B	W. Commins
Bathurst		Gloucester ... N B	Helen J. Waitt
Bathurst Village W. O		Gloucester ... N B	John Ferguson, jun.
Batiscan	Ste. Geneviéve	Champlain ... Q	D. Lacourcière
Batiscan Bridge	St. Francois Xavier.	Champlain ... Q	Narcisse Fugère
Battersea	Storrington	Frontenac ... O	W. J. Anglin
Bay du Vin, W. O.		Northumberland ... N B	Alex. Williston
Bay du Vin Mills, W. O		Northumberland ... N B	James Graham
**Bayfield*	Stanley	Huron, S. R ... O	James Gairdner
Bayfield, W. O.		Westmoreland ... N B	C. Van Buskirk
Bayfield, W. O		Antigonishe ... N S	E. W. Randall
Bay Fortune	No. 56	King's ... P E I	J. Needham
Bayside, W. O.		Charlotte ... N B	F. W. Bradford
Bayham	Bayham	Elgin, E. R ... O	George Laing
Bay St. Lawrence, W. O		Victoria ... N S	Angus McIntosh
Bayview	St. Vincent	Grey, E. R ... O	Whitney Wait
Beachburg	Westmeath	Renfrew, N. R ... O	George Surtees
Beachville	Oxford, West	Oxford, S. R ... O	Charles Mason

NAME OF POST OFFICE.	TOWNSHIP OR PARISH.	ELECTORAL COUNTY OR DIVISION.	NAME OF POSTMASTER.
Bealton	Townsend	Norfolk, N. R ... O	Frank Turner
**Beamsville*	Clinton	Lincoln ... O	J. B. Osborne
Bear Brook	Cumberland	Russell ... O	John Rogers
Bear Island, W. O.		York ... N B	Isaiah Parent
Bear Point, W. O.		Shelburne ... N S	David Smith
Bear River (West Side)		Digby ... N S	V. T. Hardwick
Beatrice	Watt	Muskoka ... O	Richard Lance
**Beauharnois*	St. Clement	Beauharnois ... Q	Crosbie McArthur
Beaulac	Rawdon	Montcalm ... Q	George Mason
Beaulieu	St. Pierre d'Orleans.	Montmorency ... Q	Prudent Blais
Beaumont	Beaumont	Bellechasse ... Q	George Couture
Beauport	Beauport	Quebec ... Q	Margaret O'Brien
Beaurivage	St. Sylvester East	Lotbinière ... Q	Owen Loughrey
Beaver Bank, W. O.		Halifax ... N S	Daniel Hallisey
Beaver Brook, W. O.		Albert ... N B	W. R. Brewster
Beaver Cove, W. O., late Boisdale, W. O.		Cape Breton ... N S	Stephen McNeill
Beaver Harb'r, W. O.		Charlotte ... N B	Leonard Best
Beaver River, W. O.		Digby ... N S	S. P. Raymond
Beaver River Corner		Digby ... N S	W. S. Raymond
**Beaverton*	Thora	Ontario, N. R ... O	Donald Cameron
Becancour	Becancour	Nicolet ... Q	Miss M. E. Rivard.
Becancour Station	Ste. Julie	Megantic ... Q	Richard St. Pierre
Becher	Sombra	Bothwell ... O	
Bedeque	No. 26	Prince ... P E I	Major Wright
Bedford	Stanbridge	Missisquoi ... Q	George Clayes, jun.
Bedford Basin, W. O		Halifax ... N S	Wm. Stevens, jun.
Beebe Plain	Stanstead	Stanstead ... Q	J. L. House
Beech Hill, W. O.		King's ... N S	Edmund Quigley
Bégon	Bégon	Temiscouata ... Q	H. Boucher
Belfast	Ashfield	Huron, N. R ... O	William Phillips
Belfast	No. 57	Queen's ... P E I	James Moore
Belford	Markham	York, E. R ... O	Israel Burton
Belfountain	Caledon	Cardwell ... O	Noah Herring
Belgrave	Morris	Huron, N. R ... O	Simon Armstrong

NAME OF POST OFFICE.	TOWNSHIP OR PARISH.	ELECTORAL COUNTY OR DIVISION.	NAME OF POSTMASTER.
Belhaven	North Gwillimbury	York, N. R. ... O	Daniel Prosser
Belle Creek	No. 62	Queen's ... P E I	James Cook
Belle Alodie	St. Valentin	St. John's ... Q	Ambroise Messier
Belledune, W. O.		Gloucester ... N B	John Chalmers
Belledune Riv'r, W.O		Gloucester ... N B	M. Killoran
Belleisle, W. O	Granville	Annapolis ... N S	Valentine Troop
Belleisle Bay, W. O.		King's ... N B	Thos. Davis
Belleisle Creek, W.O		King's ... N B	Cosmo F. McLeod
Belle Rivière		Two Mountains ... Q	William McCubbin
**Belleville*	Thurlow	Hastings, W. R. ... O	J. H. Meacham
Belleville, W. O		Carleton ... N B	James Martin
Bell Ewart	Innisfil	Simcoe, S. R. ... O	P. Ed. Drake
Belliveaux Cove, W. O		Digby ... N S	Urbain Belliveaux
Belliveaux Village, W O		Westmoreland ... N B	Lewis Richard
Bellrock	Portland	Addington ... O	Edward Walker
Bell's Corners	Nepean	Carleton ... O	George Arnold
Belmont	Westminster	Middlesex, E. R ... O	W. H. Odell
Belmore	Turnbury	Huron, N. R ... O	Peter Terriff
Belœil Station	Belœil	Verchères ... Q	William Goullette
Belœil Village	Belœil	Verchères ... Q	J. B. Brillon
Belyea's Cove, W.O.		Queen's ... N B	George N. Belyea
Benmiller	Colborne	Huron, C. R. ... O	Jonathan Miller
Bennie's Corners	Ramsay	Lanark, N. R. ... O	Robert Philip
Bensfort	South Monaghan	Peterborough, W. R ... O	Alexr. D. Galloway
Bentley	Harwich	Kent ... O	Julius Guild
Benton, late Rankin's Mills, ... W. O		Carleton ... N B	John E. Murchie
Beresford	Beresford	Terrebonne ... Q	V. Charbonneau
Bentonville	Cambridge	Russell ... O	John Benton
Bergerville	St. Colomb de Sillery	Quebec ... Q	Mrs. C. Petitclerc
Berkeley	Holland	Grey, N. R ... O	John Fleming
**Berlin*	Waterloo, North	Waterloo, N. R ... O	William Jaffray
Berne	Hay	Huron, S. R. ... O	John Grandy
Berryton, W. O.		Albert ... N B	Edward Berry

NAME OF POST OFFICE.	TOWNSHIP OR PARISH.	ELECTORAL COUNTY OR DIVISION.		NAME OF POSTMASTER.
Bersimis	Bersimis	Saguenay	Q	W. S. Church
Berthier	Berthier	Montmagny	Q	P. S. Joncas
***Berthier, en haut*	Berthier	Berthier	Q	Miss Annie Kitson
Bervie	Kincardine	Bruce, S. R	O	Nichol McIntyre
Berwick	Finch	Stormont	O	Moses A. Tobin
Berwick		King's	N S	J. M. Parker
Berwick Station, W. O		King's	N S	S. J. Nichols
Bethany	Manvers	Durham, E. R	O	W. M. Graham
Bethel	Ely	Shefford	Q	G. Bartlett
Bewdley	Hamilton	Northumberland, W. R	O	John Sidey
Bexley	Bexley	Victoria, N. R	O	George Boadway
Bic	Bic	Rimouski	Q	J. R. Colclough
Bienville	Lauzon	Levis	Q	P. Morin
Big Bank, W. O		Victoria	N S	Donald McLean
Big Bras d'Or, W. O		Victoria	N S	J. A. Fraser
Big Brook, W. O		Inverness	N S	Malcolm McLeod
Big Cove, W. O		Queen's	N B	Jas. Umphrey
Big Harbor, W. O		Inverness	N S	D. McKay
Big Intervale (Grand Narrows, W. O		Inverness	N S	Donald Gillis
Big Intervale (Margaree), W. O	Margaree	Victoria	N S	Malcolm McLeod
Big Island, W. O		Pictou	N S	Alexander McGregor
Big Lorraine, W. O		Cape Breton	N S	
Big Marsh	No. 42	King's	P E I	D. McDonald
Big Pond, W. O		Cape Breton	N S	Hugh McLellan
Big Port'leBear, W. O		Shelburne	N S	Thomas Richardson
Big Tracadie, W. O		Antigonishe	N S	William Genoir
Billings' Bridge	Gloucester	Russell	O	William Smith
Bill Town, W. O		King's	N S	Stubbard Sweet
Binbrook	Binbrook	Wentworth, S. R	O	Henry Hall
Bingham Road	Cayuga South	Haldimand	O	Joseph Goehringer
Birchton	Eaton	Compton	Q	George N. Hodge
Birdton, W. O		York	N B	Robert Bird
Birkhall	Moore	Lambton	O	F. McKenzie

NAME OF POST OFFICE.	TOWNSHIP OR PARISH.	ELECTORAL COUNTY OR DIVISION.	NAME OF POSTMASTER.
Birmingham........	Pittsburg...........	Frontenac ....O	Mrs. E. Birmingham
Birr......	London	Middlesex, E. R ....O	Joseph M. Young...
Bishop's Mills	Oxford	Grenville, N. R ....O	Asa W. Bishop. ....
Bismarck...........	Gainsborough.......	Monck ....O	Christian Trumm ...
Black Bank	Mulmur	Simcoe, S. R............O	John Newel ....
Black Brook, W. O.	....	Northumberland......N B	Robert Blake.......
Black Creek........	Willoughby	Welland ....O	Isaac H. Allen......
Black Heath	Binbrook	Wentworth, S. R ....O	Alexander Simpson .
Black Land, W. O..	....	Restigouche ....N B	William Cook ......
Black Point, W. O..	....	Restigouche ....N B	H. Connacher ......
Black Point, W. O..	....	Halifax................N S	James Hubley......
Black River, W. O..	....	Northumberland ......N B	Robert McNaughton
Black River, W. O..	....	St. John..............N B	Robert Stewart.....
Black River, W. O..	....	Antigonishe...........N S	Colin McDonald....
Black River Bridge, W. O	....	Northumberland ...N B	Mrs. I. Cameron ...
Black River Station.	St. Giles	Lotbiniere ....Q	Louis Olivier ....
Black Rock, W. O ..	....	Cumberland ....N S	Jas. Williger ....
Blackville, W. O....	....	Northumberland......N B	W. H. Grindley ....
Blair	Waterloo, ...	Waterloo, S. R ....O	J. Renshaw ....
Blairton...........	Belmont............	Peterboro', E. R ....O	Roger Bates ....
Blanchard Road, W O	....	Pictou................N S	Donald Ross.......
Blandford	St. Louis de Blandf'rd	Arthabaska.............Q	D. Bergeron........
Blandford, W. O....	....	Lunenburg........ ...N S	....
Blantyre	Euphrasia..........	Grey, E. R ....O	James C. Patterson.
Blayney Ridge, W. O	Prince William	York..................N B	Josiah Davis ....
Blessington.........	Tyendinaga	Hastings, E. R ....O	Isaac Mott ....
Blissfield, W. O	....	Northumberland......N B	John A. Arbo ......
Blissville	....	Sunbury..............N B	John E. Smith......
Bloomfield........	Hallowell	Prince Edward..........O	Jonathan Striker ...
Bloomfield..........	No. 5	Prince.............P E I	M. Gavin ....
Bloomfield, W. O....	....	Carleton ....N B	Reuben Allerton....
Bloomfield, W. O...	....	King's................N B	John Leavitt ......
Bloomingdale.......	Waterloo	Waterloo, N. R.........O	J. G. Moyer........
Bloomington	Whitchurch	York, N. R.............O	Maxon Jones ....

NAME OF POST OFFICE.	TOWNSHIP OR PARISH.	ELECTORAL COUNTY OR DIVISION.	NAME OF POSTMASTER.
Bloomsburg	Townsend	Norfolk, N. R .... O	L. W. Kitchen .....
Blue Mountain, W. O	....	Pictou .... N S	Wm. McDonald ....
Blue's Mill, W. O ...	....	Inverness .... N S	Malcolm Blue ......
Bluevale	Morris	Huron, N. R .... O	John Messer ....
Blyth	Morris	Huron, N. R .... O	P. J. Rooney.......
Blytheswood	Mersea............	Essex.................. O	John Miller ....
Bobcaygeon	Verulam	Victoria, S. R .... O	R. La T. Tupper....
Bocabec, W. O	....	Charlotte............ N B	Wm. Erskine.... ..
Bogart	Hungerford	Hastings, E. R.......... O	John Longman .....
Boiestown, W. O ...	....	Northumberland...... N B	Miles McMillen ....
Boisdale Chapel, W. O	.. ..	Cape Breton .... N S	Michael McIntyre ..
Bolingbroke	S. Sherbrooke	Lanark, S. R .... O	John Korry ....
Bolsover	Eldon	Victoria, N. R .... O	Duncan McRae.....
Bolton Centre	Bolton	Brome.................. Q	John Blaisdell......
Bolton Forest	Bolton	Brome.................. Q	James T. Channell..
Bomanton	Haldimand	Northumberland, W. R.. O	Richard Knight ....
Bonaventure River..	Hamilton	Bonaventure............ Q	Frederic Forest.....
**Bondhead*	W. Gwillimbury...	Simcoe, S. R............ O	A. H. Carter ....
Bongard's Corners ..	Marysburg	Prince Edward.......... O	Job. D. Bongard....
Bonshaw	No. 30	Queen's .... P E I	A. Robertson.......
Bookton............	Windham	Norfolk, N. R .... O	P. N. McIntosh ....
Boom, W. O........	....	Inverness .... N S	Alex. McEachern...
Bord à Plouffe......	St. Martin	Laval .... Q	V. Lemay..........
Bornholm	Logan..............	Perth, N. R .... O	Robert Keys ....
Boscobel	Ely	Shefford .... Q	Wm. Hackwell .....
Boston	Townsend	Norfolk, N. R .... O	Oliver C. Rouse ....
Bosworth...........	Peel	Wellington, C. R........ O	....
Botany.............	Howard	Bothwell .... O	C. McBrayne.......
**Bothwell*	Zone	Bothwell .... O	John Taylor........
Bothwell	No. 47...	King's .... P E I	David McVane .....
Botsford Portage, W. O	....	Westmoreland .... N B	Wm. Farrow ....
Boucherville........	Boucherville........	Chambly .... Q	Louis Normandin...
Boudreau Village, W. O	....	Westmoreland .... N B	Alex. Boudreau ....
Boulardarie	....	Victoria .... N S	A. Munro ....

NAME OF POST OFFICE.	TOWNSHIP OR PARISH.	ELECTORAL COUNTY OR DIVISION.	NAME OF POSTMASTER.
Boulter	Carlow	Hastings, N. R ... O	James Wilson, sen.
Boundary Creek, W. O		Westmoreland ... N B	Merritt D. Harris
Boundary, Présqu'le. W. O		Carleton ... N B	John D. Baird
Bourgeois, W. O		Kent ... N B	John Bourgeois
Bourg Louis	Bourg Louis	Portneuf ... Q	John Hewton
Bowling Green	Amaranth	Wellington, N. R ... O	William B. Jelly
**Bowmanville*	Darlington	Durham, W. R ... O	J. B. Fairbairn
Box Grove	Markham	York, E. R ... O	John McCaffrey
Boyne	Trafalgar	Halton ... O	
Boynton	Stanstead	Stanstead ... Q	Hollis Libbey
**Bracebridge*	Macaulay	Muskoka ... O	Robert E. Perry
Brackley Point	No. 33	Queen's ... P E I	J. B. McCallum
Brackley Point Road	No. 33	Queen's ... P E I	W. L. Rodd
**Bradford*	W. Gwillimbury	Simcoe, S. R ... O	Mrs. Anne Douglas
Brae	No. 9	Prince ... P E I	J. McLean
Braemar	E. Zorra	Oxford, N. R ... O	Alex. Anderson
Braeside	McNab	Renfrew, S. R ... O	John Gillies
Bramley	Innisfil	Simcoe, S. R ... O	James Black, jun.
**Brampton*	Chinguacousy	Peel ... O	K. Chisholm
Branchton	Dumfries North	Waterloo, S. R ... O	Robert McLeish
Brandy Creek	Windham	Norfolk, N. R ... O	E. R. Crombie
**Brantford*	Brantford	Brant, S. R ... O	A. D. Clement
Breadalbane, W. O		Restigouche ... N B	John McMillan
Brechin	Mara	Ontario, N. R ... O	John Bernard
Brentwood	Sunnidale	Simcoe, N. R ... O	L. E. Dubois
Breslaw	Waterloo	Waterloo, N. R ... O	Moses Moyer
Brewer's Mills	Pittsburg	Frontenac ... O	Robert Anglin
Brewster	Stephen	Huron, S. R ... O	W. McDougall
Bridgedale, W. O		Albert ... N B	Millidge Steeves
Bridgenorth	Smith	Peterborough, W. R ... O	Marcus S. Dean
Bridgeport	Waterloo, North	Waterloo, N. R ... O	Elias Eby
Bridgeport, W. O		Cape Breton ... N S	George Burchell
Bridgetown		Annapolis ... N S	Enoch Dodge, jun.
Bridgeville, W. O		Pictou ... N S	John Forbes

NAME OF POST OFFICE.	TOWNSHIP OR PARISH.	ELECTORAL COUNTY OR DIVISION.		NAME OF POSTMASTER.
**Bridgewater*	Elzevir	Hastings, N. R	O	Edwin James
Bridgewater		Lunenburg	N S	R. A. Newcomb
Brigg's Corner, W. O.		Queen's	N B	Joel F. Estabrooks
Brigham	Farnham, East	Brome	Q	E. O. Brigham
**Bright*	Blenheim	Oxford, N. R	O	John Cameron
**Brighton*	Brighton	Northumberland, E. R	O	Joseph Lockwood
Briley's Brook, W.O.	Dorchester	Antigonishe	N S	
Brinkworth	Rawdon	Hastings, N. R	O	Allen Williams
Brinsley	McGillivray	Middlesex, N. R	O	George Brown
Brinston's Corners	Matilda	Dundas	O	Charles Lock
Brisbane	Erin	Wellington, S. R	O	G. J. Mackelcan
Bristol	Bristol	Pontiac	Q	Wm. King
Britannia	Toronto	Peel	O	Joseph Gardner
Britannia Mills	St. Dominique	Bagot	Q	William Twohey
Britonville	Morin	Argenteuil	Q	Geo. Hamilton
Broad Cove Chapel, W. O		Inverness	N S	Alexander McLellan
Broad Cove, (Intervale), W. O		Inverness	N S	Isaac McLeod
Broad Cove, (Lunenburg), W. O		Lunenburg	N S	Elkanah Teel
Broad Cove, (Marsh), W. O		Inverness	N S	Donald Macleod
Broadlands		Bonaventure	Q	Melvin Adams
Brockton	York	York, W. R	O	Mrs. Ann Church
**Brockville*	Elizabethtown	Brockville	O	John Crawford
Brodhagen	Logan	Perth, N. R	O	Chas. Brodhagen
Brome	Brome	Brome	Q	Walter Lynch
Bromemere	Brome	Brome	Q	C. H. Jones
Brompton	Brompton	Richmond	Q	Henry Addison
Brompton Falls	Brompton	Richmond	Q	J. R. McDonnell
Bronte	Trafalgar	Halton	O	Chas. K. Jones
Brookbury	Bury	Compton	Q	R. Rowe
Brookfield		Colchester	N S	James Graham
Brookfield, W. O		Queen's	N S	W. Hendry
**Brooklin*	Whitby	Ontario, S. R	O	Robert Darlington
Brooklyn	No. 61	King's	P E I	H. Compton

NAME OF POST OFFICE.	TOWNSHIP OR PARISH.	ELECTORAL COUNTY OR DIVISION.	NAME OF POSTMASTER.
Brooklyn, W. O. ..	....	Queen's.................N S	J. R. Hall...... ...
Brooksdale	West Zorra.........	Oxford, N. R ....O	John Bagrie........
Brookvale, W. O...	....	Queen's...............N B	Mrs. Milcha Fowlie.
Brookvale, W. O...	....	Halifax.... ....N S	Hugh Hannah......
Brookville, W. O...	....	Cumberland.......... N S	J. A. Hatfield......
Brookville, W. O...	....	Pictou ....N S	Jas. McDonald.....
Brougham	Pickering	Ontario, S. R ....O	John B. Burke......
Broughton...	Broughton....	Beauce ....Q	C. H. J. Hall ......
Brown's Brook, W.O	....	Cumberland ....N S	Hiram Brown.......
Brownsburg	Chatham	Argenteuil...............Q	Alex. McGibbon....
Brownsville.........	Dereham	Oxford, S. R ....O	Mrs. E. Sponenburg.
Brucefield	Tuckersmith........	Huron, C. R ....O	Robert Marks ......
Bruce Mines...... .	....	Algoma.................O	John Hancock......
Brudenell...........	Brudenell	Renfrew, S. R ....O	James Costello......
Brunner............	Ellice	Perth, N. R ....O	Henry Gropp.......
Brunswick..........	Manvers	Durham, E. R .... O	S. R. Beamish .....
**Brussels*, late Dingle	Grey...............	Huron, C. R ....O	John R. Grant......
Bryanston	London	Middlesex, E. R ....O	John Stansfield .....
Bryson, late Hargrave............	Litchfield	Pontiac.................Q	W. G. Le Roy......
Buckhorn	Harwich	Kent ....O	....
**Buckingham*	Buckingham........	Ottawa..................Q	James Wilson ......
Buckland...........	Buckland..........	Bellechasse ....Q	Eusèbe Couture.....
Bucklaw, W. O.....	....	Victoria ....N S	Malcolm McLeod...
Buckley's, W. O....	....	King's........... ...N S	Thos. Buckley......
Buckshot...........	Clarendon	Addington..............O	Elisha Playfair .....
Buctouche..........	....	Kent.................N B	B. H. Foley ... .
Bull Creek	No. 46.............	King's ....P E I	James McAulay ....
Bulstrode...........	Bulstrode...........	Arthabaska............Q	George Dauth ......
Bulwer......	Eaton.....	Compton ....Q	Robert Cairns ......
Burford	Burford	Brant, S. R.............O	John Catton........
Burgessville	Norwich, North	Oxford, S. R....... ....O	E. W. Burgess......
Burgoyne...........	Arran..............	Bruce, N. R ....O	Alfred Shell ....
Burleigh	Burleigh	Peterborough, E. R .....O	John McDonald ...
Burlington	No. 18	Prince...... ....P E I	Joseph Davison.....

NAME OF POST OFFICE.	TOWNSHIP OR PARISH.	ELECTORAL COUNTY OR DIVISION.	NAME OF POSTMASTER.
Burlington, W. O...	....	King's...... ... .N S	Charles Hall.......
Burnbrae...........	Seymour	Northumberland, E. R...O	Alex. Donald.......
Burnhamthorpe.....	Toronto	Peel ....O	George Savage.... .
Burnley	Haldimand.........	Northumberland, W. R..O	William Lawler ....
Burns	Mornington.........	Perth, N. R ....O	Oran Phillips.......
Burnside	Portage La Prairie..	Marquette............. M	Kenneth McKenzie .
Burnstown	McNab	Renfrew, S. R ....O	Donald McRae .....
Burnt Church, W. O.	....	Northumberland ......N B	F. H. McKnight ...
Burntcoat, W. O....	....	Hants ....N S	Robt. Faulkner.....
Burnt River	Somerville..........	Victoria, N. R..........O	Simon Moore . .....
Burrard Inlet.......	....	New Westminster ....B C	Maximilian Michaud
Burritt's Rapids	Oxford	Grenville, N. R.........O	Thos. A. Kidd......
Burtch	Brantford	Brant, S. R.............O	George Taylor ......
Burton	Manvers...........	Durham, E. R ....O	James McGill ......
Burton, W. O	....	Sunbury.............N B	M. E. A. Burpee....
Bury's Green	Somerville.....	Victoria, N. R..........O	John Fell ....
Bushfield....... ...	Morris	Huron, N. R..... ......O	James Lynn........
Bute	Somerset	Megantic ....Q	D. McKinnon ......
Butternut Ridge....	....	King's., ...N B	Charles Israel Keith
Buttonville	Markham	York, E. R.............O	T. Thomson ....
Buxton.............	Raleigh	Kent ....O	D. C. Echlin ....
Byng...............	Dunn	Monck ....O	James M. Thomson.
Byng Inlet	Wallbridge	Muskoka ....O	Pulaski Clark.......
Byron..............	Westminster........	Middlesex, E. R ....O	Robert Sadler ......

NAME OF POST OFFICE.	TOWNSHIP OR PARISH.	ELECTORAL COUNTY OR DIVISION.	NAME OF POSTMASTER.
Cable Head........	No. 41.............	King's........ ....P E I	John McIntyre. ...
Cache Creek........	.. ..	Yale...............B C	James Campbell....
Cacouna	St. George.........	Temiscouata...........Q	J. B. Beaulieu......
Cadmus	Cartwright	Durham, W. R.........O	John McKinnon....
Cæsarea	Cartwright	Durham, W R..........O	John Elliott........
Cain's River...W. O	....	Northumberland..... N B	Mrs. C. A. Murdoch
Cainsville	Brantford, E	Brant, N. R............O	Henry Gawler......
Caintown...........	Yonge	Leeds, S. R......... . O	W. Tennant, jun....
Cairngorm	Metcalfe	Middlesex, W. R........O	Francis Brown. ...
Caistorville	Caistor	Monck ....O	Adam Spears, jun...
Calabogie	Bagot	Renfrew, S. R..........O	D. Dillon..........
Calder	Delaware..........	Middlesex, W. R........O	William Campbell ..
Caldwell.	Caledon...........	Cardwell ....O	Patrick Murphy....
Caledon....	Caledon	Cardwell ....O	George Bell ....
Caledon East	Caledon	Cardwell ....O	James Munsie......
Caledonia	No. 60	Queen's ....P E I	James Walker.....
Caledonia Corner....	....	Queen's...............N S	George Middlemas..
Caledonia Mills, W.O	....	Antigonishe ....N S	John Boyle.........
Caledonia, St. Mary's, W. O............	....	Guysboro'..... .....N S	Angus McDonald...
Caledonia Settlement W. O	....	Albert.............. N B	James Reid ....
Caledonia Springs...	Caledonia	Prescott ....O	John D. Cameron...
Calton.............	Bayham...........	Elgin, E. R............O	Duncan M'Laughlan
Calumet Island.....	Calumet...........	Pontiac ....Q	John Cahill ....
Cambray	Fenelon	Victoria, N. R.........O	Thomas Douglas....
Cambria	St. Columbin.......	Argenteuil............Q	William Stuart .....
Cambridge, W. O....	. ...	Queen's ....N B	William H. White..
Cambridge, W. O...	....	Halifax..............N S	Handly Starrat.....
Cambridge Station, W. O	....	King's...............N S	John C. Neiley ... .
Camden East.......	Camden East.......	Addington .. ..O	Benjamin Clark....
Cameron	Fenelon	Victoria, N. R.........O	James Bryson ......
Camerontown	Charlottenburg	Glengarry ....O	Andrew Cameron...
Camilla	Mono	Cardwell ....O	Hugh Currie ....
Camlachie..........	Plympton	Lambton...............O	Thomas Houston ...

NAME OF POST OFFICE.	TOWNSHIP OR PARISH.	ELECTORAL COUNTY OR DIVISION.	NAME OF POSTMASTER.
Campbellford	Seymour	Northumberland, E. R . . **O**	James M. Ferris....
Campbell's Cross.	Chinguacousy	Peel............... ....**O**	E. T. Hagyard .....
CampbellSettlement, W. O............	....	King's...............**N B**	D. K. Campbell . .
CampbellSettlement, W. O.	....	York.................**N B**	Henry McFarlane ..
Campbellton.........	....	Restigouche ....**N B**	A. W. Kendrick....
Campbellville.	Nassagiweya	Halton ....**O**	James H. Cooper...
Campden...........	Clinton............	Lincoln...............**O**	H. W. Moyer ......
Campo Bello........		Charlotte............**N B**	Luke Byron ....
Canaan, W. O......	....	King's...............**N S**	Adolphus Bishop ...
Canaan Road, W. O.	....	King's...............**N S**	Reuben R. Baker...
Canada Creek, W. O.	....	King's..... ....**N S**	C. Eaton ....
Canard, W. O	....	King's...... ....**N S**	J. E. Lockwood ....
Canard River.......	Sandwich...........	Essex.................**O**	Louis Drouillard....
Canboro'	Canboro'	Monck ....**O**	John Folmsbee ....
Candasville.........	Gainsborough.......	Monck ....**O**	John M. Culp ......
Canfield	Cayuga, North......	Haldimand ....**O**	Ambrose Pattison...
Cannifton	Thurlow	Hastings, E. R ....**O**	Jonas Canniff, jun..
Canning	Blenheim...........	Oxford, N. R..........**O**	Samuel Allchin.....
Canning	....	King's...............**N S**	J. W. Borden ......
**Cannington*	Brock	Ontario, N. R ....**O**	Charles Gibbs ......
Cannonville, W. O..	....	Cumberland ....**N S**	Edward D. Fullarton
Canoe Creek........	....	Cariboo..............**B C**	Robert P. Ritchie...
Canrobert	....	Rouville...............**Q**	Francois Meunier...
Canso	....	Guysboro'............**N S**	Charl'te Cunningham
Canterbury.........	Bury	Compton ....**Q**	Robert Clark ......
Canterbury........	....	York................**N B**	C. E. Grosvenor ....
Canterbury Station..	....	York................**N B**	William Main .....
Cantley	Hull	Ottawa ....**Q**	Alex. Prudhomme ..
Canton	Hope	Durham, E. R ....**O**	Samuel Stephenson .
Cap à l'Aigle (sub)..	Mount Murray	Charlevoix ....**Q**	Joseph Lavard......
Cap Chat...........	St. Norbert de Cap Chat	Gaspé ....**Q**	Telesphore Roy.....
Cap des Rosiers.....	Cap des Rosiers.....	Gaspé ....**Q**	Peter Whalan . . ..
Cape Cove..........	Percé	Gaspé ....**Q**	William Tilly.......

NAME OF POST OFFICE.	TOWNSHIP OR PARISH.	ELECTORAL COUNTY OR DIVISION.	NAME OF POSTMASTER.
Cape George........	... .	Antigonishe..........N S	Robt. McDonald....
Cape George, (North side,) W. O.	....	Antigonishe. ....N S	Donald McDonald..
Cape John, W. O...	....	Pictou................N S	Hugh McLeod......
Capelton	Ascott	Sherbrooke ....Q	John Lafontaine....
Cape Mabou, W. O.	....	Inverness ....N S	A. McQuarrie ......
Cape Negro, W. O..	....	Shelburne............N S	Josiah Smith ....
Cape North, W. O..	....	Victoria ....N S	Arch. McDonald. ..
Cape Rich..........	St. Vincent.........	Grey, E. R ....O	Donald McLaren ...
Cape Sable Island, W. O	....	Shelburne............N S	W. Cunningham....
Cape Spear, W. O ..	....	Westmoreland ....N B	John McKay.......
Cape Traverse......	No. 28	Prince ....P E I	J. L. Muttart ......
Cape Wolfe	No. 7	Prince ....P E I	Matthew Howard...
Caplin	. ...	Bonaventure ....Q	David Kerr.........
Cap Magdeleine	....	Champlain.............Q	Theodore Beaumier.
Cap Rouge	St. Foy	Quebec ....Q	Dominique Thivierge
Cap St Ignace	St. Ignace	Montmagny ....Q	Miss H. C. Larue...
Cap Santé..........	Cap Santé..........	Portneuf ....Q	J. Bernard ....
Caraquet	....	Gloucester.. ....N B	J. G. C. Blackhall..
Carden	Carden	Victoria, N. R ....O	Jacob Belfrey ......
Cardigan Bridge....	No. 53.............	King's ....P E I	George F. Owen .....
Cardigan Road	No. 38.............	King's ....P E I	P. Bambrick........
Cariboo Cove, W. O.	....	Cape Bre[illegible]......N S	Malcolm Ferguson ..
Carillon	Chatham	Argent[illegible]........Q	William Fletcher ...
Carleton............	Carleton...........	Bonaven[illegible]........Q	Joseph Meagher ....
Carleton	....	St. John..[illegible]....N B	James R. Reed .....
Carleton	No. 28............	Prince [illegible]..P E I	D. Morrison........
Carleton Place	Beckwith...........	Lanark, [illegible]......O	Patrick Struthers...
Carlingford	Fullarton...........	Perth, [illegible].... .O	James Hamilton ....
Carlisle	Flamboro East......	Wentw[illegible]R.......O	O. Livingston ......
Carlow.............	Colborne	Huron, [illegible]..........O	W. R. Clayton .....
Carlow, W. O......	....	Carleton..[illegible]........N B	S. Cummins........
Carlsruhe	Carrick	Bruce, S. R............O	Jacob Knechtel, jun.
Carlton, W, O......	....	Yarmouth ....N S	John P. Miller .....
Carluke	Ancaster	Wentworth, S. R........O	James Calder.......

NAME OF POST OFFICE.	TOWNSHIP OR PARISH.	ELECTORAL COUNTY OR DIVISION.	NAME OF POSTMASTER.
Carnarvon	Stanhope	Peterborough, E. R. O	Alfred Moore
Carnegie	Elderslie	Bruce, N. R. O	Thomas Ewart
Carp	Huntley	Carleton O	W. J. Featherstone
Carriboo Cove, W.O.		Richmond N S	John Malcolm, sen.
Carroll's Corners, W. O		Halifax N S	Jane Heffernan
Carronbrook	Hibbert	Perth, S. R O	G. J. Kidd
Carrville	Vaughan	York, W. R O	William Cook
Carsonby	North Gower	Carleton O	Benjamin Eastman
Carsonville, W. O		King's N B	John McLeod
Carthage	Mornington	Perth, N. R. O	Samuel Patterson
Cartwright	Cartwright	Durham, W. R. O	Hugh McPhail
Cascades	Hull	Ottawa Q	Thomas M. Reid
Case Settlement, W O		King's N B	George Case
Cashel	Markham	York, E. R O	Colin Shell
Cashmere	Mosa	Middlesex, W. R. O	George Mansfield
Casselman	Cambridge	Russell O	Martin Casselman
Castile	Algona, South	Renfrew, N. R. O	Edmund Bennett
Castlebar	Shipton	Richmond Q	David U. Graveline
Castleford	Horton	Renfrew, S. R O	John Warnock
Castlemore	Gore of Toronto	Peel O	
Castleton	Cramahe	Northumberland, E. R. O	John C. Pennock
Catalone, W. O.		Cape Breton N S	Allan Macdonald
Cataract	Caledon	Cardwell O	Richard Church
Cataraqui	Kingston	Frontenac O	Joseph Northmore
Cathcart	Burford	Brant, S. R. O	Alex. Kennedy
Caughnawaga	Sault St. Louis	Laprairie Q	W. D. Lorimier
Causapscal	Causapscal	Rimouski Q	Edwin L. Strange
Cavan	Cavan	Durham, E. R O	David Walker
Cavendish	No. 23	Queen's P E I	A. M. McNeill
Cavendish Road	No. 23	Queen's P E I	George W. McKay
**Cayuga*	Cayuga	Haldimand O	G. A. Messenger
Cazaville	St. Anicet	Huntingdon Q	Oliver Quenneville
Cedar Grove	Markham	York, E. R. O	John Schnell
Cedar Hall	**Matapedia**	**Rimouski Q**	**E. B. Martin**

NAME OF POST OFFICE.	TOWNSHIP OR PARISH.	ELECTORAL COUNTY OR DIVISION.	NAME OF POSTMASTER.
Cedar Hill....	Pakenham	Lanark, N. R...........O	James Connery.....
Cedar Lake, W. O..	....	Digby ....N S	Ambrose Poole ...
Cedars	Soulanges	Soulanges ....Q	T. Marcoux.........
Cedarville	Proton	Grey, E. R ....O	Thomas Rogers.....
Central Blissville, W. O...............	....	Sunbury....... .....N B	Luke E. Bailey.....
Central Cambridge, W. O	....	Queen's ....N B	Amos Mott.........
Central Chebogue, W. O	....	Yarmouth ....N S	Saml. Trask........
Centralia, late Devon	Stephen	Huron, S. R ....O	William Greenway..
Central Kingsclear, W. O	....	York.................N B	....
Central Norton, W. O	....	King's................N B	Silas Raymond......
Central Onslow, W. O	....	Colchester ....N S	Hugh Dickson.....
Centre Augusta... .	Augusta...........	Grenville, S. R..........O	A. B. Commins....
Centreton	Haldimand	Northumberland, W. R..O	T. H. McAulay.....
Centre Village, W. O	....	Westmoreland........N B	Timothy Copp......
Centreville	Camden East......	Addington ....O	Cyrus Ash..........
Centreville, W. O...	....	Albert...... ....N B	Wm. Woodworth...
Centreville	....	Carleton..............N B	Ludlow B. Clark....
Centreville, W. O....	....	King's...............N S	J. M. Rosco ....
Chambly Basin	Chambly	Chambly ....Q	Wm. Vallée ....
**Chambly Canton* ...	West Chambly	Chambly ....Q	John Hackett ......
Chambord	Metabechouan......	Chicoutimi ....Q	Job Bilodeau . ...
Champlain	Champlain	Champlain..............Q	N. Hardy ....
Chance Harbor, W. O......	....	St. John. ....N B	James Boyle.......
Chandos.	Chandos............	Peterborough, E. R..... O	Thomas Kemp ....
Chantelle..........	Chertsey	Montcalm ....Q	Delphin Morin......
Chantry........ ...	Bastard	Leeds, S. R.............O	Samuel Chant ......
Chapman	Hungerford	Hastings, E. R ....O	Alexander Chapman
Chapman, W. O....	....	Westmoreland........N B	Bowden Chapman ..
Charing Cross	Harwich	Kent . ... .O	Mrs. M. Payne.....
Charlemagne	St. Chas de Lachenaie......	L'Assomption ....Q	Antoine Desparois .. dit Champagne .
Charlesbourg	Quebec.	Quebec ....Q	M. Tremblay.......

NAME OF POST OFFICE.	TOWNSHIP OR PARISH.	ELECTORAL COUNTY OR DIVISION.	NAME OF POSTMASTER.
Charleston	Escott	Leeds, S. R. . . . O	P. F. Green
Charleston, W. O		Carleton . . . N B	John Lipsett
Charleville	Augusta	Grenville, S. R . . . O	Rufus S. Throop
Charlo's Cove, W.O.	Wilmot	Guysboro' . . . N S	Henry Lindon
Charlottetown		Queen's . . . P E I	A. A. McDonald
Charrington	Clifton	Compton . . . Q	Louis Ricard
Chatboro	Chatham	Argenteuil . . . Q	Chas. A. Bradford
Chateauguay	Chateauguay	Chateauguay . . . Q	N. Mallett
Chateauguay Basin	Chateauguay	Chateauguay . . . Q	Robert Lang
Chateau Richer	Chateau Richer	Montmorency . . . Q	Mdme. L. B. Rousseau
**Chatham*	Raleigh	Kent . . . O	S. Barfoot
Chatham		Northumberland . . . N B	Thos. Vondy, jun.
Chatillon	St. Zépherin	Yamaska . . . Q	Louis Beauchemin
Chatsworth	Holland	Grey, N. R . . . O	Henry Cardwell
Chaudiere Mills	St. Jean Chrysostome	Levis . . . Q	Antoine Lemieux
Cheapside	Walpole	Haldimand . . . O	William Pugsley
Chebogue, W. O		Yarmouth . . . N S	Ansell Robbins
Cheddar	Cardiff	Peterborough, E. R . . . O	Edward Bates
**Chelsea*	Hull	Ottawa . . . Q	H. B. Prentiss
Chelsea, W. O		Lunenburg . . . N S	H. Kedy
Cheltenham	Chinguacousy	Peel . . . O	C. H. King
Chemainus		Vancouver . . . B C	Thomas G. Askew
Chepstow	Greenock	Bruce, S. R. . . . O	Wm. Henesy
Cherry Cheek	Innisfil	Simcoe, S. R . . . O	William Maine
Cherry Grove	No. 45	King's . . . P E I	Joseph McAulay
Cherry Valley	Athol	Prince Edward . . . O	Thomas Colliver
Cherry Valley	No. 50	Queen's . . . P E I	A. McLellan
Cherrywood	Pickering	Ontario, S. R . . . O	Charles Petty
Chesley	Elderslie	Bruce, N. R . . . O	Mark McManus
Chesley's Corners, W O		Lunenburg . . . N S	Nelson Chesley
Chester	Chester	Arthabaska . . . Q	Thomas Booth
Chester		Lunenburg . . . N S	Chas. A. Brown
Chester Basin, W.O.		Lunenburg . . . N S	Jos. Eisenhaur
Chesterfield	Blenheim	Oxford, N. R . . . O	Wm. Brown

NAME OF POST OFFICE.	TOWNSHIP OR PARISH.	ELECTORAL COUNTY OR DIVISION.	NAME OF POSTMASTER.
Cheticamp, W. O...	Cheticamp	Inverness .... N S	Ed. Briard. ....
Cheverie, W. O.....	....	Hants .... N S	John Burgess......
Cheviot	Culross............	Bruce, S. R............ O	Andrew McLean ...
Chezzetcook, W. O..	....	Halifax............ N S	Donald McLaren ...
Chichester..........	Chichester..........	Pontiac. .... Q	Horace Landon.....
Chicoutimi	Chicoutimi	Chicoutimi .... Q	Jean O. Tremblay ..
Chigacnaise River, W. O............	....	Colchester .... N S	Thos. Lindsay ... ..
Chilliwack	....	New Westminster..... B C	J. McCutcheon.....
Chimney Corner, W. O	....	Inverness .... N S	Allan McKenzie ....
Chipman, W. O.....	....	Queen's .. .. N B	Geo. G. King.......
Chipman's Brook, W. O	....	King's. .... N S	Thomas Murphy....
Chipman's Corners W. O............	....	King's............... N S	Samuel Chipman ...
**Chippawa*	Stamford.	Welland .... O	J. S. Macklem......
Chlorydormes	Chlorydormes	Gaspé .... Q	Celestin Belanger...
Chockfish, W. O....	....	Kent................ N B	M. McEwen........
Christmas Island....	....	Cape Breton .... N S	M. McDougall .....
Churchill...........	Innisfil............	Simcoe, S. R........... O	H. Sloane ....
Church Hill, W. O..	....	Albert .... N B	Alex. Bayley ......
Church Point, W. O	....	Northumberland...... N B	W. M. Salter. .....
Churchstreet, W. O.	....	King's .... N S	Wm. Gilliatt ....
Churchville.........	Toronto	Peel .... O	James E. Pointer...
Churchville, W. O..	....	Pictou .. .. N S	Allan Weir.........
Chute au Blondeau..	East Hawkesbury...	Prescott .... O	James McAllister...
Chute's Cove, W. O.	....	Annapolis .... N S	H. M. Foster.......
Clachan	Orford	Bothwell .... O	Duncan McColl, jun
Clandeboye.........	Huntley............	Carleton .... O	Robert McKinlay...
Clairvaux (sub).....	St. Placide	Charlevoix .... Q	E. Larouche........
Clapham	Inverness.	Megantic .... Q	S. Johnston ....
Clare, W. O	....	Digby .... N S	A. F. Comeau ......
Claremont	Pickering	Ontario, S. R .... O	J. McM. McNab ...
Claremont, W. O ...	. ...	Cumberland.......... N S	J. C. Black.........
Clarence	Clarence	Russell .... O	Thomas Wilson.....
Clarence Creek	Clarence	Russell .... O	S. G. A. Raiche ....

NAME OF POST OFFICE.	TOWNSHIP OR PARISH.	ELECTORAL COUNTY OR DIVISION.	NAME OF POSTMASTER.
Clarenceville	Noyan	Missisquoi **Q**	Charles Stewart
Clarendon Centre	Clarendon	Pontiac **Q**	James Shaw
Clarendon Front (sub)	Clarendon	Pontiac **Q**	William Heath
Clarendon, W. O.		Charlotte **N B**	John McCutcheon
Clareview	Sheffield	Addington **O**	Robert T. McDonnell
Clarina	Granby	Shefford **Q**	Nazaire Giroux
Clarke	Clarke	Durham, W. R **O**	James Lockhart
Clarke's Harb'r, WO.		Shelburne **N S**	Beverly Smith
**Clarksburg*	Collingwood	Grey, E. R **O**	Walter Hunter
Claude	Chinguacousy	Peel **O**	Peter T. McCollum
Clavering	Keppel	Grey, N. R **O**	Henry Cammidge
Clayton	Ramsay	Lanark, N. R **O**	O. Banning, jun
Clear Creek	Houghton	Norfolk, S. R **O**	Jonathan Bridgman
Clearville	Orford	Bothwell **O**	Henry Watson
Clementsport		Annapolis **N S**	James P. Roop
Clementsvale, W. O.		Annapolis **N S**	Richard Sandford
Clifford	Minto	Wellington, N. R **O**	Francis Brown
**Clifton*	Stamford	Welland **O**	W. W. Woodruff
a Clifton House (sub)	Stamford	Welland **O**	J. Shears
Clifton, W. O.		Gloucester **N B**	A. J. Seaman
Clifton, W. O.		King's **N B**	G. H. Flewelling
Clinch's Mills, W. O		St. John **N B**	Charles F. Clinch
Clinton		Cariboo **B C**	Charles E. Pope
**Clinton*	Tuckersmith	Huron, S. R **O**	Thomas Fair
Clones, W. O.		Queen's **N B**	Andrew Corbett
Clontarf	Sebastopol	Renfrew, S. R **O**	J. R. McDonald
Clover Hill	Tecumseth	Simcoe, S. R **O**	T. M. Banting
Cloyne	Anglesea	Addington **O**	Bibins Clark
Clyde	Beverley	Wentworth, N. R **O**	George Hall
Clyde River		Shelburne **N S**	George Thompson
Coal Branch, W. O.		Kent **N B**	Charles Walker
Coal Mines, W. O		Queen's **N B**	James Brown
Coates' Mills, W. O.		Kent **N B**	Thos. Coates
**Coaticook*	Barnston	Stanstead **Q**	Horace Cutting
Cobden	Ross	Renfrew, N. R **O**	John R. McDonald

[illegible] Winter.

NAME OF POST OFFICE.	TOWNSHIP OR PARISH.	ELECTORAL COUNTY OR DIVISION.	NAME OF POSTMASTER.
**Cobourg*	Hamilton	Northumberland, W. R. . O	William Sykes
Cocaigne		Kent . . . N B	James Lucas
Cocaigne River, W.O		Kent . . . N B	Sylvan S. Le Blanc
Codrington	Brighton	Northumberland, E. R . . O	James B. Lay
Cody's, W. O		Queen's . . . N B	Charles F. Cody
Cogmagun River, WO		Hants . . . N S	Chas. Thomas
Colbeck	Luther	Wellington, N. R. . . . O	William Colbeck
**Colborne*	Cramahe	Northumberland, E. R . . O	C. R. Ford
Colchester	Colchester	Essex . . . O	Alex Hackett
Cold Brook Station, W. O		King's . . . N S	Henry Porter
Coldsprings	Hamilton	Northumberland, W. R. . O	D. McIntosh
Coldstream	Lobo	Middlesex, N. R. . . . O	Jacob Marsh
Coldstream, W. O		Carleton . . . N B	Saml. Dickinson
**Coldwater*	Medonte	Simcoe, N. R. . . . O	Saml. Drew Eplett
Colebrook	Camden East	Addington . . . O	Charles Warner
Cole Harbor, W. O.		Guysboro' . . . N S	George Jamieson
Coleraine	Toronto Gore	Peel . . . O	Mrs. Mary St. John
Cole's Island, W. O.		Queen's . . . N B	David Lawson
Colinville	Moore	Lambton . . . O	John Butler
Collfield	Litchfield	Pontiac . . . Q	M. Hughes
Collina, W. O		King's . . . N B	James M. Gibbon
**Collingwood*	Nottawasaga	Simcoe, N. R. . . . O	W. B. Hamilton
Collin's Bay	Kingston	Frontenac . . . O	Joseph Losie
Collin's Inlet		Algoma . . . O	Silas Staples
Colpoy's Bay	Albemarle	Bruce, N. R . . . O	John Shackleton
Columbus	Whitby	Ontario, S. R. . . . O	Robert Ashton
Comber	Tilbury, West	Essex . . . O	D. McAlister
Combermere	Radcliffe	Renfrew, S. R. . . . O	Daniel Johnson
Como	Vaudreuil	Vaudreuil . . . Q	John Hodgson
Comox		Vancouver . . . B C	Alexander Rodell
**Compton*	Compton	Compton . . . Q	A. W. Kendrick
Concord	Vaughan	York, W. R . . . O	Henry McElroy
Concord, W. O		Pictou . . . N S.	A Nicholson
Condon Settlement, W. O		K ng's . . . N S	W. McConnell

NAME OF POST OFFICE.	TOWNSHIP OR PARISH.	ELECTORAL COUNTY OR DIVISION.	NAME OF POSTMASTER.
Conestogo	Woolwich	Waterloo, N. R. **O**	Charles Hendry
Coningsby	Erin	Wellington, S. R. **O**	John W. Burt
Connaught	Winchester	Dundas **O**	Patrick Jordan
Connor	Adjala	Cardwell **O**	Robert Lee
Conquerall Bank, W. O		Lunenburg **N S**	James McFarlane
Conroy	Downie	Perth, S. R. **O**	Edward Flynn
Consecon	Ameliasburgh	Prince Edward **O**	A. Marsh
Constance	Hullett	Huron, C. R. **O**	R. Thompson
Contrecœur	Contrecœur	Verchères **Q**	Olivier Lamoureux
Conway	SouthFredericksburg	Lennox **O**	G. B. Sills
Cook's Brook, W. O.		Colchester **N S**	Mrs. M. Mitchell
Cookshire	Eaton	Compton **Q**	Thomas B. Terrill
**Cookstown*	Tecumseth	Simcoe, S. R. **O**	John Ferguson
Cooksville	Toronto	Peel **O**	John Peaker
Cooper	Madoc	Hastings, N. R **O**	Thomas Allen
Copenhagen	Malahide	Elgin, E. R **O**	George Winnecott
Copetown	Beverley	Wentworth, N. R. **O**	Thomas Milne
Copleston	Enniskillen	Lambton **O**	J. D. Carscaden
Corbett	McGillivray	Middlesex, N. R **O**	John F. Macey
Corbin	Hemmingford	Huntingdon **Q**	Alex. Fiddes
Corinth	Bayham	Elgin, E. R. **O**	F. A. Best
Cork Station, W. O.		York **N B**	John Sullivan
Corn Hill, W. O		King's **N B**	Ariel Keith
**Cornwall*	Cornwall	Cornwall **O**	George McDonnell
Cornwall	No. 32	Queen's **P E I**	John Frizzle
Cornwallis East, W. O		King's **N S**	Clement B. Dickey
Corunna	Moore	Lambton **O**	H. J. Miller
Côteau du Lac	Soulanges	Soulanges **Q**	Gédéon Deguire
Côteau Landing	St. Zotique	Soulanges **Q**	Anicet B. Prieur
Côteau Station	Soulanges	Soulanges **Q**	Roger Ducket
Côteaux Rivière Ouelle	Rivière Ouelle	Kamouraska **Q**	E. M. A. Boucher
Côte des Neiges	Montreal	Hochelaga **Q**	Odile Malboeuf
Côte St. Paul	Montreal	Hochelaga **Q**	Edmond Latour

NAME OF POST OFFICE.	TOWNSHIP OR PARISH.	ELECTORAL COUNTY OR DIVISION.	NAME OF POSTMASTER.
Cotswold	Minto	Wellington, N. R. O	A. McKillop
Coulson	Medonte	Simcoe, N. R. O	James Coulson
Courtland	Middleton	Norfolk, N. R. O	C. S. Harris
Covehead	No. 34	Queen's P E I	D. Lawson
Covehead Road	No. 34	Queen's P E I	Thomas McGrath
Coventry	Albion	Cardwell O	William McKee
Coverdale, W. O.		Albert N B	David Smith
Coverley	Bentinck	Grey, S. R. O	James Grant
Covey Hill	Havelock	Huntingdon Q	Alexander Brisbin
Cowal	Dunwich	Elgin, W. R O	Grant Silcox
Cowansville	Dunham	Missisquoi Q	Dr. Charles Brown
Cow Bay		Cape Breton N S	Anthony Martel
Cowichan		Vancouver B C	Samuel Harris
Coxheath, W. O		Cape Breton N S	P. T. Clarke
Craighurst	Medonte.	Simcoe, N. R. O	Thomas Craig
Craigleith	Collingwood	Grey, E. R. O	A. G. Fleming
Craigsholme	Garafraxa	Wellington, C. R. O	Murdoch Craig
Craigs Road Station.	St. Etienne de Lauzon	Levis Q	Nazaire Frechette
Craigvale	Innisfil	Simcoe, S. R. O	Robert Black
Cranbourne	Cranbourne	Dorchester Q	John Colgan
Cranworth	Burgess	Leeds, S. R. O	Peter Jones
Crapaud	No. 29	Queen's P E I	William Worth
Crawford	Bentinck	Grey, S. R. O	Hector McRae
Credit	Toronto	Peel O	Emerson Taylor
Crediton	Stephen	Huron, S. R O	John Parsons
Creek Bank	Peel	Wellington, C. R. O	James Graham
**Creemore*	Nottawasaga	Simcoe, N. R O	Alexander Gillespie
Creighton	Medonte	Simcoe, N. R O	Michael Cavanagh
Cressy	Marysburg	Prince Edward O	S. W. Carson
Crieff	Puslinch	Wellington, S. R. O	Lewis Gregor
Crinan	Aldboro'	Elgin, W. R O	D. McIntyre
Crofton	Sophiasburg	Prince Edward O	Henry Covert
Cromarty	Hibbert	Perth, S. R O	Joseph Reading
Cromwell, W. O		King's N B	Susannah Wetmore
Crosshill	Wellesley	Waterloo, N. R O	James McCutcheon

NAME OF POST OFFICE.	TOWNSHIP OR PARISH.	ELECTORAL COUNTY OR DIVISION.	NAME OF POSTMASTER.	
Crosspoint..........	Restigouche	Bonaventure............ Q	John Fraser........	
Cross Roads, Country Harbor..........	....	Guysborough......... N S	Donald Gunn.......	
Cross Roads, Lake Ainslie, W. O.....	....	Inverness........... N S	Charles Fraser......	
Cross Roads, Middle Melford, W. O....	....	Guysborough.......... N S	Jesse Anderson.....	
Cross Roads, Ohio, W. O............	....	Antigonishe.......... N S	John McPherson....	
Cross Roads, Saint George's Channel, W. O............	....	Inverness .... N S	Alexander Hill.. ...	
Crow Harbor, W. O.	....	Guysborough.......... N S	John Ehler.........	
Crowland	Crowland...........	Welland .... O	Luther Boardman...	
Croydon............	Camden, East.......	Addington .... O	Ira Williams........	
Cruickshank........	Keppel.............	Grey, N. R .... O	James Cruickshank .	
Crumlin	Dorchester, North ..	Middlesex, E. R......... O	Robert Dreany......	
Crysler...........	Finch	Stormont .... O	Chas. W. Bingham..	
Culloden	Dereham	Oxford, S. R........... O	Andrew Smart......	
Cumberland.........	Cumberland	Russell .... O	William Wilson.. .	
Cumberland Bay, W. O...............	....	Queen's.............. N B	A. Branscomb, sen..	
Cumberland Point, W. O............	....	Queen's............. N B	William Smith......	
Cumminsville..	Nelson	Halton.................. O	Robert Thomson.....	
Cumnock...........	Nichol.............	Wellington, C. R........ O	John Anderson	
Curran	Plantagenet.........	Prescott .... O	Philippe Gareau	
Curryville, W. O ..	... .	Albert............... N B	John Beaumont.....	
Cushing	Chatham	Argenteuil............. Q	James B. Cushing...	

NAME OF POST OFFICE.	TOWNSHIP OR PARISH.	ELECTORAL COUNTY OR DIVISION.	NAME OF POSTMASTER.	
Dacre.....	Brougham..........	Renfrew, S. R..........O	John Morrow.......	
Daillebout..........	Daillebout..........	Joliette ....Q	L. I. Déziel........	
Dalesville...........	Rear of Chatham...	Argenteuil............Q	Peter McArthur....	
Dalhousie	....	Restigouche ....N B	H. A. Johnson.....	
Dalhousie East, W.O	....	King's...............N S	Melissa Sterratt	
Dalhousie Mills.....	Lancaster...........	Glengarry ....O	William Chisholm ..	
Dalhousie Road, W. O.....	....	Lunenburg............N S	Robert Frayney....	
Dalhousie Settlement W. O............	....	Pictou ....N S	W. Ross...........	
Dalibaire...........	Dalibaire...........	Rimouski..... ....Q	O. A. Lamontagne..	
Dalkeith............	Lochiel............	Glengarry.............O	William Robertson..	
Dalrymple..........	Carden.............	Victoria, N. R..........O	....	
Dalston............	Vespra.............	Simcoe, N. R...........O	George Lawson	
Danby	Durham............	Drummond ....Q	John R. Reece......	
Danford Lake	Alleyn	Pontiac...............Q	Henry Heney.......	
Danforth	Scarboro'...........	York, E. R ....O	Henry Hogarth.....	
**Danville*	Shipton............	Richmond ....Q	J. W. Stockwell	
Darlington.....	No. 31.............	Queen's .P E I	J. McInnis.........	
Darnley	No. 18.............	Prince.............P E I	George Thompson...	
Darrell	Chatham	Kent ....O	Edward Hall	
Dartford............	Percy	Northumberland, E. R...O	William Bailey	
Dartmoor...........	Dalton	Victoria, N. R..........O	John Gardiner......	
Dartmouth..........	....	Halifax..............N S	Luther Sterns.......	
Dashwood	Hay...............	Huron, S. R ....O	Noah Fried.........	
Davenport	York..............	York, W. R.... ....O	Joseph Green.	
Davisville	York..............	York, E. R.............O	John Davis.........	
Dawn Mills.........	Gore of Camden.....	Bothwell ....O	W. A. Ward........	
Dawson Settlement, W. O.............	....	Albert................N B	Isaac Dawson......	
Daywood..........	Sydenham	Grey, N. R .... O	A. S. Cameron... .	
Dealtown	Raleigh............	Kent ....O	Isaac Lambert......	
Debeck Station, W. O	....	Carleton......... ....N B	Alex. Harron	
De Cewsville........	Cayuga............	Haldimand.............O	John Hudson.......	
Deep Brook, W. O..	....	Annapolis...........N S	C. Purdy	
Deerdock..........	Oso	Addington ....O	John Warren.......	

NSHIP OR ARISH.	ELECTORAL COUNTY OR DIVISION.	NAME OF POSTMASTER.
....	Yarmouth............N S	Richard Crosby.....
wwillimbury..	Simcoe, S. R...........O	Samuel Walker.....
dia	Bonaventure...........Q	John Mowat........
....	King's.............P E I	H. McLean.........
re..........	Middlesex, W. R........O	C. J. Ladd ....
ton	Norfolk, N. R..........O	James Whitsides....
l	Leeds, S. R............O	W. H. Danaut......
burg	Prince Edward.. ....O	B. Smith ....
....	King's...............N S	Hector Graves......
h..	Addington ....O	Samuel Lane........
....	Middlesex, E. R.... ....O	B. H. Rosser ....
....	Richmond ....Q	Joseph R. Denison..
nbrooke......	Addington ....O	B. C. Freeman......
....	Hants................N S	John Fraser ....
....	Hants ....N S	R. T. Densmore.....
msay........	Joliette................Q	James Read ....
....	Northumberland......N B	William Hartt......
....	Ontario, N. R..........O	Thomas Allin.......
o	Peel ....O	L. D. Sanderson....
inster	Middlesex, E. R. ....O	William Dibb.......
....	Queen's.......... ..P E I	A. McCalder ....
n...........	Grey, N. R ....O	George Smith.......
mbault	Portneuf...............Q	A. Damase Hamelin.
borough	Addington ....O	John M. Snook.....
n, East, ...	Addington ....O	William Irvine......
vaska........	Temiscouata...........Q	Mdme A. Cloutier..
....	District of Nipissing.....O	Robert Ranson......
n...........	Middlesex, E. R.........O	....
anchester	Huntingdon............Q	John Oliver.........
outh	Elgin, E. R............O	Nelson Parker ......
y	Carleton ....O	R. Walker, jun .....
....	Leeds, S. R............O	L. N. Phelps ....
ruck.....	Stormont...............O	Peter Forbes........
	.......N S	G. W. Nelson.... .

NAME OF POST OFFICE.	TOWNSHIP OR PARISH.	ELECTORAL COUNTY OR DIVISION.	NAME OF POSTMASTER.
Digby	....	Digby .... N S	Mrs. C. W. Bent....
Dillonton..........	Bolton.............	*Bromo* .... Q	George Cairns .....
Dipper Harbor, W. O.	....	St. John............. N B	D. Belmore.........
Discoose, W. O	.. ..	Richmond....... .... N S	David Grouchy.. ..
Dixie	Toronto	Peel .... O	John Kennedy......
Dixon's Corners.....	Matilda	Dundas................ O	William Wood......
Doaktown, W. O....	....	Northumberland...... N B	Hiram Freeze.......
Dobbinton..........	Elderslie...........	Bruce, N. R.... . ..... O	James Dobbin ......
Doherty's Mills, W. O	....	Kent......... .... N B	Joseph G. Cormier..
Dog Creek..........	....	Cariboo.... .... B C	William Wycott...
Dollar.......... ...	Markham..........	York, E. R .... O	Agnes Heron ....
Domaine de Gentilly	Gentilly	Arthabaska........... Q	T. Laflèche.........
Don................	York	York, E. R .... O	John Hogg ....
Doncaster	York...............	York, E. R .... O	James Young.......
Donegal	Elma	Perth, N. R............ O	Mary Mason........
Donegal, W. O	....	King's.... .... N B	John Lockhart.....
Doon...............	Waterloo, South....	Waterloo, S. R.... ..... O	Thomas Slee........
Doran.....	Bathurst	Lanark, S. R.. .... O	William Doran .....
Dorchester........	....	Westmoreland..... ... N B	S. W. Tingley ......
Dorchester Station..	Dorchester..........	Middlesex, E. R......... O	J. N. Hardy.........
Dorking............	Maryboro'..........	Wellington, N R .... O	Adam Deitz ....
Douglas............	Bromley	Renfrew, N. R.......... O	Duncan Ferguson...
Douglas, W. O......	....	York................ N B	Edward Dunphy....
Douglas Harbor, W. O	....	Queen's... .... N B	Abner Balmain .....
Douglastown........	Douglas	Gaspé .... Q	Samuel A. Veit.....
Douglastown, W. O.	....	Northumberland...... N B	Wm. Russell, jun...
Dover, W. O	....	Westmoreland .... N B	William Steeves.....
Dover, South	Dover	Kent .... O	Alexis Robert ......
Downeyville........	Emily..	Victoria, S. R.......... O	Michael O'Neill....
Downsview	York............ .	York, W. R............ O	Robert Clarke ......
Doyle Settlement, W. O	....	Restigouche.......... N B	Donald Murchie ....
Drayton	Peel..	Wellington, C. R..... .. O	W. C. Wortley .....
Dresden	Gore of Camden	Bothwell............... O	C. P. Watson.......
Drew...............	Minto	Wellington, N. R........ O	William Cardwell...

NAME OF POST OFFICE.	TOWNSHIP OR PARISH.	ELECTORAL COUNTY OR DIVISION.		NAME OF POSTMASTER.
Drew's Mills	Barford	Stanstead	Q	R. C. Baldwin
Dromore	Egremont	Grey, S. R	O	Alexander Taylor
Drum	Manvers	Durham, E. R	O	Isabella Harrison
Drumbo	Blenheim	Oxford, N. R	O	Joseph L. Burgess
Drummondville, East	Grantham	Drummond	Q	Miss C. M. Millar
Drummondville, West	Stamford	Welland	O	Luke Brokenshaw
Drumquin	Trafalgar	Halton	O	James Mason
Dryden	Wallace	Perth, N. R	O	Richard Johnston
Drysdale	Stanley	Huron, S. R	O	Robert Drysdale
Duart	Orford	Bothwell	O	James Tait
Dublin Shore, W. O.		Lunenburg	N S	Thomas Smith
Duck and Pringle		Yale	B C	James Duck
Dudswell	Dudswell	W[illegible]e	Q	Zerah Evans
Dufferin	Oneida	Haldimand	O	Mrs. James Cossar
Dumbarton, R. R. Station, W. O		Charlotte	N B	James Trenholm
Dumblane	Saugeen	Bruce, N. R	O	Donald Fraser
Dumfries, W. O		York	N B	Wm. Whitehead
Dunany	Wentworth	Argenteuil	Q	Samuel Smith
Dunbar	Williamsburg	Dundas	O	A. C. Allison
Dunbarton	Pickering	Ontario, S. R	O	John Parker
Duncan	Euphrasia	Grey, E. R	O	William McRae
Duncan, W. O.		Lunenburg	N S	Daniel Duncan
Duncrief	Lobo	Middlesex, N. R.	O	Christopher Walker
Dundalk	Melancthon	Grey, E. R.	O	James May
**Dundas*	Flamborough, West.	Wentworth, N. R.	O	J. M. Thornton
Dundas	No. 55	Kings	P E I	Richard Burdett
Dundee	Dundee	Huntingdon	Q	David Baker
Dundee, W. O.		Restigouche	N B	Alexander Laing
Dundee Centre	Dundee	Huntingdon	Q	Rev. D. Ross
Dundela	Matilda	Dundas	O	J. E. Tuttle
Dundonald	Cramahe	Northumberland, E. R.	O	John Barker
Dunedin	Nottawasaga	Simcoe, N. R.	O	Thomas H. Best
Dungannon	Wawanosh	Huron, N. R.	O	R. Clendinning
Dungiven, W. O		Westmoreland	N B	John McVey

NAME OF POST OFFICE.	TOWNSHIP OR PARISH.	ELECTORAL COUNTY OR DIVISION.		NAME OF POSTMASTER.
Dunham	Dunham	Missisquoi	Q	Edward Baker
Dunkeld	Brant	Bruce, S. R.	O	Thomas Whitehead
Dunkeld		Cariboo	B C	Allan Graham
**Dunnville*	Moulton	Monck	O	Thomas Armour
Dunphy, W. O.		Northumberland	N B	George Dunphy
Dunraven	Calumet Island	Pontiac	Q	John Letts
Dunrobin	Torbolton	Carleton	O	Hy. Younghusband
Dunsford	Verulam	Victoria, S. R.	O	William Graham
Duntroon	Nottawasaga	Simcoe, N. R.	O	James Russell
Dunvegan	Kenyon	Glengarry	O	Hector McLean
**Durham*	Bentinck	Grey, S.R.	O	Arch'd McKenzie
Durham		Pictou	N S	John McCoul
Dwyer Hill	Goulburn	Carleton	O	A. T. Rothwell
Eagle	Aldborough	Elgin, W. R.	O	Colin Gillies
Eagle's Nest	St. Peter's	Lisgar*	M	John Monkman
Eardley	Eardley	Ottawa	Q	W. H. McLean
Earltown, W. O.		Colchester	N S	W. J. McKay
East Arthabaska	St. Norbert	Arthabaska	Q	P. N. Pacaud
East Bay		Cape Breton	N S	Hugh McGillivray
East Bay, North side, W. O.		Cape Breton	N S	J. P. McKinnon
East Bolton	Bolton	Brome	Q	Alex. Sargent
East Broughton	Broughton	Beauce	Q	Louis Beaudouin
East Chester	St. Hélène de Chester	Arthabaska	Q	Joseph Jutras
East Clifton	Clifton	Compton	Q	Hugh E. Cairns

NAME OF POST OFFICE.	TOWNSHIP OR PARISH.	ELECTORAL COUNTY OR DIVISION.		NAME OF POSTMASTER.
East Dunham	Dunham	Missisquoi	Q	Robert A. Wales
Eastern Harbor, W. O.		Inverness	N S	W. Lawrence
East Farnham	Farnham, East	Brome	Q	Rodney Hutchins
East Glassville, W. O.		Carleton	N B	David Smith
East Hawkesbury	Hawkesbury East	Prescott	O	Michael Maneely
East Hereford	Hereford	Compton	Q	Elijah Purington
East Jeddore, W.O.		Halifax	N S	David Webber
East Magdala	Nelson	Megantic	Q	William J. Smyth
Eastman's Springs	Gloucester	Russell	O	D. H. Eastman
Easton's Corners	Wolford	Grenville, N. R	O	H. S. Easton
East Oro	Oro	Simcoe, N.R.	O	William Simpson
East Point	No. 47	King's	P E I	Alexander Beaton
East Port Medway, W.O.		Queen's	N S	F. P. Armstrong
East River, St. Mary's W. O.		Pictou	N S	Geo. Campbell
East River, St. Mary's W. O.		Guysborough	N S	A. W. Sutherland
East Scotch Settlement, W. O.		King's	N B	Donald McLachlan
East side of Chezzetcook, W. O.		Halifax	N S	
East side of Pubnico Harbor, W. O.		Yarmouth	N S	Byron Hines
East side of Ragged Island, W. O.		Shelburne	N S	George Craig
East side of West Branch East River of Pictou, W. O.		Pictou	N S	Daniel Shaw
East Templeton	Templeton	Ottawa	Q	Levi E. Dunning
Eastville, W. O.		Colchester	N S	James R. Ellis
East Williamsburgh	Williamsburgh	Dundas	O	Herbert E. Snyder
Eastwood	Oxford, East	Oxford, S.R.	O	John Shaw
Eaton	Eaton	Compton	Q	Moses Lebourveau
Economy		Colchester	N S	W. A. Fulmer
Eddystone	Haldimand	Northumberland, W.R.	O	M. Bradley
Eden	Bayham	Elgin, E.R	O	John Nethercott
Eden Mills	Eramosa	Wellington, S.R.	O	Anthony Jackson

NAME OF POST OFFICE.	TOWNSHIP OR PARISH.	ELECTORAL COUNTY OR DIVISION.	NAME OF POSTMASTER.
Edgar	Oro	Simcoe, N.R... .... O	John Smith ....
Edgecombe	Mornington	Perth, N.R............O	U. McFadden .. ...
Edgeley............	Vaughan	York, W.R............O	John Barnes........
Edgett's Landing, W. O.............	....	Albert ....N B	Ward Edgett .....
Edgeworth	Tilbury, East	Kent ....O	....
Edina	Chatham	Argenteuil ....Q	Wm. Tomalty......
Edmonton..........	Chinguacousy	Peel ....O	Ewen Cameron .. ..
Edmundston	....	Victoria..............N B	J. T. Hodgson.....
Edwardsburgh......	Edwardsburgh......	Grenville, S.R ..O	William S. Aiken ..
Eel Brook, W. O....	....	Yarmouth ....N S	J. B. Leblanc......
Eel Lake, W. O. ...	....	Yarmouth ....N S	Leon Porter ....
Eel River, W. O....	... .	Restigouche ....N B	Mrs. James Craig ..
Effingham	Pelham	Monck ....O	George Redpath....
Eganville	Grattan	Renfrew, S.R...........O	John Quealy ....
Egerton	Luther	Wellington, N.R. ......O	James Hunter......
Eglington	York	York, E.R. ... .O	Joseph Hargrave....
Egmondville	Tuckersmith...	Huron, C. R............O	George E. Jackson..
Egmont Bay	No. 15	Prince.............P E I	S. Arseneaux... ...
Egremont	Egremont	Grey, S. R.............O	Thomas Smith......
Egypte	Milton	Shefford ....Q	J. Depot . ...
Eig Mountain, W.O.	....	Antigonishe ....N S	Mrs. Mary Smith..
Elba	Mono	Cardwell ... .O	Charles Smith ......
Elder	Mono	Cardwell ....O	C. Conn........ ..
Eldorado	Madoc	Hastings, N. R..........O	John Blackburn ....
Elfrida	Saltfleet............	Wentworth, S. R. ......O	Hamilton Sweazie ..
Elgin	Crosby, South	Leeds, S. R.............O	Philemon Pennock..
Elgin	....	Albert.......... ....N B	R. D. Robinson ...
Elginburg	Kingston...........	Frontenac ....O	Eli Meecham.......
Elginfield	London	Middlesex, E.R.... ...O	Matthew Glass .....
Elimville	Usborne....	Huron, S. R............O	James Crocker. ....
Elizabethville	Hope	Durham, E. R..........O	Johnston Beatty....
Ellengowan.........	Brant	Bruce, S. R.............O	James Brownlee ....
Ellershausen, W. O..	....	Hants ....N S	J. Beckman ....
Ellesmere	Scarboro'..........	York, E.R.. ....O	Arch. Glendinning..

NAME OF POST OFFICE.	TOWNSHIP OR PARISH.	ELECTORAL COUNTY OR DIVISION.		NAME OF POSTMASTER.
Elliott	Bathurst	Lanark, S. R.	O	Wm. McClellan
Elm	Huntley	Carleton	O	Thomas Smith
Elmbank	Toronto	Peel	O	John Trueman
Elmgrove	Essa	Simcoe, S. R.	O	Thomas Gordon
Elmira	Woolwich	Waterloo, N. R.	O	Peter Winger
Elmsdale		Hants	N S	Alex. Dunbar
Elmsville, W. O.		Pictou	N S	D. McDonald
Elmvale	Flos	Simcoe, N. R.	O	William Harvey
Elmwood	Brant	Bruce, S. R.	O	John Reinhardt
**Elora*	Pilkington	Wellington, C. R.	O	W. H. La Pinotiere.
Elphin	North Sherbrooke	Lanark, N. R.	O	Isaac Bloomberg
Elsinore	Arran	Bruce, N. R.	O	
Embro	Zorra, West	Oxford, N. R	O	D. Matheson
Embrun	Russell	Russell	O	Joseph Lalonde
Emerald	Amherst Island	Lennox	O	John Hitchins
Emerald, W. O.		Inverness	N S	Thomas Tomkins
Emerson	Sutton	Brome	Q	N. P. Emerson
Emigrant Road, W. O.		Westmoreland	N B	Charles Mulrine
Emigrant Settlement W. O.		Westmoreland	N B	B. Carrigan
Emyvale	No. 30	Queen's	P E I	P. McCardle
Enfield	Darlington	Durham, W. R.	O	William Martyn
Enfield		Hants	N S	Henry F. Donaldson.
English Corner, W.O.		Halifax	N S	James Thomson
English Settlement, W. O.		Queen's	N B	Dougald Cormichael.
English Town		Victoria	N S	Donald Buchanan
Enniskillen	Darlington	Durham, W. R.	O	D. W. McLeod
Enniskillen Station, W. O.		Queen's	N B	C. H. Kingston
Ennismore	Ennismore	Peterboro', W. R.	O	Francis J. Daly
Enterprise	Camden, East	Addington	O	Robert Graham
Epping	Euphrasia	Grey, E. R	O	James Stewart
Epsom	Reach	Ontario, N. R.	O	Joseph C. Huckins.
Eramosa	Eramosa	Wellington, S. R	O	Robert Dryden
Erbsville	Waterloo	Waterloo, N. R.	O	John L. Erb

NAME OF POST OFFICE.	TOWNSHIP OR PARISH.	ELECTORAL COUNTY OR DIVISION.		NAME OF POSTMASTER.
Erie	Walpole	Haldimand	O	R. McBurney
**Erin*	Erin	Wellington, S R.	O	William Cornock
Erinsville	Sheffield	Addington	O	Patrick Walsh
Erinville, W. O		Guysboro'	N S	Charles Kenny
Ernestown Station	Ernestown	Lennox	O	James R. Hewson
Erroll	Plympton	Lambton	O	George Whiting
Escott	Escott	Leeds, S.R	O	Joseph L Dowsley
Escuminac (sub.)	Nouvelle	Bonaventure	Q	John Campbell
Escuminac, W. O		Northumberland	N B	James McLean
Eskasoni, W. O		Cape Breton	N S	Henry V. Brown
Esquesing	Esquesing	Halton	O	John Murray
Esquimalt		Victoria	B C	John T. Howard
Esquimaux Point		Saguenay	Q	D. B. McGie
Etang du Nord (sub)	Magdalen Island	Gaspé	Q	Damase V. Bourque
Ethel	Grey	Huron, C.R	O	James Spence
Etobicoke	York	York, W.R.	O	F. A. Howland
Eugenia	Artemesia	Grey, E.R	O	R. McLean Purdy
Evelyn	Nissouri, West	Middlesex, E.R	O	John Burns
Everett	Tosorontio	Simcoe, S.R	O	W. C. Bradshaw
Eversley	King	York, N.R.	O	James Tinline
Everton	Eramosa	Wellington, S.R	O	J. Tovell
**Exeter*	Stephen	Huron, S.R	O	William Sanders
Essex Centre	Colchester	Essex	O	Thomas Rush

NAME OF POST OFFICE.	TOWNSHIP OR PARISH.	ELECTORAL COUNTY OR DIVISION.	NAME OF POSTMASTER.
Factory Dale, W.O.	....	King's................ N S	Robert R. Ray......
Fafard	St. Sylvester	Lotbiniere .... Q	William J. Cryan ..
Fairfield	Harwich	Kent .... O	David R. Watson ..
Fairfield	No. 47	King's .... P E I	A. Cavanagh.......
Fairfield, East......	Elizabethtown	Brockville .... O	Alonzo C. Johns....
Fairfield, W.O......	....	St. John............. N B	J. A. Floyd ....
Fairfield Plain......	Burford	Brant, S. R. .... O	Elijah Forsyth......
Fairhaven, W.O. ...	....	Charlotte............ N B	Caleb Greene ....
Fairview	Gore of Downie	Perth, S. R. .... O	Richard Forrest ....
Fairville	....	St. John .... N B	C. F. Tilton ....
Falding	Foley	Muskoka .... O	Matthew Rankin ...
Falkenburg	Macauley	Muskoka .... O	Mathias Moore ....
Falkirk	Williams, East	Middlesex, N. R........ O	Thomas Stephenson.
Falkland	Brantford	Brant, S. R. .... O	M. Stally...........
Fallbrook	Bathurst	Lanark, S. R .... O	William Smith .....
Fallowfield	Nepean	Carleton .... O	....
Falmouth, W.O. ...	....	Hants .... N S	James Wolf ....
Falmouth, Windsor Bridge, W. O.....	....	Hants .... N S	William Armstrong.
False Bay Beach, W. O....	....	Cape Breton .... N S	Angus McAuley ....
Farley's Mills, W.O.	....	Carleton............. N B	James Lawson.....
Farmerston, W. O. .	....	Carleton............. N B	W. E. Estey........
Farmersville	Yonge	Leeds, S. R........... O	Arza Parish ....
Farmington*........	Amaranth..........	Wellington, N. R. ...... O	John Curry ....
Farmington	No. 56.............	King's............ P E I	L. Doyle...........
Farnboro'	Farnham, East.....	Brome.................. Q	Leonard Wells......
Farndon	Farnham	Missisquoi............. Q	Seth N. Ross ....
Farnham Centre....	Farnham...........	Brome.................. Q	John Johnston......
Farquhar..........	Usborne...........	Huron, S. R. .... O	Robert Monteith ...
Farran's Point......	Osnabruck	Stormont .... O	James Roddy.......
Father Point	St. Luce	Rimouski .... Q	Pierre D. Rouleau ..
Fenaghvale..	Caledonia	Prescott .... O	Jas. Proudfoot, jun..
Fenella.......	Haldimand..	Northumberland, W. R.. O	John W. Mather ...
Fenelon Falls	Fenelon	Victoria, N. R. .... O	Robert B. Jameson .
Fennells.....	Innisfil	Simcoe, S. R. .... O	J. G. F[illegible]gehan .....

NAME OF POST OFFICE.	TOWNSHIP OR PARISH.	ELECTORAL COUNTY OR DIVISION.	NAME OF POSTMASTER.
Fenwick	Pelham	Monck O	James W. Taylor
Fenwick, W. O.		King's N B	Joseph Wiley
Fenwick, W. O.		Cumberland N S	John D. Davidson
**Fergus*	Nichol	Wellington, C. R. O	James McQueen
Ferguson's Falls	Drummond	Lanark, S.R. O	Chas. Hollinger, jun.
Fergusonvale	Flos	Simcoe, N.R. O	John Cumming
Fermoy	Bedford	Addington O	Joseph C. Rogers
Fernhill	Lobo	Middlesex, N.R. O	Jenkin Owen
Ferris, W.O		Queen's N B	R. O'Donell
Ferryville, W.O		Carleton N B	James Hemphill
Feversham	Osprey	Grey, E.R. O	Mary Sproul
Fifteen Point	No. 15	Prince P E I	Aimé Richard
**Fingal*	Southwold	Elgin, W.R. O	Samuel Tubby
Fintona	Adjala	Cardwell O	Robert J. Lamon
Fisherville	Rainham	Haldimand O	Jacob Lemmer
Fitch Bay	Stanstead	Stanstead Q	E. V. Maloney
Fitzroy Harbour	Fitzroy	Carleton O	W. A. Shirreff
Fire Islands		Colchester NS	Andrew K. Graham
Five Mile River, W.O		Hants N S	Joseph McLearn
Flatlands		Restigouche N B	Archd. McKenzie
Flat River	No. 60	Queen's PE I	R. K. McKenzie
Fleetwood	Manvers	Durham, E.R. O	James Morrow
Flesherton	Artemesia	Grey, E.R. O	Robert J. Sproul
Fletcher's Station, W. O.		Halifax N S	Edward Largie
Fleurant		Bonaventure Q	William Gray
Flinton	Kaladar	Addington O	E. J. Matthews
Flora	Woolwich	Waterloo, N.R. O	Isaac Devitt
Florence	Euphemia	Bothwell O	John A. Young
Florenceville		Carleton N B	Stephen G. Burpee
Florenceville, East, W.O.		Carleton N B	John Lovely
Foley	Whitby	Ontario, S.R. O	Thomas Williamson
Folly Lake, W.O.		Colchester N S	
Folly Mountain, W. O.		Colchester N S	

NAME OF POST OFFICE.	TOWNSHIP OR PARISH.	ELECTORAL COUNTY OR DIVISION.	NAME OF POSTMASTER.
Fontenoy	Melbourne	Richmond .... Q	R. Fraser ....
Fonthill	Pelham	Monck .... O	Danson Kinsman ...
Forbes, W.O.	....	Colchester .... N S	John Forbes........
Fordwich, Late Lisadel	Howick	Huron, N.R............ O	Arthur Mitchell ....
Fordyce	Wawanosh	Huron, N.R............. O	Wm. Farquharson ..
Forest	Plympton	Lambton .... O	R. Dier ....
Forest City, W.O..	....	York.................... N B	George R. Gibson.
Forester's Falls	Ross	Renfrew, N.R.......... O	Oliver Forester .....
Forest Mills	Richmond	Lennox....... .... O	William Breeze....
Foreston, W. O.....	... .	Carleton .... N B	Daniel B. Gray.....
Forestville	Charlotteville.......	Norfolk, S. R.......... O	C. A. White ....
Forfar	Bastard	Leeds, S. R............ O	Richard Hales......
Forks, W. O..	....	Queen's .... N B	J. Kierstead........
Forks, Baddeck, W. O.	....	Victoria .... N S	A. R. Watson .....
Formosa	Carrick	Bruce, S. R............ O	F. X. Mesner.......
Forristall's, W. O...	....	Guysborough.......... N S	John Forristall.....
Fort Coulonge	Mansfield	Pontiac .... Q	Thomas Bryson.. ..
Fort Augustus......	No. 36	Queen's .... P E I	Hon. F. Kelly......
**Fort Erie*...... ...	Bertie..............	Welland .... O	George Lewis.......
Fort Garry.........	St. John	Selkirk................ M	A. G. B. Bannatyne.
Fort William.......	....	Algoma... .... O	Miss C. McVicar...
Fort William.......	Sheen	Pontiac .... Q	James McCool .....
Foster's, W. O......	....	Lunenberg .... N S	Henry Foster ......
Foster's Cove, W. O.	....	Victoria........ ..... N B	Abner Turner ......
Fouchie, W. O	....	Richmond .... N S	Albert B. Hooper...
Fournier	Plantagenet South..	Prescott .... O	A. S. McLennan....
Foxboro'	Thurlow............	Hastings, E. R......... O	Edward Philpot ....
Fox Creek, W. O...	....	Westmoreland........ N B	Eustache Burke ....
Fox Harbor, W. O..	....	Cumberland .... N S	Arch'd Robertson...
Fox River..........	Fox	Gaspé.................. Q	J. C. Parent........
Fox River, W. O....	....	Cumberland .... N S	J. L. Hatfield ......
Framboise, W. O...	....	Richmond .... N S	Kenneth Strachan ..
Frampton	West Frampton.....	Dorchester .... Q	M. Fitzgerald ......
Frankford	Sidney	Hastings, W. R......... O	John Chapman .....

NAME OF POST OFFICE.	TOWNSHIP OR PARISH.	ELECTORAL COUNTY OR DIVISION.	NAME OF POSTMASTER.
Frank Hill	Emily......	Victoria, S. R.......... O	Thomas Franks.....
Franklin	Manvers	Durham, E. R.......... O	William Maguire ...
Franklin Centre.....	Franklin	Huntingdon .. .. Q	William Cantwell...
Franktown	Beckwith...........	Lanark, S. R............ O	E. McEwen ....
Frankville..........	Kitley	Leeds, N. R............ O	Christopher Richards
Fraser's Grant, W.O.	....	Antigonishe........... N S	John Fraser........
Fraser's Mills, W. O.	....	Pictou................ N S	Alexander Grant ...
Frederickton	....	York................. N B	A. S. Phair........
Fredericton Junction	....	Sunbury............ N B	....
Fredericton Road, W. O...............	....	Westmoreland........ N B	J. O. Sullivan......
Freelton............	Flamborough, West.	Wentworth, N. R....... O	James Hirst.......
Freeport............	Waterloo, South....	Waterloo, S. R.......... O	Elias B. Snyder.....
Freetown...........	No. 25......... ...	Prince....... ...... P E I	D. Auld...........
Freiburg............	Waterloo, North ...	Waterloo, N. R......... O	Ferdinand Rombach.
**Freliyhsburg*	St. Armand.........	Missisouoi............. Q	W. M. Patterson....
French Lake, W. O.	....	Sunbury............. N B	Arthur H. Smith.....
French River, W. O.	....	Pictou.... .... N S	Mrs. C. McDonald..
French River......	No. 21..............	Queen's............ P E I	Jane McKay ....
French Vale, W.O.	....	Cape Breton..... ..... N S	Belloni Gonthro.....
French Village......	Kngsey	Drummond .... Q	Francois Pothier....
French Villagee.....	No. 37........	Queen's............ P E I	C. McIntyre. ......
French Village, W.O	....	King's .. . . N B	Geo Beattie. ....
Frogmore..........	Toronto	Peel .... O	Henry Cartledge...
Frome..............	Southwold.........	Elgin, W. R............ O	William Silcox.....
Frost Village.......	Shefford	Shefford................ Q	John Williams.. ...
Fulford.............	Brome	Brome.................. Q	Philo England......
Fullarton..........	Fullarton..........	Perth, S. R. .... O	John Buchan.......
Fulton..............	Grimsby............	Lincoln .... O	John Grassie.......

NAME OF POST OFFICE.	TOWNSHIP OR PARISH.	ELECTORAL COUNTY OR DIVISION.	NAME OF POSTMASTER.
Gaberouse, W. O...	....	Cape Breton..........N S	....
Gad's Hill..........	Ellice	Perth, N. R............O	....
Gagetown......	....	Queen's..............N B	Edward Simpson....
Gailey, W. O	... .	Kent........ ....N B	Simon Daigle.......
**Galt*.........	Dumfries, North....	Waterloo, S. R.........O	John Davidson.....
Galway.......... ...	Somerville..........	Victoria, N R..........O	Thomas Shields.....
Gamebridge	Thorah.......... ..	Ontario, N. R...........O	William Glover.....
**Gananoque*........	Leeds	Leeds, S. R............O	D. F. Britton.......
**Garafraxa*.........	Garafraxa	Wellington, C. R . .....O	Andrew Lightbody..
Garden Hill.........	Hope....	Durham, E. R...........O	James Dyre.........
Garden Island	Garden Island	Frontenac ....O	George Cumming ...
Garden of Eden, W. O...............	....	Picton................N S	Mrs. D. McGregor..
Garden River.......	Garden River.......	Algoma.................O	Edmund J. Penny ..
Gardiner Mines, W. O...............	....	Cape Breton.........N S	William Rutledge...
Gardner's Creek, W. O...............	....	St. John..............N B	John J. Wallace...
Garneau......	Garneau.......... .	L'Islet . ... Q	Elie Chouinard .....
Garthby............	Garthby............	Wolfe ....Q	David Grenier ......
Gaspé Basin	Gaspé..............	Gaspé..................Q	J. J. Kavanagh.....
Gaspereaux.........	Number 61	King's........ .....P E I	William Lewelleyn .
Gaspereaux, W. O .	....	Queen's ....N B	Charles E. Langin ...
Gaspereaux, W. O..	....	King's................N S	Sherman Caldwell ..
Gaspereaux Station, W. O	....	Queen's ... .N B	Thomas Trott. ......
Gay's River, W. O..	....	Halifax... ....N S	M. Frame..........
Gay's River Road, W. O	....	Halifax............. N S	Robert B. Taylor ...
Geary, W. O.	....	Sunbury..............N B	Asa Carr.... ......
Gemley	Miller	Addington ....O	James Stalker .....
Geneva	Argenteuil	Argenteuil.............Q	G. A. Hooker ......
Genoa..............	St. Jerusalem	Argenteuil..............Q	James Gordon ......
Gentilly...	Gentilly.....	Nicolet.................Q	L. Brunelle.........
Georgetown	....	King's..... ....P E I	William Wightman .
**Georgetown*	Esquesing	Halton . ...O	Lafayette Goodenow
Georgeville	Stanstead	Stanstead..............Q	Increase Bullock...

NAME OF POST OFFICE.	TOWNSHIP OR PARISH.	ELECTORAL COUNTY OR DIVISION.	NAME OF POSTMASTER.
**Georgina*	Georgina	York, N. R. ....O	J. R. Bourchier.....
Germantown, W.O .	....	Albert.. ....N B	William Fillmore...
Getson's Point, W. O...............	....	Lunenburg..... ..... N S	George McKean ....
Giant's Lake	....	Guysborough... ..... N S	John McNeil.. ....
Gibralter...........	Collingwood	Grey, E. R.............O	John Glen..........
Gilbert Cove, W. O.	....	Digby ....N S	H. S. Mallet ..... .
Gilbert's Mills.....	Sophiasburgh.......	Prince Edward... ......O	John D. Gilbert ....
Gilford.......	Gwillimbury, West .	Simcoe, S. R...........O	Thomas Maconchy..
Girvan Settlement, W. O...........	....	Kent..................N B	Thomas D. Holmden
Gladstone	Dorchester	Middlesex, E. R... .....O	L. McMurray ......
Glammis	Kincardine	Bruce, N. R ....O	Richard W. Harrison
Glanford	Glanford	Wentworth, S. R........O	John Atkinson.....
Glanmire...........	Tudor	Hastings, N. R..........O	John Ray ....
Glanworth	Westminster	Middlesex, E. R ....O	John Turnbull.....
Glascott......	Glenelg	Grey, S. R..............O	Dennis Quirk... ...
Glasgow......	Uxbridge...........	Ontario, N. R. ....O	Benjamin Parker ...
Glassville W. O....	....	Carleton.............N B	Hugh Miller... ....
Glastonbury........	Kaladar............	Addington ....O	J. A. Carscallen ....
Glen, W. O.........	....	Antigonishe...........N S	D. McMillan.......
Glenallan	Peel	Wellington, C. R........O	George Allan ....
Glen Alpine, W. O..	....	Antigonishe...........N S	
Glenarm	Fenelon	Victoria, N. R... ......O	Seth Rickaby.......
Glenburnie	Kingston	Frontenac ....O	George Hunter .....
Glencairn	Tosorontio..........	Simcoe, S. R...........O	M. N. Stephens....
Glencoe............	Ekfrid	Middlesex, W. R........O	W. G. Lumley......
Glendower	Bedford	Addington ....O	Richard Howes.....
Glenedale, W. O....	....	Inverness............. N S	John McKinnon...
Glenelg	St. Mary's..........	Guysborough..........N S	Matthew Archibald.
Glengarry Station ..	....	Pictou................N S	John Fraser ....
Glen Huron	Nottawasaga	Simcoe, N. R ....O	H. M. Frame. .....
Glenloyd	Inverness.....	Megantic ....Q	Joseph Rockingham.
Glen Major	Uxbridge...........	Huron, N. R....... ..... O	Edward Major.... .
Glenmeyer	Houghton	Norfolk, S.R ....O	George E. Meyer...
Glen Morris	Dumfries..........	Brant, N.R.... ....O	Christopher Latshaw

NAME OF POST OFFICE.	TOWNSHIP OR PARISH.	ELECTORAL COUNTY OR DIVISION.	NAME OF POSTMASTER.
Glen Murray	Inverness...........	Megantic ....Q	John Murray.......
Glennevis	Lancaster	Glengarry ....O	Alexander E. McRae
Glen Road, W. O...	....	Antigonishe...........N S	C. McGillivry . ...
Glen Sutton........	Sutton	Brome ....Q	....
Glen Tay...........	Bathurst	Lanark, S.R............O	James Kearns ......
Glenvale	Kingston...........	Frontenac......... .....O	Robert Gibson.....
Glen Williams	Esquesing	Halton ....O	Charles Williams ..
Goble's Corners.....	Blenheim...........	Oxford, N.R ....O	William L. Goble....
Goderich...........	Goderich	Huron, C. R............O	A. Dickson ....
Golden Grove, W. O.	....	St. John..............N B	Peter Brennan......
Goldenville.........	....	Guysborough..........N S	Jesse Cumminger. .
Gold Fields, W. O..	....	Colchester ....N S	George Corbett .....
Gold River, W. O...	....	Lunenburg............N S	Benjamin Reddy....
Goldstone	Peel................	Wellington, C. R........O	John Gibbons.......
Good Corner, W. O.	....	Carleton..............N B	Archibald Good.....
Goodwood..........	Uxbridge.........	Ontario, N. R ....O	Michael Chapman...
Goose Creek, W. O..	....	St. John ....N B	John Prescott.......
Goose River	....	Cumberland...........N S	David Patterson ....
Goose River	Number 42	King's.............P E I	Michael McDonald..
Gordonsville, W. O..	....	Carleton..............N B	Moses Crosby.......
Gore, W. O.........	....	Hants ....N S	Daniel Thompson...
Gore's Landing	Hamilton	Northumberland, W. R...O	Sarah Gabetis. .....
Gormley	Markham	York, E.R..............O	James Gormley.....
Gorrie	Howick	Huron, N. R.......... O	Henry Besanson ....
Goshen, W. O......	....	Albert................N B	E. A. Robinson.....
Goshen, W. O......	....	Antigonishe...........N S	Donald Sinclair.....
Gosport	Adolphustown	Lennox .... O	George Germain ....
Gould	Lingwick...........	Compton ....Q	Alexander Ross.....
Gourock	Guelph............	Wellington, S. R... ....O	James Cunningham.
Gowanstown	Wallace............	Perth, N. R............O	....
Gower Point	Westmeath.........	Renfrew, N. R..... ....O	Thomas M. Carswell.
Gowland Mountain, W. O	....	Albert................N B	William McKenzie..
Grafton	Haldimand.	Northumberland, W. R..O	J. Gillard ....
Graham's Road.....	Number 20	Queen's............P E I	Eneas Brenan.....

NAME OF POST OFFICE.	TOWNSHIP OR PARISH.	ELECTORAL COUNTY OR DIVISION.	NAME OF POSTMASTER.
Grahamsville	Toronto Gore	Peel ... O	Peter Lamphier
Granboro'	Granby	Shefford ... Q	S. W. Tracy
**Granby*	Granby	Shefford ... Q	Horace Lyman
Grand Anse, W. O.		Richmond ... N S	Allan McLean
Grand Aunce, W. O.		Gloucester ... N B	Francis LeGresley
Grand Bay, W. O.		St. John ... N B	David Hamm
Grand Bend	Bosanquet	Lambton ... O	John Ironside
Grande Baie	St. Alexis	Chicoutimi ... Q	Miss D. Nugent
Grande Greve	Cap Rosier	Gaspé ... Q	Charles Esnouf
Grande Ligne		St. John's ... Q	R. A. Girardin
Grand Tracadie	Number 35	Queen's ... P E I	Stephen McDonald
Grandes Coudées	Jersey	Beauce ... Q	Jean Lambert dit Champagne
Grand Etang, W. O.		Inverness ... N S	Zephirin Collerette
Grande Vallée		Gaspé ... Q	Louis Fournier
Grand Falls		Victoria ... N B	Patrick McMillan
Grand Falls, Portage, W. O		Victoria ... N B	W. Roach
Grand Harbour, W. O		Charlotte ... N B	Turner Wooster
Grandigue, W. O.		Kent ... N B	Fidèle Legere
Grandigue Ferry, W. O		Richmond ... N S	David Fraser
Grand Manan		Charlotte ... N B	E. Daggett
Grand Mira, North, W. O		Cape Breton ... N S	Donald McDougall
Grand Mira, South, W. O		Cape Breton ... N S	Donald Gillies
Grand Narrows, W. O		Cape Breton ... N S	J. S. McNeil
Grand Pabos	Pabos	Gaspé ... Q	Thomas Soucy
Grand River	Grand River	Gaspé ... Q	Joseph O. Sirois
Grand River, W. O.		Victoria ... N B	Edwin Akerly
Grand River, W. O.		Richmond ... N S	Hector Murchison
Granville	Number 21	Queen's ... P E I	R. Corbett
Granville Centre, W. O		Annapolis ... N S	W. B. Troop
Granville Ferry		Annapolis ... N S	Alfred Troop
Grant	Cambridge	Russell ... O	James Edmonstone

NAME OF POST OFFICE.	TOWNSHIP OR PARISH.	ELECTORAL COUNTY OR DIVISION.		NAME OF POSTMASTER.
Grantley	Williamsburg	Dundas	O	John C. Munro.....
Granton	Biddulph	Middlesex, N. R	O	James Jamieson ....
Gravel Hill........	Roxborough	Stormont	O	John Crawford .....
Gravelotte.........	Middleton	Norfolk, N. R..........	O	Robert Quance......
Gravenhurst...... ..	Muskoka	Muskoka	O	....
Graystock	Otanabee	Peterborough, E. R......	O	Mark Graystock....
Great Shemogue....	....	Westmoreland........	N B	William Avard .....
Great Village	....	Colchester.............	N S	A. W. McLellan ...
Greenbank	Reach..............	Ontario, N. R...........	O	George Flint, jun...
Greenbush	Elizabethtown	Brockville	O	Daniel Blanchard...
Greenfield	Kenyon	Glengarry	O	Alex. McDougald...
Greenfield, W. O....	....	Carleton...	N B	Thomas Wakem ....
Greenfield, W. O ...	....	Queen's...............	N S	Nath. Freeman.....
Green Hill, W. O...	....	Pictou................	N S	Mrs. Jessie McKenzie
Greenock...........	Greenock...	Bruce, S. R........	O	Henry Touchburn...
Green River	St. Antonin	Temiscouata	Q	George April ....
Green River........	Pickering	Ontario, S. R	O	J. H. Smith........
Green River, W. O..	....	Victoria.............	N B	John Lynch ....
Green's Creek, W. O.	....	Colchester	N S	Daniel Dart ....
Greensville	West Flamborough .	Wentworth, N. R.......	O	William J. Mordan.
Greenville, W. O ...	....	Cumberland...........	N S	Allan G. Purdy.....
Greenwich Hill, W.O	....	King's................	N B	Albert McKiel......
Greenwood	Pickering	Ontario, S. R	O	Frederick Meen.....
Grenville	Grenville...........	Argenteuil.............	Q	Edward Pridham ...
Gresham	Bruce	Bruce, N. R	O	E. J. Brown .. ....
Gretna	N. Fredericksburg ..	Lennox	O	W. J. Mellow ......
Grey	Grey	Huron, C. R............	O	John Leckie........
Griersville..........	St. Vincent.........	Grey, E. R.............	O	Robert Burdett.....
Griffith............	Griffith............	Renfrew, S. R	O	....
**Grimsby*	Grimsby	Lincoln.................	O	H. E. Nelles ....
Grondines	Grondines..........	Portneuf	Q	F. X. Thibodeau ...
Grosvenor, W. O ...	....	Guysboro'............	N S	Samuel O'Niel ......
Grouse Creek.......	.. ..	Cariboo........	B C	Samuel A. Rodgers.
Grovesend.........	Malahide.	Elgin, E. R............	O	Wm. Bothwell......
Groves Point, W. O.	....	Victoria	N S	Murdoch McDonald.

NAME OF POST OFFICE.	TOWNSHIP OR PARISH.	ELECTORAL COUNTY OR DIVISION.	NAME OF POSTMASTER.
Gueguen, W. O.	....	Kent .... N B	Magloire Gueguen..
**Guelph*	Guelph	Wellington, S. R. .... O	Wm. Kingsmill ....
Gulf Shore, W. O.	....	Cumberland .... N S	W. Waugh........
Gunning Cove, W. O.	....	Shelburne .... N S	Mrs. Mary Doane...
Guysborough	Middleton	Norfolk, N. R .... O	J. W. Doyle. ......
Guysborough	....	Guysborough .... N S	E. J. Cunningham..
Guysborough Intervale, W. O.	....	Guysborough .... N S	Robert McKay .....
Hackett's Cove, W. O.	....	Halifax .... N S	Elias Grono ....
Hagersville	Walpole	Haldimand .... O	Charles Hager......
Half Island Cove, W. O.	....	Guysborough .... N S	John Digdon ......
Halfway Brook, W. O.	....	Colchester .... N S	Wm. Fisher ....
Halfway River, W. O.	....	Cumberland .... N S	G. D. Fullerton.....
**Haliburton*	Dysart	Peterborough, E. R. .... O	Daniel McFarlane ..
Halifax	....	Halifax .... N S	Benj. W. Cochran..
Hallerton	Hemmingford	Huntingdon .... Q	James Blair ....
Halloway	Thurlow	Hastings, E. R. .... O	James P. Hopkins..
Hall's Bridge	Harvey	Peterborough, E. R. .... O	Henry C. Hall......
Hall's Harbor, W. O.	....	King's .... N S	Sidney R. Thorp....
Hamburg	SouthFredericksburg	Lennox .... O	A. D. Fraser ......
**Hamilton*	Barton	Hamilton .... O	Frederick E. Ritchie
Hamilton	Number 18	Prince .... P E I	Charles Stewart ....
Hamlet	Burgess, N.	Lanark, S. R. .... O	Michael Stanley ....
Hammond	Elma	Perth, N. R. .... O	Jas. Hammond, jun.

NAME OF POST OFFICE.	TOWNSHIP OR PARISH.	ELECTORAL COUNTY OR DIVISION.	NAME OF POSTMASTER.
Hammond River, W. O		King's N B	W. W. Dodge
Hammondvale		King's N B	W. Fowler
Hampstead	North Easthope	Perth, N.R. O	John Snyder
Hampstead, W.O		Queen's N B	E. W. Slipp
Hampton	Darlington	Durham, W.R. O	H. Elliott
Hampton, W.O		King's N B	John Flewelling
Hamtown, W.O		York N B	Nath. Smith
Hanford Brook, W.O		King's N B	Henry Handron
Hannon	Barton	Wentworth, S. R. O	Thomas Cowie
Hanover	Bentinck	Grey, S.R O	Thos. S. Coppinger
Hantsport		Hants N S	Wm. Davison
Hanwell, W.O		York N B	
Harbor au Bouche, W.O		Antigonishe N S	Edmd. Corbet
Harbor Road, W.O		Antigonishe N S	Hugh McGillivray
Harborville, W.O		King's N S	
Harcourt	Horton	Renfrew, S. R. O	Mrs. A. R. Hutton
Hardinge	Barrie	Addington O	Thomas Tapping
Hardwicke, W.O		Northumberland N B	Robert Noble
Hardwood Lands, W. O		Colchester N S	James Grant
Harewood, W.O		Westmoreland N B	Maurice Healy
Harlem	Bastard	Leeds, S. R. O	William Kincaid
Harley	Burford	Brant, S. R. O	John Dinby
Harlock	Hullett	Huron, C. R. O	Thomas Neilans
Harlowe	Barrie	Addington O	David W. Wait
Harmony	South Easthope	Perth, S. R. O	Edmund Corbett
Harmony, W.O		King's N S	Austin Spinney
Harold	Rawdon	Hastings, N. R. O	Albert McWilliams
Harper	Bathurst	Lanark, S. R. O	Joseph Warren
Harpley	Stephen	Huron, S. R. O	Thos. N. Hayter
Harrietsville	Dorchester	Middlesex, E. R. O	John McMillan
Harrigan Cove, W.O.		Halifax N S	John Fraser
Harrington, East	Harrington	Argenteuil Q	Donald B. Campbell
Harrington, West	Zorra, West	Oxford, N. R O	Donald Reid

NAME OF POST OFFICE.	TOWNSHIP OR PARISH.	ELECTORAL COUNTY OR DIVISION.	NAME OF POSTMASTER.
Harrisburg	Dumfries, South....	Brant, N. R ....O	James Galloway ....
Harrison's Corners ..	Cornwall...........	Cornwall ....O	Angus D. McGillis..
Harriston...........	Minto	Wellington, N. R.......O	A. Macready. .....
Harrow	Colchester...	Essex...................O	Frederick Goble ....
Harrowsmith.	Portland	Addington..............O	Samuel F. Stewart.
Hartford	Townsend...........	Norfolk, N. R...........O	B. W. Thomas.....
Hartington	Portland	Addington..............O	William Kennedy...
Hartland	....	Carleton.... ....N B	S. H. Shaw.......
Hartley	Eldon	Victoria, N. R. ....O	Archd. Campbell ...
Hartman	Gwillimbury, East..	York, N. R.............O	....
Hart's Mills, W.O..	....	Sunbury......... ....N B	T. Coleman ....
Hartsville	Number 67.	Queen's .... P. E I	M. McLeod ....
Harvey	....	Albert..............N B	J. M. Stevens....
Harvey Creek.......	....	Cariboo ....B C	Samuel Smith ......
Harvey Station......	....	York ....N B	.. ..
Harvey Hill Mines..	Leeds	Megantic...............Q	J. L. Brown.......
Harwich.	Harwich	Kent ....O	James Hutchinson..
Harwood	Hamilton	Northumberland, W.R..O	R. Drope...........
Haseville	Stanbridge	Missisquoi ....Q	Thomas Hase... ...
**Hastings*....... ..	Asphodel.....	Peterborough, E. R......O	Henry M. Fowlds ..
Hastings, W.O......	....	Cumberland .... N S	G. H. Chapman....
Hastings, W.O	... .	Albert ....N B	J. C. McQuaid.....
Hatley	Hatley	Stanstead .... Q	J. B. Le Baron.....
Haultain	Burleigh............	Peterborough, E.R......O	Giles Stone........
Havelock...........	Belmont	Peterborough, E. R......O	J. W. Pearce ......
Havelock, W.O....	... .	Digby ....N S	John G. Nowlan....
**Hawkesbury*........	Hawkesbury, West..	Prescott ... .O	James G. Higginson.
Hawkestone	Oro	Simcoe, N. R...........O	James Houston.....
Hawkesville	Wellesley	Waterloo, N. R....... .O	Robert Morrison....
Hawtrey	Norwich, South.....	Oxford, S. R............O	George Southwick ..
Hay	Hay........... ..	Huron, S. R............O	James Murray......
Haydon	Darlington	Durham, W. R.........O	Wm. Broad ....
Hayesland.........	West Flamboro'	Wentworth, N. R.......O	Michael Hayes......
Hay's River, W.O..	....	Inverness .... N S	Rod. McDougall....
Haysville...	Wilmot	Waterloo, S. R.........*O	Margaret Somerville

NAME OF POST OFFICE.	TOWNSHIP OR PARISH.	ELECTORAL COUNTY OR DIVISION.	NAME OF POSTMASTER.
Hazel Grove........	Number 22.........	Queen's .. .. P E I	Richard Bagnall....
Hazledean...	Goulbourn..........	Carleton.............. O	Adam Abbott.......
Headford..........	Markham	York, E. R............ O	....
Headingly..........	Headingly..........	Selkirk .... M	John Taylor ....
Head Lake.........	Laxton.............	Victoria, N. R.......... O	W. A. Maxwell....
Head of Amherst, W. O...............	....	Cumberland .... N S	Ephraim Finlay ....
Head of Jordan River W.O..........	....	Shelburne .... N S	Thomas Holden ....
Head of Millstream, W.O..........	....	King's...... .... N B	J. Little...........
Head of St. Margaret's Bay, W.O...	....	Halifax........... ... N S	Samuel Shatford....
Head of St. Margaret's Bay (Middle District), W.O...	....	Halifax......... ..... N S	Jessie McG. Fraser.
Head of St. Mary's Bay, W.O	....	Digby........ ... .. N S	Wm. H. Young ....
Head St. Peter's Bay	Number 41.........	King's............. P E I	Edward Drain ......
Head of South River Lake, W.O.......	....	Antigonishe .... N S	Hugh McNeil ......
Head of Tatamagouche Bay, W.O.	....	Colchester .... N S	Wm. Dobson.......
Head of Tide, W.O.	....	Restigouche ... . N B	Thomas Barclay ....
Head of Wallace Bay W.O...	....	Cumberland .... N S	G. H. D. Forshner.
Head of Wallace Bay (North Side), W.O.	....	Cumberland .... N S	George Brown ......
Heathcote..........	Euphrasia.........	Grey, E. R.... .... O	Thomas J. Rorke...
Hebb's Cross, W.O..	....	Lunenburg........... N S	Johnson Manning...
Hebron, W.O.......	....	Albert............... N B	James Smyth, sen...
Hebron	....	Yarmouth .... N S	C. Cahan ....
Heckston...........	South Gower	Grenville, N.R. .... O	Hugh Hughes ......
Heidelburg	Woolwich	Waterloo, N. R......... O	John Krassler ......
Helena............	Godmanchester	Huntingdon .... Q	J. Holbrooke... ..
Hemison	East Frampton	Dorchester .... Q	Miss Lumina Bernard
Hemmingford	Hemmingford	Huntingdon .... Q	John Edwards......
Henry.............	Longueuil	Prescott .... O	William Dickson....
Henrysburg	Lacolle.............	St. John's .... Q	William Cockerline.
Henryville	St. George de Henryville.	Iberville............... Q	Telesphore Larocque

NAME OF POST OFFICE.	TOWNSHIP OR PARISH.	ELECTORAL COUNTY OR DIVISION.	NAME OF POSTMASTER.
Hepworth	Keppel.............	Grey, N. R.............O	Thomas Briggs ....
Herbert	Potton	Brome ....Q	M. Geer ....
Herdman's Corners..	Hinchinbrooke......	Huntingdon ....Q	Rev. Hugh Niven ..
Hereford	Hereford	Compton ....Q	Aaron Workman....
Hereward	Garafraxa	Wellington, C. R. ......O	George Brown......
Heron'sIsland, W.O.	....	Restigouche ....N B	George Dutch ......
**Hespeler*.	Waterloo, South	Waterloo, S. R.. ......O	John Chapman .....
Heyworth	Eardley	Ottawa..................Q	Robert Breckenridge
Hiawatha	Otonabee	Peterborough, E. R.....O	Hugh Kent.........
Hibernia, W.O.....	....	Queen's ....N B	David Gardner .....
Higgin's Road	Number 13	Prince...... . .....P E I	William Henry.....
High Bluff	High Bluff..........	Marquette..............M	J. McD. Sweetman.
High Falls	Blithfield...........	Renfrew, S. R..........O	....
Highfield..........	Etobicoke	York, W. R............O	H. Dutchburn......
Highfield, W.O.....	....	Hants .... N S	William Crowell...
Highgate	Orford	Bothwell ....O	John Beattie ....
Highland Creek.....	Scarborough	York, E. R.............O	William Tredway...
Hilda	Thurlow............	Hastings, E. R..........O	Benjamin Palmer...
Hillier	Hillier	Prince Edward..........O	Richard Noxen .....
Hillsborough	Plympton	Lambton .... O	Thomas L. Hill ....
Hillsborough, C. B., W.O............	....	Inverness... ....N S	Malcolm McNeil....
Hillsborough	....	Albert ....N B	R. E. Steves ......
Hillsburgh	Erin	Wellington, S. R........O	William Howe, sen..
Hillsdale	Medonte	Simcoe, N. R............O	Mrs. E. P. Faragher
Hillsdale, W.O.....	....	King's.. ....N B	N. P. Wanamake ..
Hill's Green........	Hay	Huron, S. R............O	Hugh Love, sen.....
Hillside, W.O......	....	Albert........ ....N B	P. Collicutt........
Hilton	Brighton	Northumberland, E. R..O	A. A. Becker .....
Hinch........	Camden, East	Addington.... ....O	William Hinch .....
Hoasic.	Williamsburg.......	Dundas.................O	Lewis Schwedfeger..
Hoath Head	Sydenham..........	Grey, N. R.............O	R. Hoath ....
Hochelaga..........	Island of Montreal..	Hochelaga..............Q	F. Painchaud .. ...
Hockley............	Adjala	Cardwell ....O	....
Holbrook..........	Norwich, North	Oxford, S. R...........O	A. M. Whitfield ...

NAME OF POST OFFICE.	TOWNSHIP OR PARISH.	ELECTORAL COUNTY OR DIVISION.	NAME OF POSTMASTER.
Holland Landing	Gwillimbury, East	York, N. R. .... O	Miss E. B. Sloane.
Hollen	Maryborough	Wellington, N. R. .... O	S. Robertson
Holmesville	Goderich	Huron, N. R. .... O	Edward Kelly
Holmesville, W. O.		Carleton .... N B	Isaac Broad
Holstein	Egremont	Grey, S. R. .... O	N. D. McKenzie
Holt	Gwillimbury, East	York, N. R. .... O	John Quibell
Holyrood	Kinloss	Bruce, S. R. .... O	A. T. Campbell.
Homer	Grantham	Lincoln .... O	Peter A. Cavers
Honeywood	Mulmur	Simcoe, S. R. .... O	George Lawrence
Hope		Yale .... B C	John G. Wirth
Hopetown	Lanark	Lanark, N. R. .... O	John White, jun.
Hopefield	Radcliffe	Renfrew, S. R .... O	Joseph Daly
Hope River	Number 22	Queens .... P E I	Felix Murphy
Hopewell, W.O		Albert .... N B	James Wright
Hopewell, W.O		Pictou .... N S	John Gunn.
Hopewell Cape		Albert .... N B	M. B. Palmer
Hopewell Corner, W. O		Albert .... N B	John C. Calhoun
Hopewell Hill, W.O.		Albert .... N B	John R. Russell
Hornby	Esquesing	Halton .... O	John McMillan
Horning's Mills	Melancthon	Grey, E. R. .... O	William Airth
Hornsey, W. O.		Cumberland .... N S	George Reeve
Horton Landing, W. O		King's .... N S	Frederic G. Curry
Houghton	Houghton	Norfolk, S. R. .... O	George Bundy
House Harbor (sub).	Magdalen Islands	Gaspé .... Q	Edward D. Paquet
Howe Island	Pittsburgh	Frontenac .... O	Thomas Thompson
Howick	Georgetown, South	Chateauguay .... Q	Thomas Gebbie
Hubbard's Cove		Halifax .... N S	J. E. Stratford
Hudson	Vaudreuil	Vaudreuil .... Q	David Ray
**Hull*	Hull	Ottawa .... Q	H. L. Loucks
Hullsville	Walpole	Haldimand .... O	John Hull
Humber	Etobicoke	York, W. R .... O	John Linton
Humberstone	Humberstone	Welland .... O	John Thompson
Hunsdon	Albion	Cardwell .... O	Henry Fry
Hunter's Mountain, W.O.		Victoria .... N S	John McDonald

NAME OF POST OFFICE.	TOWNSHIP OR PARISH.	ELECTORAL COUNTY OR DIVISION.	NAME OF POSTMASTER.
Hunterstown	Hunterstown	Maskinongé............ Q	Wilbert Newhall....
Huntersville........	Ramsay	Lanark, N. R.......... O	John Hunter .... ..
**Huntingdon*........	Godmanchester	Huntingdon .... Q	W. Marshall.......
Huntingville	Ascot	Sherbrooke .... Q	John W. Gamsby...
Huntley............	Huntley...........	Carleton .... O	John Hueston .....
Huntsville..........	Chaffey	Muskoka .... O	James F. Hanes ....
Huston.............	Maryboro'.........	Wellington, N. R. ...... O	David Callaway ....
Huttonsville........	Chinguacousy	Peel................... O	George James ......
Hyde Park Corner..	London	Middlesex, E. R .... O	Peter C. Thompson .

Ida	Cavan.............	Durham, E. R .... O	Alexander Baptie...
Ilderton	London	Middlesex, E. R......... O	George Ord........
Indiana	Seneca	Haldimand............. O	....
Indian Brook, W.O.	....	Victoria .... N S	Donald McLennan..
Indian Cove	....	Lévis....... .... Q	Patrick Wallace ....
Indian Harbor, W.O.	....	Halifax.......... .... N S	....
Indian Harbor, W.O.	....	Guysboro'............ N S	David Suttis........
Indian Island, W. O.	....	Charlotte............. N B	J. B. W. Chaffey ..
Indian Point, W. O.	....	Lunenburg .... N S	James Moser ....
Indian River	Number 18	Prince.............. P E I	J. McLellan........
Indian Road, W. O.	....	Hants .. .. N S	.. ..
Indian Town.......	....	St. John............. N B	William G. Brown..
**Ingersoll*..........	Oxford, North.....	Oxford, S. R... .... O	Joseph Thirkell.....
Ingoldsby	Minden	Peterboro', E. R .... O	Richard Smith......
Ingonish, W.O.....	....	Victoria .... N S	J. W. Burke. .....
Inistioge	Proton	Grey, E. R.... .... O	Henry Armstrong...

NAME OF POST OFFICE.	TOWNSHIP OR PARISH.	ELECTORAL COUNTY OR DIVISION.	NAME OF POSTMASTER.
Inkerman	Mountain	Dundas .... O	John Rennick ......
Innerkip	East Zorra..........	Oxford, N. R. .... O	Mrs. Sarah Begg ...
Innisfil	Innisfil	Simcoe, S. R .... O	Benjamin Ross.....
Innisville...........	Drummond.........	Lanark, S. R. .... O	Thomas Code.......
Intervale, W.O.....	....	Westmoreland........ N B	David Horseman....
Inverary	Storrington	Frontenac .... O	D. J. Walker.......
Inverhuron	Bruce	Bruce, N. R .... O	....
Invermay..........	Arran	Bruce, N. R .... O	Abraham Neelands .
**Inverness*	Inverness..........	Megantic .... Q	John McKinnon....
Inverness...........	Number 11	Prince .... P E I	Frederick McDonald
Iona	Dunwich	Elgin, W. R ... . O	Edmund Roche.....
Irish Cove, W.O....	....	Cape Breton.......... N S	Michael McDonald .
Irishtown, W.O	....	Westmoreland........ N B	John Larracey......
Iron Hill	Brome	Brome................. Q	John D. Shufelt ....
Ironside	Hull	Ottawa................ Q	Thomas Shehan.....
**Iroquois*	Matilda	Dundas....... .... O	James Grier ....
Irving Settlement, W.O	....	Albert............... N B	William E. Bishop .
Irvine	Inverness.	Megantic. .... Q	S. B. Thurber......
Isaac's Harbor, W.O.	....	Guysboro'........... N S	Allan McMillan,junr
Island Brook	Newport	Compton .... Q	W. W. Bailey......
Islay	Fenelon	Victoria, N. R .... O	Angus McEachern..
Isle aux Coudres(sub)	Isle aux Coudres...	Charlevoix............. Q	....
Isle aux Grues	Isle aux Grues	L'Islet .... Q	B. G. Lachaine dit Jolicœur ....
Isle Dupas..........	Isle Dupas	Berthier .... Q	Rev. V. Plinguet...
Isle Perrot	Isle Perrot	Vaudreuil .... Q	Marie S. Jobin .....
Isle Verte	Isle Verte	Témiscouata .... Q	Louis A. Bertrand ..
Islington	Etobicoke	York, W. R ... . O	Thomas Musson ....
Ivanhoe	Huntingdon	Hastings, N. R. .... O	Thomas Emo . .....
Ivy	Essa	Simcoe, S. R............ O	William H. Davis..

NAME OF POST OFFICE.	TOWNSHIP OR PARISH.	ELECTORAL COUNTY OR DIVISION.	NAME OF POSTMASTER.
Jackson, W.O	....	Cumberland..... .....**N S**	Wm. Jackson.......
Jackson	Derby....	Grey, N. R. ....**O**	G. R. Wright......
Jackson Road, W.O	....	King's................**N S**	Alexander Nichol...
Jacksontown, W. O	... .	Carleton. ....**N B**	F. L. Palmer ......
Jacksonville, W. O..	....	Carleton..............**N B**	James Simonson ...
Janetville	Manvers	Durham, E. R ....**O**	David McGill ......
Janeville, W. O.....	....	Gloucester............**N B**	Robert C. Caie......
Jarratt's Corners....	Oro	Simcoe, N.R............**O**	Charles Jarratt.....
Jarvis	Walpole...........	Haldimand ....**O**	Robert Sill ....
Jasper	Wolford......	Grenville, N. R. ....**O**	William S. Ralph ..
Jeddore, W. O......	....	Halifax...............**N S**	William Blakeny ...
Jemseg, W. O	....	Queen's...............**N B**	N. B. Cottle......
Jenkins, W. O......	....	Queen's...............**N B**	Joel Jenkins........
Jersey, River Chaudière.	St. George.........	Beauce ....**Q**	Michael Cahill......
Jerseyville	Ancaster	Wentworth, S. R. .. ...**O**	A. Hendershot .....
Joggin Mines, W. O.	....	Cumberland...........**N S**	B. B. Boggs ......
Johnson............	Sydenham	Grey, N. R. ....**O**	William Johnstone..
Johnson's Mills.....	Hay...............	Huron, S. R ....**O**	Henry Hayrock ....
Johnson Mills, W. O.	....	Westmoreland ....**N B**	Edward Babcock ....
Johnston's River	Number 48	Queen's............**P E I**	P. Gormley .... ..
Johnston, W. O.....	....	Queen's ....**N B**	Thomas Mason ....
Johnville	Eaton	Compton ....**Q**	Charles Smith ......
Johnville, W. O	....	Carleton..............**N B**	John Boyd ....
Jolicure, W. O....	....	Westmoreland ....**N B**	Rufus C. Wry .....
**Joliette*	....	Joliette...............**Q**	Eusèbe Asselin . ..
Jonquières..........	Jonquières	Chicoutimi ....**Q**	Xavier Brassard ....
Jordan	Louth	Lincoln. ....**O**	Clark Snure ... .
Jordan Bay, W. O...	....	Shelburne............**N S**	John Downie.......
Judique, W. O.	....	Inverness ....**N S**	Hugh McDonnell...
Jura	Bosanquet..........	Lambton . ...**O**	James McCordie....
uvenile Settlement, W. O..........	....	Sunbury..............**N B**	Arthur Graham.....

NAME OF POST OFFICE.	TOWNSHIP OR PARISH.	ELECTORAL COUNTY OR DIVISION.	NAME OF POSTMASTER.
Kaladar	Kaladar	Addington ... O	C. F. Dunham
Kamloops		Yale ... BC	W. B. Wilson
Kamouraska	St. Louis de Kamouraska	Kamouraska ... Q	Louis Chas. Bégin
Kars	North Gower	Carleton ... O	W. J. Wood
Kars, W.O.		King's ... NB	Wm. Worden
Katevale	Hatley	Stanstead ... Q	L. C. A. T. de Lagorgendiere
Kazubazua	Aylwin	Ottawa ... Q	
Kay Settlement, W. O.		Westmoreland ... NB	Alexander Hughes
Keady	Derby	Grey, N.R. ... O	James Gilchrist
Keenansville	Adjala	Cardwell ... O	G. P. Hughes
**Keene*	Otonabee	Peterborough, E.R. ... O	W. J. Hall
Keith	Chatham	Kent ... O	Lewis Huff
Keithley Creek		Cariboo ... B C	George Keith
Kelly's Cross	No. 29	Queen's ... P E I	William Heard
Kelso	Elgin	Huntingdon ... Q	Peter MacFarlane
Kelvin	Windham	Norfolk, N.R. ... O	John Armour, jun.
Kemble	Keppel	Grey, N.R. ... O	P. McQuaid
Kempt, W.O.		Queen's ... N S	
Kempt Bridge, W.O.		Yarmouth ... N S	Elkanah Travis
Kempt Head, W.O.		Victoria ... N S	K. McKenzie
Kempt Road, W.O.		Richmond ... N S	Hugh Cameron
Kempt Town, W.O.		Colchester ... N S	A. S. Hingley
**Kemptville*	Oxford	Grenville, N.R. ... O	Robert Leslie
Kemptville, W.O.		Yarmouth ... N S	J. H. Hamilton
Kendal	Clarke	Durham, W.R. ... O	J. R. Anderson
Kennebec Line	Marlowe	Beauce ... Q	George Bartley
Kenilworth	Arthur	Wellington, N.R. ... O	Robert Hayward
Kenmore	Osgoode	Russell ... O	John B. Brannen
Kennetcook, W.O.		Hants ... N S	I. S. Sanford
Kennetcook Corner, W.O.		Hants ... N S	Mrs L. Densmore
Kent Bridge	Chatham	Kent ... O	John B. Shaw
Kent's Island, W.O.		Halifax ... N S	John Naufts
Kentville		King's ... N S	G. E. Calkin

NAME OF POST OFFICE.	TOWNSHIP OR PARISH.	ELECTORAL COUNTY OR DIVISION.	NAME OF POSTMASTER.
Kepler	Kingston	Frontenac ... O	Isaac J. Coglan
Kerrwood	Adelaide	Middlesex, N.R. ... O	James Irving
Kerry	Plantagenet, S	Prescott ... O	Magloire Parent
Kertch	Plympton	Lambton ... O	
Keswick	North Gwillimbury	York, N.R. ... O	Henry Stennett
Keswick Ridge, W. O.		York ... N B	Abraham McKeen
Ketch Harbor, W.O.		Halifax ... N S	
Kettleby	King	York, N. R. ... O	Jacob Walton
Kewstoke, W.O.		Inverness ... N S	Alex McQuain
Keyser	Adelaide	Middlesex, N. R. ... O	Samuel Cooper
Kilbride	Nelson	Halton ... O	Robert Parker
Kildare	Kildare	Joliette ... Q	O. Vigneault
Kildare	No. 3	Prince ... P E I	John Wade
Kildonan	Kildonan	Selkirk ... M	John Fraser
Kilkenny	Kilkenny	Montcalm ... Q	Damase Thouin
Killarney		Algoma ... O	Chas. Lamorandière
Killean	Puslinch	Wellington, S. R. ... O	D. Ferguson
Killerby	Yarmouth	Elgin, E. R. ... O	John Hicks
Kilmanagh	Caledon	Peel ... O	Thos. Sanderson
Kilmarnock	Wolford	Grenville, N. R. ... O	George Newsome
Kilmartin	Metcalfe	Middlesex, W. R. ... O	D. McKellar
Kilmaurs	Torbolton	Carleton ... O	William Munro
Kilsyth	Derby	Grey, N. R. ... O	Thomas Sloan
Kimberley	Euphrasia	Grey, E. R. ... O	Alex. Hy. McLean
Kinburn	Fitzroy	Carleton ... O	
**Kincardine*	Kincardine	Bruce, S.R. ... O	M. McKendrick
Kincardine, W.O.		Victoria ... N B	— Taylor
King	King	York, N.R. ... O	Benjamin Lloyd
King Creek	King	York, N. R. ... O	
Kinglake	Houghton	Norfolk, S. R. ... O	Saml. Leybourne
Kingsbridge	Ashfield	Huron, N. R. ... O	Francis L. Eagan
Kingsbury	Melbourne	Richmond ... Q	George Williamson
Kingsbury, W. O.		Lunenburg ... N S	Edward Mossman
Kingsclear, W.O.		York ... N B	J. A. Hammond

NAME OF POST OFFICE.	TOWNSHIP OR PARISH.	ELECTORAL COUNTY OR DIVISION.		NAME OF POSTMASTER.
Kingsey	Kingsey	Drummond	Q	
Kingsey Falls	Kingsey	Drummond	Q	Smith Leith
Kingsford	Tyendinaga	Hastings, E. R.	O	
Kingsley, W.O.		York	N B	George N. Foster
**Kingston*	Kingston	Kingston	O	Robert Deacon
Kingston		King's	N B	Samuel Foster
Kingston		Kent	N B	John Harnett
Kingston Mills	Kingston	Frontenac	O	Charles Harrison
Kingston Village, W. O.		King's	N S	John Wheelock
**Kingsville*	Gosfield	Essex	O	Jas. H. Smart
Kinkora	Ellice	Perth, N. R.	O	James Moriarty
Kinloss	Kinloss	Bruce, S. R.	O	John Harrison
Kinlough	Kinloss	Bruce, S.R.	O	
Kinmount	Somerville	Victoria, N. R.	O	Charles Moffitt
Kinnear's Mills	Leeds	Megantic	Q	James Kinnear
Kinross	No. 50	Queen's	P E I	David Ross
Kinsale	Pickering	Ontario, S. R.	O	Levi Mackey
Kinsman's Corner, W.O		King's	N S	Benjamin Kinsman
Kintail	Ashfield	Huron, N. R.	O	William Grant
Kintore	East Nissouri	Oxford, N. R.	O	William Easson
Kippen	Tuckersmith	Huron, C. R.	O	Robert Mellis
Kippewa		Pontiac	Q	Thomas Anderson
Kirby	Clarke	Durham, W. R.	O	James Jackson
Kirkdale	Durham	Drummond	Q	William Burril
**Kirkfield*	Eldon	Victoria, N. R.	O	John McTaggart
Kirkhill	Lochiel	Glengarry	O	William McLeod
Kirkhill, W. O.		Cumberland	N S	William Smith
Kirk's Ferry	Hull	Ottawa	Q	John Kirk
Kirkton	Usborne	Huron, S. R.	O	John McCurdy
Kirkwall	Beverley	Wentworth, N. R.	O	W. McMillan
Klineburg	Vaughan	York, W. R.	O	Thomas White
Knapdale	Mosa	Middlesex, W. R.	O	Hector McLean
Knatchbull	Nassagiweya	Halton	O	William Reid
Knowlesville, W. O.		Carleton	N B	R. Ricker

NAME OF POST OFFICE.	TOWNSHIP OR PARISH.	ELECTORAL COUNTY OR DIVISION.	NAME OF POSTMASTER.
*_Knowlton_	Brome	Brome Q	Albert Kimball
Knowlton Landing	Potton	Brome Q	J. F. Tuck
Knoxford, W. O.		Carleton N B	Thomas Fulton
Knoydart, W. O.		Pictou N S	John McGilleroy
Komoka	Lobo	Middlesex, N. R. O	Robert Hord
Kootenay (sub)		Yale B C	James Normansell
Kossuth	Waterloo	Waterloo, S. R. O	
Kouchibouguac		Kent N B	
La Baie	La Baie des Febvres	Yamaska Q	J. L. Belcourt
Labarre	Labarre	Chicoutimi Q	C. Hébert
La Beauce	St. Marie	Beauce Q	Mme. C. Bonneville
L'Acadie	L'Acadie	St. John's Q	C. T. Charbonneau
Lachenaie	Lachenaie	L'Assomption Q	J. O. Laurier
*_Lachine_	Montreal	Jacques Cartier Q	Napoléon Duquet
*_Lachute_	Argenteuil	Argenteuil Q	George L. Meikle
Lac Masson	Wexford	Terrebonne Q	C. C. Lajeunesse
Lac Noir	Fournier	L'Islet Q	J. B. Pelletier
Lacolle	Lacolle	St. John's Q	T. Van Vliet
Lafontaine	Tiny	Simcoe, N. R. O	Charles Picotte
Laggan	Kenyon	Glengarry O	Donald Cattanach
La Guerre	St. Anicet	Huntingdon Q	John McDonald
La Have Cross Roads W. O		Lunenburg N S	Isaac Heckman
La Have River, W. O.		Lunenburg N S	Mrs. M. A. Cronan
Lake Ainslie, W. O.		L[illegible]	[illegible]

NAME OF POST OFFICE.	TOWNSHIP OR PARISH.	ELECTORAL COUNTY OR DIVISION.	NAME OF POSTMASTER.
Lake Ainslie (East side), W.O.	....	Inverness............N S	Charles McDonald..
Lake Ainslie (South side), W. O.......	....	Inverness... ....N S	John McKinnon .. .
Lake Aylmer.......	Stratford	Wolfe...... ....Q	George Champoux ..
Lake Beauport	St. Dunstan	Quebec................Q	A. Simmons ....
Lake Doré	Wilberforce.........	Renfrew, N. R..........O	John Shaw, jun.....
Lake Etchemin.....	Ware	Dorchester ....Q	Joseph Begin.......
Lakefield	Gore	Argenteuil.............Q	George Rogers......
Lakefield, W.O....	... .	King's ....N B	Charles M. Sherwood
Lake George W.O..	....	York................ N B	Leveret S, Tilley ...
Lake George, W.O..	... .	King's...............N S	A. P. Hudgens .....
Lake George, W.O..	....	Yarmouth ....N S	Charles Crosby .....
Lakehurst..........	Harvey	Peterborough, E. R.....O	John Tarlington ....
Lake La Hache.....	....	Cariboo..............B C	Patrick Gannon ...
Lakelands, W.O....	....	Cumberland...... ....N S	James E. Brown....
Lake Law, W.O....	....	Inverness............N S	James Fortune......
Lakelet	Howick	Huron, N. R. ....O	Myles Young.......
Lake Megantic	Whitton............	Compton ....Q	J. McDonald.......
Lake Opinicon......	Storrington.........	Frontenac ....O	Bryce T. Davidson .
Lake Road, W O...	....	Cumberland..... .....N S	Gains Lewis ....
Lake Settlement, W.O............	....	Kent.................N B	M. Flannigan ......
Lakeside	Nissouri, East	Oxford, N. R. ... .O	Robert Armstrong ..
Lake Temiscamingue	....	Pontiac ....Q	Charles Stuart .....
Lakevale, W.O.....	....	Antigonishe..........N S	A. McGillivray.....
Lakeville, W.O.....	....	Carleton.......... ...N B	J. S. Carvell.......
Lakeville, W.O.....	....	King's...............N S	Reuben Chase ......
Lakeville Corner, W.O.	... .	Sunbury.............N B	James Thompson ...
Lake Weedon	Weedon	Wolfe..................Q	Francois Briére .....
L'Amable	Dungannon.........	Hastings, N. R.........O	John R. Tait ......
L'Amaroux........	York...............	York, W. R............O	William Long ......
Lambeth	Westminster........	Middlesex, E. R........O	George Kelley ......
Lambton	St. Vital de Lambton	Beauce ....Q	Dr. Louis Labrècque
**Lanark*...........	Lanark.............	Lanark, N. R ....O	Alexander Munro .
Lancaster	Lancaster	Glengarry ....O	John Fraser ....

NAME OF POST OFFICE.	TOWNSHIP OR PARISH.	ELECTORAL COUNTY OR DIVISION.	NAME OF POSTMASTER.
Lang..............	Otonabee.........	Peterboro', E. R....... O	Richard Short, sen..
Langevin...........	Langevin	Dorchester ....Q	Louis Vermette.....
Langford'...........	Brantford	Brant, N. R............O	Alex. Milne ....
Langley............	....	New Westminster.....B C	W. W. Gibb........
Langside	Kinloss...........	Bruce, S. R.........O	Wm. Gleeson......
Langstaff (sub)......	Markham	York, E. R. ....O	John Langstaff .....
Langton	Walsingham	Norfolk, S. R...........O	James Fulton.......
Lanoraie	Lanoraie	Berthier............... Q	T. D. Latour ......
Lansdown	Lansdown	Leeds, S. R............O	Jos. A. Bradley....
L'Anse à Giles......	L'Islet	L'Islet ....Q	J. F. Giasson ......
L'Anse au Foin.....	Tremblay..........	Chicoutimi.............Q	P. Potvin ....
Lansing	York	York, E. R. ....O	Joseph Shepard.....
Lantz, W.O	....	Lunenburg............N S	Harvey B. Lantz...
La Petite Rivière St. François (sub)	Petite Rivière	Charlevoix ....Q	....
La Pigeonnière	La Salle..	Napierville ....Q	M. Blain. ....
**Laprairie*.........	Laprairie	Laprairie...............Q	Julien Brosseau.....
La Présentation	La Présentation	St. Hyacinthe ....Q	Alexis Millet ....
Lapum.	Loughborough	Frontenac ....O	Calvin H. Knowlton
L'Ardoise, W.O.....	....	Richmond ....N S	Michael McNiel ....
Largie	Dunwich...........	Elgin, W. R............O	Allan McPherson...
Larochelle	Halifax	Megantic.... .... Q	J. T. Hébert.......
Larry's River, W.O,	Wilmot	Guysboro'............N S	Jos. Fougére ....
Laskay	King...........	York, N. R..... ....O	Henry Baldwin.....
**L'Assomption*	St. Sulpice	L'Assomption ....Q	Louis Guilbault.....
Laterrière	Notre Dame de Laterrière	Chicoutimi ....Q	George McKenzie...
Latona.............	Glenelg............	Grey, S. R.............O	Mark Appleby.....
Laugill's, W.O......	....	Lunenburg...........N S	J. S. Laugill.......
Laurel	Amaranth	Wellington, N. R.......O	James Hamilton....
Lauzon	Lauzon............	Lévis............... .....Q	Charles Bourget ....
Laval	Laval	Montmorency..... .. ..Q	John Keough.......
Lavaltrie	Lavaltrie	Berthier................Q	Joseph Charland....
Lavant............	Lavant	Lanark, N. R ....O	Archd. Browning...
Lavender..........	Mulmur...........	Simcoe, S. R...... .....O	I. B. Mastin.......
L'Avenir	Durham ..., ...	Drummond ....Q	C. Gagnon ....

NAME OF POST OFFICE.	TOWNSHIP OR PARISH.	ELECTORAL COUNTY OR DIVISION.		NAME OF POSTMASTER.
Lawrence Factory, W.O.		Cumberland	N S	Charles Lawrence
Lawrence Station, W.O.		Charlotte	N B	H. M. Mercer
Lawrencetown		Annapolis	N S	J. W. James
Lawrencetown, W.O.		Halifax	N S	Samuel Hiltz
Lawrenceville	South Ely	Shefford	Q	E. Lawrence
Layton	Brock	Ontario, N. R	O	John Sornberger
Leamington	Mersea	Essex	O	Warren Kimball
Learned Plain	Newport	Compton	Q	E. Learned
Leaskdale	Scott	Ontario, N. R	O	George Leask
Leclercville	Ste. Emélie	Lotbinière	Q	Joseph Lord
Ledge, W.O		Charlotte	N B	Bridget Leary Couley
**Leeds*	Leeds	Megantic	Q	Sarah Jiggens
Leeds Village	Leeds	Megantic	Q	Hugh McCutcheon
Lefroy	Innisfil	Simcoe, S. R	O	David Davidson
Leicester, W.O		Cumberland	N S	D. Lockhart
Leinster	Richmond	Lennox	O	M. Jordan
Leitch's Creek, W.O.		Cape Breton	N S	Alex. McDonald
Leith	Sydenham	Grey, N. R	O	James Ross, jun.
Lemesurier	Leeds	Megantic	Q	John Wilkin
Lemonville	Whitchurch	York, N. R	O	W. L. White
Lennox	Innisfil	Simcoe, S. R	O	Isaac Lennox
Lennox Ferry, W.O.		Richmond	N S	Daniel Clough
**Lennoxville*	Ascot	Sherbrooke	Q	Ephraim W. Abbott
Leonard's Hill	Wickham	Drummond	Q	M. Leonard
L'Epiphanie	St. Sulpice	L'Assomption	Q	F. Le Blanc
Lepreaux		Charlotte	N B	William R. Reynolds
Lequille, W.O		Annapolis	N S	Alfred Hoyt
Les Eboulemens	Eboulemens	Charlevoix	Q	Cleophe Coté
Les Ecureuils	Ecureuils	Portneuf	Q	Pierre Pagé
Les Escoumains	Escoumains	Saguenay	Q	John C. Barry

NAME OF POST OFFICE.	TOWNSHIP OR PARISH.	ELECTORAL COUNTY OR DIVISION.	NAME OF POSTMASTER.
**Lévis*	Lauzon	Lévis ... Q	Francois Bertrand
Lewis Bay, W.O		Cape Breton ... N S	Donald Gillis
Lewis Head, W.O		Shelburne ... N S	Wm. Herkins
Lewis Mountain, W.O		Westmoreland ... N B	James Lounsbury
Lewisville, W.O		Westmoreland ... N B	Stephen Mills
Lieury	McGillivray	Middlesex, N. R ... O	Alexander Smith
Lifford	Manvers	Durham, E. R ... O	Miss Jane Fowler
Lilley's Corners (sub)	London	London ... O	Charles Lilley
Lilloet		Cariboo ... B C	Alfred Smith
Limehouse	Esquesing	Halton ... O	John Newton
Lime Lake	Hungerford	Hastings, E. R ... O	James Jarmin
Lime Rock, W.O		Pictou ... N S	Mrs. Mary McDonald
Lincoln, W.O		Sunbury ... N B	Isaac S. Taylor
Linda	Westbury	Compton ... Q	Daniel B. Hall
**Lindsay*	Ops	Victoria, S. R ... O	Thomas Adam
Lindsay, W.O		Carleton ... N B	Alex. Lindsay
Lineboro'	Stanstead	Stanstead ... Q	James W. House
Lingan		Cape Breton ... N S	Ronald McDonald
Linton	King	York, N. R ... O	Joseph Lynn
Linton's, W.O		Sunbury ... N B	Adam Johnson
Linwood	Wellesley	Waterloo, N. R ... O	Robert Y. Fish
Lisbon	North Easthope	Perth, N. R ... O	John Zinkann
Lisburn	Huron	Bruce, S. R ... O	Daniel Teskey
Liscomb, W.O		Guysborough ... N S	James Hemlow
L'Islet	L'Islet	L'Islet ... Q	Mrs. M. E. Ballantine
**Listowel*	Wallace	Perth, N. R ... O	W. H. Hacking
Little Branch, W.O		Northumberland ... N B	Alex. Cameron
Little Bras d'Or		Cape Breton ... N S	John H. Christie
Little Britain	Mariposa	Victoria, S. R ... O	John Broad
Little Current	Howland	Algoma ... O	G. B. Abrey
Little Glace Bay		Cape Breton ... N S	Daniel McDonald
Little Harbor	Number 46	King's ... P E I	Andrew Mooney
Little Harbor, W.O		Pictou ... N S	James Stewart
Little Judique, W.O		Inverness ... N S	Angus Beaton

NAME OF POST OFFICE.	TOWNSHIP OR PARISH.	ELECTORAL COUNTY OR DIVISION.	NAME OF POSTMASTER.
Little Lepreaux, W.O	....	Charlotte.. ....N B	W. McGowan......
Little Lorraine, W.O	. ...	Cape Breton.........N S	Joseph McDonald...
LittleNarrows, W.O	....	Inverness........ ....N S	Hugh McAskil... ..
Little Rideau.......	Hawkesbury, East..	Prescott ....O	Thomas Ross ....
Little Ridge, W.O...	....	Albert...............N B	....
Little River (Coverdale), W.O......	... .	Albert...............N B	William Leemans...
Little River (Elgin), W.O	... .	Albert.............. .N B	Hiram Killam ......
Little River, W.O...	....	Sunbury.............N B	M. H. Coburn. ..
Little River, W.O...	....	Antigonishe..........N S	Levi Irish ....
Little River, W.O...	....	Cumberland..........N S	J. Lawrence Purdy.
Little River, W.O...	....	Digby ....N S	P. W. Frost........
Little River (Mid. Musquodoboit), W. O...............	....	Halifax..............N S	W. G. Cole.........
Little Rocher, W.O.	....	Albert ....N B	John Richardson....
Little Sands........	Number 64	King's.............P E I	D. Munn ....
Little Shemogue, W. O........	....	Albert..... ......N B	Thomas Oulton.....
Little Shippegan, W. O...............	....	Gloucester...........N B	Mary Wilson. .....
Little Tignish......	Number 2..	Prince.............P E I	Stephen S. Arseneaux
Little Tracadie, W.O	. ...	Antigonishe..........N S	Joseph Symonds....
Littlewood, W.O....	....	Shelburne............N S	James Littlewood...
Little York	Number 31	Queen's. ....P E I	Robert Lawson .....
Liverpool	....	Queen's... ....N S	Archd. J. Campbell.
Livingston's Cove, W. O...............	....	Antigonishe......... N S	John Livingston....
Lloydtown	King.....	York, N. R............O	Anthony Eastwood .
Lobo.........	Lobo..............	Middlesex, N. R........O	T. S. Edwards......
Lochaber, W.O.....	.. ..	Antigonishe..... .....N S	Mrs. M. Sears ......
Lochaber Bay	Lochaber..........	Ottawa ....Q	Archibald Campbell.
Lockhartville, W.O.	....	King's.... ....N S	William Glenn.....
Loch Garry	Kenyon	Glengarry ....O	James Fraser.......
Lochiel.............	Lochiel............	Glengarry ....O	Angus Chisholm....
Lochinvar..........	Lochiel............	Glengarry .... .O	Simon Fraser.......
Loch Lomond, W.O.	....	St. John ....N B	Daniel Robertson...

NAME OF POST OFFICE.	TOWNSHIP OR PARISH.	ELECTORAL COUNTY OR DIVISION.	NAME OF POSTMASTER.
Loch Lomond, W.O.	... .	Richmond ....N S	Roderick Bethune...
Lochside, W.O	....	Richmond ....N S	D. McDougall. ...
Locke Port..........	.. ..	Shelburne ....N S	....
Locksley	Alice...............	Renfrew, N. R..........O	W. M. Walford.....
Lockton......	Albion	Cardwell .... O	....
Lockville	Mountain	Dundas.............. ......O	Isaac Dillabough....
Loganville, W.O ...	....	Pictou .... N S	Dugal Logan ....
Logierait	Moore...	Lambton ....O	D. Hossie ....
Lombardy, late South Elmsley	South Elmsley......	Leeds, N. R...... ......O	James O. Mara .....
Londesborough	Hullett.............	Huron, C. R.............O	Hugh Wallace ......
**London*....	London	London........ ....O	Lawrence Lawless .
Londonderry, W.O .	....	King's.......... ......N B	James Douglas......
Londonderry	....	Colchester ....N S	Robert S. Crowe....
Long Creek.........	Number 65	Queen's............P E I	H. McEwen........
Long Creek, W.O...	....	Queen's ....N B	John Secord, jun....
Long Island	....	Digby ....N S	J. W. Eldrige ......
Long Island Locks..	Gloucester....	Russell .... O	Thomas May.......
Long River.........	Number 20.	Queen's............P E I	Archibald Cousins ..
Long Lake	Olden...............	Addington ....O	James Bender ......
Long Point.	....	Hochelaga.... ....Q	....
Long Point, W.O. .	....	King's................N B	John Coulter ....
Long Point, W.O...	....	Inverness.............N S	Duncan McDonald..
Long Point, W.O...	....	King's.... .. ..N S	Henry Ogilvie ......
Long Reach, W.O ..	....	King's................N B	James M. Smith....
Long Settlement, WO	. ...	Carleton...............N B	James H. Sproul....
Longueuil	Longueuil	Chambly .... Q	P. Lesperance . ....
Longwood...........	Ekfrid	Middlesex, W. R........O	Thomas Gordon ....
Longwood Station ..	Caradoc	Middlesex, W. R........O	Mrs. J. A. White...
Lonsdale	Tyendinaga	Hastings, E. R..........O	Richard Wildman...
Lord's Cove, W.O...	....	Charlotte. ....N B	Thomas K. Parker..
Lorette.............	St. Ambroise	Quebec ....Q	J. G. Vincent .....
Loretto	Adjala	Cardwell .... .O	P. D. Kelly ... .
**L'Orignal*	Longueuil	Prescott ....O	C. Johnson ....
Lorne	Kincardine	Bruce, S. R.............O	James Jack.........

NAME OF POST OFFICE.	TOWNSHIP OR PARISH.	ELECTORAL COUNTY OR DIVISION.	NAME OF POSTMASTER.
Lorraine	Mono	Cardwell ... O	John Mills
Lorway Mines, W.O		Cape Breton ... N S	James Corbett
Lotbinière	Lotbinière	Lotbinière ... Q	M. Lemay
Lot 1	Number 1	Prince ... P E I	P. Dalton
„ 4	do 4	Prince ... P E I	Dennis Carrol
„ 6	do 6	Prince ... P E I	W. Hardy
„ 8	do 8	Prince ... P E I	A. Ramsey
„ 10	do 10	Prince ... P E I	William Vincent
„ 11	do 11	Prince ... P E I	J. Henderson
„ 12	do 12	Prince ... P E I	William Hayes
„ 14	do 14	Prince ... P E I	John O'Connor
„ 16	do 16	Prince ... P E I	D. Campbell
„ 30	do 30	Prince ... P E I	Patrick Trainer
„ 35	do 35	Queen's ... P E I	H. McLeod
„ 45	do 45	King's ... P E I	Herman McDonald
„ 56	do 56	King's ... P E I	William Norton
„ 67	do 67	Queen's ... P E I	M. McDonald
Lotus	Manvers	Durham, E. R ... O	David Bingham
Loughborough	Loughborough	Addington ... O	Hugh Madden
Louisburg, W.O		Cape Breton ... N S	Joseph Kennedy
Louisville	Chatham	Kent ... O	R. C. Struthers
Lovat	Greenock	Bruce, S. R ... O	Thomas Allen
Low	Low	Ottawa ... Q	Caleb Brooks
Lowbanks	Moulton	Monck ... O	Isaac Michener
Lower Argyle, W.O.		Yarmouth ... N S	J. H. McLaren
LowerBarney's River W.O.		Pictou ... N S	David Patterson
LowerBrighton, W.O		Carleton ... N B	
Lower Canterbury, W.O.		York ... N B	George Ingraham
Lower Cape, W.O.		Albert ... N B	Joseph Taylor
Lower Cove, W.O		Cumberland ... N S	Amos Seaman
Lower Coverdale, W. O		Albert ... N B	James Rogers
Lower Fort Garry	St. Andrews, N.	Lisgar ... M	Donald Gunn
Lower Freetown	Number 25	Prince ... P E I	George Burns

NAME OF POST OFFICE.	TOWNSHIP OR PARISH.	ELECTORAL COUNTY OR DIVISION.	NAME OF POSTMASTER.
Lower French Village W.O	....	York.................N B	George Risteen .....
Lower Granville, W. O	....	Annapolis ....N S	J. C. Shafner.......
Lower Hayneville, W.O	....	York.................N B	George J. Sharp....
Lower Horton.......	....	King's...............N S	E. McLatchy.......
Lower Ireland......	Ireland............	Megantic........ ......Q	Edward Redman....
Lower La Have, W. O	....	Lunenburg..... ......N S	Joseph Oxner .....
Lower L'Ardoise, W. O	....	Richmond ....N S	James Matheson....
Lower Line, Queensbury, W.O	....	York.................N B	J. H. Tupper.......
Lower Montague ...	Number 59.........	King's........... ..P E I	Sarah McNeill......
Lower Newcastle, W O	....	Northumberland .....N B	John Delany........
Lower Pereaux, W.O	....	King's...............N S	Philip Brown.......
Lower Pockmouche, W.O	....	Gloucester...........N B	P. Robicheau ......
Lower Prince William W.O	....	York.................N B	John Wasson.......
Lower Prospect, W. O	....	Halifax..............N S	Samuel F. Blackburn
Lower Queensbury, W.O	....	York.................N B	James W. Brown...
Lower River Inhabitants, W.O	....	Richmond ....N S	Jos. McCarthy ....
Lower Selmah, W.O	....	Hants ....N S	William Creelman ..
Lower Settlement, Middle River, W.O	....	Victoria ....N S	Finlay McRae......
Lower Settlement, South River, W.O	....	Antigonishe..........N S	Daniel Fraser........
Lower Southampton, W.O	....	York.................N B	George Grosvenor...
Lower Stewiacke	....	Colchester ....N S	F. H. Holesworth ..
Lower Turtle Creek, W.O	....	Albert................N B	G. A. Fillmore.....
Lower Wakefield, W. O	....	Carlton..............N B	Stephen Brittain....
Lower Ward, Ste. Marguerite's Bay, W.O	....	Halifax..............N S	James A. Nickerson.
Lower Wood Harbor, W.O	....	Shelburne .... N S	S. K. Mood ....

NAME OF POST OFFICE.	TOWNSHIP OR PARISH.	ELECTORAL COUNTY OR DIVISION.	NAME OF POSTMASTER.
Lower Woodstock, W.O.	....	Carleton........N B	John Riordon......
Low Point, W.O ...	....	Inverness ....N S	Angus McMaster ...
Lowville	Nelson	Halton ....O	Francis E. Morse...
**Lucan*..........	Biddulph........	Middlesex, N. R........O	William Porte......
Lucerne	Wakefield	Ottawa ....Q	Robert Blackburn ..
**Lucknow*.	Kinloss........	Bruce, S. R........O	M. Campbell ....
Ludlow, W.O.......	....	Northumberland......N B	John Nelson........
Lumley..........	Usborne........	Huron, S. R........O	William Dinnin ....
Lunenburg	Osnabruck	Stormont ....O	F. Kirkpatrick .....
Lunenburg........	....	Lunenburg........N S	Mrs. A. M. Rudolph
Lurgan..........	Huron	Bruce, S. R........O	James McCrindle...
Lutes Mountain W.O	....	Westmoreland........N B	Alfred M. Bunnell..
Luther	Luther........	Wellington, N. R. ......O	William Dawson....
Luton	Malahide........	Elgin, E. R........O	L. R. Tyrell ......
**Lyn*	Elizabethtown	Brockville ....O	John S. Bell........
Lynden..........	Beverley	Wentworth, N. R. .. ..O	James E. Orr.......
Lyndhurst..........	Lansdowne	Leeds, S. R........O	John Roddick ......
Lynedock	Charlotteville.......	Norfolk, S. R........O	George Gray........
Lynnfield, W.O	....	Charlotte........N B	John J. Getchell....
Lynnville	Windham	Norfolk, N. R........O	Wellington Axford..
Lyons	Dorchester, South ..	Elgin, E. R........O	James Armstrong...
Lyster	Nelson	Megantic ....Q	John King ....
Lyttleton, W.O	....	Northumberland.... N B	David Somers ......
Lytton	....	Yale........ ..B C	John Boyd ....

NAME OF POST OFFICE.	TOWNSHIP OR PARISH.	ELECTORAL COUNTY OR DIVISION.	NAME OF POSTMASTER.
McAdam Junction, W.O.		York ... N B	James Haddock ....
McDonald's Corner, W.O.		Queen's ... N B	Hiram Humphries..
McDonald's Corners,	Dalhousie ...	Lanark, N. R. ... O	Wm. Lock ...
McDonald's Point, W.O.		Queen's ... N B	D. N. Smith...
McDougall Settlement, W.O		Westmoreland ... N B	Col. McDougall ....
McGillivray ...	McGillivray ...	Middlesex, N. R ... O	D. Shoff...
McIntyre ...	Osprey ...	Grey, E. R . ... O	Edward Potts .....
McKay's Point, W.O		Victoria ... N S	Malcolm McLean...
McKellar ...	McKellar ...	Muskoka ... O	Samuel Armstrong..
McKenzie's Corner, W.O.		Carleton ... N B	John Y. Hoyt.....
McLaughlan Road, W.O.		Kent ... N B	Ira Hicks ...
McLellan's Mountain, W.O.		Pictou ... N S	Donald Fraser....
McLennan's Brook, W.O.		Pictou ... N S	Alexander Fraser ...
McLeod's Mills, W.O.		Kent ... N B	George McLeod ....
McPherson's Ferry, W.O.		Richmond ... N S	James Smith ......
Maberly...	Sherbrooke, South..	Lanark, S.R. ... O	Richard Mayberry..
Mabou ...		Inverness ... N S	William Grant.....
Mabou Coal Mines, W.O.		Inverness ... N S	...
Mabou Harbor, W.O		Inverness ... N S	Donald McDonald..
Maccan, W.O		Cumberland ... N S	Robert Roach .....
Maccan Mountain, W.O.		Cumberland ... N S	W. B. Lodge .. ....
Mace's Bay...		Charlotte ... N B	Robert V. Hanson..
Macnider...	L'Assomption	Rimouski ... Q	F. Saucier...
Mactaquack, W.O..		York ... N B	James Mitchell....
Macton ...	Peel...	Wellington, C.R. ... O	J. M. McCormick ..
Macville ...	Albion ...	Cardwell... O	Seth Wilson ...
Maddington ...	Maddington ...	Arthabaska ... Q	F. H. St. Germain..
Madisco, W.O...		Gloucester ... N B	Mrs. Des Brisay....
**Madoc* ...	Madoc ...	Hastings, N.R. ... O	E. D. O'Flynn.....

...SHIP OR ...RISH.	ELECTORAL COUNTY OR DIVISION.	NAME OF POSTMASTER
....	York .... N B	Solomon Vail.......
....	Gaspé .... Q	John D. Tuzo ......
...a	Muskoka .... O	James Miller ....
....	Stanstead .... Q	Calvin Abbot.......
...d	Stanstead .... Q	Aaron Magoon .....
....	Saguenay .... Q	Peter Skelton ......
....	York .... N B	James Henry.......
....	Lunenburg............ N S	Lewis Knaut ....
...h	Essex .... O	Thomas Moran. ....
....	Cape Breton............ N S	Clara Rigby ....
....	Grenville, S.R .... O	George C. Longley..
....	Hants .... N S	Adam Roy ....
....	Annapolis .... N S	W. H. Dukeshire...
....	Yarmouth .... N S	Charles Steele ......
....	Cumberland .... N S	Robert McDonald ..
....	Inverness .... N S	L. McDonald ......
...ough	Carleton .... O	W. J. Pierce ......
....	Bruce, S.R .... O	Daniel Sullivan.....
....	Antigonishe .... N S	Donald McLean ....
....	Leeds, S.R............ O	Frederick F. Lee ...
...lge	Missisquoi .... Q	A. Lanthier ....
...a	Hastings, N.R............ O	George Richardson..
....	Peel .... O	J. B. Allen.........
...ough	York, E.R .... O	Smith Thomson.....
....	Ontario, N.R .... O	John Taylor........
....	Guysborough............ N S	James M. Whitman.
...on	Lambton .... O	Albert F. Clarke....
...sa............	Victoria, S.R .... O	Mary Douglas ......
...ack	Algoma............ O	Alexander McGregor Ironside ....
....	York .... N B	George Lister.......
....	Waterloo, S.R .... O	Charles Lederman ..
...Gower............	Carleton .... O	G. L. Dickinson ....
...:	Simcoe, S. R............ O	William Gilbert ....
	.... Q	David A. Manson...

NAME OF POST OFFICE	TOWNSHIP OR PARISH.	ELECTORAL COUNTY OR DIVISION.	NAME OF POSTMASTER.
Maple Bay		Vancouver B C	William Beaumont
Maple Green, W.O.		Restigouche N B	James Fraser
Maple Grove	Ireland	Megantic Q	Henry Cross, jun
Maple Hill	Brant	Bruce, S.R O	George Inglis, jun
Maple Leaf	Newport	Compton Q	William G. Planch
Mapleton	Yarmouth	Elgin, E.R O	William Appleford
Mapleton	St. Peter's.	Lisgar M	Alex. McKenzie
Mapleton, W.O		Albert N B	W. A. Colpits
Maple Valley	Nottawasaga	Simcoe, N.R. O	James Dick
Maquapit Lake, W.O		Queen's N B	John Stone
Mar	Albemarle	Bruce, N.R O	Thos. H. Lee
Marathon	Fitzroy	Carleton O	
Marble Mountain, W O		Inverness N S	Nicholas J. Brown
Marble Rock	Leeds	Leeds, S.R O	George Emery
Marbleton	Dudswell	Wolfe Q	J. B. Bishop
March	March	Carleton O	W. H. Berry
Marchmont	Orillia, North	Simcoe, N.R O	Charles Powley
Marden	Guelph	Wellington, S.R O	C. Mc D. Blyth
Margaree, W.O	Margaree	Inverness N S	Collin Gillies
Margaree (Forks)	Margaree	Inverness N S	Donald Campbell
Margaretsville, W.O		Annapolis N S	T. A. Margeson
Margate	No. 19	Prince P E I	Reuben Tuplin
Maria	Maria	Bonaventure Q	François S. Cyr
Marie Bridge	No. 40	King's P E I	William Bowley
Marie Joseph, W.O.		Guysboro' N S	David Mitchell
Marion Bridge, W.O		Cape Breton N S	Hector McNeil
Maritana	Franklin	Huntingdon Q	William Edwards
Markdale.	Glenelg	Grey, S.R O	W. J. McFarland
**Markham*	Markham	York, E.R O	James J. Barker
Markhamville, W.O.		King's N B	Alfred Markham
Marlbank	Hungerford	Hastings, E.R O	W. G. Allan
Marlow	Linière	Beauce Q	Joseph Thompson
Marmion	Sullivan	Grey, N.R O	John Hislop
Marmora	Marmora	Hastings, N.R O	Benjamin Johnson
Marnoch	Wawanosh		

NAME OF POST OFFICE.	TOWNSHIP OR PARISH.	ELECTORAL COUNTY OR DIVISION.	NAME OF POSTMASTER.
Marshall's Cove, W. O	....	Annapolis .... N S	James P. Foster ....
Marshall's Town, W. O	....	Digby .... N S	E. J. Haines ....
Marsh Hill.........	Reach	Ontario, N.R...... ....O	William Tomlinson .
Marsh Settlement, McLellan's Mountain, W.O........	.. ..	Pictou........... ....N S	W. McLean........
Marshville	Wainfleet	Monck ....O	Edward Lee........
Marshy Hope, W.O.	. . ..	Antigonish ....N S	James McDougall ..
Marston............	Walsingham.......	Norfolk, S.R............O	Archibald Henderson
Marsville..........	Garafraxa.........	Wellington, C.R ....O	William McCormack
Martin's River, W.O	....	Lunenburg............N S	Joseph Strum ......
Martintown	Charlottenburg	Glengarry ....O	Robert Blackwood ..
Martinville.........	Clifton............	Compton ....Q	Amasa Martin......
Marydale, W.O	....	Antigonishe...........N S	Colin Chisholm .....
Mary Lake	Stephenson.	Muskoka ....O	Henry C. Ladell....
Marysville	Tyendinaga	Hastings, E.R ....O	Daniel Black ....
Marysville, W.O...	....	York.................N B	Hazer Ponds........
Maryvale, W.O	....	Antigonishe... ... N S	James C. Ross......
Mascouche Rapids..	Mascouche	L'Assomption ....Q	M. Delfause........
Mascouche	Mascouche	L'Assomption ... .Q	J. O. Lamarche......
Masham Mills......	Masham......	Ottawa............ ....Q	William Bennett....
Maskinongé	Maskinongé	Maskinongé ....Q	J. O. Belanger......
Massawippi	Hatley, West	Stanstead ....Q	Luther Abbot ......
Massie	Holland............	Grey, N.R..............O	John Small ....
Mast Town, W.O...	....	Colchester ....N S	....
Matane	Matane	Rimouski ....Q	L. N. Blais........
Matapédia..........	Restigouche	Bonaventure ....Q	D. Fraser ....
Matawatchan.......	Matawatchan	Renfrew, S.R ....O	John McGregor ....
Matlock............	Plympton	Lambton ....O	John P. Jarmain....
Mattawa..	Mattawa	District of Nipissing.....O	John Bangs ....
Maugerville, W.O ..	....	Sunbury.............N B	....
Mawcock...........	Granby	Shefford ....Q	L. N. Hungerford ..
Maxwell............	Osprey	Grey. E.R.............O	Wesley Long ....
Mayfair	Ekfrid	Middlesex, W.R ....O	John Dalton........
Mayfield	Chinguacousy	Peel...... .... .O	William Spiers ....

NAME OF POST OFFICE.	TOWNSHIP OR PARISH.	ELECTORAL COUNTY OR DIVISION.	NAME OF POSTMASTER.	
Maynooth	Monteagle..........	Hastings, N.R.......... **O**	William Fitzgerald .	
Mayo	Lochaber	Ottawa .... **Q**	T. Bourke..........	
Meadowvale.........	Toronto	Peel .... **O**	C. H. Gooderham...	
**Meaford*.	St. Vincent	Grey, E.R.............. **O**	D. L. Layton.......	
Meagher's Grant, W. O................	....	Halifax............... **N S**	Daniel Dillman.....	
Mechanics' Settlement, W.O.......	....	King's......... ......**N B**	Alexander Moore...	
Medford, W.O	....	King's......... ......**N S**	William West	
Medina	Nissouri, E.........	Oxford, N.R .... **O**	J. H. Beck... ...	
Medonte	Medonte	Simcoe, N.R........... **O**	Robert J. Moon	
Melancthon	Melancthon	Grey, E.R.............. **O**	James Brown.......	
**Melbourne*	Melbourne	Richmond .... **Q**	Richd. F. Woodburn	
Melbourne Ridge ...	Melbourne	Richmond .... **Q**	William Beattie	
Melocheville........	Beauharnois	Beauharnois .... **Q**	George Ellis........	
Melrose	Tyendinga..........	Hastings, E.R .... **O**	George Duncan	
Melrose	St. Mary's..........	Guysborough, ...**N S**	James Stewart......	
Melvern Square, WO	....	Annapolis ....**N S**	B. Spinney	
Melville	Hillier	Prince Edward.......... **O**	Caleb Johnson	
Memramcook........	....	Westmoreland... ..**N B**	S. C. Charters	
Menie	Seymour	Northumberland, E.R... **O**	James Mather.....	
Merigonish, W.O...	....	Pictou................**N S**	Edward Finlayson..	
Merivale	Nepean	Carleton .... **O**	E. B. Hopper	
Merlin	Raleigh	Kent .... **O**	Patrick Sullivan	
**Merrickville*........	Wolford....	Grenville, N.R...... ... **O**	Samuel Jakes......	
Meritton	Grantham	Lincoln .... **O**	S. Stephens	
Mermaid Farm	No. 48......	Queen's ....**P E I**	J. Farquharson.....	
Metabechouan	Metabechouan	Chicoutimi . ... **Q**	Jacques Bergeron...	
Metaghan, W.O....	....	Digby ....**N S**	George Gorman.....	
Metaghan River, WO		Digby **N S**	Justinian Comeau	

NAME OF POST OFFICE.	TOWNSHIP OR PARISH.	ELECTORAL COUNTY OR DIVISION.	NAME OF POSTMASTER.
Middle Church....	St. Paul's..........	Lisgar.... ....**M**	James Clouston. ...
Middle Clyde River, W.O............	....	Shelburne ....**N S**	G. D. McKay ......
Middle Coverdale, W.O............	....	Albert................**N B**	James Ryan........
Middlefield, W.O ..	....	Queen's...............**N S**	E. Morton.... .....
Middle La Have Ferry, W.O......	....	Lunenburg ....**N S**	C. R. Pernette .. ..
Middle Musquodoboit............	....	Halifax.... ....**N S**	R. A. Kaulbeck ....
Middle Ohio, W.O.	....	Shelburne ....**N S**	James McKay.....
Middle Pereaux, W.O. (late Pereaux, WO).	....	King's...............**N S**	Elijah C. West .....
Middle River, W.O.	....	Pictou...............**N S**	George McLeod ....
Middle River, W.O.	....	Victoria..............**N S**	Charles L. McLeod.
Middle St. Francis, W.O............	....	Victoria.............**N B**	Andrew Douglas....
Middle Section of N. E. Margaree, W.O	Margaree	Inverness........ ....**N S**	J. G. Crowdis ......
Middle Settlement—River Inhabitants, W.O......... ..	....	Inverness ... ...**N S**	Donald McDonald ..
Middle Settlement of South River, W.O.	....	Antigonishe ....**N S**	James McDonnell ..
Middle Simmonds, W.O............	....	Carleton.. ....**N B**	David N. Raymond.
MiddleSouthampton, W.O............	....	York......... ......**N B**	George W. McKay .
Middle Stewiacke, W.O............	....	Colchester ....**N S**	John Dickie ....
Middleton	....	Annapolis ....**N S**	Albert Beals........
Middleton..........	No. 27..............	Prince......... ... **P E I**	William Roberts....
Middleville.........	Lanark..............	Lanark, N.R . ...**O**	William Croft ......
Midgic, W.O	....	Westmoreland........**N B**	Mariner Hicks .....
Midhurst	Vespra.............	Simcoe, N.R............**O**	George Smeath .....
Midland...........	Tay................	Simcoe, N.R ....**O**	Thomas B. Gladstone
Midland, W.O......	....	King's............. ..**N B**	W. M. Case ....
Mildmay	Carrick.	Bruce, S.R............**O**	Malcolm Campbell..
Mile End..........	....	Hochelaga ....**Q**	Jos. Robin Lapointe.
Milford	Marysburg	Prince Edward..........**O**	James Cooke ....
Milford, W.O......	....	Annapolis ....**N S**	S. Charlton.........

NAME OF POST OFFICE.	TOWNSHIP OF PARISH.	ELECTORAL COUNTY OR DIVISION.	NAME OF POSTMASTER.
Millbank	Mornington	Perth, N.R. .... **O**	William Rutherford.
Mill Bridge.........	Tudor	Hastings, N.R. .... **O**	R. M. Norman .....
**Mill Brook*	Cavan....	Durham, E.R. .... **O**	William Vance .....
Mill Brook, W.O ...	....	Pictou .... **N S**	M. G. Ross. ....
Mill Cove, W.O ...	....	Lunenburg .... **N S**	J. W. Jollymore....
Mill Cove, W.O	....	Queen's .... **N B**	Mrs. Nancy Sparks.
Mill Creek, W.O ...	....	Kent............... **N B**	N. Beckwith ....
Milledgeville, W.O .	....	St. John .... **N B**	John G. Tobin......
Mille Isles.....	Mille Isles..........	Argenteuil .... **Q**	Solomon Pollock....
**Mille Roches*	Cornwall	Cornwall .... **O**	Peter N. Tait . ...
Miller's Creek, W.O.	....	Hants .... **N S**	Hiram Miller.......
Mille Vaches	....	Saguenay .... **Q**	Rev. Pierre Boily...
Millfield	Inverness	Megantic............... **Q**	Thomas McKenzie ..
Mill Grove	Flamborough, West.	Wentworth, N.R. .... **O**	W. H. Berney......
Mill Haven	Ernestown	Lennox .... **O**	Anderson Venton...
Milliken	Markham	York, E.R. .... **O**	W. Gorvett.........
Mill Point..........	Tyendinga	Hastings, E.R. .... **O**	James Bowen ......
Millstream, W.O...	....	King's .... **N B**	J. A. Fenwick......
Millsville, W.O.....	....	Pictou.... .... **N S**	John McKay.......
Milltown	....	Charlotte............ **N B**	Patrick Curran.....
Mill Village	....	Queen's .... **N S**	J. N. Mack ....
Millville, W.O......	....	York .... **N B**	Henry Blaney ......
Milnesville	Markham	York, E.R. .... **O**	H. H. Read........
Milton	....	Queen's............. **N S**	E. Kempton........
Milton, East	Milton	Shefford .... **Q**	Charles Gillespie ...
**Milton, West*	Trafalgar	Halton .... **O**	W. D. Lyon........
Milverton	Mornington	Perth, N.R. .... **O**	John Pierson......
Mimico	Etobicoke	York, W.R. .... **O**	George Scott........
Miminegash	Number 3	Prince............. **P E I**	Richard Costain ....
Mimosa	Erin	Wellington, S.R. .... **O**	Nathaniel Read ....
Minden	Snowdon	Peterboro', E.R. .... **O**	S. S. Peck.........
Minesing	Vespra.............	Simcoe, N.R .... **O**	Mrs. Mary Ronald..
Mingan	....	Saguenay.............. **Q**	Benjamin Scott.....
Minudie, W.O	....	Cumberland .... **N S**	Gilbert Seaman.....
Mira Gut, W.O.....	....	Cape Breton.... ..... **N S**	Charles Martell.....

NAME OF POST OFFICE.	TOWNSHIP OR PARISH.	ELECTORAL COUNTY OR DIVISION.	NAME OF POSTMASTER.
Miscouche	Number 17	Prince P E I	H. V. Desroches
Mispec, W.O.		St. John N B	
Mitchell	Logan	Perth, S.R. O	William W. Hicks
Mitchell's Bay	Dover East	Kent O	Seth Turner
Moe's River	Compton	Compton Q	David F. Brown
Moffat	Nassagiweya	Halton O	Peter Little
Mohawk	Brantford, West	Brant, S.R. O	Thomas Racey
Mohr's Corners (late Hubbell's Falls)	Fitzroy	Carleton O	Chas. Mohr
Moria	Huntingdon	Hastings, N.R. O	Henry Ostrom
Moisic		Saguenay Q	Thomas Darling
Molesworth	Wallace	Perth, N.R. O	Samuel Longheed
Monck	Luther	Wellington, N. R. O	William Segsworth
Monaghan	Number 36	Queen's P E I	James Wisner
Monckland	Roxborough	Stormont O	John Brown
Moncton		Westmoreland N B	Jos. Crandall
Moncton Road, W.O.		Westmoreland N B	William G. Bateman
Moneymore	Hungerford	Hastings, E. R. O	John Harigan
Mongenais	Newton	Vaudreuil Q	J. Sicart
Mongolia	Markham	York, E. R. O	Robert Curtis
Monkton	Elma	Perth, N. R. O	Edward Greensides.
Mono Centre	Mono	Cardwell O	John Wilson
Mono Mills	Albion	Cardwell O	John Allen
Mono Road Station.	Chinguacousy	Peel O	John Judge
Montague	Montague	Lanark, S. R. O	Peter Clark
Montague Bridge	Number 52	King's P E I	William Annear
Montague Cross	Number 57	Queen's P E I	W. Callaghan
Montague Gold Mines W.O.		Halifax N S	Mrs. Vasey Barker
Montcalm	Rawdon	Montcalm Q	E. Copping
Monte Bello	Petite Nation	Ottawa Q	Charles Major, jun.
Mont Elie, late St. Elie.	Caxton	St. Maurice O	Otis Chamberlin
Mont Louis	Mont Louis	Gaspé Q	Joseph Lemieux
*Montmagny	St. Thomas	Montmagny Q	J. S. Vallée
Montmorency Falls.	Beauport	Quebec Q	Joseph Cazeau
Montmorin	Morin	Terrebonne Q	Joseph Belisle
		Q	E. S Freer

NAME OF POST OFFICE	TOWNSHIP OR PARISH.	ELECTORAL COUNTY OR DIVISION.	NAME OF POSTMASTER.
Montrose..........	Stamford..........	Welland................ **O**	Archd. Thompson...
Montrose..........	Number 3....	Prince.............. **P E I**	Thomas Hockin.....
Mont St. Hilaire....	St. Hilaire	Rouville................ **Q**	Alexis Brouillette...
Monument Settlement, W.O.......	....	Carleton.............. **N B**	James Kennedy.....
Moore	Moore..............	Lambton .... **O**	John Morrison......
Moorefield..........	Maryborough	Wellington, N.R......... **O**	Henry Maudsley....
Moore's Mills, W.O.	....	Charlotte............. **N B**	Joseph Cormick ....
Moore's Station.....	St. Armand	Missisquoi............. **Q**	P.C. Moore.........
Moose Brook, W. O.	....	Hants . ... **N S**	Thomas M. Reid....
Moose Creek........	Roxborough	Stormont .... **O**	William McKillican.
Moray..............	McGillivray	Middlesex, N.R .... **O**	H. Hagerman.......
Morden, W.O	....	King's................ **N S**	Thomas Farnsworth.
Morell	Number 39..........	King's............... **P E I**	W. Sterns..........
Morell Rear	do 39.........	King's.............. **P E I**	James Phelan ......
Morewood	Winchester	Dundas................. **O**	A. McKay..........
Morganston	Cramahe	Northumberland, E.R .. **O**	Wm. J. Newman ...
Morley	St. Vincent	Grey, E.R.............. **O**	James Lemon.......
Morningdale Mills ..	Mornington.........	Perth, N.R............. **O**	J. Nicklin..........
**Morpeth*	Howard	Bothwell............... **O**	J. C. Nation........
Morrisbank.........	Morris..	Huron, N.R .... **O**	James Orr .. ..
**Morrisburg*	Williamsburg	Dundas... .... **O**	James Holden ......
Morriston...........	Puslinch............	Wellington, S.R .... **O**	R. B. Morrison......
Morristown, W.O...	. ...	King's.......... ....**N S**	John Palmer ....
Morrisvale..........	Essa	Simcoe, S.R............ **O**	Archibald Thom ....
Morton	Crosby, South	Leeds, S.R............. **O**	James R. Leake.....
Morton's Corner, W.O	....	Lunenburg........... **N S**	James Morton ......
Mortonville, W.O...	....	Hants ....**N S**	Josiah Smith ....
Morven	Ernestown..........	Lennox.. .... **O**	J. L. P. Gordanier..
[illegible]	[illegible]	[illegible]	[illegible]

NAME OF POST OFFICE.	TOWNSHIP OR PARISH.	ELECTORAL COUNTY OR DIVISION.	NAME OF POSTMASTER.
Mountain View.....	Ameliasburg	Prince Edward..........O	W. H. Way........
Mount Albert	Gwillimbury, East ..	York, N.R..............O	Mrs. E. Wilson.....
Mount Albion	Saltfleet	Wentworth, S.R........O	James R. Cook ... .
**Mount Brydges*.....	Caradoc	Middlesex, W.R ....O	Edward Handy.....
Mount Carmel......	Notre Dame du Mont Carmel	Kamouraska. ....Q	R. Lavois ....
Mount Charles......	Toronto	Peel......................O	Robert McLeod.....
Mount Denison, W.O	.. . .	Hants...............N S	Mrs. J. E. Shaw....
Mount Elgin........	Dereham	Oxford, S.R............O	Isaac M. Elliott.....
**Mount Forest*.......	Arthur	Wellington, N.R. ......O	T. G. Smith ....
Mount Hanly, W.O.	....	Annapolis .... N S	Caleb Miller........
Mount Healy	Oneida	Haldimand ....O	Wm. Russell ....
Mount Horeb	Ops..................	Victoria, S.R. ....O	William Reynolds....
Mount Hurst	Albion	Cardwell ....O	John Wallace ......
Mount Johnson	St. Grégoire.........	Iberville...............Q	Louis A. Auger......
Mountjoy	....	Soulanges ....Q	Camille Lalonde....
Mount Loyal	Rawdon.............	Montcalm ....Q	William Smiley ....
Mount Oscar	Rigaud............	Vaudreuil ....Q	Leandre Lapointe ..
Mount Pleasant	Cavan...............	Durham, E.R. ....O	Abraham Bets......
Mount Pleasant	Number 12	Prince.............P E I	D. Campbell........
Mount Pleasant, WO	....	Cumberland ....N S	Isaac Simpson......
Mount Pleasant, WO	....	King's...............N B	Merritt Jones ......
Mount St. Louis....	Medonte	Simcoe, N.R. ....O	J. P. Hussey ....
Mount St. Patrick..	Brougham..	Renfrew, S.R. ....O	Bridget Brady.......
Mount Salem	Malahide....	Elgin, E.R. ....O	George Hillaker ....
Mountsberg	Flamborough, East .	Wentworth, N.R ....O	William Emmans...
Mount Stewart	Number 37	Queen's.. .... P E I	D. Egan ....
Mount Thom, W.O.	....	Pictou.......... .... N S	George McKay ....
Mount Uniacke.....	....	Hants................ N S	Richard McLean....
Mount Vernon......	Brantford, West....	Brant, S. R. ....O	William Perrin ....
Mount Whatley, W. O.........	....	Westmoreland......... N B	Dixon Chapman....
Mount Wolfe.......	Albion.............	Cardwell..................O	John Wolfe, jun....
Mouth of Jemseg, W O	....	Queen's............... N B	Elias Scribner ......
Mouth of Keswick, W.O............	....	York .... N B	George Miles ......

NAME OF POST OFFICE.	TOWNSHIP OR PARISH.	ELECTORAL COUNTY OR DIVISION.	NAME OF POSTMASTER.
Mouth of Nerepis...	....	King's..............N B	J. M. Nase ....
Muddy Creek	Number 17	Prince............P E I	John Dickie ....
Mulgrave...........	Bertie.............	Welland ....O	P. Learn, sen.......
Mull River, W.O...	....	Inverness ....N S	Donald McIsaac....
Mulmur...........	Mulmur	Simcoe, S. R. ....O	John Murphy ......
Muncey	Caradoc	Middlesex, W. R. ......O	R. E. Whiting......
Munro's, W.O......	....	Victoria ....N S	M. Munro..........
Munster...........	Goulbourn..........	Carleton ....O	Thomas Tubman....
Murray	Murray............	Northumberland, E. R...O	....
**Murray Bay*.......	Mountmurray......	Charlevoix.............Q	J. A. J. Kane ......
Murray Harbor, N..	Number 63...	King's.............P E I	....
Murray Harbor, Rd.	do 57...	Queen's.... ......P E I	M. McPherson .....
Murray Harbor, S..	do 64.........	King's.. ....P E I	C. T. Brehaut ......
Murray River.......	do 64....	King's..............P E I	Robert Saunders...
Murray's Corner, W. O	....	Westmoreland ....N B	Joseph Murray ......
Murvale...........	Portland...........	Addington ....O	Michael Davy ...
Muskoka Falls......	Draper	Muskoka ....O	Hy. A. Clifford.....
Musquash, W.O....	....	St. John ....N B	L. D. Carman ......
Musquodoboit Harbor, W.O.........	.. ..	Halifax..............N S	James Gardner .....
Musselburg.........	Mornington.........	Perth, N. R............O	George Shearer .....
Myrehall...........	Tyendinaga.........	Hastings, E. R. ....O	Mrs Elizabeth Harris
Myrtle.............	Whitby	Ontario, S. R. ....O	Reuben Hurlburt...
Mystic.............	Stanoridge.........	Missisquoi ....Q	....
Nackawick, W. O..	....	York ....N B	William H. Clark ..
Nanaimo	... .	Vancouver...........B C	James Harvey......
Nairn.............	Williams, East	Middlesex, N. R ....O	Archibald Bell.. ...
Nanticoke....	Walpole............	Haldimand . ...O	C. E. Bourne ......
Napanee	Richmond	Lennox ....O	Gilbert Bogart......
Napanee Mills......	**Camden, East**	Addington ....O	H. M. Wright .....

'NSHIP OR ARISH.	ELECTORAL COUNTY OR DIVISION.	NAME OF POSTMASTER.
'e	Middlesex, W. R........O	John Arthurs ......
orien	Napierville ....Q	Lucien Dubé ....
....	Cumberland ....N S	Samuel E. Freeman.
le	Middlesex, N. R. ....O	Thomas Jury ......
....	Queen's ....N B	Henry Todd........
....	York.................N B	James Young ......
... .	York.................N B	Peter McFarlane....
....	York.................N B	John L. Fletcher ..
iweya.	Halton .. ..O	Elias Easterbrook ..
....	Saguenay ....Q	C. A. Deschamps ..
rland........	Russell ....O	M. O'Meara........
....	Halifax ....N S	William Smith ....
....	Northumberland .....N B	David Petrie ......
gèle	Rimouski ....Q	Francois X Gagnier.
. ...	Halton ....O	D. W. Springer.....
nby	Grey, S. R. ....O	Thomas Duignan ..
.. ..	King's................N B	David McKenzie ...
rstone	Welland ....O	Lewis House ....
nby	Grey, S. R............ O	D. Winkler ....
....	Simcoe, N. R. ....O	James Greenshields.
oo, South....	Waterloo, S. R.........O	William Key ......
....	Annapolis ....N S	Albert Oaks........
....	Colchester ....N S	Gavin Bell.........
h, North	Oxford, S. R ... .O	Henry Henderson ..
....	Gloucester............N B	John Kerr ....
....	Leeds, N.R. ....O	John Edgar ....
, North... ..	Leeds, S.R. ....O	Thomas Webster ...
d............	Leeds, S.R. ....O	James Lytle.........
k............	Huron, N.R.............O	Mrs. Sarah Carson..
....	Inverness.............N S	Donald M. Lord....
n, East	Addington..............O	Robert Hope ......
....	Carleton.............N B	Richard McKinney .
....	Middlesex, W.R.........O	Thomas Robinson...
....	Halifax...............N S	John Hattee........

NAME OF POST OFFICE.	TOWNSHIP OR PARISH.	ELECTORAL COUNTY OR DIVISION.	NAME OF POSTMASTER.
New Campbelton		Victoria ... N S	Chas. C. Campbell, jr.
New Canaan, W.O.		Queen's ... N B	Lewis Keith
New Canada, W.O.		Lunenburg ... N S	Jeremiah Mader
New Carlisle	Cox	Bonaventure ... Q	Matthew Caldwell
Newcastle	Clarke	Durham, W.R. ... O	Hiram Hodges
Newcastle		Northumberland ... N B	Samuel Johnston
NewcastleBridge, W. O.		Queen's ... N B	R. P. Yeomans
Newcastle Creek, W. O.		Queen's ... N B	G. D. Bailey
Newcombe	Hagerman	Muskoka ... O	Arthur Millin
Newcomb Corner, W O.		Halifax ... N S	John Barron
New Cornwall, W.O		Lunenburg ... N S	S. E. Hallamore
New Dublin	Elizabethtown	Brockville ... O	J. A. Browne
New Dundee	Wilmot	Waterloo, S.R. ... O	Jacob G. Wegenast.
New Durham	Burford	Brant, S.R. ... O	Charles Cochran
* *New Edinburgh*	Gloucester	Russell ... O	J. W. Proctor
New Gairloch, W.O.		Pictou ... N S	John McPherson
New Germany, W.O		Lunenburg ... N S	William Nichols
New Glasgow	No. 23	Queen's ... P E I	Sarah Nisbet
New Glasgow	Lacorne	Terrebonne ... Q	James Furse
New Glasgow		Pictou ... N S	William Fraser
* *New Hamburg*	Wilmot.	Waterloo, S.R. ... O	Christian Ernst.
New Harbor, W.O.		Guysborough ... N S	Daniel Kirby
New Haven	No. 31	Queen's ... P E I	H. McMillan
New Horton, W.O.		Albert ... N B	M. Cannon
Newington	Osnabruck.	Stormont. ... O	Ferguson Jordine
New Ireland	Ireland	Megantic ... Q	Richard C. Porter
New Ireland, W.O.		Albert ... N B	John Carrens
New Ireland Road, W. O		Albert ... N B	M. McFadden
New Jerusalem, W.O		Queen's ... N B	Albert M. Short
New Larig, W. O.		Pictou ... N S	Robert G. McLeod
New Liverpool	St. Romuald	Lévis ... Q	Damase Roberge
New London	No. 21	Queen's ... P E I	D. McIntyre
New Lowell	Sunnidale	Simcoe, N. R ... O	P. Patton

NAME OF POST OFFICE.	TOWNSHIP OR PARISH.	ELECTORAL COUNTY OR DIVISION.	NAME OF POSTMASTER.
**New Market*	Whitchurch	York, N. R. O	William Roe
New Maryland, W. O		York N B	Lewis Fisher
New Mills		Restigouche N B	Donald McAlister
New Minas, W. O.		King's N S	John A. Fuller
New Perth	No 52	King's P E I	Roland H. Plummer
Newport	Brantford	Brant, S. R O	Colin Milloy
Newport		Gaspé Q	Clovis Desforges
Newport		Hants N S	J. F. Cochrane
Newport Corner, W. O.		Hants N S	James Brown
Newport Landing		Hants N S	J. W. Allison
Newport Point		Gaspé Q	Philip Hamon
Newport Station		Hants N S	J. L. Sweet
New Richmond	New Richmond	Bonaventure Q	Richard Brash
New River, W. O.		Charlotte N B	J. E. Knight
New Ross	Matilda	Dundas O	Thomas Currie
New Ross		Lunenburg N S	John Pratt
New Ross Road, W. O.		King's N S	Owen McGarry
Newry	Elma	Perth, N. R O	R. L. Alexander
New Sarum	Yarmouth	Elgin, E. R. O	Johnson Smith
Newton	No. 27	Prince P E I	J. T. Murphy
Newton Brook	York	York, W. R. O	W. W. Cummer
Newton Mills, W. O.		Colchester N S	James Creelman
Newton Robinson	Tecumseth	Simcoe, S. R O	James G. Chantler
Newtown, W. O.		King's N B	J. B. Pearce
New Town, W. O.		Guysboro' N S	Thomas McBain
New Tusket, W. O.		Digby N S	Charleton Sabean
New Westminster		New Westminster B C	Valentine B. Tait
New Wiltshire	No. 31	Queen's P E I	G. Easter
**Niagara*	Niagara	Niagara O	Robert Warren
Nichol's Corner, W. O		Annapolis N S	D. Nichols
Nicola Lake		Yale B C	John Clapperton
Nicolet	Nicolet	Nicolet Q	Miss Margaret Chillas
Nicolston	Essa	Simcoe, S. R O	John Nichol
Nictaux Falls, W. O.		Annapolis N S	Charles Berteaux

NAME OF POST OFFICE.	TOWNSHIP OR PARISH.	ELECTORAL COUNTY OR DIVISION.	NAME OF POSTMASTER.
Niel's Harbor, W.O.	....	Victoria .... N S	John McDonald ....
Niely Road	....	King's .... N S	Thaddeus Allison...
Nile...............	Colborne	Huron, C. R.......... O	Samuel Pollock.....
Nilestown	Dorchester, N.......	Middlesex, E. R.... .... O	James R. L. Waugh.
Nine Mile Creek...	No. 65	Queen's .... P E I	Gilbert Bell ....
Nile Mile River, W.O	....	Hants .... N S	Evan Thompson ....
Nipissingan	. .. .	District of Nipissing..... O	John Shaw ....
Nissouri............	Nissouri East.......	Oxford, N. R... ...... O	Archibald McBrayne
Nithburg	North Easthope.....	Perth, N. R............ O	James Brown.......
Nobleton	King	York, N. R. .... O	William Munsie ...
Noel, W. O.........	....	Hants .... N S	Osmond O'Brien....
Noel Shore, W. O...	....	Hants .... N S	Samuel McLellan...
Norham	Percy	Northumberland, E. R... O	Alexander Douglas..
Norland............	Laxton.............	Victoria, N. R. .. .. O	A. A. McLauchlin..
Normandale	Charlotteville......	Norfolk, S. R. .... O	John W. Sheppard .
Normanton	Saugeen	Bruce, N. R............. O	Mrs. Mary Roy.....
Northampton, W. O.	....	Carleton.............. N B	Aaron Tomkins.....
North Augusta......	Augusta...	Grenville, S. R.......... O	John Chapman .....
North Bedeque	No. 25	Prince .... P E I	H. Clark...........
North Bristol	Bristol	Pontiac .... Q	William Shirley ....
North Brookfield, W. O................	... .	Queen's.............. N S	George M. Fraser...
North Bruce........	Bruce	Bruce, N. R............. O	D. McCarrol ....
North Douro	Douro..............	Peterborough, E. R...... O	Robert Casement ...
North East Branch Margaree, W. O...	Margaree...........	Inverness..... ..... N S	John Rose..........
North East Harbor, W. O............	....	Shelburne .... N S	A. R. Greenwood...
North Esk Boom, W. O.	....	Northumberland...... N B	James Hutchinson .
Northfield	Cornwall	Cornwall .... O	George McDonald ..
Northfield, W. O....	....	Sunbury .... N B	Jonathan Welton...
Northfield, W. O....	....	Lunenburg........... N S	Heli Mackey ......
North Georgetown..	Beauharnois	Chateauguay . ... Q	Joseph Turcot......
North Glanford.....	Glanford	Wentworth, S. R........ O	Edward Dickenson..
North Gower	North Gower.......	Carleton............... O	Hiram Scott........
North Ham	North Ham		[illegible]

NAME OF POST OFFICE.	TOWNSHIP OR PARISH.	ELECTORAL COUNTY OR DIVISION.	NAME OF POSTMASTER.
North Hatley	Hatley	Stanstead ... Q	B. Le Baron
North Joggins, W. O.		Westmoreland ... N B	William McHaffey
North Keppel	Keppel	Grey, N. R. ... O	David Dewar
North Lake, W. O.		Westmoreland ... N B	
North Lake	No. 47	King's ... P E I	William Morrow
North Lake, W.O.		York ... N B	William Foster
North Lancaster	Lancaster	Glengarry ... O	Charles Leclair
North Mountain	Mountain	Dundas ... O	James Cleland
North Mountain, W. O.		King's ... N S	William Bennett
North Nation Mills	Petite Nation	Ottawa ... Q	Thomas Cole
North Onslow	Onslow	Pontiac ... Q	John O'Donnell
North Pelham	Pelham	Monck ... O	Mrs. M. A. McQueen
North Pinnacle	St. Armand	Missisquoi ... Q	V. Barnes
North Port	Sophiasburg	Prince Edward ... O	W. H. Morden
North Range Corner, W.O.		Digby ... N S	Charles McNiel
North Ridge	Gosfield	Essex ... O	William E. Wagstaff
North River	No. 22	Queen's ... P E I	John Sellars
North River, W. O.		Westmoreland ... N B	J. Taylor
North River, W. O.		Colchester ... N S	W. H. Higgins
North River Bridge, W. O.		Colchester ... N S	Henry Blair
North River Bridge, W. O.		Victoria ... N S	John McKenzie
North River Platform, W. O.		Westmoreland ... N B	Patrick Hopkins
North Rustico	No. 24	Queen's ... P E I	George Budd
North Salem, W.O.		Hants ... N S	N. Nelson
North Section of Earltown, W. O.		Colchester ... N S	
North Seneca	Seneca	Haldimand ... O	
North Shore, W. O.		Cumberland ... N S	Duncan McKinnon
North Shore, W. O.		Victoria ... N S	Donald McDonald
North Side of Basin, River Dennis, W.O.		Inverness ... N S	Malcolm McNiel
North Stanbridge	Stanbridge	Missisquoi ... Q	A. M. Stone
North Stoke	Stoke	Richmond ... Q	F. H. Lothrop

NAME OF POST OFFICE.	TOWNSHIP OR PARISH.	ELECTORAL COUNTY OR DIVISION.		NAME OF POSTMASTER.
North Stukely......	Stukely	Shefford	Q	Antoine Audette....
North Sutton	Sutton.............	Brome	Q	S. Sweet ....
North Sydney.......	....	Cape Breton	N S	John Forbes........
North Tryon	No. 28	Prince.............	P E I	A. Reid ....
North Wakefield ...	Wakefield..........	Ottawa	Q	A. Pritchard ....
North West Arm, W. O.............	....	Cape Breton	N S	G. K. Ball ....
North West Bridge, W. O............	....	Northumberland	N B	Edward Sinclair ....
North West Cove, W. O............	....	Lunenburg............	N S	Daniel Noonan......
North Williamsburg,	Williamsburg.......	Dundas......	O	William Gordon ....
North Winchester ..	Winchester	Dundas.................	O	Joseph S. Kyle.....
Norton, W. O........	....	King's.........	N B	John Hayes ....
Norton Creek..	Beauharnois	Chateauguay	Q	William Dinnigan ..
Norton Dale, W. O.	....	York.................	N B	William Cox ....
Norton Station	... .	King's	N B	Joseph D. Baxter..
Norval	Esquesing	Halton	O	William Clay.......
Norway	York.....	York, E. R.	O	James Smith . ....
**Norwich*...........	Norwich, North	Oxford, S. R.	O	Gilbert Moore ......
**Norwood*..........	Asphodel	Peterborough, E. R	O	J. A. Butterfield....
Notfield............	Kenyon	Glengarry	O	Peter Kennedy .....
Notre Dame du Portage.............	Notre Dame du Portage	Témiscouata............	Q	Miss Adée Michaud.
Nottawa	Nottawasaga	Simcoe, N. R...........	O	Andrew Melville....
Nouvelle	Nouvelle	Bonaventure............	Q	Archibald Kerr.....
Noyan	Sabrevois...........	Missisquoi........	Q	T. B. Derrick.......
Nutt's Corners......	Clarenceville	Missisquoi.............	Q	David Nutt .. ..

NAME OF POST OFFICE.	TOWNSHIP OR PARISH.	ELECTORAL COUNTY OR DIVISION.	NAME OF POSTMASTER
Oak Bay, W. O.	....	Charlotte............**N B**	Walter Gilley ......
Oakfield, W. O......	....	Halifax....... ....**N S**	Mrs. Francis Laurie.
Oakham, W. O.....	....	Queen's ....**N B**	James W. Starkey..
Oak Hill	Laxton.............	Victoria, N. R..........**O**	Robert Staples......
Oak Hill, W. O.....	....	Charlotte............**N B**	William McCan ....
Oakland...........	Oakland............	Brant, S. R...... .....**O**	John Toyne ....
Oak Park, W. O....	. ...	Shelburne............ **N S**	Nehemiah N. Adams
Oak Point, W. O...	....	King's........... .. .**N B**	J. L. Flewelling ....
Oak Point, W. O...	....	Northumberland ......**N B**	Alexander Davidson
Oak Point..........	....	Marquette ....**M**	William Clarke.....
Oak Ridges...	Whitchurch	York, N. R. ....**O**	Edward Curtis......
**Oakville*..........	Trafalgar..........	Halton ... .**O**	R. Balmer..........
Oakwood......	Mariposa	Victoria, S. R.. ....**O**	Richard P. Butler...
Oban...............	Sarnia	Lambton ....**O**	William Carrick....
**Odessa*............	Ernestown	Lennox ....**O**	P. S. Timmerman..
Offa................	Stephen	Huron, S. R. ....**O**	John G. Quarry....
Ogilvie, W. O......	....	King's ....**N S**	Thomas Anthony...
Ohio, W. O........	....	Antigonishe....... ...**N S**	John McDonald...
Ohsweken	Tuscarora..........	Brant, S. R. ....**O**	James Styres.......
**Oil Springs*	Enniskillen.........	Lambton................**O**	James Keating......
Oka................	. ...	Two Mountains.........**Q**	Cyprien Chaurette..
Okanagon	....	Yale.................**B C**	Cornelius O'Keefe...
Okanagon Mission..	....	Yale.......... ....**B C**	Eli Lequin...... ..
Old Barns, W. O....	....	Colchester ....**N S**	Ebenezer Archibald.
Oldham, W. O.....	....	Halifax ....**N S**	....
Old Montrose.......	Romney............	Kent .... **O**	....
O'Leary's Road.....	Number 8	Prince............ **P E I**	William Smallman..
Olinda	Gosfield	Essex ....**O**	John C. Fox ....
Olinville, W. O.	....	Queen's...............**N B**	William Tilley......
Omagh	Trafalgar..........	Halton ....**O**	Thomas Little ......
**Omemee*...........	Emily......	Victoria, S. R...........**O**	Robert Grandy.....
Omineca...........	....	Cariboo...............**B C**	Francis Page ....
Ompah	Palmerston.........	Addington .... **O**	Henry Dunham ....
150 Mile House.....	....	Cariboo............... **B C**	....
Oneida	Oneida	Haldimand.. ....**O**	J. T. Mutchmore...

NAME OF POST OFFICE.	TOWNSHIP OR PARISH.	ELECTORAL COUNTY OR DIVISION.	NAME OF POSTMASTER.
Ongley	Brighton	Northumberland, E. R. . . O	Albert H. Smith
Onondaga	Onondaga	Brant, N. R. . . O	William S. Buckwell
**Onslow*	Onslow	Pontiac . . Q	Walton Smith
Onslow, W. O.		Colchester. . . N S	Samuel McKinlay
**Crangeville*	Garafraxa	Wellington, C. R. . . O	Guy Leslie
Orchard	Egremont	Grey, S. R. . . O	J. G. Orchard
**Orillia*	Orillia	Simcoe, N. R. . . O	Wesley Bingham
Orleans	Gloucester, North	Russell . . O	Hugh Dupuis
Ormond	Winchester	Dundas . . O	Ira Morgan
Ormstown	Beauharnois	Chateauguay . . Q	R. N. Walsh
Oromocto		Sunbury . . N B	Charles McPherson
**Orono*	Clarke	Durham, W. R. . . O	Joseph L. Tucker
Orwell	Yarmouth	Elgin, E. R. . . O	D. Sutherland
Orwell	Number 57	Queen's . . P E I	B. Loughran
Orwell Cove	Number 57	Queen's . . P E I	E. Morrisey
Osaca	Hope	Durham, E. R . . O	David Gordon
**Osceola*	Bromley	Renfrew, N. R. . . O	Alexander McLaren
Osgoode	Osgoode	Russell . . O	Adam J. Baker
**Oshawa*	Whitby	Ontario, S. R. . . O	David Smith
Ospringe	Erin	Wellington, S. R. . . O	William Symon
Ossekeag		King's . . N B	Allan McN. Travis
Ossian	Enniskillen	Lambton . . O	George S. McPherson
Otnabog, W. O.		Queen's . . N B	Joseph B. Slipp
**Ottawa*	Nepean	Ottawa . . O	G. P. Baker
Otter Lake	Leslie	Pontiac . . Q	John Mather
Otterville	Norwich, South	Oxford, S. R. . . O	Wm. F. Kay
Oungah	Chatham	Kent . . O	Thomas Kinny
Oustic	Eramosa	Wellington, S. R. . . O	Robert Scott
Outram	Brant	Bruce, S. R. . . O	David Smith
Overton	Camden, East	Addington . . O	S. D. Fox
**Owen Sound*	Sydenham	Grey, N. R . . O	John G. Francis
Oxenden	Keppel	Grey, N. R. . . O	John P. Benwell
Oxford		Cumberland . . N S	Henry S. Smith
Oxford Centre	Oxford, East	Oxford, S. R. . . O	Nelson Schooley
Oxford Mills	Oxford	Gren[illegible]	[illegible]

NAME OF POST OFFICE.	TOWNSHIP OR PARISH.	ELECTORAL COUNTY OR DIVISION.	NAME OF POSTMASTER.
Oxford Station	Oxford	Grenville, N. R. O	Andrew Holmes
Oxley	Colchester	Essex O	Robert Ivison
Oyster Ponds, W.O.		Guysborough N S	James W. Carr
Oznabruck Centre	Oznabruck	Stormont O	Jacob J. Poaps
Painsec, W. O	Shediac	Westmoreland N B	Eustache Babin
Painswick	Innisfil	Simcoe, S. R. O	John Huggard
**Paisley*	Elderslie	Bruce, N. R. O	James Saunders
**Pakenham*	Pakenham	Lanark, N. R. O	
Palermo	Trafalgar	Halton O	H. M. Switzer
Palestine		Marquette M	George West
Palgrave	Albion	Cardwell O	
Palmer Rapids	Raglan	Renfrew, S. R. O	H. F. McLachlin
Palmer's Road, W.O.		King's N S	George W. Eaton
Palmerston, W. O.		Kent N B	Honoré Landry
Panmure	Fitzroy	Carleton O	James King
Papineauville	Petite Nation	Ottawa Q	F. S. McKay
Paquette	Hereford Gore	Compton Q	F. Paquette
Paradise Lane		Annapolis N S	W. H. Troop
Parham	Hinchinbrooke	Addington O	John Griffith
Park Corner	Number 20	Queen's P E I	James Doyle
**Paris*	Dumfries, South	Brant, N. R. O	George Stanton
Paris Station	Dumfries, South	Brant, N. R. O	M. X. Carr
Parker	Peel	Wellington, C. R. O	
Parker's Cove, W.O.		Annapolis N S	Thos. Milner
Park Head	Amabel	Bruce, N. R. O	Wm. Simpson
Park Hill	West Williams	Middlesex, N. R. O	John Noble

NAME OF POST OFFICE.	TOWNSHIP OR PARISH.	ELECTORAL COUNTY OR DIVISION.	NAME OF POSTMASTER.
arkhurst	St. Sylvester	Lotbinière .... Q	Thomas Walker ....
ark's Creek	St. Andrews........	Lisgar................. M	John Tait ....
arma	SouthFredericksburg	Lennox .... O	David Griffith......
arrsborough	....	Cumberland.......... N S	John W. Jinks.....
arrsborough Shore, W. O............	....	Cumberland.......... N S	William Grant......
arry Sound.... ...	McDougall	Muskoka............... O	John McClelland...
aspébiac..........	Cox	Bonaventure .... Q	D. Bisson.........
atterson	Vaughan	York, W. R............ O	W. C. Patterson....
attersonSettlement, W. O............	....	Sunbury.... .... N B	Nelson White.....
audash............	Cardiff	Peterborough, E. R...... O	John Dixon........
avillion	....	Cariboo........ ...... B C	....
eabody	Sullivan...........	Grey, N. R............ O	John Milburn......
earceton	Stanbridge	Missisquoi .... Q	James Briggs......
eel, W. O.........	....	Carleton............. N B	Charles A. Harmon.
eepabun	Luther	Wellington, N. R .... O	Robert Dickson.....
efferlaw..........	Georgina	York, N. R.... .... O	George Johnson.....
eggy's Cove, W.O.	....	Halifax .... N S	W. Crooks.. .. ...
elham Union......	Pelham	Monck........... ..... O	Joseph Johnson.....
emberton Ridge, W. O............	....	York .... N B	Cyrus B. McKenney.
Pembroke	Pembroke	Renfrew, N. R.......... O	Alex. Moffatt .....
endleton	Plantagenet, South.	Prescott.............. O	Henry Moffatt......
Penetanguishene	Tiny	Simcoe, N. R............ O	J. S. Darling.......
eninsula-Gaspé....	Gaspé Bay, North..	Gaspé .... Q	William Miller.....
ennfield, W. O	....	Charlotte........ .... N B	Jesse Prescott......
ennfieldRidge,W.O	....	Charlotte..... ... ... N B	John B. Young.....
enobsquis	....	King's.............. N B	George Morton .....
entland	Pilkington	Wellington, C. R........ O	George Ford........
enville	Tecumseth	Simcoe, S. R............ O	Edward T. Turner..
ercé..	Percé	Gaspé.................. Q	J. E. Tuzo.........
erch Station	Sarnia	Lambton............... O	John Irwin.........
erkins	Templeton	Ottawa .... Q	John Freney ....
erm	Mulmur......	Simcoe, S. R........... O	Paul Gallagher.....
erretton	Westmeath.........	Renfrew, N. R.......... O	H. W. Perrett.....

NAME OF POST OFFICE.	TOWNSHIP OR PARISH.	ELECTORAL COUNTY OR DIVISION.	NAME OF POSTMASTER.
Perryboro'..........	Hereford	Compton...............Q	Calvin Perry ....
Perry Settlement, W. O	....	King's...............N B	R. Elders ....
Perrytown..........	Hope	Durham, E. R.... ......O	R. A. Corbett......
**Perth*..............	Drummond.........	Lanark, S. R............O	Thomas Cairns .....
Perth, W. O........	....	Victoria...... ....N B	James Bishop ......
Petawawa..........	Petewawa	Renfrew, N. R.... ......O	Solomon Devine....
**Peterborough*.......	North Monaghan...	Peterborough, W. R.....O	Hy. C. Rogers .....
Petersburg	Wilmot	Waterloo, S. R......... O	John Ernst.........
Peterson	Minden	Peterborough, E. R......O	William Jarvis.....
Peter's Road	Number 63..... ..	King's.............P E I	William Johnston...
Petersville, W. O...	....	Queen's............ .N B	Timothy Malone...
Petersville (sub.)....	London	City of London.... .....O	W. Loughrey ......
Petersville Church, W. O...........	....	Queen's ....N B	A. Hamilton ....
Petherton	Arthur	Wellington, N. R. ......O	Thomas Bunston....
Petitcodiac	....	Westmoreland ....N B	W. W. Price.......
Petite de Grat, W.O.	....	Richmond............N S	George M. Jean....
Petite Passage, W.O.	....	Digby................N S	John Smith ....
PetiteRivière Bridge, W. O...........	....	Lunenburg.......... .N S	William Holden ....
Petit Métis.........	Macnider...........	Rimouski ... .Q	John MacNider ....
**Petrolea*	Enniskillen.........	Lambton...............O	Patrick Barclay ....
Petworth............	Portland	Addington ....O	Alfred Knight......
Peveril	Newton	Vaudreuil ....Q	Alexander Morrison.
Phelpston	Flos................	Simcoe, N. R...... .....O	Robert H. Platt....
Philipsburg, East....	St. Armand	Missisquoi ....Q	D. T. R. Nye......
Philipsburg, West..	Wilmot	Waterloo, S. R..........O	Daniel Lohr........
Philipsville.........	Bastard	Leeds, S. R............O	George Brown.....
Pickering	Pickering	Ontario, S. R. ....O	Eliza Whitney.....
Picton...........	Hallowell	Prince Edward..........O	Thomas Shannon ...
Pictou..............	....	Pictou ....N S	Alexander McPhail.
Piedmont Valley, W. O	....	Pictou ....N S	James McDonald...
Pierreville.	Pierreville.........	Yamaska ....Q	H. Pitt ....
Pierreville Mills....	Pierreville.........	Yamaska ....Q	Henry Vassal ......
Pig Brook.....	Number 1..........	Prince...... ......P E I	Peter Richard......

NAME OF POST OFFICE.	TOWNSHIP OR PARISH.	ELECTORAL COUNTY OR DIVISION.	NAME OF POSTMASTER.
Pigeon Hill	St. Armand	Missisquoi Q	Noah Sager
Pigeon Lake	St. François Xavier	Marquette M	J. M. House
Pike River	Stanbridge	Missisquoi Q	A. L. Taylor
Pinedale	Brock	Ontario, N. R O	John Barker
Pine Grove	Vaughan	York, W. R O	A. L. Gooderham
Pine Orchard	Whitchurch	York, N. R O	
Pine River	Huron	Bruce, S. R O	D. McDermid
Pineo Village		King's N S	J. P. Pineo
Pinkerton	Greenock	Bruce, S. R O	Samuel A. King
Piopolis	Marston	Compton Q	Chas. F. Y. Langlois
Pirate Harbor		Guysboro' N S	J. Hartley
Pisarinco, W. O		St. John N B	Thomas Galbraith
Pisquid	Number 37	Queen's P E I	R. McDonald
Pisquid Road	Number 49	Queen's P E I	M. Curran
Pittsferry	Pittsburg	Frontenac O	Daniel Root
Pittston	Edwardsburg	Grenville, S. R O	William Pitt, sen
Plainfield	Thurlow	Hastings, E. R O	Edward N. Gould
Plainfield, W. O		Pictou N S	A. Sutherland
Plantagenet	Plantagenet, North	Prescott O	Henry Smith
Plattsville	Benheim	Oxford, N. R O	John Smart
Playfair	Bathurst	Lanark, S. R O	G. C. Mills
Pleasant Bay, W.O.	Grand Anse	Inverness N S	P. R. Johnson
Pleasant Hill	Walsingham	Norfolk, S. R O	William Morgan
Pleasant Ridge, W.O.		Charlotte N B	Thomas Steen
Pleasant River, W.O.		Queen's N S	Jos. M. Freeman
Pleasant Vale, W.O.		Albert N B	R. A. Colpitts
Pleasant Valley, W.O.		Digby N S	Leslie M. Craig
Plum Hollow	Bastard	Leeds, S. R O	Daniel Derbyshire
Plymouth, W.O.		Yarmouth N S	Wilson G. Sims
Pockmouche, W.O.		Gloucester N B	Thomas Maher
Pockshaw, W.O.		Gloucester N B	
Point Abino	Bertie	Welland O	Ralph Disher
Point Alexander	Rolph	Renfrew, N. R O	Foster Armstrong
Point Bruley, W.O.		Colchester N S	M. P. Hogan

NAME OF POST OFFICE.	TOWNSHIP OR PARISH.	ELECTORAL COUNTY OR DIVISION.	NAME OF POSTMASTER.
Point Clear, W.O...	....	Victoria .... **N S**	Niel Gillis ....
Pointe à Pic (sub)...	Mount Murray	Charlevoix .... **Q**	Archibald McLean..
Pointe au Bouleau ..	Saguenay	Saguenay.............. **Q**	O. Savard ....
Pointe aux Pins.....	Park	Algoma .... **O**	W. G. Foot.........
Pointe aux Trembles	....	Hochelaga .... **Q**	Antoine Lamoureux.
Pointe aux Trembles	Neuville............	Portneuf .... **Q**	Narcisse Blais ......
Pointe Claire	Montreal...........	Jacques Cartier .... **Q**	L. B. Daoust.......
Pointe du Chêne....	St. Ann	Provencher .... **M**	Alex. Chisholm ....
Pointe du Chêne, W.O	....	Westmoreland........ **N B**	Wm. J. M. Hanington
Pointe du Lac	Pointe du Lac......	St. Maurice .... **Q**	Louis Comeau, jun..
Point Edward	Sarnia	Lambton .... **O**	Louis Ernst .... ..
Point Fortune.	Rigaud.............	Vaudreuil .... **Q**	E. A. St. Denis ....
Point Kaye.........	Monck	Muskoka .... **O**	Charles Kaye.......
Point la Nim, W.O.	....	Restigouche .... **N B**	Peter Stewart ......
Point of Cape, W.O.	....	Antigonishe ... . **N S**	Hugh McInnis .....
Point Petre	Athol	Prince Edward .... **O**	James Scott.......
Point Platon	Lotbinière..........	Lotbinière .... **Q**	Joseph Angé ....
Point Prim.........	Number 58	Queen's .... **P E I**	M. N. Murchison...
**Point St. Charles*...	....	Jacques Cartier .... **Q**	Thomas Akin.......
Point St. Peter.....	Malbaie	Gaspé .... **Q**	George Packwood...
Point Sapin, W.O..	....	Kent................. **N B**	Nicholas Merzeroll..
Point Traverse	Marysburg	Prince Edward.... ..... **O**	Geo. A. Ostrander..
Point Wolfe, W.O..	... .	Albert........... .... **N B**	William McGibbon.
Pollett River, W.O.	....	Westmoreland .... **N B**	B. R. Colpitts .....
Pomeroy Ridge, W. O.......	....	Charlotte....... ..... **N B**	John McEvoy ......
Pomona	Glenelg	Grey, S. R....... ...... **O**	William Purdy .....
Pomquet Chapel, W. O..	....	Antigonishe........... **N S**	.. ..
Pomquet Forks, W. O	....	Antigonishe........... **N S**	Mrs. M. Chisholm..
Ponds, W.O........	....	Pictou .... **N S**	A. S. Gray.........
Ponsonby	Pilkington..........	Wellington, C. R........ **O**	James L. Halley....
Pont Chateau	Soulanges	Soulanges............... **Q**	J. B. Besner.. .....
Pont de Maskinongé	Maskinongé	Maskinongé .... **Q**	A. J. Lefrenière....
Pont Rouge	St. Jeanne de Neuville.............	Portneuf .... **Q**	Thos. Larivière.....

NAME OF POST OFFICE.	TOWNSHIP OR PARISH.	ELECTORAL COUNTY OR DIVISION.	NAME OF POSTMASTER.
Poodiac, W.O......	Hammond..........	King's................N B	James Faulkner ....
Poole	Mornington	Perth, N. R.............O	Charles Beck ....
Poplar Grove, W.O.	....	Gloucester....... .. N B	Joseph Aubé ....
Poplar Hill, W.O..	....	Pictou................N S	George Morrison....
Poplar Point	Poplar Point	Marquette........ .....M	David Tait ....
Poquiock, W.O....	....	York..................N B	Michael Doherty ...
Pork Hill..........	Number 13	Prince..............P E I	John G. Hopgood...
Port Acadie, W.O..	....	Digby ....N S	M. Melançon.......
**Portage du Fort....	Litchfield	Pontiac ....Q	John Amey ....
Portage la Prairie...	Portage la Prairie ..	Marquette..............M	Charles Mair ....
Portage River, W.O.	....	Northumberland ......N B	Alex. McDermitt...
Port Albert	Ashfield............	Huron, N. R............O	Thomas Hawkins...
Portapique, W.O...	....	Colchester ....N S	....
PortapiqueMountain W.O............	....	Colchester ....N S	Daniel Giddens.....
Port au Persil	Mount Murray	Charlevoix ....Q	W. McLaren ....
Port Bruce.........	Malahide...........	Elgin, E. R.............O	Thomas Thompson..
**Port Burwell.......	Bayham...........	Elgin, E. R.............O	Thomas Pilcher.....
PortCaledonia,W.O.	....	Cape Breton ....N S	Miss Mary Boutilier
Port Carling........	Medora.............	Muskoka ....O	B. H. Johnston.....
a Port Clyde, W.O.,	....	Shelburne......... ...N S	William Greenwood.
**Port Colborne	Humberstone	Welland ....O	L. G. Carter........
Port Credit..........	Toronto	Peel ....O	Robert Cotton......
**Port Dalhousie.....	Grantham..........	Lincoln.................O	Richard Wood .....
Port Daniel	Port Daniel	Bonaventure ....Q	Patrick Sweetman ..
**Port Dover.........	Woodhouse.........	Norfolk, S. R. ....O	David Abel.........
Port Elgin	....	Westmoreland........N B	Calvin T. Bent .....
Port Elmsley	North Elmsley	Lanark, S. R...... .....O	John Elliott........
Porter's Hill........	Goderich	Huron, S. R...... ......O	James Hendry.....
Porter's Lake, W.O.	....	Halifax...............N S	George Orman......
Port Felix, W.O....	....	Guysboro'............N S	Stephen Boudrot...
Port George, W.O..	....	Annapolis. ....N S	G. B. Reid ......
Port Granby........	Clarke	Durham, W. R. ....O	David March.......
Port Greville, W.O.	....	Cumberland..........N S	Jane Elderkin ......

a Late "Lyle's Bridge," W.O.

NAME OF POST OFFICE.	TOWNSHIP OR PARISH.	ELECTORAL COUNTY OR DIVISION.	NAME OF POSTMASTER.
Port Hastings		Inverness ... N S	J. G. McKeen
Port Hawkesbury		Inverness ... N S	Angus Grant
Port Hood		Inverness ... N S	F. D. Tremaine
Port Hood Island, W. O.		Inverness ... N S	Mrs. Joshua Smith
Port Hoover	Mariposa	Victoria, S. R. ... O	Fred. C. Shaver
**Port Hope*	Hope	Durham, E. R ... O	Robert W. Smart
Port Jolly, W.O.		Shelburne ... N S	L. Robertson
Port Lambton	Sombra	Bothwell ... O	John H. Sewell
Portland	Bastard	Leeds, S. R. ... O	S. S. Scovil
Port la Tour, W.O.		Shelburne ... N S	Nancy H. Snow
Port Lewis	St. Anicet	Huntingdon ... Q	B. B. Carson
Port Maitland	Sherbrooke	Monck ... O	James Moss
Port Matoon, W.O		Queen's ... N S	William T. Leslie
Port Medway		Queen's ... N S	Freeman Cohoon
Port Mulgrave		Guysborough ... N S	G. B. Hadley
Port Nelson	Nelson	Halton ... O	George H. Green
Portneuf	Portneuf	Portneuf ... Q	Charles Gaulin
Port Perry	Reach	Ontario, N. R. ... O	H. Gordon
Port Philip, W.O., late Great Bridge, W.O.		Cumberland ... N S	George King
Port Richmond, W.O	Port Richmond	Richmond ... N S	John G. Murray
**Port Robinson*	Thorold	Welland ... O	James McCoppen
**Port Rowan*	Walsingham	Norfolk, S. R. ... O	Miss M. McLennan.
Port Royal	Walsingham	Norfolk, S. R. ... O	Robert Abbott
Port Royal, W.O		Richmond ... N S	J.M. Adèle LeBlanc
Port Ryerse	Woodhouse	Norfolk, S. R. ... O	Wm. H. Ryerse
Port Severn (sub)	Tay	Simcoe, N. R. ... O	Alex. R. Christie
Portsmouth	Kingston	Frontenac ... O	George McLeod
**Port Stanley*	Yarmouth	Elgin, E. R. ... O	Manuel Payne
Portuguese Cove, W. O		Halifax ... N S	T. Sullivan
Port Union	Pickering	Ontario, S. R. ... O	Cranswick Craven
Port Williams		King's ... N S	Albert Chase
Port Williams Station		King's ... N S	Enoch A. Forsyth

NAME OF POST OFFICE.	TOWNSHIP OR PARISH.	ELECTORAL COUNTY OR DIVISION.	NAME OF POSTMASTER.	
Powell	Huntley	Carleton ... O	Denis Egan	
Powerscourt	Hinchinbrooke	Huntingdon ... Q	David W. Johnson	
Pownal	Number 49	Queen's ... P E I	J. I. Gray	
**Prescott*	Augusta	Grenville, S. R ... O	John Dowsley	
**Preston*	Waterloo, South	Waterloo, S. R ... O	Conrad Nispel	
Preston Road, W.O.		Halifax ... N S	J. S. Griffin	
Priceville	Artemesia	Grey, E. R ... O	D. A. Ghent	
Primrose	Mono	Cardwell ... O	George Dodds	
**Prince Albert*	Reach	Ontario, N. R ... O	H. H. McCaw	
Prince of Wales, W.O		St. John ... N B	John Cairns	
Princeport, W. O.		Colchester ... N S	Mrs. M. Ambrose	
Princeton	Blenheim	Oxford, N. R ... O	Hezekiah C. Forsyth	
Princetown	Number 18	Prince ... P E I	H. E. McKay	
Princetown Road	Number 23	Queen's ... P E I	Allan R. Spence	
Prince William, W.O		York ... N B	T. W. Saunders	
Prospect	Beckwith	Lanark, S. R ... O	William Burrows	
Prospect, W.O		Halifax ... N S	Mrs. M. J. Booth	
Prosser Brook, W.O.		Albert ... N B	David H. Beeman	
Pubnico Beach, W.O		Shelburne ... N S	John McConnisky	
Pubnico Harbor, W. O		Yarmouth ... N S	John Carland	
Pugwash		Cumberland ... N S	Levi Borden	
Pugwash River, W.O		Cumberland ... N S	Thomas A. Frazer	
Purdy	Bangor	Hastings, N. R ... O	W. Lake	
Purpleville	Vaughan	York, W. R ... O		
Puslinch	Puslinch	Wellington, S. R ... O	William Leslie	
Putnam	Dorchester, North	Middlesex, E. R ... O	Seth Barr	

NAME OF POST OFFICE.	TOWNSHIP OR PARISH.	ELECTORAL COUNTY OR DIVISION.	NAME OF POSTMASTER.
Quaco Road, W.O..	....	St. John............ .N B	B. D. Kirkpatrick..
**Quebec*..........	Quebec.......	Quebec ....Q	P. G. Huot.........
Queensborough	Elzevir............	Hastings, N.R..........O	Daniel Thompson...
Queenston..........	Niagara............	Niagara................O	James Wynn.......
Queensville.........	East Gwillimbury...	York, N. R. ....O	James H. Aylward,.
Queensville, W.O...	....	Inverness... ....N S	D. J. McMasters ..
Quesnelle..........	....	Cariboo........... ..B C	Alexander Barlow...
Quesnelle Forks.....	....	Cariboo..............B C	W. P. Barry ....
Radstock......... ...	Kildare...	Joliette ....Q	William Job.. . ...
Ragged Head, W.O.	....	Guysboro'............N S	R. Bruce ....
Ragged Island, W.O.	....	Shelburne ....N S	George Wall........
Raglan	Whitby	Ontario, S. R... .. ....O	Mrs. Mary Still.....
Railton.	Loughboro'.........	Addington ....O	John Walsh........
Rainham...........	Rainham	Haldimand ....O	Isaac Honsberger...
Rainham Centre....	Rainham	Haldimand ....O	W. J. Thompson...
Rama	Rama.............	Ontario, N. R..........O	James McPherson ..
Ramsay's Corners, late Taylorholme .	Gloucester..........	Russell......... ....O	Robert Ramsay.....
Ranelagh..........	Windham	Norfolk, N. R......... .O	Benjamin Lake.....
Rankin............	Wilberforce...	Renfrew, N. R........ O	William P. Edwards
Rapides des Joachims	Aberdeen	Pontiac................Q	William Spence.....
Rathburn..........	Mara..............	Ontario, N. R..........O	Timothy Cuddahee...
Ratho....	Blandford	Oxford, N. R...........O	Joseph Morrow.....
Ratter's Corner, W.O	....	King's...............N B	....
Ravenna	Collingwood	Grey, N. R ....O	William Reid... ...
Ravenscliffe	Chaffey.....	Muskoka ....O	James Sharp........
Ravenshoe..........	East Gwillimbury ..	York, N. R............O	George Glover ......
Ravenswood	Bosanquet..........	Lambton ....O	Paul Jarvis..... ...

NAME OF POST OFFICE.	TOWNSHIP OR PARISH.	ELECTORAL COUNTY OR DIVISION.	NAME OF POSTMASTER.
Rawdon	Rawdon	Montcalm Q	Michael Skelly
Rawdon, W. O		Hants N S	Thomas Moxon
Raymond	Watt	Muskoka O	Anthony Suffern
Reaboro	Ops	Victoria S. R. O	John Holbert
Read, W. O,		Westmoreland N B	Eliphalet Read
Read	Tyendinaga	Hastings, E. R. O	John C. Hanley
Reading	Garafraxa	Wellington, C. R. O	Robert Donaldson
Rear of Black River, W.O.		Richmond N S	John Morrison
Rear Lands, Sporting Mountain, W.O		Richmond N S	William Urquhart
Red Bank, W. O		Northumberland N B	W. S. Brown
Red Islands, W. O		Richmond N S	Alexander McKenzie
Rednersville	Ameliasburg	Prince Edward O	James Redner
Red Rocks		Algoma O	Robert Crawford
Red Point	Number 46	King's P E I	D. Robertson
Reedsdale	Inverness	Megantic Q	James Reed
Relessey	Mono	Cardwell O	Robert Wilson
Renforth	Ancaster	Wentworth, S. R O	Robert Mahew
**Renfrew*	Horton	Renfrew, S. R. O	William Mackay
Renfrew, W. O		Hants N S	
Renous Bridge, W. O		Northumberland N B	R. Jardine
Renton	Townsend	Norfolk, N. R. O	Mrs. Ann Renton
Repentigny	L'Assomption	L'Assomption Q	F. X. O'Brien
Reserve Mines, W. O		Cape Breton N S	John McDonald
Rhodes, W. O		King's N S	William Rhodes
Riceburg	Stanbridge	Missisquoi Q	Simon Lambkin
Riceville	Plantagenet, South	Prescott O	P. McLaurin
Richby	Compton	Compton Q	William Howard
Richibucto		Kent N B	Jean C. Vautour
Richibucto Village, W.O		Kent N B	Urbain Breau
Richmond Corner		Carleton N B	Ivory Kilburn
**Richmond, East*	Cleveland	Richmond Q	G. K. Foster
Richmond, West	Goulbourn	Carleton O	W. H. Butler
**Richmond Hill*	Vaughan	York, W. R O	Matthew Teefy

NAME OF POST OFFICE.	TOWNSHIP OR PARISH.	ELECTORAL COUNTY OR DIVISION.	NAME OF POSTMASTER.
Richmond Station ..	Cleveland	Richmond ....Q	Philip Maher.......
Richmond Terminus, W.O............	....	Halifax...............N S	J. Foot ....
Richview...........	Toronto	Peel.................. O	Robert M. Burgess..
Richwood...........	Blenheim...........	Oxford, N. R.......... O	David Kyte.........
Ridgetown.	Howard....	Bothwell...............O	L. S. Hancock......
Ridgeville	Pelham...	Monck...................O	Jonas Steele.. ......
Rigaud.............	Rigaud............	Vaudreuil ....Q	A. W. Charleboise..
Riley Brook, W.O..	....	Victoria..............N B	....
Rimington	Madoc.............	Hastings, N. R..........O	John Rimington ....
**Rimouski*	St. Germain de Rimouski..........	Rimouski...............Q	Paschal G. St. Pierre
Ringwood	Whitchurch	York, N. R ....O	G. H. Silvester .....
Ripley..............	Huron.............	Bruce, S. R............O	William Carter .....
River Beaudette	....	Soulanges..............Q	Stephen Leblanc ....
River Bourgeoise, W.O.............	....	Richmond.... ....N S	George H. Bissett ..
River Charlo, W.O.	....	Restigouche..........N B	Alex. McPherson...
River David.........	....	Yamaska...............Q	J. B Commeault....
River Debert........	....	Colchester ....N S	Philip Fulmore. ....
River de Chute, W.O	....	Carleton..............N B	F. A. De Wolf.....
River Dennis, W.O.	....	Inverness........... N S	A. McIntyre. ......
River Dennis Road, W.O............	....	Inverness............N S	John Morrison......
River Désert........	Maniwaki......... ...	Ottawa................Q	J. Backus . ...
River Gilbert.......	St. Francois........	Beauce .. ..Q	Geo. W. Chapman..
River Hebert, W.O.	....	Cumberland.... ......N S	Michael Pugsley....
River John	....	Pictou................N S	John D. Gauld......
River Louison, W.O.	....	Restigouche..........N B	Donald Stewart.....
River Philip.........	....	Cumberland..........N S	Mrs. Grace Phillips.
Riversdale	Greenock...........	Bruce, S. R ....O	H. B. O'Connor....
Riversdale, W.O....	....	Colchester ....N S	....
River Side, W.O...	....	Albert ....N B	Hiram Edgett ......
Riverstown.........	Arthur	Wellington, N. R ......O	Alexander Allan...
Rivière aux Vaches.	Deguire	Yamaska ... . .Q	Edouard Côté ......
Rivière Bois Clair...	St. Edouard.........	Lotbinière ....Q	George Bernard ....
Rivière des Prairies	Montreal	Hochelaga............ ....Q	Louis Belanger .....

NAME OF POST OFFICE.	TOWNSHIP OR PARISH.	ELECTORAL COUNTY OR DIVISION.	NAME OF POSTMASTER.
**Rivière du Loup (en bas)*	St. Patrice de la Rivière du Loup	Témiscouata Q	Charles A. Gaudry
Rivière du Loup (en haut)	Rivière du Loup	Maskinongé Q	Louis A. Baribeau
Rivière la Madeleine		Gaspe Q	Edward Vachon
Rivière Ouelle	Rivière Ouelle	Kamouraska Q	John Belleau
Rivière Raisin	Lancaster	Glengarry O	James McPherson
Rivière Trois Pistoles	Trois Pistoles	Témiscouata Q	Edwin Marchement
Roach's Point	North Gwillimbury	York, N. R. O	Richard Flood
Robert's Island, W.O		Yarmouth N S	J. Roberts
Roberval	Roberval	Chicoutimi Q	Theodule Bolduc
Robinson	Bury	Compton Q	Lemeul Pope
Roblin	Richmond	Lennox O	Wm. M. Paul
Rob-Roy	Osprey	Grey, E. R O	Wm. Holden
Rochelle	Stukely	Shefford Q	Augustin Desautels
Rochester	Rochester	Essex O	P. Demouchelle
Rochesterville	Nepean	Carleton O	Leander Booth
Rockburn	Hinchinbrooke	Huntingdon Q	A. Oliver
Rockford	Townsend	Norfolk, N. R. O	W. C. Thompson
Rock Forest	Orford	Sherbrooke Q	Gerard J. Nagle
**Rockingham*	Brudenell	Renfrew, S. R. O	J. S. J. Watson
Rock Island	Stanstead	Stanstead Q	A. A. Barry
Rockland	Clarence	Russell O	Wm. C. Edwards
Rockland, W.O		Westmoreland N B	Jonas Taylor
Rockliffe (sub)	Head	Renfrew, N. R O	W. H. McIntyre
Rocklin, W.O		Pictou N S	Robert Fraser
Rockport	Escott	Leeds, S. R. O	William Cornwall
Rockport, W.O		Westmoreland N B	Rufus Ward
Rockside	Caledon	Cardwell O	D. Kirkwood

NAME OF POST OFFICE.	TOWNSHIP OR PARISH.	ELECTORAL COUNTY OR DIVISION.	NAME OF POSTMASTER.
Rogerville	Usborne	Huron, S. R. O	James Bontaron
Rodney	Alderboro'	Elgin, W. R. O	A. Mumphrey
Roebuck	Augusta	Grenville, S. R. O	
Roger's Hill, W.O.		Picton N S	Angus McKay
Rokeby	Sherbrooke South	Lanark, S. R. O	
Rollo Bay	No. 43	King's P E I	R. McDougall
Rollo Bay Cross	No. 44	King's P E I	L. Chaisson
Rolling Dam, W.O.		Charlotte N B	
Romans Valley, W. O		Guysboro' N S	Patrick Rogers
Romney	Romney	Kent O	
Ronaldsay	Proton	Grey, E.R. O	Joseph McArdle
Rona	Number 60	Queen's P E I	M. McKenzie
Rondeau	Harwich	Kent O	J. K. Morris
Rondeau Harbor	Harwich	Kent O	Robert Brigham
Ronson	Middleton	Norfolk, N.R. O	James Cowan
Rosa	Murray	Northumberland, E.R. O	H. Fieldhouse
Rosebank	South Dumfries	Brant, N.R. O	Almon Almas
Rosedale	Fenelon	Victoria, N.R O	Moses McNeil
Rosedene	Gainsboro'	Monck O	Cornelius McKay
Rosehall	Hillier	Prince Edward O	Isaac G. Ferguson
**Rosemont*	Mulmur	Simcoe, S.R O	George Cumming
Roseneath	Alnwick	Northumberland, W.R. O	Alfred Metcalfe
Rosetta	Lanark	Lanark, N.R. O	Robert McFarlane
Rose Vale, W.O		Albert N B	John Stevens
Rose Valley	Number 67	Queen's P E I	M. Matheson
Roseville	Dumfries, North	Waterloo, S.R O	Moses Gingrich
Roseway, W.O.		Shelburne N S	Elijah Hagar
Roslin	Thurlow	Hastings, E.R O	Barnard C. Carnohan
Roslin, W.O		Cumberland N S	David Stewart
Ross	Ross	Renfrew, N.R. O	
Ross' Corner, W.O.		King's N S	D. G. Ross
Rosseau	Humphrey	Muskoka O	William Ditchburn
Rossway, W.O.		Digby N S	David Cowan
Rothsay	Maryboro'	Wellington, N.R. O	William Smith

NAME OF POST OFFICE.	TOWNSHIP OR PARISH.	ELECTORAL COUNTY OR DIVISION.	NAME OF POSTMASTER.	
Rothsay, W.O.....	....	King's.......... .....N B	....	
Rouge Hill	Pickering...........	Ontario, S.R...... .....O	Hugh Graham......	
Rougemont.........	St. Césaire	Rouville................ Q	D. Bachelder	
Round Hill, W.O...	....	King's................N B	William McLeod....	
Round Hill, W.O...	....	Annapolis............N S	C. E. Spurr.........	
Round Plains.......	Townsend	Norfolk, N.R...........O	George Gillesby.....	
Rowanton	....	Pontiac .... Q	David West.........	
Roxburgh, W.O.....	....	Albert................N B	John Kelly	
Roxham.............	Lacolle...	St. John's .... Q	Thomas Wallis	
Roxton Falls........	Roxton.............	Shefford .... .Q	A. O. T. Beauchemin	
Roxton Pond	Roxton.............	Shefford ....Q	R. A. Kimpton	
Royal Road, W.O..	....	York ....N B	Charles W. Estey...	
Rugby	Oro	Simcoe, N. R.......... O	James Ball	
Ruisseau des Chênes	Upton	Drummond ....Q	C. Paradis..........	
Runnymede	Matapedia	Bonaventure............Q	Mrs.Barbara Wheeler	
Rupert............	Masham	Ottawa............ ....Q	W. D. Leslie	
Rusagornis, W. O....	....	Sunbury.............N B	Holland Smith......	
Rusagornis Station, W.O	....	Sunbury.............N B	John McGill........	
Russell.............	Russell............	Russell ....O	W. R. Petrie	
Russeltown..... ...	....	Chateauguay ....Q	Cyrille Turcotte ...	
Rustico	Number 24.........	Queen's..............P E I	Joseph Gallant	
Rutherford..	Dawn....	Bothwell ....O	John Brown	
Ruthven	Gosfield	Essex.... ....O	Hugh Ruthven	
Ryckman's Corners .	Barton	Wentworth, S. R..... ..O	....	
Ryegate.......... .	Sandwich, East.....	Essex...................O	Joseph Christie.....	
Rylstone...........	Seymour	Northumberland, E. R..O	D. Allan	

NAME OF POST OFFICE.	TOWNSHIP OR PARISH.	ELECTORAL COUNTY OR DIVISION.		NAME OF POSTMASTER
Ste. Adéle	Abercrombie	Terrebonne	Q	Odile Lafleur
St. Agatha	Wilmot	Waterloo, S. R.	O	Anthony Kaiser
Ste. Agathe	Ste. Agathe	Lotbinière	Q	L. Boulanger
Ste. Agnès	Ste. Agnès	Charlevoix	Q	Rev. J. A. Bureau
St. Agnes de Dundee	St. Agnes de Dundee	Huntingdon	Q	Pierre Tremblay
St. Aimé		Richelieu	Q	S. Cartier
St. Alban	St. Alban	Portneuf	Q	John D. McCormick.
St. Albert	Warwick	Arthabaska	Q	Prudent Lainesse
St. Alexandre de Kamouraska	St. Alexandre	Kamouraska	Q	E. Lévèque
St. Alexandre d'Iberville		Iberville	Q	A. A. L. Brien
St. Alexis	St. Sulpice	Montcalm	Q	Léandre Le Bau
St. Alphonse	St. Alphonse	Joliette	Q	Esdras Genereux
St. Anaclet	St. Anaclet	Rimouski	Q	O. Couture
St. André	St. André	Kamouraska	Q	P. C. Marquis
St. André Avelin	Petite Nation	Ottawa	Q	Jos. E. Lévis
St. Andrews		Charlotte	N B	G. F. Campbell
St. Andrews		Antigonishe	N S	Duncan Chisholm
St. Andrews, W.O.		Colchester	N S	
**St. Andrews, East*	Argenteuil	Argenteuil	Q	Thomas Lamb
St. Andrews, West	Cornwall	Cornwall	O	Laekey Masterson
St. Andrews	St. Andrews	District of Lisgar	M	Andrew Mowat
St. Andrew's	Number 38	Kings	P E I	John Ryan
Ste. Angéle de Monnoir	Monnoir	Rouville	Q	Michael O. Caron
Ste. Angéle de Laval	Ste. Angéle de Laval	Nicolet	Q	Olivier Désilets
St. Anicet	St. Anicet	Huntingdon	Q	F. S. Bourgeault
Ste. Anne Bout de l'Isle	Montreal	Jacques Cartier	Q	Adelme Dugal, M.D
Ste. Anne de la Pérade	Ste. Anne	Champlain	Q	Joseph U. Marcotte.
Ste. Anne des Monts	Ste. Anne des Monts	Gaspé	Q	J. Perré
Ste. Anne des Plains	Ste. Anne	Terrebonne	Q	D. Gaudette, M.D.
Ste. Anne la Pocatière	Ste. Anne	Kamouraska	Q	Joseph Dionne
St. Ann's, W.O.		Victoria	N S	M. McKenzie
St. Ann's	Number 22	Queens	P E I	Michael Murphy

NAME OF POST OFFICE.	TOWNSHIP OR PARISH.	ELECTORAL COUNTY OR DIVISION.	NAME OF POSTMASTER.
St. Ann's........ .	Gainsborough......	Monck................O	Mrs. P. E. Upper..
St. Anselme........	St. Anselme........	Dorchester.. .... Q	Pierre Fortier......
St. Anthony, W.O..	....	Kent......... .. ....N B	Cyprien Dionne.....
St. Antoine, Lotbinière	St. Antoine de Tilly.	Lotbinière.............Q	Edmond Larue......
St. Antoine, River Richelieu.........	.. ..	Verchéres............. Q	Narcisse Cartier ....
St. Antonin	St. Antonin........	Témiscouata .... Q	....
St. Apollinaire	St. Apollinaire	Lotbinière .... Q	E. Boucher...... .
St. Armand Centre.	St. Armand.........	Missisquoi .... Q	Abram Titemore....
St. Armand Station.	St. Armand	Missisquoi .... Q	Peter Smith ....
St. Arséne	St. Arséne	Témiscouata .... Q	Elie Martin.........
St. Athanase........	St. Athanase	Iberville................Q	P. Regnier ....
St. Aubert.....,.....	St. Aubert..	L'Islet... .. ..Q	Alexis Blais ....
St. Augustin Portneuf	St. Augustin	Portneuf.............. Q	C. East ....
St. Augustin, Two Mountains........	....	Two Mountains..... ...Q	Louis Paquette. ...
St. Barnabé, River Yamaska.........	St. Barnabé........	St. Hyacinthe..........Q	Joseph P. Gendron.
St. Barnabé, St. Maurice	St. Barnabé.........	St. Maurice.............Q	J. B. L. Duaime....
St. Barthélemi......	St. Barthélemi......	Berthier................Q	J. Fauteux.. .. ..
St. Bazile...........	St. Bazile.....	Portneuf.................Q	G. Jobin......... ..
St. Bazile le Grand..	St. Bazile le Grand..	Chambly ....Q	Eusébe Lalumier ...
Ste. Beatrix	Ste. Beatrix.........	Joliette ....Q	G. Lemire dit Marsolait... ....
St. Benoit..........	Two Mountains.....	Two Mountains..... ...Q	Ernest Lemaire.....
St. Bernard	St. Bernard.........	Dorchester..............Q	Pierre Plante.....
St. Bonaventure	Upton............ .	Drummond ....Q	O. Salois...... ....
St. Boniface........	St. Boniface........	Selkirk ....M	Joseph Dubugue....
Ste. Brigide..... ...	Mounoir............	Iberville ....Q	William Murray....
St. Brigitte des Saults	St. Brigitte des Saults	Nicolet ... .Q	Narcisse Rivet......
St. Bruno...........	Montarville.........	Chambly............. .Q	A. P. Paré.........
St. Camille	St. Camille....	Wolfe ....Q	Guillaume Crepeau..
St. Canute..........	St. Canute	Two Mountains.........Q	John Makereth. ....
St. Casimir	St. Casimir.........	Portneuf ....Q	François X Gingras.
St. Catherine's, East	Fossambault.......	Portneuf ....Q	....
**St. Catherine's West.*	Grantham,....... .	Lincoln.................O	W. L. Copeland... .

NAME OF POST OFFICE.	TOWNSHIP OR PARISH.	ELECTORAL COUNTY OR DIVISION.	NAME OF POSTMASTER.
St. Célestin	St. Célestin	Nicolet Q	C. E. Houde
**St. Césaire*	St. Césaire	Rouville Q	G. A. Gigault
St. Charles	St. Charles	Selkirk M	Mary Adshead
St. Charles de Stanbridge	Stanbridge	Missisquoi Q	Louis Chas. Gauvin
St. Charles, River Boyer	Beauchamp	Bellechasse Q	T. Montminy
St Charles, River Richelieu	St. Charles	St. Hyacinthe Q	J. E. LeBlanc
St. Christophe d'Arthabaska	Arthabaska	Arthabaska Q	James Goodhue
Ste. Claire	Ste. Claire	Dorchester Q	L. V. Royer
St. Clements	Wellesley	Waterloo, N. R O	John Stroh
St. Clet	Soulanges	Soulanges Q	A. Borque
Ste. Clothilde	Horton	Arthabaska Q	C. Gélinas
St. Columbin		Two Mountains Q	M. J. Phelan
St. Côme	Cathcart	Joliette Q	
St. Constant	Lapraire	Laprairie Q	Joseph E. Paradis
St. Croix, W.O		Hants N S	Daniel Mosher
St. Croix, W.O		York N B	Alfred H. Bruning
Ste. Croix	Ste. Croix	Lotbinière Q	J. Hamel
St. Cuthbert		Berthier Q	P. Tellier
St. Cyriac	Kenogami	Chicoutimi Q	Jean Dèschene
St. Cyrille	St. Cyrille	L'Islet Q	J. B. Cloutier
St. Damase	St. Damase	St. Hyacinthe Q	P. H. Petit
St. Damien de Brandon	Brandon	Berthier Q	J. A. Ecremont
St. David's	Niagara	Niagara O	C. Fisher
St. Denis de la Bouteillerie	St. Denis	Kamouraska Q	Paschal Dionne
St. Denis, River Richelieu	St. Denis	St. Hyacinthe Q	Joseph E. Mignault
St. Didace	Lanaudière	Maskinongé Q	Elzéar Germain
St. Dominique		Bagot Q	Treflé Lapalme
St. Dominique, des Cedres	Soulanges	Soulanges Q	L. Cown
Ste. Dorothee	Ste. Dorothee	Laval Q	Emélion Charron
St. Edouard		Napierville Q	J. Blain

NAME OF POST OFFICE.	TOWNSHIP OR PARISH.	ELECTORAL COUNTY OR DIVISION.	NAME OF POSTMASTER.
St. Edouard de Frampton, (sub)...	Frampton	Dorchester ....Q	James Butler ......
St. Edwidge........	Clifton	Compton ....Q	F. Courtemanche...
St. Elie	Caxton............	St. Maurice ....Q	C. H. Coutu ....
St. Eleanors	Number 17	Prince............. P E I	J. T. Fraser........
Ste. Elizabeth......	....	Berthier....... ....Q	P. L. Hudon dit Beaulieu ....
St. Eloi	St. Eloi...........	Témiscouata....... ....Q	Jacques Theriault...
St. Elzéar	St. Elzéar	Beauce ....Q	Jean Bilodeau ......
Ste. Emelie de l'Energie	Joliette	Joliette ....Q	Rev. M. Lussier....
St. Ephrem de Tring	Tring	Beauce ....Q	Olivier Begin ....
St. Ephrem d'Upton	Upton.............	Bagot ....Q	S. B. Warner.......
St. Esprit...... ...	....	Montcalm ....Q	C. Dalpédit Pariseau
St. Esprit, W.O....	....	Richmond ....N S	John Matheson......
St. Etienne de Beauharnois	Beauharnois	Beauharnois ....Q	T. Vernor.... .....
St. Etienne de Bolton...........	Bolton.......	Brome.................Q	Louis Poulin........
St. Etienne des Grés	St. Etienne des Grés.	St. Maurice...........Q	Uldoric Brunelle ...
St. Eugène	Hawkesbury, East..	Prescott ....O	Simon Labrosse.....
St. Eustache	....	Two Mountains........Q	Philias Gauthier ....
St. Evariste de Forsyth	Forsyth	Beauce ....Q	....
St. Fabien	St. Fabien	Rimouski...... ....Q	Vital Roy dit Lauzon
Ste. Famille..... ..	Ste. Famille.......	Montmorency..........Q	Joseph Prémont ....
St. Felicité	St. Denis....	Rimouski.......... ....Q	J. B. LeBel.........
St. Félix de Valois..	....	Joliette. ....Q	Max. Crepeau ... ..
St. Ferdinand.......	Halifax	Megantic .. ..Q	Louis I. Frechette..
St. Féréol (sub-office)	St. Féréol	Montmorency..........Q	....
St. Fidèle	Mount Murray .. .	Charlevoix.............Q	Archille Bhérour...
St. Flavie	St. Flavie	Rimouski..............Q	A. A. St. Laurent..
St. Flavien.........	St. Flavien	Lotbinière ... .Q	L. Bédard.. ....
Ste. Flore	Cap de la Madelaine	Champlain.............Q	F. Vincent dit Maheux ....
St. Foy	St. Foy	Quebec ....Q	Felix Belleau . ...
St. François, Beauce	St. François, Beauce	Beauce ....Q	Hiliare Poulin ......
St. François de Sales	St. François de Sales	Laval ....Q	....

NAME OF POST OFFICE.	TOWNSHIP OR PARISH.	ELECTORAL COUNTY OR DIVISION.	NAME OF POSTMASTER.
St. Francoisd'Orleans	St. Françoisd'Orleans	Montmorency........Q	Emilien Pepin dit Lachance.........
St. François du Lac.	....	Yamaska..............Q	O. H. Coutu.... .
Ste. Françoise	Bégon............	Temiscouta. ....Q	Rev. A. Duval......
St. François, Montmagny..........	St. François........	Montmagny ....Q	E. C. Boulet.......
St. François Xavier.	St. François Xavier.	Marquette.. ....M	J. B. Thibeault.....
St. Frédéric........	St. Frédéric........	Beauce................Q	L. G. A. Legendre..
St. Gabriel de Brandon............	Brandon...........	Berthier..............Q	M. O'Heir.........
Ste. Geneviéve	Montreal.	Jacques Cartier........Q	Godfroi Boileau.....
St. George..........	....	Charlotte ....N B	E. R. O'Brien.......
St. George, Beauce..	St. George....	Beauce. ....Q	Hubert Catellier....
St. George, Brant....	Dumfries, South....	Brant, N. R ....O	C. Batty.. .. ..
St. GeorgedeWindsor	Windsor..	Richmond..............Q	Edward Millette....
St. George's Channel, W.O............	....	Richmond...........N S	William McKenzie..
St. Germain de Grantham....	Grantham	Drummond............Q	H. P. Paré.........
Ste. Gertrude.......	Ste. Gertrude.......	Nicolet............... Q	Léon Champoux....
St. Gervais.........	St. Gervais.........	Bellechasse............Q	Marcel Aubé.......
St. Giles..........	St. Giles....	Lotbinière.............Q	George Coté........
St. Grégoire........	St. Grégoire........	Nicolet...... ....Q	J. A. Poirier ......
St. Guillaume d'Upton.............	Upton.....	Drummond..... ....Q	H. Mercier....... ..
Ste. Héléne	Ste. Héléne.......	Kamouraska...........Q	B. Michaud........
Ste. Héléne de Bagot	....	Bagot................. Q	Pierre Fafard......
St. Helen's.........	Wawanosh........	Huron, N. R ....O	Robert Murray.....
Ste. Hénédine......	Ste. Hénédine......	Dorchester... ....Q	Joseph Mercier.....
St. Henri..........	Lauzon............	Lévis..................Q	Charles A. Collet...
St. Henri Station...	St. Henri..........	Lévis........... ......Q	George Demers.....
St. Hermas....	....	Two Mountains........Q	P. E. Clairoux.....
St. Hermenegilde...	Barford	Stanstead.............O	Calixte Duquis.....
*a*St. Hilaire, W.O.	....	Victoria............N B	Peter Michaud......
St. Hilaire Station..	St. Hilaire.........	Rouville...............Q	Thomas Valiquet...
St. Hilaire Village.	St. Hilaire.........	Rouville...............Q	E. Goulet.........
St. Hippolyte de Kilkenny............	Kilkenny..........	Montcalm............. Q	Rev. F. X. Laberge
St. Honoré.........	Shenley	Beauce............ ....Q	Pierre Boucher.....

*a*Late Baker's Creek, W. O.

NAME OF POST OFFICE.	TOWNSHIP OR PARISH.	ELECTORAL COUNTY OR DIVISION.	NAME OF POSTMASTER.
St. Hubert.........	....	Chambly. .... Q	Francois Robert.....
St. Hugues.........	....	Bagot..... ....Q	Emery Lafontaine ..
**St. Hyacinthe*......	St. Hyacinthe......	St. Hyacinthe..........Q	E. L. R. C. Després
St. Irénée..........	St. Irénée....	Charlevoix .... Q	Joseph Gosselin.....
St. Isidore, Dorchester............ ...	St. Isidore.	Dorchester ....Q	B. Morin...........
St. Isidore, Laprairie	....	Laprairie .... Q	F. T. Langevin.....
St. Ives............	West Nissouri......	Middlesex, E. R.........O	Thomas Howard....
St. Jacob's..........	Woolwich	Waterloo, N. R..........O	John L. Wideman..
St. James..........	St. James.........	Selkirk.............. ..M	James McKay......
St. Jaques	St. Sulpice.........	Montcalm ....Q	J. F. Ecrement....
St. Jaques le Mineur	....	Laprairie...............Q	Joseph O. Poirier....
St. James Park (sub)	Westminster.	Middlesex, E. R....... O	John Taylor........
St. Janvier....... .	St. Janvier.........	Terrebonne............ Q	David Desroches....
St. Jean Baptiste de Montreal.........	Côte St. Louis......	Hochelaga.............Q	Gilbert Filiatreault.
St. Jean Baptiste de Rouville..........	Rouville...........	Rouville......... ......Q	L. G. E. Goulet ...
St. Jean Chrysostome, Chateauguay....	... .	Chateauguay ....Q	I. J. L. Derome...
St. Jean Chrysostome Levis.............	Lauzon....	Lévis...................Q	Louis Goslin ....
St. Jean des Chaillons	St. Jean des Chaillons	Lotbinière.............Q	P. C. Levasseur ....
St. Jean de Matha..	Brandon...........	Joliette ....Q	F. X. Lasalle.......
St. Jean d'Orléans ..	St. Jean d'Orleans..	Montmorency ....Q	F. X. Turcotte .....
St. Jean Port Joli ..	St. Jean Port Joli...	L'Islet ....Q	Marie Fournier .....
**St. Jérome*.........	....	Terrebonne............Q	Edouard Marchand..
St. Joachim	St. Joachim	Montmorency .. ..Q	Isaie Simard........
St. Joachim de Shefford.........	Roxton............	Shefford...............Q	Joseph Bachand.....
St. John............	....	St. John ....NB	John Howe... .....
**St. John's, East*	....	St. John's.............Q	W. A. Osgood......
St. John's, West....	Thorold	Welland................O	A. B. Brown ....
St. Joseph	St. Joseph	Beauce ....Q	Miss F. A. A. Arcand
St. Joseph, W.O....	....	Westmoreland ....N B	Daniel Ethier.......
St. Joseph du Lac ..	Two Mountains.....	Two Mountains.........Q	John McColl.. .....
St. Jude	St. Jude............	St. Hyacinthe ... .Q	Hubert Lemay......
St. Julie............	Belœil..............	Verchéres ....Q	Joseph Collette .....

NAME OF POST OFFICE.	TOWNSHIP OR PARISH.	ELECTORAL COUNTY OR DIVISION.	NAME OF POSTMASTER.
Ste. Julie de Somerset	Somerset	Megantic . . . . Q	Louis Roberge
St. Julienne		Montcalm . . . . Q	Jos. Racette
St. Justin		Maskinongé . . . . Q	Louis St. Antoine
St. Justine de Newton	Newton	Vaudreuil . . . . Q	V. J. Lalonde
St. Lambert	Lauzon	Lévis . . . . Q	M. Brochu
St. Lambert, Montreal	Laprairie	Chambly . . . . Q	Andrew Irving
St. Laurent d'Orléans	St. Laurent d'Orléans	Montmorency . . . . Q	Jean Bte. Gosselin
St. Laurent, Montreal	Montreal	Jacques Cartier . . . . Q	Joseph Le Cavalier
*a*St. Laurent		Marquette . . . . M	Rev. J. Mulvihill
St. Lazare	St. Lazare	Bellechasse . . . . Q	Rev. E. Dufour
St. Léon	Dumontier	Maskinongé . . . . Q	F. X. A. Rivard
St. Leonard	Aston	Nicolet . . . . Q	Ludger Désilets
St. Leonard's, W.O.		Victoria . . . . N B	Frank Kearney
St. Liboire	St. Liboire	Bagot . . . . Q	J. C. Bachand
St. Liguori		Montcalm . . . . Q	Ulric B. Desrochers
St. Lin		L'Assomption . . . . Q	Thomas Garault
St. Louis de Gonzague		Beauharnois . . . . Q	Léandre Vachon
Ste. Louise	Ste. Louise	L'Islet . . . . Q	Nazaire Caron
St. Luc	Longueuil	St. John's . . . . Q	Samuel Hamilton
Ste. Luce	Lessard	Rimouski . . . . Q	James Miller
St. Magloire	Rioux	Bellechasse . . . . Q	Pierre Tanguay
St. Malachie	East Frampton	Dorchester . . . . Q	George Duncan
St. Malo	Auckland	Compton . . . . Q	Moyse Roy
St. Marc	St. Marc	Verchères . . . . Q	
St. Marcel		Richelieu . . . . Q	Anselme Plamondon
St. Margaret's Bay		Halifax . . . . N S	J. S. Brine
St. Margaret's	Number 43	King's . . . . P E I	James McCormack
Ste. Marguerite	Ste. Marguerite	Dorchester . . . . Q	F. E. Genest
Ste. Marie de Monnoir	Ste. Marie	Rouville . . . . Q	G. H. Gatien
Ste. Marthe	Rigaud	Vandreuil . . . . Q	E. H. Lalonde
St. Martin	Isle Jésus	Leval . . . . Q	Léon Sauriol
St. Martine	St. Martine	Chateauguay . . . . Q	Antoine Hébert
St. Martin's		St. John . . . . N B	Andrew S. Killen

*a*Late Indian Mission

NAME OF POST OFFICE.	TOWNSHIP OR PARISH.	ELECTORAL COUNTY OR DIVISION.	NAME OF POSTMASTER.
St. Martin's, W. O.	....	St. John .... N B	J. Berry............
St. Mary's Bay, W. O	....	Digby .... N S	Edward Everett ....
**St. Mary's*	Blanchard	Perth, S. R............ O	Peter M. Nichol ....
St. Mary's, W. O...	....	Kent .... N B	Olivier Le Blanc....
St. Mary's Ferry, W. O	....	York................ N B	C. L. Estabrook ....
St. Mary's Road	Number 61	King's.. .... P E I	James Gormley.....
St. Mathias.........	East Chambly	Rouville................ Q	Paul Bertrand ......
St. Mathieu	St. Mathieu	Rimouski.............. Q	T. Leveque.........
St. Maurice	Cap de la Magdelaine	Champlain . ... Q	G. E. Bistodeau.....
St. Maurice Forges..	St. Etienne..... ...	Maurice .... Q	J. B. Beauchemin...
St. Michel..........	St. Michel.........	Bellechasse .... Q	E. S. Belleau.......
St. Michel des Saints	Brassard...........	Berthier... . ... Q	Rev. J. A. Dagnaul
St. Modeste	Wentworth	Témiscouata............ Q	Narcisse Miville ....
St. Moise..........	Cabot	Rimouski .... Q	George Blais........
St. Monique	St. Monique........	Nicolet .... Q	Godfroi Rosseau ....
St. Monique des deux Montagnes.......	St. Monique des deux Montagnes	Two Mountains.... .... Q	Damase Leonard....
St. Narcisse	Champlain	Champlain .... Q	D. Hamelin ....
St. Nicholas	St. Nicholas	Lévis..... .... Q	Morris Scott........
St. Norbert	Berthier	Berthier................ Q	N. Roch............
St. Norbert.........	St. Norbert, North..	Provencher. .... M	Joseph Lemay ......
St. Octave....	Métis	Rimouski.............. Q	....
St. Ola	Limerick	Hastings, N. R......... O	William Morton ....
St. Onézime	St. Onézime	Kamouraska .... Q	L. Oulette..........
St. Ours...........	St. Ours............	Richelieu............... Q	L. Chapelaine ......
St. Pacôme...... ..	Rivière Ouelle.....	Kamouraska........... Q	Alexander Hudon ..
St. Paschal.........	St. Paschal.........	Kamouraska........... Q	E. Chapleau........
St. Patrick, W.O...	....	Charlotte............ N B	Richard Dyer.......
St. Patrick's Channel W. O............	....	Victoria .... N S	John McNaughton..
St. Patrick's Hill ...	Tingwick	Arthabaska.. .... Q	Joseph S. Beaudette
St. Paul d'Industrie.	....	Joliette .... Q	Joseph Guilbault ....
St. Paul du Buton ..	Montmini	Montmagny .... Q	Rev. W. Couture ...
St. Paulin	St. Paulin..........	Maskinongé .... Q	Olivier Lafond......
St. Paul l'Hermite..	L'Assomption.......	L'Assomption .... Q	Joseph Marion......

NAME OF POST OFFICE.	TOWNSHIP OR PARISH.	ELECTORAL COUNTY OR DIVISION.	NAME OF POSTMASTER.
St. Paul's, W.O.		Pictou N S	William Thompson
St. Paul's, W.O.		Kent N B	Pacifique Belliveau
**St. Paul's Bay*	St. Paul's Bay	Charlevoix Q	Ovide A. Clement
St. Perpetue	St. Perpetue	Nicolet Q	Onésime Rousseau
St. Peter's		Richmond N S	R. G. Morrison
St. Peter's	St. Peter's	Lisgar M	Edward Thomas
St. Philippe	St. Philippe	Laprairie Q	Z. Mayrand
St. Philippe d'Argenteuil	Chatham	Argenteuil Q	Fernandez Naubert.
St. Philippe de Nery	St. Philippe de Nery	Kamouraska Q	François Deschène
Ste. Philomêne		Chateauguay Q	Mrs. M. J. D'Amour
St. Pie		Bagot Q	A. Gauthier dit Landerville
St. Pierre Baptiste	Inverness	Megantic Q	P. A. Drolet
St. Pierre d'Orleans	St. Pierre d'Orleans	Montmorency Q	F. Fortin
St. Pierre les Becquets	St. Pierre les Becquets	Nicolet Q	Thomas Phillips
St. Pierre Montmagny	St. Pierre Montmagny	Montmagny Q	Sarah D. Bacon
St. Placide		Two Mountains Q	Zephirin Raymond
St. Polycarpe	New Longueuil	Soulanges Q	John Taylor
St. Prime	Ashuapmouchouan	Chicoutimi Q	Rev. E. Auclair
St. Prosper	St. Prosper	Champlain Q	Joseph Frigon
St. Raphael, East	St. Raphael	Bellechasse Q	P. C. A. Fournier
St. Raphael, West	Charlottenburg	Glengarry O	Mrs. Mary McDonell
St. Raymond	Bourg Louis	Portneuf Q	Edouard Plamondon
St. Regis	St. Regis	Huntingdon Q	Robert Tyre
St. Remi	La Salle	Napierville Q	Charles Bedard
St. Robert		Richelieu Q	Olivier Dupré
**St. Roch de Québec*	St. Roch de Québec	Quebec City, East Q	Louis P. Huot
St. Roch de Richelieu	St. Roch de Richelieu	Richelieu Q	J. B. Paquette
St. Roch des Aulnaies	St. Roch des Aulnaies	L'Islet Q	A. Morin
St. Roch l'Achigan		L'Assomption Q	O. Peltier
St. Romaine	Winslow	Compton Q	E. Bélanger
St. Rosalie	St. Rosalie	Bagot O	Ant. Cabana
Ste. Rose	[illegible]	[illegible] Q	Adelard E. Leonard.

NAME OF POST OFFICE.	TOWNSHIP OR PARISH.	ELECTORAL COUNTY OR DIVISION.		NAME OF POSTMASTER.
St. Sauveur	St. Sauveur	Terrebonne	Q	L. L. J. Loranger ..
St. Sauveur de Québec	Banlieue de Québec .	Quebec	Q	J. L. Saucier.......
St. Scholastique	....	Two Mountains.........	Q	A. Fortier... .....
St. Sebastien	St. George de Henryville............	Iberville........	Q	Luc Lamoureux ....
St. Sévère	....	St. Maurice	Q	Adolphe Lamy......
St.Simon deRimouski	....	Rimouski.	Q	Antoine Bernier....
St.Simon deYamaska	De Ramsey.........	Bagot	Q	Alfred Brien..... .
Ste. Sophie.........	Halifax............	Megantic..............	Q	Joseph Vigneau.....
Ste. Sophie de Lacorne............	Lacorne	Terrebonne	Q	Ulric Leveque ......
St. Stanislas........	Batiscan...	Champlain	Q	A. Jos. Lacourcière.
St.StanislasdeKostka	....	Beauharnois	Q	Onésime Dorais.....
St. Stephen	....	Charlotte.	N B	James A. Grant ....
St. Sulpice	L'Assomption.......	L'Assomption	Q	Jacques Royal.....
St. Sylvester	St. Sylvester	Lotbinière	Q	John Machell ......
St. Sylvester, East..	St. Sylvester	Lotbinière	Q	Joan Lessard ....
St. Théodore	Acton	Bagot	Q	Paul Decelle ....
St. Théodore de Chertsey	Chertsey	Montcalm	Q	Marcel Lepine......
Ste. Thérèse de Blainville	Blainville	Terrebonne	Q	David Morris.......
St. Thomas, East ...	Lanoraie	Joliette	Q	Joseph Latour, *dit* Forget ....
**St. Thomas, West*...	Yarmouth	Elgin, E. R.	O	F. E. Ermatinger...
St. Timothée	....	Beauharnois	Q	J. B. Scott.. ......
St. Tite	Batiscan............	Champlain	Q	....
St. Tite desCaps (sub. office)	St. Tite	Montmorency	Q	Rev.G.E. Savaugeau
St. Urbain	....	Chateauguay	Q	J. B. Matthieu.....
St. Urbain	St. Urbain	Charlevoix	Q	Onésime Gauthier ..
Ste. Ursule.........	....	Maskinongé	Q	L. Lupien..........
St. Valentine.......	....	St. John's	Q	J. H. Lamarche ..
St. Valérien.... ...	Milton	Shefford	Q	P. S. Grandpré.....
St. Vallier	St. Vallier..........	Bellechasse	Q	F. Belanger ....
Ste. Victoire	....	Richelieu..	Q	C. P. Clotier. ...
St. Victor de Tring..	Tring	Beauce	Q	François Gosselin,jun
St. Vincent de Paul.	Isle Jésus	Laval	Q	C. Germain, jun....

NAME OF POST OFFICE.	TOWNSHIP OR PARISH.	ELECTORAL COUNTY OR DIVISION.	NAME OF POSTMASTER.
St. Wenceslas.......	Ashton	Nicolet .... Q	Ferdinand Thèrien..
St. Williams........	Walsingham........	Norfolk, S. R...... .... O	Harriet L. Kitchen.
St. Zenon...........	Provost	Berthier .... Q	Felix M. Trudeau ..
St. Zephirin........	Courval	Yamaska.............. Q	Nestor Duguay .....
St. Zotique.........	....	Soulanges .... Q	O. F. Prieur........
Sable.............	West Williams	Middlesex, N. R........ O	A. McDonald .....
Sable River, W. O..	....	Shelburne............ N S	....
Sabrevois..........	Sabrevois	Iberville.............. Q	Thomas Jones ......
Sackville..........	....	Westmoreland .... N B	Jos. Dixon.........
Saintfield....	Reach......	Ontario, N.R.......... O	Donald McKay.....
Salem..............	Nichol	Wellington, C.R........ O	John R. Wissler....
Salem, W.O...	....	Albert................ N B	Joshua Steeves.....
Salem, W.O.... ..	....	Cumberland.......... N S	E. Black ....
Salford	Dereham	Oxford, S. R........... O	William Boon ......
Salisbury	....	Westmoreland .... N B	... .
Salmon Beach, W.O.	....	Gloucester........... N B	R. Buttemer ....
Salmon Creek, W.O.	....	Sunbury.............. N B	James Fowler .... .
Salmon Hole, W. O.	....	Halifax .. .. N S	Jacob Sellis ....
Salmon River, W.O.	....	St. John..... .... N B	Edward H. Foster ..
Salmon River, W.O.	....	Cape Breton.......... N S	J. Huntington......
Salmon River, W.O.	....	Digby................ N S	E. Shehan.... ......
Salmon River, W.O.	....	Guysboro'............ N S	D. Lawlor ....
Salmon River, W.O.	....	Halifax .... N S	Ann Gallagher......
Salmon River (Lake Settlement), W.O.	....	Guysboro'............ N S	Thomas O'Neil......
Salmonville.........	Chinguacousy......	Peel .... O	Simon Plewes.......
Salt Springs, W. O.	....	King's............... N B	George McEwan....
Sambro, W.O	....	Halifax .... N S	E. Smith ... .

NAME OF POST OFFICE.	TOWNSHIP OF PARISH.	ELECTORAL COUNTY OR DIVISION.	NAME OF POSTMASTER.
Sanborn............	Wolfeston	Wolfe .... Q	Thomas Hurley, jun.
Sand Beach, W.O...	....	Yarmouth............N S	Wm. R. Pinkney...
Sandfield	Lochiel.............	Glengarry ....O	Mrs. McRae.. ....
Sandford	Scott...............	Ontario, N. R...........O	Edward Taylor .....
Sandhill	Chinguacousy..... .	Peel ....O	W. C. Hughes......
Sandhurst	S. Fredericksburg...	Lennox ....O	William Hill........
Sand Point	McNab..............	Renfrew, S. R.... ......O	Edward Derenzy....
Sand Point, W.O...	....	Guysboro'............N S	Alexander J. Fox...
**Sandwich*	Sandwich, West	Essex ....O	C. St. Louis........
Sandy Beach........	South Gaspé Bay ...	Gaspé ....Q	Nicholas Bailey.....
Sandy Beaches, W. O	....	Halifax ....N S	Isaac Cleveland.....
Sandy Cove	... .	Digby..................N S	John C. Morse......
Sandy Point, W.O..	....	Shelburne ....N S	John Purney... ....
Sarawak............	Sarawak...........	Grey, N. R.............O	John McKenzie.....
Sarepta..............	Hay	Huron, S. R............O	William Reynolds...
**Sarnia*	Sarnia..............	Lambton.......... .....O	William Murphy...
**Saugeen*	Saugeen	Bruce, N. R............O	Thomas Lee ....
Saulnierville, W.O..	....	Digby..... .... N S	Samuel McCormack.
Sault au Récollet ...	Montreal	Hochelaga ....Q	Edward Dauphin....
Sault Ste. Marie....	....	Algoma. ....O	Mrs. Pim..... .....
Savage's Mill	Shefford	Shefford ....Q	A. H. Savage.......
Saw Mill Creek, W.O	....	Annapolis............N S	Richardson Harris ..
Sawyerville.........	Newport	Compton...............Q	W. S. Scholefield....
**Scarboro'*..........	Scarboro'	York, E. R ....O	Donald McLean....
Scarboro' Junction ..	Scarboro'	York, E. R ....O	George Taylor, Sr ..
Schomberg..........	King..........	York, N. R ....O	J. McGinnis.. .....
Scone............. ..	Elderslee	Bruce, N. R ....O	Thomas Bearman...
Scotch Settlement, W.O.	....	Westmoreland........N B	Niel McDougall ....
Scotch Town, W.O..	....	Queen's ....N B	John R. Carle .....
Scotch Village, W.O	....	Hants .... .N S	John T. Cochran....
Scotchfort	Number 36	Queen's .. ..P E I	A. McDonald.......
Scotland	Oakland............	Brant S. R ....O	H. Lyman..........
Scott's Bay, W.O...	....	King's... ....N S	A. C. Ells..........
Scovill's Mills, W.O.	....	Kent....... ....N B	L. M. White......

NAME OF POST OFFICE.	TOWNSHIP OR PARISH.	ELECTORAL COUNTY OR DIVISION.		NAME OF POSTMASTER.
Scugog	Scugog	Ontario, N. R	O	Isaac Finley
**Seaforth*	Tuckersmith	Huron, C. R.	O	Samuel Dickson
Seaton	York	York, W. R	O	Allan Orr
Searletown	Number 27	Prince	P E I	Hiram Trueman
Sebringville	Ellice	Perth, N. R	O	
Second Falls, W.O.		Charlotte	N B	James C. Pratt
Section 7, W. O.		Cumberland	N S	
Seeley's Bay	Leeds	Leeds, S. R.	O	William Coleman
Seeley's Mill's, W.O.		King's	N B	Andrew McAfee
Seely	Brunel	Muskoka	O	Obadiah Seely
Segeun Falls	Monteith	Muskoka	O	D. F. Burk
Selby	Richmond	Lennox	O	David Wartman
Selkirk	Walpole	Haldimand	O	R. J. Winyard
Selkirk Road	Number 60	Queen's	P E I	John Dogherty
Selmah, W.O.		Hants	N S	Archibald Frame
Selton	Howard	Bothwell	O	James Robinson
Selwyn	Smith	Peterborough, W. R	O	Richard Northey
**Seneca*	Seneca	Haldimand	O	John Scott
Settrington	Settrington	Charlevoix	Q	Rev. M. E. Roy
Severn Bridge	Morrison	Muskoka	O	James H. Jackson
Sevigné	Hartwell	Ottawa	Q	Hercule Chénier
Shag Harbour, W.O		Shelburne	N S	[illegible]. W. Nickerson
Shakespeare	South Easthope	Perth, S. R	O	George Brown
Shamrock	Admaston	Renfrew, S. R	O	
Shanick	Marmora	Hastings, N. R	O	James Bailey
Shanklin, W.O		St. John's	N B	Samuel J. Shanklin
Shanly	Edwardsburgh	Grenville, S. R.	O	William Clark
Shannonvale, W. O.		Restigouche	N B	Nathaniel Ferrett
Shannonville	Tyendinaga	Hastings, E. R.	O	Hiram Holden
Shanty Bay	Oro	Simcoe, N.R.	O	Thomas Fletcher
Sharon	Gwillimbury, East	York, N. R	O	John J. Stokes
Sharpton	Kingston	Frontenac	O	[illegible] McKechnie
Shawbridge	Abercrombie	Terrebonne	Q	William Shaw
Shawenegan	Shawenegan	St. Maurice	Q	Joseph Desaulniers
Shea's River, W.O.		Inverness	N S	Alex. McDonald

NAME OF POST OFFICE.	TOWNSHIP OR PARISH.	ELECTORAL COUNTY OR DIVISION.	NAME OF POSTMASTER.
*a*Shedden........ ...	Bexley	Victoria, N. R.......... **O**	Mrs. Nancy Leroy ..
Shediac............	....	Westmoreland .... **N B**	A. R. Weldon ....
Shediac Bridge, W.O	....	Westmoreland .... **N B**	Athanase Gallant ...
Shediac Road, W.O.	....	Westmoreland.. ...... **N B**	James Rodgerson....
Sheenboro'..........	Sheen	Pontiac . ... **Q**	....
Sheet Harbor	....	Halifax............... **N S**	W. Hall............
Sheffield	Beverley...........	Wentworth, N. R. ...... **O**	Edwin Bond........
Sheffield............	....	Sunbury............ **N B**	C. J. Burpee.... .
Sheffield Academy, W.O	....	Sunbury............. **N B**	Whitehead Barker ..
Sheffield Mills, W. O.	....	King's............... **N S**	Watson Ells ....
Shefford Mountain ..	Shefford	Shefford .... **Q**	William Saxby ... .
Shelburne	Melancthon.........	Grey, E. R.............. **O**	Edward Berwick...
Shelburne...........	....	Shelburne............ **N S**	R. R. Thomson....
Sheldon	Adjala	Cardwell.......... ..... **O**	M. Webster ....
Sheldrake	....	Saguenay .... **Q**	Philip Touzel.......
Shepody Road, W.O.	....	King's .... **N B**	Jos. Wallace........
**Sherbrooke*	Ascot	Sherbrooke. .... **Q**	Samuel J. Foss ....
Sherbrooke	St. Mary's..........	Guysborough .... **N S**	Jas. H. McDonald ..
Sheridan	Trafalgar.	Halton .... **O**	....
Sherkston	Humberstone	Welland .... **O**	H. B. Zavitz.......
Sherrington.........	Sherrington...	Napierville .... **Q**	Raymond Robert....
Sherwood Spring....	Yonge	Leeds, S. R. .... **O**	James Simpson......
Shetland............	Euphemia	Bothwell .... **O**	Richard Laird ......
Shigawake..........	Hope...............	Bonaventure........... **Q**	Andrew Young ....
Shiktehawk, W. O ..	....	Carleton.... .... **N B**	Edwin Phillips... .
Shinemicas Bridge ..	....	Cumberland........... **N S**	John Moore ....
Ship Harbor, W. O..	....	Halifax............... **N S**	Charles Dean ....
Shipley.......... ..	Wallace	Perth, N. R.... .... **O**	Edward Bristow ....
Shippigan	....	Gloucester........... **N B**	John Dorron........
Shoolbred	Shoolbred	Bonaventure.. .... **Q**	Jean Trottier ......
Short Beach, W. O.	. ...	Yarmouth .... **N S**	James Bent....... .
Shrewsbury	Chatham, West Gore	Argenteuil............... **Q**	John Chambers.....
Shrigley.	Melancthon	Grey, E. R. .... **O**	George Bailey ......
Shubenacadie	....	Colchester .... **N S**	Andrew Kirkpatrick

*a*Late Coboconk.

NAME OF POST OFFICE	TOWNSHIP OR PARISH.	ELECTORAL COUNTY OR DIVISION.	NAME OF POSTMASTER.
Shulie, W. O........	....	Cumberland ....N S	A. W. Grant.......
Sidney Crossing.....	Sidney	Hastings, W.R..........O	N. R. Vandervoort.
Sierra	Charlottenburg	Glengarry .... O	C. J. McRea......
Sight Point, W.O...	....	Inverness.............N S	D. McEachean .....
Sillery Cove	St. Columba.........	Quebec ....Q	Peter McNeil.......
Sillsville	Fredericksburg	Lennox ....O	Samuel [illegible]. Mellow .
Siloam	Uxbridge...........	Ontario, N. R...........O	Samuel Widderfield.
Silver Hill	Charlotteville.......	Norfolk, S. R...........O	Henry C. Gifford ...
Silver Islet	....	Algoma...............O	John Livingstone ...
Silverstream, W. O.	....	Victoria ....N B	Baptiste Guimond ..
**Simcoe*	Woodhouse.........	Norfolk, N. R ....O	Henry Mulkins.....
Singhampton........	Nottawasaga	Simcoe, N.R. ....O	James Hamilton....
Six Mile Brook, W.O	.. ..	Pictou ....N S	John McKay ....
Six Mile Road, W.O	....	Cumberland ....N S	Albert Angevine....
Six Portages	Bouchette	Ottawa.................Q	John Sproule.......
Skeena.............	....	Cariboo..... ....B C	Thomas Hankin ....
Skinner's Pond	Number 1	Prince.............P E I	J. Doyle . ...
Skipness	Amabel	Bruce, N. R............O	Wm. Hall..... ...
Skye...............	Kenyon	Glengarry..............O	J. R. McKenzie ....
Sky Glen, W.O.....	....	Inverness ....N S	T. H. Smith........
Sleswick	Caledon	Cardwell...............O	....
Sligo	Caledon	Cardwell...............O	....
Smithfield..........	Brighton	Northumberland, E. R..O	S. D. Smith ....
Smithfield, W. O...	... .	Guysboro ....N S	John W. Archibald.
Smith's, W. O......	....	Westmoreland ....N B	William Hannington
Smith's Cove, W.O.	....	Digby ....N S	E. W. Potter ......
Smith's Creek, W.O.	....	King's................N B	Thomas H. Coates..
**Smith's Falls*	North Elmsley......	Lanark, S. R...........O	James Shaw, jun....
Smith's Mills.......	Stanstead	Stanstead..............Q	William Knight ....
Smith Town, W. O.	....	King's..............N B	David Smith........
Smithurst	Minto	Wellington, N. R.......O	Thomas B. Patterson
**Smithville, Lincoln*.	Grimsby	Lincoln.................O	Robert Thompson...
Soda Creek..... ...	....	Cariboo..............B C	Robert McLesse ....
Solina....	Darlington	Durham, W. R......... O	James C. Groat.....
Sombra	Sombra.............	Bothwell...............O	P. Cattanach.......

NAME OF POST OFFICE	TOWNSHIP OR PARISH.	ELECTORAL COUNTY OR DIVISION.	NAME OF POSTMASTER.
Somenos	District of Somenos.	Vancouver............ B C	Archd. R. Kier....
Somerset...........	St. Calixte de Somerset	Megantic............... Q	H. Jutras ....
Somerset, W. O.....	....	King's................ N S	C. W. Bertaux .....
Somerset	Number 27....... .	Prince...... .... P E I	John B. Strong.....
Somerville, W.O. ..	.. ..	Carleton.............. N B	Wm. P. Boyer .....
Sonora, W.O.	....	Guysborough.... ..... N S	James McCutcheon.
Sonya........... ...	Mariposa...........	Victoria, N. R .... O	Charles E. Black....
Sooke	....	Vancouver...... ..... B C	Michael Muir ......
Soperton	Lansdown....... ..	Leeds, S. R......... ... O	....
**Sorel*	Sorel...............	Richelieu .... Q	J. O. Duplessis .....
Souris, East	Number 45	King's.............. P E I	J. McInnis.........
Souris, West........	Number 44	King's.............. P E I	Thomas Kickham ..
Southampton, W. O.	....	Cumberland........... N S	Michael L. Tucker..
Southampton, W. O.	....	York.................. N B	Asa D. Brooks......
South Bar of Sydney River, W.O.......	....	Cape Breton.......... N S	James Fraser.......
South Barnston. ...	Barnston	Stanstead.............. Q	Francis Cooper .....
South Bay..........	Marysburgh	Prince Edward.......... O	W. H. Sloan........
South Bay, W.O....	.. ..	Victoria............. N S	Thomas Donovan...
South Bay, W.O. ..	Lancaster	St. John.............. N B	E. J. Sheldon ......
South Bolton.	Bolton	Brome... .... Q	John McMannis....
South Branch, W. O	....	Colchester.... .... N S	C. B. Cox..........
South Branch (Ken), W. O	....	King's......... ..... N B	Daniel Godard......
South Cayuga	South Cayuga	Haldimand .... O	Isaac Fry ....
South Douro........	Douro..............	Peterboro, E. R......... O	Thomas Hanrahan ..
South Dummer.....	Dummer	Peterboro, E. R... ..... O	William Speer......
South Durham	Durham..........	Drummond............. Q	F. Prefontaine......
South-East Passage, W.O.............	....	Halifax..... .... N S	Mrs. L. Williams...
South Ely..........	Ely	Shefford .... Q	Ira Jimerson. .....
South Finch........	Finch	Stormont .... O	Duncan G. McMillan
South Gloucester ...	Osgoode............	Russell .... O	Thomas Stanley ....
South Gower	South Gower	Grenville, N. R.... ..... O	David McGregor....
South Granby	Granby	Shefford .... Q	Elias Clow.........
South Gut of Saint Ann's, W. O......	....	Vi[illegible]	[illegible]

NAME OF POST OFFICE.	TOWNSHIP OR PARISH.	ELECTORAL COUNTY OR DIVISION.	NAME OF POSTMASTER.
South Ham.........	Ham...............	Wolfe ....Q	E. S. Darche ....
South La Graisse....	Lochiel	Glengarry .. ..O	H. R. McDonald ...
South Lake.........	Leeds	Leeds, S. R.............O	W. Bermingham.. .
South McLellan's Mountain, W. O..	....	Pictou ....N S	Marion Webster ....
South March	March	Carleton ....O	Samuel Scisson .....
South Middleton...	Middleton..........	Norfolk, N. R...........O	Robert McKim.....
South Monaghan....	South Monaghan....	Peterborough, W. R.... O	Robert Waddell .....
South Mountain	Mountain	Dundas ....O	S. H. Richardson...
South Nelson, W.O.	....	Northumberland ......N B	John Kain..........
South Ohio, W. O..	....	Yarmouth ....N S	William Crosby.....
Southport	Number 38	Queen's .. ..P E I	Henry Beer ....
**South Quebec*.	Notre dame de la Victoire	Lévis........ ....Q	John Ritchie ....
South Rawdon, W. O..	....	Hants ....N S	George Creed.......
SouthRockland,W.O	....	Westmoreland ....N B	Robert A. Chapman.
South Roxton... ...	Roxton.	Shefford ....Q	Wright Ball........
South Side Basin of River Denis, W.O	....	Inverness ....N S	M. McAuley ....
South Side of Boulardorie, W. O	....	Victoria .... N S	R. McKenzie.......
South Side of Whycocomagh Bay, W.O	... .	Inverness ....N S	John McEachen ....
South Side of West Margaree W. O....	Margaree.....	Inverness . ...N S	D. E. McKay......
a South Stukely	Stukely	Shefford ....Q	Luke H. Knowlton .
South West Mabou, W. O......... ...	....	Inverness ....N S	Allan McDonald....
South West, Lot 16.	Number 16	Prince.... ....P E I	Alexander McLean.
South Wiltshire	,, 31.........	Queen's............ P E I	Thomas Yeo........
South Zorra	Zorra, East.	Oxford, N. R...........O	Thomas Cross ......
Spaffordton.........	Loughboro'	Addington ....O	Henry Counter.....
Spanish River	....	Algoma. ....O	William A. Gorrell.
**Sparta*	Yarmouth	Elgin, E. R......... ....O	John A. Eakins ....
Spa Springs, W. O..	Wilmot	Annapolis. ....N S	Egbert S. Woodbury
Speedie............	Sydenham..........	Grey, N. R.............O	William Speedie....
Speedside.....	Eramosa	Wellington, S. R........O	James Loughrin ....
Sneitches Cove. W.O	....	Digby ....N S	L. McKay ....

NAME OF POST OFFICE.	TOWNSHIP OR PARISH.	ELECTORAL COUNTY OR DIVISION.	NAME OF POSTMASTER.
Spence	Spence	Muskoka .... O	F. W. Ashdown....
Spence, W. O.......	....	Westmoreland .... N B	George Spence .....
Spencer Cove..	St. Colomb de Sillery	Quebec .... Q	Mrs. Anne Flanagan.
Spencer's Island, W O	....	Cumberland.......... N S	W. H. Bigelow.....
Spencerville	Edwardsburgh	Grenville, S. R.......... O	Mrs. Mary Imrie ....
Spences Bridge	....	Yale................. B C	John Murray.......
Speyside	Esquesing	Halton .... O	Robert McPherson..
Sprague's Point, W. O.............	....	King's.. .... N B	F. D. Genong ......
Spring Arbor.......	Walsingham........	Norfolk, S. R.......... O	J. W. Hazen.......
Springbank.........	East Williams	Middlesex, N. R.. ..... O	Robert Cowie. .....
Spring Brook.. ...	Rawdon	Hastings, N. R......... O	Joshua Green.......
Springfield	Dorchester, South...	Elgin, E. R....... .... O	W. H. Graves......
Springfield.........	....	King's................ N B	A. Fairweather.....
Springfield, W O...	....	York... .... N B	Jessie Clarke ....
Springfield, W. O...	....	Annapolis............. N S	C. Grimm.... .....
Springfield	Number 67	Queen's............. P E I	Richard P. Bagnall..
Springford	Norwich, South.....	Oxford, S. R............ O	....
Spring Hill, W.O...	. ...	Cumberland..... ..... N S	J. Hewitt ....
Spring Hill Mines, W O....	. ...	Cumberland.......... N S	H. S. Ross.........
Springvale	Walpole............	Haldimand .... O	Joseph Anderson ...
Springville	North Monaghan ...	Peterboro', W. R.. ..... O	A. Goodfellow.. ..
Springville, W. O...	....	Pictou .... N S	C. A. Holmes ......
Spruce Lake, W.O..	... .	St. John....... ..... N B	John Kelly.........
Spry Bay, W. O....	....	Halifax.............. N S	Henry Leslie ......
Staffa	Hibbert	Perth, S. R............ O	James Hamilton....
Stafford	Stafford	Renfrew, N. R.... ..... O	Robert Childerhose.
Stamford.....	Stamford	Welland .... O	Mrs. Phebe A. Correl
Stanbridge, East....	Stanbridge	Missisquoi .... Q	J. M. Jones........
Stanbridge Station..	Stanbridge	Missisquoi .... Q	Benjamin Selby ....
Stanbury	Stanbridge	Missisquoi ... . Q	Porter Beattie......
Standon	Standon...........	Dorchester............. Q	....
Stanfold....	St. Eusèbe..... ...	Arthabaska .... Q	James Huston . ....
Stanhope...........	Barnston	Stanstead............. Q	David Young.......
Stanley, W. O......	....	York .... N B	William Plant......

NAME OF POST OFFICE	TOWNSHIP OR PARISH.	ELECTORAL COUNTY OR DIVISION.	NAME OF POSTMASTER.
Stanley Bridge......	Number 21	Queen's............**P E I**	Robert Brown .....
Stanley's Mills......	Chinguacousy	Peel ....**O**	C. Burrell..... ....
**Stanstead*.........	Stanstead	Stanstead........ ....**Q**	B. F. Hubbard.....
Stanton	Mulmur...........	Simcoe, S.R ....**O**	William H. Beatty.
Starkey's, W. O....	....	Queen's....... ....**N B**	S. M. Starkey......
Starnesboro'........	St. Antoine Abbé...	Huntingdon ... . **Q**	C. Meunier.........
**Stayner*	Nottawassaga	Simcoe, N. R...........**O**	James H. McKeggie
Steam Mill Village, W. O............	....	King's ....**N S**	H. Patterson.......
Steele	Oro	Simcoe, N. R...........**O**	John C. Steele......
Steep Creek, W. O...	....	Guysboro'.............**N S**	John Maguire ......
Steeve's Mountain, W.O............	....	Westmoreland .... **N B**	Amos Wilson......
Stella	Amherst	Lennox ....**O**	George Wright .....
Steeve's Settlement, W. O............	....	Westmoreland (late Head of Ridge, W.O......**N B**	W.E. Fowler ....
Stellarton......	....	Pictou ....**N S**	H. McKenzie .....
Stevensville	Bertie..............	Welland ....**O**	William T. House..
Stewartville	McNab........	Renfrew, S. R..........**O**	Alexander Duff .....
Stewiacke Cross Roads, W.O......	....	Colchester .... **N S**	....
Still Water, W. O..	....	Guysboro'........... .**N S**	W. C. Elliot. ......
**Stirling*	Rawdon............	Hastings, N. R . ...**O**	Mrs. Agnes Judd...
Stirton	Peel...........	Wellington, C. R........**O**	Joseph Sanderson...
Stisted	Walsingham.........	Norfolk, S. R..........**O**	Moses M. Harris ...
Stittsville	Goulburn..	Carleton ....**O**	J. S. Argue ....
Stockdale....	Murray	Northumberland, E. R..**O**	Peter Milligan .....
Stockwell...	St. Antoine Abbé...	Chateauguay............**Q**	M. Patenoude ......
Stoco...	Hungerford.........	Hastings, E. R..........**O**	Patrick Murphy....
Stoddart's, W. O....	....	Annapolis ....**N S**	John Stoddart ......
Stoke Centre........	Stoke	Richmond ....**Q**	Anthony Byron.....
Stoketon	Stoke	Richmond ....**Q**	Asa Hall ....
Stonefield...........	Chatham	Argenteuil ....**Q**	William Owens .....
Stoneham...........	Stoneham	Quebec ....**Q**	William Corrigan...
Stony Creek.........	Saltfleet	Wentworth, S. R.......**O**	Alva G. Jones......
Stony Creek, W.O..	....	Albert.. ....**N B**	John Scott ....

NAME OF POST OFFICE	TOWNSHIP OR PARISH.	ELECTORAL COUNTY OR DIVISION.	NAME OF POSTMASTER.
Stony Point	Tilbury, West	Essex.................. O	H. Desjardins ......
Stormont, W. O.....	....	Guysborough.......... N S	Thomas F. Milward.
Stornoway..........	Winslow	Compton .... Q	Colin Noble ....
Stottville..........	....	St. John's .... Q	William Burland....
**Stouffville*	Whitchurch	York, N. R............ O	Edward Wheler.....
Stowe	Grey	Huron, C. R........... O	Robert Ferguson..
Strabane...........	Flamborough West	Wentworth, N R........ O	Matthew Peebles....
Straffordville...	Bayham.	Elgin, E. R............ O	R. W. Smuck ......
**Stratford*	South Easthope.....	Perth N.R .... O	L. T. O'Loane.....
Strathallan	East Zorra..........	Oxford, N. R.......... O	Miss S. J. Lappin ..
Strathburn	Mosa.	Middlesex, W. R........ O	Hugh McRae......
Strathnairn.	St. Vincent.........	Grey, E. R... .... O	Joseph Inglis ....
**Strathroy*	Adelaide	Middlesex, W. R........ O	H. B. Macintosh..
**Streetville*	Toronto	Peel .... O	Robert Graydon ....
Stromness	Sherbrooke	Monck....... .... O	Albert Benson ......
Stronach Mountain, W. O	....	Annapolis .... N S	George Stronach....
Stroud	Innisfil.............	Simcoe, S. R........... O	Thomas Webb.....
Sturgeon	Number 61	King's..... .... P E I	R. A. Thornton ....
Suffolk Road	Number 34	Queen's............ P E I	W. W. Duck. ......
Sugar Loaf, W. O ..	....	Victoria .... N S	George Wilkie.....
Sullivan...	Holland...	Grey, N. R............ O	William Buchanan..
Sumas	....	New Westminster..... B C	David W. Miller....
Summerville, W.O..	....	Pictou............. . N S	C. McDonald......
Summer Hill, W.O..	....	Queen's............... N B	James Kerr ....
Summerside	....	Prince............. P E I	H. C. Green........
Summerstown	Charlottenburg	Glengarry............ O	Andrew J. Baker...
Summerville........	Toronto	Peel..... .... O	Bernard Morris....
Summerville.... ..	Number 51	King's............. P E I	N. Edmonds........
Summerville, W.O..	....	Hants.... .... N S	B. Sandford ....
Sunbury..........	Storrington.........	Frontenac .... O	John McBride ......
Sunderland.........	Brock	Ontario, N. R.......... O	John Jones.... ...
Sunnidale	Sunnidale	Simcoe, N. R.......... O	Alexander Gillespie.
Sussex Corner, W.O.	....	King's................ N B	John A. Humphreys
Sussex Portage, W.O	....	King's...... .... N B	William S. Teakles..

NAME OF POST OFFICE.	TOWNSHIP OR PARISH.	ELECTORAL COUNTY OR DIVISION.	NAME OF POSTMASTER.
Sussex Vale ...	...	King's ... N B	H. McMonagle ...
Sutherland's Corners	Euphemia ...	Bothwell ... O	James W. McKeown
Sutherland's Mills, W. O ...	...	Pictou ... N S	R. Chisholm ...
Sutherland's River, W. O ...	...	Pictou ... N S	D. Rankin ...
Sutton ...	Sutton ...	Brome ... Q	G. C. Dyer ...
Swan Creek, W. O ...	...	Sunbury ... N B	H. A. Eastabrook ...
Sweaburg ...	West Oxford ...	Oxford, S. R ... O	H. Flood ...
Sweetsburg ...	Dunham ...	Missisquoi ... Q	Curtis S. Boright ...
Switzerville ...	Ernestown ...	Lennox ... O	Peter E. R. Miller ...
Sydenham Mills ...	Sydenham ...	Grey, N. R ... O	Peter Quance ...
Sydenham Place ...	Kingsey ...	Drummond ... Q	Joseph Millington ...
Sydney ...	...	Cape Breton ... N S	Robert Martin ...
Sydney Mines ...	...	Cape Breton ... N S	Miss H. F. Rigby ...
Sylvan ...	Williams, West ...	Middlesex, N. R ... O	John Dawson ...
Sypher's Cove, W.O.	...	Queen's ... N B	Jacob Syphers ...
Tabucintac, W.O ...	...	Northumberland ... N B	Horatio Lee ...
Tadousac ...	Tadousac ...	Saguenay ... Q	Joseph Radford ...
Talbotville Royal ...	Southwold ...	Elgin, W. R ... O	John Stacy ...
Tamworth ...	Sheffield ...	Addington ... O	James Aylesworth ...
Tancook Islands, W. O ...	...	Lunenburg ... N S	Henry Hutt ...
Tangier ...	...	Halifax ... N S	John M. Forest ...
Tannery, West ...	Montreal ...	Hochelaga ... Q	Pierre Chicoine ...
Tapleytown ...	Saltfleet ...	Wentworth, S. R ... O	S. G. Harris ...
Tara ...	Arran ...	Bruce, N. R ... O	John Tobey ...
Tarbert ...	Luther ...	Wellington, N. R ... O	M. McMurchy ...
Tatamagouche ...	...	Colchester ... N S	Robert Purves, jun ...
Tatamagouche Mountain, W. O. ...	...	Colchester ... N S	John Drysdale ...

NAME OF POST OFFICE.	TOWNSHIP OF PARISH.	ELECTORAL COUNTY OR DIVISION.	NAME OF POSTMASTER.
Tatlock	Darling	Lanark, N. R. **O**	Peter Guthrie
Taunton	Whitby	Ontario, S. R **O**	Wm. Willard
Tavistock	South Easthope	Perth, S. R. **O**	George Matheson
Taylor Village, W.O.		Westmoreland **N B**	Charles Taylor
Tay Mills, W. O.		York **N B**	
Tay Settlement, W.O		York **N B**	William Tomlinson
Tecumseth	Tecumseth	Simcoe, S. R. **O**	D. A. Jones
Tedish, W. O.		Westmoreland **N B**	George E. Mills
**Teeswater*	Culross	Bruce, S. R. **O**	Samuel Waldo
Teeterville	Windham	Norfolk, N. R **O**	Darcy Hooker
Telfer	London	Middlesex, E. R **O**	Adam Telfer
Temperance Vale, W. O		York **N B**	Richard R. Carvell
Temperanceville	King	York, N. R **O**	William Bruce
Templeton	Templeton	Ottawa **Q**	James Hagan
Tempo	Westminster	Middlesex, E. R **O**	A. Remey
Tenecape, W. O.		Hants **N S**	William Stephens
Ten Mile Creek, W. O		St. John **N B**	John S. Parker
Tennant's Cove, W. O		King's **N B**	James G. Worden
Tennyson	Drummond	Lanark, S. R. **O**	D. McGregor
Terence Bay, W. O.		Halifax **N S**	J. W. Shaumwhite
Terrebonne	Terrebonne	Terrebonne **Q**	Arthur M. McKenzie
Tessierville	Matane	Rimouski **Q**	Hermyle Parent
Teston	Vaughan	York, W. R. **O**	George Wilson
Teviotdale	Minto	Wellington, N. R **O**	M. G. Miller
Teviotdale Station, W. O.		Colchester **N S**	
Thamesford	Nissouri, East	Oxford, N. R. **O**	N. C. McCarty
Thamesville	Camden	Bothwell **O**	James Duncan
Thanet	Wollaston	Hastings, N. R. **O**	B. McKillican, jun.
The Range, W. O.		Queen's **N B**	Robert Snell
Thiers	Thetford	Megantic **Q**	Joachim Delisle
Thistletown	Etobicoke	York, W. R. **O**	Richard Johnston
Thomasburg	Hungerford	Hastings, E. R. **O**	John Robertson
Thompsonville	Tecumseth	Simcoe, S. R. **O**	J. T. Schmietendorf.
Thompson's Mills		Cumberland **N S**	Joseph Jones

NAME OF POST OFFICE.	TOWNSHIP OR PARISH.	ELECTORAL COUNTY OR DIVISION.	NAME OF POSTMASTER.
Thornbrook, W. O..	....	King's...............N B	David A. Wright...
Thornbury	Collingwood	Grey, E. R............O	Thomas McKenny..
Thornby............	Thorne..	Pontiac ....Q	Joseph Hill ....
Thorndale	Nissouri, West	Middlesex, E. R........O	Thomas Harrison . .
Thorne Centre......	Thorne............	Pontiac .. . .Q	C. A. Smith .. .
Thornetown, W. O..	....	Queen's........ . ...N. B	Butler Thorne......
**Thornhill*	Vaughan	York, W.R......... ...O	Josiah Purkiss. ....
Thornton....... ...	Innisfil	Simcoe, S. R...........O	John Scott ....
**Thorold*	Thorold	Welland................O	Jacob Keefer.......
Three Brooks, W.O	... .	Victoria.............N B	John Edgar ....
**Three Rivers*	Three Rivers..... ..	Three Rivers ....Q	C. K. Ogden ....
Three Sisters, W. O.	.. ..	Cumberland...........N S	.. ..
Thunder Bay	....	Algoma....... ....O	Chas. W. Blackwood
Thurlow............	Thurlow...........	Hastings, E. R.........O	....
**Thurso*	Lochabar.....	Ottawa ....Q	George Edwards ....
Tidnish, W.O	... .	Cumberland ....N S	Oliver King ....
Tidnish Bridge, W. O	.. ..	Westmoreland.... . .N B	William Davidson ..
Tigmish	Number 1	Prince ....P E I	R. M. Carroll ......
Tilbury East........	Tilbury, East	Kent ....O	James Smith ....
**Tilsonburg*	Dereham	Oxford, S. R. ....O	E. D. Tillson.......
Tintern..	Clinton............ .	Lincoln.................O	....
Titusville, W.O	....	King's... ....N B	Alexander Simpson .
Tiverton	Kincardine	Bruce, S. R. ....O	N. McInnes ....
Toledo	Kitley.............	Leeds, N. R............O	Mrs. C. A. McLean
Toney River, W.O..	....	Pictou...............N S	Alexander Fraser...
Topping...........	North Easthope	Perth, N. R ....O	S. Crosier .. . .
Torbay, W.O.......	....	Guysboro'. ....N S	William Webber....
Torbrook, W. O.....	....	Annapolis............N S	John H. Banks.....
Tormore	Albion	Cardwell ....O	....
**Toronto*...........	York.............	Toronto ....O	Joseph Lesslie .....
Tottenham	Tecumseth	Simcoe, S. R ....O	John Wilson... ....
Tower Hill, W. O...	....	Charlotte.......... .N B	John Irons ....
Townsend Centre ...	Townsend	Norfolk, N. R ....O	Israel Slaght ....
Tracadie, W.O	....	Gloucester...........N B	John Young.. .....

NAME OF POST OFFICE.	TOWNSHIP OR PARISH.	ELECTORAL COUNTY OR DIVISION.	NAME OF POSTMASTER.
Tracadie...........	....	Antigonishe........... N S	H. H. Harrington..
Tracadie Cross......	Number 36	Queen's .... P E I	Augustus Johnson ..
Tracey's Mills, W. O	....	Carleton....... ..... N B	Isaac Adams ....
Tracey Station, W.O	....	Sunbury............. N B	D. S. Duplisea ....
Trafalgar...........	Trafalgar...........	Halton .... O	James Applebe .....
Trafalgar, W.O.....	... .	Halifax.. .... N S	John Nelson........
Traverston	Glenelg	Grey, S. R. .... O	John Travers ....
Traveller's Rest.....	Number 19.	Prince............. P E I	J. Townsend ....
Treadwell	Plantagenet, North .	Prescott .... O	James McGauvran..
Trecastle	Wallace	Perth, N. R .... O	James Shields ......
Tremblay	Tremblay	Chicoutimi .... Q	Marcel Coté........
Trenholm	Kingsey............	Drummond .... Q	Simon Stevens......
**Trenton*	Sydney	Hastings, W. R......... O	James B. Christie ..
Trois Pistoles.......	Trois Pistoles.. ..	Témiscouata .... Q	T. P. Pelletier... ..
Trois Saumons......	St. Jean Port Joli ..	L'Islet .... Q	G. C. Caron........
Trout Cove, W.O...	....	Digby .... N S	....
Trout Lake.........	Humphrey	Muskoka .... O	George Elliot.......
Trout River	Godmanchester	Huntington............ Q	James Marshall.....
Trowbridge.........	Elma...	Perth, N.R .... O	G. Code ....
Troy	Beverley	Wentworth, N.R........ O	John R. Neff... ...
Trudell	Tilbury, West.......	Essex........... ...... O	Henry Richardson ..
Truro	....	Colchester .... N S	William McCully ...
Tryon..............	Number 28	Prince.... .... P E I	J. B. Laird.........
Tuam	Tecumseth	Simcoe, S.R .. .. O	P. H. Derham......
Tullamore	Chinguacousy.......	Peel .... O	George Dodds ......
Tupperville, W.O...	....	Annapolis .... N S	W. F. Willett ......
Turtle Creek, W.O.	....	Albert............... N B	Solomon Berry .....
Turtle Lake.........	Humphrey	Muskoka .... O	Alexander Ross....
Tuscarora	Onondaga	Brant, N. R .... O	Dennis L. Dennis...
Tusket.............	....	Yarmouth .... N S	J. M. Lent.........
Tusket Forks, W.O..	....	Yarmouth .... N S	Simeon Gardner ....
Tusket Wedge, W.O	....	Yarmouth ... . N S	M. LeBlanc ....
**Tweed*	Hungerford.........	Hastings E. R.......... O	James Reid... .....
Tweedside	Saltfleet	Wentworth, S. R........ O	T. Stewart Johnson.
Tweedside, W.O	....	[illegible] N B	John Rutherford

NAME OF POST OFFICE.	TOWNSHIP OR PARISH.	ELECTORAL COUNTY OR DIVISION.	NAME OF POSTMASTER.
Tyne Valley	Number 13	Prince ... P E I	Allan McLean
Tyneside	Seneca	Haldimand ... O	
Tyrconnell	Dunwich	Elgin W. R ... O	Meredith Conn
Tyrone	Darlington	Durham, W. R ... O	John T. Welsh
Tyrrell	Townsend	Norfolk, N. R ... O	Samuel Heath
Udora	Scott	Ontario, N. R ... O	S. Umphrey
Uffington	Draper	Muskoka ... O	John Doherty
Ufford	Watt	Muskoka ... O	H. W. Gill
Ullswater	Watt	Muskoka ... O	George Bunn
Ulster	Wawanosh	Huron, N. R ... O	George McKay
Ulverton	Durham	Drummond ... Q	James Miller
Umfraville	Dungannon	Hastings, N. R ... O	D. Kavanagh
Underwood	Bruce	Bruce, N. R ... O	J. H. Coultard
Undine, W. O		Victoria ... N B	Alex. L. Watson
Union	Yarmouth	Elgin, E. R ... O	James McKenzie
Union Corner, W.O.		Carleton ... N B	Charles A. Chase
Union Hill	London	Middlesex, E. R ... O	John Mossip
Unionville	Markham	York, E. R ... O	George Eakin
Upham, W. O		King's ... N B	N. H. Upham
Uphill	Dalton	Victoria, N. R ... O	Joseph Calhoun
Upper Bay du Vin, W. O		Northumberland ... N B	William Dickens
Upper Bedford	Stanbridge	Missisquoi ... Q	N. C. Martin
Upper Branch, W.O.		Lunenburg ... N S	A. Knack
Upper Buctouche, W. O		Kent ... N B	Samuel Jerway
Upper Caledonia, W. O		Halifax ... N S	J. D. Cameron

NAME OF POST OFFICE.	TOWNSHIP OR PARISH.	ELECTORAL COUNTY OR DIVISION.	NAME OF POSTMASTER.
Upper Cape, W. O.		Westmoreland........N B	
Upper Caraquet, W. O		Gloucester........N B	S. Cormier
Upper Caverhill, W. O		York........N B	G. W. Knox
Upper Clyde River, W. O		Shelburne........N S	Jesse Bowers
Upper Cross Roads, St. Mary's, W.O		Guysborough........N S	J. A. Jordan
Upper Dyke Village, W. O		King's........N S	A. Beckwith
Upper Economy, W. O		Colchester........N S	J. L. Moore
Upper Gagetown, W. O		Queen's........N B	Thomas Crothers
Upper Gaspereaux, W. O		Queen's........N B	Isaac C. Burpee
Upper Greenwich, W. O		King's........N B	Zebulon Connor
Upper Hampstead, W. O		Queen's........N B	Reuben G. Cameron.
Upper Haynesville, W. O		York........N B	C. Manuel
Upper Kennetcook, W. O		Hants........N S	Jacob Hannegar
Upper Kent, W.O		Carleton........N B	A. Hawthorn
Upper Keswick, W. O		York........N B	James E. Smith
UpperKeswickRidge W. O		York........N B	Thomas Coburn
Upper LaHave, W. O		Lunenburg........N S	Josiah Rudolf
Upper Loch Lomond W.O		St. John........N B	James Robinson
UpperMagaguadavic W.O		York........N B	Andrew Ray
Upper Margaree, W. O		Inverness........N S	John McLennan
Upper Maugerville, W.O		Sunbury........N B	James Shields
Upper Mills		Charlotte........N B	Alice M. Morrison
Upper Musquodoboit		Halifax........N S	S. L. Henry
Upper Neguac, W.O		Northumberland........N B	Vital Alaine
Upper New Horton, W.O		Albert........N B	Minor Reid

NAME OF POST OFFICE.	TOWNSHIP OR PARISH.	ELECTORAL COUNTY OR DIVISION.	NAME OF POSTMASTER.
Upper Newport, W. O.	....	Hants ....N S	John Davison.......
Upper Peel, W.O...	....	Carleton.. ....NB	W. B. Tomkins ....
Upper Pereaux, W.O	....	King's...............N S	J. S. Newcomb.....
Upper Queensbury, W.O..	....	York................N B	David C. Parent....
Upper Rawdon, W. O..............	....	Hants ....N S	William Masters....
Upper St. Bazil, W. O..............	....	Victoria.............N B	H. Gagnon ....
Upper St. Francis, W.O...	....	Victoria.............N B	Richard Tobin......
Upper Sackville, W. O..........	....	Westmoreland ....N B	Arthur G. Chase ...
Upper Settlement of Baddeck River, W O..........	....	Victoria.............N S	Donald McMillan...
Upper Settlement of Barney's River, W O..............	....	Pictou.... ....N S	John McKay ....
Upper Settlement of Middle River, W. O	....	Victoria ....N S	John McLennan....
Upper Settlement of River Dennis, W. O..............	....	Inverness ....N S	Michael McDonald .
Upper Settlement of South River, W.O	....	Antigonishe ....N S	C. A. Cameron.....
Upper Settlement of West River, W.O.	....	Pictou.............. N S	Donald Livingstone.
Upper Sheffield, W. O..............	....	Sunbury.............N B	W. A. Garrison.....
Upper Southampton, W. O...	....	York...... ....N B	....
Upper Stewiacke ...	....	Colchester............N S	Francis Cox ....
Upper Wakefield ...	Wakefield	Ottawa .. ..Q	Patrick Farrell .....
Upper Washabuck, W.O	....	Victoria..............N S	Angus McDonald ...
Upper Wicklow, W. O	....	Carleton ....N B	Matthew Hutchinson
Upper Wood Harbour W.O............	....	Shelburne............N S	W. H. Matheson.....
Upper Woodstock, W.O..............	....	Carleton.......... .N B	William H. Sisson ..
Upsalquitch, W. O..	....	Restigouche...... . ..N B	George Croswell.....
Uptergrove	Mara................	Ontario, N. R..........O	Thomas Byrne... ..

NAME OF POST OFFICE.	TOWNSHIP OR PARISH.	ELECTORAL COUNTY OR DIVISION.	NAME OF POSTMASTER.
Urbania, W. O......	Maitland..........	Hants ....N S	Alexander Cameron.
Urquharts, W. O...	... .	King's..............N B	Nathaniel Urquhart.
Usher, W. O......	....	Antigonishe..........N S	Richard Carroll.....
Utica	Reach............	Ontario, N. R..........O	Jacob Dafoe........
Utopia	Essa	Simcoe, S. R...........O	Thomas Dawson....
Utterson ......,...	Stephenson........	Muskoka... .. ..O	Erastus Hanes.....
Uttoxeter	Plympton	Lambton.... ... O	S. Shepherd ....
**Uxbridge*	Uxbridge..........	Ontario, N. R.... ....O	George Wheeler.....
Vachell....	Georgina	York, N. R,...........O	Hugh Cooper .....
Vaillancourt........	Dionne............	L'Islet ....Q	W. F. Vaillancourt.
Valcartier	Valcartier	Quebec........ ....Q	Charles S. Wolff....
Valcourt.	South Ely	Shefford ....Q	F. X. David........
Valentia	Mariposa...........	Victoria, S. R..... .... O	W. McCracken .....
Valetta	Tillbury, East......	Kent ....O	J. Richardson ......
Vallentyne	Brock	Ontario, N.R ....O	Samuel Brethour....
Valletort...........	Aylmer	Beauce ....Q	Louis Paradis, jun.
**Valleyfield*	Beauharnois	Beauharnois ....Q	Marc C. Despocas ..
Valleyfield	Number 59........	King's............P E I	Alexander McLeod .
Valmont	Notre Dame de Mont Carmel	Champlain ....Q	Pierre Bédard ......
Vanatter	Garafraxa	Wellington, C. R........O	J. C. Reid..........
Vanbrugh	Sebastopol..........	Renfrew, S. R..........O	C. F. Holterman....
Vandecar	Oxford, East..	Oxford, S. R .... O	W. J. Davis........
Vandeleur.........	Artemesia	Grey, E. R.............O	James W. Henderson
**Vankleek Hill*.....	Hawkesbury, West .	Prescott ....O	Duncan McDonnell.
Vanneck	London	Middlesex, E. R ....O	John W. Robson....
Vanvlack	Flos................	Simcoe, N. R...........O	John Vanvlack.....
Van Winkle........	....	Cariboo..............B C	Julius L. Lindhard.

NAME OF POST OFFICE.	TOWNSHIP OR PARISH.	ELECTORAL COUNTY OR DIVISION.	NAME OF POSTMASTER.
Varennes..........	Varennes..	Verchères.............. Q	Joseph T. L. Archambeault.........
Varna.............	Stanley	Huron, S. R........... O	Josiah B. Secord....
Varney............	Normanby..........	Grey, S. R.............O	Francis Eden.......
Vasey.............	Tay...........	Simcoe, N.R............O	Mark Vasey........
Vauban	Armand............	Temiscouala......... ...Q	Alexis Morin.......
Vaudreuil	Vandreuil	Vandreuil ....Q	Dieudonné Brulé....
Vaughan's, W.O....	....	Hants ....N S	Joseph Vaughan....
Veighton	Cumberland	Russell ....O	James Lowrie ......
Vellore............	Vaughan	York, W.R.............O	John MacDonald ..
Venice	St. George...	Missisquoi..............Q	Thomas Hunter.....
Vennachar	Abinger.......	Addington........... .O	William Hames.....
Venosta	Low	Ottawa ....O	John Macauley. ....
Ventnor............	Edwardsburg.	Grenville, S. R........ O	John McAulay .....
Ventry.............	Preton	Grey, E. R............ O	Carby Johnson .....
Verchéres	Verchères	Verchères ....Q	Treffié Lussier .....
Verdun	Huron	Bruce, S. R.............O	J. Colling ....
Vereker	Colchester.........	Essex.................. O	Tancred Caya ......
Vernal, W. O..	....	Antigonishe...........N S	....
Vernon.............	Osgoode	Russel .... .O	Duncan McDonald..
Vernon Mines, W. O	....	King's... ....N S	John R. Ilsley... ..
Vernon River......	Number 49	Queen's.... ....P E I	George O'Neill......
Vernon River Bridge	Number 50	Queen's .... P E I	George Forbes......
Vernonville	Haldimand	Northumberland, W.R. O	Henry Terry . .....
Verona............	Portland	Addington..............O	Alexander Grant ...
Versailles.....	St. Grégoire........	Iberville...............Q	Isidore Marcoux....
Vesta	Brant	Bruce, S. R............O	Robert Cannon .....
Vicars.............	Havelock...........	Huntingdon ....Q	James Wilson ......
Victoria	....	Victoria ....B C	Henry Wootton.....
Victoria, W. O	....	Carleton..............N B	George R. Boyer....
Victoria, W. O	....	Cumberland ....N S	J. M. Henny.......
Victoria...........	Number 29	Queens.............P E I	A. C. Leard. .... ..
Victoria Cross......	Number 51	King's.............P E I	A. R. McQueen ....
Victoria Corners....	Reach	Ontario, N. R.......... O	James Phair.....
Victoria Harbor, W.O	....	King's................ N S	John Brown.

NAME OF POST OFFICE.	TOWNSHIP OR PARISH.	ELECTORAL COUNTY OR DIVISION.	NAME OF POSTMASTER.
Victoria Harbor	Tay	Simcoe, N. R. O	John Kean
Victoria Mines, W. O		Cape Breton N S	Alexander C. Ross
Victoria R'd Station	Carden	Victoria, N. R. O	Michael Heaphy
Victoria Square	Markham	York, E. R. O	Daniel V. Heise
**Vienna*	Bayham	Elgin, E. R. O	Samuel Brasher
Viger	Viger	Témiscouata Q	Virginie Gagne
Viger Mines	Chester	Arthabaska Q	Guillaume Lamothe
Vigo	Flos	Simcoe, N. R. O	Dennis Gallagher
**Village des Aulnaies*	St. Rochdes Aulnaies	L'Islet Q	A. Dupuis
Village Richelieu	St. Mathias	Rouville Q	N. D. D. Bessette
Villanova	Townsend	Norfolk, N. R. O	John McLaren
Villette	Hereford	Compton Q	Farrell McConney
Villiers	Otonabee	Peterborough O	W. Brotherston, sen.
Vincennes	St. Luc	Champlain Q	P. Lacourcière
Vine	Innisfil	Simcoe, S. R. O	James Goodfellow
Vinoy	Suffolk	Ottawa Q	Joseph Leduc
Vinton	Litchfield	Pontiac Q	
Violet	Ernestown	Lennox O	W. A. Rockwell
Virgil	Niagara	Niagara O	James S. Clement
Vittoria	Charlotteville	Norfolk, S. R. O	George D. McCall
Vivian	Witchurch	York, N. R. O	Robert McCormick
Voglers's Cove, W.O		Lunenburg N S	J. H. R. Fayle
Vroomanton	Brock	Ontario, N. R. O	John Tesky
Vyner	Sarnia	Lambton O	John Gates

NAME OF POST OFFICE.	TOWNSHIP OR PARISH.	ELECTORAL COUNTY OR DIVISION.	NAME OF POSTMASTER.
Waasis Station, W.O	....	Sunbury..............N B	George Grass . .....
Wabashene.........	Tay...............	Simcoe, N. R... ....O	T. W. Buck........
Wakefield..........	Wakefield	Ottawa..................Q	James McLaren ....
Waldemar..........	Amaranth..........	Wellington, N. R ....O	David Jenkins......
Wales	Osnabruck...	Stormont ....O	William Baker .. .
**Walkerton*	Brant	Bruce, S. R.......... ...O	Malcolm McLean...
Walkerville	Sandwich, East.....	Essex....................O	Henry McAfee .....
Wallace............	Wallace	Perth, N. R .... O	James Taggart .....
Wallace	.. ..	Cumberland ....N S	M. B. Huestis......
Wallace Bridge, W. O................	....	Cumberland ....N S	Richard J. Scott....
**Wallaceburg*	Chatham	Kent ....O	Lionel H. Johnson.
Wallace Ridge, W.O	....	Cumberland...........N S	John McNiel.......
Wallace River, W.O	....	Cumberland........ ..N S	David Purdy ....
Wallacetown........	Dunwich	Elgin, W. R............O	A. E. S. K. Barclay
Wallbridge	Sidney	Hastings, W. R.........O	F. B. Prior ....
Wallenstein	Wellesley...........	Waterloo, N. R .... O	Henry Powell .....
Walmer	East Zorra	Oxford, N. R...........O	Robert Parker......
Walsh	Charlotteville.......	Norfolk, S. R.. ....O	D. W. McCall......
Walter's Falls	Holland............	Grey, N. R.............O	Thomas P. Walker .
Waltham...........	Waltham...........	Pontiac.................Q	John Landon.......
Walton	McKillop	Huron, C. R............O	Robert Pattison ....
Walton	....	Hants.................N S	J. W. Stephens ....
Wanstead	Plympton	Lambton .... O	Maurice McVicar...
Warburton	Lansdown	Leeds, S. R.............O	J. H. Keating......
Warden	Shefford	Shefford ....Q	E. D. Martin .. ...
Ward's Creek Road, W. O	....	King's.................N B	A. Stapleford ......
**Wardsville*.........	Mosa..............	Middlesex, W. R....... O	W. D. Hammond...
Wareham	Osprey....	Grey, E. R..............O	George Wright .....
Warkworth	Percy	Northmberland, E. R ...O	Israel Humphries.
Warminster	Medonte	Simcoe, N. R...........O	W. George Deacon..
Warner	Caistor........... .	Monck....... ....O	Jonas R. Melick....
Warren, W. O	....	Cumberland....... ...N S	[illegible]
Warsaw	Dummer	Peterboro', E. R ..... .O	Thomas [illegible] ....
Wartburg	Ellice	Perth, N. R............O	E. Frommhagen ....

NAME OF POST OFFICE.	TOWNSHIP OR PARISH.	ELECTORAL COUNTY OR DIVISION.	NAME OF POSTMASTER.
Warwick, East	St. Medard	Arthabaska Q	Onésime Tessier
Warwick, West	Warwick	Lambton O	John H. Morris
Washademoak, W.O.		Queen's N B	Nevine McAlpine
Washago	Orilla	Simcoe, N. R O	Abial Marshall
Washington	Blenheim	Oxford, N. R O	William Dunn
Waterborough, W.O		Queen's N B	C. H. Fanjoy
**Waterdown*	Flamboro', East	Wentworth, N. R. O	James B. Thompson
**Waterford*	Townsend	Norfolk, N. R O	David Wilson
**Waterloo, East*	Shefford	Shefford Q	Gardner Stevens
**Waterloo, West*	Waterloo, North	Waterloo, N. R. O	C. Kumpf
Waterside, W. O		Albert N B	George Coonan
Waterville	Compton	Compton Q	L. W. Wyman
Waterville, W. O		Carleton N B	J. H. Seely
Waterville, W. O		King's N S	Thomas Jacques
Watford	Warwick	Lambton O	Murdo McLeay
Watson's Corners	Dalhousie	Lanark, N. R. O	John Munro
Watson Settlement, W. O		Carleton N B	John Watson
Waubamik	Ferguson	Muskoka O	Robert Reid
Waubuno	Moore	Lambton O	Thomas Moore
Waugh's River, W.O		Colchester N S	J. Murphy
Waupoos	Marysburg	Prince Edward O	Morgan L. Ketchum
Waverley	Tay	Simcoe, N. R O	John Bannister
Waverley		Halifax N S	John Lingley
Waweig, W. O		Charlotte N B	Margaret Ruddick
Way's Mills	Barnston	Stanstead Q	E. S. Southmayd
Weaver Settlement, W. O		Digby N S	Michael Weaver
Webber's W. O		Annapolis N S	Mrs. S. A. Webber
Webster's Creek, W.O		Victoria N B	M. Albert
Weedon	Weedon	Wolfe Q	Siméon Fontaine
Welcome	Hope	Durham, E. R. O	William Hill
Weldford, W. O		Kent N B	Charles Cummins
**Welland*	Crowland	Welland O	Thomas Burgar
Welland Port	Gainsboro'	Monck O	Samuel Holmes
	Wellesley	Waterloo, N. R. O	John Zoeger

NAME OF POST OFFICE.	TOWNSHIP OR PARISH.	ELECTORAL COUNTY OR DIVISION.	NAME OF POSTMASTER.
Wellington	Number 16	Prince ... P E I	Patrick Ayers
Wellington	Hillier	Prince Edward ... O	Donald Campbell
Wellington, W. O.		Albert ... N B	William Beatty
**Wellington, Square*	Nelson	Halton ... O	Walter S. Bastedo
Wellington, W. O		Yarmouth ... N S	Jacob Landers
Wellman's Corners	Rawdon	Hastings, N. R. ... O	Andrew Sherman
Welsford		Queen's ... N B	F. Woods
Wendover	Plantagenet, N.	Prescott ... O	William Lamb
Wentworth, W. O		Cumberland ... N S	Lemuel Bigney
West Arichat, W.O.		Richmond ... N S	Gilbert Paon
West Arran	Saugeen	Bruce, N. R ... O	
West Bay		Inverness ... N S	James McDonald
West Bolton	Bolton	Brome ... Q	Martin Duboyce
b Westbourne	Portage la Prairie	Marquette ... M	Peter Garrioch
West Branch, East River of Pictou, W. O		Pictou ... N S	William Dunbar
West Branch Nicholas River, W. O		Kent ... N B	T. Curran
West Branch, River John, W. O		Pictou ... N S	Mrs. J. McKay
West Branch, River Philip, W. O		Colchester ... N S	R. F. Black
West Brome	Brome	Brome ... Q	S. L. Hungerford
West Brook	Kingston	Frontenac ... O	Andrew Bridge
*a*West Brook W. O		Cumberland ... N S	Henry Jeffers
West Broughton	Broughton	Beauce ... Q	Cyrille Vallée
Westbury	Westbury	Compton ... Q	Allan Lothrop
West Cape	Number 7	Prince ... P E I	A. McWilliams
West Chester, W. O.		Cumberland ... N S	Mrs. Mary J. Purdy
West Chester Lake, W. O		Cumberland ... N S	Mrs. N. Pequignot
Western Covehead	Number 33	Queen's ... P E I	J. K. Beariste
Western Road	do 6	Prince ... P E I	J. McNaught
Westcock, W. O.		Westmoreland ... N B	
West Ditton	Ditton	Compton ... Q	Pierre Gendreau
West Dublin, W. O.		Lunenburg ... N S	R. B. Currie
West Essa	Essa	Simcoe, S. R ... O	David Henderson

*b*Late White Mud River.

NAME OF POST OFFICE.	TOWNSHIP OR PARISH.	ELECTORAL COUNTY OR DIVISION.		NAME OF POSTMASTER.
**West Farnham*	Farnham	Missisquoi............	Q	William Donahue...
Westfield...........	Wawanosh, East....	Huron, N. R	O	Mrs. Helps.........
Westfield, W. O....	....	King's..	N B	N. H. Deveber .....
West Flamboro......	Flamboro', W	Wenthworth, N. R......	O	J. B. Irving ....
West Glassville, W.O	....	Carleton..............	N B	J. R. Ronald ... ...
West Gore, W. O. .	....	Hants.................	N S	M. Wallace ....
West Huntingdon ..	Huntingdon	Hastings, N. R	O	....
West Huntley	Huntley......	Carleton	O	Edward Horan .....
West Lake	Hallowell	Prince Edward.	O	Henry Lambert....
a West Lorne	Aldborough	Elgin, W. R...	O	Duncan McKillop ..
b West Lynne	St. Agathe	Provencher	M	F. F. Bradley.....
West McGillivray ..	McGillivray	Middlesex, N. R	O	Wm. Fraser........
West Magdala......	Southwold..........	Elgin, W. R	O	Donald Turner .....
Westmeath	Westmeath	Renfrew, N. R..........	O	Alexander Fraser ...
West Merigonish, W. O	....	Pictou......	N S	James McDonald ...
West Montrose	Woolwich	Waterloo, N. R.........	O	N. F. Simons.......
Westmoreland Point.	....	Westmoreland	N B	Thos. E. Oulton ....
West Newdy Quoddy W. O	....	Halifax..............	N S	Michael O'Leary....
**Weston*	York.............	York, W. R...........	O	Robert Johnston....
West Osgoode	Osgoode	Russell...............	O	John C. Bower .....
Westover..........	Beverley	Wentworth, N, R.......	O	B. McIntosh.......
Westport..........	North Crosby	Leeds, S. R	O	John H. Whelan....
Westport	... .	Digby	N S	Benjamin H. Ruggles
West Point.........	Number 8	Prince.............	P E I	Angus Stewart ....
West Potton...... .	Potton	Brome................	Q	M. L. Elkins.......
West Quaco	....	St. John.............	N B	Mrs. C. Nugent ....
West River.........	....	Pictou...............	N S	William Munro.....
West River Station .	. ...	Pictou...............	N S	W. S. Graham......
West Shefford	Shefford....	Shefford	Q	George Tait.......
West Side of Lochbar, W. O..........	....	Antigonish	N S	Alexander Stewart...
West Side of Middle River, W. O......	....	Victoria	N S	Hector Campbell ...
Westville..........	......	Pictou.........	N S	Duncan Balfour.....
**West Winchester* ...	Winchester	Dundas	O	William Bow.......

a Late Dutton, Late West C[illegible] *b* Late Pembina.

NAME OF POST OFFICE.	TOWNSHIP OR PARISH.	ELECTORAL COUNTY OR DIVISION.		NAME OF POSTMASTER.
Westwood..........	Asphodel..........	Peterborough, E. R	O	Cristopher Lancaster
Wexford	Scarboro'..........	York, E. R	O	J. T. McBeath .....
Weymouth	.. ..	Digby	N S	Cereno D. Jones ....
Weymouth Bridge..	....	Digby	N S	Jasper Journeay ...
Whalen	Biddulph...........	Middlesex, N. R........	O	J. H. Milson ......
Wheatland	Wickham	Drummond	Q	Edward McCabe ....
Wheatley	Mersea............	Essex..................	O	George Middleton...
Wheatley River	Number 24	Queen's.............	P E I	James Power.......
Wheaton Settlement, W. O	....	Westmoreland	N B	John M. Killam....
Whim Road	Number 59	King's.............	P E I	John Martin ....
•*Whitby*	Whitby	Ontario, S. R	O	R. H. Lauder .....
Whitehead, W. O...	....	Guysborough..........	N S	....
Whitehurst....	Elizabethtown	Brockville	O	....
White Lake	McNab..	Renfrew, S. R	O	Alexander Stirling..
White Point, W. O.	....	Queen's..............	N S	J. Challoner........
White Rock Mills, W. O	....	King's........	N S	Augustus Freeman..
White Rose.........	Whitchurch	York, N. R.....	O	Jared Lloyd........
White's Cove, W. O.	....	Queen's..............	N B	S. V. White........
Whitevale	Pickering..........	Ontario, S. R	O	Donald McPhee ...
Whitefield..........	Mulmur	Simcoe, S. R............	O	P. D. Henry........
Whitney, W, O	....	Northumberland.....	N B	James Russell ......
Whittier'sRidge, W. O	....	Charlotte............	N B	Merrill Whittier ....
Whittington	Amaranth	Wellington, N. R	O	R. Bowsfield........
Whitton	Whitton.....	Compton	Q	Donald Beaton......
Whycocomagh	....	Inverness............	N S	Peter McDonald....
Wiarton............	Amabel	Bruce, N. R............	O	B. B. Miller........
Wick	Brock	Ontario, N. R	O	John Chambers.....
Wickham, W. O....	....	Queen's	N B	G. N. Golding ......
Wicklow	Haldimand	Northumberland, W. R..	O	Caleb Southon......
Wicklow	....	Carleton............	N B	Thomas H. Estey...
Wickwire Station, W. O ...	....	Halifax.............	N S	Samuel Key ....
Widder	Bosanquet.........	Lambton	O	Adam Duffus.. ...
Widder Station	Bosanquet	Lambton	O	Thomas Kirkkpatrick

NAME OF POST OFFICE.	TOWNSHIP OR PARISH.	ELECTORAL COUNTY OR DIVISION.	NAME OF POSTMASTER.
Wilfrid	Brock	Ontario, N. R. O	John Chambers
Wilkesport	Sombra	Bothwell O	William Kinball
Willetsholme	Pittsburgh	Frontenac O	Josiah Abrams
Williamsdale, W. O.		Cumberland N S	Andrew Taylor
Williamstown	Charlottenburg	Glengarry O	Albert McGillis
Williamstown, W.O.		Carleton N B	Thomas Lindsay
Williscroft	Elderslie	Bruce, N. R. O	George Williscroft
Willowdale	York	York, W. R. O	Jacob Cumner
Willowgrove	Oneida	Haldimand O	Hugh Stewart
Willowgrove, W. O.		St. John N B	William Francis
Wilmot		Annapolis N S	J. A. Gibbon
Wilmot Valley	Number 19	Prince P E I	D. Dickieson
Wilmur	Loughborough	Addington O	William Northy
Wilson's Beach, W. O		Charlotte N B	
Wilton	Ernestown	Lennox O	Sydney Warner
Winchelsea	Usborne	Huron, S. R. O	John Smith
Winchester	Winchester	Dundas O	C. T. Casselman
Winchester Springs	Williamsburg	Dundas O	James Greer
Windermore	Watt	Muskoka O	Thomas Aitkin
Windham Centre	Windham	Norfolk, N. R. O	John Lindabury
Windham Hill, W.O		Cumberland N S	John Bragg
**Windsor*	Sandwich, East	Essex O	Alex. H. Wagner
Windsor, W. O.		Carleton N B	William H. Britton.
Windsor		Hants N S	Peter S. Burnham
Windsor Junction, W. O		Halifax N S	Williams Rennells
Windsor Mills	Windsor	Richmond Q	C. E. Wurtell
Wine Harbor, W. O.		Guysboro N S	
Winfield	Peel	Wellington, C. R. O	John Hambly
Winger	Wainfleet	Monck O	Jacob Winger
Wingham	Turnberry	Huron, N. R. O	Peter Fisher
Winona	Saltfleet	Wentworth, S. R. O	Joseph Carpenter
Winterbourne	Woolwich	Waterloo, N. R. O	P. S. Kilborne
Winthrop	McKillop	Huron, C. R. O	Alex. Murchie
Wisbeach	Warwick	Lambton O	Joanna Bowes

NAME OF POST OFFICE.	TOWNSHIP OR PARISH.	ELECTORAL COUNTY OR DIVISION.	NAME OF POSTMASTER.
Woburn	Scarborough	York, E. R. O	H. M. Campbell
Wolfe Island	Wolfe Island	Frontenac O	Edward Baker
Wolfstown	Wolfstown	Wolfe Q	Norbert Roy
Wolfville		King's N S	George V. Rand
Wolvertown	Blenheim	Oxford, N. R. O	Thomas Dawson
**Woodbridge*	Vaughan	York, W. R. O	C. H. Dunning
Woodburn	Binbrook	Wentworth, S. R. O	William Ptolemy
Woodford	Sydenham	Grey, N. R. O	John Thompson
Woodham	Blanchard	Perth, S. R. O	Jonathan Shier
Woodhill	Toronto Gore	Peel O	Thomas Ward
Woodlands	Osnabruck	Stormont O	R. H. Stewart
Wood Islands	Number 62	Queen's P E I	John Kennedy
Wood Point, W. O.		Westmoreland N B	S. Outhouse
Woodside	Halifax	Megantic Q	Thomas Wood
Woodslee	Maidstone	Essex O	W. S. Lindsay
**Woodstock*	Blandford	Oxford, N. R. O	G. Alexander
Woodstock		Carleton N B	John C. Winslow
Woodstock Road Station, W. O.		Carleton N B	John S. Leighton
**Woodville*	Eldon	Victoria, N. R. O	John C. Gilchrist
Woodville, W. O.		Hants N S	Shubael Parker
Wooler	Murray	Northumberland, E. R. O	Lorenzo F. Gould
Wotton	Wotton	Wolfe Q	Benjamin Milette
Wreck Cove, W. O.		Victoria N S	John Morrison
Wright	Wright	Ottawa Q	Joshua Ellard
**Wroxeter*	Howick	Huron, N. R. O	George A. Powell
Wyandot	Maryboro'	Wellington, N. R. O	
Wyebridge	Tiny	Simcoe, N. R. O	Daniel McGregor
**Wyoming*	Plympton	Lambton O	John Anderson

NAME OF PO OFFICE.	TOWNSHIP OR PARISH.	ELECTORAL COUNTY OR DIVISION.	NAME OF POSTMASTER.
Yale		Yale B C	Benj. Douglas
Yamachiche	Machiche	St. Maurice Q	Arthur Lacerte
Yamaska	Yamaska	Yamaska Q	Honoré Lafleur
Yarker	Camden, East	Addington O	J A. Shibley
Yarm	Clarendon	Pontiac Q	Robert McJanet
Yarmouth		Yarmouth N S	A. J. Hood
Yarmouth Centre	Yarmouth	Elgin, E. R. O	William Mann
Yelverton	Manvers	Durham, E. R O	James A. Curry
Yeovil	Egremont	Grey, S. R. O	Joseph Bunston
Yoho, W.O		York N B	William Speedy
**York*	Seneca	Haldimand O	Hy. A. Duggan
York Mills	York	York, E. R O	William Hogg
York River	Faraday	Hastings, N. R O	J. C. George
**Yorkville*	York	York, E. R. O	James Dobson
Young's Cove, W.O.		Queen's N B	R. Snodgrass
Young's Point	Smith	Peterborough, W. R. O	Patrick Young
Zealand	Oso	Addington O	Joseph Davis
Zephyr	Scott	Ontario, N. R O	Manuel N. Dafoe
Zetland	Turnbury	Huron, N. R. O	L. J. Brace
Zimmerman	Nelson	Halton O	Robert Miller
Ziska	Monck	Muskoka O	W. H. Spencer
Zurich	Hay	Huron, S. R. O	Robert Brown

LIST of Post Offices closed, and not subsequently re-opened, between the 1st o July, 1872, and the 1st of July, 1873.

NAME OF OFFICE.	ELECTORAL DISTRICT.	DATE OF CLOSING.
Aboushagan Road, W. O.	Westmoreland .... N B	1st June, 1873.
Arthur Gold Mines, W.O.	Halifax .... N S	1st July, 1873.
Bangor	Ontario, S. R. .... O	1st April, 1873.
Burleigh	Peterboro, E. R. .... O	1st December, 1872.
Canning, W. O.	Queen's .... N B	1st December, 1872.
Coleridge	Wellington, N. R. .... O	1st April, 1873.
Croton	Bothwell .... O	1st April, 1873.
Felton	Russell .... O	1st September, 1872.
Glenlyon	Bruce, S. R. .... O	1st April, 1873.
L'Anse St. Jean	Chicoutimi .... Q	1st January, 1873.
La Tortue	Laprairie .... Q	1st September, 1872.
Lisgar	Peel .... O	1st April, 1873.
Lower Maccan, W. O	Cumberland .... N S	1st February, 1873.
Maccan Intervale, W. O	Cumberland .... N S	1st March, 1873.
Madrid	Renfrew, S. R. .... O	1st January, 1873.
Mortlake	York, E. R. .... O	1st November, 1872.
Mount Irwin	Peterboro' W. R. .... O	1st January, 1873.
Napan, W. O.	Northumberland .... N B	1st February, 1873.
New Zealand, W. O.	York .... N B	1st February, 1873.
Otter Creek	Bruce, S. R. .... O	1st April, 1873.
Pointe au Chene	Argenteuil .... Q	1st Febuary, 1873.
Poland	Lanark, N. R. .... O	1st January, 1873.
Scotch Block	Halton .... O	1st April, 1873.
Spring Hill, W. O	York .... N B	1st July, 1873.
Strangford	York, E. R. .... O	1st July, 1873.
Tabucintac River, W. O.	Gloucester .... N B	1st November, 1872.
Verschoyle	Oxford, S. R. .... O	1st January, 1873.
Walpole Island	Kent .... O	1st January, 1873

LIST of changes in the names of Post Offices, between the 1st of July, 1872, and the 1st of July, 1873, inclusive.

LATE NAME OF OFFICE.	ELECTORAL DISTRICT.		NEW NAME OF OFFICE.
Boisdale, W. O	Cape Breton	N S	Beaver Cove, W. O
Coboconk	Victoria, N. R	O	Shedden
Devon	Huron, S. R	O	Centralia
Dingle	Huron, C. R	O	Brussels
aDutton	Elgin, W. R	O	West Lorne
Great Bridge, W. O	Cumberland	N S	Port Philip, W. O
Hargrave	Pontiac	Q	Bryson
Head of Ridge, W. O	Westmoreland	N B	Steeves' Settlement, W.O
Hubbel's Fall's	Carleton	O	Mohrs Corners
Indian Mission	Marquette	M	St. Laurent
Lisadel	Huron, N. R	O	Fordwich
Lyles Bridge, W. O	Shelburne	N S	Port Clyde, W. O
Maccan, W. O	Cumberland	N S	Westbrook, W. O
Mascouche	L'Assomption	Q	Mascouche Rapids
Muddy Branch	Argenteuil	Q	St. Philippe d'Argenteuil.
Pereaux, W. O	King's	N S	Middle Pereaux, W. O.
Pembina	Provencher	M	West Lynne
Rankin's Mills, W. O	Carleton	N B	Benton
Salmon River, W. O	Albert	N B	Alma
South Elmsley	Leeds, N. R	O	Lombardy
Stukely	Shefford	Q	South Stukely
St. Elie	St. Maurice	Q	Mont Elie
White Mud River	Marquette	M	Westbourne

aOpened under name of West Clayton.

POST OFFICE TRANSACTIONS FOR THE MONTH OF AUGUST, 1873.

NEW POST OFFICES ESTABLISHED.

NAME OF OFFICE.	TOWNSHIP OR PARISH.	ELECTORAL COUNTY.	POSTMASTER.
†Aldouane, W.O.		Kent ..N B	F. J. Daigle.
†Burleigh (re-opened)	Burleigh	Peterborough, E.R. ..O	John McDonald.
Conn	Arthur	Wellington, N.R. ...O	Robert W. Conn.
Dupey's Corner, W.O.		Westmoreland ....N B	F. J. Hebert.
Eel Creek, W.O		Cumberland ....N S	John Fraser.
Enon, W.O.		Cape Breton ....N S	Alex. McDonald.
Fortie's Settlement, W.O.		Lunenburg ....N S	John A. Hiltz.
George's River, W.O.		Cape Breton ....N S	Campbell McQuarrie.
Glidden	Compton	Compton ....Q	Alfred Draper.
Goshen, W.O.		Colchester ....N S	William Fraser.
Hillside, W.O.		Cape Breton ....N S	Walter D. Hill.
Kolbeck, W.O.		Cumberland ....N S	W. B. Henley.
Little Ridge, W.O.		Charlotte ....N B	Robert Thompson.
Monteagle Valley	Monteagle	Hastings, N. R. ....O	Robert T. Bartlott.
Mosers River, W.O.		Halifax ....N S	J. H. Dimock.
South Cove, W.O.		Victoria ....N S	Alex. S. McDonald.
South Range, W.O		Digby ....N S	Isaac J. White.
Wagram	Arthur	Wellington, N. R. ....O	James Craig.
Hallville	Mountain	Dundas ....O	Joseph Wallace.

†Opened on the 16th June last, but not reported.
†Re-opened on the 1st of April last, but not reported.

CHANGES IN POST OFFICES ALREADY ESTABLISHED.

Offices Closed.

Inverhuron, Co. Bruce, N.R., **O.**
Kingsford, Co. Hastings, E.R., **O.**
Thurlow, Co. Hastings, E.R., **O.**

Names Changed.

Etobicoke, Co. York, N.R., **O.**, to Lambton Mills.
Baker's Creek, W.O., Co. Victoria, **N. B.**, to St. Hilaire, W.O.
Lakevale, W.O., Co. Antigonishe, **N. S.**, to Morristown, W.O.

POST OFFICE TRANSACTIONS FOR THE MONTH OF SEPTEMBER, 1878.

NEW POST OFFICES ESTABLISHED.

NAME OF OFFICE.	TOWNSHIP OR PARISH.	ELECTORAL COUNTY.	POSTMASTER.
Allenwood	Flos	Simcoe, N. R. ... O	John G. Dickinson.
Blanche	Mulgrave	Ottawa ... Q	John A. Cameron.
Caron Brook, W.O		Victoria ... N B	Theodore Pelletier.
Eagle Lake	Guilford	Peterborough, E.R. ... O	Charles Wensley.
Ecum Secum, W. O		Halifax ... N S	David Fraser.
Glenshee, W. O		Pictou ... N S	Donald Campbell.
†Grand Entry		Gaspé ... Q	Neil McPhael.
Grenfell	Vespra	Simcoe, N. R. ... O	Duncan McIntosh.
Gribbin	Toronto Gore	Peel ... O	Daniel Boyle.
Indian River (re-opened)	Otonabee	Peterborough, E.R. ... O	John Fox.
Ingram River, W. O		Halifax ... N S	Joseph G. Dimock.
Melissa	Chaffey	Muskoka ... O	William H. Buker.
Pointe à Grouette		Provencher ... M	Miss Lacerte.
Round Lake	Belmont	Peterborough, E.R. ... O	Henry N. Cooper.
St. Agathe		Provencher ... M	Pierre Cyr.
Scanterbury		Lisgar ... M	James Seter.
Shirley	Reach	Ontario, N. R. ... O	William Martyn.
Soldier's Cove, W. O		Richmond ... N S	Donald Gillies.
Stony Lake	Dummer	Peterborough, E.R. ... O	James Robb.
Thurlow (re-opened)	Thurlow	Hastings, E.R. ... O	George Phillips.

CHANGES IN POST OFFICES ALREADY ESTABLISHED.

NAMES CHANGED.

Dryden, Co. Perth, N. R., O. to Palmerston.
Pointe du Chêne, Co., Provencher, M. to St. Anne's.

†Established on 1st ultimo, but not reported.

POST OFFICES IN CANADA,

ON THE 1st JULY, 1873,

ARRANGED ACCORDING TO

PROVINCES AND ELECTORAL DISTRICTS.

POST OFFICES

IN THE

PROVINCE OF ONTARI

ARRANGED ACCORDING TO

ELECTORAL DISTRICTS AND TOWNSHIPS.

—‡—

ADDINGTON

Abinger.

Vennachar.

Anglesea.

Cloyne.

Ashby.

—

Barrie.

Hardinge
Harlowe,

Bedford.

Fermoy,
Glendower,

Camden, East.

Camden, East,
Centreville,
Colebrook,
Croydon,
Desmond,
Enterprise,
Hinch,
Moscow,
Napanee Mills,
Newburgh,
Overton,
Yarker,

Canonto, South.

—

Clarendon.

Ardoch,
Buckshot,

Denbigh.

Denbigh.

Effingham.

—

Hinchinbrooke.

Deniston,
Parham,

Kaladar.

Flinton,
Glastonbury,
Kaladar.

Kennebec.

Arden.

Loughboro'.

Desert Lake,
Lapum,
Loughboro',
Railton,
Spaffordton,
Wilmur.

Miller.

Gemley.

Olden.

Long Lake,
Mountain Grove.

Oso.

Deerdock,
Zealand.

Palmerston

Ompah.

Portland.

Bellrock,
Harrowsmith,
Hartington,
Murvale,
Petworth,
Verona.

Sheffield.

Clareview,
Erinsville,
Tamworth.

Post Offices in the Province of Ontario, arranged according to Electoral Districts and Townships.—Continued.

ALGOMA.

Assiginack.	Korah.	Tekermagh
Manitowaning.	Sault Ste. Marie.	Michael's Bay.
Fisher.		**Neebing.**
Batchewana.		Fort William.
Howland.		**Parke.**
Little Current.		Pointe aux Pins.

The following Post Offices are in the unsurveyed portion of Algoma:—

Bruce Mines,
Collin's Inlet,
Garden River.
Killarney,
Michipicoten River.
Red Rocks.
Silver Islet,
Spanish River,
Thunder Bay.

BOTHWELL.

Camden.

Dawn Mills, *Dresden*, *Thamesville.*

Dawn.

Rutherford.

Euphemia.

Florence, Shetland, Sutherland's Corners.

Howard.

Botany, **Morpeth*, *Ridgetown*, Selton.

Orford.

Clachan, Clearville, *Duart*, Highgate.

Sombra.

Baby's Point, Becher, Port Lambton, *Sombra*, Wilkesport.

Zone.

**Bothwell.*

BRANT, NORTH RIDING.

Brantford, East.

Cainsville.

Dumfries, South.

Glen Morris, Harrisburg,

Dumfries, South.—*Continued.*

**Paris*, Paris Station, Rosebank, *St. George.*

Onondaga.

Onondaga, Tuscarora.

BRANT, SOUTH RIDING.

BRANTFORD, WEST.

**Brantford*, *Mohawk*, Burtch, *Mount Vernon*, Falkland, Newport. Langford.

BURFORD.

Burford, Fairfield Plain, Cathcart, Harley.

BURFORD.—*Continued.*

New Durham.

OAKLAND.

Oakland, Scotland.

TUSCARORA.

Ohsweken.

BROCKVILLE, TOWN.

ELIZABETHTOWN.

Addison, Fairfield, East, **Brockville*, Greenbush.

ELIZABETHTOWN.—*Continued.*

**Lynn*, Whitehurst. New Dublin,

BRUCE, NORTH RIDING.

ALBERMARLE.

Colpoy's Bay, Mar.

AMABEL.

Allenford, Skipness, Park Head, *Wiarton*.

ARRAN.

Arkwright, *Invermay*, Burgoyne, *Tara*. Elsinore,

BRUCE.

Glammis, North Bruce, Gresham, Underwood. *Inverhuron*,

BURY.

—

EASTNOR.

—

ELDERSLIE.

Carnegie, **Paisley*, Chesley, Scone, Dobbington, Williscroft.

LINDSAY.

—

SAUGEEN.

Dumblane, **Saugeen*, *Normanton*, West Arran.

BRUCE, SOUTH RIDING.

BRANT.

Dunkeld, Maple Hill, Ellengowan, Outram, Elmwood, Vesta, Malcolm, **Walkerton*.

CARRICK.

Ambleside, Formosa, Carlsruhe, *Mildmay*.

CULROSS.

Cheviot, **Teeswater*.

Post Offices in the Province of Ontario, arranged according to Electoral Districts and Townships.—Continued.

BRUCE, SOUTH RIDING.—*Concluded.*

Greenock.

Chepstow,
Greenock,
Lovat,
Pinkerton,
Riversdale,

Huron.

Lisburn,
Lurgan,
Pine River,
Ripley,
Verdun.

Kincardine.

Armow,
Bervie,
**Kincardine,*
Lorne,
Tiverton.

Kinloss.

Holyrood,
Kinloss,
Kinlough,
Langside,
**Lucknow.*

CARDWELL.

Adjala.

Arlington,
Athlone,
Ballycroy,
Connor,
Fintona,
Hockley,
Keenansville,
Loretto,
Sheldon.

Albion.

**Albion,*
Coventry,
Hunsdon,
Lockton,
Macville,
Mono Mills,
Mount Hurst,
Mount Wolfe,
Palgrave,
Tormore.

Caledon.

Alton,
Belfountain,
Caldwell,
Caledon,
Caledon, East.
Cataract,
Rockside,
Sleswick,
Sligo.

Mono.

Camilla,
Elba,
Elder,
Lorraine,
Mono Centre,
Primrose,
Relessey.

CARLETON.

Fitzroy.

Antrim,
Diamond,
Fitzroy Harbor,
Kinburn,
Marathon,
Panmure,
Mohr's Corners.

Goulbourn.

Ashton,
Dwyer Hill
Hazledean,
Munster,
Richmond, West.
Stittsville.

Gower, North.

Carsonby,
Kars.
Manotic,
North Gower,

Huntley.

Clandeboye,
Carp,
Elm,
Huntley.

Huntley.—*Continued.*

Powell,
West Huntley.

March.

March,
South March.

Marlborough.

Malakoff.

Nepean.

Bells Corners,
Fallowfield,
Merivale,
Rochesterville.

Torbolton.

Dunrobin,
Kilmaurs.

Post Offices in the Province of Ontario, arranged according to Electoral Districts and Townships.—Continued.

CORNWALL, TOWN.

Cornwall.

**Cornwall,*
Harrison's Corners,
**Mille Roches,*
Northfield,
St. Andrew's, West.

DUNDAS.

Matilda.

Dixon's Corners,
Dundela,
**Iroquois,*
New Ross.

Mountain.

Inkerman,
North Mountain.
South Mountain.

Williamsburg.

Dunbar,
East Williamsburg,
Grantley,
Hoasic,
**Morrisburg,*
North Williamsburg.

Winchester.

Connaught
Morewood,
North Winchester,
Ormond,
**West Winchester,*
Winchester,
Winchester Springs.

DURHAM, EAST RIDING.

Cavan.

Bailleboro',
Cavan,
Ida,
**Mill Brook,*
Mount Pleasant.

Hope.

Canton,
Elizabethville,
Garden Hill,
Osaca,
Perrytown.

Hope.—*Continued.*

**Port Hope*
Welcome.

Manvers.

Ballyduff,
Bethany,
Brunswick,
Burton,
Drum,
Fleetwood,
Franklin,
Janetville,
Lifford,
Lotus,
Yelverton.

DURHAM, WEST RIDING.

Cartwright.

Cadmus,
Cæsarea,
Cartwright.

Clarke.

Clarke,
Kendal,
Kirby,
Leskard.

Clarke.—*Continued.*

**Newcastle,*
**Orono,*
Port Granby.

Darlington.

**Bowmanville,*
Enfield,
Enniskillen,
Hampton,
Haydon,
Solina,
Tyrone.

Post Offices in the Province of Ontario, arranged according to Electoral Districts an Townships.—Continued.

ELGIN, EAST RIDING.

Bayham.

Bayham,
Calton,
Corinth,
Eden,
**Port Burwell,*
Straffordville,
**Vienna.*

Dorchester, South.

Lyons,
Springfield.

Malahide.

Aylmer, West,
Copenhagen,

Malahide.—*Continued.*

Grovesend,
Luton,
Mount Salem,
Port Bruce.

Yarmouth.

Dexter,
Mapleton,
New Sarum,
Orwell,
**Port Stanley,*
**St. Thomas, West,*
Killerby,
**Sparta,*
Union,
Yarmouth Centre.

ELGIN, WEST RIDING.

Aldboro'.

Aldboro',
Crinan,
Eagle,
Rodney,
West Lorne.

Dunwich.

Iona,
Largie.

Dunwich.—*Continued.*

Tyrconnell,
Wallacetown.

Southwold.

Cowal,
**Fingal,*
Frome.
Talbotville, Royal,
West Magdala,

ESSEX.

Anderdon.

—

Colchester.

Colchester,
Harrow,
Essex Centre,
Oxley,
Vereker.

Gosfield.

**Kingsville,*
North Ridge,
Olinda,
Ruthven.

Maidstone.

Woodslee.

Malden.

**Amherstburg.*

Mersea.

Blytheswood,
Leamington,
Wheatly.

Rochester.

Rochester.

Sandwich, East.

Maidstone,
Ryegate,
Walkerville
**Windsor.*

Sandwich, West.

Canard River,
**Sandwich.*

Tilbury, West.

Comber,
Stoney Point,
Trudell.

Post Offices in the Province of Ontario, arranged according to Electoral Districts and Townships—Continued.

FRONTENAC.

GARDEN ISLAND.

Garden Island.

HOWE ISLAND.

Howe Island.

KINGSTON.

Cataraqui,
Collin's Bay,
Elginburg,
Glenburnie,
Glenvale,
Kepler,
Kingston Mills,
Portsmouth,
Sharpton,
West Brooke.

PITTSBURG.

Ballantyne Station,
Birmingham,
Brewer's Mills,
Pittsferry,
Willetsholme,

STORRINGTON.

Battersea,
Inverary,
Lake Opinicon,
Sunbury.

WOLFE ISLAND.

Wolfe Island.

GLENGARRY.

CHARLOTTENBURG.

Camerontown,
Martintown,
St. Raphael, West,
Sierra,
Summerstown,
Williamstown.

KENYON.

Athol,
Dunvegan,
Greenfield,
Laggan,
Loch Garry,
Notfield,
Skye,

LANCASTER.

Dalhousie Mills,
Glennevis,
Lancaster,
North Lancaster,
Riviére Raisin.

LOCHIEL.

**Alexandria,*
Dalkeith,
Kirkhill,
Lochiel,
Lochinvar,
Sandfield,
South La Graisse.

ST. REGIS.

—

GRENVILLE, SOUTH RIDING.

AUGUSTA.

Algonquin,
Centre Augusta,
Charleville,
Maitland,
Maynard,
North Augusta,
**Prescott,*
Roebuck.

EDWARDSBURG.

Edwardsburg,
Pittston,
Shanly,
Spencerville,
Ventnor.

GREY, EAST RIDING.

ARTEMESIA.

Eugenia,
Flesherton,
Inistioge.
Priceville,
Vandeleur.

COLLINGWOOD.

**Clarksburg,*
Craigleith,
Gibraltar.
Ravenna,
Thornbury.

EUPHRASIA.

Blantyre,
Duncan,
Epping.
Heathcote,
Kimberley.

MELANCTHON.

Dundalk,
Horning's Mills,
Melancthon-
Shelburne,
Shrigley.

OSPREY.

Feversham,
McIntyre,
Maxwell,
Rob Roy,
Wareham.

PROTON.

Cedarville,
Ronaldsay,
Ventry.

ST. VINCENT.

Bayview,
Cape Rich,
Griersville,
**Meaford,*
Morley,
Strathnairn.

Post Offices in the Province of Ontario, arranged according to Electoral Districts Townships.—Continued.

GREY, NORTH RIDING.

DERBY.

Alvanley,
Ashley,
Jackson,
Keady,
Kilsyth.

HOLLAND.

Arnott,
Berkeley,
Chatsworth,
Massie,
Sullivan,
Walter's Falls.

KEPPEL.

Clavering,
Cruickshank,
Hepworth,
Kemble,
North Keppel,
Oxenden.

SARAWAK.

Sarawak.

SULLIVAN.

Desboro',
Marmion,
Peabody.

SYDENHAM.

Daywood,
Hoath Head,
Johnson,
Leith,
**Owen Sound,*
Speedie,
Woodford,
Sydenham Mills.

GREY, SOUTH RIDING.

BENTINCK.

Allan Park,
Coverley,
Crawford,
Hanover.

EGREMONT.

Dromore,
Egremont,
Holstein,
Orchard,
Yeovil.

GLENELG.

**Durham,*
Glascott,
Latona,
Markdale,
Pomona,
Traverston.

NORMANBY.

Ayton,
Nenagh,
Neustadt,
Varney.

HALDIMAND.

CAYUGA, NORTH.

Canfield.
**Cayuga.*

CAYUGA, SOUTH.

Bingham Road,
De Cewsville,
South Cayuga.

ONEIDA.

Dufferin,
Mount Healey,
Oneida,
Willowgrove.

Post Offices in the Province of Ontario, arranged according to Electoral Districts and Townships.—Continued.

HALDIMAND.—*Continued.*

Rainham.

Balmoral,
Fisherville,
Rainham,
Rainham, Centre.

Seneca.

Indiana,
North Seneca,
**Seneca,*
Tyneside,
**York.*

Walpole.

Cheapside,
Erie,
Hagersville,
Hullsville,
Jarvis,
Nanticoke,
Selkirk,
Springvale.

HALTON.

Esquesing.

Acton,
Ashgrove,
Esquesing,
**Georgetown,*
Glen Williams,
Hornby,
Limehouse,
Norval,
Speyside.

Nassagiweya.

Campbelleville,
Knatchbull,
Moffatt,
Nassagiweya.

Nelson.

Appleby,
Cumminsville,
Kilbride,
Lowville,
Nelson,
Port Nelson,
**Wellington Square,*
Zimmerman.

Trafalgar.

Boyne,
Bronte,
Drumquin,
**Milton, West,*
**Oakville,*
Omagh.
Palermo,
Sheridan,
Trafalgar.

HAMILTON CITY.

**Hamilton.*

HASTINGS, EAST RIDING.

Hungerford.

Bogart,
Chapman,
Lime Lake,
Marlbank,
Moneymore,
Stoco,
Thornbury,
Tweed.

Thurlow.

Cannifton,
Foxboro',
Halloway.
Plainfield.

Thurlow.—*Continued.*

Roslin,
Thurlow.

Tiendinaga.

Blessington,
Kingsford,
Lonsdale,
Marysville,
Melrose,
Mill Point,
Myrehall,
Read,
Shannonville,

Post Offices in the Province of Ontario, arranged according to Electoral Districts Townships.—Continued.

HASTINGS, NORTH RIDING.

AIREY.

—

BANGOR.

Purdy.

CARLOW.

Boulter.

CASHEL.

—

DUNGANNON.

L'Amable,
Umfraville.

ELZIVER.

**Bridgewater*,
Queensborough.

FARADAY.

York River.

GRIMSTHORPE.

—

HERSCHEL.

—

HUNTINGDON.

Ivanhoe,
West Huntingdon.
Moira.

LAKE.

—

LIMERICK.

St. Ola.

LYELL.

—

M'CLURE.

—

MADOC.

Bannockburn,
Cooper,
Eldorado,
**Madoc*,
Rimington.

MARMORA.

Malone,
Marmora,
Shanick.

MAYO

—

MONTEAGLE.

Maynooth.

MURCHISON.

—

RAWDON.

Brinkworth,
Harold,
Spring Brook,
**Stirling*,
Wellman's Corners.

SABINE.

—

TUDOR.

Glanmire,
Millbridge.

WICKLOW.

—

WOOLLASTON.

Thanet.

HASTINGS, WEST RIDING.

SIDNEY.

**Belleville*,
Frankford.

SIDNEY.—*Continued.*

**Trenton*,
Sidney Crossing.
Wallbridge.

HURON, CENTRE RIDING.

COLBORNE.

Benmillier,
Carlow,
**Goderich*,
Nile.

GREY.

Brussels,
Ethel,
Grey,
Stowe.

HULLETT.

Bandon,
Harlock,

HULLETT.—*Continued.*

Constance,
Londesborough.

McKILLOP.

Walton,
Winthrop.

TUCKERSMITH.

Brucefield,
Egmondville,
Kippen,
**Seaforth*.

Post Offices in the Province of Ontario, arranged according to Electoral Districts and Townships.—Continued.

HURON, NORTH RIDING.

Ashfield.

Amberley,
Belfast,
Kingsbridge,
Kintail,
Port Albert.

Howick.

Fordwich,
Gorrie,
Lakelet,
Newbridge,
**Wroxeter.*

Morris.

Belgrave,
Bushfield,

Morris.—*Continued.*

Bluevale,
Blyth,
Morrisbank.

Turnberry.

Belmore,
Wingham,
Zetland.

Wawanosh, East and West.

Auburn,
Dungannon,
Fordyce,
Marnoch,
St. Helen's,
Ulster,
Westfield.

HURON, SOUTH RIDING.

Goderich.

**Clinton,*
Holmesville,
Porter's Hill.

Hay.

Berne,
Dashwood,
Hay,
Hill's Green,
Johnson's Mills,
Sarepta,
Zurich.

Stanley

**Bayfield,*
Drysdale,
Varna.

Stephen.

Brewster,
Crediton,
Centralia,
**Exeter,*
Harpley,
Offa.

Usborne.

Elimville,
Farquhar,
Kirkton,
Lumley,
Rodgerville,
Winchelsea.

KENT.

Chatham.

Darrell,
Keith,
Kent Bridge,
Louisville,
Oungah,
**Wallaceburg.*

Dover, East and West.

Mitchell's Bay,
Dover, South.

Harwich.

Bentley,
Buckhorn,
Charing Cross,
Fairfield,
Harwich,
Rondeau,
Rondeau Harbor.

Raleigh.

Buxton,
**Chatham,*
Dealtown,
Merlin.

Romney.

Old Montrose,
Romney

Tilbury, East.

Edgeworth,
Tilbury, East,
Valetta.

Post Offices in the Province of Ontario, arranged according to Electoral Dis Townships.—Continued.

KINGSTON, CITY.

**Kingston*.

LAMBTON.

Bosanquet.

Grand Bend,
Jura,
Ravenswood,
Widder,
Widder Station.

Brooke.

Alvinston,
Aughrim.

Enniskillen.

Copleston,
**Oil Springs*,
Ossian,
Petrolea.

Moore.

Birkhall,
Colinville,
Corunna,
Logierait,
Moore,
Waubuno.

Plympton.

Aberarder,
Camlachie,
Erroll,
Forest.
Hillsborough,
Kertch,
Mandamin,
Matlock,
Uttoxeter,
Vyner,
Wanstead,
**Wyoming.*

Sarnia.

Oban,
Perch Station,
Point Edward,
**Sarnia.*

Warwick.

**Arkona*,
Warwick,
Watford,
Wisbeach.

LANARK, NORTH RIDING.

Dalhousie.

McDonald's Corners,
Watson's Corners.

Darling.

Tatlock.

Lanark.

Hopetown,
**Lanark.*
Middleville,
Rosetta.

Lavant.

Lavant.

Pake

Cedar Hill,
**Pakenham.*

Ramsay.

**Almonte*,
Appleton,
Bennie's Corne
Clayton,
Huntersville.

Sherbrooke, North.

Elpin.

LANARK SOUTH RIDING.

Bathurst.

Doran,
Elliott,
Fallbrook,
Glen Tay,
Harper,
Playfair.

Beckwith.

**Carleton Place*
Frankton,
Prospect.

Post Offices in the Province of Ontario, arranged according to Electoral Districts and Townships.—Continued.

LANARK, SOUTH RIDING.—*Continued.*

BURGESS, NORTH.

Allan Mills.
Hamlet.

DRUMMOND.

Balderson,
Ferguson's Falls,
Innisville,
**Perth,*
Tennyson.

ELMSLEY, NORTH.

Port Elmsley.
**Smith's Falls.*

MONTAGUE.

Montague.

SHERBROOKE, SOUTH.

Bolingbroke,
Maberley,
Rokeby.

LEEDS AND GRENVILLE, NORTH RIDING.

ELMSLEY, SOUTH.

Lombardy.

GOWER, SOUTH.

Heckston,
South Gower.

KITLEY.

Frankville,
Newbliss,
Toledo.

OXFORD.

Bishop's Mills,
Burritt's Rapids,
**Kemptville,*
Oxford Mills,
Oxford Station.

WOLFORD.

Easton's Corners,
Jasper,
Kilmarnock,
Merrickville.

LEEDS, SOUTH RIDING.

BASTARD.

Chantry,
Delta,
Forfar,
Harlem.
Newboyne,
Philipsville,
Plum Hollow,
Portland.

BURGESS.

Cramworth.

CROSBY, NORTH.

**Newborough,*
Westport.

CROSBY, SOUTH.

Elgin,
Morton.

ESCOTT, FRONT AND REAR.

Charleston,
Escott,
Rockport.

LANSDOWN, FRONT AND REAR.

Lansdown,
Lyndhurst,
Soperton,
Warburton.

LEEDS, FRONT AND REAR.

**Gananoque*
Marble Rock,
Seeley's Bay,
South Lake.

YONGE, FRONT AND REAR.

Caintown,
Dickins,
Farmersville,
Mallorytown,
Sherwood Spring.

Post Offices in the Province of Ontario, arranged according to Electoral Districts and Townships.—Continued.

LENNOX.

ADOLPHUSTOWN.

Adolphustown,
Gosport.

AMHERST ISLAND.

Emerald,
Stella.

ERNESTOWN.

Bath,	Ernestown Station,
Mill Haven,	Switzerville,
Morven,	Violet,
**Odessa*,	Wilton.

FREDERICKSBURG, NORTH AND SOUTH.

Conway,	Parma,
Gretna,	Sandhurst,
Hamburg,	Sillsville.

RICHMOND

Forest Mills,	Roblin,
Leinster,	Selby.
**Napanee*,	

LINCOLN.

CLINTON.

**Beamsville*,	Campden.
Tintern,	

GRANTHAM.

Homer,	**Port Dalhousie*,
Merritton,	**St. Catharine's, West*.

GRIMSBY.

Fulton,	**Smithville*.
**Grimsby*,	

LOUTH.

**Jordan*.

LONDON, CITY.

**London*.

MIDDLESEX, EAST RIDING.

Post Offices in the Province of Ontario, arranged according to Electoral Districts and Townships.—Continued.

MIDDLESEX, NORTH RIDING.

Adelaide.

Adelaide,
Kerrwood,
Keyser,
Napperton.

Biddulph.

Granton,
**Lucan*,
Whalen.

Lobo.

Amiens,
Coldstream,
Duncrief,
Fernhill,
Komoka
Lobo.

McGillivray.

Adare,
Brinsley,
Lieury,
McGillivray,
Moray,
West McGillivray.

Williams, East.

Ailsa Craig,
Falkirk,
Nairn,
Springbank.

Williams, West.

Park Hill,
Sable.
Sylvan.

MIDDLESEX, WEST RIDING.

Caradoc.

Longwood Station,
**Mount Brydges*,
Muncey,
**Strathroy*.

Delaware

Calder,
Delaware.

Ekfrid.

Appin,
Glencoe,
Longwood,
Mayfair.

Metcalfe.

Cairngorm,
Kilmartin,
Napier.

Mosa.

Cashmere,
Knapdale,
**Newbury*,
Strathburn,
**Wardsville*.

MONCK.

Caistor.

Abingdon,
Attercliffe,
Caistorville,
Warner.

Canboro.

Canboro.

Dunn.

Byng.

Gainsboro'.

Bismark,
Candasville,
Rosedene,
St. Ann's,
Welland Port,

Moulton.

**Dunnville*,
Lowbanks.

Pelham.

Effingham,
Fenwick,
Fonthill,
North Pelham,
Ridgeville

Sherbrooke.

Port Maitland,
Stromness.

Wainfleet.

Marshville.
Winger.

Post Offices in the Province of Ontario, arranged according to Electoral Districts and Townships.—Continued.

MUSKOKA.

AUMICK LAKE TERRITORY.

BLAIR.

BROWN.

BRUNEL.
Seely.

CARDWELL.

CARLING.

CHAFFEY.
Huntsville,
Ravenscliffe.

CHAPMAN.
Magnetawan.

CHRISTIE.

CONGER.

COWPER.

CROFT.

DRAPER.
Muskoka Falls,
Uffington.

FERGUSON.
Waubamik.

FERRIE.

FOLEY.
Falding.

HAGERMAN.
Newcombe.

HUMPHREY.
ahdown,
osseau,
Trout Lake,
Turtle Lake.

LOUNT.

McDOUGALL.
Parry Sound.

McKELLAR.
McKellar.

McKENZIE.

McLEAN.

McMURRICH.

MACAULEY.
* *Bracebridge,*
Falkenburg.

MAGANETAWAN.

MATCHITT.

MEDORA.
Bala,
Port Carling.

MONCK.
Bardsville,
Point Kaye,
Ziska.

MONTEITH.
Segeun Falls.

MORRISON.
Severn Bridge.

MOWAT.

MUSKOKA.
Alport,
Gravenhurst.

OAKLEY.

PARRY ISLAND.

PARRY SOUND.

RYDE.

RYERSON.

SPENCE.
Spence.

STEPHENSON.
Allensville,
Mary Lake,
Utterson.

STISTED.

WALLBRIDGE.
Byng Inlet.

WATT.
Beatrice,
Raymond,
Ufford,
Ullswater,
Windermere.

WILSON

WOOD.

Post Offices in the Province of Ontario, arranged according to Electoral Districts an Townships.—Continued.

NIAGARA TOWN.

NIAGARA.

**Niagara*, Queenstown, St. David's, Virgil.

NIPISSING DISTRICT.

Deux Rivières, Mattawa, Nippissingau.

NORFOLK, NORTH RIDING.

MIDDLETON.

Acacia, Courtland, *Delhi*, Gravelotte, Guysborough, Ronson, South Middleton.

TOWNSEND.

Bealton, Bloomsburg, Boston, Hartford, Renton, Rockford, Round Plains, Townsend Centre.

TOWNSEND.—*Continued.*

Tyrrell, Villa Nova, **Waterford.*

WINDHAM.

Atherton, Bookton, Brandy Creek, Kelvin, Lynnville, Ranelagh, **Simcoe*, Teeterville, Windham, Centre.

NORFOLK, SOUTH RIDING.

CHARLOTTEVILLE.

Forestville, *Lynedoch*, Normandale, Silver Hill, *Vittoria*, Walsh.

HOUGHTON.

Clear Creek, Glen Meyer, Houghton, Kinglake.

WALSINGHAM.

Langton, Marston, Pleasant Hill, **Port Rowan*, Port Royal, *St. Williams*, Spring Arbour, Stisted.

WOODHOUSE.

Port Dover, *Port Ryerse.*

NORTHUMBERLAND, EAST RIDING.

BRIGHTON.

**Brighton*, Codrington, Hilton, Ongly, Smithfield.

CRAMAHE.

Castleton, **Colborne*, Dundonald, Morganston.

MURRAY.

Murray, [illegible].

MURRAY.—*Continued.*

Stockdale, Wooler.

PERCY.

Dartford, Norham, *Warkworth.*

SEYMOUR.

Burn-brae. **Campbellford*, Menie, Meyersburg, Rylstone.

Post Offices in the Province of Ontario, arranged according to Electoral Districts and Townships.—Continued.

NORTHUMBERLAND, WEST RIDING.

ALNWICK.

Alderville,
Roseneath.

HALDIMAND.

Bomanton,
Burnley,
Centreton,
Eddystone,
Fenella,
Grafton.

HALDIMAND.—*Continued.*

Vernonville,
Wicklow.

HAMILTON.

Baltimore,
Bewdley,
**Cobourg*,
Coldsprings,
Gore's Landing.
Harwood.

ONTARIO, NORTH RIDING.

BROOK.

**Cannington*,
Derryville,
Layton,
Pinedale,
Sunderland,
Valentyne,
Vroomanton,
Wick,
Wilfrid.

MARA.

Atherly,
Brechin,
Rathburn,
Uptergrove.

RAMA.

Rama.

REACH.

Epsom,
Greenbank,
**Manchester*,
Marsh Hill,
Port Perry,
**Prince Albert*,
Saintfield.

REACH.—*Continued.*

Utica,
Victoria Corners.

SCOTT.

Ashworth,
Athens,
Leaskdale,
Sandford,
Udora,
Zephyr.

SCUGOG.

Scugog.

THORAH.

**Beaverton*,
Gamebridge.

UXBRIDGE.

Glasgow,
Goodwood,
Glen Major.
Siloam,
**Uxbridge.*

ONTARIO, SOUTH RIDING.

PICKERING.

Altona,
Atha,
Audley,
Balsam,
Brougham,
Cherrywood.
Claremont,
Dunbarton,
Green River,
Greenwood,
Kinsale,
Pickering,
Port Union,
Rouge Hill,
Whitevale,

WHITBY, EAST AND WEST.

Ashburn,
**Brooklin*,
Columbus,
Foley,
Myrtle,
**Oshawa*,
Raglan,
Taunton,
**Whitby.*

OTTAWA CITY.

**Ottawa*,

Post Offices in the Province of Ontario, arranged according to Electoral Distric and Townships.—Continued.

OXFORD, NORTH RIDING.

Blandford.

Ratho,
**Woodstock.*

Blenheim.

**Bright,*
Canning,
Chesterfield,
Drumbo,
Goble's Corners,
Plattsville,
Princeton,
Richwood,
Washington,
Wolverton.

Nissouri, East.

Kintore,
Lakeside.

Nissouri, East.—*Continued.*

Medina,
Nissouri,
Thamesford.

Zorra, East.

Braemar,
Innerkip,
South Zorra,
Strathallen,
Walmer.

Zorra, West.

Brooksdale,
Embro,
Harrington, West.

OXFORD, SOUTH RIDING.

Dereham.

Brownsville,
Culloden,
Mount Elgin,
Salford,
**Tilsonburg.*

Norwich, North.

Burgessville,
Holbrook,
Newark,
**Norwich.*

Norwich, South.

Hawtrey,
Otterville,
Springford,

Oxford, East.

Eastwood,
Oxford Centre,
Vandecar.

Oxford, North.

**Ingersoll.*

Oxford, West.

Beachville,
Sweaburg.

PEEL.

Chinguacousy.

**Alloa,*
Brampton,
Campbell's Cross,
Cheltenham,
Claude,
Edmonton,
Kilmanagh,
Mayfield,
Mono Road Station,
Salmonville,
Sandhill,
Stanley's Mills.

Toronto.

Britannia,
Burnhamthorpe,
Churchville,
Cooksville.

Toronto.—*Continued.*

Credit,
Derry, West,
Dixie,
Elmbank,
Frogmore,
Malton,
Meadowvale.
Mount Charles,
Port Credit,
Richview,
**Streetsville,*
Summerville.

Toronto Gore.

Castlemore,
Coleraine,
Grahamsville.
Tullemore,
Woodhill.

Post Offices in the Province of Ontario, arranged according to Electoral Districts and Townships.—Continued.

PERTH, NORTH RIDING.

Easthope, North.

Hampstead,
Lisbon,
Nithburg,
Stratford,
Topping.

Ellice.

Brunner,
Gad's Hill,
Kinkora.
Sebringville,
Wartburg.

Elma.

Donegal,
Hammond,
Monkton,
Newry,
Trowbridge.

Logan.

Bornholm,
Brodhagen.

Mornington.

Burns,
Carthage,
Edgecombe,
Millbank,
Milverton
Morningdale Mills,
Musselburg,
Poole.

Wallace.

Dryden,
Gowanstown,
**Listowel,*
Molesworth,
Shipley,
Trecastle,
Wallace.

PERTH, SOUTH RIDING.

Blanshard.

Anderson,
**St. Mary's,*
Woodham.

Downie.

Avonbank,
Avonton,
Conroy,
Fairview.

Easthope, South.

Harmony.
Shakespeare
Tavistock.

Fullarton.

Carlingford,
Fullarton,
Mitchell,
Motherwell.

Hibbert.

Carronbrook,
Cromarty,
Staffa.

PETERBORO', EAST RIDING.

Anstruther.

Apsley.

Asphodel.

**Hastings,*
**Norwood,*
Westwood.

Belmont.

**Blairton,*
Haverlock,

Bruton.

—

Burleigh.

Haultain.

Cardiff

Cheddar,
Pandash.

Post Offices in the Province of Ontario, arranged according to Electoral Districts and Townships.—Continued.

PETERBORO', EAST RIDING.—*Continued.*

CAVENDISH.

—

CHANDOS.

Chandos.

CLYDE.

—

DOURO.

North Douro,
South Douro.

DUDLEY.

—

DUMMER.

South Dummer,
Warsaw.

DYSART.

**Haliburton.*

EYRE.

—

GALWAY.

—

GLAMORGAN.

—

GUILFORD.

HARBURN.

—

HARCOURT.

—

HARVEY.

Hall's Bridge,
Lakehurst.

HAVELOCK.

—

LAWRENCE.

—

LIVINGSTON.

—

MC. CLINTOCH.

—

METHUEN.

—

MINDEN.

Ingoldsby,
Peterson.

MONMOUTH.

—

NIGHTINGALE.

—

OTONABEE.

Ashburnham,
Graystock,
Hiawatha,
**Keene,*
Lang,
Villiers.

PAPINEAU.

—

SHERBURNE.

—

SNOWDON.

Minden.

STANHOPE.

Carnarvon.

PETERBORO', WEST RIDING.

ENNISMORE.

Ennismore.

MONAGHAN, NORTH.

**Peterborough,*
Springville.

MONAGHAN, SOUTH.

Bensfort,
South Monaghan.

SMITH.

Bridgenorth,
Selwyn,
Young's Point.

Post Offices in the Province of Ontario, arranged according to Electoral Districts and Townships.—Continued.

PRESCOTT.

ALFRED.

Alfred.

CALEDONIA.

Caledonia Springs, Fenaghvale.

HAWKESBURY, EAST.

Chute au Blondeau, East Hawkesbury, Little Rideau, St. Eugène, **Vankleek Hill.*

HAWKESBURY, WEST.

**Hawkesbury.*

LONGUEUIL.

Henry, **L'Orignal.*

PLANTAGENET, NORTH.

Curran, *Plantagenet*, Treadwell, Wendover.

PLANTAGENET, SOUTH.

Fournier, Kerry, Pendleton, Riceville.

PRINCE EDWARD.

AMELIASBURG.

Albury, Ameliasburg, *Consecon*, Mountain View, Rednersville.

ATHOL.

Cherry Valley, Point Petre.

HALLOWELL.

Allisonville, Bloomfield, **Picton*, West Lake.

HILLIER.

Hillier, Melville, Rosehall, Wellington.

MARYSBURG.

Bongard's Corners, Cressy, *Milford*, Point Traverse, South Bay, Waupoos.

SOPHIASBURG.

Crofton, Demorestville. Gilbert's Mills, *Northport*.

RENFREW, NORTH RIDING.

ALGONA, NORTH & SOUTH.

Castile.

ALICE.

Locksley.

BROMLEY.

Douglas, **Osceola.*

BUCHANAN.

—

CLARA.

—

FRASER.

—

HEAD.

Rockliffe, (sub).

McKAY.

—

MARIA.

—

Post Offices in the Province of Ontario, arranged according to Electoral Districts and Townships.—Continued.

RENFREW, NORTH RIDING.—*Continued.*

PEMBROKE.

**Pembroke.*

PETAWAWA.

Petawawa.

ROLPH.

Point Alexander.

ROSS.

Cobden,
Forester's Falls,

Ross.

STAFFORD.

Stafford.

WESTMEATH.

Beachburg,
Gower Point,
Perretton,
Westmeath.

WILBERFORCE.

Lake Doré,
Rankin.

WYLIE.

—

RENFREW, SOUTH RIDING.

ADMASTON.

Admaston,
Shamrock.

BAGOT.

Bagot,
Calabogie.

BLITHFIELD.

High Falls.

BROUGHAM

Dacre,
Mount St. Patrick.

BRUDENELL.

Broden ell,
**Rckin gham.*

BURNS.

—

GRATTAN.

Eganville.

GRIFFITH.

Griffith.

HAGARTY.

—

HORTON.

Castleford,
Harcourt,
Renfrew.

JONES.

Bark Lake.

LYNEDOCH.

—

M'NAB.

**Arnprior,*
Braeside,
Burnstown,
Sand Point,
Stewartville,
White Lake.

MATAWATCHAN.

Matawatchan.

RADCLIFFE.

Combermere,
Hopefield.

RAGLAN.

Palmer Rapids.

RICHARDS.

—

SEBASTOPOL.

Clontarf,
Vanbrugh.

SHERWOOD.

—

Post Offices in the Province of Ontario, arranged according to Electoral Districts and Townships.—Continued.

RUSSELL.

CAMBRIDGE.

Casselman,
Grant.

CLARENCE.

Clarence,
Clarence Creek,
Rockland.

CUMBERLAND.

Bear Brook,
Cumberland,
Navan,
Veigton.

GLOUCESTER.

Billings' Bridge,
Eastman's Springs,
Long Island Locks,
**New Edinburgh,*
Orleans,
Rock Village.

OSGOODE.

Kenmore,
Osgoode,
South Gloucester,
Vernon,
West Osgoode.

RUSSELL.

Embrun,
Russell.

SIMCOE, NORTH RIDING.

BALAKLAVA.

—

FLOS.

Apto,
Elmvale,
Fergusonvale,
Phelpston,
Vanvlack,
Vigo.

MATCHEDASH.

—

MEDONTE.

**Coldwater,*
Coulson,
Craighurst,
Creighton,
Hillsdale,
Medonte,
Mount St. Louis,
Warminster.

NOTTAWASAGA.

Avening,
**Collingwood,*
**Creemore,*
Dunedin,
Duntroon,
Glen Huron,
Maple Valley,
Nottawa,
Singhampton,
**Stayner.*

ORILLIA

Ardtrea,
Marchmont,
Orillia,
Washago.

ORO.

East Oro,
Edgar,
Hawkstone,
Jarrat's Corners,
Nevis,
Rugby,
Shanty Bay,
Steele.

ROBINSON.

—

SUNNIDALE.

Brentwood,
New Lowell,
Sunnidale.

TAY.

Midland,
Port Severn, (sub),
Vasey,
Victoria Harb
Wabashene,
Waverley.

TINY.

Lafontaine,
**Penetanguishene,*
Wyebridge.

VESPRA.

**Barrie,*
Dalston,
Midhurst,
Minesing.

Post Offices in the Province of Ontario, arranged according to Electoral Districts and Townships.—Continued.

SIMCOE, SOUTH RIDING.

ESSA.

Angus, Egbert, Elm Grove, Ivy, Nicolston, Utopia, West Essa.

GWILLIMBURY, WEST.

**Bondhead*, **Bradford*, Deerhurst, Gilford.

INNISFIL.

Allendale, *Bell Ewart*, Bramley, Cherry Creek, Churchill, Craigvale, Fennells, Innisfil, *Lefroy*, Lennox, Painswick, Stroud, Thornton, Vine.

MULMUR.

Banda, Black Bank, Honeywood, Lavender, Mansfield, Mulmur, Perm, **Rosemont*, Stanton, Whitfield.

TECUMSETH.

Alliston, *Clover Mill*, **Cookstown*, Newton Robinson, Penville, Tecumseh, Thompsonville, *Tottenham*. Tuam.

TOSORONTIO.

Airlie, Everett, Glencairn.

STORMONT.

FINCH.

Berwick, Crysler, South Finch.

OSNABRUCK.

Aultsville, *Dickinson's Landing*, Newington, Osnabruck Centre.

OSNABRUCK.—*Continued.*

Farran's Point, Lunenburg, *Wales*, Woodlands.

ROXBOROUGH.

Avonmore, Gravel Hill, Monckland, Moose Creek.

TORONTO CITY, CENTRE, EAST AND WEST.

**Toronto.*

VICTORIA, NORTH RIDING.

Post Offices in the Province of Ontario arranged according to Electoral Districts and Townships.—Continued.

VICTORIA, NORTH RIDING.—*Continued.*

DALTON.

Dartmoor,
Uphill.

DIGBY.

—

ELDON.

Argyle,
Bolsover,
Hartley,
**Kirkfield*,
**Woodville*.

FENELON.

Cambray,
Cameron,
Fenelon Falls,
Glenarm,
Islay,
Rosedale.

FRANKLIN.

—

HINDON.

—

LAXTON.

Head Lake,
Norland,
Oak Hill.

LONGFORD.

—

LUTTERWORTH.

—

RIDOUT.

—

SOMERVILLE.

Bury's Green,
Galway,
Kinmount,
Shedden.

VICTORIA, SOUTH RIDING.

EMILY.

Downeyville,
Frank Hill,
**Omemee*.

MARIPOSA.

Little Britain,
Manilla,
Oakwood,
Port Hoover,
Valentia.
Sonya,

OPS.

**Lindsay*,
Mount Horeb,
Reaboro.

VERULAM.

Bobcaygeon,
Dunsford.

WATERLOO, NORTH RIDING.

Waterloo, North.

*Berlin,
Bloomingdale,
Breslau,
Bridgeport,
Erbsville,
Freiburg,
Kossuth,
**Waterloo.*

Wellesley.

Bamberg,
Crosshill,
Dorking,
Hawkesville.

Wellesley.—*Continued.*

Linwood,
St. Clements,
Wallenstein,
**Wellesley.*

Woolwich.

Conestogo,
Elmira,
Flora,
Heidelberg,
St. Jacob's,
West Montrose,
Winterbourne.

WATERLOO, SOUTH RIDING.

Dumfries, North.

**Ayr,*
Branchton,
**Galt,*
Roseville.

Waterloo, South.

Blair,
Doon.

Waterloo, South.—*Continued.*

Freeport,
**Hespeler,*
New Aberdeen,
**Preston,*

Wilmot.

Baden,
Haysville,
Mannheim,
New Dundee,
**New Hamburg,*
Petersburg,
Philipsburg, West,
St. Agatha.

WELLAND.

Bertie.

**Fort Erie,*
Mulgrave,
Point Abino,
Stevensville.

Crowland.

Crowland,
**Welland.*

Humberstone.

Humberstone,
Netherby,
**Port Colborne,*
Sherkston.

Stamford.

**Chippawa,*
**Clifton,*
Clifton House (sub.),
Drummondville, West,
Montrose,
Stamford.

Thorold.

Allanburg,
**Port Robinson,*
St. John's, West,
**Thorold.*

Willoughby.

Black Creek.

Post Offices in the Province of Ontario, arranged according to Electoral Districts and Townships.—Continued.

WELLINGTON, CENTRE RIDING.

Garafraxa, East and West.

Craigsholme,
Garafraxa,
Hereward,
Metz,
Marsville,
+*Orangeville*
Reading,
Vanatter.

Nichol.

Barnett
Cumnock,
Fergus
Salem.

Peel.

Alma,
Bosworth,
Creek Bank,
Drayton,
Glenallan,
Goldstone,
Macton,
Parker,
Stirton,
Winfield.

Pilkington.

+*Elora,*
Pentland,
Ponsonby.

WELLINGTON, NORTH RIDING.

Amaranth.

Bowling Green,
Farmington,
Laurel,
Waldemar,
Whittington.

Arthur.

+*Arthur*
Kenilworth,
+*Mount Forest,*
Petherton,
Riverstown.

Luther.

Colbeck,
Monck.

Luther.—*Continued.*

Egerton,
Luther,
Peepabun,
Tarbert.

Marlboro'.

Hollen,
Huston,
Moorefield,
Rothesay,
Wyandott.

Minto.

Clifford,
Cotswold,
Drew,
Harriston,
Smithurst,
Teviotdale.

WELLINGTON, SOUTH RIDING.

Eramosa.

Eden Mills,
Eramosa,
Everton,
Oustic,
Rockwood,
Speedside.

Erin.

Ballinafad,
Brisbane,
Coningsby,
**Erin.*
Hillsburgh,
Mimosa,
Ospringe.

Guelph.

Gourock,
**Guelph,*
Marden.

Puslinch.

Aberfoyle,
Arkell,
Crieff,
Killean,
Morriston,
Puslinch.

Post Offices in the Province of Ontario, arranged according to Electoral Districts and Townships.—Continued.

WENTWORTH, NORTH RIDING.

Beverley.

Clyde,
Copetown,
Kirkwall,
Lynden,
Rockton,
Sheffield,
Troy,
Westover.

Flamboro', East.

Aldershot,
Carlisle.

Flamboro', East.—*Continued.*

Mountsberg,
**Waterdown*.

Flamboro', West.

**Dundas*,
Freelton,
Greensville,
Hayesland,
Mill Grove.
Strabane,
West Flamboro'.

WENTWORTH, SOUTH RIDING.

Ancaster.

Alberton,
Ancaster,
Carluke,
Jerseyville,
Renforth.

Barton.

Bartonville,
Hannon,
Ryckman's Corners.

Binbrook.

Binbrook,
Black Heath.

Binbrook,—*Continued.*

Woodburn.

Glanford.

Glanford,
North Glanford.

Saltfleet.

Elfrida,
Mount Albion,
Stony Creek,
Tapleytown,
Tweedside,
Winona.

YORK, EAST RIDING.

Markham.

Almira,
Belford,
Boxgrove,
Buttonville,
Cashel,
Cedar Grove,
Dollar,
Gormley,
Headford,
Langstaff (sub.),
**Markham*,
Milliken,
Milnesville,
Mongolia,
Unionville,
Victoria Square.

Scarboro'.

Agincourt,
Armadale.

Scarboro'.—*Continued.*

Danforth
Ellesmere,
Highland Creek,
Malvern,
**Scarboro'*,
Wexford,
Woburn.

York, East.

Davisville,
Don,
Doncaster,
Eglinton,
Lansing,
Leslie,
Norway,
York Mills,
Yorkville.

YORK, NORTH RIDING.

Georgina.

Georgina,
Pefferlaw,
Vachell.

Gwillimbury, East.

Hartman,
Holland Landing,
Holt,
Mount Albert,
Queensville,
Sharon.

Post Offices in the Province of Ontario, arranged according to Electoral Districts an Townships.—Concluded.

YORK, NORTH RIDING.—*Continued.*

GWILLIMBURY, NORTH.

Belhaven,
Keswick.
Ravenshoe,
Roache's Point.

KING.

Everaly,
Kettleby,
King,
Linton,
Lloydtown,
Nobleton.

KING.—*Continued.*

King Creek,
Laskay,
Schomburg,
Temperanceville,

WHITCHURCH.

**Aurora*,
Ballantrae,
Bloomington,
Lemonville,
**New Market*,
Oak Ridges,
Pine Orchard,
Ringwood,
**Stouffville*,
Vivian,
White Rose.

YORK, WEST RIDING.

ETOBICOKE.

Etobicoke,
Highfield,
Humber,
Islington,
Mimico,
Thistletown.

VAUGHAN.

Carrville,
Concord,
Edgely,
Klineburg,
Maple,
Patterson,
Pinegrove,
Purpleville,
**Richmondhill*.

VAUGHAN.—*Continued.*

Teston,
**Thornhill*,
Vellore,
Woodbridge,

YORK, WEST.

Brockton,
Davenport,
Downsview,
Etobicoke,
L'Amaroux,
Newton Brook,
Seaton,
**Weston*,
Willowdale.

POST OFFICES

IN THE

PROVINCE OF QUEBEC,

ARRANGED ACCORDING TO ELECTORAL DISTRICTS.

ARGENTEUIL.

Arundel, Avoca, Britonville, Brownsburg, Cambria, *Carillon,*	Chatboro, Cushing, Dalesville, Dunany, Edina, Geneva,	Genoa, *Grenville,* Harrington, East, Lachute, Lakefield,	Mille Isles, **St. Andrew's, East,* Shrewsbury, Stonefield, St. Philippe d'Argenteuil

BAGOT.

**Actonvale,* Britannia Mills, St. Dominique,	St. Ephrem d'Upton, Ste. Hélène de Bagot, *St. Hugues,*	St. Liboire, St. Pie, Ste. Rosalie,	St. Simon de Yamaska, St. Theodore.

BEAUCE.

Broughton, East Broughton, Grandes Coudées, Jersey, River Chaudiere, Kennebec, Line,	La Beauce, Lambton, Marlow, River Gilbert, St. Elzéar,	St. Ephrem de Tring, St. Evariste de Forsyth, St. François, St. Frédéric, St. George,	St. Honoré, St. Joseph, St. Victor de Tring, Vallotort, West Broughton.

BEAUHARNOIS

**Beauharnois,* Melocheville,	St. Etienne de Beauharnois St. Louis de Gonzague,	St. Stanislas de Kostka, St. Timothée,	**Valleyfield.*

BELLECHASSE.

Armagh, Beaumont, Buckland,	St. Charles, River Boyer, St. Gervais, St. Lazare,	St. Magloire, St. Michel,	St. Raphael, East, St. Vallier.

Post Offices in the Province of Quebec, arranged according to Electoral Districts.—Continued.

BERTHIER.

**Berthier (en haut)*,	Lavaltrie,	St. Damien de Brandon,	St. Norbert,
Isle Dupas,	St. Barthélemi,	St. Gabriel de Brandon,	St. Zenon.
Lanoraie,	St. Cuthbert,	St. Michel des Saints,	

BONAVENTURE.

Assametquagan,	*Carleton*,	Maria,	*Paspebiac*,
Avignon,	Cross Point,	*Matapédia*,	Port Daniel,
Bonaventure (sub),	Dee Side,	New Carlisle,	Runnymede,
Bonaventure River,	Escuminac (sub),	New Richmond,	Shigawake,
Broadlands,	Fleurant,	Nouvelle,	Shoolbred.
Caplin,			

BROME.

Abercorn,	*Dillonton*,	Herbert,	St. Etienne de Bolton,
Adamsville,	East Bolton,	Iron Hill,	South Bolton,
Bolton, Centre,	East Farnham,	**Knowlton*,	**Sutton*,
Bolton Forest,	Emerson,	Knowlton Landing,	West Bolton,
Brigham,	Farnham, Centre,	*Mansonville—Potton*,	West Brome,
Brome,	Fulford,	North Sutton,	West Potton.
Bromemere,	Glen Sutton,		

CHAMBLY.

Boucherville,	**Chambly Canton*,	St. Bazil le Grand,	St. Hubert,
Chambly Basin,	*Longueuil*,	St. Bruno,	St. Lambert, Montreal.

CHAMPLAIN.

Batiscan,	Ste. Anne de la Pèrede,	St. Narcisse,	St. Tite,
Batiscan Bridge,	Ste. Flore,	St. Prosper,	Valmont,
Cap. Magdeleine,	St. Maurice,	St. Stanislas,	Vincennes.
Champlain,			

CHARLEVOIX.

Cap à l'Aigle (sub),	Les Eboulemens,	Ste. Agnes,	**St. Paul's Bay*,
Clairvaux (sub),	**Murray Bay*,	St. Fidèle,	Settrington,
Isle aux Coudres (sub),	Pointe à Pic (sub),	St. Irénée,	St. Urbain.
La Petite Rivière St. François (sub),	Port au Persil,		

Post Offices in the Province of Quebec, arranged according to Electoral Districts.—Continued.

CHATEAUGUAY.

Allan's Corners,	Howick,	Russeltown,	Ste. Philomène,
Aubrey,	North Georgetown,	*St. Jean Chrysostôme,*	St. Urbain,
Chateauguay,	Norton Creek,	St. Martine,	Stockwell.
Chateauguay Basin,	*Ormstown,*		

CHICOUTIMI AND SAGUENAY.

Chicoutimi.		Saguenay.	
Bagotville,	L'Anse St. Jean,	Bersimis,	Moisic,
Chambord,	Laterrière,	Esquimaux Point,	Natashquan,
Chicoutimi,	Metabechouan,	Les Escoumains,	Pointe au Bouleau,
Grande Baie,	Roberval,	Les Petites Bergeronnes,	Sheldrake,
Jonquieres,	St. Cyriac,	Magpie,	*Tadousac.*
Labarre,	Tremblay,	Mille Vaches,	
L'Anse au Foin,	St. Prime,	Mingan,	

COMPTON.

Birchton,	Gould,	Martinville,	St. Malo,
Brookbury,	Hereford,	Moe's River,	St. Romaine,
Bulwer,	Island Brook,	Paquette,	Sawyerville,
Canterbury,	Johnville,	Perryboro',	Stornoway,
**Compton,*	Lake Megantic,	Piopolis,	Villette,
Cookshire,	Learned Plain,	Richby,	Waterville,
East Clifton,	Linda,	*Robinson,*	Westbury,
East Hereford,	Maple Leaf,	St. Edwige,	West Ditton,
Eaton,			Whitton,

DORCHESTER.

Cranbourne,	Langevin,	St. Edouard de Frampton	St. Malachie,
Frampton,	St. Anselme,	Ste. Hénédine,	Ste. Marguerite,
Hemison,	St. Bernard,	St. Isidore,	Standon.
Lake Etchemin,	Ste. Claire,		

DRUMMOND AND ARTHABASKA.

Drummond.		Arthabaska.	
Danby	St. Bonaventure,	Arthabaska Station,	St. Albert,
Drummondville, East,	St. Germain de Grantham,	Blandford,	St. Christophe d'Arthabaska,
French Village,	St. Guillaume d'Upton,	Bulstrode,	St. Clothilde,
Kingsey,	South Durham,	Chester,	St. Patrick's Hill,
Kingsey Falls,	Sydenham Place,	Domaine de Gentilly,	*Stanfold,*
Kirkdale,	Trenholm,	East Arthabaska,	Viger Mines,
L'Avenir,	*Ulverton,*	East Chester,	Warwick, East.
Leonard's Hill,	Wheatland,	Maddington,	
Ruisseau des Chênes,			

Post Offices in the Province of Quebec, arranged according to
Continued.

GASPÉ.

Barachois de Malbay, Cap Chat, Cap des Rosiers, Cape Cove, Chlorydormes, Douglastown,	Etang du Nord (sub.), Fox River, *Gaspé Basin,* Grande Grêve, Grande Vallée, Grande Pabos,	Grand River, House Harbor (sub), Magdalen Islands, Mont Louis, Newport, Newport Point,

HOCHELAGA.

Cote des Neiges, Cote St. Paul, Hochelaga,	Long Point, Mile End, Pointe aux Trembles,	Rivière des Prairies, St. Jean Baptiste de Montreal,

HUNTINGDON.

Anderson's Corners, Athelstan, Barrington, Cazaville, Corbin, Covey Hill, Dewittville,	Dundee, Dundee, Centre, *Franklin, Centre,* Hallerton, Helena, *Hemmingford,* Herdman's Corners.	*Huntingdon,* Kelso, La Guerre, Maritana, Port Lewis, Powerscourt,

IBERVILLE.

Henryville, Mount Johnson,	St. Alexandre, *St. Athanase,*	Ste. Brigide, St. Sebastian,

JACQUES CARTIER.

**Lachine,* Pointe Claire,	**Point St. Charles,* Ste. Anne Bout de L'Isle.	Ste. Geneviève,

JOLIETTE.

Dailleboút, De Ramsay, **Joliette,* Kildare,	Radstock, St. Alphonse, Ste. Beatrix, St. Côme,	Ste. Elizabeth, Ste. Emelie de l'Energ St. Félix de Valois, St. Jean de Matha,

Post Offices in the Province of Quebec, arranged according to Electoral Districts.—Continued.

KAMOURASKA.

Coteaux Rivière Ouelle *Kamouraska,* Mount Carmel, Rivière Ouelle, St. Alexandre,	St. André, *Ste. Anne la Pocatière,* St. Denis de la Bouteillerie,	Ste. Hélène, St. Onézime, St. Pacôme,	St. Paschal, St. Philippe de Néry.

LAPRAIRIE.

Caughnawaga, **Laprairie,*	St. Constant, St. Isidore,	St. Jacques le Mineur,	St. Philippe.

L'ASSOMPTION.

Charlemagne, Lachenaie, **L'Assomption,*	L'Epiphanie, Mascouche, Mascouche Rapids,	Repentigny, St. Lin, St. Paul l'Hermite,	St. Roch l'Achigan, St. Sulpice.

LAVAL.

Bord à Plouffe, St. Dorothee,	St. Francois de Sales, St. Martin,	Ste. Rose,	St. Vincent de Paul.

LEVIS.

Baillargeon, Bienville, Chaudiere Mills, Craig's Road Station,	Indian Cove, *Lauzon,* **Levis,* New Liverpool,	St. Henri, St. Henri Station, St. Jean Chrysostôme,	St. Lambert, St. Nicholas, **South Quebec.*

L'ISLET.

Garneau, Isle aux Grues, Lac Noir, L'Anse à Giles,	L'Islet, St. Aubert, St. Cyrille,	St. Jean, Port Joli, Ste. Louise, St. Roch des Aulnaies,	Trois Saumons, Vaillancourt, *Village des Aulnaies.*

LOTBINIÈRE.

Beaurivage, Black River Station, Fafard, Leclercville, Lotbinière,	Méthot's Mills, Parkhurst, Point Platon, Rivière Bois Claire, Ste. Agathe,	St. Antoine, St. Apollinaire, *Ste. Croix,* St. Flavien,	St. Giles, St. Jean des Chaillons, St. Sylvester, St. Sylvester, East.

Post Offices in the Province of Quebec, arranged according to Electoral Districts.—Continued.

MASKINONGÉ.

Hunterstown	*River du Loup (en haut),*	St. Justin,	St. Paulin,
Maskinongé	St. Didace,	St. Léon,	Ste. Ursule.
Pont de Ma[illegible]inongé,			

MEGANTIC.

Adderley	Harvey Hill Mines,	Lemesurier,	*St. Ferdinand,*
Bécancou[illegible] Sta[illegible]n,	**Inverness,*	Lower Ireland,	Ste. Julie de Somerset,
Bute,	Irvine,	Lyster,	St. Pierre Baptiste,
Clapham,	Kinnear's Mills,	Maple Grove,	Ste. Sophie,
East Ma[illegible]lala,	Larochelle,	Millfield,	*Somerset,*
Glenloyd,	**Leeds,*	New Ireland,	Thiers,
Glen M[illegible]rray	Leeds Village,	Redesdale,	Woodside.

MISSISQUOI.

Abbott's Corners,	**Frelighsburg,*	Nutt's Corners,	St. Charles de Stanbridge,
Aird,	Haseville,	Pearceton,	Stanbridge, East,
Bedford,	Malmaison,	*Philipsburg, East,*	Stanbridge Station,
Clarenceville,	Miranda,	Pigeon Hill,	Stanbury,
Cowansville,	Moore's Station,	*Pike River,*	*Sweetsburg,*
Dunham,	Mystic,	Riceburg,	Upper Bedford,
East [illegible]unham,	North Pinnacle,	St. Armand, Centre,	Venice,
Far[illegible]	North Stanbridge,	St. Armand Station,	**West Farnham.*
Farn[illegible],	Noyan,		

MONTCALM.

Beaulac,	Mount Loyal,	St. Esprit,	Ste. Julienne,
Chant[illegible],	Rawdon,	St. Hippolyte de Kilkenny	St. Liguori,
Kilk[illegible]	St. Alexis,	St. Jacques,	St. Theodore de Chertsey.
Montcalm,			

MONTMAGNY.

Berthier (*en bas*),	**Montmagny,*	St. Paul du Buton,	St. Pierre.
Cap St. Ignace,	St. François,		

MONTMORENCY.

Ange Gardien,	Laval,	St. François d'Orleans,	St. Laurent d'Orleans,
Beaulien,	St. Famille,	St. Jean d'Orleans,	St. Pierre d'Orleans,
Ch[illegible]au Richer,	St. Féréol (*sub*)	St. Joachim,	St. Tite des Caps (*sub*).

Post Offices in the Province of Quebec, arranged according to Electoral Districts.—Continued.

MONTREAL, CITY, CENTRE, EAST AND WEST.

**Montreal.*

NAPIERVILLE.

La Pigeonnière, *Napierville,*	St. Edouard,	*St. Rémi,*	Sherrington.

NICOLET.

Aston Station, *Bécancour,* Gentilly, *Nicolet,*	Ste. Angele de Laval, Ste. Brigitte des Saults, St. Célestin, Ste. Gertrude,	St. Grégoire, St. Leonard, Ste. Monique,	St. Perpetue, St. Pierre les Becquets, St. Wenceslas.

OTTAWA.

Angers, Aubigny, **Aylmer, East,* Aylwin, **Buckingham,* Cantley, Cascades **Chelsea,* Eardley, East Templeton,	Heyworth, **Hull,* Ironside, *Kazubazua,* Kirk's Ferry, Lochaber Bay, Low, Lucerne, Masham Mills,	Mayo, Montebello, North Nation Mills, North Wakefield, Papineauville, Perkins, River Desert, Rupert, St. André Avellin,	Sevigné, Six Portages, Templeton, **Thurso,* Upper Wakefield, Venosta, Vinoy, Wakefield, Wright.

PONTIAC.

Allumette Island, Bristol, *Bryson,* Calumette Island, Chichester, Clarendon Centre, Clarendon Front (sub),	Collfield, Danford Lake, Dunraven, Fort Coulonge, Fort William, Lake Temiscamingue, North Bristol,	North Onslow, **Onslow,* Otter Lake, **Portage du Fort,* Rapides des Joachims, Rowanton,	Sheenboro', Thornby, Thorne Centre, Vinton, Waltham, Yarm.

PORTNEUF.

Post Offices in the Province of Quebec, arranged according to Electoral Districts.—Continued.

QUEBEC CITY, CENTRE, EAST AND WEST.

**Quebec,*	*St. Roch de Quebec,*	*St. Sauveur de Quebec.*	

QUEBEC COUNTY.

Ancienne Lorette, Ancienne Lorette (sub), Beauport, Bergerville,	Cap Rouge, Charlesbourg, Lake Beauport, Lorette,	Montmorency Falls, St. Foy, Sillery Cove,	Spencer Cove, Stoneham, Valcartier,

RICHELIEU.

St. Aimé, St. Marcel,	St. Ours, St. Robert,	St. Roch de Richelieu St. Victoire,	**Sorel.*

RICHMOND AND WOLFE.

Richmond.		Wolfe.	
Brompton, *Brompton Falls,* Castlebar, *Danville,* Denison's Mills, Fontenoy, Kingsbury, **Melbourne,*	Melbourne Ridge, North Stoke. **Richmond, East,* Richmond Station, St. George de Windsor, Stoke, Centre, Stoketon, Windsor Mills.	Dudswell, Garthby, Lake Aylmer, Lake Weedon, Marbleton, North Ham,	St. Camille, Sanborn, South Ham, Weedon, Wolfstown, Wotton.

RIMOUSKI.

Bic, Causapscal, Cedar Hall, Dalibaire, Father Point,	Macnider, *Matane,* *Metis,* Neigette, Petit Metis,	**Rimouski,* St. Anaclet, St. Fabien, Ste. Félicité, Ste. Flavie,	Ste. Luce, St. Mathieu, St. Moïse, St. Octave, St. Simon de Rimouski, Tiessierville.

ROUVILLE.

Abbotsford, Angeline, Canrobert, Mont St. Hilaire,	Rougemont, Ste. Angèle, **Ste. Césaire,*	St. Hilaire Station, St. Hilaire Village, St. Jean Baptiste de Rouville,	Ste. Marie de Monnoir, St. Mathias, Village Richelieu.

Post Offices in the Province of Quebec, arranged according
Continued.

ST. HYACINTHE.

La Présentation, St. Barnabé, River Yamaska,	St. Charles, River Richelieu,	St. Damase, St. Denis, River Richelieu,

ST. JOHN'S.

Belle Alodie, Grand Ligne, Henrysburg,	L'Acadie, *Lacolle,* Roxham,	**St. John's East,* St. Luc,

ST. MAURICE.

Mont Elie, Pointe du Lac, St. Barnabé,	St. Elie, St. Etienne des Grés,	St. Maurice Forges, St. Sévère,

SHEFFORD.

Bethel, Boscobel, Clarina, Egypte, Frost Village, Granboro', **Granby,*	Lawrenceville, Mawcook, Milton, East, North Stukely, Rochelle, *Roxton Falls,* Roxton Pond,	St. Joachim de Sheff St. Valérien, Savage's Mills, Shefford Mountain, South Ely, South Granby,

SHERBROOKE TOWN.

Ascot Corner, Capelton,	Huntingville,	**Lennoxville,*

SOULANGES.

Cedars, Coteau du Lac, *Coteau Landing,*	Coteau Station, Mountjoy, Pont Château,	River Beaudette, St. Clet, St. Dominique des Ced

STANSTEAD.

Post Offices in the Province of Quebec, arranged according to Electoral Districts.—Concluded.

TEMISCOUATA.

Armand, Bégon, *Cacouna*, Détour du Lac,	Green River, Isle Verte, Notre Dame du Portage, **River du Loup (en bas)*,	River Trois Pistoles, St. Antonin, St. Arsène, St. Eloi,	Ste. Françoise, Ste. Modeste, Trois Pistoles, Viger.

TERREBONNE.

Beresford, Lac Masson, Montmorin, New Glasgow,	Ste. Adèle, Ste. Anne des Plaines, St. Janvier,	*St. Jérome*, St. Sauveur, St. Sophie de Lacorne,	*Ste Thérèse de Blainville*, Shawbridge, **Terrebonne*.

THREE RIVERS, CITY.

**Three Rivers*.

TWO MOUNTAINS.

Belle Rivière, Oka, St. Augustin, St. Benoit,	St. Canute, St. Columbin, *St. Eustache*,	St. Hermas, St. Joseph du Lac, St. Monique de Deux Montagnes,	Ste Placide, *Ste. Scholastique*.

VAUDREUIL.

Como, Hudson, Isle Perrot,	Mongenais, Mount Oscar, Peveril,	Point Fortune, Rigaud, Ste. Justine de Newton,	Ste. Marthe, Vaudreuil.

VERCHÈRES.

Belœil Station, Belœil Village,	Contrecœur, St. Antoine,	Ste. Julie, St. Marc,	Varennes, Verchères.

YAMASKA.

Chatillon, La Baie, Pierreville,	Pierreville Mills, Rivière aux Vaches,	*River David*, St. François du Lac,	St. Zéphirin, Yamaska.

POST OFFICES AND WAY OFFICES

IN THE

PROVINCE OF NOVA SCOTIA

ARRANGED ACCORDING TO ELECTORAL DISTRICTS.

ANNAPOLIS.

Annapolis,
Belleisle, W. O.,
Bridgetown,
Chute's Cove, W. O.,
Clementsport,
Clementsvale, W. O.,
Deep Brook, W. O.,
Granville Centre, W. O.,
Granville Ferry,
Lawrencetown,
Lequille, W. O.,
Lower Granville, W. O.,
Maitland, W. O.,
Margaretsville, W. O.,
Marshall's Cove, W. O.,
Melvern Square, W. O.,
Middleton,
Milford, W. O.,
Saw Mill Creek, W. O.,
Mount Hanly, W. O.,
New Albany, W. O.,
Nicholl's Corner, W. O.,
Nictaux Falls, W. O.,
Paradise Lane, W. O.,
Parker's Cove, W. O.,
Port George, W. O.,
Round Hill, W. O.,
Spa Springs, W. O.,
Springfield, W. O.,
Stoddart's, W. O.,
Stronach Mountain, W
Torbrook, W. O.,
Tupperville, W. O.,
Webber's, W. O.,
Wilmot.

ANTIGONISHE.

Antigonishe Harbour, W. O
Addington Forks, W. O.,
Antigonishe,
Arisaig, W. O.,
Back Lands, W. O.,
Barrio's Beach, W. O.,
Bayfield, W. O.,
Big Tracadie, W. O.,
Black River, W. O.,
Briley's Brook, W. O.,
Caledonia Mills, W. O.,
Cape George,
Cape George, North side, W.O.,
Cross Roads, Ohio, W. O.,
Eig Mountain, W. O.,
Fraser's Grant, W. O.,
Glen, W. O.,
Glen Alpine, W. O.,
Glen Road, W. O.,
Goshen, W. O.,
Harbor au Bouche, W. O.,
Harbor Road, W. O.,
Head of South River Lake, W. O.,
Lakevale, W. O.,
Little River, W. O.,
Little Tracadie, W. O.,
Livingston's Cove, W. O.,
Lochaber, W. O.,
Lowe Settlement South River, W. O.,
Malignant Cove, W. O.,
Marshy Hope, W. O.,
Marydale, W. O.,
Maryvale, W. O.,
Middle Settlement of South River, W. O.,
Ohio, W. O.,
Point of Cape, W. O.
Pomquet Chapel, W.,
Pomquet Forks, W.
St. Andrews,
Tracadie,
Upper Settlement South River, W. O
Usher, W. O.,
Vernal, W. O.,
West side of Locha W. O.,

CAPE BRETON.

Albert Bridge, W. O.,
Beaver Cove, W. O.,
Big Lorraine, W. O.,
Big Pond, W. O.,
Boisdale Chapel, W. O.,
Bridgeport, W. O.,
Cariboo Cove, W. O.,
Catalone, W. O.,
Christmas Island, W. O.,
Cow Bay,
Cox Heath, W. O.,
East Bay, W. O.,
East Bay, North side, W. O.,
Eskasoni, W. O.,
False Bay Beach, W. O.,
Frenchvale, W. O.,
Gabarus, W. O.,
Gardiner Mines, W. O.,
Grand Mira, North,
Grand Mira, South,
Grand Narrows, W. O.,
Irish Cove, W. O.,
Leitches Creek,
Lewis Bay, W. O.,
Lingan,
Little Bras d'Or.
Little Glace Bay,
Little Lorraine, W. O.,
Lorway Mines, W. O.,
Louisburg, W. O.,
Mainadieu, W. O.,
Marion Bridge, W. O.,
Mira Gut, W. O.,
North Sydney,
North West Arm, W.
Port Caledonia, W.
Reserve Mines, W. O
Salmon River, W. O.
South Bar of Syd River, W. O.,
Sydney,
Sydney Mines,
Victoria Mines, W. C

Post Offices and Way Offices in the Province of Nova Scotia, arranged according to Electoral Districts.—Continued.

COLCHESTER.

Acadia Mines,
Bass River, W.O.,
Brookfield,
Central Onslow, W.O.,
Chigonaise River, W.O.,
Cook's Brook, W.O.,
Dickson's Store, W.O.,
Earltown, W.O.,
Eastville, W.O.,
Economy,
Five Islands,
Folly Lake, W.O.,
Folly Mountain, W.O.,
Forbes, W.O.,
Gold Fields, W.O.,
Great Village,
Green's Creek, W.O.,
Halfway Brook, W.O.,
Hardwood Lands, W.O.,
Head of Tatamagouche, W.O.
Kempt Town, W.O.,
Londonderry,
Lower Stewiacke,
Mast Town, W.O.,
Middle Stewiacke, W.O.
New Annan, W.O.,
Newton Mills, W.O.,
North River, W.O.,
NorthRiverBridge, W.O.
North Section of Earltown, W.O.,
Old Barns, W.O.,
Onslow, W.O.,
Point Bruley, W.O.,
Portapique, W.O.,
Portapique Mountain, W.O.,
Princeport, W.O.,
River De Bert,
Riversdale, W.O.,
St. Andrew's, W.O.,
Shubenacadie,
South Branch, W.O.,
Stewiacke Cross Roads, W.O.,
Tatamagouche,
TatamagoucheMountain, W.O.,
Teviotdale Station, W.O.
Truro,
Upper Economy, W.O.,
Upper Stewiacke,
Waugh's River, W.O.,
West Branch, River Philip, W.O.

CUMBERLAND.

Advocate Harbor,
Amherst,
Amherst Hill, W.O.,
Amherst Point, W.O.,
Apple River, W.O.,
Athol, W.O.,
Barronsfield, W.O.,
Black Rock, W.O.,
Brookville, W.O.,
Brown's Brook, W.O.,
Cannonville, W.O.,
Claremont, W.O.,
Fenwick, W.O.,
Fox Harbor, W.O.,
Fox River, W.O.,
Goose River,
Greenville, W.O.,
Gulf Shore, W.O.,
Halfway River, W.O.,
Hastings, W. O.,
Head of Amherst, W.O.,
Head of Wallace Bay, W.O.,
Head of Wallace Bay, North Side, W.O.,
Hornsey, W.O.,
Joggin Mines, W.O.,
Kirk Hill, W.O.,
Lakelands, W.O.,
Lake Road, W.O.,
Lawrence Factory, W.O.
Leicester, W.O.,
Little River, W.O.,
Lower Cove, W.O.,
Maccan, W.O.,
Maccan Mountain, W.O.
Malagash, W.O.,
Middleboro', W.O.
Minudie, W.O.,
Mount Pleasant, W.O.,
Nappan, W.O.,
North Shore, W.O.,
Oxford,
Parrsborough,
Parrsborough Shore, W.O.,
Port Greville, W.O.,
Port Philip, W.O.,
Pugwash,
Pugwash River, W.O.,
River Hebert, W.O.,
River Philip,
Rockwell Settlement, W.O.
Roslin, W.O.,
Salem, W.O.,
Section 7, W.O.,
Shinemicas Bridge,
Shulie, W.O.,
Six Mile Road, W.O.,
Southampton, W.O.,
Spencer's Island, W.O.,
Spring Hill, W.O.,
Springhill Mines, W.O.
Thompson's Mills,
Three Sisters, W.O.,
Tidnish, W.O.,
Victoria, W.O.,
Wallace,
Wallace Bridge, W.O.,
Wallace Ridge, W.O.,
Wallace River, W.O.,
Warren, W.O.,
Wentworth, W.O.,
Westbrook, W.O.,
West Chester, W.O.,
West Chester Lake, W.O.,
Williamsdale, W.O.,
Windham Hill, W.O.,

DIGBY

Bear River, (West Side),
Beaver River, W.O.,
Beaver River Corner,
Belliveaus Cove, W.O.,
Cedar Lake, W.O.,
Clare, W.O.,
Digby,
Gilbert Cove, W.O.,
Havelock, W.O.,
Head of St. Mary's Bay, W.O.,
Little River, W.O.,
Long Island,
Marshall's Town, W.O.,
Metaghan, W.O.,
Metaghan River, W.O.,
New Tusket, W.O.,
North Range Corner, W.O.,
Petite Passage, W.O.,
Pleasant Valley, W.O.,
Rossway, W.O.,
St. Mary's Bay, W.O.,
Salmon River, W.O.,
Sandy Cove,
Saulnierville, W.O.,
Smith's Cove, W.O.
Speitche's Cove, W.O.
Trout Cove, W.O.,
WeaverSettlement, W.O.
Westport,
Weymouth,
Weymouth Bridge.

GUYSBOROUGH.

Caledonia, St. Mary's, W.O
Canso,
Charlo's Cove, W.O.,
Cole Harbor, W.O.,
Cross Roads (Country Harbor),
Cross Roads, Middle Melford, W.O.,
Crow Harbor, W.O.,
East River, St. Mary's, W.O.,
Erinville, W.O.,
Forristalls, W.O.,
Giant's Lake, W.O.,
Glenelg,
Goldenville.

Post Offices and Way Offices in the Province of Nova Scotia, arranged according to Electoral Districts.—Continued.

GUYSBOROUGH.—*Continued.*

Grosvenor, W.O.,
Guysborough,
Guysborough Intervale, W.O.
Half Island Cove, W.O.,
Indian Harbor, W.O.,
Isaac's Harbor, W.O.,
Larry's River, W.O.,
Liscomb, W.O.,
Manchester, W.O.,
Marie Joseph, W.O.,
Melrose,
Milford Haven Bridge, W.O.,
New Harbor, W.O.,
New Town, W.O.,
Oyster Ponds, W.O.,
Pirate Harbor,
Port Felix, W.O.,
Port Mulgrave,
Ragged Head, W.O.,
Roman's Valley, W.O.,
Salmon River, W.O.,
Salmon River, Lake Settlement, W.O.,
Sand Point, W.O.,
Sherbrooke,
Smithfield, W.O.,
Sonora, W.O.,
Steep Creek, W.O.,
Still Water, W.O.,
Stormont, W.O.,
Torbay, W.O.,
Upper Cross Roads, St. Mary's, W.O.,
White Head, W.O.,
White Harbor, W.O.,

HALIFAX CITY AND HALIFAX COUNTY.

Antrim, W.O.,
Beaver Bank, W.O.,
Bedford Basin, W.O.,
Black Point, W.O.,
Brookvale, W.O.,
Cambridge, W.O.,
Carroll's Corners, W.O.,
Chezzetcook, W.O.,
Dartmouth,
East Jeddore, W.O.,
East Side of Chezzetcook, W.O.,
English Corner, W.O.,
Fletcher's Station, W.O.,
Gay's River, W.O.,
Gay's River Road, W.O.,
Hackett's Cove, W.O.,
Halifax,
Harrigan Cove, W.O.,
Head of St. Margaret's Bay, W.O.,
Head of St. Margaret's Bay, Middle District, W.O.
Hubbard's Cove,
Indian Harbor, W.O.,
Jeddore, W.O.,
Kent's Island, W.O.,
Ketch Harbor, W.O.,
Lawrencetown, W.O.,
Little River, (Middle Musquodoboit), W.O.,
Lower Prospect, W.O.,
Lower Ward, St. Margaret's Bay, W.O.,
Meagher's Grant, W.O.,
Middle Musquodoboit,
Montague Gold Mines, W.O.,
Musquodoboit, Harbor, W.O.
Necum Tench, W.O.,
New Caledonia, W.O.,
Newcomb Corner, W.O.,
Oakfield, W.O.,
Oldham, W.O.,
Peggy's Cove, W.O.,
Porter's Lake, W.O.,
Portuguese Cove, W.O.,
Preston Road, W.O.,
Prospect, W.O.,
Richmond Terminus, W.O.
St. Margaret's Bay,
Salmon Hole, W.O.,
Salmon River, W.O.,
Sambro, W.O.,
Sandy Beaches, W.O.,
Sheet Harbor,
Ship Harbor, W.O.,
South-East Passage, W.O.,
Spry Bay, W.O.,
Tangier,
Terence Bay, W.O.,
Trafalgar, W.O.,
Upper Caledonia, W.O.,
Upper Musquodoboit,
Waverley,
West Newdy Quoddy,
Wickwire Station, W.O.,
Windsor Junction, W.O.,

HANTS.

Burnt Coat, W.O.,
Cheverie, W.O.,
Cogmagun River, W.O.,
Densmores, W.O.,
Densmores Mills, W.O.,
Ellershausen, W.O.,
Elmsdale,
Enfield,
Falmouth, W.O.,
Falmouth (Windsor Bridge, W.O.,)
Five Mile River, W.O.,
Gore, W.O.,
Hantsport,
Highfield, W.O.,
Indian Road, W.O.,
Kennetcook, W.O.,
Kennetcook Corner, W.O.,
Lower Selmah, W.O.,
Maitland,
Millers Creek, W.O.
Moose Brook, W.O.,
Mortonville, W.O.,
Mosherville, W.O.,
Mount Denison, W.O.,
Mount Uniacke,
Newport,
Newport Corner, W.O.,
Newport Landing,
Newport Station,
Nine Mile River, W.O.,
Noel, W.O.,
Noel Shore, W.O.,
North Salem, W.O.,
Rawdon, W.O.,
Renfrew,
St. Croix, W.O.,
Scotch Village, W.O.,
Selmah, W.O.,
South Rawdon, W.O.,
Summerville, W.O.,
Tenecape, W.O.,
Three Mile Plains, W.O.,
Upper Kennetcook, W.O.,
Upper Newport, W.O.,
Upper Rawdon, W.O.,
Urbania, W.O.,
Vaughans, W.O.,
Walton,
West Gore, W.O.,
Windsor, W.O.
Woodville, W.O.,

INVERNESS.

Big Brook, W.O.,
Big Harbor, W.O.,
Big Intervale, Grand Narrows, W.O.,
Blue's Mill, W.O.,
Boom, W.O.,
BroadCoveChapel, W.O.,
Broad Cove Intervale, W.O.
BroadCove Marsh, W.O.,
Cape Mabou, W.O.,
Cheticamp, W.O.,
Chimney Corner, W.O.,
Cross Roads, Lake Ainslie, W.O.,
Cross Roads, St. George's Channel, W.O.,

Post Offices and Way Offices in the Province of Nova Scotia, arranged according to Electoral Districts.—Continued.

INVERNESS.—*Continued.*

Eastern Harbor, W. O.
Emerald, W. O.
Glenedale, W. O.
Grand Etang, W. O.
Hay's River, W. O.,
Hillsborough, C.B., W. O.
Judique, W. O.
Kewstoke, W. O.
Lake Ainslie, W. O.
Lake Ainslie (East side), W. O.,
Lake Ainslie (South side), W. O.,
Lake Law, W. O.
Little Judique, W. O.
Little Narrows, W. O.
Long Point, W. O.
Low Point, W. O.
Mabou,
Mabou Coal Mines, W.O.
Mabou Harbor, W. O.
Malagawatch, W. O.,
Marble Mountain, W.O.
Margaree, W. O.
Margaree, (Forks),
Middle section of North East Margaree, W. O.
Middle Settlement of River Inhabitants, W. O.
Mull River, W. O.
New Bridge, W. O.
North-East Branch, Margaree, W. O.
North Side of Basin, River Dennis, W. O.
Pleasant Bay, W. O.
Port Hastings,
Port Hawkesbury,
Port Hood,
Port Hood Island, W. O.
Queensville, W. O.
River Dennis, W. O.
Shea's River, W. O.
Sight Point, W. O.
Sky Glen, W. O.
South Side of Basin, (River Dennis), W. O.
South side of Whycocomagh Bay, W. O.
South Side of West Margaree, W. O.
South-West Mabou, WO.
Upper Margaree, W. O.
Upper Settlement of River Dennis, W. O.
West Bay,
Whycocomagh.

KING'S.

Avonport, W. O.
Avonport Station, W. O.
Aylesford.
Beech Hill, W. O.
Berwick,
Berwick Station, W.O.
Bill Town, W. O.
Buckley's, W. O.
Burlington, W. O.
Cambridge Station, W.O.
Canaan, W. O.
Canaan Road, W. O.
Canada Creek, W. O.
Canard, W. O.
Canning,
Centreville, W. O.
Chipman's Brook, W. O.
Chipman's Corners, W. O.
Church Street, W. O.
Cold Brook Station, W. O.
Condon Settlement, W. O.
Cornwallis, East, W. O.
Dalhousie, East, W. O.
Dempsey's Corner, W. O.
Factory Dale, W. O.
Gaspereaux, W. O.
Hall's Harbor, W. O.
Harborville, W. O
Harmony, W. O.
Horton Landing, W. O.
Jackson Road, W. O.
Kentville.
Kingston Village, W. O.
Kinsman's Corner, W. O.
Lake George, W O.
Lakeville, W. O.
Lockhartville, W. O.
Long Point, W. O.
Lower Horton,
Lower Pereaux, W. O.
Medford, W. O.
Middle Pereaux, W. O.
Morden, W. O.
Morristown, W. O.
Nerepis Station, W. O.
New Minas, W. O.
New Ross Road,
Niely Road.
North Mountain, W. O.
Ogilvie, W. O.
Palmer's Road, W. O.
Pineo Village
Port Williams.
Port Williams Station.
Rhodes, W. O.
Ross' Corner, W. O.
Scott's Bay, W. O.
Sheffield Mills, W. O.
Somerset, W. O.
Steam Mills Village, W. O.
Upper Dyke Village, W. O.
Upper Pereaux, W. O.
Vernon Mines, W. O.
Victoria Harbor, W. O.
Waterville, W. O.
White Rock Mills,
Wolfville.

LUNENBURG.

Blandford, W. O.
Bridgewater,
Broad Cove, W. O.
Chelsea, W. O.
Chesley's Corners, W. O.
Chester.
Chester Basin, W. O.
Conquerall Bank, W. O.
Dalhousie Road, W. O.
Dublin Shore, W. O.
Duncan, W. O.
Foster's, W. O.
Getson's Point, W. O.
Gold River, W. O.
Hebb's Cross, W. O.
Indian Point, W. O.
Kingsbury, W. O.
La Have Cross Roads, W. O.
La Have River, W. O.
Laugill's, W. O.
Lantz, W. O.
Lower La Have, W. O.
Lunenburg.
Mahone Bay.
Marriott's Cove, W O.
Martin's River, W. O.
Middle La Have Ferry, W. O.
Mill Cove, W. O.
Morton's Corner, W. O.
Mossmans Grant, W. O.
New Canada, W. O.
New Cornwall, W. O.
New Germany, W. O.
New Ross,
Northfield, W. O.
North-West Cove, W. O.
Petite Reviére Bridge, W. O.
Tancook Islands, W. O.
Upper Branch, W. O.
Upper La Have, W. O.
Vogler's Cove, W. O.
West Dublin, W. O.

PICTOU.

Alma, W. O.
Avondale, W.O.
Bailey's Brook, W. O.
Barney's River, W. O.
Big Island, W. O.
Blanchard's Road, W. O.
Blue Mountain, W O.
Bridgeville, W. O.
Brookville, W. O.
Cape John, W. O.
Churchville, W. O.
Concord, W. O.
Dalhousie Settlement, W. O.
McLellan's Mountain, W. O.,
Poplar Hill, W. O.,
West Merigonishe, W. O.

Post Offices and Way Offices in the Province of Nova Scotia, arranged according to Electoral Districts.—Continued.

PICTOU.—*Continued.*

Durham,
East River, St. Mary's, W.O.,
East side of West Branch East River of Pictou, W. O.,
Elmsville, W. O.,
Fraser's Mills, W. O.,
French River, W. O.,
Garden of Eden, W. O.,
Glengarry Station,
Green Hill, W. O.,
Hopewell, W. O.,
Knoydart, W. O.,
Lime Rock, W. O.,
Little Harbor, W. O.,
Loganville, W. O.,
Lower Barney's River, W. O.,
McLellan's Brook, W. O.,
Marsh Settlement, (McLellan's Mountain, W. O.,)
Merigonish, W. O.,
Middle River, W. O.,
Mill Brook, W. O.,
Millsville, W. O.,
Mount Thom,
New Gairloch, W. O.,
New Glasgow,
New Lairg, W. O.,
Pictou,
Piedmont Valley, W. O.,
Plainfield, W. O.,
Ponds, W. O.,
River John,
Rocklin, W. O.,
Roger's Hill, W. O.,
St. Paul's, W. O.,
Six Mile Brook, W. O.,
South McLellan's Mountain, W. O.,
Springville, W. O.,
Stellarton,
Sumerville, W. O.,
Sutherland's Mills, W. O.,
Sutherland's River, W. O.,
Toney River, W. O.,
Upper Settlement of Barney's River, W. O.,
Upper Settlement of West River, W. O.
West Branch, East River, of Pictou, W. O.,
West Branch, River John, W. O.,
West River,
West River Station,
Westville.

QUEEN'S.

Brookfield, W. O.,
Brooklyn, W. O.,
Caledonia Corner,
East Port Medway, W. O.,
Greenfield, W. O.,
Kempt, W. O.,
Liverpool,
Middlefield, W. O.,
Mill Village,
Milton,
North Brookfield, W. O.,
Pleasant River, W. O.,
Port Matoon, W. O.,
Port Medway,
White Point, W. O.

RICHMOND.

Arichat,
Cariboo Cove, W. O.,
Discoose, W. O.,
Fourche, W. O.,
Framboise, W. O.,
Grand Anse, W. O.,
Grandigue Ferry, W. O.,
Grand River, W. O.,
Kempt Road, W. O.,
L'Ardoise, W. O.,
Lennox Ferry, W. O.,
Loch Lomond, W. O.,
Lochside, W. O.,
Lower L'Ardoise, W. O.,
Lower River Inhabitants, W. O.,
McPherson's Ferry W. O.,
Petite de Grat, W. O.,
Port Richmond, W. O.,
Port Royal, W. O.,
Rear of Black River, W. O.,
Rear Lands' Sporting Mountain, W. O.,
Red Islands, W. O.,
River Bourgeois, W. O.
St. Esprit, W. O.,
St. George's Channel, W. O.,
St. Peter's,
West Arichat, W. O.

SHELBURNE.

Barrington,
Barrington Passage, W. O.,
Bear Point, W. O.,
Big Port le Bear, W. O.,
Cape Negro, W. O.,
Cape Sable Island, W. O.,
Clarke's Harbor, W. O.,
Clyde River, W. O.,
East side of Ragged Island, W. O.,
Gunning Cove, W. O.
Head of Jordan River, W. O.,
Jordan Bay, W. O.,
Lewis Head, W. O.,
Littlewood, W. O.,
Locke Port,
Lower Wood Harbor, W. O.,
Middle Clyde River, W. O.,
Middle Ohio, W. O.
North-east Harbor, W. O.
Oak Park, W. O.,
Port Clyde, W. O.,
Port Jolly, W. O.,
Port la Tour, W. O.,
Pubnico Beach, W. O.,
Ragged Island, W. O.,
Roseway, W. O.,
Sable River, W. O.,
Sandy Point, W. O.,
Shag Harbor, W. O.,
Shelburne.,
Upper Wood Harbor, W. O.
Upper Clyde River, W. O.

VICTORIA.

Baddeck,
Baddeck Bay,
Baddeck Bridge, W. O.,
Bay St. Lawrence, W. O.
Big Bank, W. O.,
Big Bras d'Or, W. O.,
Big Intervale, Margaree, W. O.,
Boulardarie,
Cape North, W. O.,
Englishtown,
Forks, Baddeck, W. O.

Post Offices and Way Offices in the Province of Nova Scotia, arranged according to Electoral Districts.—Concluded.

VICTORIA.—*Continued.*

Bucklaw, W.O. Groves Point, W.O., Hunter's Mountain, W.O. Indian Brook, W. O., Ingonish, W. O., Kempt Head, W. O., Lower Settlement, Middle River, W. O., McKay's Point, W. O.,	Middle Rive W.O. Munro's, W. O., New Campbelton Niel's Harbor, W. O., North River Bridge, W. O., North Shore, W. O., Point Clear, W.O.,	St. Ann's, W.O., St. Patrick's Channel, W.O., South Bay, W.O. South Gut of St. Ann's, W. O., South side of Boulardarie, W. O., Sugar Loaf, W.O.,	Upper Settlement of Baddeck River, W. O., Upper Settlement of Middle River, W. O., Upper Washabuck, W. O. West Side of Middle River, W.O. Wreck Cove, W.O.

YARMOUTH.

Argyle, W. O., Carlton, W. O., Central Chebogue, W. O., Chebogue, W. O., Deerfield, W.O., Eel Lake, W. O.,	East side of Pubnico Harbor, W. O., Eel Brook, W. O. Hebron, Kemptville, W.O., Kempt Bridge, W.O., Lake George, W.O.	Maitland, W. O., Plymouth, W.O., Port Acadie, W.O. Pubnico Harbor, W. O. Robert's Island, W. O. Rockville, Sand Beach, W.O.,	Short Beach, W.O., South Ohio, W.O. *Tusket*, Tusket Wedge, W.O., Tusket Forks, *Yarmouth*. Wellington, W.O.

POST OFFICES AND WAY OFFICES

IN THE

PROVINCE OF NEW BRUNSWICK.

ARRANGED ACCORDING TO ELECTORAL DISTRICTS.

ALBERT.

Alma,
Albert Mines, W. O.,
Beaver Brook, W. O.,
Berryton, W. O.,
Bridgedale, W. O.,
Caledonia Settlement, W. O.,
Centreville, W. O.,
Church Hill, W. O.,
Coverdale, W. O.,
Curryville, W. O.,
Dawson Settlement, W. O.,
Edgett's Landing, W. O.,
Elgin,
Germantown, W. O.,
Goshen, W. O.,
Gowland Mountain, W. O.
Harvey,
Hastings, W. O.,
Hebron, W. O.,
Hillsborough,
Hillside,
Hopewell, W. O.,
Hopewell Cape,
Hopewell Corner, W. O.,
Hopewell Hill, W. O.,
Irving Settlement, W. O.
Little Ridge, W. O.,
Little River (Coverdale), W. O.,
Little River (Elgin), W. O.,
Little Rocher, W. O.,
Little Shemogue, W. O.,
Lower Cape, W. O.,
Lower Coverdale, W. O.,
Lower Turtle Creek, W. O.,
Mapleton, W. O.,
Middle Coverdale, W. O.,
New Horton, W. O.,
New Ireland, W. O.,
New Ireland Road, W. O.,
Pleasant Vale, W. O.,
Point Wolfe, W. O.,
Prosser Brook, W. O.,
River Side, W. O.,
Rosevale, W. O.,
Roxburgh, W. O.,
Salem, W. O.,
Stoney Creek, W. O.,
Upper New Horton, W. O.,
Waterside, W. O.,
Wellington, W. O.

CARLETON.

Avondale, W. O.,
Bairdsville, W. O.,
Bath,
Belleville, W. O.,
Benton, W. O.,
Bloomfield, W. O.,
Boundary Presqu' isle, W. O.,
Carlow, W. O.,
Centreville, W. O.,
Charlestown, W. O.,
Coldstream, W. O.,
Debeck Station, W. O.,
East Glassville, W. O.,
Farley's Mills, W. O.,
Farmerston, W. O.,
Ferryville, W. O.,
Florenceville,
Florenceville, East, W. O.,
Foreston, W. O.,
Glassville, W. O.,
Good Corner, W. O.,
Gordonsville, W. O.,
Greenfield, W. O.,
Hartland,
Holmsville, W. O.,
Jacksontown, W. O.,
Jacksonville, W. O.,
Johnville, W. O.,
Knowlesville, W. O.,
Knoxford, W. O.,
Lakeville, W. O.,
Lindsay, W. O.,
Long Settlement, W. O.,
Lower Brighton, W. O.,
Lower Wakefield, W. O.,
Lower Woodstock, W. O.,
McKenzie's Corner, W. O.,
Middle Simonds, W. O.,
Monument Settlement, W. O.
Newburgh, W. O.,
Northampton, W. O.,
Peel, W. O.,
Richmond Corner,
River de Chute, W. O.,
Shiktehawke, W. O.,
Somerville, W. O.,
Tracey's Mills, W. O.,
Turtle Creek, W. O.,
Union Corner, W. O.,
Upper Kent, W. O.,
Upper Peel, W. O.,
Upper Wicklow, W. O.,
Upper Woodstock, W. O.,
Victoria, W. O.,
Waterville, W. O.,
Watson Settlement, W. O.
West Glassville, W. O.,
Wicklow,
Williamstown, W. O.,
Windsor, W. O.,
Woodstock,
Woodstock Road Station, W. O.

Post Offices and Way Offices in the Province of New Brunswick, arranged according to Electoral Districts.—Continued.

CHARLOTTE.

Back Bay, W.O.
Baillie, W.O.
Basswood Ridge, W.O.
Bayside, W.O.
Beaver Harbor, W.O.
Bocabec, W.O.
Campo Bello.
Clarendon, W.O.
Dumbarton, R. R. Station, W.O.
Fairhaven, W.O.
Grand Harbor, W.O.
Grand Manan,
Indian Island, W.O.
Lawrence Station, W.O.
L'Edge, W.O.
Lepreaux,
L'Etete, W.O.
Little Lepreaux, W.O.
Lord's Cove, W.O.
Lynnfield, W.O.
Mace's Bay,
Mascarene, W.O.
Milltown,
Moore's Mills, W.O.
New River, W.O.
Oak Bay, W.O.
Oak Hill, W.O.
Pennfield, W.O.
Pennfield Ridge, W.O.
Pleasant Ridge, W.O.
Pomery Ridge, W.O.
Rolling Dam, W.O.
St. Andrews,
St. George,
St. Patrick, W.O.
St. Stephen,
Second Falls, W.O.
Tower Hill, W.O.
Upper Mills,
Waweig, W.O.
Whittier's Ridge, W.O.
Wilson's Beech, W.O.

GLOUCESTER.

Alexander's Point, W.O.
Bathurst,
Bathurst Village, W.O.
Belledune, W.O.
Belledune River, W.O.
Caraquet,
Clifton, W.O.
Grand Anse, W.O.
Janeville, W.O.
Little Shippigan, W.O.
Lower Pockmouche, W.O.
Madisco, W.O.
New Bandon, W.O.
Pockmouche, W.O.
Pockshaw, W.O.
Poplar Grove, W.O.
Salmon Beach, W.O.
Shippigan,
Tracadie, W.O.
Upper Caraquet, W.O.

KENT.

Bourgeois, W.O.
Buctouche,
Chuckfish, W.O.
Coal Branch, W.O.
Coate's Mills, W.O.
Cocaigne,
Cocaigne River, W.O.
Doherty's Mills, W.O.
Gailey, W.O.
Girvan Settlement, W.O.
Grandigue, W.O.
Gueguen, W.O.
Kingston,
Kouchibouguac,
Lake Settlement, W.O.
McLaughlan Road, W.O.
McLeod's Mills, W.O.
Mill Creek, W.O.
Moulie's River, W.O.
Palmerston, W.O.
Point Sapin, W.O.
Richibucto,
Richibucto Village, W.O.
St. Anthony, W.O.
St. Mary's, W.O.
St. Paul's, W.O.
Scovil's Mills, W.O.
Upper Buctouche, W.O.
Welford, W.O.
West Branch, Nicholas River, W.O.

KING'S.

Anagance,
Apohaqui,
Barnesville, W.O.
Bass River, W.O.
Belleisle Bay, W.O.
Belleisle Creek, W.O.
Bloomfield, W.O.
Butternut Ridge,
Campbell Settlement, W.O.
Carsonville, W.O.
Case Settlement, W.O.
Central Norton, W.O.
Clifton, W.O.
Collina, W.O.
Cornhill, W.O.
Cromwell, W.O.
Donegal, W.O.
East Scotch Settlement, W.O.
Round Hill, W.O.
Salt Springs, W.O.
Fenwick, W.O.
French Village, W.O.
Greenwich Hill, W.O.
Hammond River, W.O.
Hammond Vale,
Hampton, W.O.
Hanford Brook, W.O.
Head of Millstream, W.O.
Hillsdale, W.O.
Kars, W.O.
Kingston
Lakefield, W.O.
Londonderry, W.O.
Long Point, W.O.
Long Reach, W.O.
Markhamville, W.O.
Mechanic's Settlement, W.O.
Midland, W.O.
Millstream, W.O.
Mouth of Nerepis,
Mount Pleasant, W.O.
Nerepis Station,
Newtown, W.O.
Norton, W.O.
Norton Station,
Oak Point, W.O.
Ossekeag,
Penobsquis,
Perry Settlement, W.O.
Poodiac, W.O.
Ratter's Corner, W.O.
Rockville, W.O.
Rothsay, W.O.
Seeley's Mills, W.O.
Shepody Road, W.O.
Smith Creek, W.O.
Smith Town, W.O.
South Branch, W.O.
Sprague's Point, W.O.
Springfield,
Sussex Corner, W.O.
Sussex Portage, W.O.
Sussex Vale,
Tenant's Cove, W.O.
Thorne Brooke, W.O.
Titusville, W.O.
Upham, W.O.
Upper Greenwich, W.O.
Urquhart's, W.O.
Ward's Creek Road, W.O.
Westfield, W.O.

Post Offices and Way Offices in the Province of New Brunswick, arranged according to Electoral Districts.—Continued.

NORTHUMBERLAND.

Barnaby River, W.O.
Bartibog, W.O.
Bay du Vin, W.O.
Bay du Vin Mills, W.O.
Black Brook, W.O.
Black River, W.O.
Black River Bridge, W.O.
Blackville, W.O.
Blissfield, W.O.
Boiestown, W.O.
Burnt Church, W.O.
Cains River, W.O.
Chatham.
Church Point, W.O.
Derby, W.O.
Doaktown, W.O.
Douglastown, W.O.
Dumphy, W.O.
Escuminac, W.O.
Hardwick, W.O.
Little Branch, W.O.
Lower Newcast, W.O.
Ludlow, W.O.
Lyttleton, W.O.
Neguac, W.O.
Newcastle.
North Esk Boom, W.O.
NorthWestBridge, W.O.
Oak Point, W.O.
Portage River, W.O.
Red Bank, W.O.
Renou's Bridge, W.O.
South Nelson, W.O.
Tabucintac, W.O.
Upper Bay du Vin, W.O
Upper Neguac, W.O.
Whitney, W.O.

QUEEN'S

Armstrong's Corner, W.O.
Belyea's Cove, W.O.
Big Cove, W.O.
Brigg's Corner, W.O.
Brookvale, W.O.
Cambridge, W.O.
Central Cambridge, W.O.
Chipman, W.O.
Clones, W.O.
Coal Mines, W.O.
Cody's, W.O.
Cole's Island, W.O.
Cumberland Bay, W.O.
Cumberland Point, W.O.
Douglas Harbor, W.O.
English Settlement, W.O.
Enniskillen Station, W.O.
Ferris, W.O.
Fork's, W.O.
Gagetown.
Gaspereaux, W.O.
Gaspereaux Station, W.O.
Hampstead, W.O.
Hibernia, W.O.
Jemseg, W.O.
Jenkins, W.O.
Johnson, W.O.
Long Creek, W.O.
McDonald's Corner, W.O.
McDonald's Point, W.O.
Macquapit Lake, W.O.
Mill Cove, W.O.
Mouth of Jemseg, W.O.
Narrows.
New Canaan, W.O.
Newcastle Bridge, W.O.
Newcastle Creek, W.O.
New Jerusalem, W.O.
Oakham, W.O.
Olinville, W.O.
Otnabog, W.O.
Petersville, W.O.
Petersville Church, W.O.
Scotch Town, W.O.
Starkeys, W.O.
Summer Hill, W.O.
Sypher's Cove, W.O.
The Range, W.O.
Thorne Town, W.O.
Upper Gagetown, W.O.
Upper Gaspereaux, W.O.
Upper Hampstead, W.O.
Washademoak, W.O.
Waterborough, W.O.
Welsford.
White's Cove, W.O.
Wickham, W.O.
Young's Cove, W.O.

RESTIGOUCHE.

Archibald Settlement, W.O.
Armstrong's Brook, W.O.
Black Land, W.O.
Black Point, W.O.
Breadalbane, W.O.
Campbelltown.
Dalhousie.
Doyle Settlement, W.O.
Dundee, W.O.
Eel River, W.O.
Flatlands.
Head of Tide, W.O.
Heron Island, W.O.
Maple Green, W.O.
New Mills.
Point la Nim, W.O.
River Charlo, W.O.
River Louison, W.O.
Shannonvale, W.O.
Upsalquitch, W.O.

ST. JOHN CITY, AND ST. JOHN CITY AND COUNTY.

Black River, W.O.
Carleton.
Chance Harbor, W.O.
Clinch's Mills, W.O.
Dipper Harbor, W.O.
Fairfield, W.O.
Fairville.
Gardner's Creek, W.O.
Golden Grove, W.O.
Goose Creek, W.O.
Grand Bay, W.O.
Indian Town.
Loch Lomond, W.O.
Milledgeville, W.O.
Mispec, W.O.
Musquash, W.O.
Pisarinco, W.O.
Prince of Wales, W.O.
Quaco Road, W.O.
St. John's.
St. Martin's.
St. Martin's, W.O.
Salmon River, W.O.
Shanklin, W.O.
South Bay, W.O.
Spruce Lake, W.O.
Ten Mile Creek, W.O.
Upper Loch Lomond, W.O.
West Quaco.
Willow Grove, W.O.

SUNBURY.

Blissville.
Burton, W.O.
Central Blissville, W.O.
Frederickton Junction.
French Lake, W.O.
Geary, W.O.
Harts Mills, W.O.
Juvenile Settlement, W.O.
Lakeville Corner, W.O.
Lincoln, W.O.
Lintons, W.O.
Little River, W.O.
Maugerville, W.O.
Northfield, W.O.
Oromocto.
Patterson Settlement, W.O.
Rusagornis, W.O.
Rusagornis Station, W.O.
Salmon Creek, W.O.
Sheffield.
Sheffield Academy, W.O.
Tracey Station, W.O.
Upper Maugerville, W.O.
Upper Sheffield, W.O.
Waasis Station, W.O

Post Offices and Way Offices in the Province of New Brunswick, arranged according to Electoral Districts.—Concluded.

VICTORIA.

Andover,
Aroostook, W.O.
Arthurst, W.O.
Baker's Creek, W.O.
Edmundston,
Grand Falls,
Grand Falls Portage, W.O.
Grand River, W.O.
Green River, W.O.
Kincardine, W.O.
MiddleSt.Francis, W.O.
Perth, W.O.
Riley Brook, W.O
St. Leonard's, W.O.
Silverstream, W.O.
Three Brooks, W.O.
Undine, W.O.
Upper St. Basil, W.O.
Upper St. Francis, W.O.
Webster's Creek, W.O.

WESTMORELAND.

Anderson, W.O.
Au Lac, W.O.
Baie Verte,
Baie Verte Road, W.O.
Barachois, W.O.
Bayfield, W.O.
Belliveaus Village, W.O.
Botsford Portage, W.O.
Boudreau Village, W.O.
Boundary Creek, W.O.
Cape Spear, W.O.
Centre Village, W.O.
Chapman, W.O.
Dorchester,
Dover, W.O.
Dungiven, W.O.
Emigrant Road, W.O.
Emigrant Settlement, W.O.
Fox Creek, W.O.
Fredericton Road, W.O.
Great Shemogue,
Harewood, W.O.
Intervale, W.O.
Irishtown, W.O.
Johnson's Mills, W.O
Jolicure, W.O.
Kay Settlement, W.O.
Lewis Mountain, W.O.
Lewisville, W.O,
Lutz Mountain, W.O.
McDougall Settlement, W.O.
Memramcook,
Midgic, W.O.
Moncton,
Moncton Road, W.O.
Mount Whatley, W.O.
Murray's Corner, W.O.
North Joggins, W.O.
North Lake, W.O.
North River,
North River Platform, W.O.
Petitcodiac,
Point du Chêne, W.O.
Pollett River, W.O.
Port Elgin,
Painsec, W.O.
Read, W.O.
Rockland, W.O.
Rockport, W.O.
St. Joseph, W.O.
Sackville,
Salisbury,
Scotch Settlement, W.O.
Shediac,
Shediac Bridge, W.O.
Shediac Road, W.O.
Smith's, W.O.
South Rockland, W.O.
Spence, W.O.
Steeves Mountain, W.O.
Steeves Settlement, W.O.
Taylor Village, W.O.
Tidish, W.O.
Tidnish Bridge, W.O.
Upper Cape, W.O.
Upper Sackville, W.O.
Westcock, W.O.
Westmoreland Point,
Wheaton Settlement, W.O.
Wood Point, W.O.

YORK.

Bear Island, W.O.
Birdton, W.O.
Blayney Ridge, W.O.
Campbell Settlement, W.O.
Canterbury,
Canterbury Station,
Central Kingsclear, W.O.
Cork Station, W.O.
Douglas, W.O
Dumfries, W.O.
Forest City, W.O.
Fredericton,
Hamtown, W.O.
Hanwell, W.O.
Harvey Station,
Keswick Ridge, W.O.
Kingsclear, W.O.
Kingsley, W.O.
Lake George, W.O.
LowerCanterbury, W.O.
Lower French Village, W.O.
Lower Haynesville, W.O.
Lower Line, Queensbury, W.O.
Lower Prince William, W.O.
Lower Queensbury, W.O.
Lower Southampton, W.O.
McAdam Junction, W.O.
Mactaquack, W.O.
Magaguadavic, W.O.
Magundy, W.O.
Manners Sutton, W.O.
Marysville, W.O.
MiddleSouthampton, W.O.
Millville, W.O.
Mouth of Keswick, W.O.
Nackawick, W.O.
Nashwaak, W.O.
Nashwaaksis, W.O.
Nashwaak Village, W.O.
New Maryland, W.O.
New Zealand, W.O.
North Lake, W.O.
Norton Dale, W.O.
Pemberton Ridge, W.O.
Poquiock, W.O.
Prince William, W.O.
Royal Road W.O.
St. Croix, W.O.
St. Mary's Ferry, W.O
Southampton, W.O.
Springfield, W.O.
Stanley, W.O.
Tay Mills, W.O.
Tay Settlement, W.O.
Temperance Vale, W.O.
Tweedside, W.O.
Upper Caverhill, W.O.
Upper Haynesville, W.O.
Upper Keswick, W.O.
Upper Keswick Ridge, W.O.
UpperMagaguadavic, W.O.
Upper Queensbury, W.O.
Upper Southampton, W.O.
Yoho, W.O.

POST OFFICES

IN THE

PROVINCE OF MANITOBA,

ARRANGED ACCORDING TO ELECTORAL DISTRICTS.

LISGAR.

Eagle's Nest. Lower Fort Garry.	Mapleton. Middle Church.	Park's Creek. St. Andrew's.	St. Peter's.

MARQUETTE.

Baie St. Paul, Burnside. High Bluff.	Oak Point. Palestine. Pigeon Lake.	Poplar Point. Portage la Prairie. St. Laurent.	St. François Xavier. Westbourne.

PROVENCHER.

Point du Chêne.	St. Norbert.	West Lynne.	——

SELKIRK.

POST OFFICES

IN THE

PROVINCE OF BRITISH COLUMBIA,

ARRANGED ACCORDING TO ELECTORAL DISTRICTS.

CARIBOO.

Barkerville, Canoe Creek, Clinton, Dog Creek,	Dunkeld, Gronse Creek. Harbor Creek. Keithley Creek.	Lac La Hache, Lilloet, Omineca, 150 Mile House,	Quesnelle, Quesnelle Forks. Soda Creek, Van Winkle.

NEW WESTMINSTER.

Burrard's Inlet,	Langley,	New Westminster,	Sumas.

VANCOUVER.

Chemainus, Comox,	Cowichan, Maple Bay,	Nanaimo, Somenns,	Sooke.

VICTORIA.

Esquimalt,	Victoria.	——	——

YALE.

POST OFFICES

IN THE

PROVINCE OF PRINCE EDWARD ISLAND,

ARRANGED ACCORDING TO ELECTORAL DISTRICTS.

PRINCE.

Albany,	Lot No. 16,	Wilmot Valley.	
Alberton,	do 30,		
Augustine Cove,	Margate,		
Barretts Cross,	Middleton,		
Bedeque,	Miminegash.		
Bloomfield,	Miscouche,		
Brae,	Montrose.		
Burlington,	Mount Pleasant,		
Cape Traverse,	Muddy Creek,		
Cape Wolfe,	Newton,		
Carleton,	North Bedeque,		
Darnley,	North Tryon,		
Egmont Bay,	O'Leary's Road,		
Fifteen Point,	Pig Brook,		
Freetown,	Pork Hill,		
Hamilton,	Princetown,		
Higgin's Road,	St. Eleanors,		
Indian River,	Searletown,		
Inverness,	Skinners Pond,		
Kildare,	Somerset,		
Little Tignish,	South-West, Lot 16,		
Lower Freetown,	Summerside,		
Lot No. 1,	Tignish,		
do 4,	Traveller's Rest,		
do 6,	Tryon,		
do 8,	Tyne Valley,		
do 10,	Wellington,		
do 11,	West Cape,		
do 12,	Western Road,		
do 14,	West Point,		

Post Offices in the Province of Prince Edward Island, arranged according to Electoral Districts.—Continued.

QUEEN'S.

Belfast,
Belle Creek,
Bonshaw,
Brackley Point,
Brackley Point Road,
Caledonia,
Cavendish,
Cavendish Road,
Charlottetown,
Cherry Valley,
Cornwall,
Covehead,
Covehead Road,
Crapaud,
Darlington,
De Sable,
Emy Vale,
Flat River,
Fort Augustus,
French River,
French Village,
Graham's Road,
Grand Tracadie,
Granville,
Hartsville,
Hazel Grove,
Hope River,
Johnston's River,
Kelly's Cross,
Kinross,
Little York,
Long Creek,
Long River,
Lot 35,
,, 67,
Mermaid Farm,
Monaghan,
Montague Cross,
Mount Stewart,
Murray Harbor Road,
New Glasgow,
New Haven,
New London,
New Wiltshire,
Nine Mile Creek,
North River,
North Rustico,
Orwell,
Orwell Cove,
Park Corner,
Pisquid,
Pisquid Road,
Point Prim,
Pownal,
Princetown Road,
Rona,
Rose Valley,
Rustico,
St. Ann's,
Selkirk Road,
Scotchfort,
Southport,
Southwiltshire,
Springfield,
Stanley Bridge,
Suffolk Road,
Tracadie Cross,
Vernon River,
Vernon River Bridge,
Victoria,
Western Covehead,
Wheatley River,
Wood Islands.

KINGS.

Bay Fortune,
Big Marsh,
Bothwell,
Brooklin,
Bull Creek,
Cable Head,
Cardigan Bridge,
Cardigan Road,
Cherry Grove,
De Gros Marsh,
Dundas,
East Point,
Fairfield,
Farmington,
Gaspereaux,
Georgetown,
Goose River,
Head St., Peters Bay,
Little Harbour,
Little Sands,
Lower Montague,
Lot 45,
Lot 56,
Marie Bridge,
Montague Bridge,
Morell,
Morell Rear,
Murray Harbor, North.
do South.
Murray River,
New Perth,
North Lake,
Peters Road,
Red Point,
Rollo Bay,
Rollo Bay Cross,
St. Andrews,
St. Margaret's,
St. Mary's Road,
Souris East,
Souris West,
Sturgeon,
Summerville,
Valleyfield,
Victoria Cross,
Whim Road.

POSTAL DIVISIONS

UNDER THE CHARGE OF

THE SEVERAL INSPECTORS.

THE FOLLOWING ARE THE ELECTORAL DISTRICTS IN THE SEVERAL POSTAL DIVISIONS.

CHIEF INSPECTOR'S DIVISION.

The Provinces of

Manitoba	British Columbia,	Prince Edward Island.

OTTAWA INSPECTOR'S DIVISION.

Carleton (Ont.,)	Ottawa City (Ont.,)	Pontiac (Quebec),	Renfrew, S.R. (Ont.,)
Nipissing District (Ont.,)	Ottawa County (Quebec),	Renfrew, N.R. (Ont.,)	Russell, (Ont.,)

NOVA SCOTIA DIVISION.

Postal Divisions under the charge of the several Inspectors.—Continued.

MONTREAL DIVISION.—(Province of Quebec.)

Argenteuil,	Huntingdon.	Montreal (city),	Shefford.
Bagot,	Iberville.	Napierville.	Sherbrooke (town).
Beauharnois,	Jacques Cartier.	Richelieu.	Soulanges.
Berthier,	Joliette.	Richmond, except townships of Cleveland and Shipton.	Stanstead.
Brome,	Laprairie.	Rouville.	Terrebonne.
Chambly.	L'Assomption.	St. Hyacinthe.	Three Rivers (city),
Chateauguay.	Laval.	St. John's.	Two Mountains.
Compton.	Maskinongé.	St. Maurice.	Vaudreuil.
Drummond, except township of Kingsey.	Missisquoi.		Verchères,
Hochelaga.	Montcalm.		Yamaska.

KINGSTON DIVISION.—(Province of Ontario.)

Addington.	Grenville, S. R.	Lanark, S. R.	Peterboro', E. R.
Brockville (town).	Hastings, N. R.	Leeds, S. R.	Peterboro', W. R.
Cornwall (town).	Hastings, E. R.	Leeds & Grenville, N. R.	Prescott,
Dundas.	Hastings, W. R.	Lennox.	Prince Edward.
Frontenac.	Kingston (city).	Northumberland, N. R.	Stormont.
Glengarry,	Lanark, N. R.,	Northumberland, W. R.	

TORONTO DIVISION.—(Province of Ontario.)

Algoma.	Grey, N. R.	Simcoe, N. R.	Wellington, N. R.
Bruce, N. R.	Grey, S. R.	Simcoe, S. R.	Wellington, S. R.
Bruce, S. R.	Halton.	Toronto (city).	Wellington, C. R.
Cardwell.	Muskoka.	Victoria, N. R.	York, E. R.
Durham, E. R.	Ontario, N. R.	Victoria, S. R.	York, W. R.
Durham, W. R.	Ontario, S. R.	Waterloo, N. R.	York, N. R.
Grey, E.R.	eel.	Waterloo, S. R.	

LONDON DIVISION.—(Province of Ontario.)

Bothwell.	Huron, C. R.	Middlesex, N. R.	Oxsord, N. R.
Brant, N. R.	Huron, N. R.	Middlesex, E. R.	Oxford, S. R.
Brant, S. R.	Huron, S. R.	Middlesex, W.R.	Perth, N. R.
Elgin, E. R.	Kent.	Monck.	Perth, S. R.
Elgin, W. R.	Lambton.	Niagara.	Welland.
Essex.	Lincoln.	Norfolk, N. R.	Wentworth, N. R.
Haldimand.	London (city).	Norfolk, S.R.	Wentworth, S. R.,
Hamilton (city).			

LIST

OF

POSTMASTERS IN CANADA.

Abbott, Adam, Hazledean.. ....O
Abbott, Calvin, Magog ....Q
Abbott, Ephraim W, Lennoxville...............Q
Abbott, Luther, Massawippi ....Q
Abbott, Robert, Port Royal.....................O
Abel, David, Port Dover..........................O
Abrams, Josias, Willetsholme ....O
Abrey, G. B., Little Current......................O
Adam, Thomas, Lindsay..........................O
Adams, A., Rokeby...............................O
Adams, George, Adamsville ....Q
Adams, Isaac, Tracey's Mills, W.O............N B
Adams, Melvin, Broadlands ....Q
Adams, Nehemiah N., Oak Park, W. O.......N S
Addison, Henry, Brompton ....Q
Addshead, Mary, St. Charles.......................M
Aikin, Thomas, Point St. Charles..................Q
Akin, William S., Edwardsburgh...................O
Ainslie, James, Edgeworth..........................O
Airth, William, Horning's Mills.....................O
Aitkin, Thomas, Windermere........................O
Akerley, Edwin, Grand River, W. O..........N B
Alain, Vital, Upper Neguac, W. O............N B
Alexander, F., Alexander's Point, W. O.......N B
Alexander, G., Woodstock..........................O
Alguire, Mrs. Lydia, Plum Hollow................O
Allan, Alex., Riverstown..............................O
Allan, D., Rylstone.....................................O
Allan, W. Allan's Mills.................................O
Allan, Isaac H., Black Creek.........................O
Allan, John, Mono Mills...............................O
Allan, W. G., Marlbank.................................O
Allan, George, Glenallan...............................O
Allchin, Samuel, Canning................................O
Allen, James, Bandon...................................O
Allen, J. E., Malton.......................................O
Allen, Thomas, Cooper...................................O
Allen, Thomas, Lovat ....O
Allerton, Reuben, Bloomfield, W. O..........N S
Allin, P., Solina...O
Allin, Thos., Derryville...................................O
Allison, A. C., Dunbar....................................O
Allison, J. W., Newport Landing..............N S
Allison, Thaddeus, Neily Road..................N S
Almas, Almon, Rosebank................................O
Ambrose, Mrs. M., Princeport, W. O..........N S
Amy, John, Portage du Fort.........................Q
Anderson, Alex., Bræmar..............................O

Anderson, George, Marysville.............
Anderson, James, Anderson's Corners.....
Anderson, Jesse, Cross Roads, Middle M W. O.......................................
Anderson, John, Cumnock....................
Anderson, John, Wyoming....................
Anderson, Joseph, Springvale...............
Anderson, J. R., Kendal.......................
Anderson, Thomas, Keppewee...............
Angevine, Albert, Six Mile Road, W. O...
Anglin, Robert, Brewer's Mills..............
Anglin, W. J., Battersea.......................
Anthony, Thomas, Ogilvie, W. O...........
Applebe, John S., Ballinafad.................
Applebe, James, Trafalgar.....................
Applebee, Mark, Latona........................
Appleford, William, Mapleton...............
April, George, Green River ....
Arbo, John A., Blissfield, W. O..............
Arcand, Miss F. A. A., St. Joseph...........
Archambeault, J. T. L., Varennes.........
Archibald, Ebenezer, Old Barns, W. O...
Archibald, Janet, Alma, W. O................
Archibald, J. W., Smithfield W. O..........
Archibald, Mathew, Glenelg...................
Archibald, R., Archibald Settlement, W.O
Argue, J. S., Stittsville..........................
Armour, John, jun., Kelvin....................
Armour, Thomas, Dunville.....................
Armstrong, Foster, Point Alexander........
Armstrong, F. P., East Port Medway, W.
Armstrong, Henry, Inistioge...................
Armstrong, James, Lyons......................
Armstrong, Robert, Lakeside.................
Armstrong, Samuel, McKellar................
Armstrong, Simon, Belgrave..................
Armstrong, William, Falmouth, Windsor W. O.......................................
Arnold, George, Bell's Corners..............
Arthurs, John, Napier...........................
Ash, Cyrus, Centreville.........................
Ashdown, F. W., Spence.......................
Ashdown, James, Ashdown...................
Ashton, Robert, Columbus....................
Askew, Thos. G., Chemainees...............
Asselin, Eusèbe, Joliette......................
Atkinson, John, Glanford......................
Aubé, Joseph, Poplar Grove, W. O.........

List of Postmarters iw Canada.—Continued.

Aubé, Marcel, St. Gervais .... Q
Aubry, P. G., Aubigny .... Q
Auclair, Rev. E., St. Prime .... Q
Audette, Antoine, North Stukeley .... Q
Auger, Louis A., Mount Johnson .... Q
Ault, J. R., Aultsville .... O
Avard, William, Great Shemogue, W. O .... N B
Axford, Wellington, Lynnville .... O
Ayer, C., Ayer's Flat .... Q
Aylward, James H., Queensville .... O
Aylsworth, James, Tamworth .... O

Babcock, Edward, Johnston's Mills, W. O. .... N B
Babin, Eustache, Painsec, W. O .... N B
Bachaud, J. C., St. Liboir e .... Q
Bachelder, D., Rougemont .... Q
Backus, J., River Désert .... Q
Bacon, Sarah D., St. Pierre, Montmagny .... Q
Bagrie, John, Brooksdale .... O
Bailey, Luke E., Central Blissville, W. O .... N B
Bailey, James, Shanick .... O
Bailey, George, Shrigley .... O
Bailey, Nicholas, Sandy Beach .... Q
Bailey, Alexander, Church Hill, W. O .... N B
Bailey, G. D., Newcastle Creek, W. O .... N B
Bailey, W. W., Island Brook .... Q
Bailey, Wm., Dartford .... O
Baird, Henry, Bairdsville, W. O .... N B
Baird, John D., Boundary, Presq'uile, W. O .... N B
Baker, Andrew J., Summerstown .... O
Baker, Edward, Dunham .... Q
Baker, David, Dundee .... Q
Baker, William, Wales .... O
Baker, Edward, Wolfe Island .... O
Baker, G. P., Ottawa .... O
Baker, Adam G., Osgoode .... O
Baker, Reuben, Canaan Road, W. O .... N S
Baker, William, Barronsfield, W. O .... N S
Baldwin, Henry, Laskay .... O
Baldwin, R. C., Drew's Mills .... O
Balfour, Duncan, Westville .... N S
Ball, James, Rugby .... O
Ball, G. H., North-west Arm, W. O .... N S
Ball, Wright, South Roxton .... Q
Ballam, W. G., Arichat .... N S
Ballantyne, Mrs. E., L'Islet .... Q
Ballard, Cyprus, Middleboro, W. O .... N S
Balmain, Abner, Douglas Harbor, W. O .... N B
Balmer, R., Oakville .... O
Bannatyne, A. G. B., Fort Garry .... M
Bangs, John, Mattawa .... O
Banks, John H., Torbrook, W. O .... N S
Banning, O., jun., Clayton .... O
Bannister, John, Waverley .... O
Banting, Thomas M., Clover Hill .... O
Baptie, Alexander, Ida .... O
Barclay, A. E. S. K., Wallacetown .... O
Barclay, Thomas, Head of Tide, W. O .... N B
Barclay, Patrick, Petrolea .... O
Bard, Charles, Bardsville .... O
Barfoot, S., Chatham .... O
Baribeau, Louis A., Rivière du Loup (en haut) .... Q
Barker, Whitehead, Sheffield Academy, W. O .... N B
Barker, Mrs. Vasey, Montague Gold Mines, W. O .... N S
Barker, David, Picton .... O
Barker, John, Pinedale .... O
Barker, John, Dundonald .... O
Barker, James J., Markham .... O
Barlow, Alexander, Quesnel .... B C
Barnes, John, Edgeley .... O
Barr, Seth, Putnam .... O
Barron, John, Newcomb Corner, W. O .... N S
Barry, A. A., Rock Island .... Q

Barry, John C., Les Escoumains .... Q
Barteaux, C. W., Somerset, W. O .... N S
Bartlett, G., Bethel .... Q
Bartley, George, Kennebec Line .... Q
Bastedo, Walter S., Wellington Square .... O
Bateman, William G., Moncton Road, W. O .... N B
Bates, Ezra A., Arnprior .... O
Bates, Rodger, Blainton .... O
Bates, Edward, Cheddar .... O
Batty, C., St. George, Brant .... O
Baxter, Joseph D., Norton Station .... N B
Beals, Albert, Middleton .... N S
Beamish, S. R., Brunswick .... O
Beeman, Thomas, Scone .... O
Beaton, Donald, Whitton .... Q
Beaton, Angus, Little Judique, W. O .... N S
Beattie, Porter, Stanbury .... Q
Beattie, William, Melbourne Ridge .... Q
Beattie, George, French Village, W. O .... N B
Beattie, John, Highgate .... O
Beatty, Johnstone Elizabethville .... O
Beatty, William H., Stanton .... O
Beatty, William, Wellington, W. O .... N B
Beauchemin, A. O. T., Roxton Falls .... Q
Beauchemin, Louis, Chatillon .... Q
Beaudette, Joseph S., St. Patrick's Hill .... Q
Beaudoin, M., St. Evariste de Forsyth .... Q
Beaudoin, Louis, East Broughton .... Q
Beaulieu, J. B., Cacouna .... Q
Beaumont, John, Curryville, W. O .... N B
Beaumont, William, Maple Bay .... B C
Beaunier, Théodore, Cap Magdeléne .... Q
Beck, Charles, Poole .... O
Beck, Jacob, Baden .... O
Beck, J. H., Medina .... O
Becker, A. A., Hilton .... O
Beckman, J., Ellershausen, W. O .... N S
Beckwith, N., Mill Creek, W. O .... N B
Beckwith, A., Upper Dyke Village, W. O .... N S
Bédard Pierre, Valmont .... Q
Bédard, Charles, St. Remi .... Q
Bédard, L., St. Flavien .... Q
Beeman, David H., Prosser Brook, W. O .... N B
Begg, Mrs. Sarah, Innerkip .... O
Bégin, Oliver, St. Ephrem de Tring .... Q
Bégin, Joseph, Lake Etchemin .... Q
Bégin, Louis C., Kamouraska .... Q
Bélanger, I. O., Maskinongé .... Q
Bélanger, Celestin, Chlorydormes .... Q
Bélanger, E., St. Romaine .... Q
Bélanger, F., St. Vallier .... Q
Bélanger, Louis, Rivière des Prairies .... Q
Belcourt, J. L., La Baie .... Q
Belfour, John, Bath .... O
Belfry, Jacob, Carden .... O
Belisle, Jos., Montmorini .... Q
Bell, John M., Atha .... O
Bell, George, Caledon .... O
Bell, P. W., Michipicoton River .... O
Bell, Archibald, Nairn .... O
Bell, Gavin, New Annan, W. O .... N S
Bell, John S., Lyn .... O
Belleau, E. S., St. Michel .... Q
Belleau, Felix, St. Foy .... Q
Belleau, John, Rivière Ouelle .... Q
Belleveau, Pacifique, St. Paul's, W. O .... N B
Belleveaux, Urbain, Belleveaux Cove .... N S
Belmore, D., Dipper Harbor, W. O .... N B
Belyea, G. N., Belyea's Cove, W. O .... N B
Bender, James, Long Lake .... O
Benner, Jacob, West Montrose .... O
Bennett, Isaac, Sebringville .... O
Bennett, Wm., Masham Mills .... Q

List of Postmasters in Canada.—Continued.

Bennett, Wm., North Mountain, W. O........N S
Bennett, Edmund, Castile.........................O
Benson, Albert, Stromness............................O
Bent, Calvin, Port Elgin.........................N B
Bent, James, Short Beach, W. O.............N S
Bent, John C., Armstrong's Brook, W. O.....N B
Bent, Clara W., Digby...............................N S
Benton, John, Bentonville.........................O
Benwell, John B., Oxenden.........................O
Bergeron, D., Blanford...............................Q
Bergeron, Jacques, Metabechouan...............Q
Bermingham, W., South Lake......................O
Bernard, W. B., Arva...............................O
Bernard, George, Rivière Bois Clair...........Q
Bernard, J., Cap Sante...............................Q
Bernard, L., Hemison...............................Q
Bernard, John, Brechin...............................O
Berney, W. H., Mill Grove.........................O
Bernier, Antoine, St. Simon de Rimouski.......Q
Berry, Solomon, Turtle Creek, W. O..........N B
Berry, Edward, Berryton, W. O.................N B
Berry, J., St. Martin's, W. O...................N B
Berry, W. H., March...............................O
Berteaux, Charles, Nictaux Falls, W. O.......N S
Bertrand, François, Lévis.........................Q
Bertrand, Paul, St. Mathias.........................Q
Bertrand, Louis A., Isle Verte.....................Q
Berwick, Edward, Shelburne.........................O
Besancon, Henry, Gorrie.............................O
Besner, J. B., Pont Chateau.........................Q
Bessette, N. D. D., Village Richelieu............Q
Best, F. A., Corinth...............................O
Best, Leonard, Beaver Harbor, W. O..........N B
Best, Abraham, Mount Pleasant...................O
Best, Thomas H., Dunedin.........................O
Bethune, Roderick, Loch Lomond, W. O.......N S
Beveridge, Wm. B., Andover.......................N B
Bhérour, Archille, St. Fidèle......................Q
Bigelow, W. H., Spencer Island, W. O........N S
Bigney, Lemuel, Wentworth, W. O..............N S
Bilodeau, F. X., Bailargeon.........................Q
Bilodeau, Jean, St. Elzear.........................Q
Bilodeau, Joh, Chambord.............................Q
Bingham, Wesley, Orillia.............................O
Bingham, R., Athens.................................O
Bingham, C. W., Crysler.............................O
Bingham, David, Lotus...............................O
Bird, Robert, Birdton, W. O.......................N B
Birks, Chs., Maynard...............................O
Birmingham, Mrs. E., Birmingham...............O
Bishop, James, Perth, W. O.......................N B
Bishop, Asa W., Bishop's Mills...................O
Bishop, Adolphus, Canaan, W. O...............N S
Bishop, J. B., Marbleton.............................Q
Bishop, Wm. E., Irving's Settlement, W. O..N B
Bissett, George, River Bourgeois, W. O.......N S
Bisson, D., Paspébiac...............................Q
Bistodeau, G. E., St. Maurice.....................Q
Black, E., Salem, W. O.............................N S
Black, J. C., Claremont, W. O...................N S
Black, James, jun., Bramley.......................O
Black, R. F., West Branch, River Philip, W.O. N S
Black, Robert, Craigvale.............................O
Black, D., Marysville.................................O
Black, Chas. E., Sonya...............................O
Blackburn, John, Eldorado.........................O
Blackburn, Robert, Lucerne.........................Q
Blackburn, Samuel, Lower Prospect, W. O....N S
Blackhall, J. G. C., Caraquet.....................N B
Blackwood, Robert, Martintown...................O
Blackwood, Charles W., Thunder Bay...........O
Blain, J., St. Edouard...............................Q
Blain, M., La Pigeonnière.........................Q
Blair, Henry, North River Bridge, W. O.......N S
Blair, William, Ardtrea...............................Q
Blair, James, Hallerton.............................Q
Blais, Alexis, St. Aubert.............................Q
Blais, Patrick, North Ham...........................Q
Blais, Narcisse, Point aux Trembles.............Q
Blais, L. N., Matane.................................Q
Blais, Prudent, Beaulieu.............................Q
Blais, Geo., St. Maurice.............................Q
Blaisdell, John, Bolton Centre.....................Q
Blake, Robert, Black Brook, W. O..............N B
Blakeny, William, Joddore, W. O................N S
Blanchard, Daniel, Greenbush.....................O
Blaney, Henry, Millville, W. O..................N B
Bloomburg, Isaac, Elphin...........................O
Blue, Malcolm, Blue's Mills, W. O..............N S
Blyth, C. McD., Marden.............................O
Boadway, George, Bexley...........................O
Boardman, Luther, Crowland.......................O
Bogart, Gilbert, Napanee...........................O
Boggs, B. B., Joggin Mines, W. O..............N S
Boileau, Godfroi, St. Genevieve...................Q
Boily, Rev. P., Mille Vaches.......................Q
Boisvert, Anésime, Angeline.......................Q
Bolduc, Theodule, Roberval.........................Q
Bond, Edwin, Sheffield...............................O
Bongard, J. D., Bongard's Corners...............O
Bonneville, Caroline, La Beauce..................Q
Bonthron, James, Rodgerville.......................O
Boon, William, Salford...............................O
Booth, Mrs. M. J., Prospect, W. O.............N S
Booth, Thomas, Chester.............................Q
Booth, Leander, Rochesterville.....................O
Borden, Levi, Pugwash...............................N S
Borden, T. W., Canning.............................N S
Boright, Curtis S., Sweetsburg.....................Q
Bothwell, Wm., Grovesend...........................O
Boucher, H., Bégon...................................Q
Boucher, Et., St. Apollinaire.......................Q
Boucher, Pierre, St. Honore.........................Q
Boucher, E. M. A., Coteaux Rivière Ouelle.....Q
Boudreau, Alex., Boudreau Village, W. O.....N B
Boudrot, Benj., Barrio's Beach, W. O.........N S
Boudrot, Stephen, Port Felix.......................N S
Bouilliane, R., Les Petites Bergeronnes..........Q
Boulanger, L., St. Agathe...........................Q
Boulet, E. C., St. François Montmagny.........Q
Bourchier, J. R., Georgina...........................O
Bourgeault, F. S., St. Anicet.......................Q
Bourgeois, John, Bourgeois, W. O...............N B
Bourget, Charles, Lauzon.............................Q
Bourke, T., Mayo.....................................Q
Bourke, Thomas, Albert Bridge, W. O.........N S
Bourne, C. E., Nanticoke.............................O
Bourque, A., St. Clet.................................Q
Bourque, Damase V., Etang du Nord (sub).....Q
Boutalier, Miss M., Port Caledonia, W. O......N S
Bow, William, West Winchester...................O
Bowden, William, Second Falls, W. O.........N B
Bowen, James, Mill Point...........................O
Bower, John C., West Osgoode.....................O
Bowers, Jesse, Upper Clyde River................N S
Bowes, Joanna, Wisbeach...........................O
Bowman, John, Almira...............................O
Bowron, John, Barkerville...........................B C
Bowsfield, R. Whittington...........................O
Boyd, John Johnville, W. O.......................N B
Boyd, John Lytton.....................................B C
Boyer, George R., Victoria.........................N B
Boyer, William F., Somerville, W. O...........N B
Boyle, James, Chance Harbor, W. O............N S
Boyle, John, Caledonia Mills, W. O............N S
Brace, L. J., Zetland.................................O

List of Postmasters in Canada.—Continued

Bradford, F. W., Bayside, W. O. .... N B
Bradford, Charles A., Chatboro' .... Q
Bradley, M., Eddystone .... O
Bradley, Joseph A., Lansdown .... O
Bradley, Richard, Airlie .... O
Bradshaw, W. C., Everett .... O
Brady, Bridget, Mount St. Patrick .... O
Bragg, John, Windham Hill, W. O .... N S
Branan, J. W., Alvinston .... O
Brannen, John B., Kenmore .... O
Branscomb, A., sen., Cumberland Bay, W. O. .. N B
Brash, Richard, New Richmond .... Q
Brasher, Samuel, Vienna .... O
Brassard, Xavier, Jonquières .... Q
Bray, Benjamin, Little Ridge, W. O .... N B
Breau, Urbain, Richibucto Village, W. O .... N B
Breadner, Joshua, Athelstan .... Q
Breckenridge, Robert, Heyworth .... Q
Breeze, Wm., Forest Mills .... O
Brennan, Peter, Golden Grove, W. O .... N B
Brethour, Samuel, Valentyne .... O
Brewster, W. R., Beaver Brook, W. O .... N B
Briard, Edward, Cheticamp, W. O .... N S
Bridge, Andrew, Westbrook .... O
Bridgman, Jonathan, Clear Creek .... O
Brien, A. A. L., St. Alexandre .... Q
Brien, Alfred, St. Simon de Yamaska .... Q
Brière, François, Lake Weedon .... Q
Briggs, James, Pearceton .... Q
Briggs, Thos., Hepworth .... O
Brigham, E. O., Brigham .... Q
Brigham, Robert, Rondeau Harbor .... O
Brillon, J. B., Belœil Village .... Q
Brine, J. S., St. Margaret's Bay .... N S
Brisbin, Alexander, Covey Hill .... Q
Brittain, Wm. H., Windsor, W. O .... N B
Brittain, Stephen, Lower Wakefield, W. O .... N B
Britton, D. F., Gananoque .... O
Bristow, Edward, Shibley .... O
Broad, John, Little Britain .... O
Broad, Isaac, Holmesville, W. O .... N B
Broad, Wm., Hayden .... O
Brochu, M., St. Lambert .... Q
Brodhagen, Chas., Brodhagen .... O
Brokenshaw, Luke, Drummondville, West .... O
Brooks, Asa D., Southampton, W. O .... N B
Brooks, Caleb, Low .... Q
Brotherston, W., sen., Villiers .... O
Brouillette, Alexis, Mont St. Hilaire .... Q
Brousseau, Julien, Lapraire .... Q
Brown, Dr. Chs., Cowansville .... Q
Brown, William S., Red Bank, W. O .... N B
Brown, George, Shakespeare .... O
Brown, A. N., St. John's, West .... O
Brown, John, Rutherford .... O
Brown, James, Newport Corner, W. O .... N S
Brown, James, Coal Mines, W. O .... N B
Brown, Robert, Bass River, W. O .... N B
Brown, James, sen., Motherwell .... O
Brown, John, Monkland .... O
Brown, David F., Moe's River .... Q
Brown, James, Nithburg .... O
Brown, George, Brinsley .... O
Brown, James, Melancthon .... O
Brown, James E., Lakelands, W. O .... N S
Brown, Alexander, Aldershot .... O
Brown, James Ross, Angus .... O
Brown, Francis, Clifford .... O
Brown, Nicholas J., Marble Mountain, W. O. . N S
Brown, Philip, Lower Pereau, W. O .... N S
Brown, William, Chesterfield .... O
Brown, Chas. A, Chester .... N S
Brown, Francis, Cairngorm .... O

Brown, George, Herewa
Brown, George, Head of
Brown, H. V., Es'kaso
Brown, William G., In
Brown, John, Victoria
Brown, J. L., Harvey
Brown, Hiram, Brown's
Brown, James W., Low
Brown, E. J., Gresham
Brown, George, Philips
Brown, Robert, Zurich
Browne, J. A., New D
Browning, Archibald, 1
Brownlee, James, Ellen
Bruce, R., Ragged Hea
Bruce, Wm., Temperan
Brunelle, Uldoric, St. E
Brunelle, L., Gentilly..
Brunner, Jacob, Brunne
Brunning, A. H., St. C
Bryson, Thomas, Allan's
Bryson, Jas., Cameron.
Bryson, Thomas, Fort C
Buchan, John, Fullarto
Buchanan, Donald, Eng
Buchanan, William, Sul
Bucke, T. W., Wabash
Bucke, Richard, Harol
Buckley, Thomas, Buck
Buckwell, William S.,
Bullock, Increase, Geor
Bundy, George Hought
Bunn, George, Ullswate
Bunnell, Alfred M., Lu
Bunston, Joseph, Yeovi
Bunston, Thomas, Peth
Burchell, Geo., Bridgep
Burdett, Robert, Griers
Bureau, Rev. J. A., St
Burgar, Thomas, Wella
Burgess, Thomas, Bala..
Burgess, E. W., Burges
Burgess, John, Cheverie
Burgess, Joseph L., Dr
Burgess, Robert M., Ri
Burk, Eustache, Fox Cr
Burk, D. F., Segeun F
Burke, J. W., Ingonish,
Burke, J. G., Broughan
Burland, William, Stott
Burnham, Peter, Wind
Burns, John, Evelyn....
Burpee, C. J., Sheffield
Burpee, M. E. A., Burt
Burpee, Isaac C., Uppe
Burpee, Stephen G., Fl
Burrell, C., Stanley's M
Burrill, William, Kirkd
Burrows, William, Pros
Burt, John W., Coning
Burton, Israel, Belford
Buttemer, R., Salmon
Butler, James, St. Edo
Butler, R. P., Oakwood
Butler, W. H., Richmo
Butler, John, Colinville
Butterfield, J. A., Norv
Byrne, Thomas, Upterg
Byron, Anthony, Stoke
Byron, Luke, Campo B

Cabana, Ant., St. Rosa
Cahill, John, Calumet

List of Postmasters in Canada.—Continued.

Cahill, Michael, Jersey River, Chaudiere........Q
Caiè, Robert C., Janeville, W. O............N B
Cairns, Thomas, Perth..........................O
Cairns, John, Prince of Wales, W. O.........N B
Cairns, George, Dillonton ....Q
Cairns, Robert, Bulwer ....Q
Cairns, Hugh, East Clifton ....Q
Calder, James, Carluke.... ....O
Caldwell, Mathew, New Carlisle ....Q
Caldwell, Sherman, Gaspereaux, W.O. ...... N S
Caldwell, Samuel, Auburn ....O
Calhoun, Joseph, Uphill ....O
Calkin, G. E., Kentville ....N S
Callaway, David, Huston ....O
Cameron, Donald, Beaverton ....O
Cameron, John, Bright... ....O
Cameron, John D., Caledonia Springs. ....O
Cameron, M. A., Otnabog, W. O............N B
Cameron, Ewen, Edmonton.... ....O
Cameron, J. D., Upper Caledonia, W. O......N S
Cameron, C. A., Upper Settlement of South River, W. O .... N S
Cameron, Alexander, Little Branch, W. O....N B
Cameron, Alexander, Urbania, W. O... . ....N S
Cameron, Isabella, Black River Bridge, W. O.N B
Cameron, A. S., Daywood .. ..O
Cameron, Hugh, Kempt Road, W. O...........N S
Cameron, Andrew, Camerontown ....O
Cameron, Reuben G., Upper Hampstead, W.O.N B
Cammidge, Henry, Clavering... ....O
Campbell, Archibald, Hartley ....O
Campbell, Archibald, Lochaber Bay .... Q
Campbell, Archibald J., Liverpool.. ....N S
Campbell, Donald, Margaree Forks.............N S
Campbell, Charles C., New Campbelton. .....N S
Campbell, Donald B., Harrington East..........Q
Campbell, Geo., East River, St. Mary's W.O..N S
Campbell, G. F., St. Andrews..................N B
Campbell, Malcolm, Mildmay....................O
Campbell, William, Calder.......................O
Campbell, A. T., Holyrood.......................O
Campbell, Hector, West Side of Middle River, W.O.............. ....N S
Campbell, James, Cash Creek..................B C
Campbell, John, Escuminac, (sub.)............Q
Campbell, Donald, Wellington............. .....O
Campbell, Henry M., Woburn.....................O
Campbell, D. K., Cambpell Settlement, W.O...N B
Campbell, M., Lucknow ....O
Canniff, Jonas, jun., Cannifton..................O
Cannon, Robert, Vesta ....O
Cannon, M., New Horton, W.O...............N B
Cantwell, William, Franklin Centre..............Q
Cardwell, Henry, Chatsworth.... ....O
Cardwell, William, Drew.........................O
Carey, John, Baie Verte ....N B
Carland, John, Pubnico Harbor, W.O .. ..N S
Carle, John R., Scotch Town, W.O............N B
Carman, L. D., Musquash, W.O ....N B
Carmichael, Dougald, English Settlement, W.O.N B
Carnohan, Barnard C., Roslin....................O
Caron, G. C., Trois Saumons.....................Q
Caron, Michael, St. Angéle de Monoir..........Q
Caron, Nazaire Ste. Louise ....Q
Carpenter, Joseph, Winona.......................O
Carr, M. X., Paris Station............. ......O
Carr, James W., Oyster Ponds, W.O...........N S
Carr, Asa, Geary, W.O ....N B
Carrens, John, New Ireland, W.O..... . ...N B
Carrick, William, Oban.... . ... O
Carrigan, B., Emigrant Setlement, W.O........N B
Carroll, Richard, Usher, W.O.................N S
Carscallen, J. D., Copleston......................O

Carscallen, J. A., Glastonbury ....,...........O
Carson, Mrs. Sarah, Newbridge....................O
Carson, S. W., Cressy. .... O
Carson, D. B., Port Lewis ....Q
Carswell, Thomas M., Gower Point....... .....O
Carter, A. H., Bondhead.........................O
Carter, L. G., Port Colborne . ...O
Carter, William, Ripley ....O
Cartier S., Ste. Aimé ....Q
Cartier, Narcise, St. Antoine, River Richelieu ...Q
Cartledge, Henry, Frogmore........................O
Carvell, J. S., Lakeville W.O.... ....N B
Carvell, Richard, Temperance Vale, W.O.....N B
Case, George, Case Settlement, W.O...... ...N B
Case, W Mitchell Midland, W.O...........N B
Casselman, C. T., Winchester......................O
Casselman, Martin, Casselman......................O
Casement, Rober, North Douro......................O
Cattanach, Donald, Laggan.........................O
Cattanach, P., Somb[illegible]a.... ....O
Cattellier, Hubert St. George, Beauce ....Q
Catton, John Burford....... ....O
Cavanah, Thomas, Creighton.... ....O
Cavers, Peter A, Homer.... ....O
Cayo, Tancred, Vereker................ ....O
Cuzeau, Joseph, Montmorency Falls ... .Q
Chaffey, J. B. W., Indian Island, W.O........N B
Challoner, J., White Point, W.O.............N S
Chalmers, John, Belledune, W.O............N B
Chamberlin, Otis, Mont Elie......................Q
Chambers, John, Wick..... ....O
Chambers, John, Wilfred......................O
Chambers, John, Shrewsbury . ... Q
Champoux, Leon, St. Gertrude...................Q
Champoux, George, Lake Aylmer...............Q
Channell, James T., Bolton Forest..............Q
Chant, Samuel, Chantry... ....O
Chantler, James G., Newton Robinson...........O
Chapedelaine, L., St. Ours...... .... Q
Chapeleau, Edouard, St. Paschal.............Q
Chapman, Alexander, Chapman...................O
Chapman, Bowden, Chapman, W.O..........N B
Chapman, G. H., Hastings, W.O ... .N S
Chapman, George W., River Gilbert. ....Q
Chapman, John, North Augusta....................O
Chapman, John, Frankfort ....O
Chapman, John, Hespeler ....O
Chapman, Dixon, Mount Whatley, W.O......N B
Chapman, Michael, Goodwood.......... ......O
Chapman, Robert A., South Rockland, W.O..N B
Chapman C. S., Warren, W.O....,........N S
Charbonneau, V., Beresford.... ....Q
Charbonneau, C. T., L'Acadie .. ..Q
Charland, Joseph, Lavaltrie ....Q
Charlebois, A. W., Rigaud ....Q
Charlton, S., Milford, W.O....................N S
Charron, Emilien, St. Dorothèe ....Q
Charters, S. C., Memdomcook ....N B
Chase, Albert, Port Williams....................N S
Chase, Charles A., Union Corner, W.O.......N B
Chase, Arthur G., Upper Sackville, W.O.....N B
Chase, Reuben, Lakeville, W.O..............N S
Chaurette, Cyprien, Oka..........................Q
Chenier, Felix, Baie St. Paul....................M
Chenier, Hercule, Sevigné. ... .Q
Chesley, Nelson, Chesley's Corners, W.O......N S
Childerhose, Robert, Stafford...................O
Chillas, Miss Margaret, Nicolet.................. Q
Chipman, Samuel, Chipman's Corners, W.O...N S
Chipman, Mrs. A., Amherst.....................N S
Chisholm, Alexander, Point du Chene............M
Chisholm, Angus, Lochiel..........................O
Chisholm, Archibald, St. Andrews .... N S

List of Postmasters in Canada.—Continued.

Chisholm, John, Antigonishe Harbor, W.O ...N S
Chisholm, K., Brampton ... .O
Chisholm, Mrs. M., Pomquet Forks, W.O....N S
Chisholm, R., Sutherland's Mills, W.O.. ...N S
Chisholm, Colin, Marydale, W.O ....N S
Chisholme, William, Dalhousie Mills....O
Choat, Thomas, Warsaw....O
Chouinard, Elié, Garneau....Q
Christie, Joseph, Rycgate....O
Christie, Alex. R., Port Severn. (sub.)....O
Christie, Geo. N., Teviotdale Station, W.O...N S
Christie, John H., Little Bras d'Or....N S
Christie, John G., Apple Grove,....O
Christie, James B., Trenton....O
Church, W.S., Bersimis....Q
Church, Mrs. Ann, Brockton....O
Church, Richard, Cataract....O
Clairoux, P. E., St. Hermas....Q
Clapperton, John, Nicola Lake ....B C
Clark, Robert, Canterbury....Q
Clark, William, Shanly....O
Clark, Benjamin, Camden, East....O
Clark, William H., Nackawick, W.O....N B
Clark, William, Oak Park, W.O....N S
Clark, Peter, Montague ....O
Clark, Bibins, Cloyne....O
Clark, Jesse, Springfield, W.O....N B
Clarke, Ludlow B., Centreville....N B
Clarke, Robert, Downsview....O
Clarke, P.T., Coxheath, W.O....N S
Clarke, Albert F., Mandaman ....O
Clark, Pulaski, Byng Inlet....O
Clay, William, Norval....O
Clays, Geo., junr., Bedford....Q
Clayton, W. R., Carlow....O
Cleland, James, North Mountain....O
Clement, James S., Virgil....O
Clement, Ovide A., St. Paul's Bay....Q
Clement, A. D., Brantfort ....O
Cleminger, John, Banda....O
Clendinning, R., Dungannon....O
Cleveland, Isaac, Sandy Beaches, W.O....N S
Clifford, Henry A., Muskoka Falls ....O
Clinch, Chas. F., Clinche's Mills, W.O....N B
Clough, Daniel, Lennox Ferry, W.O....N S
Clouston, James, Middle Church.... M
Cloutier, C. P., St. Victoire....Q
Cloutier, J. B., St. Cyrille....Q
Cloutier, Mdme. A., Detour du Lac....Q
Clow, Elias, South Granby ....Q
Coates, Thos. H., Smith Creek, W.O....N B
Coates, Thos., Coates' Mills, W.O ....N B
Coburn, Thomas, Upper Keswick Ridge, W.O. N B
Coburn, M. H., Little River (Sun), W.O....N B
Cochran, B. W., Halifax ....N S
Cochran, J. T., Scotch Village, W.O....N S
Cochran, J. F., Newport....N S
Cochran, Chs., New Durham ....O
Cockerline, William, Henrysburg....Q
Code, G., Trowbridge....O
Code, Thomas, Innisville....O
Cody's, Charles, F., Cody's, W.O....N B
Coglan, Isaac J., Kepler....O
Cohan, Charles, Hebron ....N S
Cohoon, Freeman, Port Medway....N S
Colbeck, William, Colbeck....O
Colclough, J. R., Bic ....Q
Cole, Thomas, North Nation Mills....Q
Cole, W. G., Little River (Mid Musquodoboit), W.O....N S
Coleman, T., Heart's Mills, W.O....N B
Coleman, William, Seeley's Bay....O
Colgan, John, Craubourne....Q
Colhoun, John C., Hopewell Corner, W.O....N B
Collas, John, Sheldrake....Q
Collet, Charles A., St. Henri....Q
Collette, Joseph, St. Julie ....Q
Collerette, Zephirin, Grand Etang, W.O....N S
Collicut, P., Hillside, W.O ....N B
Colling, J., Verdun ....O
Colliver, Thos., Cherry Valley ....O
Colpitts, R. Alder., Plesant Vale, W.O....N B
Colpits, Robert J., Little Rivet (cov), W.O....N B
Colpitts, W. A., Mapleton, W O....N B
Comeau, Justien, Metaghan River, W.O....N S
Comeau, A. F., Clare, W.O....N S
Commeault, J. B., River David....Q
Commins, A. B., Centre Augusta....O
Commins, William, Bath....N B
Conn, C., Elder....O
Conn, Meredith, Tyrconnell....O
Connacher, H., Black Point, W.O....N B
Connery, James, Cedar Hill....O
Connor, Zebulon, Upper Greenwich, W.O ....N B
Cook, Wm., Black Land, W.O....N B
Cook, James, Milford....O
Cook, James R., Mount Albion....O
Cook, William, Carrville....O
Coonan, George, Waterside, W.O....N B
Cooper, Hugh, Vachell ....O
Cooper, Francis, South Barnston....Q
Cooper, James H., Campbellville....O
Cooper, Samuel, Keyser ....O
Cooper, Thomas, Glen Alpine, W.O....N S
Copeland, W. L., St. Catharine's, West....O
Copp, John, jun., Baie Verte Road, W.O....N B
Copp, Timothy, Centre Village, W.O....N B
Copping, E., Montcalm....Q
Coppinger, Thomas, Hanover....O
Corbett, Edmund, Harmony ....O
Corbett James, Larway Mines, W.O....N S
Corbett, Andrew, Clones, W.O....N B
Corbett, R. A., Perrytown....O
Corbett, Edmund, Harbor au Bouche, W.O....N S
Corbett, George, Gold Fields, W.O....N S
Comeau, Louis, Point du Lac....Q
Corneck, Joseph, Moor's Mills, W.O....N B
Cormier, Joseph G., Doherty Mills, W.O....N B
Cormier, S., Upper Caraquet, W.O....N B
Cornell, B., Rockton....O
Cornock, William, Erin ....O
Cornwall, William, Rockport....O
Cornwall, H. P., Ashcroft....B C
Correll, Mrs. Phoebe A., Stamford....O
Corrigan, William, Stoneham....Q
Cossar, Mrs. James, Dufferin....O
Costello, John, Brudenell....O
Coté, George, St. Giles....Q
Coté, Marcel, Tremblay ....Q
Coté, Cléophe, Les Eboulemons....Q
Coté, Edward, Rivière aux vaches....Q
Cotter, James W., Appleby....O
Cottle, N. B., Jemseg, W.O....N B
Cotton, Robert, Port Credit....O
Coulson, James, Coulson ....O
Coultard, J. H., Underwood....O
Coulter, John, Long Point, W.O....N B
Counter, Henry, Spaffordton....O
Courtemanche, F., St. Edwige....Q
Coutu, O. H., St. Francois du Lac....Q
Coutu, C. H., St. Elie....Q
Couture, O., St. Anaclet....Q
Couture, Eusèbe, Buckland....Q
Couture, Geo. Beaumont....Q
Couture, Wilbrod, St. Paul du Buton....Q
Covert, Henry, Crofton....O

List of Postmasters in Canada.—Continued.

Cowan, James, Ronson .... O
Cowan, David, Rossway, W.O .... N S
Cowie, John W., Balderson .... O
Cowie, Robert, Springbank .... O
Cowie, Thomas, Hannon .... O
Cown, L., St. Dominique des Cédres ...... Q
Cox, John, Upper Stewiacke, W.O .... N B
Cox, C. B., South Branch, W.O. .... N S
Cox, William, Norten Dale, W.O .... N B
Craig, Murdoch, Craigsholme .... O
Craig, Thomas, Craighurst .... O
Craig, Leslie M., Pleasant Valley, W.O. ...... N S
Craig, George, East side of Ragged Island ...... N S
Craig, Mrs. James, Eel River, W.O .... N B
Crandal, Joseph, Moncton .... N B
Craven, Cranswick, Port Huron .... O
rawford, John, Brockville .... O
Crawford, John, Gravel Hill .... O
Crawther, James, Attercleffe .... O
Creed, George, South Rawdon, W.O .... N S
Creelman, James, Newton Mills, W.O ...... N S
Creelman, William, Lower Selmah, W.O. ... N S
Crepeau, Guillaume, St. Camille .... Q
Crepeau, Max., St. Félix de Valois ...... Q
Crocker, James, Elimville .... O
Croft, William, Middleville .... O
Crombie, E. R., Brandy Creek .... O
Cronan, Mrs. M. A., La Have River, W.O. . N S
Crooks, W., Peggy's Cove, W.O .... N S
Crosby, Moses, Gordonsville, W.O .... N B
Crosby, Charles, Lake George, W.O .... N S
Crosby, Richard, Deerfield, W.O .... N S
Crosby, William, South Ohio, W. O .... N S
Cross, Thomas, South Zorra .... O
Cross, Henry, jun., Maple Grove .... Q
Crossfield, O., Abbotsford .... Q
Crosswell, George, Upsalquitch, W.O ..... N B
Crothers, Thomas, Upper Gagetown, W.O ... N B
Crowdis, J. G., Middle Section of N. E. Margaree, W.O. ...... N S
Crowe, R. S., Londonderry .... N S
Crowell, R. H., Barrington .... N S
Crowell, William, Hightield, W.O .... N S
Crozier, S., Topping .... O
Cruickshank, James, Cruickshank .... O
Cryan, William J. Fafard .... Q
Cuddahee, Timothy, Rathburn .... O
Cully W. R., Forrest City, W. O .... N B
Cummer, W. W., Newton Brook .... O
Cumming, John, Fergusonvale .... O
Cumming, George, Rosemont .... O
Cumming, George, Garden Island .... O
Cumminger, Jesse, Goldenville .... N S
Cummings, Charles, Milford .... N B
Cummins, S., Carlow, W. O .... N B
Cumner, Jacob, Willowdale .... O
Cunningham, Charlotte, Canso .... N S
Cunningham, E. J., Guysborough .... N S
Cunningham, James, Gourock .... O
Cunningham, W., Cape Sable Island, W. O.... N S
Curran, Patrick, Milltown .... N B
Curran, T., West Branch Nicholas River, W.O. N B
Currie, Hugh, Camilla .... O
Currie, Thomas, New Ross .... O
Currie, R. B., West Dublin, W. O .... N S
Curry, John, Farmington .... O
Curry, Frederick G., Horton Landing, W.O ... N S
Curtis, James, Alderville .... O
Curtis, Robert, Mongolia .... O
Curtis Edward, Oak Ridges .... O
Cushing, James B., Cushing .... Q
Cutting, Horace, Coaticook .... Q
Cyr, François S., Maria .... Q

Dafoe, Jocob, Utica ....
Dafoe, Manuel, Zephyr ....
Daggot, E., Grand Manan .... N
Dagnault, Rev. J. A., St. Michael des Saints ..
Daigle, Simon, Gailey, W.O .... N
Dalpé, C., dit Pariseau, St. Esprit ......
Dalton, John, Mayfair ....
Dalton, Mrs. E. J., Barnaby River, W.O .... N
Daly, Joseph, Hopefield ....
D'Amour, Marceline, Ste. Philomêne ....
D'Aoust, L. B., Point Claire ....
Darche, E. S., South Ham ....
Darling, J. S., Penetanguishene ....
Darling, Thomas, Moisic ....
Darlington, Robert, Brooklin ....
Dart, Daniel, Green Creek, W O .... N
Dauphin, Edouard, Sault au Récollet ......
Dauth, George, Bulstrode ....
David, F. X., Valcourt ....
Davidson, Alexander, Oak Point, W.O ..... N
Davidson, David, Lefroy ....
Davidson, Bryce T., Lake Opinicon ....
Davidson, William, Tidnish Bridge, W.O ..... N
Davidson, John, Galt ....
Davis, Joseph, Zealand ....
Davis, Josiah, Blayney Ridge, W. O ...... N
Davis, John, Davisville ....
Davis, Thomas, Bellisle Bay, W.O. .... N
Davis, William H., Ivy ....
Davis, William J., Vandecar ....
Davison, William, Hantsport .... N
Davison, John D., Fenwick, W. O .... N
Davison, John, Upper Newport, W.O .... N
Davy, Michael, Murvale ....
Dawson, Thomas, Wolverton ....
Dawson, Isaac, Dawson Settlement, W. O ..... N
Dawson, Thomas, Utopia ....
Dawson, William Luther ....
Dawson, John, Sylvan ....
Deacon, Robert, Kingston ....
Deacon, W. G., Warminster ....
Dean, Charles, Ship Harbor, W. O .... N
Dean, Marcus S., Bridgenorth ....
Decelle, Paul, St. Théodore ....
Deguire, Gédéon, Côteau du Lac ....
Delany, John, Lower Newcastle, W. O ..... N
De Lagorgendière, L. C. A. T., Katevale ......
Delfausse, M., Mascouche Rapids ....
Delisle, Joachim, Thiers ....
De Lorimer, W., Caughnawaga ....
Demer, George, St. Henri Station ....
Denaut, W. H., Delta ....
Denison, Joseph R., Denison's Mills ......
Dennis, Dennis L., Tuscarora ....
Densmore, R. T., Densmore's Mill, W. O ..... N
Densmore, Mrs. L., Kennetcook Corner, W.O. N
Dépot, J., Egypte ....
Dereek, S. B., Miranda ....
Derenzy, Edward, Sand Point ....
Derham, P. H., Tuam ....
Derick, T. B., Noyan ....
Derome, I. J. L., St. Jean, Chrysostôme, Chateauguay ......
Desaulniers, Joseph, Shawenegan ....
Desaultel, S., Augustin, Rochelle ....
Des Brisay, A. C. Mrs., Madisco .... N
Deschamps, C. A., Natashquan ....
Deschéne, Francois, St. Philippe de Nery ......
Deschénes, Jean, St. Cyriac ....
Deselet, Olivier, Ste. Angéle de Laval ...
Deséve, A. Tannery, West ....
Desilets, Ludger, St. Leonard ....
Desjardins, H., Stony Point ....

List of Postmasters in Canada.—Continued.

Desparais dit Champagne, Antoine, Charlemagne. Q
Desforgés, Clovis, Newport ... Q
Despocas, Marc C., Valleyfield ... Q
Després, E. L. R. C., St. Hyacinthe ... Q
Desroches, David, St. Janvier ... Q
Desroches, Ulrick B., St. Ligouri ... Q
Deveber, N. H., Westfield, W. O ... N B
Devitt, Isaac, Flora ... O
Devine, Solomon, Petawawa ... O
Dewar, David, Nort Keppel ... O
Dewolf, F. A., River de Chute ... N B
Déziel, L. I., D'Ailleboust ... Q
Dibb, William, Derwent ... O
Dick, James, Maple Valley ... O
Dick, George, sen., L'Etete, W. O ... N B
Dickens, William, Upper Bay du Vin, W. O. . N B
Dickenson, Edward, North Glandford ... O
Dickey, Mrs. Agnes, Bass River, W. O. ... N S
Dickey, John, Middle Stewiacke, W. O ... N S
Dickey, Clement B., Cornwallis East, W.O ... N S
Dickinson, Samuel, Coldstream, W.O ... N B
Dickinson, G. L., Manotic ... O
Dickson, Hugh, Central Onslow, W. O ... N S
Dickson, John, Paudash ... O
Dickson, Samuel, Seaforth ... O
Dickson, William, Henry ... O
Dickson, A., Goderich ... O
Dickson, Robert, Peepabun ... O
Dickson, Hugh H., Pakenham ... O
Dieudonné, D. Brulé, Vaudreuil ... Q
Dier, R., Forest ... O
Digdon, John, Half-Island Cove, W. O ... N S
Dillabough, Isaac, Lockville ... O
Dillon, D., Calabogie ... O
Dillon, T. H., High Falls ... O
Dillman, Daniel, Meagher's Grant, W. O ... N S
Din[illegible]y, John, Harley ... O
Dinnigan, William, Norton Creek ... Q
Dinnin, William, Lumley ... O
Dionne, Paschal, St. Denis de la Bouteillerie ... Q
Dionne, Joseph, Ste. Anne la Pocatiére ... Q
Dionne, Cyprian, St. Anthony, W. O ... N B
Disher, Ralph, Point Abino ... O
Ditchburn, William, Rosseau ... O
Ditz, Adam, Dorking ... O
Dixon, Mary C., Middleton, W.O ... N B
Dixon, Joseph, Sackville ... N B
Dixon, John, Paudash ... O
Doan, Charles, Aurora ... O
Doane, Mrs. Mary, Gunning Cove, W. O ... N S
Dobbin, James, Dobbinton ... O
Dobson, William, Head of Tatamagouche Bay, W. O ... N S
Dobson, James, Yorkville ... O
Dodd, George, Primrose ... O
Dodds, Geo., Tullamore ... O
Dodge, Enoch, jun., Bridgetown ... N S
Dodge, William W., Hammond River, W. O ... N B
Doherty, John, Uffington ... O
Doherty, Michael, Poquiock, W. O ... N B
Donahue, William, West Farnham ... Q
Donald, Alexander, Burnbrae ... O
Donaldson, Robert, Reading ... O
Donaldson, Henry F., Enfield ... N S
Donkin, F. A., Athol ... N S
Donavan, Thomas, South Bay, W. O ... N S
Dorais, Onesime, St. Stanislas de Kostka ... Q
Doran, William, Doran ... O
Dorron, John, Shippigan ... N B
Douglas, A., Middle St. Francis, W. O ... N B
Douglas, Thomas, Cambray ... O
Douglas, Mrs. Anne, Bradford ... O
Douglas, Alexander, Norham ... O
Douglas, Mary, Manilla ... O
Douglas, James, Londonderry, W. O ... N B
Downie, John, Jordon Bay, W. O ... N S
Dowsley, John, Prescott ... O
Dowsley, Joseph L., Escott ... O
Doyle, William, Back Lands, W. O ... N S
Doyle, J. W., Guysborough ... O
Drake, P. Edward, Bell Ewart ... O
Dreany, Robert, Crumlin ... O
Drolet, Pierre A., St. Pierre d'Orleans ... Q
Drope, R., Harwood ... O
Drouillard, Louis, Canard River ... O
Dryden, Robert, Eramosa ... O
Drysdale, John, Tatamagouche Mountain W.O. N S
Drysdale, Robert, Drysdale ... O
Duaine, J. B. L., St. Barnabé, St. Maurice . Q
Dubé, Lucien, Napierville ... Q
Dubois, L. E. Brentwood ... O
Duboyce, Martin, West Bolton ... Q
Dubuque, Joseph, St. Boniface ... M
Duck, James, Duck and Pringle ... B C
Ducket, Rodger, Côteau Station ... Q
Duff, Alex., Stewartville ... O
Duffus, Adam, Widder ... O
Dufour, Rev. E., St. Lazare ... Q
Dufresne, George, Ancienne Lorette (sub) ... Q
Dugal, Adelme, M. D., St. Anne, Bout de l'Isle . . Q
Duggan, Henry A., York ... O
Duguay, Nestor, St. Zephirin ... Q
Duignan, Thomas, Nenagh ... O
Dukeshire, W. H., Maitland, W. O ... N S
Dumouchelle, P., Rochester ... O
Dunbar, William, West Branch, East River of Picou, W. O ... N S
Dunbar, Alexander. Elmsdale ... N S
Dunham, Henry, Ompah ... O
Dunham, C. F., Kaladar ... O
Dunn, William, Washington ... O
Dunning, Levi E., East Templeton ... Q
Duncan, George, Melrose ... O
Duncan, James, Thamesville ... O
Duncan, Daniel, Duncan, W. O ... N S
Duncan, Geo., St. Malachie ... Q
Dumphy, Edward, Douglas, W. O ... N B
Dumphy, George, Dumphy, W. O ... N B
Duplessis, J. O., Sorel ... Q
Duplesea, D. S., Tracey Station ... N B
Dupré, Oliver, St Robert ... Q
Dupuis, A., Village des Aulnaies ... Q
Dupuis, Hugh, Orleans ... O
Dupuis, Calixte, St. Herménégilde ... Q
Duquet, Napoléon, Lachine ... Q
Dutch, George, Heron's Island, W. O ... N B
Dutchburn, H., Highfield ... O
Duval, Rev. A., St. Francoise ... Q
Dyer, Richard, St., Patrick, W. O ... N B
Dyer, G. C., Sutton ... Q
Dyer, James, Garden Hill ... O

Eaken, George, Unionville ... O
Eakens, John A., Sparta ... O
Easson, William, Kintore ... O
East, C., St. Augustin, Portneuf ... Q
Eastabrook, H. A., Swan Creek, W. O ... N B
Eastabrooks, Joel F., Brigg's Corner, W. O ... N B
Easterbrook, Elias, Nassagiweya ... O
Eastey, Charles W., Royal Road, W. O ... N B
Eastlands, Thos., Apsley ... O
Eastman, Benjamin, Carsonby ... O
Eastman, D. H., Eastman's Springs ... O
Easton, H. S., Easton's Corners ... O
Eastwood, Anthony, Lloydtown ... O
Eaton, C., Canada Creek, W. O ... N S

List of Postmasters in Canada.—Continued.

Eaton, Geo. W., Palmer's Road, W.O.........N S
Eby, Elias Bridgeport ....O
Echlin, D. C., Buxton ....O
Ecrement, J. F., St. Jacques ....Q
Ecrement, Joseph A., St. Damien de Brandon....Q
Eden, Francis, Varney ....O
Edgar, John, Newbliss..........O
Edgar, John, Three Brooks, W. O..........N B
Edgett, Hiram, River Side, W.O..........N B
Edgett, Ward, Edgett's Landing, W. O ....N B
Edmonstone, James, Grant ....O
Edwards, George, Thurso..........Q
Edward, James, Barrie ....O
Edwards, John, Hemmingford..........Q
Edwards, T. S., Lobo ....O
Edwards, W. P., Rankin ....O
Edwards, Wm. C., Rockland ....O
Edwards, William, Maritana..........Q
Egan, Denis, Powell..........O
Egan, Francis L., Kingsbridge..........O
Ehler, John, Crow Harbor, W. O ....N S
Eisenheur, Jos., Chester Basin, W. O ....N S
Elderkin, Mrs. Jane, Port Greville, W. O ....N S
Elderkin, W. R., Apple River, W. O..........N S
Elders, R., Perry Settlement, W. O..........N B
Eldridge, J. W., Long Island..........N S
Elkins, M. L., West Potton..........Q
Ellard, Joshua, Wright ....Q
Elliott, H. Hampton..........O
Elliott, Isaac M., Mount Elgin ....O
Elliott, John, Port Elmsley..........O
Elliott, George, Trout Lake..........O
Elliott, W. C., Still Water, W.O..........N S
Elliott, John, Cæsarea..........O
Ellis, George, Melocheville ....Q
Ellis, James R., Eastville, W. O..........N S
Ells, A. C., Scott's Bay, W. O..........N S
Ells, Watson, Sheffield Mills, W. O ....N S
Elmsley, R., Baddeck..........N S
Elmslie, James, Barnett ....O
Elsworth, James, Fisherville ....O
Emerson, N. P., Emerson..........Q
Emery, George, Marble Rock..........O
Emmans, William, Mountsburgh ....O
Emo, Thomas, Ivanhoe ....O
England, Philo, Fulford ....Q
Eplett, Samuel D., Coldwater..........O
Erb, John L., Erbsville ....O
Ermatinger, F. E., St. Thomas, West..........O
Ernst, Christian, New Hamburg..........O
Ernst, Louis, Point Edward..........O
Ernst, John, Petersburg ....O
Erskine, Wm., Bocabec, W O..........N B
Esnouf, Charles, Grand Grève ....Q
Estabrook, C. L., St. Mary's Ferry, W. O.....N B
Estey, Charles W., Royal Road, W.O ....N B
Estey, W. E., Farmerston, W O..........N B
Esty, Thomas H., Wicklow, W.O..........N B
Ethier, Daniel, St. Joseph, W.O..........N B
Evans, Richard J., Sleswick ....O
Evans, Miss E. M., Rock Village..........O
Evans, George, Albion ....O
Evans, Zerah, Dudswell ....Q
Everett, Edward, St. Mary's Bay, W. O....N S
Ewart, Thos. Carnegie..........O

Fafard, Pierre, St. Hélène de Bagot ....Q
Fair, Thomas, Clinton ....O
Fairburn, J. B., Bowmanville ....O
Fairweather, A., Springfield..........N B
Falconbridge, S., Aberfoyle..........O
Falconer, Daniel, Newry..........O
Fanjoy, C. H., Waterborough, W. O. ......N B
Faragher, Mrs. E. P., Hillsdale ....
Farnsworth, Thomas, Morden, W. O........N
Farquharson, Wm., Fordyce..........
Farran, John R., Farran's Point ....
Farrell, Patrick, Indiana ....
Farrel, Patrick, Upper Wakefield..........
Farrow, Wm., Botsford Portage, W. O.....N
Fauteux, J. St., Barthélemi..........
Faulkner, James, Poodiac, W. O..........N
Faulkner, Robt., Burntcoat, W. O. ....N
Fayle, J. R., Vogler's Cove, W. O. ....N
Featherstone, W. J., Carp ....
Feigehan, J. G., Fennells ....
Fell, John, Bury's Green ....
Fenwick, J. A., Millstream, W. O.........N
Ferguson, John, jun., Bathurst Village, W.O..N
Ferguson, John, Cookstown ....
Ferguson, Isaac G., Roschall ....
Ferguson, Malcolm, Cariboo Cove, W. O.....N
Ferguson, Duncan, Douglas ....
Ferguson, D. Kileau ....
Ferguson, Robert, Stowe..........
Ferris, Jas., M. Campbellford ....
Fiddes, Alexander, Corbin ....
Fieldhouse, H., Rosa ....
Filiatreault, Gilbert, St. John Babtiste de Montreal ....
Fillmore, Wm., Germantown, W. O ....N
Fillmore, G. A., Lower Turtle Creek, W. O...N
Finlay, Ephraim, Head of Amherst, W. O...N
Finlayson, Edward, Merigonish, W. O.......N
Finley, Isaac, Scugog..........
Fish, Robert Y., Linwood..........
Fisher, William, Halfway Brook, W. O. ....N
Fisher, C., St. Davids ....
Fisher, M. A. Athol..........
Fisher, Lewis, New Maryland..........N
Fisher, Peter, Wingham ....
Fitzgerald, M., Frampton ....
Fitzgerald, William, Maynooth ....
Flanagan, Mrs. Anne, Spencer Cove ....
Flannigan, M., Lake Settlement, W. O.....N
Fleming, John, Berkeley ....
Fleming, A. G., Craigleith ....
Fletcher, John L., Nashwaak Village, W. O...N
Fletcher, George, Alliston..........
Fletcher, Thomas, Shanty Bay..........
Fletcher, William, Carrillon..........
Flewelling, J. L., Oak Point, W. O........N
Flewelling, G. H., Clifton, W. O ....N
Flewelling, John, Hampton, W. O.........N
Flint, George, junr., Greenbank ....
Flood, H. Sweaburg..........
Flood, Richard, Roach's Point ....
Floyd, J. A., Fairfield, W. O. ....N
Flynn, Edward, Conroy..........
Foisy, Louis, Arthabaska Station..........
Foley, B. H., Buctouche..........N
Follis, George, Ashley ....
Folmsbee, John, Canboro' ....
Fontaine, Siméon, Weedon ....
Foot, W. G., Point-aux-Pins..........
Foot, J., Richmond Terminus, W. O..........N
Forbes, John, Bridgeville, W. O ....N
Forbes, John, North Sydney..........N
Forbes, John, Forbes, W. O. ....N
Forbes, Peter, Dickenson Landing ....
Ford, George, Pentland ....
Ford, C. R., Colborne ....
Forman, Robert, Acadia Mines ....N
Forest, Frederick, Bonaventure River..........
Forest, John M., Tangier..........N
Forester, Oliver, Forester's Falls ....

Forrest, Richard, Fairview.....................O
Forrestall, John, Forrestall's, W. O.... .....N S
Forshner, G. H. D., Head of Wallace Bay, W. O.. ....N S
Forsyth, Hezekiah C., Princeton..............O
Forsyth, Enoch, A., Fort William Station...N S
Forsyth, Elijah, Fairfield Plain ....O
Fortier, A., Ste. Scholastique ....Q
Fortier, Pierre, St. Anselme ....Q
Fortin, F., St. Pierre d'Orleans.......................Q
Fortune, James, Lake Law, W. O..........N S
Foss, Samuel J., Sherbrooke..... ....Q
Foster, Edward H., Salmon River, W. O...N S
Foster, H. M., Chute's Cove, W. O.........N S
Foster, G. K., Richmond East . ...Q
Foster, George N., Kingsley, W. O........N B
Foster, William, North Lake...... ....N B
Foster, James P., Marshall's Cove, W. O...N S
Foster, Henry, Foster's, W. O......... .. . N S
Foster, Samuel, Kingston.......... ... .N B
Fougère, Jos., Larry's River, W. O..........N S
Fournier, Marie, St. Jean Port Joli.......... Q
Fournier, Joseph, Méthot's Mills .... Q
Fournier, Louis, Grande Vallée.. ....Q
Fournier, P. C. Auguste, St. Raphael East. ..Q
Fowlds, H. M., Hastings......... ....O
Fowler, James, Salmon Creek, W. O....... N B
Fowler, Miss Jane, Lifford .... .O
Fowler, W. E., Steeve's Settlement, W. O..N B
Fowler, W., Hammondvale ....N B
Fowlie, Mrs. Micha, Brookvale, W. O......N B
Fox, Alex. J., Sand Point, W. O..........N S
Fox, S. D., Overton........................O
Fox, John C., Olinda........................O
Frame, H. M., Glen Huron .... O
Frame, Archibald, Selmah, W. O.... ...... N S
Frame, M., Gay's River, W. O.............N S
Francis, William, Willowgrove, W. O.......N B
Francis, John G., Owen Sound ....O
Frayney, Robert, Dalhousie Road, W. O.....N S
Franklin, Job., Alberton ....O
Franks, Thos., Frank Hill............. ....O
Fraser, Alex., Toney River, W. O. ....N S
Fraser, Alex, Westmeath ....O
Fraser, Donald, McLellan's Mountain, W. O...N S
Fraser, J. A., Big Bras d'Or, W. O....... N S
Fraser Robert, Rocklin, W. O. ....N S
Fraser, James, South Bar of Sydney River, W. O. .... N S
Fraser, John, Kildonan... . ... M
Fraser, John, Densmores, W. O........... .N S
Fraser, John, Harrington Cove, W. O.......N S
Fraser, Jessie McG., Head of St. Margaret's Bay (Middle District), W. O ....N S
Fraser, William, West McGillivray ....O
Fraser, John, Lancaster ... .O
Fraser, Daniel Lower Settlement, South River, W. O.... .. ..N S
Fraser, D., Matapedia ... .Q
Fraser James, Maple Green, W. O....... ...N B
Fraser, Charles Cross Roads, Lake Ainslie, W.O N S
Fraser, William, New Glasgow..............N S
Fraser, George M., North Brookfield, W. O....N S
Fraser, John, Crosspoint... .... Q
Fraser, Donald Dumblane ....O
Fraser, Alexander, McLennan's Brook, W. O..N S
Fraser, James, Loch Garry.. ....O
Fraser, David, Grandigue Ferry, W. O.. ....N S
Fraser, A. D., Hamburg ....O
Fraser, John, Glengarry Station.. ....N S
Fraser, R., Fontenoy.......................Q
Fraser, John, Fraser's Grant, W. O........ ..N S
Fraser, Simon, Lochinvar........ ....O

Fraser, Thomas A., Pugwash River, W. O.....N S
Fréchette, Louis J., St. Ferdinand......... ....Q
Fréchette, Nazaire, Craigs Road Station....... Q
Freeman, Nath, Greenfield, W. O............N S
Freeman, B. C., Deniston.....................O
Freeman, Jos. M., Pleasant River, W. O... . N S
Freeman, Samuel E., Nappan, W. O..........N S
Freeman, Augustus, White Rock Mills, W. O..N S
Freer, E. S., Montreal...... ....Q
Freney, John, Perkins........................Q
Freeze, Hiram, Doaktown, W. O......... ...N B
Freid, Noah, Dashwood........... .... O
Frigon, Joseph, St. Prosper ....Q
Frommhagen, E., Wartburg . ...O
Frost, P. W., Little River, W. O ....N S
Fry, Isaac, South Cayuga...................O
Fry, Henry, Hursdon..... .... O
Fugere, Narcisse, Batiscan Bridge............Q
Fullerton, G. D., Halfway River, W. O.......N S
Fullerton, Edward D., Cannonville....... ....N S
Fuller, J. A., New Minus, W. O..... .. ....N S
Fulmer, W. A., Economy....................N S
Fulmore, Philip, River Debert, W. O..........N S
Fulton, Thomas, Knoxford, W. O............N B
Fulton, James, Langton.......... ....O
Furse, James, New Glasgow................. .Q

Gabetis, Sarah, Gore's Landing............... O
Gage, W. J., Bartonville...... ....O
Gagné, Virginie, Viger ....Q
Gagnier, Frs. X., Neigette.....................Q
Gagnon, H., Upper St. Bazil, W. O..... .....N B
Gagnon, C., L'Avenir...... ....Q
Gairdner, James, Bayfield...... ....O
Gallagher, Dennis, Vigo.......................Q
Gallagher, Ann, Salmon River, W. O.... .....N S
Gallagher, Paul, Perm.............. ....O
Gallang, Thos, Barachois, W. O............ N B
Gallant, Athanase, Shediac Bridge, W. O.....N B
Galloway, James, Harrisburg..................O
Galloway, Alex. D., Bensfort.............. ...O
Gamsby, J. W., Huntingville ....Q
Gannan, Patrick, Lake La Hashe............B C
Gairner, Wm., Minden.........................O
Garrault, Thomas, St. Lin....................Q
Gareau, Philip, Curran.......................O
Gardiner, John, Dartmoor ....O
Gardner, Alex., Armow................. ..O
Gardner, Simeon, Tusket Forks, W. O... . N S
Gardner, Joseph, Britannia ....O
Gardner, David, Hibernia, W. O.......... N B
Gardner, James, Musquodoboit Harbor, W. O.N S
Garriock, Peter, Westbourne... .... M
Garrison, W. A., Upper Sheffield, W. O.....N B
Gates, John, Vyner............................O
Gatien, G. H., Ste. Marie de Monnoir.........Q
Gaudette, Dr. G., St. Annedes Plains..........Q
Gaudry, Charles A., Rivière du Loup (en bas)....Q
Gauld, John D., River John............. . N S
Gaulin, Charles, Portneuf. ....Q
Ganthier, dit Landerville, A., St. Pie........ Q
Gauthier, Onézime, St. Urbain.............. Q
Gauthier, Philias, St. Eustache. . ...Q
Gauvin, Louis G., St. Charles de Stanbridge.....Q
Gavaza, Thomas A., Annapolis........ ....N S
Gawler, Henry, Gainsville....................O
Gebbie, Thomas, Howick....... ....Q
Geer, M., Herbert.... ....Q
Gélinas, C., St. Clothilde... ... .Q
Gendreau, Pierre, West Ditton..... .... Q
Gendron, Joseph P., St. Barnabé, River Yamaska Q
Généreux, Esdras, St. Alphonse................ Q

Genest, F. E., St. Marguerite .... Q
Genoir, William, Big Tracadie, W. O .... N S
Genong, F. D., Spague's Point...... .... N B
George, J. C., York River .... O
George, James, Huttonsville.................. O
Germain, C., jun., St. Vincent de Paul.......... Q
Germain, Elzéar, St. Didace....... .... Q
Germain, George, Gosport.............. .... O
Getchell, John J., Lynnfield, W. O... .... N B
Ghent, D. A., Priceville... .. .. O
Giasson, G. F., L'Anse à Giles.................. Q
Gibb, W. W., Langley .... B C
Gibbon, J. A., Wilmot.......... .... N S
Gibbon, James, Collina, W. O .... N B
Gibbons, John, Goldstone..................... O
Gibbs, Chas., Cannington..................... O
Gibson, Robert, Glenvale.. .... O
Gibson, Geo. R., Forest City, W. O .... N B
Giddens, Daniel, Portapique Mountain, W. O N S
Gifford, Henry J., Silver Hill..... .... O
Gigault, G. A., St. Cesaire...................... Q
Gilbault, Joseph, St. Paul d'Industrie.......... Q
Gilbert, William, Mansfield... .... O
Gilbert, John D., Gilbert's Mills.............. O
Gilbraith, Thos., Pisarinco, W. O............ N B
Gilchrist, James, Keady .... O
Gilchrist, John C., Woodville .... O
Gill, H. W., Ufford.......... .. .. O
Gillard, J., Grafton .... O
Gillespie, Alex., Creemore .... O
Gillespie, Alexander, Sunnidale....... .... O
Gillespie, George, Round Plains................ O
Gillespie, George M., Glenarm .... O
Gillespie, Charles, Milton, East........... ... Q
Gilley, Walter, Oak Bay, W. O............. N B
Gillies, Colin, Margaree, W. O............... N S
Gillies, Donald, Grand Mira South, W. O.... N S
Gillies, John, Braeside...... .... O
Gillies, Colin, Eagle .... O
Gilliott, Wm., Churchstreet, W. O.......... N S
Gillis, Niel, Point Clear. O.................... N S
Gillis, Wm., Arisaig, W. O................. N S
Gillis, Donald, Lewis Bay, W. O............. N S
Gillis, Donald, Big Intervale, (Grand Narrows), W. O.. N S
Gilman, Francis, Parker's Creek....... .... M
Gingras, Francois X., St. Casimir........ ..... Q
Gingrich, Moses, Roseville..................... O
Girardin, R. A., Grande Ligne.....,......... O
Giroux, Nazaire, Clarina......... .... Q
Gladstone, Thos. B., Midland .... O
Glass, Matthew, Elginfield... .... O
Gleeson, William, Langside.. .... O
Glen, John, Gibralter ... . O
Glendinning, Arch., Ellesmere................. O
Glendinning, David, Harvey Station.......... N B
Glenn, William, Lochartville, W. O.......... N S
Glover, George, Ravenshoe..................... O
Glover, William, Gamesbridge........... ... O
Goble, Frederick, Harrow...................... O
Goble, Wm L., Goble's Corners. . ... O
Godard, Daniel, South Branch (Kent)......... N B
Godfrey, E. L., Mountain Grove .... O
Goehringer, Joseph, Bingham Road .... O
Golding, G. N., Wickham, W. O............. N B
Gonthro, Belloni, French Vale, W. O....... N S
Good, Archibald, Good Corner, W. O......... N B
Goodenow, Lafayette, Georgetown............. O
Gooderham, A. L., Pine Grove......... ..... O
Gooderham, C. H., Meadowvale........ ..... O
Goodeve, Chas. F., Allan Park... .... O
Goodfellow, A., Springville............. ..... O

Goodfellow, James, Vin
Goodhue, James, St. Ch
Goodhue, Saml., Barnst
Gordanier, J. L. P., Mc
Gordon, David, Osaea..
Gordon, James, Genoa.
Gordon, William, North
Gordon, Thomas, Longw
Gordon, H., Port Perry
Gordon, Thomas, Elm G
Gorman, George, Metag
Gormley, James, Gorml
Gorvell, Wm. O., Spani
Gorvett, W., Milliken..
Gosselin, François, junr.
Gosselin, Louis, St. Jean
Gosselin, Jean Baptiste,
Gosselin, Joseph, St. Iré
Gould, Lorenzo T., Woo
Gould, Edward. N., Fla
Goulet, L. G. E., St. Jér
Goulet, E., St. Hilaire V
Goulette, William, Belœ
Gow, F. G., Gravenhurst
Graham, W. M., Bethar
Graham, Andrew K. Fiv
Graham, Robert, Enterp
Graham, W. S., West Ri
Graham, Hugh, Rouge H
Graham, James, Brookfi
Graham, James, Creek I
Graham, John, Lifford..
Graham, William, Dunsf
Graham, Arthur, Juveni
Graham, Allen, Dunkelc
Graham, James, Baydu
Grandpré, P. S., St. Vale
Grandy, John, Berne....
Grandy, Robert, Omemee
Grant, Alexander, Veron
Grant, Alex., Frazer's M
Grant, James, Coverley..
Grant, A. W., Shulie, W
Grant, James A., St. Ste
Grant, William, Parrsbo
Grant, William, Kintail.
Grant, William, Mabou.
Grant, John R., Brussels
Grant, James, Harwood
Grant, Angus, Port Haw
Grass, George, Waais Sta
Grassie, John, Fulton ..
Graveline, David U., Cas
Graves, W. H., Springfie
Graves, Hector, Dempsey
Gray, George, Lynedoch.
Gray, William, Fleurant
Gray, A. S., Ponds, W.
Gray, Daniel B., Foresto
Graydon, Robert, Streets
Graystock, Mark, Grayst
Green, Joseph, Davenpor
Green, P. F., Charleston.
Green, Caleb, Fairhaven,
Green, George, H. H., Po
Green, Joshua, Spring B
Greenshields James, Ne
Greensides, Edward, Mor
Greenwood, William, Po
Greenwood, A. R., North
Greer, James, Winchester
Greenway, William, Cen

List of Postmasters in Canada.—Continued.

Gregor, Lewis, Crieff .... Q
Grenier, David, Carthby.......... Q
Grier, James, Iroquois.......... O
Griffin, J. S., Preston Road, W. O.......... N S
Griffith, David, Parma.......... O
Griffith, John, Parham.......... O
Grimm, C., Springfield, W. O.......... N S
Grindley, W. H., Blackville, W. O.......... N B
Grono, Elias, Hackett's Cove, W. O.......... N S
Gropp, Henry, Brunner.......... O
Grosvenor, C. E., Canterbury.......... N B
Grosvenor, George, Lower Southampton, W. O. N B
Grouchey, David, Discouse, W. O.......... N B
Grout, James C., Solina.......... O
Gueguen, Magloire, Gueguen, W. O.......... N B
Guilbauldt, Louis, L'Assomption.......... Q
Guild, Julius, Bentley.......... O
Guimond, Baptiste, Silver Stream, W. O.......... N B
Gunn, Donald, Lower Fort Garry.......... M
Gunn, Donald, Cross Roads, Country Harbor.. N S
Gunn, John, Hopwell, W. O.......... N S
Guthrie, Peter, Tatlock.......... N S

Hackett, Alexander, Colchester.......... O
Hackett, John, Chambly Canton.......... Q
Hacking, W. H., Listowell.......... O
Hackwell, William, Boscobel.......... Q
Haddock, James, McAdam Junction, W. O.. N B
Hadley, G. B., Port Mulgrave.......... N S
Hagan, James, Templeton.......... Q
Hagar, Elijah, Roseway, W. O.......... N S
Hager, Charles, Hagersville.......... O
Hagerman, H., Moray.......... O
Hagyard, E. T., Campbell's Cross.......... O
Haines, E. J., Marshall's Town, W. O.......... N S
Hales, Richard, Forfar.......... O
Hall, C. H. J., Broughton.......... Q
Hall, Asa, Stoketon.......... Q
Hall, Edward, Darrell.......... O
Hall, Henry, Binbrook.......... O
Hall, J. H., Brooklyn, W. O.......... N S
Hall, W., Sheet Harbor, W. O.......... N S
Hall, Henry G., Hall's Bridge.......... O
Hall, Charles, Burlington, W. O.......... N S
Hall, Daniel B, Linda.......... Q
Hall, George, Clyde.......... O
Hall, W. J., Keene.......... O
Hall, Wm., Skipness.......... O
Hallamore, S. E., New Cornwall, W. O.......... N S
Halley, James L., Ponsonby.......... O
Hallisay, Daniel, Beaver Bank, W. O.......... N S
Hambly, John, Winfield.......... O
Hamel, J., St. Croix.......... Q
Hamelin, D., St. Narcisse.......... Q
Hamelin, A. Damase, Deschambault.......... Q
Hames, William, Veunachar.......... O
Hamilton, James, Singhampton.......... O
Hamilton, Mrs. S. J., Springford.......... O
Hamilton, Samuel, St. Luc.......... Q
Hamilton, W. B., Collingwood.......... O
Hamilton, James, Carlingford.......... O
Hamilton, James, Staffa.......... O
Hamilton, George, Britonville.......... Q
Hamilton, A., Petersville Church, W. O.......... N B
Hamilton, J. H., Kempt, W. O.......... N S
Hamilton, James, Laurel.......... O
Hamm, David, Grand Bay, W. O.......... N B
Hammond, W. D., Wardsville.......... O
Hammond, James, jun., Hammond.......... O
Hammond, J. A., Kingsclear, W. O.......... N B
Hamon, Philip, Newport Point.......... Q
Hancock, L. S. Ridgetown.......... O
Hancock, John, Bruce Mines.......... O

Handron, Henry, Handford Brook, W. O.......... N B
Handy, Edward, Mount Brydges.......... O
Hanes, Erastus, Utterson.......... O
Hanes, James F., Huntsville.......... O
Hanley, J. C., Reed.......... O
Hanna, Hugh, Brookvale, W. O.......... N S
Hannegar, Jacob, Upper Kennetcook, W. O... N S
Hannington, W. J. M., Pointe du Chêne, W. O N B
Hannington, W., Smith's, W. O.......... N B
Hanrahan, Thos., South Douro.......... O
Hanson, Robert V., Mace's Bay.......... N B
Hardwicke, V. F., Bear River, (West side).... N S
Hardy, J. N., Dorchester Station.......... O
Hardy, N., Champlain.......... Q
Hargrave, Joseph, Eglington.......... O
Harigan, John, Moneymore.......... O
Harmon, Charles A., Peel, W. O.......... N B
Harnett, John, Kingston.......... N B
Harrington, H. H., Tracadie.......... N S
Harris, Richardson, Saw Mill Creek, W. O.... N S
Harris, Mrs. Elizabeth, Myrehall.......... O
Harris, C. S., Courtland.......... O
Harris, S. G., Tapleyton.......... O
Harris, Merritt D., Boundary Creek, W. O... N B
Harris, Samuel, Cowichan.......... B C
Harris, T. R., Aylesford.......... N S
Harris, John L., Albert Mines, W. O.......... N B
Harrison, J. H., Rockville, W. O.......... N B
Harrison, Isabella, Drum.......... O
Harrison, John, Kinloss.......... O
Harrison, Richard, Glammis.......... O
Harrison, Thomas, Thorndale.......... O
Harrison, Charles, Kingston Mills.......... O
Harron, Alexander, Debec Station, W. O.......... N B
Hartley, Jonathan, Pirate Harbor.......... N S
Hartt, William, Derby, W. O.......... N B
Harvey, James, Nanaimo.......... B C
Harvey, Willliam Elmvale.......... O
Hase, Thomas, Haseville.......... Q
Hatfield, J. A., Brookville, W. O.......... N S
Hatfield, J. L., Fox River, W. O.......... N S
Hattee, John, New Caledonia, W. O.......... N S
Hawkin, Thomas, Schoona.......... B C
Hawley, H. A., Aird.......... Q
Hawthorne, A., Upper Kent, W. O.......... N B
Hay, Shackleton, Ailsa Craig.......... O
Hayes, John, Norton, W. O.......... N B
Hayes, Michael, Hayesland.......... O
Hayter, Thos. N., Harpley.......... O
Hayward, Robert, Kenilworth.......... O
Hazen, J. W., Spring Arbor.......... O
Healey, Maurice, Harewood, W. O.......... N B
Heaphy, Michael, Victoria Road Station.......... O
Heard, William, Kemble.......... O
Heath, Samuel, Tyrrell.......... O
Heath, William, Clarendon Front (sub).......... Q
Hébert, Antoine, St. Martime.......... Q
Hébert, C., Labarre.......... Q
Hébert, J. T., Larochelle.......... Q
Heckman, Isaac, La Have Cross Roads, W. O. N S
Heffernan, Jane, Carroll's Corners, W. O.......... N S
Heise, Daniel V., Victoria Square.......... O
Helps, Mrs., Westfield.......... O
Henlow, James, Liscombe, W. O.......... N S
Hemphill, James, Ferryville, W. O.......... N B
Hendershot, A. Jerseyville.......... O
Henderson, David, West Essa.......... O
Henderson, James W., Vandeleur.......... O
Henderson, Henry, Newark.......... O
Henderson, Archibald, Marston.......... O
Hendry, Charles, Conestogo.......... O
Hendry, James, Porter's Hill.......... O
Hendry, W., Brookfield, W. O.......... N S

List of Postmasters in Canada.—Continued.

Henesey, Wm., Chepstow .... O
Heney, Henry, Danford Lake .... Q
Henry, S. L., Upper Musquodoboit .... N S
Henry, P. D., Whitfield .... O
Henry, James, Magundy, W. O .... N S
Herkins, William, Lewis Head, W. O .... N S
Heron, Agnes, Dollar .... O
Héroux, Moise, Mekinac .... Q
Herring, Noah, Belfountain .... O
Hewitt, J., Spring Hill, W. O .... N S
Hewson, Jas. R., Earnestown Station .... O
Hewton, John, Bourg Louis .... Q
Heyrock, Henry, Johnson's Mills .... O
Hicks, W. W., Mitchell .... O
Hicks, John, Killerby .... O
Hicks, Mariner, Midgic, W. O .... N B
Hicks, Ira, McLaughlan Road, W. O .... N B
Higgins, W. H., North River, W. O .... N S
Higginson, James G., Hawkesbury .... O
Hillaker, George, Mount Salem .... O
Hill, William, Sandurst .... O
Hill, Robert, Ballantrae .... O
Hill, William, Welcome .... O
Hill, Alexander, Cross Roads, Saint George's Channel, W. O .... N S
Hill, Joseph, Thornby .... Q
Hill, H. P., Antigonishe .... N S
Hill, Thomas L., Hillsborough .... O
Hiltz, Samuel, Lawrencetown, W. O .... N S
Hinch, William, Hinch .... O
Hines, Byron, East side of Pubnico Harbor, W. O .... N S
Hingley, A. S., Kemptown, W. O .... N S
Hirst, James, Freelton .... O
Hislop, John, Marmion .... O
Hitchin, John, Emerald .... O
Hoath, R., Hoath Head .... O
Hoare, John S., Adelaide .... O
Hodge, George N., Birchton .... Q
Hodges, Hiram, Newcastle .... O
Hodgkinson, Philip, Aylmer, West .... O
Hodgson, John, Como .... Q
Hodgson, J. T., Edmundston .... N B
Hogan, M., Point Bruléy, W. O .... N S
Hogarth, Henry, Danforth .... O
Hogg, William, York Mills .... O
Hogg, John, Don .... O
Holbert, John, Reaboro .... O
Holbrooke, J., Helena .... Q
Holden, James, Morrisburgh .... O
Holden, William, Petite Rivière Bridge, W. O .... N S
Holden, Hiram, Shannonville .... O
Holden, Thomas, Head of Jordan River, W. O .... N S
Holden, William, Rob-Roy .... O
Holesworth, F. H., Lower Stewiacke .... N S
Hollinger, Charles, J., Fergusson's Falls .... O
Holmden, Thomas D., Girvan Settlement, W. O .... N B
Holmes, Andrew, Oxford Station .... O
Holmes, Samuel, Welland Port .... O
Holmes, C. A., Springville, W. O .... N S
Holmes, Richard, Blyth .... O
Holterman, C. F., Vanburgh .... O
Honsberger, Isaac, Rainham .... O
Hood, A. T., Yarmouth .... N S
Hooker, D'Arcy, Teeterville .... O
Hooker, G. A., Geneva .... Q
Hooper, Albert B., Fourche, W. O .... N S
Hope, Robert, Newburgh .... O
Hope, Charles, Abbott's Corners .... Q
Hopkins, James P., Holloway .... O
Hopkins, Patrick, North River Platform, W. O .... N B
Hopper, E. B., Merivale .... O
Horan, Edward, West Huntley .... O
Hord, Robert, Komoka .... O
Horseman, David, Intervale, W. O .... N B
Hossie, D., Logierait .... O
Houde, C. E., St. Celestin .... Q
House, William T., Stevensville .... O
House, J. L., Beebe Plain .... Q
House, J. M., Pigeon Lake .... M
House, Louis, Netherby .... O
House, James W., Lineboro' .... Q
Houston, Thomas, Camlachie .... O
Houston, James, Hawkstone .... O
How, William, sen., Hillsburgh .... O
Howard, John T., Esquimalt .... B C
Howard, Thomas, St. Ives .... O
Howard, William, Richby .... Q
Howe, John, St. John .... N B
Howes, Richard, Glendower .... O
Howden, Richard, Millbrook .... O
Howey, William, Massey .... Q
Howland, F. A., Etobicoke .... O
Hoyt, Alfred, Lepuille, W. O .... N S
Hoyt, John Y., McKenzie's Corner, W. O .... N B
Hubbard, B. F., Stanstead .... Q
Hubley, James, Black Point, W. O .... N S
Hubley, Frederick, Indian Harbor, W. O .... N S
Huckins, Joseph C., Epsom .... O
Hudgens, A. P., Lake George, W. O .... N S
Hudon, Alexander, St. Pacome .... Q
Hudon, dit Beaulieu, St. Elizabeth .... Q
Hudson, John, Haldimand .... O
Huestis, M. B., Wallace .... N S
Hueston, John, Huntley .... O
Huff, Lewis, Keith .... O
Huggard, John, Painswick .... O
Hughes, W. C., Sandhill .... O
Hughes, G. P., Keenansville .... O
Hughes, M., Collfield .... Q
Hughes, Alexander, Kay Settlement, W. O .... N B
Hughes, Hugh, Heckston .... O
Hull, John, Hullsville .... O
Humphrey, A., Rodney .... O
Humphries, Hiram, McDonald's Corner, W. O .... N B
Humphries, Israel, Warkworth .... O
Humphries, John, Sussex Corner, W. O .... N B
Hungerford, L. N., Mawcook .... Q
Hungerford, S. L., West Brome .... Q
Hunter, Thomas, Venice .... Q
Hunter, Walter, Clarksburg .... O
Hunter, George, Glenburnie .... O
Hunter, James, Egerton .... O
Hunter, John, Hunterville .... O
Huntingdon, J., Salmon River, W. O .... N S
Huot, P. G., Quebec .... Q
Hurlburt, Reuben, Myrtle .... O
Hurly, Thomas, jun., Sanborn .... Q
Hussey, J. B., Mount St. Louis .... O
Huston, James, Stanford .... Q
Hutchins, Rodney, East Farnham .... Q
Hutchinson, Matthew, Upper Wicklow, W. O .... N B
Hutchinson, James, North Esk Boom, W. O .... N B
Hutchinson, James, Harwich .... O
Hutt, Henry, Tancook Islands, W. O .... N S
Hutton, Mrs. A. R., Harcourt .... O
Hysop, John, Ballantyne Station .... O

Ilsley, John R., Vernon Mines, W. O .... N S
Imrie, Mrs. Mary, Spencerville .... O
Ingles, Joseph, Strathnairn .... O
Ingles, George, junr., Maple Hill .... O
Irish, Levi, Little River, W. O .... N B
Irons, John, Tower Hill, W. O .... N B
Ironside, A. McGregor, Manitowaning .... O
Ironside, John, Grand Bend .... O

List of Postmasters in Canada.—Continued.

Irvine, William, Desmond ..... O
Irving, J. B., West Flamboro' ..... O
Irving, Andrew, St. Lambert, Montreal ..... Q
Irving, James, Kerrwood ..... O
Irwin, John, Perch Station ..... O
Ivison, Robert, Oxley ..... O

Jack, James, Lorne ..... O
Jackson, Anthony, Eden Mills ..... O
Jackson, James, Kerby ..... O
Jackson, James H., Severn Bridge ..... O
Jackson, Geo. E., Egmondville ..... O
Jacques, Thomas, Waterville, W.O ..... N S
Jaffray, Wm., Berlin ..... O
Jakes, Samuel, Merrickville ..... O
James, Edwin, Bridgewater ..... O
James, J. W., Laurencetown ..... N S
Jameson, Robert B., Fenison Falls ..... O
Jamieson, Geo. C., Cole Harbor, W.O ..... N S
Jamieson, James, Granton ..... O
Jardine, R., Renous Bridge, W.O ..... N B
Jardine, Ferguson, Newington ..... O
Jarmain, J. P., Matlock ..... O
Jarmin, James, Lime Lake ..... O
Jarratt, Charles, Jarratt's Corners ..... O
Jarvis, Paul, Ravenswood ..... O
Jarvis, William, Peterson ..... O
Jean, George M., Petit de Grat, W.O ..... N S
Jeffers, Henry, Westbrook, W.O ..... N S
Jelly, Wm. B., Bowling Green ..... O
Jenkins, Joel, Jenkins, W.O. ..... N B
Jenkins, David, Waldemar ..... O
Jenks, John W., Parrsborough ..... N S
Jerway, Samuel, Upper Buctouche, W.O ..... N B
Jewitt, S. C., Lower Wakefield, W.O ..... N B
Jiggens, Sarah, Leeds ..... Q
Jimerson, Ira, South Ely ..... Q
Job, William, Radstock ..... Q
Jobin, G., St. Bazile ..... Q
Jobin, Marie S., Isle Perrot ..... Q
Johns, Alonzo C., Fairfield East ..... O
Johnson, David W., Powers Court ..... Q
Johnson, Benjamin, Marmora ..... O
Johnson, Caleb, Melville ..... O
Johnson, Lionel H., Wallaceburg ..... O
Johnson, Carby, Ventry ..... O
Johnson, H. A., Dalhousie ..... N B
Johnson, T. Stewart, Tweedside ..... O
Johnson, Daniel, Cumbermere ..... O
Johnson, George, Pefferlaw ..... O
Johnson, C., L'Original ..... O
Johnson, T. W., Ballymote ..... O
Johnson, Anne, Kinlough ..... O
Johnston, S., Clapham ..... Q
Johnston, Joseph, Pelham Union ..... O
Johnston, Robert, Weston ..... O
Johnston, Richard, Dryden ..... O
Johnston, Richard, Thistletown ..... O
Johnston, B. H., Port Carling ..... O
Johnston, John, Farnham Centre ..... Q
Johnston, Samuel, Newcastle ..... N B
Johnstone, Adam, Linton's, W. O ..... N B
Johnstone, William, Johnson ..... O
Jollimore, J. W., Mill Cove, W. O ..... N S
Joncas, P. S., Berthier (*en bas*) ..... Q
Jones, Cereno D., Weymouth ..... N S
Jones, Maxon, Bloomington ..... O
Jones, C. H., Bromemere ..... Q
Jones, Joseph, Thompson's Mills ..... N S
Jones, J. M., Stanbridge, East ..... Q
Jones, Merritt, Mount Pleasant, W. O ..... N B
Jones, Charles, junr., Oxford Mills ..... O
Jones, Chas. K., Bronte ..... O

Jones, Thomas, Sabrevois .....
Jones, D. A. Tecumseth .....
Jones, John, Sunderland .....
Jones, Alva G., Stony Creek .....
Jones, Peter, Cranworth .....
Jordan, J. A., Upper Cross Roads, St. Mary's, W. O ..... N
Jordan, M., Leinster .....
Jordan, Patrick, Connaught .....
Jordine, Ferguson, Newington .....
Journeay, Jasper, Weymouth Bridge ..... N
Judd, Agnes, Stirling .....
Judge, John, Mono Road Station .....
Jury, Thomas, Napperton .....
Jutras, Joseph, East Chester .....
Jutras, H., Somerset .....

Kain, John, South Nelson, W.O ..... N
Kaiser, Anthony, Ste. Agathe .....
Kane, J. A. J., Murray Bay .....
Kaulback, R. A., Middle Musquodoboit ..... N
Kavanagh, Michael, Creighton .....
Kavanagh, D., Umfraville .....
Kavanagh, J. J., Gaspé Basin .....
Kay, W. F., Otterville .....
Kaye, Charles, Point Kaye .....
Kean, John, Victoria Harbour .....
Kearney, Frank, St. Leonard's, W.O ..... N
Kearns, James, Glen Tay .....
Keating, James, Oil Springs .....
Keating, J. H., Warburton .....
Kedy, H., Chelsea, W.O. ..... N
Keefer, Jacob, Thorold .....
Keith, Ariel, Cornhill, W.O ..... N
Keith, Lewis, New Canaan, W.O ..... N
Keith, C. I., Butternut Ridge, W.O ..... N
Keith, George, Keithley Creek ..... B
Kelley, George, Lambeth .....
Kelly, John, Spruce Lake, W.O. ..... N
Kelly, Edward, Baby's Point .....
Kelly, John, Roxborough, W.O ..... N
Kelly, Edward, Holmesville .....
Kelly, P. D., Loretto .....
Kimball, Warren, Leamington .....
Kemp, Thomas, Chandos .....
Kempton, E., Milton ..... N
Kincaid, William, Harlow .....
Kendrick, A. W., Campbellton ..... N
Kendrick, A. W., Compton .....
Kennedy, Peter, Notfield .....
Kennedy, Alexander, Cathcart .....
Kennedy, James, Monument Settlement, W.O. N
Kennedy, Patrick, Bagot .....
Kennedy, John, Dixie .....
Kennedy, Joseph, Louisburg, W.O. ..... N
Kennedy, James, Monument Settlement, W.O. N
Kennedy, William, Hartington .....
Kenny, Charles, Erinville, W.O ..... N
Kent, Hugh, Hiawatha .....
Keough, John, Laval .....
Kerr, David, New Bandon, W.O ..... N
Kerr, Samuel, Antrim, W.O ..... N
Kerr, Archibald, Nouvelle (sub) .....
Kerr, James, Summer Hill, W.O ..... N
Kerr, David, Caplin .....
Ketchum, Morgan L., Waupoos .....
Key, Samuel, Wickwire Station, W.O ..... N
Key, William, New Aberdeen .....
Keys, Robert, Bornholm .....
Kidd, John, Athlone .....
Kidd, George J., Carronbrook .....
Kidd, Thomas, Arlington .....
Kidd, Thos. A., Burritt's Rapids .....

List of Postmasters in Canada.—Continued.

Kier, Archibald R., Somenos................B C
Kierstead, George, Alma........ ....N B
Kilbank, William, Codrington ....O
Kilborne, P. S., Winterbourne..................O
Killam, J. M., Wheaton Settlement, W.O....N B
Killam, Hiram, Little River (Elgin), W.O....N B
Killen, Andrew S., St. Martin's.. .. ..N B
Killoan, M., Belledune River, W.O ....N B
Kimball, Warren, Leamington ....O
Kimball, William, Wilkesport ....O
Kimball, Albert, Knowlton.....................Q
Kimpton, R. A., Roxton Pond............ .....Q
Kincaid, William, Harlem.. ....O
King, Charles H., Cheltenham..................O
King, George G., Chipman, W.O..............N B
King, John, Lyster .... Q
King, Joshua, Port Philip, W.O. .... N S
King, Oliver Tidnish, W.O.. ....N S
King, Samuel A., Pinkerton ....O
King, Wm., Bristol... ....Q
Kingsmill, Wm., Guelph. . ... O
Kingston, C. H., Enniskillen Station, W.O ..N B
Kinnear, James, Kinnear's Mills.......... ....Q
Kinny, Thomas, Oungah. .... O
Kinsman, Benjamin, Kinsman's Corners.......N S
Kinsman, Danson, Fonthill ....O
Kipp, Joseph B., Otnabog, W.O. ....N B
Kirby, Daniel, New Harbor, W.O... ..... N S
Kirk, John, Kirk's Ferry.......................Q
Kirkpatrick, Andrew, Shubenacadie . ...N S
Kirkpatrick, B., Quaco Road, W.O ....N B
Kirkpatrick, Samuel, Aldboro .... O
Kirkpatrick, Thomas, Widder Station..........O
Kirkpatrick, F., Lunenburg.... ....O
Kirkwood, D., Rockside.......................O
Kitchen, Harriet L., St. Williams ....O
Kitchen, L. W., Bloomsburg...................O
Kittson, Annie, Berthier (*en haut*) .... Q
Knack, A., Upper Branch, W.O.... ....N S
Knaut, Lewis, Mahone Bay .... N S
Knechtel, Jacob, Carlsruhe .... O
Knight, Alfred, Petworth ....O
Knight, William, Smith's Mills ... . Q
Knight, J. E., New River, W.O...............N B
Knight, Richard, Bowmanton ....O
Knowles, Leonard, Barrington Passage, W. O.N S
Knowlton, Calvin H., Lapum. ....O
Knowlton, Luke H., South Stukely........... Q
Knox, G. W., Upper Caverhill, W.O........ N B
Korry, John, Bolingbroke ....O
Krassler, John, Heidelburgh .... O
Kumpf, C., Waterloo ....O
Kyle, Joseph S., North Winchester..............O
Kyte, David, Richwood .... O

Laberge, Rev. F. X., Ste. Hippolyte de Kilkenny Q
Labrèque, Dr. Louis, Lambton . ... Q
Labrosse, Simon, St. Eugène . ...Q
Lacerte, Arthur, Yamachiche ....Q
Lachaine, dit Jolicœur, B. G., Isle aux Grues... Q
Lacourcière, A. Jos., St. Stanislas..................Q
Lacourcière, P., Vincennes.... . . ..Q
Lacourcière, D., Batiscan ....Q
Ladell, Henry G., Mary Lake ....O
Ladd, C. J., Delaware............ ....O
Laflèche, T., Domaine de Gentilly ....Q
Lafleur, Odile, Ste. Adèle ....Q
Lafleur, Honoré, Yamaska ....Q
Lafleur, A., Aubrey ....Q
Lafond, Olivier, St. Paulin ....Q
Lafontaine, Emery, St. Hugues.. ....Q
Lafontaine, John, Capeltown........ . ...Q
Lainesse, Prudent, St. Albert.......................Q

Laing, G., Bayham..............................O
Laing, Alexander, Dundee, W.O. ....N B
Laird, Richard, Shetland............ .. ..O
Lajeunesse, C. C., Lac Masson ....Q
Lake, W., Purdy ....O
Lake, Benjamin, Ranelagh ....O
Lalonde, E. H., St. Marthe......................Q
Lalonde, R. J., Ste. Justine de Newton.........Q
Lalonde, Camille, Mountjoy....... ....Q
Lalonde, Joseph, Embrun .. ..O
Lalumière, Eusèbe, St. Bazile le Grand.........Q
Lamarche, J. O., Mascouche.......................Q
Lamb, William, Wendover ....O
Lamb, Thomas, St. Andrews, East ....Q
Lambert dit Champagne, Jean, Grand Coudées ..Q
Lambert, Henry, West Lake......................O
Lambert, Isaac Dealtown. ....O
Lambkin, Simon Riceburg.......................Q
Lamontagne, O. A., Dalibaire.....................Q
Lamothe, Guillaume, Viger Mines................Q
Lamorandiere, Chas., Killarney ....O
Lamoureux, Antoine, Pointe aux Trembles......Q
Lamoureux, Luc, St. Sébastien ....Q
Lamoureux, Olivier, Contrecœur ....Q
Lamphier, Peter, Grahamsville .... O
Lamy, Adolphe, St. Sévère. . ... Q
Lancaster, Christopher, Westwood ....O
Lance, Richard, Beatrice . ... O
Landon, John, Waltham ....Q
Landon, Horace, Chichester ....Q
Landers, Jacob, Wellington, W. O ....N S
Landry, Honoré, Palmerston, W. O...... ....N B
Lane, Samuel, Denbigh..... .... O
Lane, Reuben, Mossley...... .... O
Lang, Robert, Chateauguay Basin ....Q
Langlois, Charles, F. Y., Piopolis.... .... Q
Langin, Chas. E., Gaspereaux, W. O.........NB
Langevin, F. T., St. Isidore, Laprairie.........Q
Langman, John, Bogart ....O
Langstaff, John, Langstaff (sub.) ....O
Lantz, Harvey, Lantz, W. O.... ....N S
Lapalme, Trefflé, St. Dominique.............. Q
La Pinotière, W. H., Elora...... ....O
Lapointé, C. F., Ste. Flavie ....Q
Lapointe, Leandre, Mount Oscar.... ....Q
Lapointe, Jos., Robin, Mile End . ...Q
Lappin, Sarah Jane, Miss, Strathallan...... ....O
Largie, Edward, Fletcher's Station ....N S
Larivière, Thomas, Pont Rouge....................Q
Larocque, Telesphore, Henryville.................Q
Larouche, E., Clairvaux, (sub.) . . .. Q
Larracey, John, Irish Town, W. O............N B
Larue, Edmund, St. Antoine, Lotbinière........Q
Larue, Miss H. C., Cap St. Ignace .... Q
Lasalle, F. X. St. Jean de Matha. ....Q
Latour, dit Forget, Joseph, St. Thomas, East...Q
Latour, Edmond, Côte St. Paul .... Q
Latshaw, Christopher, Glen Morris.... ....O
Laugill, J. S. Laugill's, W. O...................N S
Laurie, Francis, Oakfield, W. O............. .N S
Laurier, J. O., Lachenaie..........................Q
Lauthier, A., Malmaison............................Q
Lavett, Agnes, Adare ....O
Lavoie, R., Mount Carmel ....Q
Lawler, D., Salmon River, W. O. ... .N S
Lawless, Lawrence, London ....O
Lawlor, Wm., Burnley. ....O
Lawrence, George, Honeywood.... ....O
Lawrence, Erastus, Lawrenceville................Q
Lawrence, W., Eastern Harbor, W. O ... ... N S
Lawrence, Chas., Lawrence Factory, W. O....N S
Lawder, R. H., Whitby.........................O
Lawlor, J. B., Alfred ....O

List of Postmasters in Canada.—Continued.

Lawson, James, Farley's Mills, W. O. ....N B
Lawson, George, Dalston ....O
Lawson, David, Cole's Island, W.O... .. ....N B
Laymen, Robert S., Fintona. ....O
Layton, D. L., Meaford ....O
Leake, James R., Morton .... .O
Leemans, Wm., Little River, Coverdale, W.O..N B
Learn, P., senr., Mulgrave.......... ....O
Learned, E., Learned Plain .... Q
Leary, Bridget, Ledge, W. O,....... ....N S
Leask, George, Leaskdale........ ....O
Leavitt, John, Bloomfield, W. O..............N B
Le Baron, B., North Hatley... ....Q
Le Baron, J. B., Hatley ....Q
Le Bau, Léandre, St. Alexis ....Q
Le Bel, J. B., St. Félicité ... .Q
Lebel, Paschal, Armand.........................Q
LeBlanc, J. B., Eel Brook .... .N S
LeBlanc, J. E., St. Charles, River Richelieu ..Q
LeBlanc, M., Tusket Wedge, W. O. ....N S
LeBlanc, F., L'Epiphanie ... ... Q
LeBlanc, J. M. A., Port Royal, W. O.... ....N S
LeBlanc, Olivier, St. Mary's, W. O............N B
LeBlanc, Sylvain, Cocaigne River, W. O. .....N B
LeBlanc, Stephen, River Beaudette ....Q
Lebourveau, Moses, Eaton. .. .. Q
Lecavallier, J. J., St. Laurent, Montreal........Q
Leckie, John, Grey.................. .. ..O
Leclair, Charles, North Lancaster........... ....O
Lederman, Chas., Mannheim ....O
Leduc, Joseph, Vinoy ....Q
Lee, Thomas, Saugeen...........................O
Lee, Horatio, Tabucintac, W. O. .. . .N B
Lee, Frederick F., Mallorytown ....O
Lee, Edward, Marshville ....O
Lee, Robert, Connor. ....O
Lee, Thomas H., Mar ... .O
Lee, Frenière, A. J., Pont de Maskinongé ......Q
Legendre, L. G. A., St. Frederick .... Q
Legère, Fidèle, Grandigue, W.O. .. ..N B
Le Gresly, Francis, Grand Anse, W. O........N B
Le Hane, Thos. S., Ennismore ....O
Leighton, John S., Woodstock Road Station, W. O. ....N B
Leith, Smith, Kingsey Falls........ .... Q
Lellis, Jacob, Salmon Hole W. O ....N S
Lemaire, Ernest, St. Benoit .... Q
Lemay, Joseph, St. Norbert...... ....M
Lemay, V., Bord à Plouffe ....Q
Lemay, M., Lotbinière ....Q
Lemay, Hubert, St. Jude...................... Q
Lemieux, Antoine, Chaudiere Mills ....Q
Lemieux, Joseph Mont Louis ....Q
Lemire dit Marsolait, G., Ste. Béatrix..........Q
Lemmer, Jacob, Fisherville.......................O
Lemon, James, Morley ....O
Lennox, Isaac, Lemon ....O
Lent, J. M., Tusket........................N S
Leonard, M., Leonard's Hill .... Q
Leonard, Adelard E., Ste. Rose.... ....Q
Leonard, Damase, St. Moniquedesdeux Montagnes Q
Lépine, Marcel, St. Théodore ....Q
Lequin, Eli, O'Kanagan Mission ....B C
LeRoy, W. C., Bryson.................... ....Q
LeRoy, Mrs. Nancy, Shedden...... ....O
Leslie Henry, Spry Bay, W. O................N B
Leslie, Guy, Orangeville..........................O
Leslie, William, Puslinch...... ....O
Leslie, W. D., Rupert ....Q
Leslie, George, junr., Leslie. ....O
Leslie, Robert, Kemptville ....O
Leslie, W. T., Port Matoon, W. O. .. ..N S
Lespérance, P., Longueuil................. .Q
Lessard, Eugéne, St. Ephrem de Tring ....
Lessard, Jean, St. Sylvester, East ....
Leslie, Joseph, Toronto. ....
Letts, John, Dunraven...... ....
Levasseur, P. C., St Jean des Chaillons ....
Lévèque, Ulric, Ste. Sophie de Lacorne..........
Lévèque, Théophile, St. Mathieu................
Lévèque, E., St. Alexandre.......................
Lévesque, E., Bagotville...........................
Lévis, Jos. E., St. André Avelin...... ... .
Lewis, Coleman, Addison.... ....
Lewis, George, Fort Erie ....
Lewis, Gains, Lake Road, W. O...............N
Leybourne, Samuel, Kinglake. ....
Lightbody, Andrew, Garafraxa .. ..
Lilley, Charles, Lillie's Corners (sub) ....
Lindabury, John, Windham Centre ....
Lindard, Julius L., Van Winkle..................B
Linden, H., Charlo's Cove, W. O. .... N
Lindsay, Alex., Lindsay, W. O. ....N
Lindsay, Thomas, Williamstown, W. O. ......N
Lindsay, W. S., Woodslee.........................
Lindsay, Thos., Chignonaise River, W.O. .....N
Lingley, John, Waverley . ...
Linton, John, Humber ....
Lipset, John, Charlestown, W. O. .... N
Lister, George, Manners Sutton, W. O..........N
Little, Peter, Moffatt.............................
Little, Thomas, Omagh........ ....
Little, J., Head of Mill Stream, W. O........N
Little, J., Aylwin............... ....
Littlewood, James, Littlewood, W. O ....N
Livingston, Donald, Upper Settlement of West River, W. O ....N
Livingston, John, Livingstone's Cove, W. O...N
Livingston, Oliver, Carlisle...... . ...
Livingston, John, Silver Islet ....
Lloyd, Jared, White Rose ....
Lloyd, Benjamin, King...........................
Lock, William, McDonald's Corners. ....
Lock, Charles, Brinston's Corners ....
Lockhart, D., Leicester, W. O ....N
Lockhart, John, Donegal, W. O .. ..N
Lockhart, James, Clarke...........................
Lockwood, J. E., Canard, W. O ....N
Lockwood, Joseph, Brighton.......................
Lodge, W. B., Maccan Mountain, W. O. ......N
Logan, Dougal, Loganville, W. O. ....N
Lohr, Daniel, Phillipsburg, West ....
Long, Wm., l'Amaroux.............................
Long, Wesley, Maxwell.............................
Longheed, Samuel, Molesworth.....................
Longley, George C., Maitland. . ...N
Loranger, L. L. J., St. Sauveur..................
Lord, Joseph, Leclercville.........................
Lord, Donald M. Newbridge, W. O ....N
Losie, Joseph, Collins Bay... ....
Lothrop, Allan, Westbury ... .
Lothrop, F. H., North Stoke ....
Loucy, Thomas, Grand Pabos ....
Loughrey, Owen, Beaurivage ....
Loughrey, W. Petersville, West (sub)... ...
Loughrin, James, Speedside ....
Loucks, H. L., Hull ....
Lounsbury, James, Lewis Mountain, W. O....N
Love, Hugh, senr., Hill's Green...................
Love, Margt., Basswood Ridge, W. O..........N
Lovely, John, Florenceville East...............N
Lowrie James, Veighton.... ....
Lucas, Jas. Cocaigne. ....N
Lumley, W. G., Glencoe.........................
Lundy, George B., Balmoral........................
Lupien, L., St. Ursule ....

List of Postmasters in Canada.—Continued.

Lussier, Trefflé, Verchères .... Q
Lussier, Revd. L., Ste. Emilie de l'Energie... .. Q
Luttis, David, Indian Harbor, W. O.......... N S
Lyman, H., Scotland.............................. O
Lyman, Horace, Granby........................... Q
Lynch, John, Green River, W. O............. N B
Lynch, Walter, Brome .... Q
Lynch, John, Allumette Island .... Q
Lynn, James, Bushfield .... O
Lynn, Joseph, Linton .... O
Lyon, R. A., Michael's Bay........................ O
Lyon, W. D., Milton West .... O
Lyttle, James, Newboyne............................ O
Lyttle, Oliver, Barrington .... Q

McAfee, Andrew, Seeley's Mills, W. O........ N B
McAfee, Henry, Walkerville........................ O
McAlister, Donald, New Mills .... N B
McAlister, D., Comber................................ O
McAllister, James, Chute à Blondeau .... O
McAlpine, Nevin, Washademoak, W. O ...... N B
McArdle, Joseph, Ronaldsay .... O
McArthur, John, Amiens............................. O
McArthur, Crosbie, Beauharnois................. Q
McArthur, Peter, Dalesville........................ Q
McAskill, Hugh, Little Narrows, W. O.... ... N S
McAulay, T. H., Centreton .... O
McAulay, John, Ventnor.............................. O
McAulay, Angus, False Bay Beach, W. O..... N S
McAulay, M., South Side Basin of River Denis, W. O.. N S
McBain, Thomas, New Town .... N S
McBean, D., Aberarder............................... O
McBeath, J. T., Wexford............................. O
McBrady, Daniel, Audley .... O
McBrane, Archibald, Missouri .... O
McBrayne, C., Botany .... O
McBride, John, Sunbury .... O
McBurney, R., Erie.................................... O
McCabe, Edward, Wheatland .... Q
McCaffery, John, Box Grove .... O
McCall, D. W., Walsh .... O
McCall, George D., Victoria........................ O
McCallum, John, Avoca.............................. Q
McCann, William, Oak Hill, W. O.......... N B
McCarroll, North Bruce.............................. O
McCarron, Charles, Assametquagan........... Q
McCarthy, Joseph, Lower River Inhabitants, W. O.. N S
McCarty, N. C., Thamesford .... O
McCaul, John, Durham .... N S
McCaw, H. H., Prince Albert .... O
McLellan, W., Elliott .... O
McLellan, A. W., Great Village .... N S
McLelland, John, Parry Sound .... O
McColl, Duncan, jun., Clachan .... O
McColl, John, St. Joseph du Lac .... O
McCollum, Peter T., Claude .... O
McConnell, W., Condon Settlement, W. O..... N S
McConney, Farrell, Villette .... Q
McConnisky, John, Pubnico Beach, W. O..... N S
McCool, James, Fort William .... Q
McCoppen, James, Port Robinson .... O
McCordie, James, Jura.............................. O
McCormack, Samuel, Saulmerville, W. O...... N S
McCormack, William, Marsville .... O
McCormick, J. D., St. Alban....................... Q
McCormick, Robert, Vivian........................ O
McCormick, J. M., Macton.......................... O
McCracken, N., Valentia............................. O
McCready, John E., Avondale, W. O......... N B
McCrindle, James, Lurgan .... O
McCubbin, William, Belle Rivière .... N S

McCully, William, Truro........................ N S
McCurdy, John, Kirkton.............................. O
McCutcheon, John, Clarendon Settlement..... N B
McCutcheon, J. Chilliwack .... B C
McCutcheon, Hugh, Leeds Village.............. Q
McCutcheon, James, Sonora, W. O. .... N S
McCutcheon, James, Crosshill .... O
McDermid, D., Pine River .... O
McDermitt, Alexander, Portage River, W. O.. N B
McDonald, Chas., Baddeck Bay, W. O........ N S
McDonald, Mrs C., French River, W. O...... N S
McDonald, Murdoch, Groves Point, W. O.... N S
McDonald, John, La Guerre .... Q
McDonald, J., Lake Megantic .... Q
McDonald, Alex., Leitch's Creek, W. O....... N S
McDonald, Mrs Mary, Lime Rock, W. O ..... N S
McDonald, John, Hunter's Mountain, W. O... N S
McDonald, Daniel, Little Glace Bay .... N S
McDonald, Joseph, Little Lorraine, W. O.... N S
McDonald, Donald, Mabou Harbor, W. O..... N S
McDonald, Robert, Malagash, W. O........... N S
McDonald, L., Malagawatch, W. O............ N S
McDonald, Angus, Caledonia, St. Mary's, W. O. N S
McDonald, James, West Bay...................... N S
McDonald, Peter, Whycocomah.................. N S
Macdonald, D. D., Bailey's Brook, W. O...... N S
McDonald, Robert, Avondale, W. O .... N S
McDonald, Duncan, Vernon......................... O
McDonald, Archibald, Cape North, W. O...... N S
McDonald, William, Blue Mountain, W. O.... N S
McDonald, Alexander, Shea's River, W. O..... N S
McDonald, James H., Sherbrooke .... N S
McDonald, A., Sable .... O
McDonald, Donald, North Shore, W. O....... N S
McDonald, John, Ohio, W. O .... N S
McDonald, George, Northfield...................... O
McDonald, John, Niel's Harbor, W. O........ N S
McDonald, Donald, Middle Settlement, River Inhabitants, W. O.................................. N S
McDonald, James, Piedmont Valley, W. O ... N S
McDonald, Colin, Black River, W. O.......... N S
McDonald, Michael, Upper Settlement of River Dennis, W. O... N S
McDonald, Angus, Upper Washabuck, W. O.. N S
McDonald, J. R., Clontarf .... O
McDonald, John R., Cobden .... O
McDonald, Allan, Catalone, W. O .... N S
McDonald, Robert, Cape George............... N S
McDonald, Donald, Cape George (North side), W. O.. N S
McDonald, Chas., Lake Ainslie (East side).... N S
McDonald, C., Sumerville, W. O .... N S
McDonald, James, Brookville, W. O .... N S
McDonald, Michael, Irish Cove, W. O .... N S
McDonald, D., Elmsville, W. O .... N S
McDonald, James, West Merigonishe .... N S
McDonnell, Allan, South West Mabou, W. O . N S
McDonnell, Duncan, Vancleek Hill .... O
McDonnell, Duncan, Long Point, W. O ...... N S
McDonnell, Hugh, Judique, W. O .... N S
McDonnell, Mrs. Mary, St. Raphael, West..... O
McDonnell, George, Cornwall .... O
McDonnell, J. R., Brompton Falls .... Q
McDonnell, James, Middle Settlement of South River, W. O .... N S
McDonnell, Robert, Clearview .... O
McDougald, Alexander, Greenfield .... O
McDougall, D., Lockside, W. O .... N S
McDougall, Col., McDougall Settlement, W. O. N B
McDougal, Rod., Hay's River, W. O .... N B
McDougall, James, Marshy Hope, W. O..... N S
McDougall, W., Brewster............................. O
McDougall, Niel, Scotch Settlement, W. O.... N B

McDougall, M., Christmas Island, W.O ......N S
McDougall, Donald, Grand Mira North, W.O.N S
McEachan, D., Sight Point, W.O...... .....N S
McEachern, John, South side of Wycocomah
Bay, W.O... ... .N S
McEachern, Archibald, Moulie's River, W.O.N B
McEachern, Angus, Islay ....O
McEachern, Alex., Boom, W.O..............N S
McElroy, Wm. Joseph, Alma ....O
McElroy, Henry, Concord ....O
McEvoy, John, Pomeroy Ridge, W.O........N B
McEwan, George, Salt Springs, W.O ....N B
McEwan, M., Chockfish, W.O......... .....N B
McEwen, E., Franktown ....O
McFadden, M., New Ireland Road, W.O.....N B
McFarland, Henry, Campbell Settlement
W.O. .... N B
McFarland, W. J., Markdale ....O
McFarlane, Peter, Nashwaaksis, W.O. ......N B
McFarlane, Robert, Rosetta ....O
McFarlane, James, Conquerall Bank, W.O....N S
McFarlane, Peter, Kelso. ....Q
McFarlane, Daniel, Haliburton........... ....O
McGarry, Owen, New Ross Road, W.O.......N S
McGauvran, James, Treadwell..................O
McGee, Joseph, Back Bay, W.O. ....N B
McGibbon, Alex., Brownsburg. ....Q
McGibbon, William, Point Wolf, W.O.......N B
McGie, D. B., Esquimaux Point..............Q
McGill, David, Janetville ....O
McGill, J., Rusagornis Station, W.O.........N B
McGill, James, Burton.. ... .O
McGillis, Angus D., Harrison Corners... ..... O
McGillis, Albert, Williamston ....O
McGillavray, C., Glen Road, W.O....... ....N S
McGillivray, Archibald, Lake Vale, W.O.....N S
McGillivray, Hugh, Harbor Road, W.O ......N S
McGillivray, Hugh, East Bay, W.O ....N S
McGilleroy, John, Knoydart, W.O...........N S
McGinnis, Donald, Schomberg...................O
McGowen, W., Little Lepreaux, W.O........N B
McGregor, Mrs. D., Garden of Eden, W.O....N S
McGregor, Daniel, Wyebridge ....O
McGregor, David, South Gower........... ... .O
McGregor, John, Matawatchan..................O
McGregor, D., Tennyson................ ......O
McGregor, Alex., Big Island, W.O...... ....N S
McHaffey, Wm., North Goggins, W.O.......N B
McHarry, H., Orleans.... .. ..O
McHenny, J., Victoria, W.O..................N S
McInnis, Charles, Aros ....O
McInnis, N., Tiverton........ ....O
McInnis, Hugh, Point of Cape, W.O..........N S
McInnis, Angus, Lake Ainslie, W.O ....N S
McIntosh, B., Westover.........................O
McIntosh, P. N., Bookton.......................O
McIntosh, Angus, Bay St. Lawrence, W.O....N S
McIntosh, D., Coldsprings........ . ...O
McIntyre, Nichol, Bervie..,... ....O
McIntyre, A., River Dennis, W.O.. ... .N S
McIntyre, W. H., Rockliffe (sub)..... ....O
McIntyre, D., Crinan ....O
McIntyre, Michael, Boisdale Chapel, W.O ....N S
McIsaac, Donald, Mull River, W.O..........N S
McJanet, Robert, Yarm..................... .. Q
McKay, George W., Middle Southampton, W.O.N B
McKay, F. S., Papineauville....................O
McKay, George, Mount Thom, W.O...........N S
McKay, A., Morewood.......... ....O
McKay, James, St. James ....M
McKay, John, Millsville, W.O ... .N S
McKay, D., Big Harbor, W.O ....N S
McKay, Robert, Guysborough Intervale, W.O.N S

McKay, Angus, Rog
McKay, Cornelieus,
McKay, John, Six M
McKay, Anna M., A
McKay, Mrs. J., W
W.O..............
McKay, John, Uppe
River, W.O.......
McKay, George, Ulst
McKay, L., Speitche
McKay, Donald, Sai
McKay, John, Argyl
McKay, John, Cape
McKay, W. J. Earl
McKay, D. E., South
McKay, G. D., Midd
McKay, James, Mid
McKee, William, Co
McKechnie, R., Sha
McKeen, Abraham,
McKeen, J. G., Por
McKeen, George, Ge
McKeggie, James H.
McKellar, D., Kilm
McKendrick, M., K
McKenney, Cyrus B
McKenney, Thomas,
McKenzie, George,
McKenzie, William,
McKenzie, N. D.,
McKenzie, Alex., R
McKenzie, M., St.
McKenzie, A. M., T
McKenzie, Angus, A
McKenzie, James, U
McKenzie Alex., M
McKenzie, Thos., M
McKenzie, David, N
McKenzie, John, N
McKenzie, Mrs. Jes
McKenzie, K., Kem
McKenzie, Wm. L.,
McKenzie, John, Sa
McKenzie, J. R., Sh
McKenzie, R., South
O. ....
McKenzie, Archibal
McKenzie, H., Stell
McKenzie, Arthur
McKenzie, William,
O. ....
McKenzie, F., Birk
McKenzie, Archiba
McKenzie, Kenneth
McKeown, James W
McKeune, J., Augl
McKie, Thomas, W
McKiel, Albert, Gr
McKillican, B., jun.
McKillican, Wm.,
McKillop, A., Cots
McKillop, Duncan,
McKim, Robert, So
McKinlay, Robert,
McKinly, Samuel, (
McKinney, Richard
McKinnon, John, G
McKinnon, John,
W.O. ....
McKinnon, John, C
McKinnon, John,
McKinnon, Duncan
McKinnon, Donald

List of Postmasters in Canada.—Continued.

McKinnon, J. P., East Bay, North Side, W. O. **N S**
McKnight, F. H., Burnt Church. W.O. **N B**
McLachlan, Donald, East Scotch Settlement W.O. **N B**
McLachlin, H. F. Palmer Rapids **O**
McLarin, Wm., Port au Persil **Q**
McLaren, J. H, Lower Argyle, W. O. **N S**
McLaren, Alex., Osceola **O**
McLaren, John, Vilanova **O**
McLaren, James, Wakefield **Q**
McLaren, Donald, Cape Rich **O**
McLaren, Donald, Chezzetcook W.O. **N S**
McLatchey, E., Lower Horton **N S**
McLaughlan, Duncan, Calton **O**
McLaughlin, A. A., Norland **O**
McLaughlin, C., Apto **O**
McLauren, P., Riceville **O**
McLean, Donald, Malignant Cove. W.O. **N S**
McLean, Donald, Big Bank, W. O. **N S**
McLean, Malcolm, McKay's Point, W O. **N S**
McLean. W. H., Eardley **Q**
McLean, Allan, Grand Anse, W. O. **N S**
McLean, Alexander Henry, Kimberley **O**
McLean, Richard, Mount Uniacke **N S**
McLean, Archibald, Point à Pic (sub) **Q**
McLean, Hector, Dunvegan **O**
McLean, Hector, Knapdale **O**
McLean, James, Escuminac, W. O. **N B**
McLean, A., Cheviot **O**
McLean, Malcolm, Walkerton **O**
McLean, Mrs. C. A., Toledo **O**
McLean, Donald, Scarboro' **O**
McLearn, Joseph, Five Mile River, W. O. **N S**
McLeay, Murdo, Watford **O**
McLees, Robert, Soda Creek **B C**
McLeish, Robert, Branchton **O**
McLellan, Alex., Broad Cove Chapel, W.O. **N S**
McLellan, Samuel, Noel Shore, W. O. **N S**
McLellan, A. W., Great Village **N S**
McLellan, Miss Margaret, Port Rowan **O**
McLennan, John, Upper Settlement of Middle River, W. O. **N S**
McLennan, Donald, Indian Brook, W. O. **N S**
McLennan, A. S., Fournier **O**
McLennan, John, Upper Margaree, W. O. **N S**
McLeod, Charles L., Middle River, W. O. **N S**
McLeod, Robert G., Mount Charles **O**
McLeod, Robert, New Larig, W. O. **N S**
McLeod, Malcolm, Bucklaw, W. O. **N S**
McLeod, William, Kirkhill **O**
McLeod, Donald, Broad Cove (Marsh), W. O. **N S**
McLeod, George, Middle River, W.O. **N S**
McLeod, John Carsonville, W. O. **N B**
McLeod, Hugh, Cape John, W. O. **N S**
McLeod, George, Portsmouth **O**
McLeod, William, Round Hill, W.O. **N B**
McLeod, George, McLeod's Mills, W. O. **N B**
McLeod, Isaac, Broad Cove (Intervale) W. O. **N S**
McLeod, D. W., Enniskillen **O**
McLeod, Malcolm, Big Brook, W. O. **N S**
McLeod, C. F., Belleisle Creek, W. O. **N B**
McLeod, Malcolm, Big Intervale (Margaree, W. O.) **N S**
McLeod, Donald, Newbridge, W. O. **N S**
McMannis, John, South Bolton **Q**
McManus, Mark, Chesley **O**
McMaster, Angus, Low Point, W. O. **N S**
McMasters, D. J., Queensville, W. O. **N S**
McMillan, D., Glen, W.O. **N S**
McMillan, John, Breadalbane, W. O. **N B**
McMillan, John, Harriettsville **O**
McMillan, Patrick, Grand Falls **N B**
McMillan, Duncan G., South Finch **O**
McMillan, Donald, Upper Settlement of Baddeck River, W. O. **N S**
McMillan, Allan, jun., Isaac's Harbor **N S**
McMillan, A., King Creek **O**
McMillan, William, Kirkwall **O**
McMillan, John, Avonbank **O**
McMillen, John, Hornby **O**
McMillen, Miles, Boiestown, W. O. **N B**
McMonagle, H., Sussex Vale **N B**
McMurchy, M., Tarbert **O**
McMurray, L., Gladstone **O**
McNab, J, McM., Claremont **O**
McNaughton, John, St. Patrick's Channel, W. O. **N S**
McNaughton, R., Black River, W. O. **N B**
McNeil, Hector, Marion Bridge, W. O. **N S**
McNeil, J. S., Grand Narrows. W. O. **N S**
McNeil, John, Giant's Lake, W. O. **N S**
McNeil, Malcolm, Hillsborough, C. B. W. O. **N S**
McNeil, Hugh, Head of South River Lake, W. O. **N S**
McNeil, Charles, North Range Corner, W. O. **N S**
McNichol, Allen, Allensville **O**
McNiel, John, Wallace Ridge, W. O. **N S**
McNiel, Michael, L'Ardoise, W. O. **N S**
McNiel, Peter, Sillery Cove **Q**
McNiel, Malcolm, North Side of Basin, River Dennis, W. O. **N S**
McNiel, Moses, Rosedale **O**
McNeill, Stephen, Beaver Cove, W. O. **N S**
McPhail, Alex., Pictou **N S**
McPhail, Hugh, Cartwright **O**
McPhee, Donald, Whitevale **O**
McPherson, James, Rama **O**
McPherson, Alexander, River Charlo, W. O. **N B**
McPherson, Allan, Largei **O**
McPherson, Charles, Oronocto **N B**
McPherson, James, Rivière Raisin **O**
McPherson, G. S., Ossian **O**
McPherson, John, New Gairloch. W. O. **N S**
McPherson, John, Cross Roads, Ohio, W. O. **N S**
McPherson, Robert, Speyside **O**
McQuaid, J. C., Hastings, W. O **N B**
McQuain, Alexander, Kewstoke **N S**
McQuarrie, A., Cape Mabou, W. O **N S**
McQueen, Mrs. M. A., North Pelham **O**
McQueen, James, Fergus **O**
McRae, Mrs., Sandfield **O**
McRae, Hugh, Strathburn **O**
McRae, Alex. E., Glennevis **O**
McRae, Donald, Burnstown **O**
McRae, Duncan, Bolsover **O**
McRae, Finlay, Lower Settlement, Middle River W.O **NS**
McRae, Hector, Crawford **O**
McRae, William, Duncan **O**
McRae, C. J., Sierra **O**
McRae, Alex., Baddeck Bridge, W. O **N S**
McTaggart, John, Kirkfield **O**
McVey, John, Dungiven. W. O. **N B**
McVicar, Miss C., Fort William **O**
McVicar, Morris, Wanstead. **O**
McWilliams, Albert, Harold **O**
Macaulay, John, Venosta **Q**
Macdonald, John, Vellore **O**
Macdonald, D. A., Alexandria **O**
Macdonald, Norman, Addington Forks, W. O. **N S**
Macfadden, Urian, Edgecombe **O**
Machell, John, St. Sylvester **Q**
Mack, I. N., Mill's Village **N S**
Mackay, William, Renfrew **O**
Mackay, Levi, Kinsale **O**
Mackelcan, G. I., Brisbane **O**

List of Postmasters in Canada.—Continued.

Millett, Benjamin, Marriott's Cove, W. O.....N S
Mackclean, G. J., Brisbane.....O
Mackereth, John, St. Canute.....Q
Mackey, Heli, Northfield, W.O.....N S
Mackintosh, Henry B., Strathroy.....O
Macklem, J. S., Chippewa.....O
MacNider, John, Petit Métis.....Q
Maconchy, Thos. Gilford.....O
Macrea, George, St. Sylvester, East.....Q
Macready, A., Harriston.....O
Macy, J. F., Corbett.....O
Maddon, Hugh, Loughborough.....O
Mader, Jeremiah, New Canada, W.O.....N S
Magoon, Aaron, Magoon's Point.....Q
Maguire, John, Steep Creek, W. O.....N S
Maguire, William, Franklin.....O
Maher, Philip, Richmond Station.....Q
Mahew, Robert, Renforth.....O
Main, William, Canterbury Station.....N B
Main, William, Cherry Creek.....O
Mair, Charles, Portage la Prairie.....M
Major, Charles, jun., Monte Bello.....Q
Major, Edward, Glen Major.....O
Maher, Thos., Pockmouche, W.O.....N B
Malbœuf, Odile, Côte des Neiges.....Q
Malcolm, John, Jun., Cariboo Cove, W.O.....N S
Mallet, H. S., Gilbert Cove.....N S
Mallet, N., Chateauguay.....Q
Malone, Timothy, Petersville, W. O.....N B
Maloney, Ernest V., Fitch Bay.....Q
Mamely, Michael, East Hawkesbury.....O
Mann, William, Yarmouth Centre.....O
Manning, Johnson, Hebb's Cross, W. O.....N S
Mansfield, Geo., Cashmere.....O
Manson, David A., Mansonville Potton.....Q
Manuel, C., Upper Haynesville, W. O.....N B
Marchand, Edouard, St. Jerome.....Q
Marchment, Edwin, Rivière Trois Pistoles.....Q
March, David, Port Granby.....O
Marcotte, Joseph U., Ste. Anne de la Pe'rad.....Q
Marcoux, Isidore, Versailles.....Q
Marcoux, T., Cedars.....Q
Margeson, T. A., Margaretsville, W. O.....N S
Marion, Joseph, St. Paul l'Hermite.....Q
Markham, Alfred, Markhamville, W.O.....N B
Marks, Robert, Brucefield.....O
Marquis, P. C., St. André.....Q
Marsh, Jacob, Coldstream.....N B
Marsh, A., Consecon.....O
Marshall, James, Trout River.....Q
Marshall, W., Huntingdon.....Q
Marshall, Obiah, Washago.....O
Martel, Anthony, Cow Bay.....N S
Martell, Charles, Mira Gut, W. O.....N S
Martin, E. B., Cedar Hall.....Q
Martin, Amasa, Martinville.....Q
Martin, Robert, Sydney.....N S
Martin, James, Belleville, W. O.....N B
Martin, E. D., Warden.....Q
Martin, N. C., Upper Bedford.....Q
Martin, Octave, Avignon.....Q
Martin, Elie, St. Arsene.....Q
Martineau, J. E., St. Alphonse.....Q
Martyn, William, Enfield.....O
Mason, Mary, Donegal.....O
Mason, George, Beaulac.....Q
Mason, Charles, Peachville.....O
Mason, James, Drumquin.....O
Mason, Thomas, Johnston, W. O.....N B
Masters, Wm., Upper Rawdon, W. O.....N S
Masterson, Lackey, St. Andrew's, West.....O
Mastin, I. B., Lavender.....O
Mather, James, Menie.....O
Mather, John, Otter Lake.....Q
Mather, John W., Fenello.....O
Matheson, George, Tavistock.....O
Matheson, D., Embro.....O
Matheson, J., St. Esprit, W. O.....N S
Matheson, James, Lower L'Ardoise, W. O.....N S
Matheson, W. H., Upper Woods Harbor, W. O.....N S
Matthews, E. J., Flinton.....O
Matthews, J., Acton.....O
Matthieu, J. B., St. Urbain.....Q
Maudsley, Henry, Moorefield.....O
Maxwell, W. A., Head Lake.....O
May, Thomas, Long Island Locks.....O
May, James, Dundalk.....O
Mayberry, Richard, Maberly.....O
Mayrand, Z., St. Phillippe.....Q
Meacham, J. H., Belleville.....O
Meagher, Joseph, Carleton.....Q
Meecham, Eli, Elginburg.....O
Meek, Agnes, Alton.....O
Meen, Frederick, Greenwood.....O
Meikle, G. L. Lachute.....Q
Melançon, M., Port Acadia, W. O.....N S
Melick, Jonas R., Warner.....O
Mellis, Robert, Kippen.....O
Mellon, Samuel H., Sillsville.....O
Mellow, W. J., Gretna.....O
Mellville, Andrew, Nottawa.....O
Menhennick, John, Putnam.....O
Mercier, H., St. Guillaume d'Upton.....Q
Mercier, Joseph, Ste. Hénédine.....O
Mercer, H. M., Lawrence Station, W. O.....N B
Merritt, John, Pelham Union.....O
Messier, Ambrose, Belle Alodie.....Q
Mesner, F. X., Formosa.....O
Messer, John, Bluevale.....O
Metcalfe, Alfred, Roseneath.....O
Meunier, C., Starnesboro'.....Q
Meunier, François, Canrobert.....Q
Meyer, George E., Glenmeyer.....O
Merzeroll, Nicholas, Point Sapin, W. O.....N B
Michaud, B., Ste. Hélène.....Q
Michaud, Peter, St. Hilaire, W.O.....N B
Michaud, Maximilian, Burrard's Inlet.....B C
Michaud, Miss Adée, Notre Dame du Portage.....Q
Micheuer, Isaac, Lowbanks.....O
Middlemas, George, Caledonia Corner.....N S
Middleton, George, Wheatley.....O
Mignault, Joseph E., St. Dennis, River Richelieu.....Q
Milburn, John, Peabody.....O
Miles, George, Mouth of Keswick, W.O.....N B
Milette, Benjamin, Wotton.....Q
Millar, James, Magnetawan.....O
Millar, Miss C. M., Drummondville, East.....Q
Miller, Hugh, Glassville, W.O.....N B
Miller, B. B., Wiarton.....O
Miller, Robert, Zimmerman.....O
Miller, M. G., Teviotdale.....O
Miller, James, Ulverton.....Q
Miller, James, St. Luce.....Q
Miller, John P., Carleton, W.O.....N S
Miller, William, Peninsula, Gaspé.....Q
Miller, H. J., Corunna.....O
Miller, Hiram, Miller's Creek, W.O.....N S
Miller, Caleb, Mount Hanly, W.O.....N S
Miller, Jonathan, Benmiller.....O
Miller, John, Blytheswood.....O
Miller, David W., Sumas.....B C
Miller, Peter, Switzerville.....O

List of Postmasters in Canada.—Continued.

Millett, Alexis, La Présentation .... Q
Millett, Edouard, St. George de Windsor...... Q
Milligan, Thos. J., Baltimore.............. O
Millin, Arthur, Newcombe .... O
Millington, Joseph, Sydenham Place .... Q
Milloy, Colin, Newport .... O
Mills, Stephen, Lewisville, W.O.............. N B
Mills, Wm. B., Arden...................... O
Mills, George E., Tedish, W.O............... N B
Mills, George, Armstrong's Corner, W.O...... N B
Mills, G. C., Playfair..................... O
Mills, John, Lorraine...................... O
Milne, Alexander, Langford.................. O
Milne, Thos., Copetown..................... O
Milne, John, Agincourt..................... O
Milner, Thomas, Parker's Cove, W.O.......... N S
Milson, J. H., Whalen...................... O
Milward, Thomas F., Stormont, W.O.......... N S
Miscampbell, Andrew, Allendale............. O
Mitchell, Mrs. M., Cook's Brook, W.O........ N S
Mitchell, Arthur, Fordwich................. O
Mitchell, David, Marie Joseph, W.O.......... N S
Mitchell, James, Mactaquack, W.O............ N B
Mitchell, John, Metz....................... O
Miville, Narcisse, Ste. Modeste............ Q
Moffatt, Alexander, Pembroke................ O
Moffatt, Henry, Pendleton.................. O
Moffitt, Chas., Kinmount.................... O
Moncion, L., Angers........................ Q
Monkhouse, Joseph, Altona.................. O
Monkman, John, Eagles Nest................. M
Monteith, Robert, Farquhar.................. O
Montminy, T. St. Charles, River Boyer....... O
Mood, S. K., Lower Wood Harbor, W.O........ N S
Moon, Robert J., Medonte................... O
Moore, Gilbert, Norwich.................... O
Moore, P. C., Moore's Station.............. Q
Moore, Alexander, Mechanics' Settlement, W.O. N B
Moore, John, Shinemicas Bridge............. N S
Moore, J. S., Upper Economy, W.O............ N S
Moore, Mathias, Falkenburg.................. O
Moore, Alfred, Carnarvon................... O
Moore, Thomas, Waubuno...................... O
Moore, Simon, Burnt River................... O
Moran, Thomas, Maidstone................... O
Morden, W. H., North Port.................. O
Morden, H J., Greensville.................. O
Morgan, William, Pleasant Hill.............. O
Morgan, Ira, Ormond........................ O
Moriarty, James, Kinkora................... O
Morin, B., St. Isidore, Dorchester.......... Q
Morin, A., St. Roch des Aulnais............. Q
Morin, P., Bienville....................... Q
Morin, Delphin, Chantelle.................. Q
Morin, Alexis, Vauban...................... Q
Morris, John H., Warwick................... O
Morris, David, Ste. Thérèse de Blainville .... Q
Morris, J. K., Rondeau..................... O
Morris, R., Avening........................ O
Morris, Nathan B., Advocate Harbor .... N S
Morrow, John, Dacre........................ O
Morrow, Joseph, Ratho'..................... O
Morse, John G., Sandy Cove.................. N S
Morse, Francis E., Lowville................ O
Morton, E., Middlefield, W.O................ N S
Morton, George, Penobsquis................. N B
Morton, James, Morton's Corner, W.O......... N S
Morton, William, St. Ola................... O
Moss, James, Indian Point, W.O.............. N S
Mosher, Daniel, St. Croix, W.O.............. N S
Mosher, Joseph, Mosherville, W.O............ N S
Moss, James, Port Maitland.................. O
Mossip, John, Union Hill................... O
Mossman, Edward, Kingsbury, W.O............. N S
Mott, Isaac, Blessington.................... O
Mott, Amos, Central Cambridge, W.O.......... N B
Mowat, Andrew, St. Andrews................. M
Mowat, John, Deeside........................ Q
Moyer, Moses, Breslaw...................... O
Moyer, H. W., Campden...................... O
Moyer, J. G., Bloomingdale.................. O
Moxon, Thomas, Rawdon, W.O.................. N S
Mulkins, Henry, Simcoe..................... O
Mulrine, Chas., Emigrant Road, W.O.......... N B
Mulvihill, Revd. J., St. Laurent............ M
Munro, Alex., Lanark....................... O
Munro, John, Watson's Corners.............. O
Munro, William, West River.................. N S
Munro, A., Boulardorie..................... N S
Munro, William, Kilmaurs.................... S
Munro, John C., Grantley.................... O
Munro, M., Munro's, W.O..................... N S
Munsie, William, Nobleton................... O
Munsie, James, Caledon, East................ O
Murchie, Alex., Winthrop.................... O
Murchie, Donald, Doyle Settlement, W.O...... N B
Murchie, J. E., Benton, W.O................. N B
Murchison, Hector, Grand River, W.O......... N S
Murdoch, Mrs. Christy A., Cain's River, W.O. N B
Muir, Michael, Sooke....................... B C
Murphy, John, Mulmer........................ O
Murphy, Patrick, Stoco..................... O
Murphy, William, Sarnia..................... O
Murphy, J., Waugh's River, W.O.............. N S
Murphy, Patrick, Caldwell................... O
Murphy, Thos., Chipman's Brook, W.O......... N S
Murray, William G., Arnott.................. O
Murray, John, Esquesing..................... O
Murray, James, Hay.......................... O
Murray, John, Glen Murray................... Q
Murray, William, Ste. Brigide............... Q
Murray, John G., Port Richmond, W.O......... N S
Murray, Joseph, Murray's Corner, W.O........ N B
Murray, Robert, St. Helen's................. O
Murray, John, Spence's Bridge............... B C
Mussells, William, Webber's, W.O............ N S
Musson, Thomas, Islington................... O
Mustard, John, Ashworth..................... O
Mutchmore, J. T., Oneida.................... O

List of Postmasters in Canada.—Continued.

Nelson, G. W., Dickson's Store, W. O. ....N S
Nelson, John, Trafalgar, W. O. ....N S
Nelson, John, Ludlow, W. O. ....N B
Nethercott, John, Eden ....O
Newcomb, J. S., Upper Perreaux, W. O. ....N S
Newcomb, R. A., Bridgewater ....N S
Newcomb, W. F., Avonport Station, W. O. ......N S
Newell, John, Black Bank ....O
Newhall, Wilbert, Hunterstown ....Q
Newman, W. J., Morganston ....O
Newsome, George, Kilmarnock ....O
Newton, John, Limehouse ....O
Nickerson, E., Wood Harbor, W. O. ....N S
Nichol, Alexander, Jackson Road, W. O. ....N S
Nichol, Peter M., St. Mary's ....O
Nichols, S. J., Berwick Station, W. O. ....N S
Nicholls, D., Nicholl's Corner, W. O. ....N S
Nicholls, William, New Germany, W. O. ....N S
Nicholson, Donald, Barney's River, W. O. .....N S
Nickerson, S. W., Shag Harbor, W. O. ....N S
Nicholson, A., Concord, W. O. ....N S
Nicklin, J., Morningdale Mills ....O
Nicol, John, Nicolston ....O
Nispel, Conrad, Preston ....O
Niven, Revd. Hugh, Herdman's Corners ....Q
Noble, John, Park Hill ....O
Noble, Colin, Stornoway ....Q
Noble, Robert, Hardwicke, W. O. ....N B
Noonan, Daniel, North-West Cove, W. O. ....N S
Norman, R. M., Mill Bridge ....O
Normandin, A., St. Jean Baptiste de Montréal ..Q
Normandin, Louis, Boucherville ....Q
Normansell, James, Kootenay ....B C
Northey, Richard, Selwyn ....O
Northy, William, Wilmur ....O
Northmore, Joseph, Cataraqui ....O
Nowlan, John G., Havelock, W. O. ....N S
Noxen, Richard, Hillier ....O
Nugent, Miss D., Grand Baie ....Q
Nugent, Mrs. C., West Quaco ....N B
Nutt, David, Nutt's Corners ....Q
Nye, D. T. R., Philipsburg, East ....Q

Oaks, Albert, New Albany, W. O. ....N S
O'Brien, E. R., St. George ....N B
O'Brien, F. X., Repentigny ....Q
O'Brien, Osmond, Noel, W. O. ....N S
O'Brien, Margaret, Beauport ....Q
O'Connor, H. B. C., Riversdale ....O
Odell, W. H., Belmont ....O
O'Donell, R. Ferris, W. O. ....N B
O'Donnell, John, North Onslow ....Q
O'Flynn, E. D., Madoc ....O
Ogden, C. K., Three Rivers ....Q
Ogilvie, Henry, Long Point, W. O. ....N S
O'Heir, M., St Gabriel de Brandon ....Q
O'Keif, Cornelius, Okanagon ....B C
O'Leary, Michael, West Newdy Quoddy ....N S
Oliver, A., Rockburn ....Q
Oliver, Edward, Ashburn ....O
Oliver, John, Dewitville ....Q
Olivier, Louis, Black River Station ....Q
Olmstead, Albert D., Aroostook, W. O. ....N B
O'Loane, L. T., Stratford ....O
O'Meara, James, Lombardy ....O
O'Meara, M., Navan ....O
O'Niel, Samuel, Grosvenor, W. O. ....N S
O'Neill, Michael, Downerville ....O
O'Neill, Thomas, Salmon River (Lake Settlement) W. O. ....N S
Orchard, John G., Orchard ....O
Ord, George, Ilderton ....O
Orman, George, Porter's Lake, W. O. ....N S

Orr, Allen, Seaton ....O
Orr, James, Morrisbank ....O
Orr, James E., Lynden ....O
Osborne, Sydney, Renton ....O
Osbornes, J. B., Beamsville ....O
Osgood, W. A., St. John's, East ....Q
Ostrander, G. A., Point Traverse ....O
Ostrom, Henry, Moira ....O
O'Sullivan, Cornelius, Meyersburg ....O
Ouellet, L., St. Onezime ....Q
Oulton, Thomas E., Westmoreland Point ....N B
Oulton, Thomas, Little Shemogue, W. O. ....N B
Outhouse, S., Wood Point, W. O. ....N B
Owen, Jenkins, Fernhill ....O
Owens, William, Stonefield ....Q
Oxner, Joseph, Lower La Have, W. O. ....N S

Pacaud, P. N., East Arthabaska ....Q
Packwood, George, Point St. Peter ....Q
Page, W. E., Métis ....Q
Page, Francis, Omineca ....B C
Pagé, Pierre, Les Ecureuils ....Q
Painchaud, F., Hochelaga ....Q
Palmer, Benjamin, Hilda ....O
Palmer, M. B., Hopewell Cape ....N B
Palmer, John Morristown, W. O. ....N S
Palmer, F. L., Jacksontown, W. O. ....N B
Palmer, Ira, Balsam ....O
Palmer, Hanford, Anagance ....N B
Paon, Gilbert, West Arichat, W. O. ....N S
Paquette, J. B., St. Roch de Richelieu ....Q
Paquette, Louis, St. Augustin, Two Mountains ..Q
Paquette, F., Paquette ....Q
Paquet, Edward D., House Harbor (sub) ....Q
Paradis, Joseph E., St Constant ....Q
Paradis, Louis, junr, Valetort ....Q
Paradis, C., Ruisseau des Chênes ....Q
Paré, A. P., St. Bruno ....Q
Paré, H. P., St. Germain de Grantham ....Q
Parent, David C., Upper Queensbury, W. O. ....N B
Parent, Hermyle, Tessierville ....Q
Parent, J. C., Fox River ....Q
Parent, Isaiah, Bear Island, W. O. ....N B
Parent, Magloire, Kerry ....O
Parish, Arza Farmersville ....O
Park, Ernest G., Amherstburgh ....O
Parker, John S., Ten Mile Creek, W. O. ....N B
Parker, Benjamin, Glasgow ....O
Parker, Robert, Kilbride ....O
Parker, J. M., Borwick ....N S
Parker, Nelson, Dexter ....O
Parker, Robert Walmer ....O
Parker, John, Dunbarton ....O
Parker, Shubael Woodville, W. O. ....N S
Parry, H. H., Copleston ....O
Parsons, John, Crediton ....O
Passmore, Robert, Rockwood ....O
Paton, P., New Lowell ....O
Pattenoude, M., Stockwell ....Q
Patterson, W. C., Patterson ....O
Patterson, Thomas B., Smithurst ....O
Patterson, H., Steam Mill Village, W. O. .....N S
Patterson, David, Goose River ....N S
Patterson, David, Lower Barney's River, W. O. N S
Patterson, Jane, Admaston ....O
Patterson, Samuel, Carthage ....O
Patterson, Ira H., Au Lac, W. O. ....N B
Patterson, James C., Blantyre ....O
Pattison, Ambrose, Canfield ....O
Pattison, Robert, Walton ....O
Pattison, W. M., Frelighsburg ....Q
Paul, W. M., Roblin ....O
Payne, Manuel, Port Stanley ....O

List of Postmasters in Canada.—Continued.

Payne, Mrs. M., Charing Cross.............. O
Peaker, John, Cooksville .... O
Pearce, J. B., Newton, W. O................ N B
Pearce, Josiah W., Havelock................ O
Pearson, Thomas, Abingdon.................. O
Peck, James H., Albury .... O
Peebles, Matthew, Strabane .... O
Pelletier, T. P., Trois Pistoles........... Q
Pelletier, J. B., Lac Noir.................. Q
Pelletier, O., St. Roch l'Achigan .... Q
Pennock, Philemon, Elgin................... O
Pennock, John C., Castleton................ O
Penny, Edmund I, Garden River.............. O
Pepin, dit Lachance, Emilien, St. François d'Orléans........................... Q
Pequignol, Mrs. Nancy, West Chester Lake, W.O.......................... N S
Percy, John, Bangor........................ O
Pernette, C. R., Middle La Have Ferry, W.O. N S
Perré, J., Ste. Anne des Monts............ Q
Perrett, H W., Perretton .... O
Perrin, John D., Bailieboro' .... O
Perrin, William, Mount Vernon.............. O
Perrott, Nathaniel, Shannonvale, W. O...... N B
Perry, Calvin, Perryboro'.................. Q
Perry, Robert E., Bracebridge.............. O
Petit, P. H., St. Damase................... Q
Petitclerc, Mrs. C., Bergeville .... Q
Petrey, W. B., Russell .... O
Petrie, David, Neguac, W. O................ N B
Petty, Charles, Cherry Wood .... O
Phair, James, Victoria Corners .... O
Phair, A. S., Fredericton.................. N B
Phelan, M. J., St. Columbia .... Q
Phelps, Linius, W., Dickens................ O
Phillips, Edwin, Shiktehawk Bridge......... N S
Phillipps, Thomas, St. Piérre les Becquets. Q
Phillipps, Mrs. Grace, River Philip........ N S
Phillips, Oran, Burns...................... O
Phillips, Robert, Bennies Corners .... O
Phillips, William, Belfast................. O
Philpott, Edward, Foxboro'................. O
Picotte, Chas., Lafontaine................ Q
Pierce, W. J., Malakoff .... O
Pierson, John, Milverton................... O
Pilcher, Thomas, Port Burwell.............. O
Pim, Mrs., Sault Ste. Marie................ O
Pineo, J. P., Pineo Village................ N S
Pinkney, W. R., Sand Beach, W. O........... N S
Pipes, Jonathan, Amherst Point, W. O....... N S
Pitt, H., Pierreville...................... Q
Pitt, William, senr., Pittson .... O
Plamondon, Edouard, St. Raymond............ Q
Plamondon, Anselme, St. Marcel............. Q
Planch, William G., Maple Leaf............. Q
Plant, William, Stanley, W. O.............. N B
Plante, Pierre, St. Bernard................ Q
Playfair, Elisha, Buckshot................. O
Plews, Simon, Salmonville .... O
Plinguet, Revd. V., Isle Dupas .... Q
Poaps, Jacob J., Oznabruck Centre.......... O
Pointer, James E., Churchville............. O
Poirier, Joseph O., St. Jacques le Mineur.. Q
Poirier, J. A., St. Grégoire............... Q
Pollock, Solomon, Mille Isles.............. Q
Pollock, Samuel, Nile .... O
Poole, Ambrose, Cedar Lake, W. O........... N S
Ponds, Hazer, Marysville, W. O............. N B
Pope, Charles E., Clinton.................. B C
Pope, Lemuel, Robinson..................... Q
Porte, William, Lucan...................... O
Porter, Richard C., New Ireland .... Q
Porter, Henry, Cold Brook Station, W. O.... N S
Porter, Leon, N. S., Eel Lake, W. O........ N S
Porterfield, P., Marnoch................... O
Pothier, François, French Village.......... Q
Potter, E. W., Smith's Cove, W. O.......... N S
Potts, Edward, McIntyre.................... O
Potvin, P., L'Anse au Foin................. Q
Polin, Hilaire, St. François, Beauce....... Q
Poulin, Louis, St. Etienne de Boulton...... Q
Powell, Henry, Wallenstein................. O
Powell, George A., Wroxeter................ O
Powley, Charles, Marchmont................. O
Pratt, John, New Ross .... N S
Pratt, James C., Second Falls, W. O........ N B
Prefontaine, Fulgence South Durham......... Q
Premont, Joseph Ste Famille................ Q
Prentiss, H. B., Chelsea .... Q
Prescott, Jesse, Pennfield, W. O .... N B
Prescott, John, Goose Creek, W. O .... N B
Price, W. W., Petitcodiac.................. N B
Pridham, Edward, Grenville................. Q
Prieur, Anicet B., Soulanges............... Q
Prieur, O. F., St. Zotique.................. Q
Prior, F. B., Wallbridge................... O
Pritchard, A., North Wakefield .... Q
Proctor, J. W., New Edinburgh .... O
Proctor, John, Leskard..................... O
Prosser, Daniel, Belhaven .... O
Proudfoot, James, junr., Fenaghvale........ O
Prudhomme, Alex., Cantley .... Q
Ptolemy, William, Woodburn................. O
Pugsley, Daniel, Amherst Hill, W. O .... N S
Pugsley, Michael, River Hébert, W. O....... N S
Pugsley, William, Cheapside................ O
Purdy, Allan G., Greenville, W. O.......... N S
Purdy, C., Deep Brook, W. O................ N S
Purdy, William, Pomona..................... O
Purdy, Joseph Lawrence, Little River, W. O.. N S
Purdy, David, Wallace River, W. O.......... N S
Purdy, Mrs. Mary J., West Chester, W. O.... N S
Purdy, R. McLean, Eugenia .... O
Purkiss, Josiah, Thornhill................. O
Purney, John, Sandy Point, W. O............ N S
Purington, Elijah, East Hereford .... Q
Purves, Robert, junr., Tatamagouche .... N S
Purves, —— Kossuth .... O

Quance, Peter, Sydenham Mills .... O
Quance, Robert, Gravelotte .... O
Quarry, John G., Offa .... O
Quealy, John, Eganville.................... O
Queenville, O., Cazaville .... Q
Quibell, John, Holt .... O
Quigley, Edmund, Beech Hill, W. O.......... N S
Quintin, dit Duboise, A., Action Vale ..... Q
Quirk, Dennis, Glascott .... O

Racette, Jos., Ste., Julienne .... Q
Racey, Thos., Mohawk .... O
Radford, Joseph, Tadousac.................. Q
Raiche, S. G. A., Clarence Creek........... O
Ralph, William S., Jasper.................. O
Ramsey, Robert, Ramsey's Corners .... O
Rand, George V., Wolfville .... N S
Randall, E. W., Bayfield, W. O .... N S
Rankin, D., Sutherland's River, W. O ...... N S
Rankin, Matthew, Falding................... O
Rannie, John, Allanburg .... O
Ranson, Robert, Deux Rivieres.............. Q
Ray, David, Hudson......................... Q
Ray, Andrew, Upper Magaguadavic, W. O...... N B
Ray, John, Glanmire........................ O
Ray, Robert R., Factory Dale, W. O......... N S
Raymond, S. P., Beaver River, W. O......... N S

Raymond, Wm. S., Beaver River Corner......N S
Raymond, David, N., Middle Simonds, W. O. N B
Raymond, George, Kouchibouguac ....N B
Raymond, Silas, Central Norton, W. O ......N B
Raymond, Zephirim, St. Placide........... .. .Q
Read, H. H., Milnesville... ....O
Read, Eliphalet, Read, W. O................N B
Read, James, De Ramsey.......................Q
Reading, Joseph, Cromarty .... O
Reardon, P., Pockshaw, W. O.............. N B
Redman, Edward, Lower Ireland...............Q
Redner, James, Rednersville...... ... .O
Redpath, Geo., Ethngham...................... O
Redy, Benjamin, Gold River, W. O...........N S
Reece, John R., Danby........ .... Q
Reed, Nathaniel, Mimosa....... ....O
Reed, William, Knatchbull.................... O
Reed, James R., Carleton...................N B
Reed, James, Reedsdale.........................Q
Reeve, George, Hornsey, W. O...............N S
Reeve, Arthur, Atherley...... ....O
Regnier, P., St. Athanase........................Q
Reid, Donald, Harrington, West.............. ..O
Reid, J. C., Vanatter...... .... O
Reid, James, Tweed.......... .... O
Reid, Robert, Waubaumik... .... O
Reid, Thomas M., Moose Brook, W. O.........N S
Reid, William, Ravenna....... .. ..O
Reid, G. B., Port George, W. O...............N S
Reid, Minor, Upper New Horton, W. O......N B
Reid, James, Caledonia Settlement, W. O.....N B
Reid, Thomas, Cascades..........................Q
Reid, W. A., Avonport, W. O..................N S
Reinhardt, John, Elmwood.. .... O
Remey, A., Tempo..... ... . .O
Rennells, William, Windsor Junction, W. O...N S
Renshaw, J., Blair... ....O
Renton, Mrs. Ann, Renton......................O
Renwick, John, Inkerman ....O
Reynolds, William, Sarepta.............. .....O
Reynolds, William, Mount Horeb .. ..O
Reynolds, W. R., Lepreaux ....O
Rhodes, William, Rhodes, W. O............. .N S
Richard, Lewis, Belliveaux Village, W. O.....N B
Richards, Christopher, Frankville...............O
Richardson, John, Little Rocher........... ..N B
Richardson, George, Malone.......... ....O
Richardson, Henry, Trudel.... ....O
Richardson, J., Valetta.............................O
Richardson, Thos., Big Port le Bear, W. O.....N B
Richardson, Samuel H., South Mountain... ....O
Rickaby, Seth, Glenarm .... O
Ricker, R., Knowlesville,. ....N B
Riddell, James, Mohrs Corners ....O
Rigby, Miss Henrietta F., Sydney Mines.. ...N S
Rigby, Clara, Mainadieu, W. O............ ..N S
Rimington, John, Rimington ....O
Ring, James, Panmure ....O
Riordon, John, Lower Woodstock, W. O.......N B
Risteen, George, Lower French Village, W. O..N B
Ritchie, Frederick, Hamilton....................O
Rivard, F. X. A., St. Léon. ....Q
Rivard, Miss M. E., Bécancour ....Q
Rivet, Narcisse, St. Brigitte des Saults........ .Q
Roach, W., Grand Falls, Portage, W. O.......N B
Roach, Robert Maccan, W. O.....................N S
Roberge, Louis, Ste. Julie de Somerset..........Q
Roberge Damase, New Liverpool....... .. ....Q
Robert, Raymond, Sherrington ....Q
Robert, François, St. Hubert.......... .. ..Q
Robert, Allenander, Dover South. ....O
Roberts, J., Robert's Island, W. O...............N S
Robertson, Arch., Fox Harbor, W. O.... ....N S

Robertson, John Thomasburg ....O
Robertson, L., Port Jolly, W. O...... ....N S
Robertson, S. Hollen.....................................O
Robertson, Daniel, Loch Lomond, W. O.......N B
Robertson, William, Dalkeith.......................O
Robbins, Ansell, Chebogue, W. O..............N S
Robicheau, P., Lower Pocmouche, W. O. .. ..N B
Robinson, James, Upper Loch Lomond, W. O..N B
Robinson, W. S., Baillie, W. O... ....N B
Robinson, James, Selton.................................O
Robinson, E. A., Goshen, W. O..................N B
Robinson, Thomas, Newbury........................O
Robinson, R. D., Elgin................ ....N B
Robitaille, Louis, Ancienne Lorette.............Q
Roblin, Owen, Ameliasburgh......... ....O
Robson, John W., Vanneck........................O
Roch, N., St. Norbert......... .. .. .Q
Roche, Edmund, Iona............................O
Rockingham, Joseph, Glenloyd....................Q
Rockwell Amon, Rockwell Settlement, W. O...N S
Roddick, John, Lyndhurst........................O
Roddy, James, Farran's Point... ....O
Rodell, Alexander, Comox.......................B C
Rodgers, Robert D., Ashburnham ....O
Rodgers, Samuel A., Grouse Creek ....B C
Rodgerson, James, Shediac Road, W. O.......N B
Roe, Frederick A., Woodbridge.... ....O
Roe, William, New Market. .... O
Rogers, George, Lakefield..........................Q
Rogers, H. C., Peterborough.... ....O
Rogers, James, Lower Coverdale, W. O........N B
Rogers, Patrick, Romans Valley, W. O........N S
Rogers, Thomas, Cedarville ....O
Rogers, John, Bearbrook ....O
Rogers, Joseph C., Fermoy....... ....O
Rombach, Ferdinand, Freigburg .. . .O
Ronald, J. R., West Glassville, W. O..........N B
Rooney, P. J., Blyth...... ....O
Roop, Jas. P., Clementsport.....................N S
Root, Daniel, Pittsferry..............................O
Rorke, Thomas J., Heathcote....... .... O
Ross, Alexander, Turtle Lake....... ....O
Ross, Benjamin Innisfil.......... ....Q
Ross, Alexander, Gould ....Q
Ross, Alexander C., Victoria Mines, W. O.....N S
Ross, D. G., Ross' Corner, W. O................N S
Ross, Seth W., Farndon..... .... Q
Ross, James G., Maryvale, W. O..... ....N S
Ross, James, Leith.......... ....O
Ross, Thomas, Little Rideau .. ..O
Ross, Revd D., Dundee Centre.....................Q
Ross, M. G., Mill Brook, W. O ....N S
Ross, John, North-East Branch Margaree, W. O N S
Ross, W Dalhousie Settlement, W. O. ......N S
Ross, Donald, Blanchard Road, W. O....... .N S
Ross, H. S., Spring Hill Mines, W. O. ..... N S
Rosser, B. H., Denfield .... O
Rothwell, A. T., Dwyer Hill.... ....O
Rouleau, Pierre D., Father Point.................Q
Rouse, Oliver C., Boston......... ....O
Rousseau, Godfroi, St. Monique...................Q
Rousseau, Onésime, St. Perpetue..................Q
Rousseau, Mdme. A. B., Chateau Richer.......Q
Routledge, William, Gardiner Mines, W. O...N S
Rowe, R., Brookbury....... ... .Q
Roy, Norbert, Wolistown.........................Q
Roy, Adam, Maitland ....N S
Roy, Mrs. Mary, Normanton...... ... .O
Roy, dit Lauzon, Vital, St. Fabien..............Q
Roy, Moyse, St. Malo .... Q
Roy, C., Armagh ....Q
Roy, M. E., Settrington.... ... .Q
Roy, Telesphore, Cap Chat.......... ....Q

Royal, Jacques, St. Sulpice .... Q
Royer, L. V., St. Claire .... Q
Ruddick, Margaret, Waiweig, W. O .... N S
Rudolf, Josiah, Upper La Have, W. O .... N S
Rudolph, Mrs. A. M., Luneuburgh .... N S
Ruggles, B H., Westport .... N B
Rupert, J. P., Maple .... O
Rusco, J. M., Centreville, W. O .... N S
Rusk, Robert, Stockdale .... O
Russell, John R., Hopewell Hill, W. O .... N B
Russell, James, Duntroon .... O
Russell, James, Whitney, W. O .... N B
Russell, Wm., Mount Healey .... O
Russell, Wm., jun., Douglastown, W. O .... N B
Rutherford, John, Tweedside, W. O .... N B
Rutherford, William, Millbank .... O
Ruthven Hugh, Ruthven .... O
Ryan, James, Middle Coverdale, W. O .... N B
Ryder, Mrs. S., Argyle, W. O .... N S
Ryerse, Wm. H., Port Ryerse .... O

Sabeans, Charleton, New Tusket, W. O .... N S
Sadler, Robert, Byron .... O
Sager, Noah, Pigeon Hill .... Q
Salois, O., St. Bonaventure .... Q
Salter, W. M., Church Point, W. O .... N B
Sanders, William, Exeter .... O
Sanderson, Joseph, Stirton .... O
Sanderson, L. D., Derry, West .... O
Sanderson, Thomas, Kilmanagh .... O
Sandford, Richard, Clementsvale, W. O .... N S
Sandford, B., Summerville, W. O .... N S
Sandford I. S., Kennetcook, W. O .... N S
Sanson, William sen., Tay Mills, W. O .... N B
Sargent, Alex., East Bolton .... Q
Saucier, J. L., St. Sauveur de Québec .... Q
Saucier, F., Macnider .... Q
Saunders, T. W., Prince William, W. O .... N B
Saunders, Jas., Paisley .... O
Sauriol, Léon, St. Martin .... Q
Savageau, Rev. G. E., St. Tite des Caps (sub-office) Q
Savage, A. H., Savage's Mill .... Q
Savage, Geo., Burnhamthorpe .... O
Savard, Joseph, Cap a l'Aigle (sub) .... Q
Savard, O., Point au Bouleau .... Q
Saxby, William, Shefford Mountain .... Q
Schnell, John, Cedar Grove .... O
Scholefield, William S., Sawyerville .... Q
Schmietendorf, J. T., Thompsonville .... O
Schneider, John, Hampstead .... O
Schooley, E. F., New Durham .... O
Schooley, Louisa, Arkona .... O
Schooley, Nelson, Oxford Centre .... O
Schwedfeger, Lewis, Hoasic .... O
Scidmore, R. P., Acacia .... O
Scisson, Samuel, South March .... O
Scott, Benjamin, Mingan .... Q
Scott, Hiram, North Gower .... O
Scott, Robert, Oustic .... O
Scott, James, Point Petre .... O
Scott, George, Mimico .... O
Scott, John, Stony Creek, W. O .... N B
Scott, John, Thornton .... O
Scott, Richard, Wallace Bridge, W. O .... N S
Scott, Mrs., Caistorville .... O
Scott, Morris, St. Nicholas .... Q
Scott, J. B., St. Timothée .... Q
Scott, John, Seneca .... O
Scott, W. J., jun., Batchewana .... O
Scovil, S. S., Portland .... O
Scribner, Elias, Mouth of Jemseg, W. O .... N B
Seaman, Guilbert, Minadie, W. O .... N S
Seaman, Amos, Lower Cove, W. O .... N S
Seaman, A. J., Clifton, W. O .... N B
Sears, Mrs. M., Lochaber, W. O .... N B
Seaton, Benjamin, Abercorn .... Q
Secord, Josiah B., Varna .... O
Secord, John, jun., Long Creek .... N B
Selby, Benjamin, Stanbridge Station .... Q
Seely, Obadiah, Seely .... O
Segsworth, William, Monck .... O
Sellis, Jacob, Salmon Hole, W. O .... N S
Setter, John, Park's Creek .... M
Sewell, J. H., Port Lambton .... O
Shackleton, John, Colpoy's Bay .... O
Shaffner, J. C., Lower Granville, W. O .... N S
Shanklin, S. J., Shanklin, W. O .... N B
Shannon, Thomas, Picton .... O
Sharp, Mrs. C. M., Sharp's Bridge, W. O .... N S
Sharp, William, Allenford .... O
Sharp, George J., Lower Hayneville, W. O .... N B
Sharp, James, Ravenscliffe .... O
Shatford, Samuel, Head of St. Margaret's Bay, W. O .... N S
Shaver, E. N., Avonmore .... O
Shaver, F. C., Port Hoover .... O
Shaw, James, jun., Smith's Falls .... O
Shaw, S. H., Hartland .... N B
Shaw, Mrs. J. E., Mount Denison, W. O .... N S
Shaw, William, Shawbridge .... Q
Shaw, James, Clarendon Centre .... Q
Shaw, John B., Kent Bridge .... O
Shaw, John, jun., Lake Doré .... O
Shaw, Daniel, East side of West Branch, East River of Pictou, W. O .... N S
Shaw, John, Eastwood .... O
Shaw, John, Nipissingan .... O
Shawnwhite, James W., Terence Bay, W. O .... N S
Shearer, George, Musselburg .... O
Shears, J., Clifton House (sub) .... O
Shehan, Terence, Salmon River, W. O .... N S
Shehan, Thomas, Ironside .... Q
Sheldon, E. J., South Bay, W. O .... N B
Shell, Alfred, Burgoyne .... O
Shell, Colin, Cashel .... O
Sheppherd, John W., Normandale .... O
Sheppherd, Joseph, Lansing .... O
Shepherd, S., Uttoxeter .... O
Sherman Andrew, Wellman's Corners .... O
Sherwood, Charles M., Lakefield, W. O .... N B
Shibley, J. A., Yarker .... O
Shields, A., Avonton .... O
Shields, James, Trecastle .... O
Shields, James, Upper Maugerville, W. O .... N B
Shields, Thomas, Galway .... O
Shier, Jonathan, Woodham .... O
Shirreff, Wm. Alex., Fitzroy Harbor .... O
Shirley, William, North Bristol .... Q
Shoff, D., McGillivary .... O
Short, Richard, sen., Lang .... O
Short, Albert M., New Jerusalem, W. O .... N B
Shufelt, J. D., Iron Hill .... Q
Sicart, J., Mongenais .... Q
Sidey, John, Bewdley .... O
Silcox, Grant, Corral .... O
Silcox, William, Frome .... O
Sill, Robert, Jarvis .... O
Sills, G. B., Conway .... O
Silverthorn, Mahlon, Alloa .... O
Silvester, G. H., Ringwood .... O
Simard, Isaie, St. Joachim .... Q
Simmons, A., Lake Beauport .... Q
Simons, S. T., West Montrose .... O
Simonson, James, Jacksonville, W. O .... N B
Simpson, William, Park Head .... O
Simpson, Isaac, Mount Pleasant, W. O .... N S

List of Postmasters in Canada,—Continued.

Simpson, William, East Ora .... O
Simpson, Alexander, Titusville, W. O .... N B
Simpson, Edward, Gagetown .... N B
Simpson, Alex., Black Heath .... O
Simpson, Archibald, Anderson, W. O .... N B
Simpson, James, Sherwood Spring .... O
Sims, Wilson G., Plymouth, W. O .... N S
Sinclair, Donald, Goshen, W. O .... N S
Sinclair, Edward, North West Bridge, W. O .... N B
Sirois, Joseph O., Grand River .... Q
Sisson, William H., Upper Woodstock, W. O .... N B
Skelly, Michael, Rawdon .... Q
Skelton, Peter, Magpie .... Q
Slaght, Israel, Townsend Centre .... O
Slee, Thomas, Doon .... O
Slipp, Edward W., Hampstead, W. O .... N B
Sloan, Thomas, Kilsyth .... O
Sloan, W. H., South Bay .... O
Sloane, H., Churchill .... O
Sloane, Miss E. B., Holland Landing .... O
Small, Janet, Arthur .... O
Small, Peter, Ballycroy .... O
Smart, Robert W., Port Hope .... O
Smart, Jas. H., Kingsville .... O
Smart, John, Platstville .... O
Smart, Andrew, Culloden .... O
Smeath, George, Midhurst .... O
Smiley, William, Mount Loyal .... Q
Smith, Albert H., Ongley .... O
Smith, Alexander, Lieury .... O
Smith, Alfred, Lilloet .... B C
Smith, William, Rothsay .... O
Smith, Samuel, Harvey Creek .... B C
Smith, Robert, Ayton .... O
Smith, John, New Sarem .... O
Smith, John, Winchelsea .... O
Smith, Thomas, Elm .... O
Smith, Andrew H., French Lake, W. O .... N B
Smith, J. H., Green River .... O
Smith, Richard, Ingoldsby .... O
Smith, Charles, Johnville .... Q
Smith, William, Kirkhill, W. O .... N S
Smith, D. A., McDonald's Point, W. O .... N B
Smith, Nathan, Hampton, W. O .... N B
Smith, T. H., Sky Glen, W. O .... N S
Smith, S. D., Smithfield .... O
Smith, David, Smith Town, W. O .... N B
Smith, James, McPherson's Ferry, W. O .... N S
Smith, James M., Long Reach, W. O .... N B
Smith, Josiah, Mortonville, W. O .... N S
Smith, George, Desboro' .... O
Smith, Beverley, Clark's Harbor, W. O .... N S
Smith, Josiah, Cape Negro, W. O .... N S
Smith, J. E., Blissville .... N B
Smith, David, Bear Point, W. O .... N B
Smith, G. C., Avon .... O
Smith, William, Billing's Bridge .... O
Smith, William, Fallbrook .... O
Smith, John, Edgar .... O
Smith, Thomas, Egremont .... O
Smith, Mrs. Mary, Big Mountain, W. O .... N S
Smith, James, Tilbury, East .... O
Smith, James E., Upper Keswick, W. O .... N B
Smith, Henry S., Oxford, W. O .... N S
Smith, David, Outram .... O
Smith, David, East Glassville, W. O .... N B
Smith, E., Sambro', W. O .... N S
Smith, Charles, Elba .... O
Smith, Thomas, Dublin Shore, W. O .... N S
Smith, John, Petite Passage, W. O .... N S
Smith, Henry, Plantagenet .... O
Smith, C. A., Thorne Centre .... Q
Smith, Samuel, Dunany .... Q
Smith, Peter, St. Armand Station .... Q
Smith, Walton, Onslow .... Q
Smith, William, Necum Tench, W. O .... N S
Smith, George, Milton, West .... O
Smith, T. G., Mount Forest .... O
Smith, Thomas E., Apohaqui .... N B
Smith, Mrs. Joshua, Port Hood Island, W. O .... N S
Smith, James, Norway .... O
Smith, David, Oshawa .... O
Smith, Holland, Rusagornis .... N B
Smith, David, Coverdale, W. O .... N B
Smith, B., Demorestville .... O
Smith, William, Cumberland Point, W. O .... N B
Smuck, R. W., Staffordville .... O
Smyth, Robert, Ashgrove .... O
Smyth, William J., East Magdala .... Q
Smyth, James, senr., Hebron W. O .... N B
Snell, Robert, The Range, W. O .... N B
Snodgrass, R., Young's Cove, W. O .... N B
Snook, John M., Desert Lake .... O
Snow, Nancy H., Port La Tour, W. O .... N S
Snure, Clark, Jordan .... O
Snyder, Elias B., Freeport .... O
Snyder, Herbert E., East Williamsburg .... O
Somers, Noah, Lyttleton, W. O .... N B
Somerville, Margaret, Haysville .... O
Sorinberger, John, Layton .... O
Southmayd, E. S., Way's Mills .... Q
Southwick, George, Hawtrey .... O
Southon, Caleb, Wicklow .... O
Sparks, Mrs. Nancy, Mill Cove, W. O .... N B
Speedie, William, Speedie .... O
Spears, Adam J., Caistorville .... O
Speedy, William, Yoho, W. O .... N B
Speer, William, South Dummer .... O
Spence, William, Rapides des Joachims .... Q
Spence, James, Ethel .... O
Spencer, W. H., Ziska .... O
Spiers, William, Mayfield .... O
Spinney, Austin, Harmony, W. O .... N S
Spinney, B., Melvern Square .... N S
Sponenburgh, Mrs. E., Brownsville .... O
Springer, D. W., Nelson .... O
Sproul, Mary, Feversham .... O
Sproul, James, Long Settlement, W. O .... N B
Sproul, John, Six Portages .... Q
Sproul, R. J., Flesherton .... O
Stacy, John, Talbotville Royal .... Q
Spurr, C. E., Round Hill, W. O .... N S
Stacey, Fred. G., Ascot Corner .... Q
Stalker, James, Gemley .... O
Stally, M., Falkland .... O
Stanfield, John, Bryanston .... O
Stanley, Michael, Hamlet .... O
Stanley, Thomas, South Gloucester .... O
Stanton, George, Paris .... O
Stapleford, A., Ward's Creek Road, W. O .... N B
Staples, Silas, Collin's Inlet .... O
Staples, Robert, Oak Hill .... O
Starkey, S. M., Starkey's, W. O .... N B
Starkey's, James, Oakham, W. O .... N B
Starrat, Handley, Cambridge, W. O .... N S
Steele, John C., Steele .... O
Steele, Jonas, Ridgeville .... O
Steele, Charles, Maitland, W. O .... N S
Steen, Thomas, Pleasant Ridge, W. O .... N B
Stephens, J. W., Walton .... N S
Stephens, William, Tenecape, W. O .... N S
Stephens, S., Merriton .... O
Stephenson, Samuel, Canton .... O
Stephenson, Thomas, Falkirk .... O
Stephens, M. N., Glencairn .... O

List of Postmasters in Canada.—Continued.

Steeves, John, Salem, W.O .... N B
Steeves, William, Dover, W.O .... N B
Stennett, Henry, Keswick .... O
Sterns, Luther, Dartmouth .... N S
Stevens, John, Rose Vale, W.O .... N B
Stevens, J. M., Harvey .... N B
Stevens, Simon, Trenholm .... Q
Stevens, Wm., Bedford Basin, W.O .... N S
Stevens, Gardner, Waterloo East .... Q
Steeves, R. E., Hillsborurgh .... N B
Steeves, Millidge, Bridgedale, W.O .... N B
Sterratt, Melessa, Dalhousie East, W.O .... N S
Stewart, Peter, Point la Nim, W.O .... N B
Stewart, Samuel F., Harrowsmith .... O
Stewart, James, Little Harbor, W.O .... N S
Stewart, James, Epping .... O
Stewart, James, Melrose .... N S
Stewart, Alexander, West side of Lochaber, W.O .... N S
Stewart, Hugh, Willogrove .... O
Stewart, Donald, River Louison, W.O .... N B
Stewart, R. H., Woodlands .... O
Stewart, Chas., Clarenceville .... Q
Stewart, Robert, Black River, W.O .... N B
Stewart, David, Roslin, W.O .... N S
Still, Mrs. Mary, Raglan .... O
Stirling, Alexander, White Lake .... O
St. Laurent, A. Amable, St. Flavie .... Q
Stockdale, Peter Milligan, Stocdale .... O
Stockwell, J. W., Danville .... Q
Stoddart, John, Stoddarts, W.O .... N S
Stokes, John J., Sharon .... O
Stone, A. M., North Stanbridge .... Q
Stone, Giles, Haultain .... O
Stone, John, Maquapit Lake, W.O .... N B
Strachan, Kenneth, Framboise W.O .... N S
Strange, Edwin L., Causapscal .... Q
Stratford, John E., Hubbard's Cove, W.O .... N S
Striker, Jonathan, Bloomfield .... O
Stroh, John, St. Clements .... O
Stronach, George, Stronach Mountain .... N S
Strum, Joseph, Martin's River, W.O .... N S
Struthers, R. C., Louisville .... N S
Struthers, P., Carleton Place .... O
Stuart, Charles, Lake Témiscamingue .... Q
Stuart, James, Epping .... O
Stuart, Wm., Cambria .... Q
Styres, James, Oshweken .... O
Suffern, Anthony, Raymond .... O
Sullivan, Patrick, Merlin .... O
Sullivan, J. O., Fredericton Road, W O .... N B
Sullivan, Daniel, Malcolm .... O
Sullivan, T., Portuguese Cove, W. O .... N S
Sullivan, John Corinth .... O
Sumner, John, Ashton .... O
Surtees, George, Beachburg .... O
Sutherland, D., Orwell .... O
Sutherland, A., Plainfield, W. O .... N S
Sutherland, A. W., East River, St. Mary's, W. O .... N S
Sweet, S., North Sutton .... Q
Sweet, J. L., Newport Station .... N S
Sweet, Stubbard, Billtown, W. O .... N S
Sweetman, Patrick, Port Daniel .... Q
Sweetman, J. McD., High Bluff .... M
Switzer, H. M., Palermo .... O
Sweazie, Hamilton, Elfrida .... O
Sykes, William, Cobourg .... O
Symon, William, Ospringe .... O
Symons, Joseph, Little Tracadie, W. O .... N S
Syphers, Jacob, Syphers' Cove, W. O .... N B
St. Antoine, Louis, St. Justin .... Q

St. Denis, A., Point Fo
St. Germain, F. H., Ma
St. Jacques, Revd. J. H.
St. John, Mary, Colerai
St. Louis, C., Sandwich
St. Pierre, Paschal G., F
St. Pierre, Richard, Bec

Taggart, James, Wallac
Tait, David, Poplar Poi
Tait, George, West Shef
Tait, Peter N., Mille Rc
Tait, John R., L'Amabl
Tait, James, Duart.....
Tait, Valantine B., New
Tarlington, John, Lakeh
Tanguay, Pierre, St. M
Tapp, Thomas, Baracho
Tapping, Thos., Hardin
Taylor, Andrew, Williar
Taylor, Isaac S., Lincol
Taylor, James W., Fen
Taylor, John, Manchest
Taylor, John, St. James
Taylor, John, Headingl
Taylor, Joseph, Lower (
Taylor, Robert B., Gay
Taylor, J., North River
Taylor, A. L., Pike Ri
Taylor, Edward Sandfc
Taylor, John, St. Polyc
Taylor, Emerson, Credi
Taylor, Alexander, Dro
Taylor, John F., Adder
Taylor, John, Bothwell.
Taylor, W. H., Alport.
Taylor, Charles, Taylor
Taylor, Geo., Burtch...
Taylor, -. Kincardine,
Taylor, Jonas, Rocklan
Taylor, George, senr., S
Teakles, William, Susse
Teefy, Matthew, Richn
Teel, Elkanah, Broad C
Telfer, Adam, Telfer...
Tellier, P., St. Cuthber
Tennant, W., junr., Ca
Terriff, Peter, Belmore
Terry, Henry, Vernonv
Terry, D., Hartman...
Teskey, John, Vrooma
Teskey, Albert, Applet
Teskey, Daniel, Lisbur
Tessier, Onezime, Warv
Tétu, Nazaire, Rivière
Theriault, Jacques, St.
Thérien, Ferdinand, St
Thibaudeau, F. X., G
Thibeault, J. B., St.
Thirkell, Joseph, Inger
Thivierge, Dominique,
Thomas, B., Hartford.
Thomas, Charles, Cogn
Thomas, Edward, St.
Thompson, Thomas, Pc
Thompson, Daniel, Gor
Thompson, John, Hum
Thompson, Evan, Nine
Thompson, George, Cly
Thompson, James B.,
Thompson, Thomas, H
Thompson, R., Smithv
Thompson, William, St

List of Postmasters in Canada.—Continued.

Thompson, Archibald, Montrose .... O
Thompson, W. J., Rainham Centre .... O
Thompson, Daniel, Queensborough .... O
Thompson, R., Constance .... O
Thompson, James, Lakeville Corner, W. O. . N B
Thompson, W. C., Rockford .... O
Thompson, Peter C., Hyde Park Corner....... O
Thomson, Smith, Malvern .... O
Thomson, Joseph, Marlow .... Q
Thomson, Robert, Cumminsville .... O
Thomson, T., Buttonville .... O
Thomson, Jas. M., Byng .... O
Thomson, R. R., Shelburne .... N S
Thomson, John, Woodford .... O
Thomson, James, English Corner, W. O..... N S
Thomson, William, Arundel .... Q
Thom, Archibald, Morrisdale .... O
Thorne, Butler, Thorn Town, W. O. .... N B
Thornton, J. M., Dundas .... O
Thorp, Sidney R., Hall's Harbour, W.O..... .
Thouin Damase, Kilkenny .... Q
Throop, Rufus S., Charleville .... O
Thurber, S. B., Irvine .... Q
Tilley, William, Glinville, W. O. .... N B
Tilley, Leveret S., Lake George, W. O..... N B
Tillson, E. D., Tilsonburg .... O
Tilly, William, Cape Cove .... Q
Tilton, C. F., Fairville .... N B
Tingley, S. W., Dorchester .... N B
Tinline, James, Eversley .... O
Timmerman, P. S., Odessa .... O
Titemore, Abram, St. Armand Centre .... Q
Titus, Benjamin, Allisonville .... O
Tobey, John, Tara .... O
Tobin, John J., Milledgeville, W. O. .... N B
Tobin, Richard, Upper St. Francis, W. O.. N B
Tobin, M. A., Berwick .... O
Todd, Henry, Narrows .... N B
Tom, John C., Welcome .... O
Tomalty, William, Edina .... Q
Tomkins, W. B., Upper Peel, W. O. .... N B
Tompkins, Thomas, Emerald, W. O. .... N S
Tompkins, Aaron, Northampton, W. O. ..... N B
Tomlinson, W., Tay Settlement, W. O. ..... N B
Tomlinson, Wm., Marsh Hill .... O
Torey, Joseph, Milford Haven Bridge, W. O.. N S
Touchburn, Henry, Greenock .... O
Tovell, J., Everton .... O
Toyne, John, Oakland .... O
Tracy, S. W., Granboro .... Q
Trask, Samuel, Central Chebogue, W.O. ..... N S
Travers, John, Traverston .... O
Travis, Allan McN., Ossekeag .... N B
Travis, Elkanah, Kempt Bridge, W.O. .... N S
Tredway, William, Highland Creek .... O
Tremaine, F. D., Port Hood .... N S
Tremblay, Jean O., Chicoutimi .... Q
Tremblay, M., Charlesbourg .... Q
Tremblay, Peter, Ste. Agnes de Dundee .... Q
Trenholm, James, Dumbarton R. R. Station, W. O. .... N B
Troop, Valentine, Belleisle, W. O. .... N S
Troop, W. B., Granville Centre, W. O. .... N S
Troop, W. H., Paradise Lane, W. O. .... N S
Troop, Alfred, Granville Ferry .... N S
Trott, Thomas, Gaspereaux Station, W. O..... N B
Trottier, Jane, Shoolbred .... Q
Trudeau, Félix M., St. Zènon .... Q
Trueman, John, Elmbank .... O
Trumm, Christian, Bismarck .... O
Tubby, Samuel, Fingal .... O
Tubman, Thomas, Munster .... O
Tuck, J. F., Knowlton Landing .... Q
Tucker, Joseph L., Orono .... O
Tucker, L. Michael, Southampton, W. O. ..... N S
Tupling, Christopher, Alvanley .... O
Tupper, J. H., Lower Line, Queensbury, W. O. N B
Tupper, R. La T., Bobcaygeon .... O
Turcot, Joseph, North Georgetown .... Q
Turcotte, F. X., St. Jean d'Orléans .... Q
Turcotte, Cyrille, Russelltown .... Q
Turnbull, John, Glanworth .... O
Turner, Abner, Foster's Cove .... N B
Turner, Seth, Mitchell's Bay .... O
Turner, Donald, West Magdala .... O
Turner, Edward T., Fenville .... O
Turner, Frank, Bealton .... O
Tuttle, J. E., Dundela .... O
Tuzo, J. E., Percé .... Q
Tuzo, John D., Magdalen Islands .... Q
Twohey, Wm., Brittania Mills .... Q
Tyre, Robert, St. Regis .... Q
Tyrell, L. R., Luton .... O
Tyrrell, Thos. B., Cookshire .... Q

Umphrey, J., Big Cove, W. O. .... N B
Upham, N. H., Upham, W. O. .... N B
Upper, Mrs. Phœbe E., St. Ann's .... O
Urquhart, Nathaniel, Urquharts, W. O. .... N B
Urquhart, William, Rear Lands, Sporting Mountain, W. O. .... N B

Vachon, Edward, Riviere la Madeleine .... Q
Vachon, Léandre, St. Louis de Gonzague .... Q
Vachon, Antoine, Aston Station .... Q
Vail, Solomon, Magaguadavic, W. O. .... N B
Valiquet, Thomas, St. Hilaire Station .... Q
Vaillancourt, W. F., Vaillancourt .... Q
Vallée, Cyrille, West Broughton .... Q
Vallée, J. S., Montmagny .... Q
Vallée, Wm., Chambly Basin .... Q
Vance, William, Mill Brook .... O
Vandervoort, N. A., Sidney Crossing .... O
Van Buskirk, C., Bayfield, W. O. .... N B
Vanluven, Zara, Moscow .... O
Vanvlack, John, Vanvlack .... O
Van Vliet, T., Lacolle .... Q
Vasey, Mark, Vasey .... O
Vassal, Henry, Pierreville Mills .... Q
Vatour, Jean C., Richibucto .... N B
Vaughan, Joseph, Vaughan's, W. O. .... N S
Veit, S. A., Douglastown .... Q
Venton, Anderson, Mill Haven .... O
Vermette, E., St. Malachie .... Q
Verner, T., St. Etienne de Beauharnois .... Q
Vigneault, O., Kildare .... Q
Vigneau, Joseph, St. Sylvester, East .... Q
Vincent dit Maheux, F., St. Flore .... Q
Vincent, J. G., Lorette .... Q
Vondy, Thos., junr., Chatham .... N B

Waddell, Robert, South Monaghan .... O
Waganost, W., New Dundee .... O
Wagner, Alex. H., Windsor .... O
Wagstaff, William E., North Ridge .... O
Wait, David W., Harlowe .... O
Wait, Whitney, Bayview .... O
Wait, Helen, Bathurst .... N B
Wakem, Thomas, Greenfield, W. O. .... N B
Waldo, Samuel, Teeswater .... O
Wales, Robert A., East Dunham .... Q
Walford, W. M., Locksley .... O
Walker, Edward, Bel'rock .... O
Walker, Christopher, Duncrief .... O
Walker, Chas., Coal Branch, W. O. .... N B
Walker, David, Cavan .... O

List of Postmasters in Canada.—Continued.

Walker, R., jun., Diamond.......... O
Walker, D. J., Inverary.......... O
Walker, Samuel, Deerhurst.......... O
Walker, Thomas, Parkhurst.......... Q
Wall, George, Ragged Island, W. O.......... N S
Wall, Robert, Bartibog, W. O.......... N B
Wallace, Hugh, Londesborough.......... O
Wallace, M., West Gore, W. O.......... N S
Wallace, Joseph, Shepody Road, W. O.......... N B
Wallace, John, Mount Hurst.......... O
Wallace, John J., Gardner's Creek, W. O.......... N B
Wallace, Patrick, Indian Cove.......... Q
Wallis, Thomas, Roxham.......... Q
Walsh, John, Railton.......... O
Walsh, Patrick, Erinsville.......... O
Walsh, R. N., Ormstown.......... Q
Walter, F., Bamberg.......... O
Walter, Thomas P., Walter's Falls.......... O
Walton, Jacob, Kettleby.......... O
Wanless, James, Wanstead.......... O
Wannemake, N. P., Hillsdale, W. O.......... N B
Ward, Rufus, Rockport.......... N B
Ward, Thomas, Woodhill.......... O
Ward, W. A., Dawn Mills.......... O
Warner, Sydney, Wilton.......... O
Warner, S. B., St. Ephrem d'Upton.......... Q
Warner, Charles, Colebrook.......... O
Warnock, John, Castleford.......... O
Warren, Joseph, Harper.......... O
Warren, Robert, Niagara.......... O
Warren, John, Deerdock.......... O
Wartman, David, Selby.......... O
Wasson, John, Lower Prince William, W. O.. N B
Watkins, Bramwell, Ardoch.......... O
Watson, Alex. L., Undine, W. O.......... N B
Watson, C. P., Dresden.......... O
Watson, David R., Fairfield.......... O
Watson, J. S. J., Rockingham.......... O
Watson, John, Watson Settlement, W. O.......... N B
Watson, A. R., Forks Baddeck, W. O.......... N S
Watson, Henry, Clearville.......... O
Watson, Wm., Arkell.......... O
Watson, J. J., Adolphustown.......... O
Watt, William, West Lynne.......... M
Waugh, William, Gulf Shore, W. O.......... N S
Waugh, James, R. L., Nilestown.......... O
Way, W. H., Mountain View.......... O
Weaver, Michael, Weaver, W. O.......... N S
Webb, James, Stroud.......... O
Webber, William, Torbay, W. O.......... N S
Webber, David, East Jeddore, W. O.......... N S
Webster, M., Sheldon.......... O
Webster, Marion, South McLellan's Mountain, W. O.......... N S
Webster, Thomas, Newborough.......... O
Weir, Allan, Churchville, W. O.......... N S
Wellard, William, Taunton.......... O
Wells, William, Rickman's Corners.......... O
Wells, Leonard, Farnboro'.......... Q
Welch, John T., Tyrone.......... O
Welton, Jonathan, Northfield, W. O.......... N B
Wensley, Susan Anne, South Quebec.......... Q
West, David, Rowanton.......... Q
West, William, Medford, W. O.......... N S
West, Elijah C., Middle Pereaux, W. O.......... N S
Weston, Nathan, Brockville, W. O.......... N S
Wetmore, Susannah, Cromwell, W. O.......... N B
Whalan, Peter, Cap des Rosiers.......... Q
Wheelock, John, Kingston Village, W. O.......... N S
Wheeler, George, Uxbridge.......... O
Wheeler, Mrs. Barbara, Runnymede.......... Q
Wheeler, Edward, Stouffville.......... O
Whelan, John H., Westport.......... O

Wheldon, A. R., Shediac.......... N B
White, C. A., Forestville.......... O
White, W. H., Springfield.......... N B
White, William H., Cambridge, W. O.......... N B
White, Thomas, Klineburg.......... O
White, John, jun., Hopetown.......... O
White, S. V., White's Cove, W. O.......... N B
White, Nelson, Patterson Settlement, W. O.. N B
White, Mrs. J. A., Longwood Station.......... O
White, Humphrey, Anderson.......... O
White, W. L., Lemonville.......... O
White, L. M., Scovil's Mills, W. O.......... N B
Whitehead, Thomas, Dunkeld.......... O
Whitehead, W., Dumfries, W. O.......... N B
Whitfield, A. M., Holbrook.......... O
Whiting, R. E., Muncey.......... O
Whiting, George, Erroll.......... O
Whitman, James M., Manchester, W. O.......... N S
Whitney, Mrs. Eliza, Pickering.......... O
Whitsides, James, Delhi.......... O
Widderfield, Samuel, Siloam.......... O
Widman, John L., St. Jacob's.......... O
Widman, Richard, Lonsdale.......... O
Wilkie, James, Amberley.......... O
Wilkie, Geo., Sugar Loaf, W. O.......... N S
Wilkin, John, Lemesurier.......... Q
Wiley, Joseph, Fenwick, W. O.......... N B
Willet, W. F., Tupperville, W. O.......... N S
Wilton, Samuel, New Sarum.......... O
Williams, Charles, Glen Williams.......... O
Williams, Allen, Brinkworth.......... O
Williams, Mrs. L., South East Passage, W. O.. N S
Williams, John, Frost Village.......... Q
Williams, Ira, Croydon.......... O
Williamson, J. C., Ballyduff.......... O
Williamson, George, Kingsbury.......... Q
Williamson, Thos., Foley.......... O
Williger, Jas., Blackrock, W. O.......... N S
Williscroft, George, Williscroft.......... O
Williston, Alexander, Baie du Vin, W. O.......... N B
Wilson, G. C., Atherton.......... O
Wilson, George, Teston.......... O
Wilson, Amos, Steeve's Mountain, W. O.......... N B
Wilson, John, Tottenham.......... O
Wilson, Robert, Rolessey.......... O
Wilson, Seth, Macville.......... O
Wilson, W. H., Bannockburn.......... O
Wilson, William, Cumberland.......... O
Wilson, W. B., Kamloops.......... B C
Wilson, Mary, Little Shippigan, W. O.......... N B
Wilson, Thos., Clarence.......... O
Wilson, James, Vicars.......... Q
Wilson, David, Waterford.......... O
Wilson, John, Autrim.......... O
Wilson, John, Mono Centre.......... O
Wilson, John, Canfield.......... O
Wilson, James, Buckingham.......... Q
Wilson, James, senr., Boulter.......... O
Winger, Jacob, Winger.......... O
Winger, Peter, Elmira.......... O
Winkler, D., Neustadt.......... O
Winnecott, George, Copenhagen.......... O
Winslow, John C., Woodstock.......... N B
Winyard, Robt. J., Selkirk.......... O
Wirth John, Hope.......... B C
Wissler, John R., Salem.......... O
Wolfe, John, junr., Mount Wolfe.......... O
Wolf, James, Falmouth, W. O.......... N S
Wolff, Charles S., Valcartier.......... Q
Wood, Thomas, Woodside.......... Q
Wood, Richard, Port Dalhousie.......... O
Wood, W. J., Kars.......... O

List of Postmasters in Canada.—Continued.

Wood, William, Dixon's Corners ....O
Woodburn, Richard F., Melbourne............Q
Woodbury, Egbert S., Spa Springs, W. O.....N S
Woodruff, W. W., Clifton.....................O
Woods, F., Welsford .... N B
Woods, J. R., Aylmer (East)......... .... Q
Woodworth, William, Centreville, W. O......N B
Wooster, Turner, Grand Harbor, W. O.......N B
Wootton, Henry, Victoria...................B C
Worden, James G., Tennant's Cove, W. O....N B
Worden, Wm., Kars, W. O ....N B
Workman, Aaron, Hereford.. .... Q
Worrell, Thomas, Barnesville, W. O..........N B
Wortley, W. C., Drayton..................... O
Wright, George, Wareham.....................O
Wright, George, Stella.......... ....O
Wright, H. M., Napanee Mills............ ... O
Wright, G. R., Jackson.......................O
Wright, James, Hopewell, W. O..............N B
Wright, David A., Thornbrook, W. O....... N B
Wry, Rufus C., Jolicure, W. O... ....N B
Wurtele, C E., Windsor Mills...............Q
Wycott, William, Dog Creek..... ....B C

Wylie, James H., junr., Almonte............. O
Wylie, Robert, Ayr.... ....O
Wyman, L. W., Waterville.................. Q
Wynn, James, Queenston ....O

Yeomans, R. P., Newcastle Bridge, W. O.....N B
Young, James, Nashwaak, W. O............ N B
Young, Myles, Lakelet.........................O
Young, William, Head of St. Mary's Bay, W. O N S
Young, Joseph, Birr........... ....O
Young, Patrick, Young's Point... ....O
Young, John A., Florence....... ... .O
Young, James, Doncaster.......................O
Young, Andrew, Shigawake.............. ....Q
Young, John, Tracadie, W. O............. N B
Young, David, Stanhope.......................Q
Young, John B., Pennfield Ridge, W. O......N B
Younghusband, Henry, Dunrobin..............O

Zavitz, H. B., Sherkston.......................O
Zinkann, John, Lisbon.... ....O
Zinger, Wm., Ambleside.... ....O
Zoeger, John, Wellesley..................... .O

TABLES

OF

RATES OF POSTAGE

IN

CANADA AND ALSO BETWEEN CANADA

AND THE

UNITED KINGDOM, BRITISH COLONIES AND FOREIGN COUNTRIES

—o—

TABLE No. 1.—Rates of Postage on Letters within the Dominion of Canada, (including the Provinces of Ontario, Quebec, New Brunswick, Nova Scotia, Manitoba, British Columbia, and Prince Edward's Island), and to the United States.

TABLE No. 2.—By mails sent to England in Mail Steam Packets sailing weekly (every Saturday), from Quebec in Summer, and from Portland in Winter; and fortnightly, from Halifax, Nova Scotia.

TABLE No. 3. By Cunard or other Steamers sailing from New York or Boston for England, (closed mail).

TABLE No. 4.—To Bermuda and West Indies, by British Mail Packet, sailing monthly from Halifax to Bermuda and St. Thomas.

TABLE No. 5.—To certain British Colonies and Foreign Countries, to be included in the United States Mails for Steamers sailing from New York for the West Indies, Panama, and South America.

TABLE No. 6.—Rates on matters transmissible by post, within Canada, and to Newfoundland, the United Kingdom, France, and the United States.

Table 1.

RATES OF POSTAGE on letters within the Dominion of Canada, (including the Provinces of Ontario, Quebec, New Brunswick, Nova Scotia, Manitoba, British Columbia, and Prince Edward's Island).

	POSTED PREPAID.	POSTED UNPAID.
On a letter weighing not more than ½ an oz	3 Cents.	5 Cents.
On a letter weighing more than ½ an oz., but not more than 1 oz	6 "	10 "
On a letter weighing more than 1 oz., but not more than 1½ oz	9 "	15 "
On a letter weighing more than 1½ oz., but not more than 2 oz	12 "	20 "
On a letter weighing more than 2 oz., but not more than 2½ oz	15 "	25 "

and so on, 3 cents or 5 cents (according as the letter is paid or unpaid), being charged for every additional ½ oz., or fraction of a ½ oz.

Letters addressed as above which are only partially prepaid, are to be rated as if *wholly* unpaid, credit being given, however, for the amount prepaid thereon. Thus, if a letter weighing more than ½ an oz., but less than 1 oz., and liable to two rates (equal to 10 cents) is prepaid only 3 cents, it is subject to a further charge of 7 cents.

The charge on local or drop letters is one cent for each letter, which must be prepaid by stamp.

The charge for the Registration of a letter is 2 cents, to be prepaid by stamp.

CANADA AND NEWFOUNDLAND.

Letters for Newfoundland are charged at the rate of 6 cents per half ounce, and must in all cases be *prepaid*.

The Registration fee to Newfoundland is the same as to places within the Dominion, viz., 2 cents.

CANADA AND THE UNITED STATES.

	POSTED PREPAID.	POSTED UNPAID.
On a letter weighing not more than ½ an ounce	6 Cents.	10 Cents.
On a letter weighing more than ½ an oz. but not more than 1 oz	12 ,,	20 ,,
On a letter weighing more than 1 oz., but not more than 1½ oz.	18 ,,	30 ,,
On a letter weighing more than 1½ oz., but not more than 2 oz.	24 ,,	40 ,,
On a letter weighing more than 2 oz., but not more than 2½ oz	30 ,,	50 ,,

and so on, 6 cents or 10 cents, (according as the letter is paid or unpaid,) being charged for every additional ½ oz., or fraction of a ½ oz.

Letters addressed as above which are only partially prepaid, are to be rated as if *wholly* unpaid.

Registration fee, 5 cents, prepaid by stamps.

TABLE No. 2.

BRITISH AND FOREIGN POSTAGE TABLE.

[*VIA ENGLAND.*]

TABLE shewing the amount of Postage, to be collected in the Dominion of Canada, upon Letters, Newspapers, and Book Packets, forwarded by Canadian Mail Steamers, to the United Kingdom, and through the United Kingdom to the undermentioned Colonies and Foreign Countries.

Mem. 1.—In all cases the postage must be prepaid. Letters for the United Kingdom, if posted unpaid, or insufficiently prepaid, will be forwarded,—but they will be charged on delivery with the amount of deficient postage, and a fine of threepence sterling each letter.

2.—Letters may be registered to all places, except those the names of which are followed by the letters *n r*, indicating that no registration can be effected.

3.—The Registration Fee on letters addressed to the United Kingdom is 8 cents each. In all other cases the Registration Fee is 16 cents from Canada to the place of destination; except to Egypt (Alexandria and Suez excepted) the registration fees to which are 30 cents each letter, and to places marked *a*, in which cases a registration fee of 8 cents each letter, and in addition double the ordinary rates of postage, as given in this table, must be collected (See note at foot of table marked A.)

4.—No Book Packet addressed to Portugal, Madeira, the Azores, or Cape de Verds, must exceed 1 lb. in weight; to Russia and Poland no such packet must exceed 8 oz. A Packet of Patterns for Germany or Belgium or any country, *via* Belgium, must not exceed 8 oz. A Book Packet for Greece must not exceed 3 lbs. in weight nor must it exceed 2 ft. in length by 1 ft. in width or depth.

5.—Upon Letters, and Book Packets, forwarded through the United States, the following additional rates must be collected, viz., 2 cents per ½ oz. on Letters, and 2 cents per 4 oz. on Book Packets.

6.—An additional postage of 6 cents per half ounce must be collected on Letters, 2 cents each on Newspapers, and 6 cents per 4 ounces on Book Packets and Patterns for places marked thus * when addressed to be sent *via* Brindisi.

7.—On Book Packets for the United Kingdom, not exceeding one oz. in weight, the postage is 2 cents. On Book Packets, weighing more than one oz., the progressive rates of postage will be found in the table below.

COUNTRIES, &c.	For a Letter.					For each Newspaper.	For a Book Packet.					
	Not exceeding ¼ oz.	Above ¼ oz. and not exceeding ½ oz.	Above ½ oz. and not exceeding ¾ oz.	For every additional ¼ oz.	For every additional ½ oz.		Not exceeding 2 ozs.	2 ozs. to 4 ozs.	4 ozs. to 8 ozs.	8 ozs. to 12 ozs.	12 ozs. to 1 lb.	For every additional 4 ozs.
	$ cts.	$ cts.	$ cts.	$ cts.	$ cts.		$ cts.	$ cts.	$ cts.	$ cts.	$ cts.	$ cts.
*Aden	0 22	0 22	0 44	—	0 22	6 cents.	0 10	0 12	0 24	0 36	0 48	0 12
Africa, West Coast of (*n r*)	0 16	0 16	0 32	—	0 16	4 cents.	0 08	0 10	0 20	0 30	0 40	0 10
Alexandria { *via* Brindisi	0 20	0 20	0 40	—	0 20	6 cents.	0 14	0 16	0 30	0 46	0 60	0 16
Alexandria { *via* Southampton	0 16	0 16	0 32	—	0 16	4 cents.	0 8	0 10	0 20	0 30	0 40	0 10
a Algeria	0 10	0 16	0 26	0 06	0 04	Book rate.	0 06	0 12	0 24	0 36	0 48	0 12
Ascension (*n r*)	0 28	0 28	0 56	—	0 28	4 cents.	0 08	0 10	0 20	0 30	0 40	0 10
*Australia, South	0 16	0 16	0 32	—	0 16	6 cents.	0 10	0 12	0 24	0 36	0 48	0 12
*Australia, Western	0 16	0 16	0 32	—	0 16	6 cents.	0 10	0 12	0 24	0 36	0 48	0 12

Austria	0 10	0 10	0 20	—	0 10	Book rate.	0 8	0 16	0 32	0 48	0 64	0 16
Azores	0 16	0 28	0 44	0 12	0 04	do	0 06	0 12	0 24	0 36	0 48	*see mem* 4
Baden	0 10	0 10	0 20	—	0 10	Book rate.	0 08	0 16	0 32	0 48	0 64	0 16
Bavaria	0 10	0 10	0 20	—	0 10	do	0 08	0 16	0 32	0 48	0 64	0 16
Belgium	0 10	0 10	0 20	—	0 10	do	0 06	0 12	0 24	0 36	0 48	0 12
Beyrout	0 24	0 24	0 48	—	0 24	12 cents.	0 14	0 16	0 32	0 48	0 64	0 16
Bolivia (*n r*)	0 40	0 40	0 80	—	0 40	6 cents.	0 10	0 12	0 24	0 36	0 48	0 12
Borneo (*n r*)	0 28	0 28	0 56	—	0 28	6 cents.	0 10	0 12	0 24	0 36	0 48	0 12
Bourbon	0 24	0 24	0 48	—	0 24	8 cents.	0 14	0 16	0 32	0 48	0 64	0 16
Brazil (*n r*)	0 28	0 28	0 56	—	0 28	4 cents.	0 08	0 10	0 20	0 30	0 40	0 10
Bremen	0 10	0 10	0 20	—	0 10	Book rate.	0 08	0 16	0 32	0 48	0 64	0 16
Brunswick	0 10	0 10	0 20	—	0 10	do	0 08	0 16	0 32	0 48	0 64	0 16
Buenos Ayres (*n r*)	0 28	0 28	0 56	—	0 28	4 cents.	0 08	0 10	0 20	0 30	0 40	0 10
Canary Islands	0 16	0 28	0 44	0 12	0 04	Book rate.	0 08	0 16	0 32	0 48	0 64	0 16
Cape de Verds	0 16	0 16	0 32	—	0 16	do	0 06	0 12	0 24	0 36	0 48	*see mem* 4
Cape of Good Hope	0 28	0 28	0 56	—	0 28	4 cents.	0 08	0 10	0 20	0 30	0 40	0 10
*Ceylon	0 22	0 22	0 44	—	0 22	6 cents.	0 10	0 12	0 24	0 36	0 48	0 12
Chili (*n r*)	0 40	0 40	0 80	—	0 40	6 cents.	0 10	0 12	0 24	0 36	0 48	0 12
*China—(except Hong Kong)—(*n r*)	0 28	0 28	0 56	—	0 28	6 cents.	0 10	0 12	0 24	0 36	0 48	0 12
Constantinople	0 12	0 12	0 24	—	0 12	Book rate.	0 08	0 16	0 32	0 48	0 64	0 16
Costa Rica (*n r*)	0 28	0 28	0 56	—	0 28	4 cents.	0 08	0 10	0 20	0 30	0 40	0 10
Cuba (*n r*)	0 28	0 28	0 56	—	0 28	4 cents.	0 08	0 10	0 20	0 30	0 40	0 10
*a*Dardanelles	0 16	0 28	0 44	0 12	0 04	Book rate.	0 06	0 12	0 24	0 36	0 48	0 12
Denmark	0 12	0 12	0 24	—	0 12	do	0 08	0 16	0 32	0 48	0 64	0 16
Ecuador (*n r*)	0 40	0 40	0 80	—	0 40	6 cents.	0 10	0 12	0 24	0 36	0 48	0 12
Egypt—Alexandria and Suez *via* Brindisi	0 24	0 24	0 48	—	0 24	8 cents.	0 14	0 16	0 32	0 48	0 64	0 16
Egypt—Cairo and all places except above, *via* Southampton	0 20	0 20	0 40	—	0 20	6 cents.	0 10	0 12	0 24	0 36	0 48	0 12
England	0 06	0 06	0 12	—	0 06	2 cents.	0 04	0 06	0 12	0 18	0 24	0 06
Falkland Islands	0 16	0 16	0 32	—	0 16	4 cents.	0 08	0 10	0 20	0 30	0 40	0 10
Fernando Po (*n r*)	0 16	0 16	0 32	—	0 16	4 cents.	0 08	0 10	0 20	0 30	0 40	0 10
*a*France	0 10	0 16	0 26	0 06	0 04	Book rate.	0 04	0 08	0 16	0 24	0 32	0 08
Frankfort	0 10	0 10	0 20	—	0 10	do	0 08	0 16	0 32	0 48	0 64	0 16
*a*Galatz	0 16	0 28	0 44	0 12	0 04	do	0 06	0 12	0 24	0 36	0 48	0 12
Gallipoli (*n r*)	0 16	0 28	0 44	0 12	0 04	do	0 06	0 12	0 24	0 36	0 48	0 12
Gambia	0 16	0 16	0 32	—	0 16	4 cents.	0 08	0 10	0 20	0 30	0 40	0 10
Gibraltar	0 16	0 16	0 32	—	0 16	4 cents.	0 08	0 10	0 20	0 30	0 40	0 10
Gold Coast	0 16	0 16	0 32	—	0 16	4 cents.	0 08	0 10	0 20	0 30	0 40	0 10
Greece	0 20	0 20	0 40	—	0 20	Book rate.	0 08	0 16	0 32	0 48	0 64	0 16
Grey Town (*n r*)	0 28	0 28	0 56	—	0 28	4 cents.	0 08	0 10	0 20	0 30	0 40	0 10
Guatemala (*n r*)	0 28	0 28	0 56	—	0 28	4 cents.	0 08	0 10	0 20	0 30	0 40	0 10
Hamburg	0 10	0 10	0 20	—	0 10	Book rate.	0 08	0 16	0 32	0 48	0 64	0 16
Hanover	0 10	0 10	0 20	—	0 10	do	0 08	0 16	0 32	0 48	0 64	0 16
Hayti (*n r*)	0 28	0 28	0 56	—	0 28	4 cents.	0 08	0 10	0 20	0 30	0 40	0 10
Hesse	0 10	0 10	0 20	—	0 10	Book rate.	0 08	0 16	0 32	0 48	0 64	0 16
Hesse Homburg	0 10	0 10	0 20	—	0 10	do	0 08	0 16	0 32	0 48	0 64	0 16
Holland	0 10	0 10	0 20	—	0 10	Book rate.	0 06	0 12	0 24	0 36	0 48	0 12
*Hong Kong	0 28	0 28	0 56	—	0 28	6 cents.	0 10	0 12	0 24	0 36	0 48	0 10
*India	0 22	0 22	0 44	—	0 22	6 cents.	0 10	0 12	0 24	0 36	0 48	0 12

BRITISH AND FOREIGN POSTAGE TABLE.—*Continued.*

COUNTRIES, &c.	For a Letter. Not exceeding ¼ oz.	Above ¼ oz. and not exceeding ½ oz.	Above ½ oz. and not exceeding ¾ oz.	For every additional ¼ oz.	For every additional ½ oz.	For each Newspaper.	For a Book Packet. Not exceeding 2 ozs.	2 ozs. to 4 ozs.	4 ozs. to 8 ozs.	8 ozs. to 12 ozs.	12 ozs. to 1 lb.	For every additional 4 ozs.
	$ cts.	$ cts.	$ cts.	$ cts.	$ cts.		$ cts.	$ cts.	$ cts.	$ cts.	$ cts.	$ cts.
Ireland	0 06	0 06	0 12	—	0 06	2 cents.	0 04	0 06	0 12	0 18	0 24	0 06
Italy	0 14	0 14	0 28	—	0 14	Book rate.	0 08	0 16	0 32	0 48	0 64	0 16
*Labuan	0 28	0 28	0 56	—	0 28	6 cents.	0 10	0 12	0 24	0 36	0 48	0 12
Larnaca	0 16	0 16	0 32	—	0 16	Book rate.	0 08	0 16	0 32	0 48	0 64	0 16
Lauenburg	0 10	0 10	0 20	—	0 10	do	0 08	0 16	0 32	0 48	0 64	0 16
Liberia	0 16	0 16	0 32	—	0 16	4 cents.	0 08	0 10	0 20	0 30	0 40	0 10
Lippe Detmold	0 10	0 10	0 20	—	0 10	Book rate.	0 08	0 16	0 32	0 48	0 64	0 16
Lubeck	0 10	0 10	0 20	—	0 10	do	0 08	0 16	0 32	0 48	0 64	0 16
Madeira	0 16	0 16	0 32	—	0 16	do	0 06	0 12	0 24	0 36	0 48	see mem 4
Malta	0 16	0 16	0 32	—	0 16	4 cents.	0 08	0 10	0 20	0 30	0 40	0 10
Mauritius	0 24	0 24	0 48	—	0 24	8 cents.	0 14	0 16	0 32	0 48	0 64	0 16
Mecklenburg	0 10	0 10	0 20	—	0 10	Book rate.	0 08	0 16	0 32	0 48	0 64	0 16
Mexico (*n r*)	0 28	0 28	0 56	—	0 28	4 cents.	0 08	0 10	0 20	0 30	0 40	0 10
Moldavia	0 14	0 14	0 28	—	0 14	Book rate.	0 08	0 16	0 32	0 48	0 64	0 16
Monte Video (*n r*)	0 28	0 28	0 56	—	0 28	4 cents.	0 08	0 10	0 20	0 30	0 40	0 10
Mytelene (*n r*)	0 16	0 28	0 44	0 12	0 04	Book rate.	0 06	0 12	0 24	0 36	0 48	0 12
Nassau, Duchy of	0 10	0 10	0 20	—	0 10	do	0 08	0 16	0 32	0 48	0 64	0 16
Natal	0 28	0 28	0 56	—	0 28	4 cents.	0 08	0 10	0 20	0 30	0 40	0 10
New Grenada (*n r*)	0 28	0 28	0 56	—	0 28	4 cents.	0 08	0 10	0 20	0 30	0 40	0 10
*New South Wales	0 16	0 16	0 32	—	0 16	6 cents.	0 10	0 12	0 24	0 36	0 48	0 12
*New Zealand	0 16	0 16	0 32	—	0 16	6 cents.	0 10	0 12	0 24	0 36	0 48	0 12
Norway	0 14	0 14	0 28	—	0 14	Book rate.	0 08	0 16	0 32	0 48	0 64	0 16
Oldenburg	0 10	0 10	0 20	—	0 10	do	0 08	0 16	0 32	0 48	0 64	0 16
*Penang	0 28	0 28	0 56	—	0 28	6 cents.	0 10	0 12	0 24	0 36	0 48	0 12
Peru (*n r*)	0 40	0 40	0 80	—	0 40	6 cents.	0 10	0 12	0 24	0 36	0 48	0 12
Poland	0 16	0 16	0 32	—	0 16	Book rate.	0 08	0 16	0 32	See	mem 4	
Porto Rico (*n r*)	0 28	0 28	0 56	—	0 28	4 cents.	0 08	0 10	0 20	0 30	0 40	0 10
Portugal	0 16	0 28	0 44	0 12	0 04	Book rate.	0 06	0 12	0 24	0 36	0 48	see mem 4
Prussia	0 10	0 10	0 20	-	0 10	do	0 08	0 16	0 32	0 48	0 64	0 16
*Queensland	0 16	0 16	0 32	—	0 16	6 cents.	0 10	0 12	0 24	0 36	0 48	0 12
Réunion	0 24	0 24	0 48	—	0 24	8 cents.	0 14	0 16	0 32	0 48	0 64	0 16
Reuss	0 10	0 10	0 20	—	0 10	Book rate.	0 08	0 16	0 32	0 48	0 64	0 16
aRhodes	0 16	0 28	0 44	0 12	0 04	do	0 06	0 12	0 24	0 36	0 48	0 12
Russia	0 14	0 14	0 28	—	0 14	do	0 08	0 16	0 32	See	mem. 4	
St. Helena	0 28	0 28	0 56	—	0 28	4 cents.	0 08	0 10	0 20	0 30	0 40	0 10

aSalonica	0 16	0 28	0 44	0 12	0 04	Book rate.	0 06	0 12	0 24	0 36	0 48	0 12
aSamsoun	0 16	0 28	0 44	0 12	0 04	do	0 06	0 12	0 24	0 36	0 48	0 12
Saxe Altenburg Saxe Coburg Gotha Saxe Meiningen Saxe Weimar Saxony Schaumburg Lippe Schwartzburg Rudolstadt Schwartzburg Sonderhausen	0 10	0 10	0 20	—	0 10	Book rate.	0 08	0 16	0 32	0 48	0 64	0 16
Scotland	0 06	0 06	0 12	—	0 06	2 cents.	0 04	0 06	0 12	0 18	0 24	0 06
Scutari	0 16	0 16	0 32	—	0 16	Book rate.	0 08	0 16	0 32	0 48	0 64	0 15
Seres	0 16	0 16	0 32	—	0 16	do	0 08	0 16	0 32	0 48	0 64	0 16
Sierra Leone	0 16	0 16	0 32	—	0 16	4 cents.	0 08	0 10	0 20	0 30	0 40	0 10
*Singapore	0 28	0 28	0 56	—	0 28	6 cents.	0 10	0 12	0 24	0 36	0 48	0 12
aSmyrna	0 16	0 28	0 44	0 12	0 04	Book rate.	0 06	0 12	0 24	0 36	0 48	0 12
Spain	0 20	0 20	0 40	—	0 20	do	0 08	0 16	0 32	0 48	0 64	0 16
Suez via Brindisi	0 20	0 20	0 40	—	0 20	6 cents.	0 14	0 16	0 30	0 46	0 60	0 16
Suez via Southampton	0 16	0 16	0 32	—	0 16	4 cents.	0 08	0 10	0 20	0 30	0 40	0 10
Surinam	0 28	0 28	0 56	—	0 28	4 cents.	0 08	0 10	0 20	0 30	0 40	0 10
Sweden	0 14	0 14	0 28	—	0 14	Book rate.	0 08	0 16	0 32	0 48	0 64	0 16
Switzerland, via Belgium	0 10	0 10	0 20	—	0 10	do	0 08	0 16	0 32	0 48	0 64	0 16
Switzerland, via France	0 14	0 24	0 38	0 10	0 04	do	0 06	0 12	0 24	0 36	0 48	0 12
Syria (n r)	0 16	0 28	0 44	0 12	0 04	do	0 06	0 12	0 24	0 36	0 48	0 12
Tasmania	0 16	0 16	0 32	—	0 16	6 cents.	0 10	0 12	0 24	0 36	0 48	0 12
Tchesme	0 16	0 16	0 32	—	0 16	Book rate.	0 08	0 16	0 32	0 48	0 64	0 16
Tenedos						do	0 08	0 16	0 32	0 48	0 64	0 16
aTrebizond	0 16	0 28	0 44	0 12	0 04	do	0 06	0 12	0 24	0 36	0 48	0 12
aTultcha	0 16	0 28	0 44	0 12	0 04	do	0 06	0 12	0 24	0 36	0 48	0 12
aTunis	0 16	0 28	0 44	0 12	0 04	do	0 06	0 12	0 24	0 36	0 48	0 12
aVarna	0 16	0 28	0 44	0 12	0 04	do	0 06	0 12	0 24	0 36	0 48	0 12
Venezuela (n r)	0 28	0 28	0 56	—	0 28	4 cents.	0 08	0 10	0 20	0 30	0 40	0 10
*Victoria	0 16	0 16	0 32	—	0 16	6 cents.	0 10	0 12	0 24	0 36	0 48	0 12
Wallachia	0 14	0 14	0 28	—	0 14	Book rate.	0 08	0 16	0 32	0 48	0 64	0 16
West Indies, British	0 28	0 28	0 56	—	0 28	4 cents.	0 08	0 10	0 20	0 30	0 40	0 10
West Indies, Foreign (n r), except places specified	0 28	0 28	0 56	—	0 28	4 cents.	0 08	0 10	0 20	0 30	0 40	0 10
Wurtemburg	0 10	0 10	0 20	—	0 10	Book rate.	0 08	0 16	0 32	0 48	0 64	0 16

A

REGISTERED LETTERS.

TABLE shewing the Postage, including Registration Fee, to be collected on Registered Letters sent from Canada to the undermentioned Countries.

COUNTRIES.	Not exceeding ¼ oz.	Over ¼ and not exceeding ½ oz.	Over ½ and not exceeding ¾ oz.	Over ¾ and not exceeding 1 oz.	Over 1 and not exceeding 1¼ oz.	Over 1¼ and not exceeding 1½ oz.
	$ cts.	$ cts.	$ cts.	$ cts.	$ cts.	$ cts.
Belgium	0 26	0 26	0 36	0 36	0 46	0 46
France	0 32	0 44	0 68	0 80	1 04	1 16
Hamburg	0 26	0 26	0 36	0 36	0 46	0 46
India	0 38	0 38	0 60	0 60	0 82	0 82
Italy	0 30	0 30	0 44	0 44	0 58	0 58
Norway	0 32	0 32	0 48	0 48	0 64	0 64
Prussia	0 26	0 26	0 36	0 36	0 46	0 46

TABLE No. 3.

RATES OF POSTAGE

From Canada to the United Kingdom, British Colonies, and Foreign Countries by Cunard or other Steamers, sailing from New York or Boston, for England.

On Letters.—If addressed to the United Kingdom, 8 cents per ½ oz. If addressed to British Colonies, or Foreign Countries, add to the rates, in Table No. 1, 2 cents per ½ oz.

Newspapers.—Addressed to the United Kingdom must be prepaid at the ordinary commuted rate, or *two cents* each paper, if *transient.* Newspapers addressed to British Colonies and Foreign Countries are not forwarded by the above Steamers.

On Book Packets and Packets of Patterns and Samples addressed to the United Kingdom, 8 cents per 4 ounces (see Table of Rates, page 258), which must be prepaid. Book Packets, and Packets of Patterns and Samples addressed to British Colonies and Foreign Countries are not forwarded by the above Steamers.

The Registration Fees are the same as by Canadian Steamers in Table No. 2.

Letters, &c., intended for despatch by the Packets sailing from New York or Boston, should be specially so addressed.

TABLE No. 4.

RATES of Postage to Bermuda and West Indies, by British Mail Packet, sailing from Halifax to Bermuda and St. Thomas, monthly.

COUNTRY.	Letters.	For each Newspaper.	On Printed Matter.
Bermuda	6 cents per ½ oz	2 cents	6 cents per 4 oz. weight.
West Indies, British and Foreign	12 cents ,,	,,	,, ,,

These Rates should in all cases be prepaid by Postage Stamps. Unpaid correspondence cannot be forwarded by this route.

TABLE No. 5.

SHEWING the Rates of Postage to be collected in Canada on Letters, Newspapers, Pamphlets, Magazines, Printed Matter and Books sent by way of the United States to the undermentioned Colonies and Foreign Countries.

COUNTRIES, &c.	Letters, per ½ oz.	Newspapers, each.	Other Printed Matter.	Registration Fees.
	cts.	cts.	cts.	cts.
Argentine Republic (Buenos Ayres)	21	6	12 per 4 oz.	....
Aspinwall (Colon)—Registered Letters	21	....	....	10
do Unregistered Letters	13	4	3 per 2 oz.	....
Bahamas	3	4	3 per 2 oz.	....
(B) Belize, British Honduras	21	6	12 per 4 oz.	10
Bermuda	10	4	3 per 2 oz.	....
Bolivia	25	6	12 per 4 oz.	10
*Brazil	18	3	2 per 2 oz.	12
Chili	25	6	12 per 4 oz.	10
(A) China (ex Hong Kong and dependant ports)	10	4	3 per 2 oz.	10
Costa Rica	13	4	3 per 2 oz.	....
Cuba	10	4	3 per 2 oz.	....
(B) East Indies (British and Straits Settlements)	13	4	10 per 4 oz.	....
Ecuador	23	4	6 per 4 oz.	....
(B) Guatemala	13	4	3 per 2 oz.	....
(C) Hawaiian Kingdom, Sandwich Islands	9	2	6 per 4 oz.	....
Honduras (not British)	13	4	3 per 2 oz.	....
(B) Hong Kong and dependant ports	13	4	....	....
Jamaica	10	4	3 per 2 oz.	10
(A) Japan	10	4	3 per 2 oz.	10
*Mexico	13	4	2 per 2 oz.	....
Nicaragua	13	4	3 per 2 oz.	....
Panama	13	4	3 per 2 oz.	10
Peru	25	6	12 per 4 oz.	10
(B) San Salvador	13	4	3 per 2 oz.	....
St. Domingo	10	4	3 per 2 oz.	....
U. S. of Columbia, ex Panama and Aspinwall (Colon)	21	6	12 per 4 oz.	10
(B) Venezuela	13	4	3 per 2 oz.	10
West Indies (Danish)	13	4	3 per 2 oz.	....
(B) do not otherwise specified, including British Guiana	21	6	12 per 4 oz.	10

(A) Letters can be registered to Shanghae, in China, and to Yokohama, in Japan, by San Francisco but to no other place in either country.

(B) Printed Prices Current and Mercantile Circulars can, where this letter is prefixed, be forwarded as Newspapers.

(C) The postage to be collected on Newspapers for the Sandwich Islands is two cents for each paper, and an additional charge of one cent for each two ounces weight or fraction thereof, thus, on a single paper weighing three ounces, collect four cents.

* Where an asterisk is prefixed, an additional charge of one cent per two ounces weight on Newspapers, and one cent per ounce on Books and other printed matter, must be collected.

Registration can be effected on correspondence for those places only to which the fee is given.

TABLE

RATES of Postage on all matter transmissible by Post—not of the character and the

NOTE.—The Postage upon all matter included in

DESCRIPTION OF MATTER.	Between any place in Canada and to Newfoundland.	To Great Britain, Mail Steam Packets sailing from Quebec or Portland and Halifax.
Books.....................	1 cent per 2 oz................	Canadian Pkt. Book Post...(a)
Cartes de visite.....................	do	do do ......
Circulars—Printed.....................	1 cent each when sent singly, or 1 cent per 2 oz..............	do do ......
Handbills.....................	1 cent per 2 oz..............	do do ......
Lithographed Letters and Circulars.......	1 cent each when sent singly, or 1 cent per 2 oz..............	do do ......
Newspapers, Canadian.....................	Once a week, 5 cts. per quarter* Twice ,, 10 ,, Thrice ,, 15 ,, Daily ,, 30 ,,	At commuted rate, if prepaid from office of publication ...
Newspapers, transient.....................	2 cents each	2 cents each ....
Pamphlets and occasional Publications...	1 cent per 2 oz................	Canadian Pkt. Book Post...(a)
"*Parcel Post*" *Packages*....	Parcels cannot be sent by post beyond the Dominion of Canada. For rates, see margin (d)	....
Patterns of Merchandize for sale........	1 cent per oz.	Canadian Pkt. Book Post....(a
Periodicals.....................	1 cent per 4 ozs., whether package contains one or more Nos. Weighing less than 1 oz. ½ cent each if sent separately......	2 cents each No. if published in Canada; Canadian Pkt. Book Post, if foreign...........
†*Photographs in Cases*......	Parcel post........	Canadian Pkt. Book Post....(a
,, on card, see *Cartes de Visite*.		
,, Albums.....................	do	do do .....
Prices Current..............	1 cent per 2 oz................	2 cents each, or in bulk at Canadian Packet Book Post....(a
Book and Newspaper Manuscript, Printers' Proof, Maps, &c.	do	Canadian Pkt. Book Post ...(
Printed Matter—of the same character as Circulars, Handbills, &c..............	do	do do .....
Sample of Merchandize—See Patterns.		
School Returns—Half-yearly...	do	do do
School Returns—by School Trustees to Superintendent, even although filled up in writing	1 cent each or 1 cent per 2 oz..	do do .....
Seeds, &c.,—samples of (including Cuttings, Bulbs, Roots, Scions, or Grafts)	1 cent per 2 oz.....	do do .....
Parliamentary Papers..................	Free	do do
Petitions and Addresses to Provincial Legislatures, Votes and Proceedings, and other papers, printed by order of said Legislatures	Free to and from places where Session is held	

No. 6.

of a Letter—within Canada, to Newfoundland, Great Britain, France, United States.

this table should be prepaid by Postage Stamps.

To Great Britain by Cunard and other Steamers sailing from New York or Boston.	To France by Mail Steam Packets sailing from Quebec, &c.	To United States.
CunardPktBookPost(*b*)	French Book Post (*c*)	1 ct. per 2 oz., subject on delivery to U.S. postage
do do	do	do
do do	do	do
do do	do	do
do do	do	do
As by Canadian Str...	do	2 cents each.
2 cents each.....	do ...	do
CunardPktBookPost(*b*)	do	1 ct. per 2 oz. as above
....	....	....
CunardPktBookPost(*b*)	French Book Post (*c*)	Cannot be sent.......
do do	do	Same as between places in Canada, subject on delivery to U.S. postage.
do do	do	
do do	do	do
4 cents each	do	do
CunardPktBookPost(*b*)	do	1 ct. per 2 oz., as above.
do do	do	do
do do	do	do
do do	do	do
do do	do	do
do do	do	do

(*a*)—CANADIAN PACKET BOOK POST.

Not exceeding 1 oz	2	cents
1 to 2 oz..................	4	"
2 to 4 oz..................	6	"
4 to 8 oz..................	12	"
8 to 12 oz..........	18	"
12 ozs. to 1 lb.	24	"

and so on.

(*b*)—CUNARD PACKET BOOK POST.

Not exceeding 1 oz	4	cents
1 to 2 oz..................	6	"
2 to 4 oz	8	"
4 to 8 oz	16	"
8 to 12 oz	24	"
12 oz to 1 lb.............	32	"

and so on.

(*c*)—FRENCH BOOK POST.

Not exceeding 2 oz........	4	cents
2 to 4 oz..................	8	"
4 to 8 oz..................	16	"
8 to 12 oz.................	24	"
12 oz to 1 lb..............	32	"

and so on.

A Book Packet may contain an number of separate books, public tions, works of literature and ar maps or prints, photographs, d gueroetypes, when not on glass, c in frames containing glass; any qua tity of paper, vellum, or parchmer (to the exclusion of letters); and th books, maps, papers, &c., may b either written, printed, or plain, c any mixture of the three; and ma be either British, colonial, or foreig

Book Packages must be open a *both ends or both sides.*

(*d*)—PARCEL POST.

Not exceeding ½ lb	12½	cents
½ lb. to 1 lb....	25	"
1 lb. to 1½ lb	37½	"
1½ lb. to 2 lbs..	50	"
2 lbs. to 2½ lbs...........	62½	"
2½ lbs. to 3 lbs.....	75	"
3 lbs. to 3½ lbs...........	87½	"
3½ lbs. to 4 lbs.... ...	$1.00.	

Registration Fee, 5 *cents*.

Parcels can only be sent by Post t places in Canada, and may contai books, daguereotypes, photograph printers' proof and copy, military r turns, states and rolls containin written figures and signatures, r turns, deeds, legal papers, and a transmissions of a like character, nc being strictly letters ....

REGISTRATION.

No letter, book, newspaper, pa cel or packet of any kind whateve can in future be received for regi tration unless both postage and regi tration fee are fully prepaid; pr payment should, if possible, be b postage stamps.

List of Post Offices,

1874.

LIST

OF

POST OFFICES IN CAN

WITH THE

NAMES OF THE POSTMASTERS

ON THE

1st JULY, 1874.

Printed by Order of the Postmaster General.

Toronto:

TABLE OF CONTENTS.

(Memorandum.)

POST OFFICE DEPARTMENT,
1st July, 1874.

Should any Postmaster discover an error in the description of his Office, as set forth in this List, he will please notify the same to this Department without delay.

A List of Rates of Postage for Foreign Countries, &c., is appended to this Li-

PRINCIPAL OFFICERS OF THE POST OFFICE DEPARTMENT.

HON. DONALD A. MACDONALD	*Postmaster General.*
WILLIAM HENRY GRIFFIN	*Deputy Postmaster General.*
HORATIO ASPREY WICKSTEED	*Accountant.*
WILLIAM WHITE	*Secretary.*
J. CUNNINGHAM STEWART	*Superintendent Savings Bank Branc*
JOHN ASHWORTH	*Cashier.*
WILLIAM HENRY SMITHSON.	*Assistant Accountant.*

MONEY ORDER BRANCH.

PETER LE SUEUR....	Chief Superintendent..............................	*Ottawa.*
J. H. THORNE	Superintendent for Nova Scotia	*Halifax*, N. S.
JAS. HALE	Superintendent for New Brunswick..............	*St. John*, N. B
ROBT. WALLACE......	Inspector, acting as Superintendent for British Columbia.....	*Victoria*, B. C.

INSPECTORS.

			STATIO
JOHN DEWE, *Chief Inspector*			...*Ottawa.*
ARTHUR WOODGATE......	in charge of	......Nova Scotia Division	...............*Halifax*
JOHN McMILLAN	"	......New Brunswick "	...............*St. John*
W. G. SHEPPARD..........	"	......Quebec "	...............*Quebec.*
E. F. KING	"	......Montreal "	.... *Montre*
ROBT. W. BARKER.......	"	......Kingston "	...............*Kingsto*
M. SWEETNAM	"	......Toronto "	...............*Toronto*
G. E. GRIFFIN................	"	......London "	...............*London*
ROBERT WALLACE	"	......British Columbia "	.... *Victoria*
T. P. FRENCH	"	..... Ottawa "	...............*Ottawa.*

LIST OF

POST OFFICES IN CANADA,

On THE 1st JULY, 1874.

The Offices printed in Italics are authorized to Grant and Pay Money Orders.

*The Offices marked * are Savings Bank Offices.*

The letters "W. O." following the name of a Post Office, signify "Way Office."

The Capital letters on the right of the County column indicate the several Provinces of the Dominion.

NAME OF POST OFFICE.	TOWNSHIP OR PARISH.	ELECTORAL COUNTY OR DIVISION.		NAME OF POSTMASTER.
Abbott's Corners	St. Armand	Missisquoi	Q	Charles Hope
Abbotsford		Rouville	Q	O. Crossfield
Aberarder	Plympton	Lambton	O	William Johnston
Abercorn	Sutton	Brome	Q	Benjamin Seaton
Aberfoyle	Puslinch	Wellington, S. R.	O	S. Falconbridge
Abingdon	Caistor	Monck	O	John Millar
Acacia	Middleton	Norfolk, N. R.	O	R. P. Scidmore
Acadia Mines		Colchester	N S	Robert Forman
Acton	Esquesing	Halton	O	J. Matthews
Acton Vale	Acton	Bagot	Q	A. Quintin-dit Dubois.
Adamsville	Farnham East	Brome	Q	George Adams
Adare	McGillivray	Middlesex, N. R.	O	Mrs. Agnes Lavett
Adderley	Inverness	Megantic	Q	John F. Taylor

NAME OF POST OFFICE.	TOWNSHIP OR PARISH.	ELECTORAL COUNTY OR DIVISION.	NAME OF POSTMASTER.
Addison	Elizabethtown	Brockville O	Coleman Lewis
Adelaide	Adelaide	Middlesex, N. R. O	John S. Hoare
Admaston	Admaston	Renfrew, S. R. O	Miss Jane Patterson
Adolphustown	Adolphustown	Lennox O	J. J. Watson
Advocate Harbor		Cumberland N S	Nathan B. Morris
Agincourt	Scarboro'	York, E. R. O	John Milne
Ailsa Craig	East Williams	Middlesex, N. R. O	Shackleton Hay
Aird	Clarenceville	Missisquoi Q	H. A. Hawley
Airlie	Mulmur	Simcoe, S. R. O	Richard Bradley
Akerly, W. O	Wickham	Queens N B	B. H. Akerly
Albany	No. 27	Prince P E I	James Donelly
Albert	Tiendinaga	Hastings, E. R. O	Richard Jones
Albert Bridge, W. O		Cape Breton N S	Thomas Bourke
Albert Mines, W. O		Albert N B	John L. Harris
Alberton	Ancaster	Wentworth, S. R O	John Prentice
Alberton	No. 4	Prince P E I	R. M. Costin
**Albion*	Albion	Cardwell O	George Evans
Albury	Ameliasburg	Prince Edward O	James H. Peck
Aldboro'	Aldboro'	Elgin, W. R. O	Samuel Kirkpatrick
Aldershot	Flamboro, E	Wentworth, N. R O	Alexander Brown
Alderville	Alnwick	Northumberland, W. R. O	
Aldouane, W. O.		Kent N B	F. J. Daigle
Alexander's Point, W. O.		Gloucester N B	F. Alexander
**Alexandria*	Lochiel	Glengarry O	Duncan A. Macdonald
Alfred	Alfred	Prescott O	John B. Lawlor
Algonquin	Augusta	Granville, S. R. O	W. L. McKenzie
Allanburg	Thorold	Welland O	Richard Tucker
Allandale	Innisfil	Simcoe, S. R. O	Andrew Miscampbell
Allan Park	Bentinck	Grey, S. R. O	Chas. F. Goodeve
Allan's Corners	Durham	Chateauguay Q	Thomas Bryson
Allan's Mills	Burgess, N	Lanark, S. R. O	William Allan
Allenford	Amabel	Bruce, N. R. O	William Sharp
Allensville	Stephenson	O	Allan McNicol

NAME OF POST OFFICE.	TOWNSHIP OR PARISH.	ELECTORAL COUNTY OR DIVISION.	NAME OF POSTMASTER.
Allenwood	Flos	Simcoe, N. R. ....O	J. G. Dickinson.........
Allisonville...............	Hallowell	Prince Edward...........O	Benjamin Titus.... ...
Alliston	Tecumseth	Simcoe, S. R...............O	George Fletcher.........
Alloa	Chinguacousy	Peel......................O	Mahlon Silverthorn ...
Allumette Island	Allumette Island	Pontiac ....Q	John Lynch ....
Alma	Peel...........................	Wellington, C. R.........O	Levi Philip ....
Alma	....	Albert ....N B	George Kiersted ......
Alma, W. O.	....	Pictou ....N S	Archibald H. Fraser...
Almira	Markham	York, E. R... ....O	John Bowman ....
Almonte	Ramsay	Lanark, N. R........ ......O	James H. Wylie, jun
Alport......................	Muskoka	Muskoka ....O	W. H. Taylor ....
Alton	Caledon	Cardwell .... O	Mrs. Agnes Meek......
Altona	Pickering	Ontario, S. R............. O	Joseph Monkhouse ...
Alvanley	Derby	Grey, N. R........... .....O	Christopher Tupling..
Alvinston	Brooke	Lambton ....O	J. W. Branan ....
Amaranth Station	Amaranth	Wellington, N. R ....O	Archibald Lamb ......
Amberley	Ashfield	Huron, N. R................O	James Wilkie ....
Ambleside	Carrick	Bruce, S. R ....O	Wm. Zinger ....
Ameliasburg	Ameliasburg	Prince Edward...........O	Owen Roblin..... ......
Amherst	....	Cumberland .... N S	Mrs. A. Chipman ......
**Amherstburgh*	Malden	Essex ... .O	Ernest G. Park.........
Amherst Hill, W.O....	....	Cumberland ....N S	Daniel Pugsley...... ..
Amherst Point, W.O..	....	Cumberland ....N S	Jonathan Pipes ....
Amiens	Lobo	Middlesex, N. R. ....O	John McArthur ....
Ancaster..................	Ancaster..................	Wentworth, S. R... ......O	Anna M. McKay ......
Ancienne Lorette	Ancienne Lorette.... .	Quebec ....Q	Louis Robitaille........
Ancienne Lorette, (sub)	Ancienne Lorette......	Quebec ....Q	George Dufresne .... ..
Anderdon	Anderdon	Essex ... .O	John G. Smith ....
Anderson	Blanchard	Perth, S. R.......... ......O	Humphrey White......
Anderson, W.O.........	....	Westmoreland.........N B	Archibald Simpson ...
Anderson's Corners...	Hinchinbrooke	Huntingdon ....Q	James Anderson.......
Andover	....	Victoria ....N B	....
Ange Gardien	Ange Gardien	Montmorency ....Q	....

NAME OF POST OFFICE.	TOWNSHIP OR PARISH.	ELECTORAL COUNTY OR DIVISION.	NAME OF POSTMASTER.
Angers	Buckingham	Ottawa ... Q	L. Moncion
**Angus*	Essa	Simcoe, S. R. ... O	J. R. Brown
Annegance		King's ... N B	Stanford Palmer
a Annan	Sydenham	Grey, N. R. ... O	William Speedie
Annapolis		Annapolis ... N S	Thos. A. Gavaza
Antigonishe		Antigonishe ... N S	H. P. Hill
Antigonishe Harbour, W. O.		Antigonishe ... N S	John Chisholm
Antrim	Fitzroy	Carleton ... O	John Wilson
Antrim, W. O.		Halifax ... N S	Samuel Kerr
Apohaqui		King's ... N B	O. A. Barberie
Appin	Ekfrid	Middlesex, W. R. ... O	Angus McKenzie
Appleby	Nelson	Halton ... O	James W. Cotter
Apple Grove	Stanstead	Stanstead ... Q	John G. Christie
Apple River, W. O.		Cumberland ... N S	W. R. Elderkin
Appleton	Ramsay	Lanark, N. R. ... O	Albert Teskey
Apsley	Anstruther	Peterborough, E. R. ... O	Henry Eastland
Apto	Flos	Simcoe, N. R. ... O	C. McLaughlin
Archibald Settlement, W. O.		Restigouche ... N B	R. Archibald
Arden	Kennebec	Addington ... O	Wm. B. Mills
Ardoch	Clarendon	Addington ... O	Ernest R. Jacobi
Ardtrea	Orillia	Simcoe, N R. ... O	William Blair, sen.
Argyle	Eldon	Victoria, N. R. ... O	John McKay
Argyle, W. O.		Yarmouth ... N S	Mrs. S. Ryder
Arichat		Richmond ... N S	W. G. Ballam
Arisaig, W. O.		Antigonishe ... N S	Wm. Gillis
Arkell	Pushlinch	Wellington, S. R. ... O	Wm. Watson
**Arkona*	Warwick	Lambton ... O	Miss Louisa Schooley
Arkwright	Arran	Bruce, N. R. ... O	W. F. Sithes
Arlington	Adjala	Cardwell ... O	Thomas Kidd
Armadale	Scarboro'	York, E R. ... O	George Stonehouse
Armagh	St. Cajetan	Belchasse ... Q	C. Roy
Armand	Armand	Temiscouata ... Q	Paschal Lebel
Armow	Kincardine	B–	

NAME OF POST OFFICE.	TOWNSHIP OR PARISH.	ELECTORAL COUNTY OR DIVISION.	NAME OF POSTMASTER.
Armstrong's Brook, W. O.		Restigouche..... N B	John C. Bent
Armstrong's Corner, W. O.		Queen's..... N B	George Mills
Arnott	Holland	Grey, N. R. ..... O	Wm. G. Murray
**Arnprior*	McNabb	Renfrew, S. R. ..... O	Ezra A. Bates
Aroostoock, W. O.		Victoria ..... N B	Albert D. Olmstead
Aros	Bexley	Victoria, N. R. ..... O	Charles McInnes
Arthabaska Station	Arthabaska	Arthabaska ..... Q	Louis Foisy
* Arthabaskaville	Arthabaska	Arthabaska ..... Q	James Goodhue
**Arthur*	Arthur	Wellington, N. R. ..... O	Mrs. Janet Small
Arthurette, W. O.		Victoria ..... N B	
Arundel	Arundel	Argenteuil ..... Q	William Thomson
Arva	London	Middlesex, E. R. ..... O	William Scarrow
Ascot Corner	Ascot	Sherbrooke ..... Q	Fred. G. Stacey
Ashburn	Whitby	Ontario, S. R. ..... O	Edward Oliver
Ashcroft		Yale ..... B C	H. P. Cornwall
Ashdown	Humphrey	Muskoka ..... O	James Ashdown
Ashgrove	Esquesing	Halton ..... O	Robert Smyth
Ashley	Derby	Grey, N. R. ..... O	George Follis
Ashton	Goulburn	Carleton ..... O	James Conn
Ashworth	Scott	Ontario, N. R. ..... O	John Mustard
Aspdin	Stisted	Muskoka ..... O	James Aspdin
Assametquagan	Assametquagan	Bonaventure ..... Q	M. J. Hogan
Aston Station	Aston	Nicolet ..... Q	
Atha	Pickering	Ontario, S. R. ..... O	John M. Pell
Athelstan	Hinchinbrooke	Huntingdon ..... Q	Joshua Breadner
Athens	Scott	Ontario, N. R. ..... O	R. Bingham
Atherley	Mara	Ontario, N. R. ..... O	
Atherton	Windham	Norfolk, N. R. ..... O	G. C. Willson
Athlone	Adjala	Cardwell ..... O	John Kidd
Athol	Kenyon	Glengarry ..... O	M. A. Fisher
Athol		Cumberland ..... N S	F. A. Donkin
Attercliffe	Caistor	Monck ..... O	James Crowther
Aubigny	Ripon	Ottawa ..... Q	P. G. Aubry

NAME OF POST OFFICE.	TOWNSHIP OR PARISH.	ELECTORAL COUNTY OR DIVISION.	NAME OF POSTMASTER.
Aubrey	South Georgetown	Chateauguay ... Q	Joachim Lefebvre
Auburn	Wawanosh	Huron, N. R. ... O	Samuel Caldwell
Audley	Pickering	Ontario, S. R. ... O	Daniel McBrady
Aughrim	Brooke	Lambton ... O	J. McKeune
Augustine Cove	No. 28	Prince ... P E I	Eliza McKenzie
Au Lac, W. O.		Westmoreland ... N B	Ira H. Patterson
Aultsville	Osnabruck	Stormont ... O	I. R. Ault
**Aurora*	Whitchurch	York, N. R. ... O	Charles Doan
Avening	Nottawasaga	Simcoe, N. R. ... O	R. Morris
Avignon	Matapedia	Bonaventure ... Q	Octave Martin
Avoca	Grenville	Argenteuil ... Q	John McCallum
Avon	Dorchester North	Middlesex, E. R. ... O	G. C. Smith
Avonbank	Downie	Perth, S. R. ... O	John McMillan
Avondale, W. O.		Carleton ... N B	John E. McCready
Avondale, W. O		Pictou ... N S	Robert McDonald
Avonmore	Roxborough	Stormont ... O	E. N. Shaver
Avonport, W. O.		King's ... N S	W. A. Reid
Avonport Station		King's ... N S	J. B. Newcomb
Avonton	Downie	Perth, S. R. ... O	John McKellar
Ayer's Flat	Hatley	Stanstead ... Q	C. Ayer
Aylesford		King's ... N S	T. R. Harris
**Aylmer (East)*	Hull	Ottawa ... Q	J. R. Woods
**Aylmer (West)*	Malahide	Elgin, E. R. ... O	Philip Hodgkinson
Aylwin	Aylwin	Ottawa ... Q	J. Little
**Ayr*	Dumfries	Waterloo, S. R. ... O	Robert Wylie
Ayton	Normanby	Grey, S. R. ... O	Robert Smith

NAME OF POST OFFICE.	TOWNSHIP OR PARISH.	ELECTORAL COUNTY OR DIVISION.	NAME OF POSTMASTER.
Baby's Point	Sombra	Bothwell **O**	Edward Keeley
Back Bay, W. O.		Charlotte **N B**	
Back Lands, W. O.		Antigonishe **N S**	William Doyle
Baddeck		Victoria **N S**	R. Elmsly
Baddeck Bay, W. O.		Victoria **N S**	C. McDonald
Baddeck Bridge, W.O.		Victoria **N S**	Alex. McRae
Baden	Wilmot	Waterloo, S. R. **O**	Jacob Beck
Bagot	Bagot	Renfrew, S, R. **O**	Patrick Kennedy
Bagotville	St. Alphonse	Chicoutimi **Q**	E. Levesque
Baie St. Paul	Baie St. Paul	Marquette **M**	Felix Chenier
Baie Verte		Westmoreland **N B**	Charles A. Read
Baie Verte Road, W. O.		Westmoreland **N B**	John Copp, jun.
Bailey's Brook, W.O.		Pictou **N S**	D. D. Macdonald
Bailieboro'	South Monaghan	Peterborough, W. R. **O**	John D. Perrin
Baillargeon	St. Etienne de Lauzon	Lévis **Q**	Frs. Xavier Bilodeau
Baillie, W. O.		Charlotte **N B**	W. S. Robinson
Bairdsville, W. O.		Victoria **N B**	Henry Baird
Bala	Medora	Muskoka **O**	Thomas Burgess
Balderson	Drummond	Lanark, S. R. **O**	John W. Cowie
Ballantrae	Whitchurch	York, N. R. **O**	Robert Hill
Ballantyne's Station	Pittsburg	Frontenac **O**	John Hysop
Ballinafad	Erin	Wellington, S. R. **O**	John S. Appelbe
Ballycroy	Adjala	Cardwell **O**	Peter Small
Ballyduff	Manvers	Durham, E. R. **O**	J. C. Williamson
Ballymote	London	Middlesex, E. R. **O**	T. W. Johnson
Balmoral	Rainham	Haldimand **O**	George B. Lundy
Balsam	Pickering	Ontario, S. R. **O**	Ira Palmer
**Baltimore*	Hamilton	Northumberland, W. R. **O**	Archibald Russell
Bamberg	Wellesley	Waterloo, N. R. **O**	F. Walter
Banda	Mulmer	Simcoe, S. R. **O**	John Cleminger
Bandon	Hullet	Huron, C. R. **O**	James Allen
Bannockburn	Madoc	Hastings, N. R. **O**	William H. Wilson
Barachois, W. O.		Westmoreland **N B**	Thomas Gallang

NAME OF POST OFFICE.	TOWNSHIP OR PARISH.	ELECTORAL COUNTY OR DIVISION.	NAME OF POSTMASTER.
Bardsville	Monck	Muskoka **O**	Charles Bard
Barkerville		Cariboo **B C**	John Bowron
Bark Lake	Jones	Renfrew, S. R. **O**	James Whelan
Barnaby River, W. O		Northumberland **N B**	Mrs. E. J. Dalton
Barnesville, W. O.		King's **N B**	Thomas Worrell.
Barnett	Nichol	Wellington, C. R. **O**	James Elmslie
Barney's River, W.O.		Pictou **N S**	Donald Nicolson
Barnston	Barnston	Stanstead **Q**	Samuel Goodhue
Barrett's Cross	No. 19.	Prince **P E I**	William Glover
Barrie	Vespra	Simcoe, N. R. **O**	James Edwards
Barrington	Hemmingford	Huntingdon **Q**	Oliver Lytle
Barrington		Shelburne **N S**	R. H. Crowell
Barrington Passage, W. O		Shelburne **N S**	Leonard Knowles
Barrio's Beach, W. O.	Antigonishe	Antigonishe **N S**	Benj. Boudrot
Barronsfield, W. O.		Cumberland **N S**	William Baker
Bartibog, W. O.		Northumberland **N B**	Robert Wall
Bartonville	Barton	Wentworth, S. R. **O**	W. J. Gage
Bassin du Lievre	Buckingham	Ottawa **Q**	Asa A. Cooke
Bass River, W. O.		Kent **N B**	Robert Brown
Bass River, W. O.	Londonderry	Colchester **N S**	Mrs. A. Dickey
Basswood Ridge, W.O.		Charlotte **N B**	Margaret Love
Batchewana	Fisher	Algoma **O**	John A. Cameron
Bath	Ernestown	Lennox **O**	John Belfour
Bath		Carleton **N B**	E. D. W. R. Phillips
Bathurst		Gloucester **N B**	Helen J. Waitt
Bathurst Village, W.O.		Gloucester **N B**	John Ferguson, jun.
Batiscan	Ste. Geneviève	Champlain **Q**	D. Lacourcière

NAME OF POST OFFICE.	TOWNSHIP OR PARISH.	ELECTORAL COUNTY OR DIVISION.	NAME OF POSTMASTER.
Bayfield, W. O.		Westmoreland ... N B	C. Van Buskirk
Bayfield, W. O.		Antigonishe ... N S	E. W. Randall
Bay Fortune	No. 56	King's ... P E I	J. Needham
Bayham	Bayham	Elgin, E. R ... O	George Laing
Bayside, W. O.		Charlotte ... N B	John Mowatt
Bay St. Lawrence, W. O.		Victoria ... N S	Angus McIntosh
Bayview	St. Vincent	Grey, E. R ... O	Whitney Wait
Bayville	McLean	Muskoka ... O	William H. Brown
Beachburg	Westmeath	Renfrew, N. R. ... O	George Surtees
**Beachville*	Oxford, West	Oxford, S. R ... O	Charles Mason
Bealton	Townsend	Norfolk, N. R. ... O	
**Beamsville*	Clinton	Lincoln ... O	J. B. Osborne
Bear Brook	Cumberland	Russell ... O	
Bear Island, W. O.		York ... N B	Isaiah Parent
Bear Point, W. O.		Shelburne ... N S	David Smith
Bear River (West Side)		Digby ... N S	V. T. Hardwick
Beatrice	Watt	Muskoka ... O	Richard Lance
**Beauharnois*	St. Clement	Beauharnois ... Q	Crosbie McArthur
Beaulac	Rawdon	Montcalm ... Q	George Mason
Beaulieu	St. Pierre d'Orleans.	Montmorency ... Q	Prudent Blais
Beaumont	Beaumont	Bellechasse ... Q	George Couture
Beauport	Beauport	Quebec ... Q	Margaret O'Brien
Beaurivage	St. Sylvester East	Lotbinière ... Q	Owen Loughrey
Beaver Bank, W. O.		Halifax ... N S	Daniel Hallisey
Beaver Brook, W. O.		Albert ... N B	W. R. Brewster
Beaver Cove, W. O.		Cape Breton ... N S	Stephen McNeill
Beaver Harbour, W. O.		Charlotte ... N B	Leonard Best
Beaver River, W. O.		Digby ... N S	S. P. Raymond
Beaver River Corner		Digby ... N S	W. S. Raymond
**Beaverton*	Thora	Ontario, N. R. ... O	Donald Cameron
Becancour	Becancour	Nicolet ... Q	Miss M. E. Rivard
Becancour Station	Ste. Julie	Megantic ... Q	Richard St. Pierre
Bedeque	No. 26	Prince ... P E I	Major Wright

NAME OF POST OFFICE.	TOWNSHIP OR PARISH.	ELECTORAL COUNTY OR DIVISION.	NAME OF POSTMASTER.
Bedford	Stanbridge	Missisquoi **Q**	George Clayes, jun.
Bedford Basin, W. O.		Halifax **N S**	Wm. Stevens, jun
Beebe Plain	Stanstead	Stanstead **Q**	J. L. House
Beech Hill, W. O.		King's **N S**	Edmund Quigley
Bégon	Bégon	Temiscouata **Q**	H. Boucher
Belfast	Ashfield	Huron, N. R. **O**	William Phillips
Belfast	No. 57	Queen's **P E I**	James Moore
Belford	Markham	York, E. R. **O**	Israel Burton
Belfountain	Caledon	Cardwell **O**	Noah Herring
Belgrave	Morris	Huron, N. R. **O**	Simon Armstrong
Belhaven	North Gwillimbury	York, N. R. **O**	Daniel Prosser
Belle Creek	No. 62	Queen's **P E I**	James Cook
Belle Alodie	St. Valentin	St. John's **Q**	Ambroise Messier
Belledune, W. O		Gloucester **N B**	John Chalmers
Belledune River, W. O		Gloucester **N B**	M. Killoran
Belleisle, W. O.	Granville	Annapolis **N S**	Valentine Troop
Belleisle Bay, W. O.		King's **N B**	Thomas Davis
Belleisle Creek, W. O.		King's **N B**	Cosmo F. McLeod
a Belle River	Rochester	Essex **O**	P. Demouchelle
Belle Riviere		Two Mountains **Q**	Charles Robertson
**Belleville*	Thurlow	Hastings, W. R. **O**	J. H. Meacham
Belleville, W. O.		Carleton **N B**	James Martin
Bell Ewart	Innisfil	Simcoe, S. R **O**	P. Ed. Drake
Belliveaux Cove, W. O.		Digby **N S**	Urbain Belliveaux
Belliveaux Village, W. O.		Westmoreland **N B**	Lewis Richard
Bellrock	Portland	Addington **O**	Edward Walker
Bell's Corners	Nepean	Carleton **O**	George Arnold

NAME OF POST OFFICE.	TOWNSHIP OR PARISH.	ELECTORAL COUNTY OR DIVISION.	NAME OF POSTMASTER.
Bennie's Corners	Ramsay	Lanark, N. R. **O**	John Crossley
Bennington	W. Zorra	Oxford, N. R. **O**	Robert Heron
Bensfort	South Monaghan	Peterborough, W. R. **O**	Alex. D. Galloway
Bentley	Harwich	Kent **O**	Julius Guild
Benton, W. O		Carleton **N B**	John E. Murchie
Beresford	Beresford	Terrebonne **Q**	V. Charbonneau
Bentonville	Cambridge	Russell **O**	John Benton
Bergerville	St. Colomb de Sillery.	Quebec **Q**	Mrs. C. Petitclerc
Berkeley	Holland	Grey, N. R. **O**	John Fleming
**Berlin*	Waterloo, North	Waterloo, N. R. **O**	William Jaffray
Berne	Hay	Huron, S. R. **O**	John Grandy
Berryton, W. O.		Albert **N B**	Edward Berry
Bersimis	Bersimis	Saguenay **Q**	W. S. Church
Berthier	Berthier	Montmagny **Q**	P. S. Joncas
**Berthier en haut*	Berthier	Berthier **Q**	Miss Zoe S. Kitson
Bervie	Kincardine	Bruce, S. R. **O**	Nichol McIntyre
Berwick	Finch	Stormont **O**	Moses A. Tobin
Berwick		King's **N S**	J. M. Parker
Berwick Station, W. O.		King's **N S**	S. J. Nichols
Bethany	Manvers	Durham, E. R. **O**	W. M. Graham
Bethel	Ely	Shefford **Q**	G. Bartlett
Bethesda	Whitchurch	York, N. R. **O**	Hezekiah Pretty
Bewdley	Hamilton	Northumberland, W. R. **O**	John Sidey
Bexley	Bexley	Victoria, N. R. **O**	George Boadway
Bic	Bic	Rimouski **Q**	J. R. Colclough
Bienville	Lauzon	Levis **Q**	P. Morin
Big Bank, W. O.		Victoria **N S**	Donald McLean
Big Bras d'Or		Victoria **N S**	J. A. Fraser
Big Brook, W. O.		Inverness **N S**	Malcolm McLeod
Big Cove, W. O.		Queen's **N B**	James Humphrey
Big Harbor, W. O.		Inverness **N S**	D. McKay
Big Intervale (Grand Narrows), W. O.		Inverness **N S**	Donald Gillis
Big Intervale (Mar-			

NAME OF POST OFFICE.	TOWNSHIP OR PARISH.	ELECTORAL COUNTY OR DIVISION.	NAME OF POSTMASTER.
Big Island, W. O		Pictou ... N S	John Cameron
Big Lorraine, W. O		Cape Breton ... N S	George Jewell
Big Marsh	No. 42	King's ... P E I	D. McDonald
Big Pond, W. O.		Cape Breton ... N S	Michael McLellan
Big Port'le Bear, W. O.		Shelburne ... N S	Thomas Richardson
Big Tracadie, W. O		Antigonishe ... N S	William Girroir
Billings' Bridge	Gloucester	Russell ... O	William Smith
Bill Town, W. O		King's ... N S	Stubbard Sweet
Binbrook	Binbrook	Wentworth, S. R. ... O	Henry Hall
Bingham Road	Cayuga South	Haldimand ... O	Joseph Goehringer
Birchton	Eaton	Compton ... Q	George N. Hodge
Birdton, W. O.		York ... N B	Robert Bird
Birkhall	Moore	Lambton ... O	F. McKenzie
Birmingham	Pittsburg	Frontenac ... O	Mrs. E. Birmingham
Birr	London	Middlesex, E. R. ... O	Joseph M. Young
Bishop's Mills	Oxford	Grenville, N. R ... O	Asa W. Bishop
Bismarck	Gainsborough	Monck ... O	W. H. Trumm
Black Bank	Mulmur	Simcoe, S. R ... O	John Newel
Black Brook, W. O		Northumberland ... N B	Robert Blake
Black Brook, W. O		Cape Breton ... N S	Hugh Livingstone
Black Creek	Willoughby	Welland ... O	Isaac H. Allen
Black Heath	Binbrook	Wentworth, S. R ... O	Alexander Simpson
Black Land, W. O		Restigouche ... N B	William Cook
Black Point, W. O		Restigouche ... N B	H. Connacher
Black Point, W. O.		Halifax ... N S	James Hubley
Black River, W. O.		Northumberland ... N B	Robert McNaughton
Black River		St. John ... N B	Robert Stewart
Black River, W. O.		Antigonishe ... N S	Colin McDonald
Black River Bridge, W. O		Northumberland ... N B	Mrs. I. Cameron
Black River Station	St. Giles	Lotbiniere ... Q	Louis Olivier
Black Rock, W. O		Cumberland ... N S	Jas. Williger
Blackville, W. O		Northumberland ... N B	W. H. Grindley
Blair	Waterloo	Waterloo, S. R ... O	J. Renshaw

NAME OF POST OFFICE.	TOWNSHIP OR PARISH.	ELECTORAL COUNTY OR DIVISION.		NAME OF POSTMASTER.
Blakeney	Ramsay	Lanark, N. R.	O	Peter McDougall
Blanchard Road, W. O.		Pictou	N S	Donald Ross
Blanche	Mulgrave	Ottawa	Q	John A. Cameron
Blandford	St. Louis de Blandford	Arthabaska	O	D. Bergeron
Blandford, W. O.		Lunenburg	N S	Mrs. E. Publicover
Bluntyre	Euphrasia	Grey, E. R.	O	James C. Patterson
Blayney Ridge, W. O.	Prince William	York	N B	Josiah Davis
Blessington	Tyendinaga	Hastings, E. R.	O	Isaac Mott
Blissfield, W. O.		Northumberland	N B	John A. Arbo
Blissville		Sunbury	N B	Hezekiah Hoyt
Bloomfield	Hallowell	Prince Edward	O	Jonathan Striker
Bloomfield	No. 5	Prince	P E I	
Bloomfield, W. O.		Carleton	N B	Charles T. Allerton
Bloomfield, W. O.		King's	N B	John Leavitt
Bloomingdale	Waterloo	Waterloo, N. R.	O	Michael Martel'
Bloomington	Whitchurch	York, N. R.	O	Maxon Jones
Bloomsburg	Townsend	Norfolk, N. R.	O	L. W. Kitchen
Blue Mountain, W. O.		Pictou	N S	Wm. McDonald
Blue's Mill, W. O.		Inverness	N S	Malcolm Blue
Bluevale	Morris	Huron, N. R.	O	John Messor
Blyh	Morris	Huron, N. R.	O	D. B. McKinnon
Blytheswood	Mersea	Essex	O	John Miller
**Boycaygeon*	Verulam	Victoria, S. R.	O	R. La T. Tupper
Bocabec, W. O.		Charlotte	N B	Wm. Erskine
Bogart	Hungerford	Hastings, E. R.	O	Abraham Bogart
Boiestown		Northumberland	N B	Miles McMillen
Boisdale Chapel, W. O.		Cape Breton	N S	Michael McIntyre
Bolingbroke	S. Sherbrooke	Lanark, S. R.	O	John Korry
Bolsover	Eldon	Victoria, N. R.	O	Duncan McRae
Bolton Centre	Bolton	Brome	Q	Mrs. E. D. Blaisdell
Bolton Forest	Bolton	Brome	Q	James T. Channell
Bomanton	Haldimand	Northumberland, W. R.	O	Richard Knight
Bonaventure River	Hamilton	Bonaventure	Q	Frederic Forest
*Bond Head	W. Gwillimbury	Simcoe, S. R.	O	A. H. Carter

NAME OF POST OFFICE.	TOWNSHIP OR PARISH.	ELECTORAL COUNTY OR DIVISION.	NAME OF POSTMASTER.
Bongard's Corners ...	Marysburg..............	Prince Edward ....O	Job D. Bongard ....
Bonshaw	No. 30....................	Queen's..... ....P E I	A. Robertson...........
Bookton	Windham	Norfolk, N. R. ....O	P. N. McIntosh........
Boom, W. O............	....	Inverness ....N S	Alex. McEachern......
Bord à Plouffe	St. Martin	Laval ....Q	V. Lemay ....
Bornholm	Logan.....................	Perth, N. R. ....O	Robert Keys ....
Bornish	E. Williams	Middlesex, N. R. ....O	John Doyle ....
Boscobel.................	Ely	Shefford ....Q	Wm. Hackwell ....
Boston	Townsend	Norfolk, N. R. ....O	Oliver C. Rouse ......
Bosworth	Peel.......................	Wellington, C. R.........O	W. H. Edwards.........
Botany	Howard	Bothwell, ...O	C. McBrayne............
Bothwell	Zone	Bothwell ....O	John Taylor ....
Bothwell......	No. 47.....................	King's.................P E I	David McVane ....
Botsford Portage, W. O	....	Westmoreland.........N B	Wm. Farrow ....
Boucherville	Boucherville	Chambly ....Q	Louis Normandin......
Bourck's Hill............	Williamsburg	Dundas .... O	Henry W. Ford.........
Boudreau Village, W. O.......	....	Westmoreland.........N B	Alex. Bourdrot ....
Boulardarie	....	Victoria..................N S	A. Munro ....
Boulter	Carlow	Hastings, N. R.......... .O	James Wilson, sen.....
Boundary Creek, W.O.	....	Westmoreland.........N B	R. B. C. Weldon........
Boundary, Présqu'le, W. O.....................	....	Carleton.................N B	John D. Baird... ......
Bourgeois, W. O.......	....	Kent ....N B	John Bourgeois ....
Bourg Louis	Bourg Louis	Portneuf..... ....Q	John Hewton ....
Bowling Green.........	Amaranth................	Wellington, N. R.........O	Robert Magwood .....
**Bowmanville*.......	Darlington..............	Durham, W. R.............O	J. B. Fairbairn.........
Box Grove..............	Markham	York, E. R............. ...O	John McCaffrey.........

NAME OF POST OFFICE.	TOWNSHIP OR PARISH.	ELECTORAL COUNTY OR DIVISION.	NAME OF POSTMASTER.
Braemar	E. Zorra	Oxford, N R. **O**	Alex. Anderson
Braeside	McNab	Renfrew, S. R. **O**	John Gillis
Bramley	Innisfil	Simcoe, S. R. **O**	James Black, jun.
**Brampton*	Chinguacousy	Peel **O**	Matthew M. Elliott
Branchton	Dumfries, North	Waterloo, S. R. **O**	William Pickering
Brandy Creek	Windham	Norfolk, N. R. **O**	E. R. Cromby
**Brantford*	Brantford	Brant, S. R. **O**	A. D. Clement
Breadalbane, W. O.		Restigouche **N B**	John McMillan
Brechin	Mara	Ontario, N. R. **O**	John Bernard
Brentwood	Sunnidale	Simcoe, N. R. **O**	James Graham
Breslaw	Waterloo	Waterloo, N. R. **O**	Moses Moyer
Brower's Mills	Pittsburg	Frontenac **O**	Robert Anglin
Brewster	Stephen	Huron, S. R. **O**	W. McDougall
Bridgedale, W. O.		Albert **N B**	Millidge Steeves
Bridgenorth	Smith	Peterborough, W. R. **O**	Marcus S. Dean
Bridgeport	Waterloo, North	Waterloo, N. R. **O**	Elias Eby
Bridgeport, W. O.		Cape Breton **N S**	George Burchell
Bridgetown		Annapolis **N S**	Enoch Dodge, jun.
Bridgeville, W. O.		Pictou **N S**	John A. Cameron
**Bridgewater*	Elzevir	Hastings, N. R. **O**	Edwin James
Bridgewater		Lunenburg **N S**	Joseph Whitford
Brigg's Corner, W. O.		Queen's **N B**	Joel F. Estabrooks
Brigham	Farnham, East	Brome **Q**	E. O. Brigham
**Bright*	Blenheim	Oxford, N. R. **O**	John Cameron
**Brighton*	Brighton	Northumberland, E. R. **O**	Thomas C. Lockwood
Briley's Brook, W.O.	Dorchester	Antigonishe **N S**	John McAdam
Brinkworth	Rawdon	Hastings, N. R. **O**	Allen Williams
Brinsley	McGillivray	Middlesex, N. R. **O**	George Brown
Brinston's Corners	Matilda	Dundas **O**	Charles Lock
Brisbane	Erin	Wellington, S. R. **O**	G. J. Mackelcan
Bristol	Bristol	Pontiac **Q**	William King
Britannia	Toronto	Peel **O**	Joseph Gardner
Britannia Mills	St. Dominique	Bagot **Q**	Mrs. H. Guilbert
Britonville	Morin	Argenteuil **Q**	George Hamilton

NAME OF POST OFFICE.	TOWNSHIP OR PARISH.	ELECTORAL COUNTY OR DIVISION.	NAME OF POSTMASTER.
Broad Cove Chapel, W.O.		Inverness N S	Alexander McLennan.
Broad Cove (Intervale), W.O.		Inverness N S	Isaac McLeod
Broad Cove (Lunenburg), W.O.		Lunenburg N S	Elkanah Teel
Broad Cove (Marsh), W.O.		Inverness N S	Donald Macleod
Broadlands		Bonaventure Q	Melvin Adams
Brockton	York	York, W. R. O	Mrs. Ann Church
Brockville	Elizabethtown	Brockville O	John Crawford
Brodhagen	Logan	Perth, N. R. O	Charles Brodhagen
Brome	Brome	Brome Q	Walter Lynch
Bromemere	Brome	Brome Q	C. H. Jones
Brompton	Brompton	Richmond Q	Henry Addison
Brompton Falls	Brompton	Richmond Q	J. R. McDonnell
Bronson	Dungannon	Hastings, N. R. O	Frederic Mullett
Bronte	Trafalgar	Halton O	Charles K. Jones
Brookbury	Bury	Compton Q	R. Rowe.
Brookfield		Colchester N S	James Graham
Brookfield, W. O.		Queen's N S	W. Hendry
**Brooklin*	Whitby	Ontario, S. R O	Robert Darlington
Brooklyn	No. 61	King's P E I	H Compton
Brooklyn, W. O.		Queen's N S	J. R. Hall
Brooksdale	West Zorra	Oxford, N. R. O	John Bagrie
Brookvale, W. O.		Queen's N B	Mrs. Milcha Fowlie
Brookvale, W. O.		Halifax N S	Hugh Hannah
Brookville, W. O.		Cumberland N S	J. A. Hatfield
Brookville, W. O.		Pictou N S	Jas. McDonald
Brougham	Pickering	Ontario, S. R. O	John B. Burke
Broughton	Broughton	Beauce Q	C. H. J. Hall
Brown's Brook, W. O.		Cumberland N S	Hiram Brown
Brownsburg	Chatham	Argenteuil Q	Alex. McGibbon
Brownsville	Dereham	Oxford, S. R. O	Mrs. E. Sponenburg
Brucefield	Tuckersmith	Huron, C. R. O	Robert Marks
Bruce Mines		Algoma O	J. B. Dobie

NAME OF POST OFFICE.	TOWNSHIP OR PARISH.	ELECTORAL COUNTY OR DIVISION.	NAME OF POSTMASTER.
Brudenell	Brudenell	Renfrew, S. R. O	James Costello
Brunner	Ellice	Perth, N. R. O	Henry Gropp
Brunswick	Manvers	Durham, E. R. O	S. R Beamish
**Brussels*	Grey	Huron, C. R, O	John R. Grant
Bryanston	London	Middlesex, E. R. O	Thomas B. Goulding
Bryson	Litchfield	Pontiac. Q	W. G. Le Roy
Buckhorn	Harwich	Kent O	T. H. Stripp
**Buckingham*	Buckingham	Ottawa Q	James Wilson
Buckland	Buckland	Bellechasse Q	Eusèbe Couture
Bucklaw, W. O		Victoria N S	Malcolm McLeod
Buckley's, W. O		King's N S	Thos. Buckley
Buckshot	Clarendon	Addington O	Elisha Playfair
Buctouche		Kent N B	B. H. Foley
Bull Creek	No. 46	King's P E I	James McAulay
a Bullock's Corners	W. Flamboro'	Wentworth, N. R. O	Wm. J. Mordan
Bulstrode	Bulstrode	Arthabaska Q	George Dauth
Bulwer	Eaton	Compton Q	Robert Cairns
Burford	Burford	Brant, S. R. O	John Catton
Burgessville	Norwich, North	Oxford, S. R. O	E. W. Burgess
Burgoyne	Arran	Bruce, N. R. O	Alfred Shell
Burleigh	Burleigh	Peterborough, E. R O	John McDonald
Burlington	No. 18	Prince P E I	Joseph Davison
Burlington, W. O		King's N S	
Burnbrae	Seymour	Northumberland, E. R. O	Alex. Donald
Burnhamthorpe	Toronto	Peel O	George Savage
Burnley	Haldimand	Northumberland, W. R. O	William Lawler
Burns	Morrington	Perth, N. R O	Oran Phillips
Burnside	Portage La Prairie	Marquette. M	
Burnstown	McNab	Renfrew, S. R O	Donald McRae
Burnt Church, W. O		Northumberland N B	F. H. McKnight
Burntcoat, W. O		Hants N S	Robert Faulkner
Burnt River	Somerville	Victoria, N. R. O	Simon Moore
Burrard Inlet		New Westminster B C	Maximilian Michaud
[illegible]	[illegible]	[illegible] N. R. O	Thomas A. Kidd

NAME OF POST OFFICE.	TOWNSHIP OR PARISH.	ELECTORAL COUNTY OR DIVISION.	NAME OF POSTMASTER.
Burtch	Brantford	Brant, S. R. **O**	George Taylor
Burton	Manvers	Durham, E R. **O**	James McGill
Burton, W. O.		Sunbury **N B**	M. E. A. Burpee
Bury's Green	Somerville	Victoria, N. R. **O**	John Fell
Bushfield	Morris	Huron, N. R. **O**	James Lynn
Bute	Somerset	Megantic **Q**	John Kelso
Butternut Ridge		King's **N B**	Charles Israel Keith
Buttonville	Markham	York, E. R **O**	T. Thomson
Buxton	Raleigh	Kent **O**	D. C. Echlin
Byng	Dunn	Monck **O**	James M. Thomson
Byng Inlet	Wallbridge	Muskoka **O**	Pulaski Clark
Byron	Westminster	Middlesex, E. R. **O**	Robert Sadler
Cable Head	No. 41	King's **P E I**	John McIntyre
Cache Creek		Yale **B C**	James Campbell
Cacouna	St. George	Temiscouata **Q**	J. B. Beaulieu
Cadmus	Cartwright	Durham, W. R. **O**	John McKinnon
Cæsarea	Cartwright	Durham, W. R. **O**	John Elliott
Cain's River, W. O.		Northumberland **N B**	Mrs. C. A. Murdoch
Cainsville	Brantford, E.	Brant, N. R. **O**	Andrew Chittenden
Caintown	Yonge	Leeds, S. R. **O**	W. Tennant, jun.
Cairngorm	Metcalfe	Middlesex, W. R. **O**	Francis Brown
Caistorville	Caistor	Monck **O**	Adam Spears, jun.
Calabogie	Bagot	Renfrew, S. R. **O**	D. Dillon
Calder	Delaware	Middlesex, W. R. **O**	William Campbell
Caldwell	Caledon	C[illegible]	[illegible]

NAME OF POST OFFICE.	TOWNSHIP OR PARISH.	ELECTORAL COUNTY OR DIVISION.	NAME OF POSTMASTER.
Caledon	Caledon	Cardwell ... O	George Bell
Caledon East	Caledon	Cardwell ... O	James Munsie
Caledonia	No. 60	Queen's ... P E I	James Walker
Caledonia Corner		Queen's ... N S	George Middlemas
Caledonia Mills, W. O.		Antigonishe ... N S	John Boyle
Caledonia, St. Mary's, W. O.		Guysboro' ... N S	Angus McDonald
Caledonia Settlement, W. O.		Albert ... N B	James Reed
Caledonia Springs	Calodonia	Prescott ... O	John D. Cameron
Calton	Bayham	Elgin, E. R. ... O	Duncan McLaughlan
Calumet Island	Calumet	Pontiac ... Q	John Cahill
Cambray	Fenelon	Victoria, N. R. ... O	Thomas Douglas
Cambria	St. Columbin	Argenteuil ... Q	William Stuart
Cambridge, W. O.		Queen's ... N B	William H. White
Cambridge, W. O.		Halifax ... N S	Handly Starrat
Cambridge Station, W. O.		King's ... N S	John C. Neiley
Camden East	Camden East	Addington ... O	Benjamin Clark
Cameron	Fenelon	Victoria, N. R. ... O	James Bryson
Camerontown	Charlottenburg	Glengarry ... O	Andrew Cameron
Camilla	Mono	Cardwell ... O	Hugh Currie
Camlachie	Plympton	Lambton ... O	Thomas Houston
Campbellford	Seymour	Northumberland, E. R. O	James M. Ferris
Campbell's Cross	Chingacousy	Peel ... O	E. T. Hagyard
Campbell Settlement, W. O.		King's ... N B	D. K. Campbell
Campbell Settlement, W. O.		York ... N B	Henry McFarlane
Campbellton		Restigouche ... N B	A. W. Kendrick
Campbellville	Nassagiweya	Halton ... O	Thos. Christie
Campden	Clinton	Lincoln ... O	H. W. Moyer
Campo Bello		Charlotte ... N B	Luke Byron
Canaan		King's ... N S	W. J. Wallace
Canaan Rapids, W. O.		Queen's ... N B	Robert Phillips
Canaan Road, W. O.		King's ... N S	Reuben R. Baker

NAME OF POST OFFICE.	TOWNSHIP OR PARISH.	ELECTORAL COUNTY OR DIVISION.	NAME OF POSTMASTER.
Canard, W. O.		King's N S	J. E. Lockwood
Canard River	Sandwich	Essex O	Louis Drouillard
Canboro'	Canboro'	Monck O	John Folmsbee
Candasville	Gainsborough	Monck O	John M. Culp
Canfield	Cayuga North	Haldimand O	Ambrose Pattison
Cannifton	Thurlow	Hastings, E. R. O	Jonas Canniff, jun.
Canning	Blenheim	Oxford, N. R. O	Samuel Allchin
Canning		King's N S	J. W. Borden
**Cannington*	Brock	Ontario, N. R. O	Robert Talbot
Cannonville, W. O.		Cumberland N S	Edward D. Fullarton
Canoe Creek		Cariboo B C	Robert P. Ritchie
Canrobert		Rouville Q	Francois Meunier
Canso		Guysboro' N S	Charlotte Cunningham
Canterbury	Bury	Compton Q	Robert Clark
Canterbury		York N B	C. E. Grosvenor
Canterbury Station		York N B	William Main
Cantley	Hull	Ottawa Q	Alex. Prudhomme
Canton	Hope	Durham, E. R. O	Samuel Stephenson
Cap à l'Aigle (sub)	Mount Murray	Charlevoix Q	Joseph Layard
Cap Ch. t	St. Norbert de Cap Chat	Gaspé Q	Telesphore Roy
Cap de Moselle Creek, W. O.		Albert N B	John Wilson
Cap des Rosiers	Cap des Rosiers	Gaspé Q	Peter Whalan
Cape Cove	Percé	Gaspé Q	William Tilly
Cape Crother	Albemarle	Bruce, N.R. O	Fred. Lamorandière
Cape George		Antigonishe N S	Robert McDonald
Cape George (North Side), W. O.		Antigonishe N S	Donald McDonald
Cape John, W. O.		Pictou N S	Hugh McLeod

NAME OF POST OFFICE.	TOWNSHIP OR PARISH.	ELECTORAL COUNTY OR DIVISION.	NAME OF POSTMASTER.
Cape Sable Island, W. O		Shelburne **N S**	W. Cunningham
Cape Spear, W. O		Westmoreland **N B**	John McKay
Cape Traverse	No. 28	Prince **P E I**	J. L. Muttart
Cape Wolfe	No. 7	Prince **P E I**	Matthew Howard
Caplin		Bonaventure **Q**	David Kerr
Cap Magdeleine		Champlain **Q**	Onesime Toupin
Cap Rouge	St. Foy	Quebec **Q**	Dominique Thivierge
Cap St. Ignace	St. Ignace	Montmagny **Q**	Miss H. C. Larue
Cap Santé	Cap Santé	Portneuf **Q**	J. Bernard
Caraquet		Gloucester **N B**	J. G. C. Blackhall
Carden	Carden	Victoria, N. R **O**	Jacob Belfrey
Cardigan Bridge	No. 53	King's **P E I**	George F. Owen
Cardigan Road	No. 38	King's **P E I**	P. Banbrick
Cardwell	Marysburg	Prince Edward **O**	George J. Hayek
Carillon	Chatham	Argenteuil **Q**	William Fletcher
Carleton	Carleton	Bonaventure **Q**	Joseph Meagher
Carleton		St. John **N B**	James R. Reed
Carleton	No. 28	Prince **P E I**	D. Morrison
Carleton Place	Beckwith	Lanark, S. R **O**	Patrick Struthers
Carlingford	Fullarton	Perth, S. R **O**	James Hamilton
Carlisle	Flamboro East	Wentworth, N. R **O**	T. W. Colcleugh
Carlow	Colborne	Huron, C. R **O**	James McDonagh
Carlow, W. O		Carleton **N B**	S. Cummins
Carlsruhe	Carrick	Bruce, S. R **O**	Jacob Knechtel, jun.
Carlton, W. O		Yarmouth **N S**	John P. Miller
Carluke	Ancaster	Wentworth, S. R **O**	James Calder
Carnarvon	Stanhope	Peterborough, E. R **O**	Alfred Moore
Carnegie	Elderslie	Bruce, N. R. **O**	Thomas Ewart
Caron Brook, W. O		Victoria **N B**	Theodore Pelletier
Carp	Huntley	Carleton **O**	W. J. Featherstone
Carriboo Cove, W.O		Richmond **N S**	John Malcolm, sen.
Carriboo Cove, W.O		Cape Breton **N S**	Malcolm Ferguson
Carroll's Corners, W.O		Halifax **N S**	Jane Heffernan
		O	G. J. Kidd

NAME OF POST OFFICE.	TOWNSHIP OR PARISH.	ELECTORAL COUNTY OR DIVISION.	NAME OF POSTMASTER.
Carrville	Vaughan	York, W. R. **O**	William Cook
Carsonby	North Gower	Carleton **O**	Benjamin Eastman
Carsonville, W. O.		King's **N B**	John McLeod
Carthage	Mornington	Perth, N. R. **O**	Charles Schneider
Cartwright	Cartwright	Durham, W. R. **O**	Hugh McPhail
Cascades	Hull	Ottawa **Q**	Thomas M. Reid
Case Settlement, W.O.		King's **N B**	George Case
Cashel	Markham	York, E. R. **O**	Colin Shell
Cashion's Glen	Charlottenburg	Glengarry **O**	Mrs. Caroline Cashion
Cashmere	Mosa	Middlesex, W. R. **O**	George Mansfield
Cass Bridge	Winchester	Dundas **O**	Joseph Cass, jun.
Casselman	Cambridge	Russell **O**	Martin Casselman
Cassel	E. Zorra	Oxford, N. R. **O**	John Loth, jun.
Cassiar		**B C**	James Pringle
Castile	Algona, South	Renfrew, N. R. **O**	Edmund Bennett
Castlebar	Shipton	Richmond **Q**	David U. Graveline
Castleford	Horton	Renfrew, S. R. **O**	John Warnock
Castlemore	Gore of Toronto	Peel **O**	George Dale
Castleton	Cramahe	Northumberland, E. R. **O**	John C. Pennock
Catalone, W. O.		Cape Breton **N S**	
Cataract	Caledon	Cardwell **O**	Richard Church
Cataraqui	Kingston	Frontenac **O**	Joseph Northmore
Cathcart	Burford	Brant, S. R. **O**	Alex. Kennedy
Caughnawaga	Sault St. Louis	Laprairie **Q**	W. D. Lorimer
Causapscal	Causapscal	Rimouski **Q**	Edwin L. Strange
Cavan	Cavan	Durham, E. **O**	David Walker
Cavendish	No. 23	Queen's **P E I**	A. M. McNeill
Cavendish Road	No. 23	Queen's **P E I**	George W. McKay

NAME OF POST OFFICE.	TOWNSHIP OR PARISH.	ELECTORAL COUNTY OR DIVISION.	NAME OF POSTMASTER.
Cedar Lake, W. O.		Digby N S	Ambrose Poole
Cedars	Soulanges	Soulanges Q	T. Marcoux
Cedarville	Proton	Grey, E. R. O	Thomas Rogers
Central Blissville, W. O.		Sunbury N B	Luke E. Bailey
Central Cambridge, W. O.		Queen's N B	Amos Mott
Central Chebogue, W. O.		Yarmouth N S	R. W. Woodworth
Centralia	Stephen	Huron, S. R. O	William Greenway
Central Kingsclear, W. O.		York N B	
Central Norton, W. O.		King's N B	Silas Raymond
Central Onslow, W. O.		Colchester N S	Hugh Dickson
Centre Augusta	Augusta	Grenville, S. R. O	A. B. Cummins
Centreton	Haldimand	Northumberland, W. R. O	T. H. McAulay
Centre Village, W. O.		Westmoreland N B	Timothy Copp
Centreville	Camden East	Addington O	Cyrus Ash
Centreville, W. O		Albert N B	Wm. Woodworth
Centreville		Carleton N B	Ludlow B. Clark
Centreville, W. O.		King's N S	J. M. Rosco
Chambly Basin	Chambly	Chambly Q	Wm. Vallée
Chambly Canton	West Chambly	Chambly Q	John Hackett
Chambord	Metabechouan	Chicoutimi Q	Job Bilodeau
Champlain	Champlain	Champlain Q	N. Hardy
Chance Harbour, W O.		St. John N B	James Boyle
Chandos	Chandos	Peterborough, E. R. O	Thomas Kemp
Chantelle	Chertsey	Montcalm Q	Delphin Morin
Chantry	Bastard	Leeds, S. R. O	Samuel Chant
Chapman	Hungerford	Hastings, E. R. O	Alexander Chapman
Chapman, W. O.		Westmoreland N B	Bowden Chapman
Charing Cross	Harwich	Kent O	John L. Brodie
Charlemagne	St. Chas. de Lachenaie	L'Assomption Q	Antoine Desparois dit Champagne
Charlesbourg	Quebec	Quebec Q	M. Tremblay
Charleston	Escott	Leeds, S. R. O	P. F. Green

NAME OF POST OFFICE.	TOWNSHIP OR PARISH.	ELECTORAL COUNTY OR DIVISION.	NAME OF POSTMASTER.
Charleston, W. O.		Carleton ..... N B	John Lipsett
Charleville	Augusta	Grenville, S. R. ..... O	Rufus S. Throop
Charlo's Cove, W. O.	Wilmot	Guysboro' ..... N S	Henry Lindon
Charlottetown		Queen's ..... P E I	A. A. McDonald
Chatboro'	Chatham	Argenteuil ..... Q	Chas. A. Bradford
Chateauguay	Chateauguay	Chateauguay ..... Q	N. Mallett
Chateauguay Basin	Chateauguay	Chateaugnay ..... Q	Robert Lang
Chateau Richer	Chateau Richer	Montmorency ..... Q	Mdme. L. B. Rousseau
**Chatham*	Raleigh	Kent ..... O	S. Barfoot
Chatham		Northumberlaad ..... N B	Thos. Vondy, jun
Chatillon	St. Zépheria	Yamaska ..... Q	Thomas N. Hart
Chatsworth	Holland	Grey, N. R. ..... O	Henry Cardwell
Chaudiere Mills	St. Jean Chrysostome	Levis ..... Q	Antoine Lemieux
Chaudiere Station		Levis ..... Q	John Ochlenschlaeger
Cheapside	Walpole	Haldimand ..... O	William Pugsley
Chebogue, W. O.		Yarmouth ..... N S	Ansell Robbins
Cheddar	Cardiff	Peterborough, E. R ..... O	Edward Bates
**Chelsea*	Hull	Ottawa ..... Q	H. B. Prentiss
Chelsea, W. O.		Lunenburg ..... N S	H. Kedy
Cheltenham	Chinguacousy	Peel ..... O	C. H. King
Chemainus		Vancouver ..... B C	Thomas G. Askew
Chepstow	Greenock	Bruce, S. R ..... O	Wm. Henesy
Cherry Creek	Innisfil	Simcoe, S. R. ..... O	William Mains
Cherry Grove	No. 45	King's ..... E P I	Joseph McAulay
Cherry Vale, W. O.		Queen's ..... N B	Allen McDonald
Cherry Valley	Athol	Prince Edward ..... O	Thomas Colliver
Cherry Valley	No. 50	Queen's ..... P E I	A. McLellan
Cherrywood	Pickering	Ontario, S. R. ..... O	Charles Petty

NAME OF POST OFFICE.	TOWNSHIP OR PARISH.	ELECTORAL COUNTY OR DIVISION.	NAME OF POSTMASTER.
Chesterfield	Blenheim	Oxford, N. R. **O**	Wm. Brown
Cheticamp, W. O.	Cheticamp	Inverness **N S**	Ed. Briard
Cheverie, W. O.		Hants **N S**	John Burgess
Cheviot	Culross	Bruce, S. R. **O**	Andrew McLean
Chezzetcook, W. O.		Halifax **N S**	Donald McLaren
Chichester	Chichester	Pontiac **Q**	Horace Landon
Chicoutimi	Chicoutimi	Chicoutimi **Q**	Jean O. Tremblay
Chicagacnaise River, W. O.		Colchester **N S**	Thos. Lindsay
Chilliwack		New Westminster **B C**	J. McCutcheon
Chimney Corner, W. O.		Inverness **N S**	Hector McKay
Chipman, W. O.		Queen's **N B**	Geo. G. King
Chipman's Brook, W. O.		King's **N S**	Thomas Murphey
Chipman's Corners, W. O.		King's **N S**	Samuel Chipman
* *Chippawa*	Stamford	Welland **O**	J. S. Macklem
Chlorydormes	Clorydormes	Gaspé **Q**	Celestin Belanger
Chockfish, W. O.		Kent **N B**	M. McEwen
Christmas Island		Cape Breton **N S**	John Mackinnon
Churchill	Innisfil	Simcoe, S. R. **O**	H. Sloane
Church Hill, W. O.		Albert **N B**	Alex. Bayley
Church Point, W. O.		Northumberland **N B**	W. M. Salter
Churchstreet, W. O.		King's **N S**	Wm. Gilliat
Churchville	Toronto	Peel **O**	James E. Pointer
Churchville, W. O.		Pictou **N S**	Allan Weir
Chute au Blondeau	East Hawkesbury	Prescott **O**	James McAllister
Chute's Cove, W. O.		Annapolis **N S**	H. M. Foster
Clachan	Orford	Bothwell **O**	Duncan McColl, jun.
Clairvaux (sub)	St. Placide	Charlevoix **Q**	E. Larouche
Clam Harbour, W. O.		Halifax **N S**	Thomas Stoddart
Clandeboye	Huntley	Carleton **O**	Robert McKinlay
Clapham	Inverness	Megantic **Q**	S. Johnston
Clare W. O.		Digby **N S**	A. F. Comeau
Claremont	Pickering	Ontario, S. R. **O**	J. McM. McNab

NAME OF POST OFFICE.	TOWNSHIP OR PARISH.	ELECTORAL COUNTY. OR DIVISION.	NAME OF POSTMASTER.
Claremont, W. O.		Cumberland **N S**	J. C. Black
Clarence	Clarence	Russell **O**	Thomas Wilson
Clarence Creek	Clarence	Russell **O**	S. G. A. Raiche
Clarenceville	Noyan	Missisquoi **Q**	Charles Stewart
Clarendon Front (sub)	Clarendon	Pontiac **Q**	William Heath
Clarendon, W. O.		Charlotte **N B**	John McCutcheon
Clareview	Sheffield	Addington **O**	Robert T. McDonnell
Clarina	Granby	Shefford **Q**	Nazaire Giroux
Clarke	Clarke	Durham, W. R. **O**	James Lockhart
Clarke's Harb'r, W.O.		Shelburne **N S**	James L. Nickerson
**Clarksburg*	Collingwood	Grey, E. R. **O**	Walter Hunter
Claude	Chinguacousy	Peel **O**	James Westervett
Clavering	Keppel	Grey, N. R. **O**	Henry Cammidge
Clayton	Ramsay	Lanark, N. R. **O**	O. Banning, jun.
Clear Creek	Houghton	Norfolk, S. R. **O**	
**Clearville*	Orford	Bothwell **O**	Henry Watson
Clementsport		Annapolis **N S**	James P. Roop
Clementsvale, W. O		Annapolis **N S**	Richard Sandford
Clifford	Minto	Wellington, N. R. **O**	Francis Brown
**Clifton*	Stamford	Welland **O**	W. W. Woodruff
a Clifton House (sub).	Stamford	Welland **O**	J. Shears
Clifton, W. O.		Gloucester **N B**	A. J. Seaman
Clifton		King's **N B**	G. H. Flewelling
Clinch's Mills		St. John **N B**	Charles F. Clinch
Clinton		Cariboo **B C**	Charles E. Pope
**Clinton*	Tuckersmith	Huron, S. R. **O**	Thomas Fair
Clones, W. O		Queen's **N B**	Andrew Corbett
Clontarf	Sebastopol	Renfrew, S. R. **O**	J. B. McDonald

NAME OF POST OFFICE.	TOWNSHIP OR PARISH.	ELECTORAL COUNTY OR DIVISION.	NAME OF POSTMASTER.
Coates' Mills, W. O.		Kent N B	Thomas Coates
**Coaticook*	Barnston	Stanstead Q	Horace Cutting
Cobden	Ross	Renfrew, N. R. O	John R. McDonald
**Cobourg*	Hamilton	Northumberland, W. R. O	William Sykes
Cocagne		Kent N B	James Lucas
Cocagne River, W. O.		Kent N B	Sylvan S. Le Blanc
Codrington	Brighton	Northumberland, E. R. O	James B. Lay
Cody's, W. O.		Queen's N B	Charles F. Cody
Cogmagun River, W. O		Hants N S	Charles Thomas
Colbeck	Luther	Wellington, N. R. O	William Colbeck
**Colborne*	Cramahe	Northumberland, E. R. O	C. R. Ford
Colchester	Colchester	Essex O	Alex. Hackett
Cold Brook Station, W. O.		King's N S	Henry Porter
Cold Springs	Hamilton	Northumberland, W. R. O	D. McIntosh
Coldstream	Lobo	Middlesex, N. R. O	Jacob Marsh
Coldstream, W. O.		Carleton N B	Samuel Dickinson
**Coldwater*	Medonte	Simcoe, N. R. O	Samuel Drew Eplett
Colebrook	Camden East	Addington O	Charles Warner
Cole Harbor, W. O.		Guysboro' N S	George Jamieson
Coleraine	Toronto Gore	Peel O	Mrs. Margaret Kelly
Cole's Island		Queen's N B	John Cole
Colinville	Moore	Lambton O	John Butler
Collfield	Litchfield	Pontiac Q	M. Hughes
Collina, W. O.		King's N B	James M. Gibbon
**Collingwood*	Nottawasaga	Simcoe, N. R. O	W. B. Hamilton
Collin's Bay	Kingston	Frontenac O	Joseph Losie
Collin's Inlet		Algoma O	Silas Staples
Colpoy's Bay	Albemarle	Bruce, N. R. O	John Shackleton
Columbus	Whitby	Ontario, S. R. O	Robert Ashton
Comber	Tilbury, West	Essex O	D. McAlister
Combermere	Radcliffe	Renfrew, S. R. O	Daniel Johnson
Como	Vaudreuil	Vaudreuil Q	John Hodgson
Comox		Vancouver B C	Alexander Rodell
		O	A. W. Kendrick

NAME OF POST OFFICE.	TOWNSHIP OR PARISH.	ELECTORAL COUNTY OR DIVISION.	NAME OF POSTMASTER.
Concord	Vaughan	York, W. R. **O**	Henry McElroy
Concord, W. O.		Pictou **N S**	A. Nicholson
Condon Settlement, W. O.		King's **N S**	W. McConnell
Conestogo	Woolwich	Waterloo, N. R. **O**	Charles Hendry
Coningsby	Erin	Wellington, S. R. **O**	John W. Burt
Conn	Arthur	Wellington, N. R. **O**	R. W. Conn
Connaught	Winchester	Dundas **O**	Patrick Jordan
Connor	Adjala	Cardwell **O**	Robert Lee
Conquerall Bank, W. O		Lunenburg **N S**	James McFarlane
Conroy	Downie	Perth, S. R. **O**	Edward Flynn
Consecon	Ameliasburgh	Prince Edward **O**	A. Marsh
Constance	Hullett	Huron, C. R. **O**	R. Thompson
Contrecœur	Contrecœur	Verchères **Q**	Olivier Lamoureux
Conway	South Fredericksburg	Lennox **O**	G. B. Sills
Cook's Brook, W. O.		Colchester **N S**	Mrs. M. Mitchell
Cook's Creek		Lisgar **M**	George Miller
Cookshire	Eaton	Compton **Q**	Thomas B. Terrill
**Cookstown*	Tecumseth	Simcoe, S. R. **O**	Henry Coleman
Cooksville	Toronto	Peel **O**	Mrs. H. Peaker
Cooper	Madoc	Hastings, N. R. **O**	Thomas Allen
Copenhagen	Malahide	Elgin, E. R. **O**	George A. Wannacott
Copetown	Beverley	Wentworth, N. R. **O**	Thomas Milne
Copleston	Enniskillen	Lambton **O**	
Corbett	McGillivray	Middlesex, N. R. **O**	John F. Macey
Corbin	Hemmingford	Huntingdon **Q**	Alex. Fiddes
Corinth	Bayham	Elgin, E. R **O**	F. A. Best
Cork Station, W. O.		York **N B**	John Sullivan
Corn Hill, W. O		King's **N B**	John Keith
**Cornwall*	Cornwall	Cornwall **O**	George McDonnell
Cornwall	No. 32	Queen's **P E I**	John Corbin
Cornwallis, East		King's **N S**	Clement B. Dickey
Corunna	Moore	Lambton **O**	H. J. Miller
Côteau du Lac	Soulanges	Soulanges **Q**	Gédéon Deguire
Côteau Landing	St. Zotique	Soul[illegible]	

NAME OF POST OFFICE.	TOWNSHIP OR PARISH.	ELECTORAL COUNTY OR DIVISION.	NAME OF POSTMASTER.
Côteau Station	Soulanges	Soulanges Q	Roger Ducket
Côte des Neiges	Montreal	Hochelaga Q	Odile Malboeuf
Côte St. Paul	Montreal	Hochelaga Q	Edmond Latour
Cotswold	Minto	Wellington, N. R. O	A. McKillop
Couchiching	S. Orillia	Simcoe, N. R. O	James Fennell
Coulson	Medonte	Simcoe, N. R. O	James Coulson
Courtland	Middleton	Norfolk, N. R. O	C. S. Harris
Courtright	Moore	Lambton O	B. Woodbury
Covehead	No. 34	Queen's P E I	D. Lawson
Covehead Road	No. 34	Queen's P E I	John Whelan
Coventry	Albion	Cardwell O	John Reynar
Coverdale, W. O.		Albert N B	David Smith
Coverley	Bentinck	Grey, S. R. O	James Grant
Covey Hill	Havelock	Huntingdon Q	Alexander Brisbin
Cowal	Dunwich	Elgin, W. R. O	Grant Silcox
Cowansville	Dunham	Missisquoi Q	Dr. Charles Brown
Cow Bay		Cape Breton N S	Anthony Martel
Cowichan		Vancouver B C	Samuel Harris
Coxheath, W. O.		Cape Breton N S	P. T. Clarke
Craighurst	Medonte	Simcoe, N. R. O	Thomas Craig
Craigleith	Collingwood	Grey, E. R. O	A. G. Fleming
Craigsholme	Garafraxa	Wellington, C. R. O	Murdoch Craig
Craigs Road Station	St. Etienne de Lauzan	Levis Q	Nazaire Frechette
Craigvale	Innifil	Simcoe, S. R. O	Robert Black
Cranbourne	Cranbourne	Dorchester Q	John Colgan
Cranworth	Burgess	Leeds, S. R. O	Peter Jones
Crapaud	No. 29	Queen's P E I	William Worth
Crathie	Adelaide	Middlesex, N. R. O	James Anderson
Crawford	Bentinck	Grey, S. R. O	Hector McRae
Credit	Toronto	Peel O	Emerson Taylor
Crediton	Stephen	Huron, S. R. O	John Parsons
Creek Bank	Peel	Wellington, C. R. O	James Graham
**Creemore*	Nottawasaga	Simcoe, N. R. O	Alexander Gillespie
[illegible]	[illegible]	[illegible] N. R. O	Michael Cavanagh

NAME OF POST OFFICE.	TOWNSHIP OR PARISH.	ELECTORAL COUNTY OR DIVISION.	NAME OF POSTMASTER.
Cressy	Marysburg	Prince Edward ... **O**	S. W. Carson
Crieff	Puslinch	Wellington, S. R. **O**	Lewis Gregor
Crinan	Aldboro'	Elgin, W. R. **O**	D. McIntyre
Crofton	Sophiasburg	Prince Edward **O**	Henry Covert
Cromarty	Hibbert	Perth, S. R. **O**	Joseph Reading
Cromwell, W. O.		King's **N B**	Susannah Wetmore
Crosshill	Wellesley	Waterloo, N. R. **O**	John Halloway
Crosspoint	Restigouche	Bonaventure **Q**	John Fraser
Cross Roads, Country Harbor		Guysborough **N S**	Donald Gunn
Cross Roads, Lake Ainslie, W. O		Inverness **N S**	Charles Fraser
Cross Roads, Middle Melford, W. O.		Guysborough **N S**	Jesse Anderson
Cross Roads, Ohio, W. O.		Antigonishe **N S**	John McPherson
Cross Roads, Saint George's Channel, W. O.		Richmond **N S**	Alexander Hill
Crowell		Shelburne **N S**	Israel Crowell
Crow Harbor, W. O.		Guysborough **N S**	John Ehler
Crowland	Crowland	Welland **O**	Luther Boardman
Croydon	Camden, East	Addington **O**	Ira Williams
Cruickshank	Keppel	Grey, N. R. **O**	James Cruickshank
Crumlin	Dorchester, North	Middlesex, E. R. **O**	Robert Dreany
Crysler	Finch	Stormont **O**	Charles W Bingham
Culloden	Dereham	Oxford, S. R. **O**	Andrew Smart
Cumberland	Cumberland	Russell **O**	G. G. Dunning
Cumberland Bay, W. O.		Queen's **N B**	A. Branscombe, sen.
Cumberland Mills	Cumberland	Russell **O**	William Lough, jun.
Cumberland Point, W. O.		Queen's. **N B**	William Smith
Cumminsville	Nelson	Halton **O**	Robert Thomson
Cumnock	Nichol	Wellington, C. R. **O**	John Anderson
Curran	Plantagenet	Prescott **O**	Philippe Gareau
Curry Hill	Lancaster	Glengarry **O**	Alexander McLeod
Curryville, W. O.		Albert **N B**	John Beaumont

NAME OF POST OFFICE.	TOWNSHIP OR PARISH.	ELECTORAL COUNTY OR DIVISION.	NAME OF POSTMASTER.
Dacre	Brougham	Renfrew, S. R. **O**	John Morrow
Daillebout	Daillebout	Joliette **Q**	L. I. Déziel
Dalesville	Rear of Chatham	Argenteuil **Q**	Peter McArthur
Dalhousie		Restigouche **N B**	H. J. Johnson
Dalhousie East, W. O.		King's **N S**	Melissa Starratt
Dalhousie Mills	Lancaster	Glengarry **O**	William Chisholm
Dalhousie Road, W. O.		Lunenburg **N S**	Robert Frayney
Dalhousie Settlement, W. O.		Pictou **N S**	W. Ross
Dalibaire	Dalibaire	Rimouski **Q**	O. A. Lamontague
Dalkeith	Lochiel	Glengarry **O**	
Dalrymple	Carden	Victoria, N. R. **O**	Joseph Fowler
Dalston	Vespra	Simcoe, N. R. **O**	J. Burge
Damascus	Luther	Wellington, N. R. **O**	James Anderson
Danby	Durham	Drummond **Q**	John R. Reece
Danford Lake	Alleyn	Pontiac **Q**	Henry Heney
Danforth	Scarboro'	York, E. R. **O**	Henry Hogarth
**Danville*	Shipton	Richmond **Q**	J. W. Stockwell
Darlington	No. 31	Queen's **P E I**	J. McInnes
Darnley	No. 18	Prince **P E I**	George Thompson
Darrell	Chatham	Kent **O**	Edward Hall
Dartford	Percy	Northumberland, E. R. **O**	William Bailey
Dartmoor	Dalton	Victoria, N. R. **O**	John Gardiner
Dartmouth		Halifax **N S**	Luther Sterns
Dashwood	Hay	Huron, S. R. **O**	Noah Fried
Davenport	York	York, W. R. **O**	Joseph Green
Davisville	York	York, E. R. **O**	John Davis
Dawn Mills	Gore of Camden	Bothwell **O**	W. A. Ward
Dawson Settlement, W. O.		Albert **N B**	Isaac Dawson
Daywood	Sydenham	Grey, N. R. **O**	A. S. Cameron
Dealtown	Raleigh	Kent **O**	Isaac Lambert
Dean, W. O.		Halifax **N S**	Charles Dean
Debeck Station, W. O.		Carleton **N B**	Alex. Harron
De Cewsville	Cayuga	Haldimand **O**	W. S. Wood

NAME OF POST OFFICE.	TOWNSHIP OR PARISH.	ELECTORAL COUNTY OR DIVISION.	NAME OF POSTMASTER.
Deep Brook, W. O.		Annapolis N S	C. Purdy
Deerdock	Oso	Addington O	John Warren
Deerfield. W. O.		Yarmouth N S	Richard N. Crosby
Deerhurst	West Gwillimbury	Simcoe, S. R. O	Samuel Walker
Dee Side	Matapedia	Bonaventure Q	John Mowat
De Gros Marsh	No. 55	King's P E I	H. McLean
Delaware	Delaware	Middlesex, W. R. O	C. J. Ladd
Delhi	Middleton	Norfolk, N. R. O	James Whitsides
Delta	Bastard	Leeds, S. R. O	W. H. Danaut
Demorestville	Sophiasburg	Prince Edward O	B. Smith
Dempsey's Corner, W. O.		King's N S	Andrew Lee
Denbigh	Denbigh	Addington O	Samuel Lane
Denfield	London	Middlesex, E. R. O	B. H. Rosser
Denison's Mills	Shipton	Richmond Q	Joseph R. Denison
Deniston	Hinchinbrooke	Addington O	B. C. Freeman
Densmore's, W. O.		Hants N S	John Fraser
Densmore's Mills, W. O.		Hants N S	R. T. Densmore
De Ramsay	De Ramsay	Joliette Q	James Read
Derby, W. O.		Northumberland N B	William Hartt
Derryville	Brock	Ontario, N. R. O	Thomas Allin
Derry, West	Toronto	Peel O	
Derwent	N. Dorchester	Middlesex, E. R. O	Mitchell Dibb
De Sable	No. 29	Queen's P E I	A. McCalder
Desboro'	Sullivan	Grey, N. R. O	George Smith
Deschambault	Deschambault	Portneuf Q	A. Damase Hamlin
Desert Lake	Loughborough	Addington O	John M. Snook
Desmond	Camden East	Addington O	William [illegible]

NAME OF POST OFFICE.	TOWNSHIP OR PARISH.	ELECTORAL COUNTY OR DIVISION.	NAME OF POSTMASTER.
Diamond	Fitzroy	Carleton **O**	R. Walker, jun.
Dickens	Yonge	Leeds, S. R. **O**	L. N. Phelps
Dickinson's Landing	Osnabruck	Stormont **O**	Peter Forbes
Dickson's Store, W. O.		Colchester **N S**	G. W. Nelson
Digby		Digby **N S**	Mrs. C. W. Bent
Dillonton	Bolton	Brome **Q**	George Cairns
a Dingwall	Huron	Bruce, S. R. **O**	Paul D. McInness
Dipper Harbor, W. O.		St. John **N B**	D. Belmore
Discoose, W. O		Richmond **N S**	David Grouchy
Dixie	Toronto	Peel **O**	John Kennedy
Dixon's Corners	Matilda	Dundas **O**	William Wood
b Dixville	Barford	Stanstead **Q**	R. C. Baldwin
Doaktown, W. O.		Northumberland **N B**	Hiram Freeze
Dobbington, W. O.	Elderslie	Bruce, N. R. **O**	James Dobbin
Doctor's Cove, W. O.		Shelburne **N S**	Herman Kelly
Doherty's Mills, W. O		Kent **N B**	Joseph G. Cormier
Dog Creek		Cariboo **B C**	William Wycott
Dollar	Markham	York, E. R. **O**	Agnes Heron
Domaine de Gentilly	Gentilly	Arthabaska **Q**	T. Laflèche
Don	York	York, E. R. **O**	John Hogg
Doncaster	York	York, E. R. **O**	James Young
Donegal	Elma	Perth, N. R. **O**	Mary Mason
Donegal, W. O.		King's **N B**	John Lockhart
Doon	Waterloo, South	Waterloo, S. R. **O**	Thomas Slee
Doran	Bathurst	Lanark, S. R. **O**	William Doran
Dorchester		Westmoreland **N B**	S. W. Tingley
Dorchester Station	Dorchester	Middlesex, E. R. **O**	J. N. Hardy
Dorking	Maryboro'	Wellington, N. R. **O**	Adam Deitz

NAME OF POST OFFICE.	TOWNSHIP OR PARISH.	ELECTORAL COUNTY OR DIVISION.	NAME OF POSTMASTER.
Dover, South	Dover	Kent **O**	T. Bourassa
Dover, West, W. O.		Halifax **N S**	William Baker
Downeyville	Emily	Victoria, S. R. **O**	Michael O'Neil
Downsview	York	York, W. R. **O**	Robert Clarke
Doyle Settlement, W. O		Restigouche **N B**	John Murchie
Drayton	Peel	Wellington, C. R. **O**	W. C. Wortley
**Dresden*	Gore of Camden	Bothwell **O**	C. P. Watson
Drew	Minto	Wellington, N. R. **O**	William Cardwell
Dromore	Egremont	Grey, S. R. **O**	Alexander Taylor
Drum	Manvers	Durham, E. R. **O**	Miss Isabella Harrison
Drumbo	Blenheim	Oxford, N. R. **O**	Joseph L. Burgess
Drummondville, East	Grantham	Drummond **Q**	Miss C. M. Millar
**Drummondville, West*	Stamford	Welland **O**	T. W. Woodruff
Drumquin	Trafalgar	Halton **O**	Thomas H. Patterson
Drysdale	Stanley	Huron, S. R **O**	Robert Drysdale
Duart	Orford	Bothwell **O**	James Tait
Dublin Shore, W. O.		Lunenburg **N S**	Thomas Smith
Duck and Pringle		Yale **B C**	James Duck
Dudswell	Dudswell	Wolfe **Q**	Zerah Evans
Dufferin	Oneida	Haldimand **O**	Mrs James Cossar
Dumbarton, R. R. Station, W. O.		Charlotte **N B**	
Dumblane	Saugeen	Bruce, N. R. **O**	Donald Fraser
Dumfries, W. O		York **N B**	Wm. Whitehead
Dunany	Wentworth	Argenteuil **Q**	Samuel Smith
Dunbar	Williamsburg	Dundas **O**	A. C. Allison
Dunbarton	Pickering	Ontario, S. R. **O**	John Parker
Duncan	Euphrasia	Grey, E. R. **O**	William McRae
Duncan, W. O.		Grey, E. R. **O**	Daniel Duncan
Duncrief	Lobo	Lunenburg **N S**	Christopher Walker
Dundalk	Melancthon	Middlesex, N. R. **O**	James May
Dundalk Station	Proton	Grey, E. R. **O**	John J. Middleton
**Dundas*	Flamborough, West	Wentworth, N. R. **O**	J. M. Thornton
Dundas	No. 55	King's **P E I**	Richard Burdett
Dundee	Dundee	Huntingdon **Q**	David Baker

NAME OF POST OFFICE.	TOWNSHIP OR PARISH.	ELECTORAL COUNTY OR DIVISION.	NAME OF POSTMASTER.
Dundee, W. O.		Restigouche... N B	James Innis
Dundee Centre	Dundee	Huntingdon Q	Rev D. Ross
Dundela	Matilda	Dundas O	J. E. Tuttle
Dundonald	Cramahe	Northumberland, E. R. O	John Barker
Dunedin	Nottawasaga	Simcoe, N. R. O	
**Dungannon*	Wawanosh	Huron, N. R. O	R. Clendinning
Dungivon, W. O.		Westmoreland N B	John McVey
Dunham	Dunham	Missisquoi Q	Edward Baker
Dunkeld	Brant	Bruce, S. R. O	Thomas Whitehead
Dunkeld		Cariboo B C	Allan Graham
**Dunnville*	Moulton	Monck O	Thomas Armour
Dunphy, W. O.		Northumberland N B	George Dunphy
Dunraven	Calumet Island	Pontiac Q	John Letts
Dunrobin	Torbolton	Carleton O	Hy. Younghusband
Dunsford	Verulam	Victoria, S. R. O	William Graham
Duntroon	Nottawasaga	Simcoe, N. R. O	James Russell
Dunvegan	Kenyon	Glengarry O	Wm. Urquhart
Dupey's Corner, W. O.		Westmoreland N B	F. J. Hebert
**Durham*	Bentinck	Grey, S. R. O	Archb'd McKenzie
Durham		Pictou N S	John McCoul
Dwyer Hill	Goulbourn	Carleton O	A. T. Rothwell
Eagle	Aldborough	Elgin, W. R. O	Philip J. Lindermann
Eagle Lake	Guildford	Peterborough, E. R. O	Charles Wensley
Eagle's Nest	St. Peter's	Lisgar M	John Monkman

NAME OF POST OFFICE.	TOWNSHIP OR PARISH.	ELECTORAL COUNTY OR DIVISION.	NAME OF POSTMASTER.
Earltown, W. O.		Colchester ... N S	W. J. McKay
East Arthabaska	St. Norbert	Arthabaska ... Q	P. N. Pacaud
East Bay		Cape Breton ... N S	Wm Chisholm
East Bay, North Side, W. O.		Cape Breton ... N S	J. P. McKinnon
East Bolton	Bolton	Brome ... Q	Alex. Sargant
East Broughton	Broughton	Beauce ... Q	Louis Beaudouin
East Chester	St. Hélène de Chester	Arthabaska ... Q	Joseph Jutras
East Clifton	Clifton	Compton ... Q	Hollis A. Cairn
East Durham	Dunham	Missisquoi ... Q	Robert A. Wales
Eastern Harbor, W. O		Inverness ... N S	W. Lawrence
East Farnham	Farnham, East	Brome ... Q	Rodney Hutchins
East Glassville, W. O		Carleton ... N B	John Smith
East Hawkesbury	Hawkesbury, East	Prescott ... O	Michael Maneely
East Hereford	Hereford	Compton ... Q	—. Holbrook
East Jeddore, W. O.		Halifax ... N S	David Webber
East Magdala	Nelson	Megantic ... Q	William J. Smyth
Eastman's Springs	Gloucester	Russell ... O	D. H. Eastman
Easton's Corners	Wolford	Grenville, N. R. ... O	H S. Easton
East Oro	Oro	Simcoe, N. R. ... O	Gilbert L. Bell
East Point	No. 47	King's ... P E I	Alexander Beaton
East Port Medway, W. O.		Queen's ... N S	F. P Armstrong
East River, St. Mary's W. O		Pictou ... N S	George Campbell
East River, St. Mary's W. O.		Guysborough ... N S	A. W. Sutherland
East Scotch Settlement, W. O.		King's ... N B	John King
East side of Chezzetcook, W. O		Halifax ... N S	Edmund Oldmixon
East side of Pubnico Harbor, W. O		Yarmouth ... N S	Byron Hines
East side of Ragged Island, W. O		Shelburne ... N S	George Craig
East side of West Branch East River of Pictou, W. O.		Pi[illegible] N S	D[illegible] Sh[illegible]

NAME OF POST OFFICE.	TOWNSHIP OR PARISH.	ELECTORAL COUNTY OR DIVISION.	NAME OF POSTMASTER.
East Templeton	Templeton	Ottawa ... Q	Levi E. Dunning
Eastville, W. O		Colchester ... N S	James R. Ellis
East Williamsburgh	Williamsburgh	Dundas ... O	Herbert E. Snyder
Eastwood	Oxford, East	Oxford, S. R. ... O	John Shaw
Eaton	Eaton	Compton ... Q	Moses Lebourveau
Economy		Colchester ... N S	W. A. Fulmer
Ecum Secum, W. O.		Halifax ... N S	
Eddystone	Haldimand	Northumberland, W. R. ... O	M. Bradley
Eden	Bayham	Elgin, E. R ... O	John Nethercott
Eden Mills	Eramosa	Wellington, S. R. ... O	Anthony Jackson
Edgar	Oro	Simcoe, N. R. ... O	
Edgeley	Vaughan	York, W. R. ... O	Jesse Smith
Edgett's Landing, W. O		Albert ... N B	Ward Edgett
Edgeworth	Tilbury, East	Kent ... O	James Waddell
Edina	Chatham	Argenteuil ... Q	William Tomalty
Edmonton	Chinguacousy	Peel ... O	Ewen Cameron
Edmundston		Victoria ... N B	J. T. Hodgson
Edwardsburgh	Edwardsburgh	Grenville, S. R. ... O	William S. Aiken
Eel Brook, W. O.		Yarmouth ... N S	
Eel Creek, W. O.		Cumberland ... N S	John Fraser
Eel Lake, W. O		Yarmouth ... N S	Leon Porter
Eel River		Restigouche ... N B	Mrs. Ellen Craig
Effingham	Pelham	Monck ... O	George Redpath
Eganville	Grattan	Renfrew, S. R. ... O	John Quealy
Egbert	Essa	Simcoe, S. R. ... O	Archibald Thom
Egerton	Luther	Wellington, N. R. ... O	James Hunter
Eglington	York	York, E. R. ... O	Joseph Hargrave
Egmondville	Tuckersmith	Huron, C. R. ... O	George E. Jackson
Egmont Bay	No. 15	Prince ... P E I	
Egremont	Egremont	Grey, S. R. ... O	Thomas Smith
Egypte	Milton	Shefford ... Q	J. Depot
Eig Mountain, W. O.		Antigonishe ... N S	Mrs. Mary Smith
Elba	Mono	Cardwell ... O	Charles Smith
[illegible]	[illegible]	[illegible] ... O	D. H. Sensabaugh

NAME OF POST OFFICE.	TOWNSHIP OR PARISH.	ELECTORAL COUNTY OR DIVISION.	NAME OF POSTMASTER.
Elder	Mono	Cardwell O	C. Conn
Elder's Mills	Vaughan	York, W. R. O	William Irvine
Eldorado	Madoc	Hastings, N. R. O	Joseph Best
Elfrida	Saltfleet	Wentworth, S. R. O	Hamilton Sweazie
Elgin	Crosby, South	Leeds, S. R. O	Philemon Pennock
Elgin		Albert N B	R. D. Robinson
Elginburg	Kingston	Frontenac O	Eli Meecham
Elginfield	London	Middlesex, E. R. O	Matthew Glass
Elimville	Usborne	Huron, S. R. O	James Crocker
Elizabethville	Hope	Durham, E. R. O	Johnston Beatty
Ellengowan	Brant	Bruce, S. R. O	James Brownlee
Ellershausen, W. O.		Hants N S	J. Beckman
Ellesmere	Scarboro'	York, E. R. O	Arch. Glendinning
Elliott	Bathurst	Lanark, S. R. O	Wm. McLellan
Elm	Huntley	Carleton O	Mrs. Nancy Smith
Elmbank	Toronto	Peel O	John Trueman
Elmgrove	Essa	Simcoe, S. R. O	Thomas Gordon
Elmira	Woolwich	Waterloo, N. R. O	Peter Winger
Elmsdale		Hants N S	Alex. Dunbar
Elmsville, W. O.		Pictou N S	D. McDonald
Elmvale	Flos	Simcoe, N. R. O	William Harvey
Elmwood	Brant	Bruce, S. R. O	John Reinhardt
**Elora*	Pilkington	Wellington, C. R. O	W. H. La Pinotiere
Elphin	North Sherbrooke	Lanark, N. R. O	Isaac Bloomberg
Elsinore	Arran	Bruce, N. R. O	Joseph Johnston
**Embro*	Zorra, West	Oxford, N. R. O	D. Matheson
Embrun	Russell	Russell O	Joseph Lalonde
Emerald	Amherst Island	[illegible]	[illegible]

NAME OF POST OFFICE.	TOWNSHIP OR PARISH.	ELECTORAL COUNTY OR DIVISION.	NAME OF POSTMASTER.
Enfield		Hants **N S**	Henry F. Donaldson
English Corner, W. O.		Halifax **N S**	James Thomson
English Settlement, W. O.		Queen's **N B**	Dougald Cormichael
English Town		Victoria **N S**	Duncan McDonald
Enniskillen	Darlington	Durham, W. R. **O**	D. W. McLeod
Enniskillen Station, W. O.		Queen's **N B**	Joseph Brittain
Ennismore	Ennismore	Peterboro', W. R. **O**	Francis J. Daly
Enon, W. O.		Cape Breton **N S**	Alexander McDonald.
Enterprise	Camden, East	Addington **O**	Robert Graham
Epping	Euphrasia	Grey, E. R. **O**	John Jinkins
Epsom	Reach	Ontario, N. R. **O**	Newbry Munro
Eramosa	Eramosa	Wellington, S. R. **O**	Robert Dryden
Erbsville	Waterloo	Waterloo, N. R. **O**	John L. Erb
Erie	Walpole	Haldimand **O**	R. McBurney
**Erin*	Erin	Wellington, S. R. **O**	William Cornock
Erinsville	Sheffield	Addington **O**	Patrick Walsh
Erinville, W. O.		Guysborough **N S**	Charles Kenny
Ernestown Station	Ernestown	Lennox **O**	James R. Hewson
Erroll	Plympton	Lambton **O**	George Whiting
Escott	Escott	Leeds, S. R. **O**	Joseph L. Dowsley
Escuminac (sub.)	Nouvelle	Bonaventure **Q**	John Campbell
Escuminac, W. O.		Northumberland **N B**	James McLean
Eskasoni, W. O.		Cape Breton **N S**	Henry V. Bown
Esquesing	Esquesing	Halton **O**	John Murray
Esquimalt		Victoria **B C**	John T. Howard
Esquimaux Point		Saguenay **Q**	D. B. McGie
Essex Centre	Colchester	Essex **O**	Thomas Rush
Etang du Nord (sub.)	Magdalen Island	Gaspé **Q**	Damase V. Bourque
Ethel	Grey	Huron, C. R. **O**	James Spence
Eugenia	Artemesia	Grey, E. R. **O**	R. McLean Purdy
Evelyn	Nissouri, West	Middlesex, E. R. **O**	John Burns
Everett	Tosorontio	Simcoe, S. R. **O**	W. C. Bradshaw
		O	James Tinline

NAME OF POST OFFICE.	TOWNSHIP OR PARISH.	ELECTORAL COUNTY OR DIVISION.	NAME OF POSTMASTER.
Everton	Eramosa	Wellington, S. R. **O**	Robert Morrison
**Exeter*	Stephen	Huron, S. R. **O**	William Sanders
Factory Dale, W. O.		King's **N S**	Robert R. Ray
Fafard	St. Sylvester	Lotbiniere **Q**	William J. Cryan
Fairfield	Harwich	Kent **O**	
Fairfield	No. 47	King's **P E I**	Edward Holland
Fairfield, East	Elizabethtown	Brockville **O**	Alonzo C. Johns
Fairfield		St. John **N B**	J. A. Floyd
Fairfield Plain	Burford	Brant, S. R. **O**	Elijah Forsyth
Fairhaven, W. O.		Charlotte **N B**	Caleb Greene
Fairview	Gore of Downie	Perth, S. R. **O**	Richard Forrest
Fairville		St. John **N B**	C. F. Tilton
Falding	Foley	Muskoka **O**	Matthew Rankin
Falkenburg	Macauley	Muskoka **O**	Mathias Moore
Falkirk	Williams, East	Middlesex, N. R. **O**	Thomas Stephenson
Falkland	Brantford	Brant, S. R. **O**	M. Stally
Fallbrook	Bathurst	Lanark, S. R. **O**	William Smith
Fallowfield	Nepean	Carleton **O**	John Leamy
Falmouth, W. O.		Hants **N S**	James Wolf
Falmouth, Windsor Bridge, W. O		Hants **N S**	William Armstrong
False Bay Beach, W. O		Cape Breton **N S**	Angus McAuley
Farley's Mills, W. O.		Carleton **N B**	James Lawson
Farmerston, W. O.		Carleton **N B**	W. E. Estey

NAME OF POST OFFICE.	TOWNSHIP OR PARISH.	ELECTORAL COUNTY OR DIVISION.	NAME OF POSTMASTER.
Farmington	Amaranth	Wellington, N. R. **O**	John Curry
Farmington	No. 56	King's **P E I**	L. Doyle
Farnboro'	Farnham, East	Brome **Q**	Leonard Wells
Farndon	Farnham	Missisquoi **Q**	Seth N. Ross
Farnham Centre	Farnham	Brome **Q**	Adam Clark
Farquhar	Usborne	Huron, S. R. **O**	N. J. Clark
Farran's Point	Osnabruck	Stormont **O**	James Roddy
Father Point	St. Luce	Rimouski **Q**	Pierre D. Rouleau
Fawkham	Rama	Ontario, N. R. **O**	Isaac S. Wardell
Fenaghvale	Caledonia	Prescott **O**	
Fenella	Haldimand	Northumberland, W. R. **O**	John W. Mather
**Fenelon Falls*	Fenelon	Victoria, N. R. **O**	Robert B. Jameson
Fennells	Innisfil	Simcoe, S. R. **O**	J. G. Foigehan
Fenwick	Pelham	Monck **O**	James W. Taylor
Fenwick, W. O		King's **N B**	Joseph Wiley
Fenwick, W. O		Cumberland **N S**	John D. Davidson
**Fergus*	Nichol	Wellington, C. R. **O**	James McQueen
Ferguson's Falls	Drummond	Lanark, S. R. **O**	
Fergusonvale	Flos	Simcoe, N. R **O**	John Cumming
Fermoy	Bedford	Addington **O**	Joseph C. Rogers
Fernhill	Lobo	Middlesex, N. R. **O**	Jenkin Owen
Ferris, W. O		Queen's **N B**	R. O'Donell
Ferryville, W. O		Carleton **N B**	James Hemphill
Feversham	Osprey	Grey, E. R **O**	Mary Sproul
Fifteen Point	No. 15	Prince **P E I**	Aimé Richard
**Fingal*	Southwold	Elgin, W. R. **O**	Samuel Tubby
Fintona	Adjala	Cardwell **O**	Robert J. Lamon
Fish Creek	Blanchard	Perth, S. R. **O**	T. W. Bell
Fisherville	Rainham	Haldimand **O**	Jacob Lemmer
Fitch Bay	Stanstead	Stanstead **Q**	S. M. Rider
Fitzroy Harbour	Fitzroy	Carleton **O**	W. A. Shirreff
Five Islands		Colchester **N S**	Andrew K. Graham
Five Mile River, W.O.		Hants **N S**	Joseph McLaren
		he **N B**	Archd. McKenzie

NAME OF POST OFFICE.	TOWNSHIP OR PARISH.	ELECTORAL COUNTY OR DIVISION.	NAME OF POSTMASTER.
Flat River	No. 60	Queen's ... P E I	R. K. McKenzie
Fleetwood	Manvers	Durham, E. R. ... O	James Morrow
Flesherton	Artemesia	Grey, E. R. ... O	Robert J. Sproul
Fletcher's Station, W. O.		Halifax ... N S	Edward Largie
Fleurant		Bonaventure ... Q	William Gray
Flinton	Kaladar	Addington ... O	E. J. Matthews
Flora	Woolwich	Waterloo, N. R. ... O	Isaac Devitt
Florence	Euphemia	Bothwell ... O	John A Young
Florenceville		Carleton ... N B	Stephen G. Burpee
Florenceville, East, W. O		Carleton ... N B	John Lovely
Foley	Whitby	Ontario, S. R ... O	Thomas Williamson
Folly Lake, W. O		Colchester ... N S	Thomas Barber
Folly Mountain		Colchester ... N S	John McLean
Folly River, W. O		Colchester ... N S	Charles M. McElman
Fontenoy	Melbourne	Richmond ... Q	R. Fraser
**Fonthill*	Pelham	Monck ... O	Danson Kinsman
Forbes, W. O		Colchester ... N S	John Forbes
Fordwich	Howick	Huron, N. R ... O	Arthur Mitchell
Fordyce	Wawanosh	Huron, N. R ... O	Wm. Farquharson
Forest	Plympton	Lambton ... O	Dr. Alex. Scott
Forest City, W. O		York ... N B	Joseph Blanchard
Forester's Falls	Ross	Renfrew, N. R. ... O	Oliver Forester
Forest Mills	Richmond	Lennox ... O	William Breeze
Foreston, W. O		Carleton ... N B	Daniel B. Gray
Forestville	Charlotteville	Norfolk, S. R. ... O	W. A. Miller
Forfar	Bastard	Leeds, S. R. ... O	Richard Haler

NAME OF POST OFFICE.	TOWNSHIP OR PARISH.	ELECTORAL COUNTY OR DIVISION.	NAME OF POSTMASTER.
Fort Garry	St. John	Selkirk M	John Macdougall
Forties Settlement, W. O		Lunenburg N S	John A. Hiltz
Fort William		Algoma O	Miss C. McVicar
Fort William	Sheen	Pontiac Q	James McCool
Foster's, W. O		Lunenberg N S	Henry Foster
Foster's Cove, W. O		Victoria N B	John Trafton
Fouchie, W. O		Richmond N S	Albert B. Hooper
Fournier	Plantagenet South	Prescott O	A. S. McLennan
Foxboro'	Thurlow	Hastings, E. R. O	Edward Philpot
Fox Creek, W. O		Westmoreland N B	Eustache Burke
Fox Harbor, W. O		Cumberland N S	Arch'd Robertson
Fox River	Fox	Gaspé Q	J. C. Parent
Fox River, W. O		Cumberland N S	J. L. Hatfield
Foymount	Sebastopol	Renfrew, S. R. O	John Foy
Framboise, W. O		Richmond N S	Kenneth Strachan
Frampton	West Frampton	Dorchester Q	M. Fitzgerald
Frankford	Sidney	Hastings, W. R. O	John Chapman
Frank Hill	Emily	Victoria, S. R. O	Thomas Franks
Franklin	Manvers	Durham, E. R. O	William Maguire
Franklin Centre	Franklin	Huntingdon Q	William Cantwell
Franktown	Beckwith	Lanark, S. R. O	E. McEwen
Frankville	Kitley	Leeds, N. R. O	W. H. Leavitt
Fraser's Grant, W. O.		Antigonishe N S	John Fraser
Fraser's Mills, W. O		Pictou N S	Alexander Grant
Fredericton		York N B	A. S. Phair
Fredericton Junction		Sunbury N B	C. H. Kingston
Fredericton Road, W. O		Westmoreland N B	J. O. Sullivan
Freelton	Flamborough, West	Wentworth, N. R. O	James Hirst
Freeport	Waterloo, South	Waterloo, S. R O	Elias B. Snyder
Freetown	No. 25	Prince P E I	D. Auld
Freiburg	Waterloo, North	Waterloo, N. R. O	Ferdinand Rombach
**Freligbsburg*	St. Armand	Missisquoi Q	Dr. Elijah Rowell
[illegible]		[illegible] N B	Arthur H. Smith

NAME OF POST OFFICE.	TOWNSHIP OR PARISH.	ELECTORAL COUNTY OR DIVISION.	NAME OF POSTMASTER.
French River, W. O...	....	Pictou......... ....N S	Mrs. C. McDonald ...
French River	No. 21.....................	Queen's ....P E I	Jane McKay.. ....
French Vale, W. O.....	....	Cape Breton ....N S	Belloni Gonthro ....
French Village.........	Kingsey	Drummond ....Q	Francois Pothier .....
French Village	No. 37....	Queen's ....P E I	C. McIntyre ....
French Village.........	....	King's ....N B	Geo. Beatty ....
Frome	Southwold	Elgin, W. R. ....O	Thomas Sharon... .....
Frost Village....	Shefforrn	Shefford ....Q	John Williams ....
Fulford	Brome	Brome ....Q	Philo England ....
Fullarton	Fullarton	Perth, S. R.................O	John Buchan...........
Fulton	Grimsby	Lincoln .... O	John Grassie...........
Gaberouse	....	Cape Breton ....N S	Roderic R. Morrison...
Gad's Hill	Ellice	Perth, N. R. .. ..O	Frederick Junker .. ...
Gagetown	....	Queen's ....N B	Edward Simpson .....
Gailey, W. O.	....	Kent ....N B	Simon Daigle...........
Galbraith	Lanark	Lanark, N. R. ....O	Joseph Matthie.........
**Galt*	Dumfries, North	Waterloo, S. R.............O	John Davidson ....
Gallingertown	Osnabruck	Stormont ....O	Edward Marshall ......
Gamebridge	Thorah	Ontario, N. R. ....O	William Glover........
**Gananoque*	Leeds	Leeds, S. R. ....O	D. F. Britton...........
**Garafraxa*	Garafraxa	Wellington, C. R......... O	Andrew Lightbody....
Garden Hill	Hope	Durham, E. R. .... O	James Dyre ....
Garden Island	Garden Island	Fr—	[illegible]

NAME OF POST OFFICE.	TOWNSHIP OR PARISH.	ELECTORAL COUNTY OR DIVISION.	NAME OF POSTMASTER.
Garden of Eden, W. O.	....	Pictou ....N S	Mrs. D. McGregor .. ..
GardenRiver............	Garden River	Algoma ....O	Malcolm McRae .....
Gardiner Mines, W. O.	....	Cape Breton............N S	William Rutledge......
Gardener's Creek	....	St John...................N B	William Wallace ... ..
Garneau	Garneau	L'Islet.........................Q	Elie Chouinard ....
*a*Garnet.............	Walpole	Haldimand...................O	W. S. Colver ....
Garthby	Garthby	Wolfe ....Q	David Grenier..........
Gaspé Basin	Gaspé	Gaspé ....Q	J. J. Kavanagh.........
Gaspereaux	No. 61......................	King's........ ....P E I	William Lewelleyn.....
Gaspereaux	....	Queen's..................N B	J. A. Caldwell ....
Gaspereaux, W. O......	....	King's ....N S	Sherman Caldwell .....
Gaspereaux Station,	....	Queen's...................N B	Thomas Trott ....
Gay's River	....	Halifax,...................N S	M. Frame ....
Gay's River Road, W. O.	....	Halifax ....N S	Robert B. Taylor ......
Geary, W. O............	....	Sunbury ... .N B	Asa Carr..................
Gemley	Miller	Addington ....O	James Stalker ....
Geneva	Argenteuil	Argenteuil .... Q	G. A. Hooker..... ......
Genoa	St. Jerusalem	Argenteuil ....Q	James Gordon ....
Gentilly	Gentilly	Nicolet ....Q	L. Brunelle .. ..
George's River, W. O.	....	Cape Breton.. ....N S	Campbell McQuarrie..
Georgetown	....	King's...... ....P E I	William Wightman ...
**Georgetown*	Esquesing	Halton ....O	Lafayette Goodenow...
Georgeville	Stanstead	Stanstead ....Q	Increase Bullock.......
**Georgina*	Georgina	York, N. R....................O	J. R. Bourchier.........
Germantown, W. O....	....	Albert ....N B	William Fillmore ......
Gesto	Colchester	Essex ....O	W. F. Marlowe ....
Getson's Point, W. O.	....	Lunenburg................N S	George McKean .....
Giant's Lake, W. O...	....	Guysborough............N S	John McNeil............
Gibraltar	Collingwood	Grey, E. R.... ....O	John Glen ....
Gibson	Tiney	Simcoe, N. R..... ....O	William Gibson .. ..
Gilbert Cove, W. O....	....	Digby ....N S	H. S. Mallet ....
Gilbert's Mills	Sophiasburgh	Prince Edward............O	John D. Gilbert ......
Gilford	Gwillimbury, West.....	Simcoe, S. R.................O	Thomas Machonchy ..

NAME OF POST OFFICE.	TOWNSHIP OR PARISH.	ELECTORAL COUNTY OR DIVISION.	NAME OF POSTMASTER.
Gladstone	Dorchester	Middlesex, E. R. O	L. McMurray
Glamis	Kincardine	Bruce, N. R. O	Richard W. Harrison
Glamorgan	Manvers	Durham, E. R. O	Kendall Kennedy
Glanford	Glanford	Wentworth, S. R. O	John Atkinson
Glanmire	Tudor	Hastings, N. R. O	John Ray
Glanworth	Westminster	Middlesex, E. R. O	John Turnbull
Glascott	Glenelg	Grey, S. R. O	Dennis Quirk
Glasgow	Uxbridge	Ontario, N. R. O	Benjamin Parker
Glassville, W. O.		Carleton N B	Hugh Miller
Glastonbury	Kaladar	Addington O	J. A. Carscallen
Glen, W. O		Antigonishe N S	D. McMillan
**Glen Allan*	Peel	Wellington, C. R. O	George Allan
Glen Alpine, W. O.		Antigonishe N S	
Glenarm	Fenelon	Victoria, N. R. O	Seth Rickaby
Glenburnie	Kingston	Frontenac O	George Hunter
Glencairn	Tosorontio	Simcoe, S. R. O	M. N. Stephens
Glencoe	Ekfrid	Middlesex, W. R. O	W. G. Lumley
Glen Donald	Charlottenburg	Glengarry O	Wm. McDonald
Glendower	Bedford	Addington O	Richard Howes
Glenedale, W. O.		Inverness N S	John McKinnon
Glenelg	St. Mary's	Guysborough N S	Matthew Archibald
Glengarry Station		Pictou N S	John Fraser
Glen Gordon	Charlottenburg	Glengarry O	A. R. McLennan
Glen Huron	Nottawasaga	Simcoe, N. R. O	H. M. Frame
Glenloyd	Inverness	Megantic Q	Joseph Rockingham
Glen Major	Uxbridge	Huron, N. R. O	Edward Major
Glenmeyer	Houghton	Norfolk, S. R. O	George E. Meyer

NAME OF POST OFFICE.	TOWNSHIP OR PARISH.	ELECTORAL COUNTY OR DIVISION.	NAME OF POSTMASTER.
a Glenshee	Charlotteville	Norfolk, S. R. **O**	Mrs. M. Smith
Glenshee, W. O		Pictou **N S**	Donald Campbell
Glen Stewart	Matilda	Dundas **O**	William Stewart
Glen Sutton	Sutton	Brome **Q**	James Esty
Glen Tay	Bathurst	Lanark, S. R **O**	James Kearns
Glenvale	Kingston	Frontenac **O**	Robert Gibson
Glen Walter	Charlottenburg	Glengarry **O**	D. J. Deruchil
Glen Williams	Esquesing	Halton **O**	Charles Williams
b Glenwood, W. O		Yarmouth **N S**	Archibald Watson
Glidden	Compton	Compton **Q**	Alfred Draper
Goble's Corners	Blenheim	Oxford, N. R **O**	J. G. Goble
* *Goderich*	Goderich	Huron, C. R **O**	A. Dickson
Golden Grove		St. John **N B**	Peter Brennan
Golden Lake	N. Algoma	Renfrew, N. R **O**	Peter Jeffrey
Goldenville		Guysborough **N S**	Jesse Cumminger
Gold Fields, W. O		Colchester **N S**	George Corbett
Gold River, W. O		Lunenburg **N S**	Benjamin Reddy
Goldstone	Peel	Wellington, C. R. **O**	John Gibbons
Good Corner, W. O		Carleton **N B**	Archibald Good
Gooderham	Glamorgan	Peterborough, E. R. **O**	Charles Way
Goodwood	Uxbridge	Ontario, N. R. **O**	Michael Chapman
Goose Creek, W. O		St. John **N B**	John Prescott
Goose River		Cumberland **N S**	David Patterson
Goose River	Number 42	King's **P E I**	Michael McDonald
Gordonsville, W. O		Carleton **N B**	
Gore, W. O		Hants **N S**	Daniel Thompson
Gore's Landing	Hamilton	Northumberland, W. R. **O**	William East
Gormley	Markham	York, E. R **O**	James Gormley

NAME OF POST OFFICE.	TOWNSHIP OR PARISH.	ELECTORAL COUNTY OR DIVISION.	NAME OF POSTMASTER.
Gourock	Guelph	Wellington, S. R. **O**	James Cunningham
Gowanstown	Wallace	Perth, N. R. **O**	Charles Smith
Gower Point	Westmeath	Renfrew, N. R. **O**	Thomas M. Carswell
Gowland Mountain, W. O.		Albert **N B**	William McKenzie
Grafton	Haldimand	Northumberland, W. R. **O**	J. Gillard
Graham's Road	Number 20	Queen's **P E I**	Eneas Brenan
Grahamsville	Toronto Gore	Peel **O**	Peter Lamphier
Granboro'	Granby	Shefford **Q**	S. W. Tracy
**Granby*	Granby	Shefford **Q**	Horace Lyman
Grand Anse, W. O.		Richmond **N S**	Allan McLean
Grand Aunce, W. O.		Gloucester **N B**	Francis LeGresley
Grand Bay		St. John **N B**	David Hamm
Grand Bend	Bosanquet	Lambton **O**	John Ironside
Grande Baie	St. Alexis	Chicoutimi **Q**	Miss D. Nugent
Grande Greve	Cap Rosier	Gaspé **Q**	Charles Esnouf
Grande Ligne		St. John's **Q**	R. A. Girardin
Grand Entry, W. O.		Gaspé **Q**	Neil McPhail
Grandes Coudeés	Jersey	Beauce **Q**	Jean Lambort dit Champagne
Grand Etang, W. O.		Inverness **N S**	Zephirin Collerette
Grande Vallée		Gaspé **Q**	Louis Fournier
Grand Falls		Victoria **N B**	Patrick McMillan
Grand Falls, Portage, W. O.		Victoria **N B**	W. Roach
Grand Harbour, W. O.		Charlotte **N B**	Turner Wooster
Grandigue, W. O		Kent **N B**	Fidèle Legere
Grandigue Ferry, W O.		Richmond **N S**	David Fraser
Grand Manan		Charlotte **N B**	B. Daggett

NAME OF POST OFFICE.	TOWNSHIP OR PARISH.	ELECTORAL COUNTY OR DIVISION.	NAME OF POSTMASTER.
Grand River, W. O....	....	Victoria..................N B	F. Violette...........
Grand River	....	Richmond..................N S	Hector Murchison ...
Grand Tracadie	No. 35................	Queen's ... .P E I	Stephen McDonald...
Granville	....	New Westminster ... B C	Henry Harvey ....
Granville	Number 21	Queen's ....P E I	R. Corbett ....
Granville Centre, W. O.	....	Annapolis ....N S	W. B. Troop ... .
Grandville Ferry	....	Annapolis ....N S	Alfred Troop...........
Grant	Cambridge	Russell .... O	James Edmonstone ...
Grantley	Williamsburg	Dundas ....O	John C. Munro ....
Granton	Biddulph	Middlesex, N. R. ....O	James Grant............
Gravel Hill	Roxborough	Stormont .... O	John Crawford ....
Gravelotte	Middleton	Norfolk, N. R. .... O	Robert Quance ....
Gravenhurst	Muskoka	Muskoka.......................O	J. P. Cockburn... ....
Graystock	Otanabee	Peterborough, E. R.......O	Mark Greystock ......
Great Shemogue	....	Westmoreland..... ...N B	William Avard ....
Great Village	....	Colchester...............N S	A. W. McLellan ....
Greenbank	Reach	Ontario, N. R. .... O	George Flint, jun.......
Greenbush	Elizabethtown	Brockville ....O	Daniel Blanchard......
Greenfield	Kenyon	Glengarry ....M	Alex. McDougald......
Greenfield, W. O.	....	Carleton .... N B	Thomas Wakem ......
Greenfield, W. O.	....	Queen's ....N S	Mrs. L. H. Freeman...
Green Hill, W. O.	....	Pictou ....N S	....
Greenock	Greenock	Bruce, S. R. ....O	Wm. Grundy........
Green Point	Sophiasburg	Prince Edward ....O	Philip Roblin...........
Green River	St. Antonin	Temiscouata .... Q	George April........ ...
Green River	Pickering	Ontario, S. R. ....O	J. H. Smith ....
Green River, W. O.....	....	Victoria ... .N B	....
Green's Creek, W. O..	....	Colchester ....N S	Daniel Dart ....
Greensville	West Flamborough ..	Wentworth, N. R. ....O	Andrew Black ....
Greenview	Monteagle	Hastings, N. R. ... .O	John Fitzgerald .....
Greenville, W. O......	....	Cumberland .. .. N S	Allan G. Purdy........
Greenville Station	....	Cumberland ....N S	John S. orshner......
Greenwich Hill, W. O	....	King's ... .N B	Albert McKiel....... .

NAME OF POST OFFICE.	TOWNSHIP OR PARISH.	ELECTORAL COUNTY OR DIVISION.	NAME OF POSTMASTER.
Grenfell	Vespra	Simcoe, N. R. ....O	Duncan McIntosh ....
Grenville.....	Grenville	Argenteuil ....Q	Edward Pridham .. ...
Gresham	Bruce	Bruce, N. R. ... .O	E. J. Brown ....
Gretna	N. Fredericksburg.....	Lennox ....O	W. J. Mellow............
Grey	Grey	Huron, C. R.................O	Alexander McNair.....
Griersville	St Vincent.	Grey, E. R. ....O	Robert Burdett.........
Gribbin	Toronto Gore............	Peel .. ..O	Daniel Boyle............
Griffith	Griffith	Renfrew, S. R. ....O	....
**Grimsby*.........	Grimsby	Lincoln ....Q	H. E. Nelles ....
Grondines	Grondines	Portneuf ....Q	F. X. Thibodeau........
Grosses Coques, W. O.	....	Digby ....N S	G. H. Lovitt ....
Grosvenor, W. O........	....	Guysboro' ....N S	Samuel O'Neil ....
Grovesend	Malahide	Elgin, E. R. ....O	William Bothwell......
Grovespoint, W. O......	....	Victoria .... N S	Murdoch McDonald...
Gueguen, W. O.........	....	Kent ....N B	Magloire Gueguen.....
**Guelph*....................	Guelph	Wellington, S. R..........O	Wm. Kingsmill.........
Gulf Shore, W. O......	....	Cumberland ....N S	W. Waugh.................
Gunning Cove, W. O..	....	Shelburne .... N S	Mrs. Mary Doane......
Guysborough......	Middleton	Norfolk, N. R. ....O	J. W. Doyle........ ....
Guysborough..............	....	Guysborough ....N S	E. J. Cunningham.....
Guysborough Intervale, W. O.	....	Guysborough .... .N S	Robert McKay ....
Hackett's Cove, W. O.	....	Halfax ....N S	Elias Grono ....
Hagersville...............	Walpole	Haldimand ....O	Charles Hager ....

NAME OF POST OFFICE.	TOWNSHIP OR PARISH.	ELECTORAL COUNTY OR DIVISION.	NAME OF POSTMASTER.
Half Island Cove, W. O.	....	Guysborough .... N S	John Digdon..........
Halfway Brook, W. O.	....	Colchester .... N S	Wm. Fisher..........
Halfway River, W. O.	....	Cumberland .... N S	G. D. Fullerton........
**Haliburton*	Dysart........	Peterborough, E. R.......O	Daniel McFarlane .....
Halifax	....	Halifax .... N S	Benj. W. Cochron.. ...
Hallerton	Hemmingford	Huntingdon .... Q	James Blair ....
Halloway	Thurlow	Hastings, E. R .... O	James P. Hopkins.....
Hall's Bridge........	Harvey	Peterborough, W. R. .. O	James Stewart ....
Hall's Harbour, W. O.	....	King's .... N S	Sidney R. Thorp .....
Hamburg	South Fredericksburg	Lennox .... O	A. D. Fraser ....
**Hamilton*........	Barton	Hamilton .... O	Frederick E. Ritchie..
Hamilton	No. 18..	Prince .... P E I	Charles Stewart........
Hamlet	Burgess, N.	Lanark, S. R. ....O	Michael Stanley ....
Hammond	Elma	Perth, N. R. .... O	Jas. Hammond, jun...
Hammond River........	....	King's .... N B	W. W. Dodge ....
Hammondvale	....	King's .... N B	W. Fowler........
Hampstead	North Easthope	Perth, N. R. ....O	John T. Schneider ..
Hampstead.....	....	Queen's............ N B	E. W. Slipp ....
Hampton........	Darlington........	Durham, W. R. ....O	H. Elliott ....
Hampton	....	King's .... N B	John Flewelling ......
Hamtown, W. O.. ...	....	York .... N B	Nath. Smith ....
Hanford Brook, W. O.	....	King's .... N B	Henry Handron .....
Hannon	Barton	Wentworth, S. R.........O	Thomas Cowie ....
Hanover	Bentinck	Grey, S. R............O	Thomas S. Coppinger
Hantsport	....	Hants .... N S	Wm. Davison ....
Hanwell, W. O........	....	York .... N B	John Kingston ....
Harbor au Bouche, W. O.	....	Antigonishe .... N S	Edmund Corbet ......
Harbor Road, W. O...	....	Antigonishe .... N S	Hugh McGillivray ...
Harborville, W. O. ...	....	King's .... N S	D. B. Parker ....
Harcourt	Horton	Renfrew, S. R........O	Mrs. A. R. Hutton ...
Hardinge	Barrie	Addington ....O	Thomas Tapping .....
Hard Ledge, W. O. ...	....	Westmoreland........ N B	George Kirk ....

NAME OF POST OFFICE.	TOWNSHIP OR PARISH.	ELECTORAL COUNTY OR DIVISION.	NAME OF POSTMASTER.
Hardwood Lands, W. O.		Colchester ... N S	James Grant
Harewood, W. O.		Westmoreland ... N B	Maurice Healy
Harlem	Bastard	Leeds, S. R. ... O	William Kincaid
Harley	Burford	Brant, S R. ... O	A. B. McWilliams
Harlock	Hullett	Huron, C. R. ... O	Thomas Neilans
Harmony	South Easthope	Perth, S. R. ... O	Edmund Corbett
Harmony, W. O.		King's ... N S	Austin Spinney
Harold	Rawdon	Hastings, N. R. ... O	Albert McWilliams
Harper	Bathurst	Lanark, S. R. ... O	Joseph Warren
Harpley	Stephen	Huron, S. R. ... O	Thomas N. Hayter
Harrietsville	Dorchester	Middlesex, E. R. ... O	John McMillan
Harrigan Cove, W. O.		Halifax ... N S	John Fraser
Harrington, East	Harrington	Argenteuil ... Q	Donald B. Campbell
Harrington, West	Zorra, West	Oxford, N. R. ... O	Donald Reid
Harrisburg	Dumfries, South	Brant, N. R. ... O	James Galloway
Harrison's Corners	Cornwall	Cornwall ... O	Angus D. McGillis
**Harriston*	Minto	Wellington, N. R. ... O	A. Macready
Harrow	Colchester	Essex ... O	Frederick Goble
Harrowsmith	Portland	Addington ... O	Samuel F. Stewart
Hartford	Townsend	Norfolk, N. R. ... O	B. W. Thomas
Hartington	Portland	Addington ... O	William Kennedy
Hartland		Carleton ... N B	S. H. Shaw
Hartley	Eldon	Victoria, N. R. ... O	Archd. Campbell
Hartman	Gwillimbury, East	York, N. R. ... O	David Terry
Hart's Mills, W. O.		Sunbury ... N B	T. Coleman
Hartsville	No. 67	Queen's ... P E I	M. McLeod
Harvey		Albert ... N B	J. M. Stevens

NAME OF POST OFFICE.	TOWNSHIP OR PARISH.	ELECTORAL COUNTY OR DIVISION.	NAME OF POSTMASTER.
Hastings, W. O		Cumberland N S	G. H. Chapman
Hastings, W. O		Albert N B	J. C. McQuaid
Hatley	Hatley	Stanstead Q	J. B. LeBaron
Haultain	Burleigh	Peterborough, E. R. O	Giles Stone
Havelock	Belmont	Peterborough, E. R. O	Thos. E. Wilde
Havelock, W. O		Digby N S	John G. Nowlan
**Hawkesbury*	Hawkesbury, West	Prescott O	James G. Higginson
Hawkestone	Oro	Simcoe, N. R. O	James Houston
Hawkesville	Wellesley	Waterloo, N. R. O	Robert Morrison
Hawthorne	Gloucester	Russell O	H. F. Graham
Hawtrey	Norwich, South	Oxford, S. R. O	George Southwick
Hay	Hay	Huron, S. R. O	John Currelly
Haydon	Darlington	Durham, W. R. O	Wm. Broad
Hayesland	West Flamboro'	Wentworth, N. R. O	Michael Hayes
Hay's River, W. O.		Inverness N S	Rod. McDougall
Haysville	Wilmot	Waterloo, S. R. O	Margaret Somerville
Hazel Grove	Number 22	Queen's P E I	Richard Bagnall
Hazledean	Goulbourn	Carleton O	Adam Abbott
Headford	Markham	York, E. R. O	
Headingly	Headingly	Selkirk M	John Taylor
Head Lake	Laxton	Victoria, N. R. O	W. A. Maxwell
Head of Amhurst, W. O		Cumberland N S	Ephraim Finlay
Head of Jordan River, W. O		Shelburne N S	Thomas Holden
Head of Millstream, W. O		King's N B	J. Little
Head of St. Margaret's Bay, W. O		Halifax N S	Samuel Shatford
Head of St. Margaret's Bay (Middle District), W. O		Halifax N S	Jessie McG. Fraser
Head of St. Mary's Bay, W. O		Digby N S	Wm. H. Young
Head St. Peter's Bay	Number 41	King's P E I	Edward Drain
Head of South River Lake, W. O		Antigonishe N S	Hugh McNeil
Head of Tatama-		ter N S	Wm. Dobson

NAME OF POST OFFICE.	TOWNSHIP OR PARISH.	ELECTORAL COUNTY OR DIVISION.	NAME OF POSTMASTER.
Head of Tide, W. O..	....	Restigouche......... ...N B	R. Gerard.... ....
Head of Wallace Bay W. O.	.. ..	Cumberland.... ....N S	G. H. D. Forshner.....
Head of Wallace Bay (North Side), W.O..	....	Cumberland ....N S	George Brown..... .....
Heathcote	Euphrasia	Grey, E. R.................O	Thomas J. Rorke......
Hebb's Cross, W. O....	....	Lunenburg.......... ...N S	Johnson Manning .....
Hebron, W. O..........	....	Albert................... N B	James Smyth, sen......
Hebron	....	Yarmouth..... ....N S	C. Caban ....
Heckston	South Gower............	Grenville, N. R ....O	Hugh Hughes...........
Hedleyville	St. Roch..................	Quebec...... ....Q	J. de Bloisdit Gregoire
Heidelburg	Woolwich	Waterloo, N. R... ....O	John Krassler...........
Helena	Godmanchester.........	Huntingdon...... ....Q	J. Holbrooke............
Hellerup, W. O	....	Victoria ....N B	R. W. L. Tibbitts......
Hemison.................	East Frampton.........	Dorchester.................Q	....
Hemmingford	Hemmingford...........	Huntingdon.................Q	John Edwards ....
Henderson Settlement, W. O...................	....	Queen's...................N B	William Henderson ...
Henderson Settlement, W. O.................. ...	....	Cumberland..............N S	John M. Henderson...
Henry	Longueuil	Prescott ....O	William Dickson ......
Henrysburg...............	Lacolle	St. John's....................Q	William Cockerline ...
Henryville	St. George de Henryville........	Iberville................ .....Q	F. Lafond................
Hepworth.................	Keppel	Grey, N. R. ... .O	Thomas Briggs.........
Herbert	Potton....................	Brome ....Q	M. Geer ....
Herdman's Corners ...	Hinchinbrooke	Huntingdon ... .Q	Rev. Hugh Niven .....
Hereford	Hereford...................	Compton ....Q	Aaron Workman ......
Hereward	Garafraxa	Wellington, C. R.. ....O	George Brown ....
Heron's Island, W. O.	....	Restigouche...........N B	George Dutch ....
**Hespeler*	Waterloo, South	Waterloo, S. R......... ...O	John Chapman ....
Heyworth.................	Eardley	Ottawa ....Q	Robert Breckenridge..
Hiawatha	Otonabee	Peterborough, E. R ......O	Hugh Kent ....
Hibernia, W. O.........	....	Queen's ....N B	David Gardner ....
Higgin's Road	No. 13......................	Prince ....P E I	William Henry.........
High Bluff	High Bluff	Marquette ....M	J. McD. Sweetman.. .

NAME OF POST OFFICE.	TOWNSHIP OR PARISH.	ELECTORAL COUNTY OR DIVISION.	NAME OF POSTMASTER.
Highfield	Etobicoke	York, W. R. O	H. Dutchburn
Highfield, W. O.		Hants N S	William Crowell
Highgate	Orford	Bothwell O	John Beattie
Highland Creek	Scarborough	York, E. R. O	William Tredway
Hilda	Thurlow	Hastings, E. R. O	Benjamin Palmer
Hillier	Hillier	Prince Edward O	Richard Noxen
Hillsborough	Plympton	Lambton O	Thomas L. Hill
Hillsborough, C. B., W. O.		Inverness N S	Malcolm McNeil
Hillsborough		Albert N B	R. E. Steves
Hillsburgh	Erin	Wellington, S. R. O	William Howe, sen.
Hillsdale	Medonte	Simcoe, N. R. O	Mrs. E. B. Faragher
Hillsdale		King's N B	N. P. Wanamake
Hill's Green	Hay	Huron, S. R. O	Hugh Love, sen.
Hillside, W. O.		Cape Breton N S	W. D. Hill
Hillside, W. O.		Albert N B	P. Collicutt
Hilton	Brighton	Northumberland, E. R. O	A. A. B[illegible]ker
Hinch	Camden, East	Addington O	William Hinch
Hoasic	Williamsburg	Dundas O	Lewis Schwedfeger
Heath Road	Sydenham	Grey, N. R. O	R. Heath
Hochelaga	Isle of Montreal	Hochelaga Q	F. Painchaud
Hockley	Adjala	Cardwell O	John Hackett
Holbrook	Norwich, North	Oxford, S. R. O	A. M. Whitfield
Holland Landing	Gwillimbury, East	York, N. R. O	Alex. Williams
Hollen	Maryborough	Wellington, N. R. O	Thomas Thompson
Holmsville	Goderich	Huron, N. R. O	Edward Kelly
Holmesville, W. O.		Carleton N B	Isaac Broad
Holstein	Egremont	Grey, S. R. O	N. D McKenzie
Holt	Gwillimbury, East	York, N. R. O	John Quibell
Holyrood	Kinloss	Bruce, S. R. O	A. T. Campbell
Homer	Grantham	Lincoln O	Peter A. Cavers
Honeywood	Mulmur	Simcoe, S. R. O	George Lawrence
Hope		Yale B C	John G. Wirth
Hopetown	Lanark	Lanark, N. R. O	John White, jun.
Hopefield	Radcliffe	Renfrew, S. R. O	Joseph Daly

NAME OF POST OFFICE.	TOWNSHIP OR PARISH.	ELECTORAL COUNTY OR DIVISION.	NAME OF POSTMASTER.
Hope River	Number 22	Queen's ... P E I	Felix Murphy
Hopewell, W. O.		Albert ... N B	James Wright
Hopewell, W. O.		Pictou ... N B	John Gunn
Hopewell Cape		Albert ... N B	G. H. Steadman
Hopewell Corner		Albert ... N B	W. C. Pipes
Hopewell Hill, W. O.		Albert ... N B	Joseph McAlmon
Hornby	Esquesing	Halton ... O	John McMillan
Horning's Mills	Melancthon	Grey, E. R. ... O	William Airth
Hornsey, W. O.		Cumberland ... N S	George Reeve
Horton Landing, W. O.		King's ... N S	Frederic G. Curry
Houghton	Houghton	Norfolk, S. R. ... O	George Bundy
House Harbor (sub)	Magdalen Islands	Gaspé ... Q	Edward D. Paquet
Howe Island	Pittsburgh	Frontenac ... O	Thomas Thompson
Howick	Georgetown, South	Chateauguay ... Q	Thomas Gebbie
Hubbard's Cove		Halifax ... N S	J. E. Stratford
Hudson	Vaudreuil	Vaudreuil ... Q	Albert Vipond
**Hull*	Hull	Ottawa ... Q	H. L. Loucks
Humber	Etobicoke	York, W. R. ... O	John Linton
Humberstone	Humberstone	Welland ... O	John Thompson
Hunsdon	Albion	Cardwell ... O	Henry Fry
Hunter's Mountain, W. O.		Victoria ... N S	John McDonald
Hunterstown	Hunterstown	Maskinongé ... Q	E. Malloc
Huntersville	Ramsay	Lanark, N. R. ... O	John Hunter
**Huntingdon*	Godmanchester	Huntingdon ... Q	W. Marshall
Huntingville	Ascot	Sherbrooke ... Q	John W. Gamsby
Huntley	Huntley	Carleton ... O	John Johnston
Hunt's Point, W. O.		Queen's ... N S	William Innis
Huntsville	Chaffey	Muskoka ... O	James F. Hanes
Hurdville	McKellar	Muskoka ... O	Isaac N. Hurd
Huston	Maryboro'	Wellington, N. R. ... O	David Callaway
Huttonsville	Chinguacousy	Peel ... O	James P. Hutton
Hyde Park Corner	London	Middlesex, E. R. ... O	Peter C. Thompson

NAME OF POST OFFICE.	TOWNSHIP OR PARISH.	ELECTORAL COUNTY OR DIVISION.	NAME OF POSTMASTER.
Ida	Cavan	Durham, E. R. **O**	Alexander Baptie
Ilderton	London	Middlesex, E. R. **O**	George Ord
Indiana	Seneca	Haldimand **O**	
Indian Brook, W. O.		Victoria **N S**	Donald McLennan
Indian Cove		Lévis **Q**	Theodore Samson
Indian Harbor, W. O.		Halifax **N S**	Charles Covey
Indian Harbor, W. O.		Guysboro' **N S**	David Suttis
Indian Island, W. O.		Charlotte **N B**	J. B. W. Chaffey
Indian Point, W. O.		Lunenburg **N S**	James Moser
Indian River	Otonabee	Peterborough, S. R. **O**	John Smith
Indian River	No. 18	Prince **P E I**	J. McLellan
Indian Road, W. O.		Hants **N S**	Peter McPhee
Indian Town		St. John **N B**	William G. Brown
**Ingersoll*	Oxford, North	Oxford, S. R. **O**	Joseph Thirkell
Ingoldsby	Minden	Peterboro', E. R. **O**	Richard Smith
Ingonish, W. O.		Victoria **N S**	J. W. Burke
Ingram River, W. O.		Halifax **N S**	J. G. Dimock
Inistioge	Proton	Grey, E. R. **O**	Henry Armstrong
Inkerman	Mountain	Dundas **O**	Alva Corrigan
Innerkip	East Zorra	Oxford, N. R. **O**	Mrs. Sarah Begg
Innisfil	Innisfil	Simcoe, S. R. **O**	Benjamin Ross
Innisville	Drummond	Lanark, S. R. **O**	Thomas Code
Intervale, W. O.		Westmoreland **N B**	David Horseman
Inverary	Storrington	Frontenac **O**	D. J. Walker
Inverhuron	Bruce	Bruce, N. R. **O**	Hugh Matheson
Invermay	Arran	Bruce, N. R. **O**	Abraham Neelands
**Inverness*	Inverness	Megantic **Q**	John McKinnon
Inverness	No. 11	Prince **P E I**	Frederick McDonald
Iona	Dunwich	Elgin, W. R. **O**	Edmund Roche
Irish Cove, W. O.		Cape Breton **N S**	Michael McDonald
Irishtown, W. O.		Westmoreland **N B**	John Larracey
Iron Hill	Brome	Brome **Q**	John D. Shufelt
Ironside	Hull	Ottawa **Q**	Napoleon Lafosse
**Iroquois*	Matilda	Dundas **O**	James Grier

NAME OF POST OFFICE.	TOWNSHIP OR PARISH.	ELECTORAL COUNTY OR DIVISION.	NAME OF POSTMASTER.
Irving Settlement, W. O.	....	Albert .... N B	William E. Bishop ...
Irvine	Inverness	Megantic .... Q	S. B. Thurber ....
Isaac's Harbor, W. O.	....	Guysboro' .... N S	Allan McMillan, jun...
Isaac's Harbor (east side), W. O	....	Guysboro' .... N S	David Buckley ....
Island Brook............	Newport	Compton................ Q	W. W. Bailey ....
Islay	Fenelon	Victoria, N. R. .... O	....
Isle aux Coudres (sub)	Isle aux Coudres	Charlevoix .... Q	....
Isle aux Grues	Isle aux Grues	L'Islet.................... Q	P. G. Lachaine, dit Jolicoeur ....
Isle Bizard..............	....	Jacques Cartier......... Q	Albert Barbeau........
Isle Dupas	Isle Dupas	Berthier .... Q	Rev. V. Plinguet ......
Isle Perrot	Isle Perrot	Vaudreuil .... Q	Marie S. Jobin ....
Isle Vert..................	Isle Verte	Témiscouata .... Q	Louis A. Bertrand .....
Islington	Etobicoke	York, W. R. .... O	Thomas Musson ......
Ivanhoe	Huntingdon............	Hastings, N. R. .... O	Thomas Emo...........
Ivy	Essa	Simcoe, S. R. .... O	William H. Davis .....
Jackson, W. O..........	....	Cumberland .... N S	Wm. Jackson...........
Jackson	Derby	Grey, N. R................ O	G. R. Wright............
Jackson Road, W. O...	....	King's.................... N S	Alexander Nichol .....
Jacksontown, W. O ..	....	Carlton................. N B	F. L. Palmer...........
Jacksonville, W. O.....	....	Carleton .... N B	James Simonson........
Janetville.................	Manvers	Durham, E. R............ O	....
Janeville, W. O.........	....	Gloucester .... N B	Robert C. Caie ....
Jarratt's Corners	Oro		

NAME OF POST OFFICE.	TOWNSHIP OR PARISH.	ELECTORAL COUNTY OR DIVISION.	NAME OF POSTMASTER.
Jarvie	Walpole	Haldimand........**O**	Robert Sill
Jasper	Wolford	Grenville, N. R........**O**	P. B. Webster
Jeddore, W. O		Halifax........**N S**	William Blakeny
Jemseg, W. O		Queen's........**N B**	N. B. Cottle
Jenkins, W. O		Queen's........**N B**	Joel Jenkins
Jersey, River Chaudière	St. George	Beauce........**Q**	Michael Cahill
Jerseyville	Ancaster	Wentworth, S. R........**O**	A. Hendershot
Joggin Mines, W. O		Cumberland........**N S**	B. B. Boggs
Johnson	Sydenham	Grey, N. R........**O**	William Johnstone
Johnson's Mills	Hay	Huron, S. R........**O**	Henry Hayrock
Johnson Mills, W.O		Westmoreland........**N B**	Edward Babcock
Johnston's River	Number 48	Queen's........**P E I**	P. Gormley
Johnston, W. O		Queen's........**N B**	Thomas Mason
Johnville	Eaton	Compton........**Q**	Charles Smith
Johnville, W. O		Carleton........**N B**	John Boyd
Jolicure, W. O		Westmoreland........**N B**	Rufus C. Wry
**Joliette*		Joliette........**Q**	Eusèbe Asselin
Jonquières	Jonquières	Chicoutimi........**Q**	Xavier Brassard
Jordan	Louth	Lincoln........**O**	Clark Snure
Jordan Bay, W. O		Shelburne........**N S**	John Downie
Judique, W. O		Inverness........**N S**	Hugh McDonnell
Jura	Bosanquet	Lambton........**O**	Byron Boyd
Juvenile Settlement, W. O		Sunbury........**N B**	Arthur Graham

NAME OF POST OFFICE.	TOWNSHIP OR PARISH.	ELECTORAL COUNTY OR DIVISION.	NAME OF POSTMASTER.
Kaladar	Kaladar	Addington O	C. F. Dunham
Kamloops		Yale B C	W. B. Wilson
Kamouraska	St. Louis de Kamouraska	Kamouraska Q	Louis Charles Bégin
Kars	North Gower	Carleton O	James Lindsay
Kars, W. O.		King's N B	William Worden
Katevale	Hatley	Stanstead Q	Joseph Sorel
Kazubazua	Aylwin	Ottawa Q	Samuel C. Kenny
Kay Settlement, W. O.		Westmoreland N B	Alexander Hughes
Keady	Derby	Grey, N. R. O	James Gilchrist
Keats		Westmoreland N B	Ronald F. Keith
Keenansville	Adjala	Cardwall O	G. P. Hughes
**Keene*	Otonabee	Peterborough, E. R. O	W. J. Hall
Keith	Chatham	Kent O	Lewis Huff
Keithley Creek		Cariboo B C	George Keith
Kelly's Cross	No. 29	Queen's P E I	P. McQuaid
Kelso	Elgin	Huntingdon Q	Peter MacFarlane
Kelvin	Windham	Norfolk, N. R. O	G. W. Phipps
Kemble	Keppel	Grey, N. R. O	William Heard
Kempt, W. O.		Queen's N S	E. P. Freeman
Kempt Bridge, W. O.		Yarmouth N S	Elkanah Travis
Kempt Head, W. O.		Victoria N S	K. McKenzie
Kempt Road, W. O.		Richmond N S	Hugh Cameron
Kempt Town, W. O.		Colchester N S	A. S. Hingley
**Kemptville*	Oxford	Grenville, N. R. O	Robert Leslie
Kemptville, W. O.		Yarmouth N S	S. W. Hamilton
Kendal	Clarke	Durham, W. R. O	J. R. Anderson
Kennebec Line	Marlowe	Beauce Q	George Bartley
Kenilworth	Arthur	Wellington, N. R. O	Robert Hayward
Kenmore	Osgoode	Russell O	John B. Brannen
Kennetcook, W. O.		Hants N S	I. S. Sanford
Kennetcook Cornor, W. O.		Hants N S	Mrs. L. Densmore
Kent Bridge	Chatham	Kent O	John A. Langford
Kentville		[illegible] N S	G. E. Calkin

NAME OF POST OFFICE.	TOWNSHIP OR PARISH.	ELECTORAL COUNTY OR DIVISION.	NAME OF POSTMASTER.
Kepler	Kingston	Frontenac **O**	Isaac J. Coglan
Keppoch, W. O.		Antigonishe **N S**	Alex. McDonald
Kerrwood	Adelaide	Middlesex, N. R. **O**	James Irving
Kerry	Plantagenet, S.	Prescott **O**	Mrs. Louisa Parent
Kertch	Plympton	Lambton **O**	Arch. McPhedrain
Keswick	North Gwillimbury	York, N. R. **O**	J. W. Montgomery
Keswick Ridge, W. O.		York **N B**	
Kertch Harbor, W. O.		Halifax **N S**	
Kettleby	King	York, N. R. **O**	Jacob Walton
Kewstoke, W. O.		Inverness **N S**	Alex. McQuain
Keyser	Adelaide	Middlesex, N. R. **O**	Samuel Cooper
Kilbride	Nelson	Halton **O**	Robert Parker
Kidare	Kildare	Joliette **Q**	O. Vigneault
Kildare	No. 3	Prince **P E I**	
Kildonan	Kildonan	Selkirk **M**	James Fraser
Kilkenny	Kilkenny	Montcalm **Q**	Damase Thouin
Killarney		Algoma **O**	P. R. de Lamorandière
Killean	Puslinch	Wellington, S. R. **O**	D. Ferguson
Killerby	Yarmouth	Elgin, E. R. **O**	John Hicks
Kilmanagh	Caledon	Peel **O**	Thos. Sanderson
Kilmarnock	Wolford	Grenville, N. R. **O**	George Newsome
Kilmartin	Metcalfe	Middlesex, W. R. **O**	D. McKellar
Kilmaurs	Torbolton	Carleton **O**	William Munro
Kilsyth	Derby	Grey, N. R. **O**	Thomas Sloan
Kimberley	Euphrasia	Grey, E. R. **O**	Alex. Hy. McLean
Kinburn	Fitzroy	Carleton **O**	
**Kincardine*	Kincardine	Bruce, S. R. **O**	M. McKendrick
Kincardine, W. O.		Victoria **N B**	— Taylor
King	King	York, N. R. **O**	Benjamin Lloyd
King Creek	King	York, N. R. **O**	William Stokes
Kingsbridge	Ashfield	Huron, N. R. **O**	Francis L. Eagan
Kingsbury	Melbourne	Richmond **Q**	George Williamson
Kingsbury, W. O.		Lunenburg **N S**	Edward Mosman

NAME OF POST OFFICE.	TOWNSHIP OR PARISH.	ELECTORAL COUNTY OR DIVISION.	NAME OF POSTMASTER.
Kingsclear		York **N B**	J. A. Hammond
Kingsey	Kingsey	Drummond **Q**	
Kingsey Falls	Kingsey	Drummond **Q**	Smith Leith
Kingsley		York **N B**	George N. Foster
Kingsmill	Malahide	Elgin, E. R. **O**	Stephen W. Tuple
**Kingston*	Kingston	Kingston **O**	Robert Deacon
Kingston		King's **N B**	Samuel Foster
Kingston		Kent **N B**	John Harnett
Kingston Mills	Kingston	Frontenac **O**	Charles Harrison
Kingston Station		Frontenac **O**	John McMillan
Kingston Village, W. O.		King's **N S**	John Wheelock
**Kingsville*	Gosfield	Essex **O**	James H. Smart
Kinkora	Ellice	Perth, N. R **O**	James Moriarty
Kinloss	Kinloss	Bruce, S. R. **O**	John Harrison
Kinlough	Kinloss	Bruce, S. R. **O**	Robert Paxton
Kinmount	Somerville	Victoria, N. R **O**	Charles Moffitt
Kinnear's Mills	Leeds	Megantic **Q**	James Kinnear
Kinross	No. 50	Queen's **P E I**	David Ross
Kinsale	Pickering	Ontario, S. R. **O**	Levi Mackay
Kinsman's Corner, W. O.		King's **N S**	Benjamin Kinsman
Kintail	Ashfield	Huron, N. R. **O**	U. T. Pellow
Kintore	East Nissouri	Oxford, N. R. **O**	William Easson
Kippen	Tuckersmith	Huron, C. R. **O**	Robert Mellis
Kippewa		Pontiac **Q**	Thomas Anderson
Kirby	Clarke	Durham, W. R. **O**	James Jackson
Kirkdale	Durham	Drummond **Q**	William Burril
**Kirkfield*	Eldon	Victoria, N. R. **O**	
Kirkhill	Lochiel	Glengarry **O**	William McLeod
Kirkhill, W. O.		Cumberland **N S**	William Smith
Kirkland, W. O.		Carleton **N B**	John Nicholson
Kirk's Ferry	Hull	Ottawa **Q**	John Kirk
Kirkton	Usborne	Huron, S. R. **O**	John McCurdy
Kirkwall	Beverley	Wentworth, N. R. **O**	W. McMillan

NAME OF POST OFFICE.	TOWNSHIP OR PARISH.	ELECTORAL COUNTY OR DIVISION.	NAME OF POSTMASTER.
Klineburg	Vaughan	York, W. R. O	Thomas White
Knapdale	Mosa	Middlesex, W. R O	Hector McLean
Knatchbull	Nassagiweya	Halton O	William Reid
Knowlesville, W. O.		Carleton N B	R. Ricker
**Knowlton*	Brome	Brome Q	Albert Kimball
Knowlton Landing	Potton	Brome Q	J. F. Tuck
Knoxford, W. O.		Carleton N B	Thomas Fulton
Knoydart, W. O.		Pictou N S	
Kolbeck, W. O.		Cumberland N S	W. B. Henley
Komoka	Lobo	Middlesex, N. R. O	Robert Hord
Kootenay (sub)		Yale B C	James Normansell
Kossuth	Waterloo	Waterloo, S. R. O	Charles Theller
Kouchibouguac		Kent N B	
La Baie	La Baie des Febvres	Yamaska Q	J. L. Belcourt
Labarre	Labarre	Chicoutimi Q	C. Hébert
La Beauce	St. Marie	Beauce Q	Mme. C. Bonneville
L'Acadie	L'Acadie	St. John's Q	C. T. Charbonneau
Lachenaie	Lachenaie	L'Assomption Q	J. O. Laurier
**Lachine*	Montreal	Jacques Cartier Q	L. J. Lefebvre
**Lachute*	Argenteuil	Argenteuil Q	George L. Meikle
Lac Masson	Wexford	Terrebonne Q	C. C. Lajeunesse
Lac Noir	Fournier	L'Islet Q	J. B. Pelletier
Lacolle	Lacolle	St. John's Q	T. Van Vliet
Lafontaine	Tiny	Simcoe, N. R O	

NAME OF POST OFFICE.	TOWNSHIP OR PARISH.	ELECTORAL COUNTY OR DIVISION.	NAME OF POSTMASTER.
La Guèrre	St. Anicet	Huntingdon Q	John McDonald
La Have Cross Roads, W. O.		Lunenburg N S	Isaac Heckman
La Have River W. O.		Lunenburg N S	Mrs M. A. Cronan
Lake Ainslie, W. O.		Inverness N S	Angus McInnis
Lake Ainslie (East Side), W. O.		Inverness N S	Charles McDonald
Lake Ainslie (South Side), W. O.		Inverness N S	John McKinnon
Lake Aylmer	Stratford	Wolfe Q	George Champoux
Lake Beauport	St. Dunstan	Quebec Q	A. Simmons
Lake Doré	Wilberforce	Renfrew, N. R. O	John Shaw, jun
Lake Etchemin	Ware	Dorchester Q	Joseph Bégin
Lakefield	Gore	Argenteuil Q	George Rogers
Lakefield, W. O		King's N B	
Lake George, W. O.		York N B	Charles L. S. Tilley
Lake George, W. O.		King's N S	A. P. Hudgens
Lake George, W. O.		Yarmouth N S	Charles Crosby
Lakehurst	Harvey	Peterborough, E. R. O	John Tarlington
Lake La Hache		Cariboo B C	Patrick Gannon
Lakelands, W. O.		Cumberland N S	James E. Brown
Lake Law, W. O.		Inverness N S	James Fortune
Lakelet	Howick	Huron, N. R. O	Myles Young
Lake Megantic	Whitton	Compton Q	J. McDonald
Lake Opinicon	Storrington	Frontenac O	Bryce T. Davidson
Lake Road, W. O.		Cumberland N S	Gains Lewis
Lake Settlement, W. O		Kent N B	M. Flannigan
Lakeside	Nissouri, East	Oxford, N. R. O	Robert Armstrong
Lake Temiscamingue.		Pontiac Q	
Lakevale, W. O		Antigonishe N S	Angus McDonald
Lakeview, W. O.	Johnstone	Queen's N B	Thomas O'Donnell
Lakeville, W. O.		Carleton N B	J. S. Carvell
Lakeville, W. O.		King's N S	Reuben Chase
Lakeville Corner, W. O		Sunbury N B	James S. Jewett
Lake Weedon	Weedon	Wolfe Q	François Brière

NAME OF POST OFFICE.	TOWNSHIP OR PARISH.	ELECTORAL COUNTY OR DIVISION.	NAME OF POSTMASTER.
L'Amaroux	York	York, E. R. **O**	William Nash
Lamartine	St. Eugene	L'Islet **Q**	Polycarpe C. Coultier
Lambeth	Westminster	Middlesex, E. R. **O**	George Kelley
Lambton	St. Vital de Lambton	Beauce **Q**	Dr. Louis Labrècque
a Lambton Mills	York	York, W. R. **O**	F. A. Howland
**Lanark*	Lanark	Lanark, N. R. **O**	Wm. Robertson
Lancaster	Lancaster	Glengarry **O**	John Fraser
Landreville		Beauharnois **Q**	Walter Bryden
Lang	Otonabee	Peterboro', E. R. **O**	Richard Short, sen.
Langevin	Langevin	Dorchester **Q**	Louis Vermette
Langford	Brantford	Brant, N. R. **O**	Alex. Milne
Langill's, W. O.		Lunenburg **N S**	J. P. Langille
Langley		New Westminster **B C**	W. W. Gibb
Langside	Kinloss	Bruce, S. R. **O**	Wm. Gleeson
Langstaff (sub)	Markham	York, E. R. **O**	John Langstaff
Langton	Walsingham	Norfolk, S. R. **O**	James Fulton
Lanoraie	Lanoraie	Berthier **Q**	T. D. Latour
Lansdown	Lansdown	Leeds, S. R. **O**	Jos. A. Bradley
L'Anse à Giles	L'Islet	L'Islet **Q**	J. F. Giasson
L'Anse au Foin	Tremblay	Chicoutimi **Q**	P. Potvin
L'Anse aux Gascons	Port Daniel	Bonaventure **Q**	Joseph Acteson
Lansing	York	York, E. R. **O**	Joseph Shepard
L'Anse St. Jean	St. Jean	Chicoutimi **Q**	Rev. M. Girard
Lantz, W. O.		Lunenburg **N S**	Harvey B. Lantz
La Petite Rivière St. François (sub)	Petite Rivière	Charlevoix **Q**	
La Pigeonnière	La Salle	Napierville **Q**	Flavien Robert
**Laprairie*	Laprairie	Laprairie **Q**	Julien Brosseau
La Présentation	La Présentation	St. Hyacinthe **Q**	Alexis Millet
L'Ardoise, W. O.		Richmond **N S**	Michael McNiel
Largie	Dunwich	Elgin, W. R. **O**	Allan McPherson
Larochelle	Halifax	Megantic **Q**	J. T. Hébert
Larry's River, W. O.	Wilmot	Guysboro' **N S**	Jos. Fougére
Laskay	King	York, N. R. **O**	Henry Baldwin

NAME OF POST OFFICE.	TOWNSHIP OR PARISH.	ELECTORAL COUNTY OR DIVISION.	NAME OF POSTMASTER.
Laterrière	Notre Dame de Laterrière	Chicoutimi .... Q	George McKenzie......
Latimer	Storrington	Frontenac .... O	Silas Coverley ....
Latona	Glenelg	Grey, S. R. .... O	Mark Appleby...........
Laurel..................	Amaranth..............	Wellington, N. R.......... O	M. S. Gray ....
Lauzon	Lauzon	Lévis .... Q	Charles Bourget ....
Laval	Laval	Montmorency .... Q	John Keough ....
Lavaltrie	Lavaltrie	Berthier .... Q	Joseph Charland ......
Lavant	Lavant	Lanark, N. R.............. O	Archd. Browning .....
Lavender	Mulmur	Simcoe, S. R............... O	I. B. Mastin ....
L'Avenir	Durham	Drummond .... Q	C. Gagnon ....
Lawrence Factory, W. O.	....	Cumberland .... N S	Charles Lawrence...
Lawrence Station, W. O.	....	Charlotte .... N B	John Taylor ....
Lawrencetown	....	Annapolis .... N S	J. W. James ....
Lawrencetown, W. O..	....	Halifax .... N S	Samuel Hiltz...........
Lawrenceville	South Ely..............	Shefford .... Q	E. Lawrence
Layton	Brock	Ontario, N. R.............. O	John Sornberger ......
**Leamington*	Mersea	Essex .... O	Warren Kimball ......
Learned Plain	Newport	Compton .... Q	E. Learned ....
Leaskdale	Scott	Ontario, N. R. .... O	George Leask ....
Lebanon	Maryboro'	Wellington, N. R.......... O	James W. Huff.........
Leclercville	Ste. Emelie	Lotbinière .... Q	Joseph Lord ....
Ledge, W. O............	....	Charlotte .... N B	Mrs. B. Conley ....
**Leeds*	Leeds	Megantic .... Q	Sarah Jiggens..........
Leeds Village	Leeds	Megantic .... Q	Hugh McCutcheon.....
Lefroy	Innisfil	Simcoe, S. R............... O	David Davidson ....
Leicester, W. O.	....	Cumberland .... N S	D. Lockhart............
Leinster	Richmond	Lennox .... O	M. Jordan ....
Leitch's Creek, W. O..	....	Cape Breton .... N S	Alex. McDonald ......
Leith	Sydenham	Grey, N. R. .... O	James Ross, jun. ......
Lemesurier............	Leeds	Megantic .... Q	John Wilkin ....
Lemonville	Whitchurch	York, N. R. .... O	W. L. White ....
Lennox	Innisfil	Simcoe, S. R............... O	....

NAME OF POST OFFICE.	TOWNSHIP OR PARISH.	ELECTORAL COUNTY OR DIVISION.	NAME OF POSTMASTER.
**Lennoxville*	Ascot	Sherbrooke **Q**	Ephraim W. Abbott
L'Epiphanie	St. Sulpice	L'Assomption **Q**	F. Le Blanc
Lepreaux		Charlotte **N B**	William K. Reynolds
Lequille, W. O.		Annapolis **N S**	Alfred Hoyt
Les Eboulemens	Eboulemens	Charlevoix **Q**	Cleophe Coté
Les Ecureuils	Ecureuils	Portneuf **Q**	Pierre Pagé
Les Escoumains	Escoumains	Saguenay **Q**	John C. Barry
Lesoard	Clarke	Durham, W. R. **O**	John Proctor
Leslie	York	York, E. R. **O**	George Leslie, jun.
Les Petites Bergeronnes		Saguenay **Q**	R. Bouilliane
L'Etete, W. O.		Charlotte **N B**	George Dick, sen.
**Lévis*	Lauzon	Lévis **Q**	Elzear Bédard
Lewis Bay, W. O.		Cape Breton **N S**	Donald Gillis
Lewis Head, W. O.		Shelburne **N S**	William Herkins
Lewis Mountain, W. O.		Westmoreland **N B**	James Lounsbury
Lewisville, W. O		Westmoreland **N B**	Stephen Mills
Lieury	McGillivray	Middlesex, N. R. **O**	Alexander Smith
Lifford	Manvers	Durham, E R. **O**	Miss Jane Fowler
Lilley's Corner's	London	Middlesex, E. R. **O**	Charles Lilley
Lilloet		Cariboo **B C**	Alfred Smith
Limehouse	Esquesing	Halton **O**	John Newton
Lime Lake	Hungerford	Hastings, E. R. **O**	John Henderson
Lime Rock, W. O.		Pictou **N S**	Mrs. Mary McDonald.
Lincoln, W. O.		Sunbury **N B**	Isaac S. Tayler
Linda	Westbury	Compton **Q**	Daniel B. Hall
**Lindsay*	Ops	Victoria, S. R. **O**	Thomas Adam
Lindsay, W. O.		Carleton **N B**	Alex. Lindsay
Lineboro'	Stanstead	Stanstead **Q**	James W. House
Lingan		Cape Breton **N S**	Ronald McDonald
Linton	King	York, N. R. **O**	Joseph Lynn
Linton's, W. O.		Sunbury **N B**	Adam Johnson
Linwood	Wellesley	Waterloo, N. R. **O**	Robert Y. Fish
[redacted]		. R.' **O**	John Zinkann

NAME OF POST OFFICE.	TOWNSHIP OR PARISH.	ELECTORAL COUNTY OR DIVISION.	NAME OF POSTMASTER.
Liscombe..................	....	Guysborough ....N S	James Hemlow ....
L'Islet.........	L'Islet.....	L'Islet............ .. ..Q	Mrs. M. E. Ballantine.
Listowel..................	Wallace	Perth, N. R. ....O	W. H. Hacking..........
Little Branch, W. O...	....	Northumberland......N B	Alex. Cameron ....
Little Bras d'Or	....	Cape Breton ....N S	John H. Christie .....
Little Britain............	Mariposa	Victoria, S. R. ....O	John Broad..............
Little Current	Howland	Algoma ....O	G. B. Abrey ....
Little Grace Bay	....	Cape Breton........... N S	Daniel McDonald......
Little Harbor...........	No. 46	King's ....P E I	Andrew Mooney........
Little Harbor, W. O...	....	Pictou ....N S	James Stewart ....
Little Judique, W. O...	....	Inverness ....N S	Angus Beaton...........
Little Lepreaux, W. O.	....	Charlotte .... N B	W. McGowan............
Little Lorraine, W. O.	....	Cape Breton .... N S	....
Little Narrows, W. O.	....	Inverness ....N S	Hugh McAskil . . ..
Little Rideau...........	Hawkesbury, East.....	Prescott ... .O	Thomas Ross......... ..
Little Ridge, W. O.....	....	Albert........ ....N B	George Bartlett.........
Little Ridge, W. O.....	....	Charlotte ....N B	Robert Thompson......
Little River (Coverdale), W. O.	....	Albert ....N B	William Leemans......
Little River (Elgin), W. O.	....	Albert....................N B	Hiram Killam ....
Little River, W. O. ...	....	Sunbury................N B	M. H. Coburn...........
Little River, W. O. ...	....	Antigonishe ....N S	Levi Irish .. ..
Little River, W. O. ..	....	Cumberland ....N S	J. Lawrence Purdy ...
Little River, W. O. ...	....	Digby ....N S	P. W. Frost..............
Little River (Mid. Musquodoboit), W. O.......................	....	Halifax ... .N S	Thomas McMullen
Little Rocher, W. O...	....	Albert .... .N B	John Richardson ......

NAME OF POST OFFICE.	TOWNSHIP OR PARISH.	ELECTORAL COUNTY OR DIVISION.	NAME OF POSTMASTER.
Little York	Number 34	Queen's ... **P E I**	Robert Lawson
Liverpool		Queen's ... **N S**	Archd. J. Campbell
Livingston's Cove, W. O.		Antigonishe ... **N S**	John Livingston
Lloydtown	King	York, N. R. ... **O**	Anthony Eastwood
Lobo	Lobo	Middlesex, N. R. ... **O**	T. S. Edwards
Lochabar, W. O.		Antigonishe ... **N S**	Mrs. M. Sears
Lochaber Bay	Lochaber	Ottawa ... **Q**	Archibald Campbell
Lockhartville, W. O.		King's ... **N S**	George King
Loch Garry	Kenyon	Glengarry ... **O**	James Fraser
Lochiel	Lochiel	Glengarry ... **O**	D. B. McMillan
Lochinvar	Lochiel	Glengarry ... **O**	Simon Fraser
Loch Lomond		St. John ... **N B**	Daniel Robertson
Loch Lomond, W. O.		Richmond ... **N S**	Roderick Bethune
Lochside, W. O.		Richmond ... **N S**	D. McDougall
Locke Port		Shelburne ... **N S**	Ross Hammond
Locksley	Aliee	Renfrew, N. R. ... **O**	W. M. Walford
Lockton	Albion	Cardwell ... **O**	William Wallace
Lockville	Mountain	Dundas ... **O**	Isaac Dillabough
Loganville, W. O.		Pictou ... **N S**	Dugald Logan
Logierait	Moore	Lambton ... **O**	D. Hossie
Lombardy	South Elmsley	Leeds, N. R. ... **O**	James O. Mara
Londesborough	Hullett	Huron, C. R. ... **O**	Hugh Wallace
London	London	London ... **O**	Lawrence Lawless
Londonderry, W. O.		King's ... **N B**	James Douglas
Londonderry		Colchester ... **N S**	Robert S. Crowe
Londonderry Station		Colchester ... **N S**	John C. Spencer
Long Creek	Number 65	Queen's ... **P E I**	Wm. McKinnon
Long Creek, W. O.		Queen's ... **N B**	John Secord, jun.
Long Island		Digby ... **N S**	J. W. Eldrige
Long Island Locks	Gloucester	Russell ... **O**	
Long River	Number 20	Queen's ... **P E I**	Archibald Cousins
Long Lake	Olden	Addington ... **O**	James Bender
Long Point		Hochelaga ... **Q**	

NAME OF POST OFFICE.	TOWNSHIP OR PARISH.	ELECTORAL COUNTY. OR DIVISION.	NAME OF POSTMASTER.
Long Point, W. O.....	....	King's ....**N B**	John Coulter ....
Long Point, W. O......	....	Inverness ....**N S**	Duncan McDonald.....
Long Point, W. O. ...	....	King's..... .... **N S**	Henry Ogilvie...........
Long Reach, W. O.....	....	King's ....**N B**	James M. Smith ......
Long Settlement, W.O	....	Carleton ....**N B**	James H. Sproul ......
Longueuil	Longueuil	Chambly....................**Q**	P. Lesperance...........
Longwood	Ekfrid.....	Middlesex, W. R.........**O**	Thomas Gordon ....
Longwood Station.....	Caradoc	Middlesex, W. R.........**O**	Oliver White............
Lonsdale	Tyendinaga	Hastings, E. R..... ......**O**	Richard Wildman .....
Lord's Cove, W. O....	....	Charlotte ....**N B**	Franklin Lambert.....
Lorette	St. Ambroise............	Quebec ....**Q**	J G. Vincent ....
Loretto	Adjala..	Cardwell..... ....**O**	Wm. Casserly ....
**L'Orignal*	Longueuil	Prescott ....**O**	C. Johnson ....
Lorne	Kincardine.....	Bruce, S. R.................**O**	James Jack..............
Lorneville	Eldon	Victoria, N. R.............**O**	Thomas Morrison......
Lorraine..................	Mono......	Cardwell ....**O**	John Mills. ....
Lorway Mines, W.O...	....	Cape Breton .... **N S**	....
Lotbinière	Lotbinière	Lotbinière ... . **Q**	M. Lemay ....
Lot 1.....	Number 1	Prince.................**P E I**	P. Dalton........ .. ..
" 4...........	Do 4	Prince.................**P E I**	Dennis Carrol...........
" 6......................	Do 6	Prince.................**P E I**	W. Hardy ....
" 8...............	Do 8	Prince ....**P E I**	A. Ramsey ....
" 10.............	Do 10	Prince.................**P E I**	William Vincent........
" 11.....	Do 11	Prince.................**P E I**	....
" 12......................	Do 12	Prince.................**P E I**	William Hayes ....
" 14......................	Do 14	Prince ....**P E I**	John O'Connor ....
" 16..............	Do 16	Prince.................**P E I**	D. Campbell ....
" 30......................	Do 30	Prince...... ....**P E I**	Patrick Trainer ....
" 35......................	Do 35	Queen's ....**P E I**	H. McLeod..............
" 45....................	Do 45	King's.... ....**P E I**	Herman McDonald....
" 56......................	Do 56	King's.................'**P E I**	William Norton.........
" 67......................	Do 67	Queen's ....**P E I**	M. McDonald ....
Lotus.......................	Manvers	Durham, E. R. ....**O**	David Bingham........
Loughborough	Loughborough	Addington ....**O**	Hugh Madden..........

NAME OF POST OFFICE.	TOWNSHIP OR PARISH.	ELECTORAL COUNTY OR DIVISION.	NAME OF POSTMASTER.	
Louisburg, W. O.	....	Cape Breton .... **N S**	Joseph Kennedy........	
Louisville.........	Chatham	Kent .... **O**	R. C. Struthers	
Lovat	Greenock	Bruce, S. R. .... **O**	Thomas Allen	
Low.....	Low...	Ottawa .... **Q**	Caleb Brooks............	
Lowbanks	Moulton	Monck................. .....**O**	Isaac Michener..	
Lowor Argyle, W. O...	....	Yarmouth ....**N S**	J. F. McLarren.........	
Lower Barney's River W. O.	....	Pictou ....**N S**	....	
Lower Brighton, W.O.	....	Carleton......... ....**N B**	John L. Dow	
Lower Canterbury. W. O.	....	York ....**N B**	D. J. Langstaff	
Lower Cape, W. O......	....	Albert ....**N B**	Joseph Taylor....	
Lower Cove, W. O......	....	Cumberland ....**N S**	Amos Seaman	
Lower Coverdale, W.O	....	Albert .... **N B**	James Rogers	
Lower East Pubnico, W. O.	....	Yarmouth ....**N S**	William Killam.........	
Lower Fort Garry......	St. Andrews, N.........	Lisgar..... .... **M**	Donald Gunn..	
Lower Freetown	No. 25........................	Prince..................**P E I**	George Burns	
Lower French Village, W. O.	....	York ....**N B**	George Risteen...	
Lower Granville, W.O.	....	Annapolis ....**N S**	A. L. Delap	
LowerHayneville W.O	....	York ....**N B**	....	
Lower Horton.............	....	King's ....**N S**	E. McLatchy............	
Lower Ireland...........	Ireland	Megantic ....**Q**	Edward Redman	
Lower La Have, W.O.	. ...	Lunenburg ... .**N S**	Joseph Oxner............	
Lower L'Ardoise, W.O.	....	Richmond . ...**N S**	James Matheson	
Lower Line, Queensbury, W. O.	....	York...... ....**N B**	J. H. Tupper............	
Lower Montague	No. 59....	King's ....**P E I**	William Johnston	
Lower Newcastle, W.O.	....	Northumberland......**N B**	John Delany.....	
Lower Pereaux, W.O..	....	King's ....**N S**	Philip Brown............	
Lower Pockmouche, W. O.	....	Gloucester ....**N B**	P. Robicheau.....	
Lower Prince William, W. O.	....	York ....**N B**	John Wasson............	
Lower Prospect, W. O.	....	Halifax .... **N S**	Samuel F. Blackburn..	
Lower Queensbury, W. O.	....	York ....**N B**	James W. Brown	

NAME OF POST OFFICE.	TOWNSHIP OR PARISH.	ELECTORAL COUNTY OR DIVISION.	NAME OF POSTMASTER.
Lower River Inhabitants, W. O		Richmond N S	Jos. McCarthy
Lower Selmah, W. O.		Hants N S	William Creelman
Lower Settlement, Middle River, W.O.		Victoria N S	Finlay McRae
Lower Settlement, South River, W.O.		Antigonishe N S	Donald McKenzie
Lower Ship Harbor, W. O.		Halifax N S	Mrs. Mary O'Brien
Lower Southampton, W. O.		York N B	George Grosvenor
Lower Stewiacke		Colchester N S	F. H. Holesworth
Lower Turtle Creek, W. O.		Albert N B	G. A. Fillmore
Lower Wakefield, W.O		Carleton N B	Stephen Brittain
Lower West Pubnico, W. O.		Yarmouth N S	Mark D'Entremont
Lower Wood Harbor, W. O.		Shelburne N S	S. K Mood
Lower Woodstock, W. O		Carleton N B	John Riordon
Low Point, W. O.		Inverness N S	Angus McMaster
Lowville	Nelson	Halton O	Wm. J. Hawkins
Lucan	Biddulph	Middlesex, N. R. O	William Porte
Lucerne	Wakefield	Ottawa Q	Robert Blackburn
Lucknow	Kinloss	Bruce, S. R. O	M. Campbell
Ludlow, W. O.		Northumberland N B	John Nelson
Lumley	Usborne	Huron, S. R. O	William Dinnin
Lunenburg	Osnabruck	Stormont O	F. Kirkpatrick
Lunenburg		Lunenburg N S	Mrs. A. M. Rudolph
Lurgan	Huron	Bruce, S. R. O	James McCrindle
Lutes Mountain, W. O.		Westmoreland N B	Alfred M. Bunnell
Luther	Luther	Wellington, N. R. O	William Dawson
Luton	Malahide	Elgin, E. R. O	L. R. Tyrell
Lyn	Elizabethtown	Brockville O	Joshua Lillie
Lynden	Beverley	Wentworth, N. R. O	James E. Orr
Lyndhurst	Lansdowne	Leeds, S. R. O	John Roddick
Lynedoch	Charlotteville	Norfolk, S. R. O	Wm. A. Charlton
Lynnfield, W. O.		Charlotte N B	John J. Getchell

NAME OF POST OFFICE.	TOWNSHIP OR PARISH.	ELECTORAL COUNTY OR DIVISION.	NAME OF POSTMASTER.
Lynnville	Windham	Norfolk, N. R. ... O	E. B. Myers
Lyons	Dorchester, South	Elgin, E. R. ... O	
Lyster	Nelson	Megantic ... Q	John King
Lyster Station	Nelson	Megantic ... Q	Francois Leclerc
Lyttleton, W. O		Northumberland ... N B	David Somers
Lytton		Yale ... B C	John Boyd
McAdam Junction, W. O		York ... N B	James Haddock
McAdam's Lake, W. O		Cape Breton ... N S	Daniel McIsaac
a McAlpine, W. O		Queen's ... N B	Nevine McAlpine
McAulay's, W. O.		Victoria ... N S	N. McAulay
McDonald's Corner, W. O.		Queen's ... N B	Hiram Humphries
McDonald's Corners	Dalhousie	Lanark, N. R. ... O	Wm. Lock
McDonald's Point, W. O		Queen's ... N B	D. N. Smith
McDougall Settlement, W. O		Westmoreland ... N B	Col. McDougall
McGillivray	McGillivray	Middlesex, N. R. ... O	D. Shoff
McIntyre	Osprey	Grey, E. R ... O	Edward Potts
McKay's Point, W. O.		Victoria ... N S	Michael McLean
McKellar	Mckellar	Muskoka ... O	Samuel Armstrong
McKenzie's Corner, W. O,		Carleton ... N B	John Y. Hoyt
McLaughlin Road, W. O		Kent ... N B	Ira Hicks
McLellan's Mountain, W. O		... N S	Donald Fraser

NAME OF POST OFFICE.	TOWNSHIP OR PARISH.	ELECTORAL COUNTY OR DIVISION.	NAME OF POSTMASTER.
McLellan's Brook, W. O		Pictou **N S**	Alexander Fraser
McLeod's Mills, W. O.		Kent **N B**	George McLeod
McPherson's Ferry, W. O		Richmond **N S**	James Smith
Maberly	Sherbrooke, South	Lanark, S. R. **O**	Richard Mayberry
Mabou		Inverness **N S**	William Grant
Mabou Coal Mines, W O.		Inverness **N S**	Donald Beaton
Mabou Harbor, W. O.		Inverness **N S**	Donald McDonald
Macbeth	Hawkesbury, East	Prescott **O**	Archibald McBean
Maccan, W. O		Cumberland **N S**	Robert Roach
Maccan Mountain, W. O.		Cumberland **N S**	W. B. Lodge
Mace's Bay		Charlotte **N B**	Robert V. Hanson
Macnider	L'Assomption	Rimouski **Q**	F. Saucier
Mactaquack, W. O.		York **N B**	James Mitchell
Macton	Peel	Wellington, C. R. **O**	J. M. McCormick
Macville	Albion	Cardwell **O**	Seth Wilson
Maddington	Maddington	Arthabaska **Q**	F. H. St. Germain
Madisco, W. O.		Gloucester **N B**	Mrs. Des Brisay
**Madoc*	Madoc	Hastings, N. R. **O**	Wm. H. O'Flynn
Magaguadavic. W. O.		York **N B**	Solomon Vail
Magdalen Islands		Gaspé **Q**	John D. Tuzo
Magenta	Ange Gardien	Rouville **Q**	Jacques Fournier
Magnetawan	Chapman	Muskoka **O**	James Miller
Magog	Magog	Stanstead **Q**	George O. Somers
Magoon's Point	Stanstead	Stanstead **Q**	Aaron Magoon
Magpie		Saguenay **Q**	Philippe Bisson
Magundy, W. O		York **N B**	James Henry
Mahone Bay		Lunenburg **N S**	Lewis Knaut
Maidstone	Sandwich	Essex **O**	
Mainadieu, W. O		Cape Breton **N S**	Clara Rigby
Maitland	Augusta	Grenville, S. R. **O**	George C. Longley
Maitland		Hants **N S**	Alexander Roy
Maitland, W. O		Annapolis **N S**	W. H. Dukeshire

NAME OF POST OFFICE.	TOWNSHIP OR PARISH.	ELECTORAL COUNTY OR DIVISION.	NAME OF POSTMASTER.
Maitland, W. O		Yarmouth N S	Charles Steele
Malagash, W. O.		Cumberland N S	Robert McDonald
Malagawatch, W. O		Inverness N S	L. McDonald
Malakoff	Marlborough	Carleton O	W. J. Pierce
Malcolm	Brant	Bruce, S. R. O	Daniel Sullivan
Malignant Cove, W.O.		Antigonishe N S	Donald McLean
Mallorytown	Yonge	Leeds, S. R. O	Frederick F. Lee
Malmaison	Stanbridge	Missisquoi Q	
Malone	Marmora	Hastings, N. R. O	George Richardson
Malton	Toronto	Peel O	J. B. Allen
Malvern	Scarborough	York, E. R. O	Smith Thomson
Manchester	Reach	Ontario, N. R. O	John Taylor
Manchester, W. O		Guysborough N S	James M. Whitman
Mandamin	Plympton	Lambton O	R. S. Dunlop
Manilla	Mariposa	Victoria, S. R. O	Mary Douglas
Manitowaning	Assiginack	Algoma O	Alexander McGregor Ironside
Manners Sutton, W.O.		York N B	
Mannheim	Wilmot	Waterloo, S. R. O	Charles Lederman
Manotic	North Gower	Carleton O	G. L. Dickinson
Mansfield	Mulmur	Simcoe, S. R. O	William Gilbert
Mansonville-Potton	Potton	Brome Q	David A. Manson
Maple	Vaughan	York, W. R. O	J. P. Rupert
Maple Bay		Vancouver B C	William Beaumont
Maple Green, W. O		Restigouche N B	James Fraser
Maple Grove	Ireland	Megantic Q	Henry Cross, jun.
Maple Hill	Brant	Bruce, S. R. O	George Inglis, jun.
Maple Leaf	Newport	Compton Q	William G. Planch
Mapleton	Yarmouth	Elgin, E. R. O	William Appleford
Mapleton	St. Peter's	Lisgar M	John Peers
Mapleton, W. O.		Albert N B	W. A. Colpits
Maple Valley	Nottawasaga	Simcoe, N. R O	James Dick
Maplewood	West Zorra	Oxford, N. R. O	Christopher G. Bean
Maquapit Lake, W. O.		Queen's N B	John Stone
Mar	Albermarle	Bruce, N. R. O	Thomas H. Lee

NAME OF POST OFFICE.	TOWNSHIP OR PARISH.	ELECTORAL COUNTY OR DIVISION.	NAME OF POSTMASTER.
Marathon...........	Fitzroy	Carleton ....**O**	....
Marble Mountain, W. O......	....	Inverness ....**N S**	Nicholas J. Brown ...
Marble Rock...........	Leeds	Leeds, S. R......... ....**O**	George Emery........
Marbleton	Dudswell	Wolfe ....**Q**	J. B. Bishop ....
March......................	March....................	Carleton ....**O**	W. H. Berry ....
Marchmont	Orillia, North	Simcoe, N. R...............**O**	Charles Powley.........
Marden	Guelph	Wellington, S. R.........**O**	C. Mc D. Blyth.........
Margaree, W. O.......	Margaree	Inverness .... **N S**	Collin Gillies............
Margaree (Forks)......	Margaree	Inverness ....**N S**	Donald Campbell ......
Margaretsville, W. O.	....	Annapolis ....**N S**	T. A. Margeson.........
Margate	No. 19	Prince......... ....**P E I**	Reuben Tuplin.........
Maria	Maria	Bonaventure ....**Q**	François S. Cyr .....
Marie Bridge............	No. 40...............	King's..... ....**P E I**	William Bowley ......
Marie Joseph, W. O...	....	Guysboro' .... **N S**	Elisha Hawbolt ......
Marion Bridge, W. O.	....	Cape Breton ....**N S**	Hector McNeil..........
Maritana	Franklin......	Huntingdon ....**Q**	William Edwards.....
Markdale................	Glenelg	Grey, S. R........... ..... **O**	W. J. McFarland......
Markham	Markham	York, E. R................. **O**	James J. Barker........
Markhamville, W. O..	....	King's ....**N B**	Alfred Markham .....
Marlbank	Hungerford	Hastings, E. R... .... **O**	Alex. D. Allan ....
Marlow....................	Linière	Beauce ....**Q**	Joseph Thompson ...
Marmion	Sullivan	Grey, N. R............... ..**O**	John Hislop ....
Marmora	Marmora	Hastings, N. R...........**O**	D. Bentley................
Marnoch..................	Wawanosh	Huron, N. R.............. **O**	P. Poterfield ....
Marriott' Cove, W. O.	....	Lunenburg... ....**N S**	Benj. Millet..............
Marshall's Cove, W. O.........	....	Annapolis ....**N S**	James P. Foster ......
Marshall's Town, W. O...	....	Digby ....**N S**	E. J. Haines ....
Marsh Hill.........	Reach	Ontario, N. R. ....**O**	William Tomlinson ...
Marshville	Wainfleet	Monck.........................**O**	Edward Lee ....
Marshy Hope, W. O...	... .	Antigonishe ....**N S**	James McDougall......
Marston	Walsingham	Norfolk, S. R.............. **O**	Edwin Cridland ....
Marsville	Garafraxa	Wellington. C. R.........**O**	William McCormack ..
Martin's River, W. O.	....	Lunenburg	**N S**	Joseph Strum ....

NAME OF POST OFFICE.	TOWNSHIP OR PARISH.	ELECTORAL COUNTY OR DIVISION.	NAME OF POSTMASTER.
Martintown	Charlottenburg	Glengarry ... O	Robert Blackwood
Martinville	Clifton	Compton ... Q	
Marydale, W. O.		Antigonishe ... N S	Colin Chisholm
Marysville	Tyendinaga	Hastings, E. R. ... O	Daniel Black
Marysville, W. O.		York ... N B	Benjamin Dennison
Maryvale, W. O.		Antigonishe ... N S	James C. Ross
Mascouche Rapids	Mascouche	L'Assomption ... Q	M. Delfause
Mascouche	Mascouche	L'Assomption ... Q	J. O. Lamarche
Masham Mills	Masham	Ottawa ... Q	William Bennett
Maskinongé	Maskinongé	Maskinongé ... Q	J. O. Belanger
Masonville	London	Middlesex, E. R. ... O	Robert Mason
Massawippi	Hatley, West	Stanstead ... Q	Luther Abbot
Massie	Hollond	Grey, N. R. ... O	Joshua Milligan
Mast Town, W. O		Colchester	Geo. C. Stephens
Matane	Matane	Rimouski ... Q	
Matapédia	Restigouche	Bonaventure ... Q	D. Fraser
Matawatchan	Matawatchan	Renfrew, S. R. ... O	John McGregor
Matlock	Plympton	Lambton ... O	John P. Jarmain
Mattawa	Mattawa	District of Nipissing ... O	John Bangs
Maugerville		Sunbury ... N B	
Mawcook	Granby	Shefford ... Q	L. N. Hungerford
Maxwell	Osprey	Grey, E. R. ... O	Wesley Long
Mayfair	Ekfrid	Middlesex, W. R. ... O	John Dalton
Mayfield	Chingacousy	Peel ... O	William Spiers
Maynard	Augusta	Grenville, S. R. ... O	
Maynooth	Monteagle	Hastings, N. R. ... O	William Fitzgerald
Mayo	Lochaber	Ottawa ... Q	
Meadowvale	Toronto	Peel ... O	C. H Gooderham
**Meaford*	St. Vincent	Grey, E. R. ... O	D. L. Layton
Meagher's Grant, W. O.		Halifax ... N S	Daniel Dillman
Mechanics' Settlement, W. O.		King's ... N B	Alexander Moore
Medford, W. O.		King's ... N S	William West

NAME OF POST OFFICE.	TOWNSHIP OR PARISH.	ELECTORAL COUNTY OR DIVISION.	NAME OF POSTMASTER.
Medonte	Medonte	Simcoe, N. R. **O**	Robert J. Moon
Melancthon	Melancthon	Grey, E. R. **O**	James Brown
**Melbourne*	Melbourne	Richmond **Q**	William Beattie
Melbourne Ridge	Melbourne	Richmond **Q**	Richard Woodard
Melissa	Chaffey	Muskoka **O**	W. H. Buker
Melocheville	Beauharnois	Beauharnois **Q**	George Ellis
Melrose	Tyendinaga	Hastings, E. R. **O**	George Duncan
Melrose	St. Mary's	Guysborough **N S**	James Stewart
Melvern Square		Annapolis **N S**	B. Spinney
Melville	Hillier	Prince Edward **O**	Caleb Johnson
Memramcook		Westmoreland **N B**	S. C. Charters
Menie	Seymour	Northumberland, E. R. **O**	James Mather
Merigonish, W. O.		Pictou **N S**	Edward Finlayson
Merivale	Nepean	Carleton **O**	E. B. Hopper
Merlin	Raleigh	Kent **O**	Patrick Sullivan
**Merrickville*	Wolford	Grenville, N. R. **O**	Samuel Jakes
Merritton	Grantham	Lincoln **O**	Wm. Parnall
Mermaid Farm	No. 48	Queen's **P E I**	J. Farquharson
Metabechouan	Metabechouan	Chicoutimi **Q**	Jacques Bergeron
Metaghan		Digby **N S**	George Gorman
Metaghan River, W. O		Digby **N S**	Justinian Come u
Méthot's Mills	St. Flavien	Lotbinère **Q**	Joseph Fournier
Métis	Métis	Rimouski **Q**	W. E. Page
Metz	Garafraxa	Wellington, C. R. **O**	John Mitchell
Meyersburg	Seymour	Northumberland, E. R. **O**	Cornelius O'Sullivan
Michael's Bay	Tekermagh	Algoma **O**	R. A. Lyon
Michipicoton River		Algoma **O**	P. W. Bell
Middleboro, W. O.		Cumberland **N S**	Cyprian Ballard
Middle Church	St. Paul's	Lisgar **M**	James Clouston
Middle Clyde River, W. O.		Shelburne **N S**	G. D. McKay
Middle Coverdale, W. O		Albert **N B**	Sandford S. Ryan
Middlefield, W. O.		Queen's **N S**	E. Morton
Middle La Have Ferry			

NAME OF POST OFFICE.	TOWNSHIP OR PARISH.	ELECTORAL COUNTY OR DIVISION.	NAME OF POSTMASTER.
Middle Musquodoboit		Halifax N S	R. A. Kaulbeck
Middle Ohio, W. O		Shelburne N S	James McKay
Middle Pereaux, W. O		King's N S	Elijah C. West
Middle River, W. O		Pictou N S	George McLeod
Middle River, W. O		Victoria N S	Charles L. McLe...
Middle St. Francis, W. O		Victoria N B	Andrew Douglas
Middle Section of N. E. Margaree, W. O	Margaree	Inverness N S	J. G. Crowdis
Middle Settlement—River Inhabitants W. O		Inverness N S	Donald McDonald
Middle Settlement of South River, W. O		Antigonishe N S	Sames McDonnell
Middle Simmonds, W. O		Carleton N B	David N. Raymond
Middle Southampton, W. O		York N B	George W. McKay
Middle Stewiacke, W. O		Colchester N S	John Dickie
Middleton		Annapolis N S	Albert Beals
Middleton	No. 27	Prince P E I	William Roberts
Middleville	Lanark	Lanark, N. R O	William Croft
Midgic, W. O		Westmoreland N B	Mariner Hicks
Midhurst	Vespra	Simcoe, N. R O	George Smeath
Midland	Tay	Simcoe, N. R O	Thomas B. Gladstone
Midland, W. O		King's N B	W. M. Case
Milby	Ascott	Sherbrooke Q	Allan Cole
Mildmay	Carrick	Bruce, S. R O	Malcolm Campbell
Mile End		Hochelaga Q	Jos. Robin Lapointe
Milford	Marysburg	Prince Edward O	James Cooke
Milford, W. O		Annapolis N S	S. Charlton
Milford Haven Bridge, W. O		Guysborough N S	Thomas McDonald
Millbank	Mornington	Perth, N. R O	William Rutherford
Mill Bridge	Tudor	Hastings, N. R O	R. M. Norman
**Mill Brook*	Cavan	Durham, E. R O	William Vance

NAME OF POST OFFICE.	TOWNSHIP OR PARISH.	ELECTORAL COUNTY OR DIVISION.	NAME OF POSTMASTER.
Mill Brook, W. O......	....	Queen's ....N B	David Hughes ....
Mill Cove. W. O.........	....	Lunenburg...............N S	J. W. Jollymore. .....
Mill Cove, W. O.	....	Queen's............ ..... N B	Mrs. Nancy Sparks ...
Mill Creek, W. O......	....	Kent ....N B	N. Beckwith ....
Milledgeville...........	....	St. John .... N B	John G. Tobin ....
Mille Isles	Mille Isles................	Argenteuil ....Q	Solomon Pollock .....
Mille Roches	Cornwall.....................	Cornwall ....O	Wm. N. Tait ....
Miller's Creek, W. O..	....	Hants ....N S	Hiram Miller............
Mille Vaches.............	....	Saguenay ....Q	J. A. Piuze ....
Millfield	Inverness	Megantic ....Q	Thomas McKenzie.....
Mill Grove..............	Flamborough, West...	Wentworth, N. R.........O	W. H. Berney ....
Mill Haven	Ernestown	Lennox ....O	Anderson Venton......
Milliken	Markham	York, E. R..................O	W. Gorvett ....
Mill Point	Tyendinaga	Hastings, E. R............O	James Bowen ....
Millstream, W. O.....	....	King's ....N B	J. A. Fenwick ....
Millsville, W. O	....	Picton........................N S	John McKay..... ..
Milltown	....	Charlotte.. ....N B	Patrick Curran.........
Mill Village..............	....	Queen's ....N S	J. N. Mack ....
a Millville, W. O.......	....	King's.........................N S	Emerson Gates.........
Millville, W. O.........	....	York ....N B	....
Milnesville...............	Markham	York, E. R .... O	H. H. Read.............
Milton....	....	Queen's ....N S	E. Kempton ....
Milton, East	Milton.....	Shefford ....Q	Charles Gillespie ......
Milton, West	Trafalgar	Halton ....O	W. D. Lyon ....
Milverton	Mornington	Perth, N. R. ....O	John Pierson............
Mimico........	Etobicoke	York, W. R. ....O	George Scott ....
Miminegash	Number 3................	Prince ....P E I	Richard Costain ......
Mimosa	Erin	Wellington, S. R. ......O	[illegible]

NAME OF POST OFFICE.	TOWNSHIP OR PARISH.	ELECTORAL COUNTY OR DIVISION.	NAME OF POSTMASTER.
Miscouche	No. 17	Prince P E I	H. V. Desroches
Mispec, W. O.		St. John N B	
**Mitchell*	Logan	Perth, S R. O	William W. Hicks
Mitchell's Bay	Dover East	Kent O	Chas. W. Raymond
Moe's River	Compton	Compton Q	David F. Brown
Moffat	Nassagiweya	Halton O	Peter Little
Mohawk	Brantford, West	Brant, S. R. O	Thomas Racey
Mohr's Corners	Fitzroy	Carleton O	Charles Mohr
Moira	Huntingdon	Hastings, N. R. O	Henry Ostrom
Moisic		Saguenay Q	Samuel Strong
Molesworth	Wallace	Perth, N. R. O	Samuel Longheed
Monaghan	No. 36	Queen's P E I	James Wisner
Monck	Luther	Wellington, N. R. O	William Segsworth
Monckland	Roxborough	Stormont O	John Brown
Moncton		Westmoreland N B	Jos. Crandall
Moncton Road, W. O.		Westmoreland N B	William G. Bateman
Moneymore	Hungerford	Hastings, E. R. O	John Thompson
Mongenais	Newton	Vaudreuil Q	J. Sicart
Mongolia	Markham	York, E. R. O	Robert Curtis
Monkton	Elma	Perth, N. R. O	Edward Greensides
Mono Centre	Mono	Cardwell O	John Wilson
Mono Mills	Albion	Cardwell O	John Allen
Mono Road Station	Chinguacousy	Peel O	John Judge
Montague	Montague	Lanark, S. R. O	Peter Clark
Montague Bridge	No. 52	King's P E I	William Annear
Montague Cross	No. 57	Queen's P E I	W. Callaghan
Montague Gold Mines, W. O.		Halifax N S	Mrs. Vasey Barker
Montcalm	Rawdon	Montcalm Q	E. Copping
Monteagle Valley	Monteagle	Hastings, N. R. O	Robert T. Bartlett
Monte Bello	Petite Nation	Ottawa Q	Charles Major
Mont Elie	Caxton	St. Maurice Q	Otis Chamberlin
Mont Louis	Mont Louis	Gaspé Q	Joseph Lemieux
**Montmagny*	St Thomas	Montmagny Q	J. S. Vallée

NAME OF POST OFFICE.	TOWNSHIP OR PARISH.	ELECTORAL COUNTY OR DIVISION.	NAME OF POSTMASTER.
Montmorin......	Morin	Terrebonne.................. **Q**	Joseph Belisle ....
******Mc ntreal*..................	Montreal..................	Montreal .... **Q**	Guillaume La Mothe ..
Montrose	Stamford	Welland .... **O**	Archd. Thompson ...
Montrose	No. 3	Prince. . ... **P E I**	....
Mont St. Hilaire......	St. Hilaire	Rouville .... **Q**	Alexis Brouillette.....
Monument Settlement, W. O.	....	Carleton................. **N B**	James Kennedy ......
Moodyville	....	New Westminster..... **B C**	D. S. Milligan ....
Moore	Moore	Lambton .... **O**	John Morrison ....
Moorefield	Maryborough	Wellington, N. R.......... **O**	Henry Maudsley ......
Moore's Mills, W. O...	....	Charlotte .... **N B**	Joseph Cormick ....
Moore's Station	St. Armand.......	Missisquoi .... **Q**	P. C. Moore ....
Moose Brook, W. O...	....	Hants .... **N S**	Thomas M. Reid .....
Moose Creek......	Roxborough	Stormont .... **O**	William McKillican..
Moray.........	McGillivray	Middlesex, N. R........... **O**	H. Hagerman ....
Morden, W. O..........	....	King's......................... **N S**	Thomas Farnsworth..
Morell....	Number 39	King's .... **P E I**	W. Sterns................
Morell Rear	do 39	King's.................. **P E I**	James Phelan ....
Morewood	Winchester	Dundas .... **O**	A. McKay ....
Morganston -	Cramahe...................	Northumberland, E. R.. **O**	Wm. J. Newman.......
Morley	St. Vincent	Grey, E. R. .... **O**	James Lemon ....
Morningdale Mills.....	Mornington	Perth, N. R.... .... **O**	J. Nicklin ....
**Morpeth*	Howard	Bothwell..................... **O**	J. C. Nation ....
Morrisbank	Morris......................	Huron, N. R.. .... **O**	James Orr ....
**Morrisburg*	Williamsburg	Dundas .... **O**	Patrick Gormely ......
Morriston	Puslinch..................	Wellington, S. R.......... **O**	R. B. Morrison.........
*a*Morristown, W. O...	....	Antigonishe... .... **N S**	A. McGillivray.........
Morristown, W. O.... .	....	King's .... **N S**	John Palmer...... .....
Morton	Crosby South	Leeds, S. R. **O**	[illegible]

NAME OF POST OFFICE.	TOWNSHIP OR PARISH.	ELECTORAL COUNTY OR DIVISION.	NAME OF POSTMASTER.
Mossley	Dorchester, N.	Middlesex, E. R. O	Reuben Lane
Mossman'sGrant, W.O		Lunenburg N S	James Mossman
Motherwell	Fullarton	Perth, S. R. O	James Brown, sen.
Moulies River, W. O.		Kent N B	Arch. McEacheren.
Mountain Grove	Olden	Addington O	E. L. Godfrey
Mountain View	Ameliasburg	Prince Edward. O	W. H. Way
Mount Albert	Gwillimbury, East.	York, N. R. O	Andrew Clifford
Mount Albion	Saltfleet	Wentworth, S. R. O	James R. Cook
**Mount Brydges*	Caradoc	Middlesex, W. R. O	Edward Handy
Mount Carmel	Notre Dame de Mont Carmel	Kamouraska Q	R. Lavois
Mount Charles	Toronto	Peel O	Robert McLeod
Mount Denison, W.O.		Hants N S	Mrs. J. E. Shaw
Mount Elgin	Dereham	Oxford, S. R. O	James Stevens
**Mount Forest*	Arthur	Wellington, N. R. O	T. G. Smith
Mount Hanly, W. O.		Annapolis N S	Caleb Miller
Mount Healy	Oneida	Haldimand O	W. Donaldson
Mount Horeb	Ops	Victoria, S. R O	William Reynolds
Mount Hurst	Albion	Cardwell O	John Wallace
Mount Johnson	St Grégoire	Iberville Q	Louis A. Auger
Mountjoy		Soulanges Q	Camille Lalonde
Mount Loyal	Rawdon	Montcalm Q	William Smiley
Mount Oscar	Rigaud	Vaudreuil Q	Leandre Lapointe
Mount Pleasant	Cavan	Durham, E. R. O	Abraham Bets
Mount Pleasant	Number 12	Prince P E I	D. Campbell
Mount Pleasant, W.O		Cumberland N S	Isaac Simpson
Mount Pleasant, W.O.		King's N B	Merritt Jones
Mount St. Louis	Medonte	Simcoe, N. R. O	J. P. Hussey
Mount St. Patrick	Brougham	Renfrew, S. R. O	Bridget Brady
Mount Salem	Malahide	Elgin, E. R. O	George Hillaker
Mountsberg	Flamborough, East	Wentworth, N. R. O	Oron Thompson
Mount Stewart	Number 37	Queen's P E I	D. Egan
Mount Thom, W. O.		Pictou N S	George McKay
Mount Uniacke		Hants N S	Richard McLean
[illegible]	[illegible]	S. R O	William Perrin

NAME OF POST OFFICE.	TOWNSHIP OR PARISH.	ELECTORAL COUNTY OR DIVISION.	NAME OF POSTMASTER.
Mount Whatley, W.O.	....	Westmoreland ....N B	Dixon Chapman.......
Mount Wolfe...........	Albion.....................	Cardwell....... ....O	John Wolfe, jun. ......
Mouth of Jemseg, W. O........................	....	Queen's.............. ...N B	Elias Scribner..........
Mouth of Keswick, W. O........................	....	York ....N B	Mrs. Margaret Zerxa.
Mouth of Nerepis......	....	King's ....N B	J. M. Nase...............
Muddy Creek	Number 17..............	Prince ....P E I	John Dickie . ...
**Muir*	London.....	Middlesex, E. R..........O	William Mills ....
Mulgrave	Bertie	Welland.........................O	P. Learn, sen.........
Mull River, W. O.....	....	Inverness ....N S	Donald McIsaac.......
Mulmur	Mulmur	Simcoe, S. R ....O	John Murphy ....
Muncey	Caradoc	Middlesex, W. R..........O	R. E. Whiting.. ....
Munroe's Mills	Charlottenburg.........	Glengarry ....O	Malcolm Munroe .....
Munro's, W. O..........	....	Victoria ....N S	M. Munro.................
Munster	Goulbourn	Carleton ....O	Thomas Tubman .....
Murray.....................	Murray	Northumberland, E. R...O	Peter Rowe...............
**Murray Bay*....	Mount Murray.........	Charlevoix................ Q	Elie Angers..............
Murray Harbor, N.....	Number 63..............	King's...............P E I	David Maclure ....
Murray Harbor, Rd...	do 57.........	Queen's ....P E I	John McPherson ......
Murray Harbor, S......	do 64................	King's................P E I	C. T. Brehaut ....
Murray River..	do 64...............	King's...............P E I	Robert Saunders........
Murray's Corner, W. O.........	....	Westmoreland ....N B	Joseph Murray ....
Murvale	Portland...	Addington ....O	Michael Davy ....
Muskoka Falls	Draper	Muskoka ....O	Hy. A. Clifford... ....
Musquash, W. O........	....	St. John ....N B	L. D. Carman ..., ...
Musquodoboit Harbor W. O.....................	....	Halifax ....N S	....
Musselburg.............	Mornington	Perth, N.R.................O	George Shearer.........
Myrehall	Tyendinaga......	Hastings, E. R.............O	Mrs. Elizabeth Harris
Myrtle.....................	Whitby....................	Ontario, S. R............. O	Reuben Hurlburt .....
Mystic.....................	Stanbridge	Missisquoi ....Q	Joseph A. Phelps.....

NAME OF POST OFFICE.	TOWNSHIP OR PARISH.	ELECTORAL COUNTY OR DIVISION.	NAME OF POSTMASTER.
Nackawick, W. O.. ...	....	York ... .N B	William H. Clark......
Nanaimo..................	....	Vancouver......... .....B C	Charles Wormesley ...
Nairn	Williams, East	Middlesex, N. R ....O	Archibald Bell ....
Nanticoke................	Walpole	Haldimand....................O	W. M. Alderson........
Napanee...................	Richmond	Lennox ....O	Gilbert Bogart ....
Napanee Mills...........	Camden, East	Addington ....O	H. M. Wright ....
Napier	Metcalfe	Middlesex, W. R..........O	John Arthurs.............
Napierville.....	St. Cyprien	Napierville....................Q	Amable Brassard, jun.
Nappan, W. O...........	....	Cumberland .... N S	Samuel E. Freeman...
Napperton	Adelaide.....................	Middlesex, N. R. ....O	Thomas Jury............
Narrows	....	Queen's.................. .N B	Henry Todd ....
Nashwaak Station, W. O......	....	York ....N B	James Young...........
Nashwaak, W. O.........	....	York ....N B	James R. Garden .....
Nashwaaksis	... .	York .... N B	....
NashwaakVillage,W.O	....	York ....N B	John L. Fletcher ......
Nassagiweya	Nassagiweya.............	Halton ....O	Elias Easterbrook......
Natashguan	. ...	Saguenay ....Q	Rev. Jacob Gagné ....
Navan	Cumberland	Russell ....O	M. O'Meara ....
Necum Tench, W. O...	....	Halifax ....N S	William Smith ....
Neigette	St. Angèle	Rimouski ....Q	François X. Gagnier..
Nelson..............	Nelson	Halton . ...O	D. W. Springer.........
Nenagh.....................	Normanby	Grey, S. R.....................O	Thomas Duignan ......
Nerepis Station, W. O.	....	King's ....N B	David McKenzie ......
Netherby	Humberstone.....	Welland ....O	Joshua Fares............
Neustadt...................	Normanby	Grey, S. R......................O	D. Winkler................
Nevis	Oro	Simcoe, N. R.................O	James Greenshields. .
New Aberdeen	Waterloo, South	Waterloo, S. R...... .....O	William Key ....
New Albany, W. O. ...	....	Annapolis ....N S	Albert Oaks ....
New Annan, W. O. ...	....	Colchester ....N S	Wellington Blair .. ...
Newark......................	Norwich, North	Oxford, S. R,...... ....O	E. F. Schooley ....
New Bandon, W. O....	....	Gloucester ....N B	John Kerr ....
Newbliss..................	Kitley	Leeds, N. R. . ...O	John Edgar ....
Newbois	St. Narcisse de Beaurivage	Lotbinière ....Q	Eugene Boisonneau ..

NAME OF POST OFFICE.	TOWNSHIP OR PARISH.	ELECTORAL COUNTY OR DIVISION.	NAME OF POSTMASTER.
**Newborough*	Crosby, North	Leeds, S. R. **O**	Thomas Webster
Newboyne	Bastard	Leeds, S. R. **O**	James Lytle
Newbridge	Howick	Huron, N. R. **O**	Mrs. Sarah Carson
New Bridge, W. O		Inverness **N S**	Donald L. McDonald
**Newburgh*	Camden, East	Addington **O**	Robert Hope
Newburgh, W. O.		Carleton **N B**	Richard McKinney
**Newbury*	Mosa	Middlesex, W. R. **O**	Thomas Robinson
New Caledonia, W. O.		Halifax **N S**	John Hattee
New Campbelton, W. O.		Victoria **N S**	Chas. C. Campbell, jr
New Canaan, W. O.		Queen's **N B**	Lewis Keith
New Canada, W. O.		Lunenburg **N S**	Jeremiah Mader
New Carlisle	Cox	Bonaventure **Q**	Matthew Caldwell
**Newcastle*	Clarke	Durham, W. R. **O**	Hiram Hodges
Newcastle		Northumberland **N B**	Samuel Johnston
Newcastle Bridge		Queen's **N B**	R. P. Yeomans
Newcastle Creek, W. O		Queen's **N B**	G. D. Bailey
Newcombe	Hagerman	Muskoka **O**	Arthur Millin
Newcomb Corner, W. O		Halifax **N S**	John Barron
Newcombe Mills	Brighton	Northumberland, E. R. **O**	Edward Clark
New Cornwall, W. O.		Lunenburg **N S**	S. E. Hallamore
New Dublin	Elizabethtown	Brockville **O**	J. A. Browne
New Dundee	Wilmot	Waterloo, S. R. **O**	Lyman Beach
New Durham	Burford	Brant, S. R. **O**	Charles Cochran
**New Edinburgh*	Gloucester	Russell **O**	J. W. Proctor
New Gairloch, W. O.		Pictou **N S**	John McPherson
New Germany, W. O.		Lunenburg **N S**	William Nichols
New Glasgow	No. 23	Queen's **P E I**	R. G. McCoutrey
New Glasgow	Lacorne	Terrebonne **Q**	James Furse
New Glasgow		Pictou **N S**	William Fraser
**New Hamburg*	Wilmot	Waterloo, S. R. **O**	Christian Ernst
New Harbor, W. O.		Guysborough **N S**	David Kirby
New Haven	No. 31	Queen's **P E I**	H. McMillan
New Horton, W. O.		Albert **N B**	M. Cannon
Newington	Osnabruck	Storm—	

NAME OF POST OFFICE.	TOWNSHIP OR PARISH.	ELECTORAL COUNTY OR DIVISION.	NAME OF POSTMASTER.
New Ireland	Ireland	Megantic Q	Richard C. Porter
New Ireland, W. O		Albert N B	John Carrens
New Ireland Road, W. O		Albert N B	M. McFadden
New Jerusalem, W. O		Queen's N B	Albert M. Short
New Larig, W. O		Pictou N S	Robert G. McLeod
New Liverpool	St. Romuald	Lévis Q	Damase Roberge
New London	No. 21	Queen's P E I	D. McIntyre
New Lowell	Sunnidale	Simcoe, N. R O	P. Patton
**New Market*	Whitchurch	York, N. R O	William Roe
New Maryland, W.O		York N B	Lewis Fisher
New Mills		Restigouche N B	Donald McAlister
New Minas, W. O		King's N S	John A. Fuller
New Perth	No. 52	King's P E I	Roland H. Plummer
Newport	Brantford	Brant, S. R O	Colin Milloy
Newport		Gaspé Q	Clovis Desforges
Newport		Hants N S	J. F. Cochrane
Newport Corner, W.O		Hants N S	James Brown
Newport Landing		Hants N S	J. W. Allison
Newport Point		Gaspé Q	Philip Hamon
Newport Station		Hants N S	J. L. Sweet
New Richmond	New Richmond	Bonaventure Q	Richard Brash
New River, W. O		Charlotte N B	J. E. Knight
New Ross	Matilda	Dundas O	Thomas Currie
New Ross		Lunenburg N S	John Pratt
New Ross Road, W.O		King's N S	Owen McGarry
Newry	Elma	Perth, N. R O	R. L. Alexander
New Sarum	Yarmouth	Elgin, E. R O	Wm. H. Elliott
Newton	No. 27	Prince P E I	J. T. Murphy
Newton Brook	York	York, W. R O	W. W. Cummer
Newton Mills, W. O		Colchester N S	James Creelman
Newton Robinson	Tecumseth	Simcoe, S. R O	James G. Chantler
Newtown, W. O		King's N B	J. B. Pearce
New Town, W. O		Guysboro' N S	Thomas McBain
		N S	Charleton Sabean

NAME OF POST OFFICE.	TOWNSHIP OR PARISH.	ELECTORAL COUNTY OR DIVISION.	NAME OF POSTMASTER.
New Westminster.....	....	New Westminster......**B C**	Valentine B. Tait......
New Wiltshire..........	No. 31....................	Queen's..............**P E I**	G. Easter..................
**Niagara*	Niagara	Niagara ....**O**	Robert Warren ....
Nichol's Corner, W.O.	....	Annapolis...............**N S**	D. Nichols................
Nicola Lake..............	....	Yale.........................**B C**	John Clapperton ......
Nicolet	Nicolet	Nicolet....... ....**Q**	Miss Margaret Chillas
Nicolston	Essa	Simcoe, S. R.......... ....**O**	John Nichol........ ...
Nictaux Falls...........	....	Annapolis................**N S**	Charles Berteaux ...
Niel's Harbor, W. O...	....	Victoria ....**N S**	John McDonald ......
Niely Road	....	King's . ... **N S**	Thaddeus Allison......
Nile	Colborne...........	Huron, C. R......... .....**O**	Samuel Pollock.........
Nilestown................	Dorchester, N.	Middlesex, E. R. ....**O**	James R. L. Waugh...
Nine Mile Creek	No. 65....................	Queen's ....**P E I**	Gilbert Bell ....
Nine Mile River, W.O	....	Hants ....**N S**	Evan Thompson .....
Nipissingan	....	District of Nipissing .....**O**	John Shaw ....
Nissouri	Nissouri East	Oxford, N. R. ....**O**	Archibald McBrayne..
Nithburg.................	North Easthope.........	Perth, N. R. ....**O**	James Brown....... ....
Nobleton	King	York, N. R. .... **O**	William Munsie ......
Noel, W. O..............	....	Hants .... **N S**	Osmond O'Brien ......
Noel Shore, W. O......	....	Hants ....**N S**	....
Norham	Percy	Northumberland, E. R.. **O**	Alexander Douglas ...
Norland	Laxton	Victoria, N. R. ....**O**	A. A. McLauchlin .....
Normandale	Charlotteville	Norfolk, S. R. ....**O**	John W. Sheppard.....
Northampton, W. O....	....	Carleton ....**N B**	Aaron Tomkins.........
North Augusta	Augusta	Grenville, S. R. ....**O**	John Chapman ....
North Bedeque	No. 25	Prince...... . ...**P E I**	H. Clark........... ......
North Bristol............	Bristol	Pontiac ....**Q**	William Shirley........
North Brookfield, W.O	....	Queen's ....**N S**	George M. Fraser......
North Bruce	Bruce	Bruce, N. R. .... **O**	Arnold Ross ....
North Douro	Douro	Peterborough, E. R..... **O**	Robert Casement ......
North East Branch Margaree, W. O......	Margaree	Inverness .... **N S**	John Rose ....
North East Harbor, W. O.	....	Shelburne ....**N S**	A. R. Greenwood .. ...
North Esk Boom, W.O	....	Northumberland......**N B**	James Hutchinson.....

NAME OF POST OFFICE.	TOWNSHIP OR PARISH.	ELECTORAL COUNTY OR DIVISION.	NAME OF POSTMASTER.
Northfield	Cornwall	Cornwall ... O	Benjamin G. Runions.
Northfield, W. O.		Sunbury ... N B	Jonathan Welton
Northfield, W. O.		Lunenburg ... N S	Heli Mackey
North Georgetown	Beauharnois	Chateauguay ... Q	Joseph Turcot
North Glanford	Glanford	Wentworth, S. R. ... O	Edward Dickenson
North Gower	North Gower	Carleton ... O	Hiram Scott
North Ham	North Ham	Wolfe ... Q	Patrick Blais
North Hatley	Hatley	St nstead ... Q	B. Le Baron
North Joggins, W. O.		Westmoreland ... N B	John G. Read
North Keppel	Keppel	Grey, N. R. ... O	David Dewar
North Lake, W. O.		Westmoreland ... N B	
North Lake	No. 47	King's ... P E I	William Morrow
North Lake, W. O.		York ... N B	William Foster
North Lancaster	Lancaster	Glengarry ... O	Charles Leclair
North Mountain	Mountain	Dundas ... O	James Cleland
North Mountain, W. O.		King's ... N S	William Bennett
North Nation Mills	Ste. Angelique	Ottawa ... Q	Thomas Cole
North Onslow	Onslow	Pontiac ... Q	John O'Donnell
North Pelham	Pelham	Monck ... O	Mrs. M. A. McQueen
North Pinnacle	St. Armand	Missisquoi ... Q	V. Barnes
North Port	Sophiasburg	Prince Edward ... O	W. H. Morden
North Range Corner, W. O.		Digby ... N S	Charles McNiel
North Ridge	Gosfield	Essex ... O	William E. Wagstaff
North River	No. 32	Queen's ... P E I	John Sellars
North River, W. O.		Westmoreland ... N B	J. Taylor
North River, W. O.		Colchester ... N S	W. H. Higgins
North River Bridge, W. O.		Colchester ... N S	Henry Blair
North River Bridge, W. O.		Victoria ... N S	John McKenzie
North River Platform, W. O.		Westmoreland ... N B	Patrick Hopkins
North Rustico	No. 24	Queen's ... P E I	George Budd
North Salem, W. O.		Hants ... N S	N. Nelson
North Section of Earl-		... N S	William Ross

NAME OF POST OFFICE.	TOWNSHIP OR PARISH.	ELECTORAL COUNTY OR DIVISION.	NAME OF POSTMASTER.
North Seneca..........	Seneca	Haldimand .... O	John Fuchor...........
North Shore, W. O. ..	....	Cumberland .... N S	Duncan McKinnon ...
North Shore, W. O. ...	....	Victoria ....N S	Donald McDonald ...
North Side of Basin, River Dennis, W. O	....	Inverness ....N S	Malcolm McNiel ......
North Stanbridge	Stanbridge	Missisquoi ....Q	A. M. Stone ....
North Stoke	Stoke.......	Richmond ....Q	F. H. Lothrop ....
North Stukely..........	Stukely..................	Shefford ....Q	Antoine Audette........
North Sutton....	Sutton.....	Brome............. ....Q	S. Sweet ....
North Sydney	....	Cape Breton ....N S	John Forbes ....
North Tryon............	No. 28.....................	Prince.....................P E I	A. Reid............. ......
North Wakefield.........	Wakefield.....	Ottawa ....Q	A. Pritchard ....
North West Arm	. ...	Cape Breton ....N S	G. K. Ball ....
North West Bridge W. O....................	....	Northumberland.......N B	Edward Sinclair.......
North West Cove, W. O........................	....	Lunenburg................N S	Daniel Noonan.........
North Williamsburg...	Williamsburg	Dundas......... ....O	J. S. Whittaker.........
North Winchester......	Winchester	Dundas...... ....O	Joseph S. Kyle.........
Norton, W. O............	....	King's......................N B	John Hayes.............
Norton Creek...........	Beauharnois............	Chateauguay ....Q	William Dinnigan .....
Norton Dale, W. O....	....	York...... .. ..N B	William Cox ....
Norton Station	....	King's.....................N B	Samuel McCready .....
Norval......................	Esquesing	Halton .... O	William Clay...........
Norway..	York	York, E. R.....................O	....
**Norwich*	Norwich, North.........	Oxford, S. R................O	Gilbert Moore .. ..
**Norwood*..........	Asphodel	Peterborough, E. R......O	J. A. Butterfield.. .....
Notfield.....................	Kenyon.................. ..	Glengarry ....O	Peter Kennedy...........
Notre Dame du Portage	Notre Dame du Portage.	Témiscouata ....Q	Miss Adée Michaud...
Nottawa	Nottawasaga	Simcoe, N. R...............O	Andrew Melville........
Nouvelle (sub)..........	Nouvelle..................	Bonaventure................Q	Archibald Kerr. ......
Noyan..........	Sabrevois	Missisquoi ....Q	T. B. Derrick............
Nutt's Corners..........	Clarenceville	Missisquoi ....Q	David Nutt ....

NAME OF POST OFFICE.	TOWNSHIP OR PARISH.	ELECTORAL COUNTY OR DIVISION.	NAME OF POSTMASTER.
Oak Bay, W. O.		Charlotte **N B**	Walter Gilley
Oakfield, W. O.		Halifax **N S**	Mrs. Francis Laurie
Oakham, W. O.		Queen's **N B**	Andrew Lammon
Oak Hill	Laxton	Victoria, N. R. **O**	Robert Staples
Oak Hill, W. O		Charlotte **N B**	William McCan
Oakland	Oakland	Brant, S. R. **O**	John Toyne
Oak Park, W. O.		Shelburne **N S**	Nehemiah N. Adams
Oak Point, W. O.		King's **N B**	J. L. Flewelling
Oak Point, W. O.		Northumberland **N B**	Alexander Davidson
Oak Point		Marquette **M**	William Clarke
Oak Ridges	Whitchurch	York, N. R. **O**	Edward Curtis
**Oakville*	Trafalgar	Halton **O**	R. Balmer
Oakwood	Mariposa	Victoria, S. R. **O**	Richard P. Butler
Oban	Sarnia	Lambton **O**	William Carrick
**Odessa*	Ernestown	Lennox **O**	P. S. Timmerman
Offa	Stephen	Huron, S. R. **O**	John G. Quarry
Ogilvie, W. O.		King's **N S**	Thomas Anthony
Ohio, W. O.		Antigonishe **N S**	John McDonald
Ohsweken	Tuscarora	Brant, S. R. **O**	James Styres
Oil City	Enniskillen	Lambton **O**	James A. Thompson
**Oil Springs*	Enniskillen	Lambton **O**	James Keating
Oka		Two Mountains **Q**	Cyprien Chaurette
Okanagon		Yale **B C**	Cornelius O'Keefe
Okanagon Mission		Yale **B C**	Eli Lequin
Old Barns, W. O.		Colchester **N S**	Ebenezer Archibald
Oldham, W. O.		Halifax **N S**	Edward Sheffer
Old Montrose	Romney	Kent **O**	Horatio Mills
O'Leary's Road	No. 8	Prince **P E I**	William Smallman
Olinda	Gosfield	Essex **O**	John C. Fox
Olinville, W. O		Queen's **N B**	William Tilley
Omagh	Trafalgar	Halton **O**	Thomas Little
Omemee	Emily	Victoria, S. R. **O**	Robert Grandy
Omineca		Cariboo **B C**	Francis Page
Omnah	Palmerston	Addington **O**	Henry Dunham

NAME OF POST OFFICE.	TOWNSHIP OR PARISH.	ELECTORAL COUNTY OR DIVISION.	NAME OF POSTMASTER.
150 Mile House........	....	Cariboo ....**B C**	George W. Cook........
Oneida	Oneida.....	Haldimand....................**O**	J. T. Mutchmore ....
Ongley	Brighton	Northumberland, E. R..**O**	....
Onondaga	Onondaga	Brant, N. R. .... **O**	Wm. S. Buckwell.....
**Onslow*	Onslow	Pontiac ....**Q**	Walton Smith........
Onslow, W. O.............	....	Colchester ....**N S**	Samuel McKinlay ...
**Orangeville*	Garafraxa	Wellington, C. R.... .....**O**	Guy Leslie ... .
Orchard	Egremont	Grey, S. R ....**O**	J. G. Orchard..........
**Orillia*	Orillia	Simcoe, N. R......... ......**O**	Wesley Bingham .....
Orleans	Gloucester, North ...	Russell ....**O**	Hugh Dupuis ....
Ormond	Winchester	Dundas ....**O**	Ira Morgan ....
Ormstown	Beauharnois	Chateauguay ....**Q**	R. N. Walsh ....
Oromocto	....	Sunbury ....**N B**	Charles McPherson...
**Orono*	Clarke........................	Durham, W. R.............**O**	Joseph L. Tucker......
Orwell............	Yarmouth	Elgin, E. R................. **O**	D. Sutherland ....
Orwell........................	No. 57.........	Queen's ....**P E I**	B. Loughran ....
Orwell Cove	No. 57..	Queen's ....**P E I**	E. Morrisey ....
Osaca	Hope	Durham, E. R...... ......**O**	David Gordon ....
**Osceola*	Bromley	Renfrew, N. R... ....**O**	Alexander McLaren..
Osgoode	Osgoode	Russell ....**O**	Zachariah McMillan..
**Oshawa*	Whitby	Ontario, S. R. .. ..**O**	David Smith ....
Ospringe	Erin	Wellington, S R........ **O**	Wm. Symon ....
Ossekeag	....	King's ....**N B**	Allan McN. Travis ...
Ossian....	Enniskillen	Lambton ....**O**	George S. McPherson
Otnabog, W. O..........	....	Queen's................. **N B**	Joseph B. Slipp ......
**Ottawa*	Nepean	Ottawa ....**O**	G. P. Baker ....
Otter Lake	Leslie	Pontiac ....**Q**	John Mather............
**Otterville*	Norwich, South	Oxford, S. R. **O**	Wm. E. W...

NAME OF POST OFFICE.	TOWNSHIP OR PARISH.	ELECTORAL COUNTY OR DIVISION.	NAME OF POSTMASTER.
Oxford	......	Cumberland ... N S	Henry S. Smith
Oxford Centre	Oxford, East	Oxford, S. R. ... O	Nelson Schooley
Oxford Mills	Oxford	Grenville, N. R. ... O	Charles Jones, jun.
Oxford Station	Oxford	Grenville, N. R. ... O	Andrew Holmes
Oxley	Colchester	Essex ... O	Robert Ivison
Oyster Ponds, W. O.		Guysborough ... N S	James W. Carr
Oznabruck Centre	Oznabruck	Stormont ... O	Jacob J. Poaps
Painsec, W. O.	Shediac	Westmoreland ... N B	Eustache Babin
Painswick	Innisfil	Simcoe, S. R. ... O	John Huggard
**Paisley*	Elderslie	Bruce, N. R. ... O	James Saunders
**Pakenham*	Pakenham	Lanark, N. R. ... O	Richard H. Davie
Palermo	Trafalgar	Halton ... O	H. M. Switzer
Palestine		Marquette ... M	
Palgrave	Albion	Cardwell ... O	Robert Wylie
Palmer Rapids	Raglan	Renfrew, S. R. ... O	H. F. McLachlin
Palmer's Road, W. O.		King's ... N S	George W. Eaton
*a*Palmerston	Wallace	Perth, N. R. ... O	Richard Johnston
Palmerston, W. O.		Kent ... N B	Honoré Landry
Panmure	Fitzroy	Carleton ... O	James Ring
Papineauville	St. Angelique	Ottawa ... Q	F. S. McKay
Paquette	Hereford Gore	Compton ... Q	F. Paquette
Paradise Lane		Annapolis ... N S	W. F. Morse
Parham	Hinchinbrooke	Addington ... O	John Griffith
Park Corner	No. 20	Queen's ... P E I	James Doyle
[illegible]	[illegible]	[illegible] ... O	George Stanton

NAME OF POST OFFICE.	TOWNSHIP OR PARISH.	ELECTORAL COUNTY OR DIVISION.	NAME OF POSTMASTER.
Paris Station	Dumfries, South	Brant, N. R. **O**	M. X. Carr
Parker	Peel	Wellington, C. R. **O**	William McKim
Parker's Cove, W. O.		Annapolis **N S**	Thomas Milner
Park Head	Amabel	Bruce, N. R. **O**	Wm. Simpson
Park Hill	West Williams	Middlesex, N. R. **O**	John Noble
Parkhurst	St. Sylvester	Lotbinière **Q**	Thomas Walker
Park's Creek	St. Andrews	Lisgar **M**	John Tait
Parma	South Fredericksburg	Lennox **O**	David Griffith
Parrsborough		Cumberland **N S**	John W. Jinks
Parrsborough Shore, W. O		Cumberland **N S**	William Grant
Parry Sound	McDougall	Muskoka **O**	John McClelland
Partridge Island, W. O		Cumberland **N S**	Isaac Wason
Paspébiac	Cox	Bonaventure **Q**	P. de N. Loisel
Patillo	Maidstone	Essex **O**	William Richardson
Patterson	Vaughan	York, W. R. **O**	W. C. Patterson
Patterson Settlement, W. O		Sunbury **N B**	Nelson White
Paudash	Cardiff	Peterborough, E. R. **O**	John Dickson
Peabody	Sullivan	Grey, N. R. **O**	John Millburn
Pearceton	Stanbridge	Missisquoi **Q**	James Briggs
Pearson's, W. O.		King's **N B**	W. W. Pearson
Peel, W. O		Carleton **N B**	Charles A. Harmon
Peepabun	Luther	Wellington, N. R. **O**	Robert Dickson
Pefferlaw	Georgina	York, N. R **O**	George Johnson
Peggy's Cove, W. O.		Halifax **N S**	W. Crooks
Pelissier	Wakefield	Ottawa **Q**	P. N. E. Pelissier
Pelham Union	Pelham	Monck **O**	Joseph Johnson
Pemberton Ridge, W. O		York **N B**	Cyrus B. McKenney
**Pembroke*	Pembroke	Renfrew, N. R. **O**	Alex. Moffatt
Pendleton	Plantagenet, South	Prescott **O**	Henry Moffatt
**Penetanguishene*	Tiny	Simcoe, N. R **O**	J. S. Darling
Peninsula-Gaspé	Gaspé Bay, North	Gaspé	William Miller
Pennfield, W. O		Charlotte **N B**	Jesse Prescott
Pennfield Ridge, W. O.		Charlotte **N B**	John R. Young

NAME OF POST OFFICE.	TOWNSHIP OR PARISH.	ELECTORAL COUNTY OR DIVISION.	NAME OF POSTMASTER.
Penobsquis		King's N B	George Morton
Pentland	Pilkington	Wellington, C. R. Q	George Ford
Penville	Tecumseth	Simcoe, S. R. O	Edward T. Turner
Percé	Percé	Gaspé Q	J. E. Tuzo
Perch Station	Sarnia	Lambton O	John Irwin
Perkins	Templeton.	Ottawa Q	John Freney
Perm	Mulmur	Simcoe, S. R. O	Paul Gallagher
Perretton	Westmeath	Renfrew, N. R. O	Mrs. E. McCracken
Perryboro'	Hereford	Compton Q	Calvin Perry
Perry Settlement, W.O		King's N B	R. Elders
Perrytown	Hope	Durham, E. R. O	R. A. Corbett
**Perth*	Drummond	Lanark, S. R. O	Thomas Cairns
Perth, W. O.		Victoria N B	James Bishop
a Perth Road	Loughborough	Frontenac O	James Stoneness
Petawawa	Petawawa	Renfrew, N. R. O	Solomon Devine
**Peterborough*	North Monaghan	Peterborough. W. R. O	Hy. C. Rogers
Petersburg	Wilmot	Waterloo, S. R O	John Ernst
Peterson	Minden	Peterborough, E. R. O	William Jarvis
Peter's Road	No. 63	King's P E I	William Johnston
Petersville, W. O.		Queen's N B	Timothy Malone
Petersville (sub)	London	City of London O	W. Loughrey
Petersville Church, W. O.		Queen's N B	Thomas Leonard
Petherton	Arthur	Wellington, N. R. O	Thomas Bunston
Petitcodiac		Westmoreland N B	W. W. Price
Petite de Grat, W. O.		Richmond N S	George M. Jean
Petite Passage, W. O.		Digby N S	Charles Outhouse
Petite Rivière Bridge, W. O.		Lunenburg N S	William Holden
Petit Métis	Macnider	Rimouski Q	John MacNider
**Petrolea*	Enniskillen	Lambton O	Patrick Barclay
Petworth	Portland	Addington O	Alfred Knight
Peveril	Newton	Vaudreuil Q	Alexander Morrison
Phelpston	Flos	Simcoe, N. R. O	Robert H. Platt
Philipsburg, East	St. Armand	Missisquoi Q	D. T. R. Nye

NAME OF POST OFFICE.	TOWNSHIP OR PARISH.	ELECTORAL COUNTY OR DIVISION.	NAME OF POSTMASTER.
Philipsburg, West......	Wilmot........	Waterloo, S. R... ....O	Daniel Lohr.. ....
a Philipston	Thurlow	Hastings, E. R...........O	George Philips ....
Philipsville	Bastard	Leeds, S. R. ....O	George Brown..........
Pickering..............	Pickering	Ontario, S. R. ....O	Eliza Whitney..........
**Picton*	Hallowell	Prince Edward ....O	Thomas Shannon ...
Pictou	....	Pictou ....N S	Alexander McPhail ...
Piedmont Valley, W.O	....	Pictou ....N S	James McDonald ......
Pierreville	Pierreville	Yamaska ....Q	H. Pitt ....
Pierreville Mills	Pierreville	Yamaska ....Q	Henry Vassal ....
Pig Brook	No. 1......	Prince.................P E I	Peter Richard ....
Pigeon Hill	St. Armand	Missisquoi ....Q	Noah Sager. ....
Pigeon Lake	St. François Xavier...	Marquette .... M	J M. House ....
Pike River	Stanbridge	Missisquoi ....Q	A. L. Taylor.... ......
Pinedale..................	Brock	Ontario, N. R.............O	Charles Will ....
Pine Grove	Vaughan	York, W. R. ....O	A. L. Gooderham.....
Pine Orchard	Whitchurch	York, N. R........... .....O	Nelson May.............
*b*Pine Ridge, W. O. ...	....	Kent .... .N B	T. D. Holmden.........
Pine River........	Huron..................	Bruce, S. R......... .. ...O	D. McDermid ....
Pinkerton......	Greenock	Bruce, S. R................O	Samuel A. King.......
Piopolis	Marston	Compton....................Q	Chas. F. X. Langlois..
Pirate Harbor..........	....	Guysboro' ....N S	J. Hartley ....
Pisarinco, W. O.......	....	St. John ....N B	Thomas Galbraith ...
Pisquid	Number 37..............	Queen's .... P E I	....
Pisquid Road	Number 49.........	Queen's ....P E I	M. Curran ....
Pitts Ferry	Pittsburg...............	Frontenac ....O	Lewis Root ....
Pittston	Edwardsburg	Grenville, S. R...........O	Wm. Pitt, sen..........
Plainfield	Thurlow	Hastings, E. R.............O	Edward N. Gould......
Plainfield, W. O.......	....	Pictou......................N S	A. Sutherland ....
**Plantagenet*	Plantagenet, North ...	Prescott ....O	Henry Smith..........
Plattsville	Blenheim	Oxford, N. R..............O	John Smart ....
Playfair	Bathurst	Lanark, S. R..............O	Jones Grant ....
Pleasant Bay, W. O...	Grand Anse	Inverness ....N S	Angus McIntosh ......
Pleasant Hill............	Walsingham	Norfolk, S. R..............O	William Morgan......
*b*Pleasant Point, W. O	....	Halifax ....N S	John Naufts...........

NAME OF POST OFFICE.	TOWNSHIP OR PARISH.	ELECTORAL COUNTY OR DIVISION.	NAME OF POSTMASTER.
Pleasant Ridge, W. O	....	Charlotte ..... N B	Thomas Steen........
Pleasant River, W. O.	....	Queen's .... N S	Jos. M. Freeman .....
Pleasant Vale, W. O.	....	Albert .... N B	R. A. Colpitts ....
Pleasant Valley, W. O......	....	Digby .... N S	Leslie M. Craig........
Plum Hollow	Bastard	Leeds, S. R........ O	Daniel Derbyshire.....
Plymouth, W. O..	....	Yarmouth .... N S	Wilson G. Sims........
Pockmouche, W. O...	....	Gloucester........ N B	Thomas Maher ....
Pookshaw, W. O.......	....	Gloucester .... N B	Jeremiah D. Foley ...
Point Alexander........	Rolph	Renfrew, N. R........ O	Foster Armstrong ....
Point Bruley, W. O...	....	Colchester .... N S	James W. Cassidy ...
Point Clear, W. O......	....	Victoria........ N S	Niel Gillis ....
Pointe à Grouette......	....	Provencher .... M	Miss Lacerte ....
Pointe à Pic	Mount Murray	Charlevoix........ Q	J. M. Bouchard........
Pointe au Bouleau. ...	Saguenay	Saguenay .... Q	O. Savard........
Pointe aux Pins........	Park	Algoma........ O	W. G. Foot........
Pointe aux Trembles..	....	Hochelaga .... Q	Antoine Lamoureux...
Pointe aux Trembles..	Neuville	Portneuf........ Q	Narcisse Blais........
Pointe Claire........	Montreal	Jacques Cartier .... Q	L. B. Daoust ....
Pointe du Chêne, W.O	....	Westmoreland........ N B	Wm. J. M. Hanington
Pointe du Lac........	Pointe du Lac........	St. Maurice........ Q	Louis Comeau, jun.....
Point Edward........	Sarnia........	Lambton........ O	Louis Ernst ....
Point Fortune........	Rigaud	Vaudreuil .... Q	E. A. St. Denis........
Point Kaye	Monck	Muskoka .... O	Charles Kaye ....
Point la Nim, W. O...	....	Restigouche .... N B	Peter Stewart ....
Point of Cape, W. O...	....	Antigonishe........ N S	Hugh McInnis ....
Point Petre........	Athol........	Prince Edward........ O	James Scott ....
Point Platon........	Lotbinière	Lotbinière .... Q	Joseph Angé........
Point Prim........	Number 58........	Queen's .... P E I	M. N. Murchison........
**Point St. Charles*	....	Jacques Cartier........ Q	John S. Keith........
Point St. Peter........	Malbaie	Gaspé .... Q	George Packwood......
Point Sapin, W. O.....	....	Kent........ N B	Nicholas Merzeroll.....
Point Traverse	Marysburg........	Prince Edward........ O	Abraham Cannon.. ...
Point Wolfe, W. O.....	....	Albert .... N B	William McGibbon ...

NAME OF POST OFFICE.	TOWNSHIP OR PARISH.	ELECTORAL COUNTY OR DIVISION.	NAME OF POSTMASTER.
Pollett River, W. O...	....	Westmoreland.........N B	B. R. Colpitts...........
Pomeroy Ridge, W.O.	....	Charlotte .... N B	Wm. Pomeroy.. ....
Pomona	Glenelg	Grey, S. R.................O	William Purdy .. ...
Pomquet Chapel, W.O	....	Antigonishe.............N S	Constant Dion...........
Pomquet Forks, W.O.	....	Antigonishe ....N S	Mrs. M. Chisholm .....
Ponds, W. O............	....	Pictou.......................N S	A. S. Gray................
Ponsonby	Pilkington	Wellington, C. R.... .....O	James L. Halley.. .....
Pont Chateau	Soulanges	Soulanges.....................Q	J. B. Besner ... .
Pont de Maskinongé..	Maskinongé.............	Maskinongé..................Q	A. J. Lefrenière ....
Pont Rouge.....	St. Jeanne de Neuville	Portneuf....................... ..Q	Thomas Larivière .....
Poodiac, W. O..........	Hammond	King's..... .... N B	James Faulkner. ......
Poole	Mornington	Perth, N. R..................O	John Engel..............
Poplar Grove, W. O...	....	Gloucester ....N B	Joseph Aubé............
Poplar Hill, W. O......	....	Pictou.......................N S	George Morrison .....
Poplar Point...........	Poplar Point...... ...	Marquette ....M	David Tait...............
Poquiock, W. O..	....	York ....N B	Michael Doherty ......
Port Hill	No. 18	Prince...................P E I	John G. Hopgood . ...
Port Acadie.....	....	Digby .... N S	C. M. Melançon ......
**Portage du Fort*	Litchfield	Pontiac ....Q	John Amey ....
Portage la Prairie ...	Portage la Prairie	Marquette ....M	Charles Mair...........
Portage River, W.O..	....	Northumberland......N B	Alex. McDermitt ......
Port Albert	Ashfield	Huron, N. R...............O	Thomas Hawkins......
Portapique, W. O	. ...	Colchester ....N S	Timothy Davidson ...
Portapique Mountain, W. O..................	....	Colchester ....N S	Daniel Giddens.........
Port au Persil....	Mount Murray	Charlevoix....................Q	Seraphin Guerin ......
Port Bruce	Malahide	Elgin, E. R.. ....O	Thomas Thompson ...
**Port Burwell*	....	Elgin, E. R. .... O	Thomas Pilcher ....
Port Caledonia, W. O..	....	Cape Breton ....N S	Miss Mary Boutilier ..
Port Carling	Medora	Muskoka ....O	B. H. Johnston.........
Port Clyde, W. O......	....	Shelburne ....N S	William Greenwood...
**Port Colborne*	Humberstone....... ...	Welland ....O	L. G. Carter ....
Port Credit	Toronto	Peel ....O	Robert Cotton..........
**Port Dalhousie*	Grantham	Lincoln ....O	Richard Wood ....

NAME OF POST OFFICE.	TOWNSHIP OR PARISH.	ELECTORAL COUNTY OR DIVISION.	NAME OF POSTMASTER.
**Port Dover*	Woodhouse	Norfolk, S. R. **O**	David Abel
a **Port Elgin*	Saugeen	Bruce, N. R. **O**	Mrs. Mary M. Roy
Port Elgin		Westmoreland **N B**	
Port Elmsley	North Elmsley	Lanark, S. R. **O**	John Elliott
Porter's Hill	Goderich	Huron, S. R. **O**	James Hendry
Porter's Lake, W O.		Halifax **N S**	George Orman
Port Felix, W.O.		Guysboro' **N S**	Stephen Boudrot
Port Franks	Bosanquet	Lambton **O**	John Dalziel
Port George, W. O.		Annapolis **N S**	G. B. Reid
Port Granby	Clarke	Durham, W. R. **O**	David March
Port Greville, W. O.		Cumberland **N S**	Jane Elderkin
Port Hastings		Inverness **N S**	J. G. McKeen
Port Hawkesbury		Inverness **N S**	Angus Grant
Port Hood		Inverness **N S**	Angus McDonald
Port Hood Island, W.O		Inverness **N S**	Mrs. Joshua Smith
Port Hoover	Mariposa	Victoria, S. R. **O**	R. C. Shaver
**Port Hope*	Hope	Durham. E. R. **O**	Robert W. Smart
Port Jolly, W. O.		Shelburne **N S**	L. Robertson
Port Lambton	Sombra	Bothwell **O**	John H. Sewell
Portland	Bastard	Leeds, S. R. **O**	S. S. Scovil
Port la Tour, W. O.		Shelburne **N S**	Nancy H. Snow
Port Lewis	St. Anicet	Huntingdon **Q**	B. B. Carson
Port Maitland	Sherbrooke	Monck **O**	James Moss
Port Matoon, W. O.		Queen's **N S**	William T. Leslie
Port Medway		Queen's **N S**	Freeman Cohoon
Port Mulgrave		Guysborough **N S**	G. B. Hadley
Port Nelson	Nelson	Halton **O**	George H. Green
Portneuf	Portneuf	Portneuf **Q**	F. X. T. Hamelin
Port Perry	Reach	Ontario, N. R. **O**	H. Gordon
Port Philip, W.O.		Cumberland **N S**	Joshua King
Port Richmond, W.O.	Port Richmond	Richmond **N S**	John G. Murray
**Port Robinson*	Thorold	Welland **O**	James McCoppen
**Port Rowan*	Walsingham	Norfolk, S. R. **O**	Miss M. McLennan
Port Royal	Walsingham	Norfolk, S. R. **O**	Robert Abbott

NAME OF POST OFFICE.	TOWNSHIP OR PARISH.	ELECTORAL COUNTY OR DIVISION.	NAME OF POSTMASTER.
Port Royal, W. O......	....	Richmond ....N S	J. M. Adèle Le Blanc..
Port Ryerse	Woodhouse	Norfolk, S. R. .... O	Wm. H. Ryerse........
Port Severn (sub)......	Tay	Simcoe, N. R. ....O	Alex. R. Christie ......
Portsmouth	Kingston	Frontenac ....O	George McLeod... .....
**Port Stanley*........ ...	Yarmouth	Elgin, E. R. ....O	Manuel Payne ....
a Port Sydney	Stephenson	Muskoka ... .O	H. C. Ladell ....
Portuguese Cove, W.O	....	Halifax ....N S	T. Sullivan...............
Port Union	Pickering	Ontario, S. R. ....O	Cranswick Craven......
Port Williams	....	King's ....N S	Albert Chase ....
Port Williams Station.	....	King's ....N S	Enoch A. Forsyth......
Powell.........	Huntley	Carleton ....O	Denis Egan ... .
Powerscourt.............	Hinchinbrooke	Huntingdon ....Q	David W. Johnson.....
Pownall	No. 49..........	Queen's ... .P E I	Samuel Brown ....
**Prescott*....	Augusta	Grenville, S. R............O	John Dowsley ....
**Preston*	Waterloo, South	Waterloo, S. R. ....O	Conrad Nispel ....
Preston Road, W. O...	....	Halifax ... .N S	J. S. Griffin ....
Price's Corner	Oro	Simcoe, N. R. ....O	George Dissette ....
Priceville..................	Artemesia................	Grey, E. R. ....O	D. A. Ghent..... ......
Primrose....	Mono........................	Cardwell.. .. ..O	George Dodds ....
**Prince Albert*	Reach	Ontario, N. R. .... O	John McPherson ......
Prince of Wales, W.O	....	St. John ....N B	John Cairns ....
Princeport, W. O......	....	Colchester ....N S	Mrs. E. R. Ambrose...
**Princeton*	Blenheim	Oxford, N. R. ....O	Hezekiah C. Forsyth...
Princetown	No. 18.....................	Prince ....P E I	H. E. McKay ....
Princetown Road	No. 23....	Queen's ....P E I	Allan R. Spence ......
Prince William, W. O.	....	York ....N B	T. W. Saunders.........
Prinyer	N. Marysburg	Prince Edward ....O	George R. German.....
Prospect	Beckwith	Lanark, S. R. ....O	William Burrows ......
Prospect, W. O.........	....	Halifax ....N S	Mrs. M. J. Booth .....
Prosser Brook, W. O..	....	Albert .... N B	David H. Beeman.....
Pubnico Beach, W. O	....	Shelburne ....N S	John McComisky .....
Pubnico Harbor, W.O	....	Yarmouth ....N S	John Carland ....
Pugwash	....	Cumberland ....N S	Levi Borden ....
Pugwash River, W. O.	....	Cumberland .... N S	Thomas A. Fraser......

NAME OF POST OFFICE.	TOWNSHIP OR PARISH.	ELECTORAL COUNTY OR DIVISION.	NAME OF POSTMASTER.
Purdy	Bangor	Hastings, N. R ....**O**	W. Lake
Purpleville	Vaughan	York, W. R. ....**O**	Samuel W. Peterman
Puslinch	Puslinch	Wellington, S. R. ....**O**	William Leslie
Putnam	Dorchester, North	Middlesex, E. R. ....**O**	Seth Barr
Quaco Road, W. O		St. John ....**N B**	B. D. Kirkpatrick
**Quebec*	Quebec	Quebec ....**Q**	Jean Bte. Pruneau
Queensborough	Elzevir	Hastings, N. R ....**O**	Daniel Thompson
Queenston	Niagara	Niagara ....**O**	James Wynn
Queensville	East Gwillimbury	York, N. R ....**O**	James H. Aylward
Queensville, W. O		Inverness ....**N S**	D. J. McMasters
Quesnelle		Cariboo ....**B C**	Alexander Barlow
Quesnelle Forks		Cariboo ....**B C**	W. P. Barry
Radstock	Kildare	Joliette ....**Q**	Thomas Luby
Ragged Head, W. O		Guysboro' ....**S**	R. Bruce

NAME OF POST OFFICE.	TOWNSHIP OR PARISH.	ELECTORAL COUNTY OR DIVISION.	NAME OF POSTMASTER.
Raglan	Whitby	Ontario, S. R. **O**	Mrs. Mary Still
Railton	Loughboro'	Addington **O**	Mrs. Mary Walsh
Rainham	Rainham	Haldimand **O**	Isaac Honsberger
Rainham Centre	Rainham	Haldimand **O**	H. Zimmerman
Rama	Rama	Ontario, N. R. **O**	James McPherson
Ramsay's Corners	Gloucester	Russell **O**	Robert Ramsay
Randwick	Mulmur	Simcoe, S. R. **O**	William Parkhill
Ranelagh	Windham	Norfolk, N. R. **O**	Benjamin Lake
Rankin	Wilberforce	Renfrew, N. R. **O**	William P. Edwards
Rapides des Joachims	Aberdeen	Pontiac **Q**	William Spence
Rathburn	Mara	Ontario, N. R. **O**	Timothy Cuddahee
Ratho	Blandford	Oxford, N. R. **O**	Joseph Morrow
Ratter's Corner, W. O.		King's **N B**	Robert Manamin
Ravenna	Collingwood	Grey, N. R. **O**	M. Stoutenburg
Ravenscliffe	Chaffey	Muskoka **O**	James Sharp
Ravenshoe	East Gwillimbury	York, N. R. **O**	George Glover
Ravenswood	Bosanquet	Lambton **O**	James Paisley
Rawdon	Rawdon	Montcalm **Q**	Michael Skelly
Rawdon, W. O.		Hants **N S**	Thomas Moxon
Raymond	Watt	Muskoka **O**	Anthony Suffern
Reaboro	Ops	Victoria, S. R. **O**	John Holbert
Read, W. O.		Westmoreland **N B**	Eliphalet Read
Read	Tyendinaga	Hastings, E. R. **O**	John C. Hanley.
Reading	Garafraxa	Wellington, C. R. **O**	Robert Donaldson
Rear of Black River, W. O.		Richmond **N S**	John Morrison
Rear Judeque, W. O.		Inverness **N S**	Duncan McMillan
Rear Lands, Sporting Mountain, W. O.		Richmond **N S**	William Urquhart
Red Bank, W. O.		Northumberland **N B**	W. S. Brown
Red Islands, W. O.		Richmond **N S**	Alexander McKenzie
Rednersville	Ameliasburg	Prince Edward **O**	James Redner
Red Rocks		Algoma **O**	Robert Crawford
Red Point	Number 46	King's **P E I**	D. Robertson

NAME OF POST OFFICE.	TOWNSHIP OR PARISH.	ELECTORAL COUNTY OR DIVISION.	NAME OF POSTMASTER.
Relessey	Mono	Cardwell ... O	Robert Wilson
Renforth	Ancaster	Wentworth, S. R. ... O	Robert Mahew
**Renfrew*	Horton	Renfrew, S. R. ... O	William McKay
Renfrew		Hants ... N S	
Renous Bridge, W. O.		Northumberland ... N B	R. Jardine
Renous River, W. O.		Northumberland ... N B	Michael Hayes
Renton	Townsend	Norfolk, N. R. ... O	Mrs Ann Renton
Renton Station	Glenford	Wentworth, S. R. ... O	Thomas Wilkinson
Repentigny	L'Assomption	L'Assomption ... Q	F. X. O'Brien
Reserve Mines, W. O.		Cape Breton ... N S	John McDonald
Rhodes, W. O.		King's ... N S	William Rhodes
Riceburg	Stanbridge	Missisquoi ... Q	Simon Lambkin
Riceville	Plantagenet, South	Prescott ... O	P. McLaurin
Richibucto		Kent ... N B	Jean C. Vautour
Richibucto Village, W. O.		Kent ... N B	Urbain Breau
Richmond Corner		Carleton ... N B	Ivory Kilburn
**Richmond, East*	Cleveland	Richmond ... Q	G. K. Foster
**Richmond, West*	Goulbourn	Carleton ... O	W. H. Butler
**Richmond Hill*	Vaughan	York, W. R. ... O	Matthew Teefy
Richmond Station	Cleveland	Richmond ... Q	Philip Maher
Richmond Terminus, W. O.		Halifax ... N S	
Richview	Toronto	Peel ... O	Robert M. Burgess
Richwood	Blenheim	Oxford, N. R. ... O	David Kyte
Ridgetown	Howard	Bothwell ... O	L. S. Hancock
Ridgeville	Pelham	Monck ... O	Jonas Steele
a Ridgeway	Bertie	Welland ... O	Ralph Disher
Rigaud	Rigaud	Vaudreuil ... Q	A. W. Charleboise
Riley Brook, W. O.		Victoria ... N B	John Mitchell
Rimington	Madoc	Hastings, N. R. ... O	John Rimington
**Rimouski*	St. Germain de Rimouski	Rimouski ... Q	A. G. Dion
Ringwood	Whitchurch	York, N. R. ... O	G. H. Silvester
River Beaudette		Soulanges ... Q	Stephen Leblanc
[illegible]	[illegible]	[illegible]ond ... N S	George H. Bissett

NAME OF POST OFFICE.	TOWNSHIP OR PARISH.	ELECTORAL COUNTY OR DIVISION.	NAME OF POSTMASTER.
River Charlo, W. O....	....	Restigouche ....N B	Alex. McPherson .....
River David	....	Yamaska............ ......Q	J. B. Commeault ......
River de Chute, W. O.	....	Carleton ....N B	Joseph B. Porter ......
River Dennis, W. O...	....	Inverness .... N S	A. McIntyre ....
River Dennis Road, W. O.	....	Inverness ....N S	John Morrison ....
River Désert	Maniwaki	Ottawa ....Q	Charles Logue.... ......
River Gilbert...........	St. Francois	Beauce ... ...Q	George W. Chapman..
River Hebert, W. O...	....	Cumberland ....N S	Michael Pugsley.... ...
River John	....	Pictou.....................N S	John D. Gauld ....
River Louison, W. O..	....	Restigouche...... .....N B	Donald Stewart.........
River Philip.............	....	Cumberland ....N S	Mrs. Grace Phillips ...
Riversdale	Greenock	Bruce, S. R. ... .O	....
Riversdale, W. O.......	....	Colchester ....N S	Robert J. Hingley .....
River Side, W. O... ...	....	Albert ....N B	Hiram Edgett...........
Riverstown	Arthur	Wellington, N. R.........O	Alexander Allan........
Rivière aux Vaches ...	Deguire	Yamaska ....Q	Edouard Coté ....
Rivière Bois Clair	St. Edouard.............	Lotbinière ....Q	George Bernard ....
Rivière des Prairies...	Montreal.....	Hochelaga ....Q	Louis Belanger . ...
**Rivière du Loup (en bas)*......................	St. Patrice de la Rivière du Loup.......	Témiscouata ....Q	Charles A. Gaudry ...
Rivière du Loup (en haut)	Rivière du Loup........	Maskinongé ....Q	Louis A. Baribeau.....
Rivière la Madeleine..	....	Gaspe .... Q	Edward Vachon ......
Rivière Ouelle	Rivière Ouelle...........	Kamouraska ....Q	John Belleau ....
Rivière Raisin	Lancaster	Glengarry ....O	James McPherson.....
Rivière Trois Pistoles	Trois Pistoles	Témiscouata ....Q	Edwin Marchement...
Roach's Point...	North Gwillimbury...	York, N. R................O	Robert McCordick ...
Roberval	Roberval	Chicoutimi..................Q	Theodule Bolduc......
Robinson	Bury	Compton .. ..Q	Lemeul Pope ....
Roblin	Richmond	Lennox ....O	Wm. M. Paul ....
Rob Roy...................	Osprey	Grey, E. R..................O	Wm. Holden ....
Rochelle	Stukely	Shefford ....Q	Augustin Desautels...
Rochesterville	Nepean......	Carleton ....O	Wm. Patterson ....
Rockburn	Hinchinbrooke	Huntingdon.......... ......Q	A. Oliver ....

NAME OF POST OFFICE.	TOWNSHIP OR PARISH.	ELECTORAL COUNTY OR DIVISION.	NAME OF POSTMASTER.
Rockford	Townsend	Norfolk, N. R. **O**	
Rock Forest	Orford	Sherbrooke **Q**	Gerard J. Nagle
Rockingham	Brudenell	Renfrew, S. R. **O**	J. S. J. Watson
Rock Island	Stanstead	Stanstead **Q**	A. A. Barry
Rockland	Clarence	Russell **O**	Wm. C. Edwards
Rockland, W. O.		Westmoreland **N B**	Jonas Taylor
Rockliffe (sub)	Head	Renfrew, N. R. **O**	W. H. McIntyre
Rocklin, W. O.		Pictou **N S**	Robert Fraser
Rockly, W. O.		Cumberland **N S**	Donald McKinnon
Rockport	Escott	Leeds, S. R. **O**	Charles Cornwall
Rockport, W. O.		Westmoreland **N B**	Rufus Ward
Rockside	Caledon	Cardwell **O**	D. Kirkwood
Rockton	Beverley	Wentworth, N. R. **O**	B. Cornell
Rock Village	Gloucester	Russell **O**	Miss E. M. Evans
Rockville, W. O.		King's **N B**	J. L. Harrison
Rockville, W. O.		Yarmouth **N S**	Wilson Haley
Rockwell Settlement, W. O.		Cumberland **N S**	Aaron Rockwell
Rockwood	Eramosa	Wellington, S. R. **O**	Robert Pasmore
Rockwood		Lisgar **M**	John Robinson
Rogerville	Usborne	Huron, S. R. **O**	James Bonthron
Rodney	Alderboro'	Elgin, W. R. **O**	A. Mumphrey
Roebuck	Augusta	Grenville, S. R **O**	Albert Lawrence
Roger's Hill		Pictou **N S**	Wm. Carson
Rokeby	Sherbrooke, South	Lanark, S. R. **O**	
Rollo Bay	No. 43	King's **P E I**	R. McDougall
Rollo Bay Cross	No. 44	King's **P E I**	L. Chaisson
Rolling Dam, W. O.		Charlotte **N B**	Jacob Styles
Roman's Valley, W.O.		Guysboro' **N S**	Patrick Rogers
Romney	Romney	Kent **O**	
Ronaldsay	Proton	Grey, E. R. **O**	Joseph McArdle
Rona	No. 60	Queen's **P E I**	Wm. McQueen
******Rondeau*	Harwich	Kent **O**	J. K. Morris
Rondeau Harbor	Harwich	Kent **O**	Robert Brigham
R		**O**	James Cowan

NAME OF POST OFFICE.	TOWNSHIP OR PARISH.	ELECTORAL COUNTY OR DIVISION.	NAME OF POSTMASTER.
Rosa	Murray	Northumberland, E. R. **O**	H. Fieldhouse
Rosebank	South Dumfries	Brant, N. R. **O**	Mrs. S. A. Durnin
Rosedale	Fenelon	Victoria, N. R. **O**	Moses McNeil
Rosedene	Gainsboro'	Monck **O**	Cornelius McKay
Rosehall	Hillier	Prince Edward **O**	Isaac G. Ferguson
**Rosemont*	Mulmur	Simcoe, S. R. **O**	George Cumming
Roseneath	Alnwick	Northumberland, W.R. **O**	Alfred Metcalfe
Rosetta	Lanark	Lanark, N. R. **O**	Robert McFarlane
Rose Vale, W. O.		Albert **N B**	John Stevens
Rose Valley	No. 67	Queen's **P E I**	Hector McDonald
Roseville	Dumfries, North	Waterloo, S. R. **O**	Moses Gingrich
Roseway, W. O.		Shelburne **N S**	Elijah Hagar
Roslin	Thurlow	Hastings, E. R. **O**	Miss Jane Hewitt
Roslin, W. O.		Cumberland **N S**	David Stewart
Ross	Ross	Renfrew, N. R. **O**	Mrs. Mary McLaren
Ross' Corner, W. O.		King's **N S**	D. E. Ross
Rosseau	Humphrey	Muskoka **O**	William Ditchburn
Rossway, W. O.		Digby **N S**	David Cowan
Rothsay	Maryboro'	Wellington, N. R. **O**	William Smith
Rothsay, W. O.		King's **N B**	Charles F. McCready
Rouge Hill	Pickering	Ontario, S. R. **O**	Hugh Graham
Rougemont	St. Césaire	Rouville **Q**	D. Bachelder
Round Hill, W. O.		King's **N B**	William McLeod
Round Hill, W. O.		Annapolis **N S**	C. E. Spurr
Round Lake	Belmont	Peterborough, E. R. **O**	Hy. N. Cooper
Round Plains	Townsend	Norfolk, N. R. **O**	George Gillesby
Rowanton		Pontiac **Q**	David West
Roxburgh, W. O.		Albert **N B**	John Kelly
Roxham	Lacolle	St. John's **Q**	Thomas Wallis
Roxton Falls	Roxton	Shefford **Q**	A. O. T. Beauchemin
Roxton Pond	Roxton	Shefford **Q**	R. A. Kimpton
Royal Road, W. O.		York **N B**	Charles W. Estey
Rugby	Oro	Simcoe, N. R. **O**	James Ball

NAME OF POST OFFICE.	TOWNSHIP OR PARISH.	ELECTORAL COUNTY OR DIVISION.	NAME OF POSTMASTER.
Runnymede	Matapedia	Bonaventure Q	Mrs. Barbara Wheeler
Rupert	Masham	Ottawa Q	W. D. Leslie
Rusagornis, W. O.		Sunbury N B	Abner Smith
Ruscom River	Rochester	Essex O	Jeremiah Duprey
Rusagornis Station, W. O.		Sunbury N B	John McGill
Russell	Russell	Russell O	W. R. Petrie
Russeldale	Fullarton	Perth, S. R. O	John Wilson
Russeltown		Chateauguay Q	Cyrille Turcotte
Rustico	No. 24	Queen's P E I	Joseph Gallant
Rutherford	Dawn	Bothwell O	John Brown
Ruthven	Gosfield	Essex O	Hugh Ruthven
Ryckman's Corners	Barton	Wentworth, S. R. O	
Ryegate	Sandwich, East	Essex O	Joseph Christie
Rylstone	Seymour	Northumberland, E. R. O	D. Allan
Ste. Adéle	Abercrombie	Terrebonne Q	Odile Lafleur
St. Agatha	Wilmot	Waterloo, S. R. O	Anthony Kaiser.
Ste. Agathe	Ste. Agathe	Lotbinière Q	L. Boulanger
Ste. Agnès	Ste. Agnès	Charlevoix Q	Rev. J. A. Bureau
St. Agnes de Dundee	St. Agnes de Dundee	Huntingdon Q	Pierre Tremblay
St. Aimé		Richelieu Q	S. Cartier
S Alban	St. Alban	Portneuf Q	John D. McCormick
St. Albert	Warwick	Arthabaska Q	Prudent Lainesse

NAME OF POST OFFICE.	TOWNSHIP OR PARISH.	ELECTORAL COUNTY OR DIVISION.	NAME OF POSTMASTER.
St. Alexandre d'Iberville	.....	Iberville ..... Q	A. A. L. Brien
St. Alexis	St. Sulpice	Montcalm ..... Q	Miss M. Omon
St. Alphonse	St. Alphonse	Joliette ..... Q	Esdras Genereux
St. Anaclet	St. Anaclet	Rimouski ..... Q	O. Couture
St. André	St. André	Kamouraska ..... Q	P. C. Marquis
St. André Avellin	St. André Avellin	Ottawa ..... Q	H. N. Raby
St. Andrews	.....	Charlotte ..... N B	G. F. Campbell
St. Andrews	.....	Antigonishe ..... N S	Duncan Chisholm
St. Andrews, W. O	.....	Colchester ..... N S	A. B. Sibley
**St. Andrews, East*	Argenteuil	Argenteuil ..... Q	Thomas Lamb
St. Andrews, West	Cornwall	Cornwall ..... O	Lackey Masterson
St. Andrews	St. Andrews	District of Lisgar ..... M	Andrew Mowat
St. Andrew's	No. 38	King's ..... P E I	John Ryan
Ste. Angéle de Monnoir	Monnoir	Rouville ..... Q	Michael O. Caron
Ste. Angéle de Laval	Ste. Angéle de Laval	Nicolet ..... Q	Olivier Désilets
St. Anicet	St. Anicet	Huntingdon ..... Q	F. S. Bourgeault
Ste. Anne Bout de l'Isle	Montreal	Jacques Cartier ..... Q	Adelme Dugal, M. D.
Ste. Anne de Beaufort	.....	Montmorency ..... Q	Adolphe Paré
Ste. Anne de la Perade	Ste. Anne	Champlain ..... Q	Joseph U. Marcotte
Ste. Anne des Monts	Ste. Anne des Monts	Gaspé ..... Q	J. Perré
Ste. Anne des Plains	Ste. Anne	Terrebonne ..... Q	D. Gaudette, M. D.
Ste. Anne la Pocatière	St. Anne	Kamouraska ..... Q	Joseph Dionne
St. Ann's, W. O	.....	Victoria ..... N S	M. McKenzie
aSt. Ann's	St. Ann's	Provencher ..... M	Alex. Cisholm
St. Ann's	Number 22	Queen's ..... P E I	Michael Murphy
St. Ann's	Gainsborough	Monck ..... O	G. Secord
St. Anselme	St. Anselme	Dorchester ..... Q	Pierre Fortier
St. Anthony, W. O	.....	Kent ..... N B	Cyprien Dionne
St. Antoine, Lotbinière	St. Antoine de Tilly	Lotbinière ..... Q	Edmond Larue
St. Antoine, River Richelieu	.....	Verchéres ..... Q	Narcisse Cartier
St. Antonin	St. Antonin	Témiscouata ..... Q	Felix Queen

NAME OF POST OFFICE.	TOWNSHIP OR PARISH.	ELECTORAL COUNTY OR DIVISION.	NAME OF POSTMASTER.
St. Armand Centre.....	St. Armand	Missisquoi ....Q	Abram Titemore..... ..
St. Armand Station ...	St. Armand	Missisquoi ....Q	Peter Smith ....
St. Arséne	St. Arséne	Témisouata ....Q	Elie Martin ....
St. Athanase	St. Athanase	Iberville ....Q	P. Regnier...............
St. Aubert	St. Aubert	L'Islet ....Q	Alexis Blais.............
St. Augustan Portneuf	St. Augustin	Portneuf ....Q	O. East ....
St. Augustan, Two Mountains	....	Two Mountains...........Q	Louis Paquetto ....
St. Barnabé River Yamaska...............	St. Barnabé	St. Hyacinthe ....Q	Alexis Bouvier ....
St. Barnabé, St. Maurice	St. Barnabé	St. Maurice ....Q	J. B. L. Duaime ....
St. Barthélemi	St. Barthélemi	Berthier ....Q	J. Fauteux..............
St. Bazile	St. Bazile	Portneuf ....Q	G. Jobin ....
St. Bazile le Grand ...	St. Bazile le Grand.....	Chambly......................Q	Eusébe Lalumier ......
Ste. Beatrix	Ste. Beatrix	Joliette ....Q	G. Lemire dit Marsolait....... ....
St. Benoit	Two Mountains.........	Two Mountains...........Q	Ernest Lemaire.........
St. Bernard	St. Bernard	Dorchester ....Q	Pierre Plante........ ...
St. Bernard (sud)......	St. B. de Laville	St. John's ....Q	J. E. Trudeau ....
St. Bonaventure	Upton	Drummond..................Q	O. Salois ....
St. Boniface	St. Boniface	Selkirk..................... .M	Joseph Dubugue........
Ste. Brigide	Monnoir	Iberville..... ....Q	William Murray........
St. Brigitte des Saults	St. Brigitte des Saults	Nicolet ....Q	Narcisse Rivet ....
St. Bruno	Montarville	Chambly ....Q	A. P. Paré...............
St. Camille........... ..	St. Camille...............	Wolfe ....Q	Guillaume Crepeau.....
St. Canute	St. Canute	Two Mountains............Q	John Makereth ....
St. Casimir......	St. Casimir	Portneuf.......................Q	François X. Gingras...
St. Catherine's, East..	Fossambault	Portneuf......... ....Q	Rev. H. Gagnon........
**St. Catherine's West* ..	Grantham	Lincoln ....O	W. L. Copeland ....
St. Célestin	St. Célestin	Nicolet ....Q	C. E. Houde ....
**St. Césaire*...	St. Césaire...............	Rouville ....Q	J. E. Gaboury...........
St. Charles...............	St. Charles.........	Selkirk........................M	Mary Adshead . ...
St. Charles de Stanbridge	Stanbridge................	Missisquoi..................Q	Louis Chas. Gauvin ...
St. Charles, River Boyer	Beauchamp..............	Bellechasse ....Q	T. Montminy ....

NAME OF POST OFFICE.	TOWNSHIP OR PARISH.	ELECTORAL COUNTY. OR DIVISION.	NAME OF POSTMASTER.
St. Charles, River Richelieu	St. Charles	St. Hyacinthe Q	J. E. LeBlanc
Ste. Claire	Ste. Claire	Dorchester Q	L. V. Royer
St. Clements	Wellesley	Waterloo, N. R. O	John Stroh
St. Clet	Soulanges	Soulanges Q	A. Borque
Ste. Clothilde	Horton	Arthabaska Q	C. Gélinas
St. Columbin	..	Two Mountains Q	M. J. Phelan
St. Côme	Cathcart	Joliette Q	Venant Gaudet
St. Constant	Laprairie	Laprairie Q	J. O. Longtin
St. Croix, W. O		Hants N S	Daniel Mosher
St. Croix, W. O		York N B	Alfred H. Bruning
Ste. Croix	Ste. Croix	Lotbinière Q	J. Hamel
St. Cuthbert		Berthier Q	F. X. R. Biron
St. Cyriac	Kenogami	Chicoutimi Q	Jean Dèschene
St. Cyrille	St. Cyrille	L'Islet Q	J. B. Cloutier
St. Damase	St. Damase	St. Hyacinthe Q	P. H. Petit
St. Damien de Brandon	Brandon	Berthier Q	J. A. Ecremont
St. David's	Niagara	Niagara O	C. Fisher
St. Denis de la Bouteillerie	St. Denis	Kamouraska Q	Paschal Dionne
St. Denis, River Richelieu	St. Denis	St. Hyacinthe Q	Joseph E. Mignault
St. Didace	Lanaudière	Maskinongé Q	Elzéar Germain
St. Dominique		Bagot Q	Treflé Lapalme
St. Dominique, des Cedres	Soulanges	Soulanges Q	L. Cown
Ste. Dorothee	Ste. Dorothee	Laval Q	Casimir Valiquette
St. Edward		Napierville Q	J. Blain
St. Edouard de Frampton (sub)	Frampton	Dorchester Q	James Butler
St. Edwidge	Clifton	Compton Q	F. Courtemanche
St. Elie	Caxton	St. Maurice Q	C. H. Coutu
St. Eleanors	Number 17	Prince P E I	J. T. Fraser
Ste. Elizabeth		Berthier Q	P. L. Hudon dit Beaulieu
St. Eloi	St. Eloi	Témiscouata Q	Jacques Theriault
St. Elzéar	St. Elzéar	Beauce Q	Jean Bilodeau

NAME OF POST OFFICE.	TOWNSHIP OR PARISH.	ELECTORAL COUNTY OR DIVISION.		NAME OF POSTMASTER.
Ste. Emelie de l'Energie	Joliette	Joliette	Q	P. A. Laporte
St. Ephrem de Tring	Tring	Beauce	Q	Olivier Begin
St. Ephrem d'Upton	Upton	Bagot	Q	S. B. Warner
St. Esprit		Montcalm	Q	C. Dalpédit Pariseau
St. Esprit, W. O		Richmond	N S	John Matheson
St. Etienne de Beauharnois	Beauharnois	Beauharnois	Q	J. B. C. de Courville
St. Etienne de Bolton	Bolton	Brome	Q	Louis Poulin
St Etienne des Grés	St. Etienne des Grés	St. Maurice	Q	Uldoric Brunelle
St. Eugène	Hawkesbury, East	Prescott	O	Simon Labrosse
St. Eustache		Two Mountains	Q	Philias Gauthier
St. Evariste de Forsyth	Forsyth	Beauce	Q	Majorique Montmigny
St. Fabien	St. Fabien	Rimouski	Q	Vital Roy dit Lauzon
Ste. Famille	Ste. Famille	Montmorency	Q	Joseph Prémont
St. Felicité	St. Denis	Rimouski	Q	J. B. LeBel
St. Felix de Valois		Joliette	Q	Max Crepeau
St. Ferdinand	Halifax	Megantic	Q	Louis I. Frechette
St. Féréol (sub-office)	St. Féréol	Montmorency	Q	
St. Fidéle	Mount Murray	Charlevoix	Q	Archille Bhérour
St. Flavie	St. Flavie	Rimouski	Q	Joseph Fournier
St. Flavien	St. Flavien	Lotbinière	Q	L. Bédard
Ste. Flore	Cap de la Madelaine	Champlain	Q	F. Vincent dit Maheux
St. Fortunat	Wolfstown	Wolfe	Q	Damase St. Pierre
St. Foy	St. Foy	Quebec	Q	Felix Belleau
St. François, Beauce	St. François, Beauce	Beauce	Q	Hiliare Poulin
St. François de Sales	St. François de Sales	Laval	Q	Syriac St. Amour
St. Francois d'Orleans	St. François d'Orleans	Montmorency	Q	Emilien Pepin dit Lachance
St. François du Lac		Yamaska	Q	O. H. Coutu
Ste. François	Bégon	Temiscouata	Q	Napoleon Beauline
St. François, Montmagny	St. François	Montmagny	Q	E. C. Boulet
St. François Xavier	St. François Xavier	Marquette	M	J. B. Thibeault
St. François Xavier		[illegible]ata	Q	Guillaume Caron

NAME OF POST OFFICE.	TOWNSHIP OR PARISH.	ELECTORAL COUNTY OR DIVISION.	NAME OF POSTMASTER.
St. Frédéric............	St. Frédéric............	Beauce........................Q	L. G. A. Legendre.....
St. Gabriel de Brandon	Brandon	Berthier...... ....Q	M. O'Heir................
Ste. Geneviéve	Montreal	Jacques Cartier...... .... Q	Godfroi Boileau ....
St. George...............	....	Charlotte ....N B	E. R. O'Br en... ... .
St George, Beauce ...	St. George...............	Beauce .... Q	Hubert Catellier.......
St. George, Brant	Dumfries, South	Brant, N. R... ....O	C. Batty................
St. George de Windsor	Windsor	Richmond .... Q	F. X. Roy. ....
St. George's Channel, W. O.................. ...	....	Richmond ....N S	William McKenzie ...
St. Germain de Grantham	Grantham.................	Drummond ....Q	Mrs. E. Paré... .... ..
Ste. Gertrude..	Ste. Gertrude............	Nicolet ....Q	Léon Champoux........
St. Gervais	St. Genvais	Bellechasse ....Q	Marshal Aubé..........
St. Giles..................	St. Giles..................	Lotbinière...... ....Q	George Coté ....
St. Grégoire	St. Grégoire............	Nicolet · ....Q	J A. Poirier..... ....
St. Guillaume d'Upton	Upton	Drummond ....Q	H. Mercier...............
Ste. Héléne.............	Ste. Héléne	Kamouraska . ...Q	B. Michaud.......... ..
Ste. Héléne de Bagot	....	Bagot ....Q	Pierre Fafard...........
St. Helen's.............	Wawanosh	Huron, N. R..... ....O	John Gordon............
Ste. Hénédine..........	Ste. Hénédine..	Dorchester.................Q	Joseph Mercier.........
St. Henri......	Lauzon	Lévis ....Q	Charles A. Collet .....
St. Henri Station	St. Henri	Lévis.............. ....Q	George Demers..... ...
St Hermas	....	Two Mountains............Q	P. E. Clairoux.. ....
St. Hermenegilde	Barford..................	Stanstead ....Q	Calixte Duquis ....
St. Hilaire, W. O......	....	Victoria........ ...... N B	Peter Michaud ....
St. Hilaire Station...	St. Hilaire	Rouville ....Q	Thomas Valiquet......
St. Hilaire Village.....	St. Hilaire	Rouville.....................Q	E. Goulet...............
St. Hippolyte de Kilkenny	Kilkenny	Terrebonne .... Q	J. Dagenais.......... ..
St. Honoré...............	Shenley	Beauce ....Q	Pierre Boucher..... ...
St. Hubert	....	Chambly ....Q	Francois Robert........
St. Hugues	....	Bagot ....Q	Emery Lafontaine......
**St. Hyacinthe*	St. Hyacinthe	St. Hyacinthe ....Q	E. L R, C. Després ...
St. Irénée	St. Irénée..	Charlevoix ....Q	Joseph Gosselin ....
St. Isidore, Dorchester	St. Isidore	Dorchester......... ......Q	B. Morin............... ..

NAME OF POST OFFICE.	TOWNSHIP OR PARISH.	ELECTORAL COUNTY OR DIVISION.		NAME OF POSTMASTER.
St. Ives	West Nissouri	Middlesex, E. R.	O	Thomas Howard
**St. Jacob's*	Woolwich	Waterloo, N. R.	O	John L. Wideman
St. James	St. James	Selkirk	M	James McKay
St. Jaques	St. Sulpice	Montcalm	Q	J. F. Ecrement
St. Jaques le Mineur		Laprairie	Q	Joseph O. Poirier
St. James Park (sub)	Westminster	Middlesex, E. R.	O	John Taylor
St. Janvier	St. Janver	Terrebonne	Q	David Desroches
St. Jean Baptiste de Montreal	Côte St. Louis	Hochelaga	Q	Gilbert Filiatreault
St. Jean Baptiste de Rouville	Rouville	Rouville	Q	L. G. E. Goulet
St. Jean Chrysostome, Chateauguay		Chateauguay	Q	I. J. L. Derome
St. Jean Chrysostome, Levis	Lauzon	Lévis	Q	Morcellin Goslin
St. Jean des Chaillons	St. Jean des Chaillons	Lotbinière	Q	Elie Chandonnais
St. Jean de Matha	Brandon	Joliette	Q	F. X. Lasalle
St. Jean d'Orléans	St. Jean d'Orléans	Montmorency	Q	F. X. Turcotte
St. Jean Port Joli	St. Jean Port Joli	L'Islet	Q	Marie Fournier
**St. Jérome*		Terrebonne	Q	Edouard Marchand
St. Joachim	St. Joachim	Montmorency	Q	Isaie Simard
St. Joachim de Shefford	Roxton	Shefford	Q	Joseph Bachand
St. John		St. John	N B	John Howe
**St. John's, East*		St. John's	Q	W. A. Osgood
St. John's, West	Thorold	Welland	O	A. B. Brown
St. Joseph	St. Joseph	Beauce	Q	Miss F. A. A. Arcand.
St. Joseph, W. O.		Westmoreland	N B	Daniel Ethier
St. Joseph du Lac	Two Mountains	Two Mountains	Q	John McColl
St. Jude	St. Jude	St. Hyacinthe	Q	Hubert Lemay
St. Julie	Belœil	Verchéres	Q	Joseph Collette
Ste Julie de Somerset	Somerset	Megantic	Q	Louis Roberge
St. Julienne		Montcalm	Q	Jos. Racette
St. Justin		Maskinongé	Q	Louis St. Antoine
St. Justine de Newton	Newton	Vaudreuil	Q	P. J. Lalonde
St. Lambert	Lauzon	Lévis	Q	M. Brochu

NAME OF POST OFFICE.	TOWNSHIP OR PARISH.	ELECTORAL COUNTY OR DIVISION.	NAME OF POSTMASTER.
St. Laurent d'Orléans	St. Laurent d'Orléans	Montmorency .... Q	Jean Bte. Gosselin.....
St. Laurent, Montreal	Montreal	Jacques Cartier .. ..Q	Joseph Le Cavalier ..
St. Laurent	....	Marquette ....M	Rev. J. Mulvihill......
St. Lazare...............	St. Lazare	Bellechasse ....Q	Rev. E. Dufour.........
St. Léon...........	Dumontier	Maskinongé ....Q	F. X. A. Rivard........
St. Leonard	Aston	Nicolet ....Q	Moise Carbonneau.....
St. Leonard's, W. O...	....	Victoria...... ....N B	Patrick Martin..... ...
St. Liboire......	St. Liboire	Bagot ....Q	J. C. Bachand...........
St. Liguori...............	....	Montcalm ....Q	Ulric B. Desrochers...
St. Lin	....	L'Assomption ....Q	Thomas Gerault ......
St. Louis de Gonzague	....	Beauharnois ....Q	Léandre Vachon ......
Ste. Louise	Ste. Louise	L'Islet......... ....Q	Nazaire Caron ....
St. Luc	Longueuil................	St. John's.... ....Q	Samuel Hamilton .. ..
Ste. Luce	Lessard	Rimouski ....Q	James Miller............
St. Magloire..............	Rioux	Bellechasse..................Q	Pierre Tanguay ....
St. Malachie	East Frampton..... ...	Dorchester ....Q	George Duncan.........
St. Malo.	Auckland	Compton.......................Q	Moyse Roy ....
St. Marc.....	St. Marc.................	Verchères ....Q	Pierre Duvernay.. ....
St. Marcel.	....	Richelieu ....Q	Anselme Plamondon ..
St. Margaret's Bay ...	....	Halifax....................N S	J. S. Brine ....
St. Margaret's...........	Number 43..............	King's ....P E I	James McCormack.....
Ste. Marguerite...	Ste. Marguerite.........	Dorchester ....Q	F. E. Genest ....
Ste. Marie de Monnoir	Ste. Marie	Rouville..... ....Q	F. H. Gatien...... .....
Ste Marthe.....	Rigaud	Vaudreuil... ....Q	E. H. Lalonde..........
St. Martin	Isle Jésus............. ...	Laval ....Q	Léon Sauriol...........
St. Martine	St. Martine	Chateauguay ....Q	Antoine Hébert.........
St. Martin's	....	St. John..................N B	Andrew S. Killen......
St. Martins, W. O......	....	St. John................N B	J. Berry...................
St. Mary's Bay	.. ..	Digby........................N S	Edward Everett ....
**St. Mary's*...............	Blanchard...............	Perth, S. R................O	Peter M. Nichol ....
St. Mary's, W. O......	....	Kent.......... ....N B	Olivier Le Blanc........
St. Mary's Ferry, W. O.....................	....	York ....N B	C. L. Estabrook ....

NAME OF POST OFFICE.	TOWNSHIP OR PARISH.	ELECTORAL COUNTY OR DIVISION.	NAME OF POSTMASTER.
St. Mathias	East Chambly..........	Rouville.................. Q	Paul Bertrand..........
St. Mathieu	St. Mathieu	Rimouski .... Q	T. Leveque............
St. Maurice....	Cap de la Magdelaine	Champlain .... Q	G. E. Bistodeau ....
St. Maurice Forges ...	St. Etienne	Maurice .... Q	J. B. Beauchemin......
St Michel	St. Michel	Bellechasse .... Q	E. S. Belleau...........
St. Michel des Saints.:	Brassard........	Berthier .... Q	Rev. J. A. Dagnaul...
St. Modeste...............	Wentworth.....	Témiscouata... .... Q	Narcisse Miville.......
St. Moise...................	Cabot	Rimouski .... Q	Macavie Morin.... ....
St. Monique...............	St. Monique.............	Nicolet.. .... Q	Godfroi Rosseau......
St. Monique des deux Montagnes........ ...	St. Monique des deux Montagnes............	Two Mountains........... Q	Damase Leonard .....
St. Narcisse.......... ...	Champlain	Champlain .... Q	D. Hamelin. ....
St. Nicholas	St. Nicholas.......	Lévis...... .... Q	Morris Scott.............
St. Norbert	Berthier....................	Berthier .... Q	N. Roch......... ....
St. Norbert	St. Norbert, North.....	Provencher .... M	Joseph Lemay...........
St. Octave	Métis......................	Rimouski .... Q	Narcisse Richard......
St. Ola	Limerick	Hastings, N. R........... O	William Morton........
St. Onezime..............	St. Onezime..	Kamouraska.............. Q	L. Oulette...............
St. Ours....................	St. Ours....................	Richelieu .... Q	L. Chapelaine...........
St. Pacôme	Rivière Ouelle..........	Kamouraska .... Q	Alexander Hudon ....
St. Paschal	St. Paschal..............	Kamouraska............... Q	E. Chapleau..............
St. Patrick, W. O......	....	Charlotte................. N B	Richard Dyer...........
St. Patrick's Channel, W. O..................	....	Victoria................... N S	John McNaughton.....
St. Patrick's Hill.....	Tingwick	Arthabaska. .... Q	Joseph S. Beaudette...
St. Paul d'Industrie...	....	Joliette . ... Q	Joseph Guilbault ......
St. Paul du Buton.....	Montmini	Montmagny.............. Q	Rev. W. Couture.. .....
St. Paulin....	St. Paulin	Maskinongé. .... Q	Olivier Lafond ....
St. Paul l'Hermite......	L'Assomption	L'Assomption.............. Q	Joseph Marion ....
St. Paul's, W. O.	....	Pictou...................... N S	William Thompson ...
St. Paul's, W. O.	....	Kent .... N B	Pacifique Belliveau ...
**St. Paul's Bay*	St. Paul's Bay..........	Charlevoix .... Q	Ovide A. Clement......
St. Perpetue.............	St. Perpetue	Nicolet........................ Q	Onésime Rousseau.....
St. Peter's.................	....	Richmond . ... N S	R. G. Morrison ....

NAME OF POST OFFICE.	TOWNSHIP OR PARISH.	ELECTORAL COUNTY OR DIVISION.	NAME OF POSTMASTER.
St. Philippe	St. Philippe	Laprairie Q	Z. Mayrand
St. Philippe d'Argenteuil	Chatham	Argenteuil Q	Fernandez Naubert
St. Philippe de Nery	St. Philippe de Nery	Kamouraska Q	François Deschène
Ste. Philomêne	....	Chateauguay Q	Mrs. M. J. D'Amour
St. Pie	....	Bagot Q	A. Gauthier dit Landerville
St. Pierre Baptiste	Inverness	Megantic Q	P. A. Drolet
St. Pierre d'Orleans	St. Pierre d'Orleans	Montmorency Q	F. Fortin
St. Pierre les Becquets	St. Pierre les Becquets	Nicolet Q	Thomas Phillips
St. Pierre Montmagny	St. Pierre Montmagny	Montmagny Q	Sarah D. Bacon
St. Placide	....	Two Mountains Q	Zephirin Raymond
St. Polycarpe	New Longueuil	Soulanges Q	John Taylor
St. Prime	Ashuapmouchouan	Chicoutimi Q	Rev. E. Auclair
St. Prosper	St. Prosper	Champlain Q	Joseph Frigon
St. Raphael, East	St. Raphael	Bellechasse Q	P. C. A. Fournier
St. Raphael, West	Charlottenburg	Glengarry O	Mrs. Mary McDonell.
St. Raymond	Bourg Louis	Portneuf Q	Edouard Plamondon
St. Regis	St. Regis	Huntingdon Q	Robert Tyre
St. Remi	La Salle	Napierville Q	Charles Bedard
St. Robert	....	Richelieu Q	Olivier Dupré
**St. Roch de Québec*	St. Roch de Québec	Quebec City, East Q	Louis P. Huot
St. Roch de Richelieu	St. Roch de Richelieu	Richelieu Q	J. B. Paquette
St. Roch des Aulnaies	St. Roch des Aulnaies	L'Islet Q	George Gagnon
St. Roch l'Achigan	....	L'Assomption Q	O. Peltier
St. Romaine	Winslow	Compton Q	E. Bélanger
St. Rosalie	St. Rosalie	Bagot Q	Ant. Cabana
Ste. Rose	Isle Jésus	Laval Q	Adelard E. Leonard
St. Sauveur	St. Sauveur	Terrebonne Q	L. L. J. Lorangor
St. Sauveur de Québec	Banlieue de Québec	Quebec Q	J. L. Saucier
St. Scholastique	....	Two Mountains Q	A. Fortier
St. Sebastien	St. George de Henryville	Iberville Q	Luc Lamoureux
St. Sévère	....	St. Maurice Q	Adolphe Lamy
St. Severin de Beaurivage	St. Sylvestre	L	[illegible]

NAME OF POST OFFICE.	TOWNSHIP OR PARISH.	ELECTORAL COUNTY OR DIVISION.	NAME OF POSTMASTER.
St. Simon de Rimouski	....	Rimouski ....Q	Antoine Bernier.......
St. Simon de Yamaska	De Ramsey	Bagot ....Q	Alfred Brien ....
Ste. Sophie	Halifax	Megantic ....Q	Joseph Vigneau ......
Ste. Sophie de Lacorne	Lacorne	Terrebonne ....Q	Ulric Leveque... ....
St. Stanislas	Batiscan	Champlain .... Q	A. Jos. Lacourcière...
St. Stanislas de Kostka	....	Beauharnois ....Q	Onésime Dorais ....
St. Stephen.....	....	Charlotte ....N B	James A. Grant ....
St. Sulpice	L'Assomption	L'Assomption ... .Q	Jacques Royal ....
St. Sylvester..............	St. Sylvester	Lotbinière ....Q	John Machell ....
St. Sylvester, East.....	St. Sylvester	Lotbinière .... Q	Jean Lessard............
St. Théodore.....	Acton	Bagot .. ..Q	Paul Decelle ....
St. Théodore de Chertsey	Chertsey..................	Montcalm ....Q	Marcel Lepine ....
Ste. Thérèse de Blainville	Blainville.......	Terrebonne ....Q	David Morris............
St. Thomas, East......	Lanoraie..................	Joliette ....Q	Joseph Latour, dit Forget........ ....
St. Thomas, West.....	Yarmouth	Elgin, E. R........ ....O	F. E. Ermatinger......
St. Timothée...........	....	Beauharnois ....Q	Auguste Lesperance...
St. Tite	Batiscan	Champlain . ...Q	P. O. Trudel ....
St. Tite des Caps	St. Tite..........	Montmorency ....Q	Rev. E. H. L. Marceau.
St. Ubalde...............	St. Ubalde.....	Portneuf.......... ....Q	André G. Trottier.....
St. Urbain	....	Chateauguay ....Q	J. B. Matthieu ....
St. Urbain	St. Urbain	Charlevoix........ ....Q	Joseph Girouard........
Ste. Ursule...............	....	Maskinongé..................Q	L. Lupien................
St. Valentin	....	St. John's ....Q	Z. O. Lamarche...... ...
St. Valérien	Milton.....................	Shefford . ...Q	P. S. Grandpré.........
St. Vallier	St. Vallier	Bellechasse ....Q	F. Belanger.............
Ste. Victoire	....	Richelieu ....Q	C. P. Clotier... ....
St. Victor de Tring ...	Tring	Beauce ....Q	François Gosselin, jun
St. Vincent de Paul...	Isle Jésus........	Laval ....Q	C. Germain, jun.........
St. Vital	....	Provencher .... M	A. Goudry ....
St. Wenceslas	Ashton	Nicolet.......... ....Q	Ferdinand Thèrien ...
St. Williams	Walsingham	Norfolk, S. R...............O	Harriet L. Kitchen ...
St. Zenon	Provost....................	Berthier .... .Q	Felix M. Trudeau .....

NAME OF POST OFFICE.	TOWNSHIP OR PARISH.	ELECTORAL COUNTY OR DIVISION.	NAME OF POSTMASTER.
St. Zephirin	Courval	Yamaska **Q**	Nestor Duguay
St. Zotique		Soulanges **Q**	O. F. Prieur
Sable	West Williams	Middlesex, N. R. **O**	A. McDonald
Sable River, W. O.		Shelburne **N S**	Wm. Dunlop
Sabrevois	Sabrevois	Iberville **Q**	Thomas Jones
Sackville		Westmoreland **N B**	Jos. Dixon
Saintfield	Reach	Ontario, N. R. **O**	Donald McKay
Salem	Nichol	Wellington, C. R. **O**	John R. Wissler
Salem, W. O.		Albert **N B**	Joshua Steeves
Salem, W. O.		Cumberland **N S**	E. Black
Salford	Dereham	Oxford, S. R **O**	John F. Snider
Salisbury		Westmoreland **N B**	J. Taylor
Salmon Beach		Gloucester **N B**	R. Buttemer
Salmon Creek, W. O.		Sunbury **N B**	James Fowler
Salmon Hole. W. O.		Halifax **N S**	Jacob Sellis
Salmon River, W O.		St. John **N B**	Edward H. Foster
Salmon River, W. O.		Cape Breton **N S**	J. Huntington
Salmon River		Digby **N S**	
Salmon River, W. O.		Guysboro' **N S**	D. Lawlor
Salmon River, W. O.		Halifax **N S**	Ann Gallagher
Salmon River (Lake Settlement) W. O.		Guysboro' **N S**	Thomas O'Neil
Salmonville	Chinguacousy	Peel. **O**	Simon Plewes
Salt Springs, W. O.		King's **N B**	George McEwan

NAME OF POST OFFICE.	TOWNSHIP OR PARISH.	ELECTORAL COUNTY OR DIVISION.	NAME OF POSTMASTER.
Sambro, W. O.		Halifax N S	E. Smith
Sanborn	Wolfeston	Wolfe Q	Thomas Hurley, jun
Sand Beach, W. O.		Yarmouth N S	Wm. R. Pinkney
Sandford	Scott	Ontario, N. R. O	Edward Taylor
Sandhill	Chinguacousy	Peel O	W. C. Hughes
Sandhurst	S. Fredericksburg	Lennox O	William Hill
Sand Point	McNab	Renfrew, S. R. O	Edward Derenzy
Sand Point, W. O.		Guysboro' N S	Alexander J. Fox
**Sandwich*	Sandwich, West	Essex O	C. St. Louis
Sandy Beach	South Gaspé Bay	Gaspé Q	Nicholas Bailey
Sandy Beaches, W. O.		Halifax N S	Isaac Cleveland
Sandy Cove		Digby N S	J. C. Morse
Sandy Point, W. O.		Shelburne N S	John Purney
Sarawak	Sarawak	Grey, N. R. O	John McKenzie
Sarepta	Hay	Huron, S. R. O	Wm. Reynolds
**Sarnia*	Sarnia	Lambton O	Wm. Murphy
**Saugeen*	Saugeen	Bruce, N. R. O	Thomas Lee
Saulnierville, W. O.		Digby N S	Samuel McCormack
Sault au Cochon		Saguenay O	Henry A. Stenton
Sault au Récollet	Montreal	Hochelaga Q	Edward Dauphin
Sault Ste. Marie		Algoma O	Mrs. Pim
Savage's Mill	Shefford	Shefford Q	A. H. Savage
Saw Mill Creek, W. O.		Annapolis N S	Richardson Harris
Sawyerville	Newport	Compton Q	W. S. Scholefield
**Scarboro'*	Scarboro'	York, E. R. O	
Scarboro' Junction	Scarboro'	York, E. R. O	George Taylor, sen.
Schomberg	King	York, N. R. O	J. McGinnis
Scone	Elderslee	Bruce, N. R. O	Thomas Bearman
Scotch Ridge	St. James	Charlotte N B	Michael D. Gleeson
Scotch Settlement, W. O.		Westmoreland N B	Niel McDougall
Scotch Town, W. O.		Queen's N B	John R. Carle
Scotch Village, W. O.		Hants N S	John T. Cochran
Scotchfort	Number 36	Queen's P E I	A. McDonald
Scotland	Oakland	Brant, S. R. O	H. Lyman

NAME OF POST OFFICE.	TOWNSHIP OR PARISH.	ELECTORAL COUNTY OR DIVISION.	NAME OF POSTMASTER.
Scott's Bay		King's ... N S	Daniel Jess
Scott's Town	Hampden	Compton ... Q	John Scott, jun
Scovill's Mills, W. O.		Kent ... N B	L. M. White
Scratching River	St. Agathe	Provencher ... M	W. C. Cowan
Scugog	Scugog	Ontario, N. R. ... O	Isaac Finley
**Seaforth*	Tuckersmith	Huron, C. R. ... O	Samuel Dickson
Seagrove	Reach	Ontario, N. R. ... O	Abram O. Coryell
Seaton	York	York, W. R. ... O	Allan Orr
Searletown	No. 27	Prince ... P E I	Hiram Trueman
Sebright	Rama	Ontario, N. R. ... O	E. L. H. Herring
Sebringville	Ellice	Perth, S. R. ... O	John Kastner
Second Falls, W. O.		Charlotte ... N B	James C. Pratt
Seely's Bay	Leeds	Leeds, S. R. ... O	William Coleman
Seely's Mills, W. O.		King's ... N B	Andrew McAfee
Seely	Brunel	Muskoka ... O	Obadiah Seely
Segeun Falls	Monteith	Muskoka ... O	D. F. Burk
Selby	Richmond	Lennox ... O	David Wartman
Selkirk	Walpole	Haldimand ... O	R. J. Winyard
Selkirk Road	No. 60	Queen's ... P E I	John Dogherty
Selmah, W. O.		Hants ... N S	Archibald Frame
Selton	Howard	Bothwell ... O	James Robinson
Selwyn	Smith	Peterborough, W. R. ... O	Richard Northey
**Seneca*	Seneca	Haldimand ... O	John Scott
Settrington	Settrington	Charlevoix ... Q	Rev. M. E. Roy
Severn Bridge	Morrison	Muskoka ... O	James H. Jackson
Sevigné	Hartwell	Ottawa ... Q	Hercule Chênier
Shag Harbor, W. O.		Shelburne ... N S	S. W. Nickerson
Shakespeare	South Easthope	Perth, S. R. ... O	George Brown
Shamrock	Admaston	Renfrew, S. R. ... O	Patrick Gormon
Shanick	Marmora	Hastings, N. R. ... O	James Bailey
Shanklin, W. O.		St. John's ... N B	Samuel J. Shanklin
Shanly	Edwardsburgh	Grenville, S. R. ... O	William Clark
Shannonvale, W. O.		Restigouche ... N B	Nathaniel Perrett
Shannonville	Tyendinaga	Hastings, E. R. ... O	Hirem Holden

NAME OF POST OFFICE.	TOWNSHIP OR PARISH.	ELECTORAL COUNTY OR DIVISION.	NAME OF POSTMASTER.
Shanty Bay	Oro	Simcoe, N. R. **O**	Thomas Fletcher
Sharon	Gwillimbury, East	York, N. R. **O**	John J. Stokes
Sharpton	Kingston	Frontenac **O**	R. McKechnie
Shawbridge	Abercrombie	Terrebonne **Q**	William Shaw
Shawenegan	Shawenegan	St. Maurice **Q**	Joseph Desaulniers
a Shawville	Clarendon	Pontiac **Q**	James Shaw
Shea's River, W. O		Inverness **N S**	Robert Frizzle
Shedden	Bexley	Victoria, N. R **O**	Mrs. Nancy LeRoy
Shediac		Westmoreland **N B**	A. R. Weldon
Shediac Bridge, W.O		Westmoreland **N B**	Athanase Gallant
Shediac Road, W. O		Westmoreland **N B**	James Rogerson
Sheenboro'	Sheen	Pontiac **Q**	
Sheet Harbor		Halifax **N S**	W. Hall
Sheffield	Beverley	Wentworth, N. R **O**	Edwin Bond
Sheffield		Sunbury **N B**	C. J. Burpee
Sheffield Academy, W. O		Sunbury **N B**	Whitehead Barker
Sheffield Mills, W.O		King's **N S**	Watson Ells
Shefford Mountain	Shefford	Shefford **Q**	William Saxby
Shelburne	Melancthon	Grey, E. R **O**	Edward Berwick
Shelburne		Shelburne **N S**	R. R. Thomson
Sheldon	Adjala	Cardwell **O**	M. Webster
Sheldrake		Saguenay **Q**	Philip Touzel
Shepody Road, W.O		King's **N B**	Jos. Wallace
*Sherbrooke	Ascot	Sherbrooke **Q**	Samuel J. Foss
Sherbrooke	St. Mary's	Guysborough **N S**	Jas. H. McDonald
Sheridan	Trafalgar	Halton **O**	Wm. R. Kelly
Sherkston	Humberstone	Welland **O**	H. B. Zavitz
Sherrington	Sherrington	Napierville **Q**	Raymond Robert
Sherwood Spring	Yonge	Leeds, S. R **O**	James Simpson
Shetland	Euphemia	Bothwell **O**	Richard Laird
Shigawake	Hope	Bonaventure **Q**	Andrew Young
Shiktehawk, W.O		Carleton **N B**	Edwin Phillips
Shiloh	Eramosa	Wellington, S. R **O**	James Mitchell
[illegible]		[illegible] **N S**	

NAME OF POST OFFICE.	TOWNSHIP OR PARISH.	ELECTORAL COUNTY OR DIVISION.	NAME OF POSTMASTER.
Ship Harbor, W. O....	....	Halifax..................N S	Charles Dean ....
Shipley	Wallace	Perth, N. R...... ....O	Edward Bristow.......
Shippigan	....	Gloucester..............N B	John Dorron...........
Shirley	Reach	Ontario, N. R..............O	William Martyn........
Shoolbred.................	Shoolbred................	Bonaventure ....Q	Jean Trottier..........
Short Beach, W. O....	....	Yarmouth................N S	James Bent..............
Shrewsbury...............	Chatham, West Gore..	Argenteuil,...................Q	John Chambers.........
Shrigley	Melancthon	Grey, E. R...................O	George Bailey..........
Shubenacadie	....	Colchester ....N S	Andrew Kirkpatrick...
Shulie, W. O.............	....	Cumberland ....N S	A. W. Grant ....
Shunacadie, W. O......	....	Cape Breton ....N S	Stephen McInnis ......
Sidney Crossing..	Sidney	Hastings, W. R. ....O	N. R. Vandervoort... .
Sight Point, W. O	....	Inverness ....N S	D. McEachean ....
Sillery Cove	St. Columba	Quebec .. ..Q	John Brown ....
Sillsville	Fredericksburg	Lennox ....O	Samuel H. Mellow.....
Siloam.....................	Uxbridge	Ontario, N. R. ....O	Samuel Widderfield ...
Silver Hill	Charlotteville	Norfolk, S. R. ....O	Henry C. Gifford........
Silver Islet...............	....	Algoma ....O	John Livingstone......
a Silver Lake	Somerville	Victoria, N. R. ....O	Joseph Clemens ......
Silverstream, W. O.....	....	Victoria..................N B	Baptiste Guimond .....
**Simcoe*	Woodhouse	Norfolk, N. R. ....O	Henry Mulkins.........
Sinclairville	Binbrook	Wentworth, S. R.... . ...O	Edward Wilson.........
Singhampton	Nottawasaga	Simcoe, N. R. ....O	James Hamilton.....
Six Mile Brook, W.O..	....	Pictou............ ....N S	John McKay............
Six Mile Road, W.O...	....	Cumberland ....N S	Charles Cook...........
Six Portages	Bouchette	Ottawa ....Q	John Sproule............
Skead's Mills............	Nepean	Carleton ....O	Rebecca Pratt ....
Skeena	....	Cariboo .. . .B C	Thomas Hankin ......
Skinner's Pond.........	No. 1	Prince..................P E I	J. Doyle...... ....
Skipness.....	Amabel	Bruce, N. R. ....O	William Hall...........
Skye	Kenyon	Glengarry ....O	J. R. McKenzie........
Sky Glen, W. O.	....	Inverness ....N S	T. H. Smith ....
Sleswick	Caledon	Cardwell ....O	James Killeen ....
Sligo	Caledon	Cardwell ....O	Thomas Bell ....

a Late (

NAME OF POST OFFICE.	TOWNSHIP OR PARISH.	ELECTORAL COUNTY OR DIVISION.	NAME OF POSTMASTER.
Smirleville	Mountain	Dundas **O**	Joseph Wallace
Smithfield	Brighton	Northumberland, E. R. **O**	S. D. Smith
Smithfield, W. O.		Guysboro' **N S**	John W. Archibald
Smith's, W. O.		Westmoreland **N B**	William Hannington
Smith's Cove, W. O.		Digby **N S**	E. W. Potter
Smith's Creek, W. O.		King's **N B**	Thomas H. Coates
**Smith's Falls*	North Elmsley	Lanark, S. R. **O**	James Shaw, jun.
Smith's Mills	Stanstead	Stanstead **Q**	William Knight
Smith Town, W. O.		King's **N B**	David Smith
Smilhurst	Minto	Wellington, N. R. **O**	Thomas B. Patterson
**Smithville, Lincoln*	Grimsby	Lincoln **O**	Robert Thompson
Soda Creek		Cariboo **B C**	Robert McLeese
Soldier's Cove, W. O.		Richmond **N S**	Donald Gillies
Solina	Darlington	Durham, W. R. **O**	James C. Groat
Sombra	Sombra	Bothwell **O**	P. Cattanach
Soixante	La Presentation	St. Hyacinthe **Q**	John Coughlin
Somenos	District of Somenos	Vancouver **B C**	Archd. R. Kier
Somerset	St. Calixte de Somerville	Megantic **Q**	H. Jutras
Somerset, W. O.		King's **N S**	C. W. Bertaux
Somerset	Number 27	Prince **P E I**	John B. Strong
Somerville, W. O.		Carleton **N B**	Wm. P. Boyer
Sonora, W. O.		Guysborough **N S**	James McCutcheon
Sonya	Mariposa	Victoria, N. R. **O**	Charles E. Black
Sooke		Vancouver **B C**	Michael Muir
Soperton	Lansdown	Leeds, S. R. **O**	Nathan Soper
**Sorel*	Sorel	Richelieu **O**	J. O. Duplessis
Souris, East	Number 45	King's **P E I**	J. McInnis
Souris, West	Number 44	King's **P E I**	Thomas Kickham
Southampton, W. O.		Cumberland **N S**	William Adams
Southampton, W. O.		York **N B**	Asa D. Brooks
South Bar of Sydney River, W. O.		Cape Breton **N S**	James Fraser
South Barnston	Barnston	Stanstead **Q**	Francis Cooper
South Bay	Marysburgh	Prince Edward **O**	W. H. Sloan

NAME OF POST OFFICE.	TOWNSHIP OR PARISH.	ELECTORAL COUNTY OR DIVISION.	NAME OF POSTMASTER.
South Bay, W. O......	....	Victoria ....N S	Thomas Donovan......
South Bay, W. O......	Lancaster	St. John ....N B	E. J. Sheldon ... .
South Bolton............	Bolton..........	Brome .. ..Q	John McMannis........
South Branch, W. O...	....	Colchester .... N S	C. B. Cox................
South Branch (Ken.), W. O.....................	....	King's ....N B	Daniel Godard ....
South Branch of St. Nicholas River, W. O	....	Kent ....N B	Charles McDonald .....
South Cayuga..........	South Cayuga	Haldimand ....O	Isaac Fry ....
South Cove, W. O.....	....	Victoria ....N S	Alex. J. McDonald.....
South Douro	Douro	Peterboro', E. R. ....O	Thomas Hanrahan.....
South Dummer........	Dummer	Peterboro', E. R. ....O	William Speer ....
South Durham	Durham..................	Drummond ....Q	F. Prefontaine..........
South-East Passage, W. O.	....	Halifax ... .N S	Mrs L. Williams .....
South Ely	Ely	Shefford ....Q	Ira Jimerson ....
South Finch	Finch	Stormont .... .O	Duncan G. McMillan..
South Gloucester	Osgoode	Russell ....O	Thomas Stanley ... .
South Gower.....	South Gower	Grenville, N. R. ....O	David McGregor ......
South Granby	Granby	Shefford ....Q	Elias Clow..............
South Gut of St. Ann's W. O....................	....	Victoria ....N S	Donald J. Morrison ...
South Ham	Ham	Wolfe ....Q	E. S. Darche ....
South La Graisse	Lochiel	Glengarry ....O	H. R. McDonald ......
South Lake..............	Leeds	Leeds, S. R. ....O	W. Bermingham.. . ..
South McLellan's Mountain, W. O.....	....	Pictou .... N S	Marion Webster.........
South March............	March	Carleton ....O	L. G. Major..............
South Middleton.......	Middleton	Norfolk, N. R. ....O	Robert McKim.........
South Monaghan	South Monaghan	Peterborough, W. R......O	Robert Waddell ....
South Mountain........	Mountain	Dundas ....O	S. H. Richardson......
South Nelson, W. O...	....	Northumberland ......N B	John Kain......... .....
South Ohio, W. O......	....	Yarmouth ....N S	William Crosby .. ..
Southport	Number 38	Queen's.............. P E I	Henry Beer ....
**South Quebec*	Notre dame de la Victoire	Lévis..........................Q	John Ritchie............
South Range, W. O...	....	Digby ....N S	Isaac J. White ....

NAME OF POST OFFICE.	TOWNSHIP OR PARISH.	ELECTORAL COUNTY OR DIVISION.	NAME OF POSTMASTER.
South Rawdon, W. O.	....	Hants .... **N S**	George Creed ....
South Rockland, W.O.	....	Westmoreland .... **N B**	Robert A. Chapman...
South Roxton..........	Roxton	Shefford ....**Q**	Wright Ball ....
South Side Basin of River Denis, W. O..	....	Inverness .... **N S**	M. McAuley ....
South Side of Boulardorie, W. O.........	....	Victoria .... **N S**	R. McKenzie...... .....
South Side of Little Narrows, W. O.....	....	Victoria .... **N S**	John Matheson ....
South Side of Whycocomagh Bay, W. O..	....	Inverness .... **N S**	John McEachen........
South Side of West Margaree, W. O.....	Margaree...............	Inverness ....**N S**	D. E. McKay ....
South Stukely...........	Stukely..............	Shefford ....**Q**	Luke H. Knowlton.....
South West Mabou, W. O.................	....	Inverness ....**N S**	Allan McDonald.......
South West, Lot 16...	Number 16...............	Prince..................**P E I**	Alexander McLean ..
South Wiltshire	Number 31......	Queen's........ ....**P E I**	Thomas Yeo ....
South Zorra.......	Zorra, East	Oxford, N. R............. **O**	Thomas Cross ....
Spaffordton	Loughboro'	Addington ....**O**	Henry Counter. ....
Spanish River..........	....	Algoma ....**O**	Wm. A. Gorrell ....
**Sparta*	Yarmouth..............	Elgin, E. R.......... ..... **O**	John A. Eakins ....
Spa Springs, W. O. ...	Wilmot	Annapolis .... **N S**	Egbert S. Woodbury..
Speedside	Eramosa	Wellington, S. R. ....**O**	James Loughrin........
Speitches Cove, W. O.	....	Digby .... **N S**	L. McKay ....
Spence	Spence	Muskoka .. ..**O**	F. W. Ashdown ....
Spence, W. O.	....	Westmoreland ....**N B**	George Spence ....
Spencer Cove...........	St. Colomb de Sillery..	Quebec ....**Q**	Mrs. Anne Flanagan...
Spencer's Island, W.O	....	Cumberland ....**N S**	W. H. Bigelow ....
Spencerville	Edwardsburgh	Grenville, S. R............**O**	Mrs. Mary Imrie........
Spences Bridge.........	....	Yale .. ..**B C**	John Murray............
Speyside............. ...	Esquesing	Halton..........................**O**	Robert McPherson.....
Sprague's Pôint, W.O.	....	King's ....**N B**	F. D. Genong ....
Spring Arbor............	Walsingham	Norfolk, S. R. ....**O**	J. W. Hazen ....
Springbank	East Williams	Middlesex, N. R. ....**O**	Robert Cowie...........
Spring Brook	Rawdon	Hastings, N. R............**O**	Joshua Green ....
Springfield	Dorchester, South	Elgin, E. R. ....**O**	W. H. Graves ....

NAME OF POST OFFICE.	TOWNSHIP OR PARISH.	ELECTORAL COUNTY OR DIVISION.	NAME OF POSTMASTER.
Springfield		Lisgar **M**	W. R. Dick
Springfield		King's **N B**	A. Fairweather
Springfield, W. O		York **N B**	Jessie Clarke
Springfield, W. O		Annapolis **N S**	G. Grimm
Springfield	No. 67	Queen's **P E I**	Richard P. Bagnall
Springford	Norwich, South	Oxford, S. R. **O**	Hy. Henderson
Spring Hill, W. O		Cumberland **N S**	J. Hewitt
Spring Hill Mines, W. O.		Cumberland **N S**	H. S. Ross
Springvale	Walpole	Haldimand **O**	Joseph Anderson
Springville	North Monaghan	Peterboro', W. R. **O**	A. Goodfellow
Springville, W. O.		Pictou **N S**	Peter Grant
Spruce Lake, W. O		St. John **N B**	John Kelly
Spry Bay, W. O.		Halifax **N S**	Henry Leslie
Staffa	Hibbert	Perth, S. R. **O**	James Hamilton
Stafford	Stafford	Renfrew, N. R. **O**	Robert Childerhose
Stamford	Stamford	Welland **O**	Mrs. Phebe A. Correl
Stanbridge, East	Stanbridge	Missisquoi **Q**	J. M. Jones
Stanbridge Ridge	Stanbridge	Missisquoi **Q**	Noble Martindale
Stanbridge Station	Stanbridge	Missisquoi **Q**	Benjamin Selby
Stanbury	Stanbridge	Missisquoi **Q**	Porter Beattie
Standon	Standon	Dorchester **Q**	
Stanfold	St. Eusèbe	Arthabaska **Q**	James Huston
Stanhope	Barnston	Stanstead **Q**	David Young
Stanley, W. O.		York **N B**	William Plant
Stanley Bridge	Number 21	Queen's **P E I**	Alex. McMillan
Stanley's Mills	Chinguacousy	Peel **O**	C. Burrell
**Stanstead*	Stanstead	Stanstead **Q**	B. F. Hubbard
Stanton	Mulmur	Simcoe, S. R. **O**	Wm. [illegible]. Beatty
Starkey's, W. O		Queen's **N B**	S. M. Starkey
Starnesboro'	St. Antoine Abbé	Huntingdon **Q**	C. Meunier
**Stayner*	Nottawassaga	Simcoe, N. R. **O**	James H. McKeggie
Steam Mill Village, W. O		King's **N S**	H. Patterson
Steele	Oro	Simcoe, N. R. **O**	John C. Steele

NAME OF POST OFFICE.	TOWNSHIP OR PARISH.	ELECTORAL COUNTY OR DIVISION.	NAME OF POSTMASTER.
Steep Creek, W. O.		Guysboro' N S	John McGuire
Steeve's Mountain, W. O.		Westmoreland N B	Amos Wilson
Stella	Amherst	Lennox O	George Wright
Steeve's Settlement, W. O.		Westmoreland N B	W. E. Fowler
Stellarton		Pictou N S	H. McKenzie
Stevensville	Bertie	Welland O	Wm. T. House
Stewartville	McNab	Renfrew, S. R. O	Alexander Duff
Stewiacke Cross Roads, W. O.		Colchester N S	F. Creelman
Still Water, W. O		Guysboro' N S	W. C. Elliot
**Stirling*	Rawdon	Hastings, N. R. O	Mrs. Agnes Judd
Stirton	Peel	Wellington, C. R. O	Joseph Sauderson
Stittsville	Goulburn	Carleton O	J. S. Argue
Stockdale	Murray	Northumberland, E. R. O	
Stockwell	St. Antoine Abbé	Chateauguay Q	M. Patenoude
Stoco	Hungerford	Hastings, E. R. O	Patrick Murphy.
Stoddart's, W. O.		Annapolis N S	John Stoddart
Stoke Centre	Stoke	Richmond Q	Anthony Byron
Stoketon	Stoke	Richmond Q	Asa Hall
Stonefield	Chatham	Argenteuil Q	William Owens
Stoneham	Stoneham	Quebec Q	William Corrigan
Stoneleigh	Macaulay	Muskoka O	Charles Piper, sen
Stony Creek	Saltfleet	Wentworth, S. R. O	Alva G. Jones
Stony Creek, W. O.		Albert N B	John Scott
Stony Lake	Dummer	Peterboro', E. R. O	James Robb
Stony Point	Tilbury, West	Essex O	H. Desjardins
Stormont, W. O.		Guysborough N S	Thomas F. Milward
Stornoway	Winslow	Compton Q	Colin Noble
Stottville	St. Valentin	St. John's Q	Daniel Salt
**Stouffville*	Whitchurch	York, N. R. O	Edward Wheler
Stowe	Grey	Huron, C. R. O	Robert Ferguson
Strabane	Flamborough, West	Wentworth, N. R. O	Matthew Peebles
Straffordville	Bayham	Elgin, E R. O	R. W. Smuck

NAME OF POST OFFICE.	TOWNSHIP OR PARISH.	ELECTORAL COUNTY OR DIVISION.	NAME OF POSTMASTER.
**Stratford*	South Easthope	Perth, N. R. **O**	L. T. O'Loane
Strathallan	East Zorra	Oxford, N. R. **O**	Miss S. J. Lappin
Strathburn	Mosa	Middlesex, W. R. **O**	Hugh McRae
Strathnairn	St. Vincent	Grey, E. R. **O**	Joseph Inglis
**Strathroy*	Adelaide	Middlesex, W. R. **O**	H. B. Macintosh
Street's Ridge, W. O.		Cumberland **N S**	Jeremiah Gehan
**Streetville*	Toronto	Peel **O**	Robert Graydon
Stromness	Sherbrooke	Monck **O**	Albert Benson
Stronach Mountain, W. O.		Annapolis **N S**	George Stronach
Stroud	Innisfil	Simcoe, S. R. **O**	Thomas Webb
Sturgeon	No. 61	King's **P E I**	R. A. Thornton
Stymast Settlement, W. O.		Northumberland **N B**	John Stymast
Suffolk Road	No. 34	Queen's **P E I**	W. W. Duck
Sugar Loaf, W. O		Victoria **N S**	George Wilkie
Sullivan	Holland	Grey, N. R. **O**	William Buchanan
Sumas		New Westminster **B C**	David W. Miller
Summer Hill, W. O.		Queen's **N B**	James Kerr
Summerside		Prince **P E I**	H. C. Green
Summerstown	Charlottenburg	Glengarry **O**	Andrew J. Baker
Summerville	Toronto	Peel **O**	Bernard Morris
Summerville, W. O.		Pictou **N S**	C. McDonald
Summerville	No. 51	King's **P E I**	N. Edmonds
Summerville, W. O.		Hants **N S**	Mrs. S. Sandford
Sunbury	Storrington	Frontenac **O**	John McBride
Sunderland	Brock	Ontario, N. R. **O**	John Jones
Sunnidale	Sunnidale	Simcoe, N. R. **O**	Alexander Gillespie
Sunshine	Morris	Huron, N. R. **O**	W. F. Cornell
Sussex Corner, W. O.		King's **N B**	John A. Humphreys
Sussex Portage, W. O.		King's **N B**	William S. Teakles
Sussex Vale		King's **N B**	
Sutherland's Corners	Euphemia	Bothwell **O**	James W. McKeown
Sutherland's Mills, W. O.		Pictou **N S**	R. Chisholm

NAME OF POST OFFICE.	TOWNSHIP OR PARISH.	ELECTORAL COUNTY OR DIVISION.	NAME OF POSTMASTER.
Sutherland's River, W. O.		Pictou N S	D. Rankin
Sutton	Sutton	Brome Q	G. C. Dyer
Swan Creek, W. O		Sunbury N B	H. A. Eastabrook
Sweaburg	West Oxford	Oxford, S. R. O	H. Flood
Sweetsburg	Dunham	Missisquoi Q	Curtis S. Boright
Switzerville	Ernestown	Lennox O	Peter E. R. Miller
Sydenham Mills	Sydenham	Grey, N. R. O	C. H. Heming
Sydenham Place	Kingsey	Drummond Q	Mrs. C. Blake
Sydney		Cape Breton N S	Robert Martin
Sydney Forks, W. O		Cape Breton N S	Charles Tobin
Sydney Mines		Cape Breton N S	Miss H. F. Rigby
Sylvan	Williams, West	Middlesex, N. R. O	John Dawson
Sypher's Cove, W. O		Queen's N B	Jacob Syphers
Tabucintac, W. O		Northumberland N B	Horatio Lee
Tadousac	Tadousac	Saguenay Q	Josepeh Radford
Talbotville Royal	Southwold	Elgin, W. R. O	John Stacey
Tamworth	Sheffield	Addington O	James Aylesworth
Tancook Island, W.O.		Lunenburg N S	Henry Hutt
Tangier		Halifax N S	John M. Forest
Tannery, West	Montreal	Hochelaga Q	Ferdinand Faure
Tapleytown	Saltfleet	Wentworth, S. R. O	S. G. Harris
Tara	Arran	Bruce N. R. O	John Tobey
Tarbert	Luther	Wellington, N. R. O	M. McMurchy
Tatamagouche		Colchester N S	Robert Purves, jun.
Tatamagouche Mountain, W. O		Colchester N S	John Drysdale
T		[illegible] O	Peter Guthrie

NAME OF POST OFFICE.	TOWNSHIP OR PARISH.	ELECTORAL COUNTY OR DIVISION.	NAME OF POSTMASTER.
Taunton	Whitby	Ontario, S. R. **O**	Wm. Willard
Tavistock	South Easthope	Perth, S. R. **O**	George Matheson
Taylor Village, W. O.		Westmoreland **N B**	Charles Taylor
Tay Mills, W. O.		York **N B**	Stephen Boon
Tay Settlement, W. O.		York **N B**	Wm. Tomlinson
Tecumseth	Tecumseth	Simcoe, S.R. **O**	D. A. Jones
Tedish, W. O.		Westmoreland **N B**	George E. Mills
**Teeswater*	Culross	Bruce, S. R. **O**	Samuel Waldo
Teeterville	Windham	Norfolk, N. R. **O**	Wm. Robinson
Telfer	London	Middlesex, E. R. **O**	
Temperance Vale, W. O.		York **N B**	Richard R. Carvell
Temperanceville	King	York, N. R. **O**	David Johnston
Templeton	Templeton	Ottawa **Q**	James Hagan
Tempo	Westminster	Middlesex, E. R. **O**	A. Remey
Tenecape, W. O.		Hants **N S**	Wm. Stephens
Ten Mile Creek, W O.		St. John **N B**	John S. Parker
Tennant's Cove, W. O.		King's **N B**	James G. Worden
T[illegible]	Drummond	Lanark, S. R. **O**	D. McGregor
Terence Bay, W. O.		Halifax **N S**	J. W. Shaumwhite
Terr bonne	Terrebonne	Terrebonne **Q**	Arthur M. McKenzie
Tessierville	Matane	Rimouski **Q**	Hermyle Parent
Teston	Vaughan	York, W. R. **O**	George Wilson
Teviotdale	Minto	Wellington, N. R. **O**	M. G. Miller
Teviotdale Station, W. O		Colchester **N S**	G. H. Hamilton
Thamesford	Nissouri, East	Oxford, N. R. **O**	N. C. McCarty
Thamesville	Camden	Bothwell **O**	James Duncan
Thanet	Wollaston	Hastings, N. R. **O**	
The Range, W. O.		Queen's **N B**	Robert Snell
Thiers	Thetford	Megantic **Q**	Joachim Delisle
Thistletown	Etobicoke	York, W. R. **O**	Richard Johnston
Thomasburg	Hungerford	Hastings, E. R. **O**	John Robertson
Thompsonville	Tecumseth	Simcoe, S. R. **O**	J. T. Schmietendorf
Thompson's Mills			

NAME OF POST OFFICE.	TOWNSHIP OR PARISH.	ELECTORAL COUNTY OR DIVISION.		NAME OF POSTMASTER.
Thornbrook, W. O.		King's	N B	David A. Wright
Thornbury	Collingwood	Grey, E. R.	O	Thomas McKenny
Thornby	Thorne	Pontiac	Q	Joseph Hill
Thorndale	Nissouri, West	Middlesex, E. R.	O	Thomas Harrison
Thorne Centre	Thorne	Pontiac	Q	C. A. Smith
Thornetown, W. O.		Queen's	N B	Butler Thorne
Thornhill	Vaughan	York, W. R.	O	Josiah Purkiss
Thornton	Innisfil	Simcoe, S. R.	O	John Scott
**Thorold*	Thorold	Welland	O	Edwin Keefer
Three Brooks, W. O.		Victoria	N B	John Edgar
**Three Rivers*	Three Rivers	Three Rivers	Q	C. K. Ogden
Three Sisters, W. O.		Cumberland	N S	
Thunder Bay		Algoma	O	Chas. W. Blackwood
**Thurso*	Lochabar	Ottawa	Q	George Edwards
Tichborne	Bedford	Addington	O	Norman Clark
Tidnish, W. O.		Cumberland	N S	Oliver King
Tidnish Bridge, W. O.		Westmoreland	N B	William Davidson
Tignish	No. 1	Prince	P E I	R. M. Carroll
Tilbury, East	Tilbury, East	Kent	O	James Smith
**Tilsonburg*	Dereham	Oxford, S. R.	O	E. D. Tillson
Tilton	Seymour	Northumberland, E. R.	O	George Gibson
Tintern	Clinton	Lincoln	O	Benoni Crumb
Titusville, W. O.		King's	N B	Alexander Simpson
Tiverton	Kincardine	Bruce, S. R.	O	N. McInnes
Toledo	Kitley	Leeds, N. R.	O	Mrs. C. A. McLean
Toney River, W. O.		Pictou	N S	Alexander Fraser
Topping	North Easthope	Perth, N. R.	O	S. Crosier
Torbay, W. O.		Guysboro'	N S	William Webber
Torbrook, W. O.		Annapolis	N S	John H. Banks
Toronto Gore	Toronto Gore	Peel	O	Thomas Shuttleworth
**Toronto*	York	Toronto	O	Joseph Leslie
Tottenham	Tecumseth	Simcoe, S. R.	O	S. E. Turner
Tower Hill, W. O.		Charlotte	N B	John Irons
Tow[illegible]	[illegible]	[illegible]	O	Israel Slaght

NAME OF POST OFFICE.	TOWNSHIP OR PARISH.	ELECTORAL COUNTY OR DIVISION.	NAME OF POSTMASTER.
Tracadie		Gloucester ... N B	Miss Harriet Dumaresque.
Tracadie		Antigonishe ... N S	H. H. Harrington
Tracadie Cross	Number 36	Queen's ... P E I	Augustus Johnson
Tracey's Mills, W. O.		Carleton ... N B	Isaac Adams
Tracey Station, W. O.		Sunbury ... N B	D. S. Duplisea
Trafalgar	Trafalgar	Halton ... O	James Applebe
Trafalgar, W. O.		Halifax ... N S	John Nelson
Tramore	Hagarty	Renfrew, N. R. ... O	Peter Foy
Traverston	Glenelg	Grey, S. R. ... O	John Travers
Traveller's Rest	Number 19	Prince ... P E I	J. Townsend
Treadwell	Plantagenet, North	Prescott ... O	James McGauvran
Trecastle	Wallace	Perth, N. R. ... O	Daniel McCaughrin
Tremblay	Tremblay	Chicoutimi ... Q	Marcel Coté
Trenholm	Kingsey	Drummond ... Q	Simon Stevens
Trent Bridge	Seymour	Northumberland, E. R. ... O	Francis E. Lee
**Trenton*	Sydney	Hastings, W. R ... O	James B. Christie
Trois Pistoles	Trois Pistoles	Témiscouata ... Q	T. P. Pelletier
Trois Saumons	St. Jean Port Joli	L'Islet ... Q	G. C. Caron
Trout Brook	Tingwisk	Arthabaska ... Q	John C. Stevens
Trout Cove, W. O.		Digby ... N S	Mrs M. J. Moorehouse
Trout Lake	Humphrey	Muskoka ... O	George Elliot
Trout River	Godmanchester	Huntingdon ... Q	James Marshall
Trowbridge	Elma	Perth, N. R. ... O	G. Code
Troy	Beverley	Wentworth, N. R. ... O	John R. Neff
Trudell	Tilbury, West	Essex ... O	Henry Richardson
Truro		Colchester ... N S	Wm. McCully
Tryon	Number 28	Prince ... P E I	J. B. Laird
Tuam	Tecumseth	Simcoe, S. R. ... O	P. H. Derham
Tullamore	Chinguacousy	Peel ... O	George Dodds
Tupperville, W. O.		Annapolis ... N S	W. F. Willett
Turtle Creek, W. O.		Albert ... N B	Solomon Berry
Turtle Lake	Humphrey	Muskoka ... O	Alexander Ross
Tuscarora	Onondaga	Brant, N. R ... O	Dennis L. Dennis.
Tusket			

NAME OF POST OFFICE.	TOWNSHIP OR PARISH.	ELECTORAL COUNTY OR DIVISION.	NAME OF POSTMASTER.
Tusket Forks, W. O.		Yarmouth ... N S	Simeon Gardner
Tusket Wedge, W. O.		Yarmouth ... N S	M. Le Blanc
**Tweed*	Hungerford	Hastings, E. R. ... O	James Reid
Tweedside	Saltfleet	Wentworth, S. R. ... O	T. Stewart Johnson
Tweedside, W. O.		York ... N B	John Rutherford
Tyne Valley	Number 13	Prince ... P E I	Allan McLean
Tyneside	Seneca	Haldimand ... O	William Geo. Hassard
Tyrconnell	Dunwich	Elgin, W. R. ... O	Samuel Harris
Tyrone	Darlington	Durham, W. R. ... O	John T. Welsh
Tyrrell	Townsend	Norfolk, N. R. ... O	Samuel Heath
Udora	Scott	Ontario, N. R. ... O	S. Umphrey
Uffington	Draper	Muskoka ... O	John Doherty
Ufford	Watt	Muskoka ... O	H. W. Gill
Ullin		Algoma ... O	Thos. L. Hilborn
Ullswater	Watt	Muskoka ... O	George Bunn
Ulster	Wawanosh	Huron, N. R. ... O	John W. Mowbray
Ulverton	Durham	Drummond ... Q	James Miller
Umfraville	Dungannon	Hastings, N. R. ... O	D. Kavanagh
Underwood	Bruce	Bruce, N. R. ... O	Donald Cameron
Undine, W. O.		Victoria ... N B	Alex. L. Watson
Union	Yarmouth	Elgin, E. R. ... O	James McKenzie
Union Corner, W. O.		Carleton ... N B	David S. Carpenter
Union Hill	London	Middlesex, E. R. ... O	

NAME OF POST OFFICE.	TOWNSHIP OR PARISH.	ELECTORAL COUNTY OR DIVISION.	NAME OF POSTMASTER.
Upper Bay du Vin, W. O.		Northumberland ...... N B	William Dickens .....
Upper Bedford	Stanbridge........	Missisquoi .... Q	N. C. Martin ....
Upper Branch, W. O...		Lunenburg .... N S	A. Knack ....
Upper Buctouche, W. O.		Kent .... N B	Samuel Jerway. ......
Upper Caledonia, W. O.		Halifax .... N S	J. D. Cameron ....
Upper Cape, W. O. ...		Westmoreland .... N B	Alfred Raworth ....
Upper Caraquet, W.O.		Gloucester............... N B	S. Cormier ....
Upper Caverhill, W. O.		York .... N B	G. W. Knox ....
Upper Clyde River, W. O.		Shelburne .... N S	Jesse Bowers...........
Upper Cross Roads, St. Mary's, W. O....		Guysborough........... N S	J. A. Jordan ....
Upper Dyke Village, W. O.		King's..................... N S	A. Beckwith ....
Upper Economy, W. O.		Colchester .... N S	J. L. Moore ....
Upper Gagetown, W. O.		Queen's .... N B	Thomas Crothers .....
Upper Gaspereaux.....		Queen's .... N B	Isaac C. Burpee .....
Upper Greenwich, W. O.		King's .... N B	Henry Walton ....
Upper Hampstead, W. O.		Queen's .... N B	E. M. Dickie ....
Upper Hayneville		York .... N B	
Upper Kennetcook, W. O.		Hants .... N S	Jacob Hannegar........
Upper Kent, W. O ...		Carleton. .... N B	A. Hawthorn...........
Upper Keswick, W. O.		York .... N B	James E. Smith ....
Upper Keswick Ridge, W. O.		York .... N B	Thomas Coburn ....
Upper La Have, W.O.		Lunenburg............... N S	Josiah Rudolf ......
Upper Loch Lomond, W. O.		St. John .... N B	
Upper Magaguadavic, W. O.		York .... N B	Andrew Ray ....
Upper Margaret, W. O.		Inverness................ N S	John McLennan .....
Upper Maugerville, W. O.		[illegible]	[illegible] Shields

NAME OF POST OFFICE.	TOWNSHIP OR PARISH.	ELECTORAL COUNTY OR DIVISION.	NAME OF POSTMASTER.
Upper Mills		Charlotte N B	Alice M. Morrison
Upper Musquodoboit		Halifax N S	S. L. Henry
Upper Neguac, W. O.		Northumberland N B	Vital Alaine
Upper New Horton, W. O.		Albert N B	Minor Reid
Upper Newport, W. O.		Hants N S	John Davison
Upper Peel, W. O.		Carleton N B	W. B. Tomkins
Upper Pere[illegible]x, W. O.		King's N S	J. L. Newcomb
Upper Queensbury, W. O.		York N B	D. C. Parent
Upper Rawdon, W. O.		Hants N S	Wm. Marsters
Upper St. Bazil		Victoria N B	H. Gagnon
Upper St. Francois, W. O		Victoria N B	Richard Tobin
Upper Sackville, W. O.		Westmoreland N B	Arthur G. Chase
Upper Settlement of Baddeck River, W. O		Victoria N S	Donald McMillan
Upper Settlement of Barney's River, W. O		Pictou N S	John McKay
Upper Settlement of Middle River, W. O		Victoria N S	John McLennan
Upper Settlement of River Dennis, W. O.		Inverness N S	Michael McDonald
Upper Settlement of South River, W. O.		Antigonishe N S	C. A. Cameron.
Upper Settlement of West River, W. O.		Pictou N S	Donald Livingstone
Upper Sheffield, W. O.		Sunbury N B	W. A. Garrison
Upper Southampton, W. O.		York N B	
Upper Stewiacke		Colchester N S	Francis Cox
Upper Wakefield	Wakefield	Ottawa Q	Patrick Farrell
Upper Washabuck, W. O.		Victoria N S	Angus McDonald
Upper Wicklow, W. O.		Carleton N B	Matthew Hutchinson
Upper Wood Harbour, W. O.		Shelburne N S	W. H. Matheson
Upper Woodstock, W. O.		Carleton N B	Wm. H. Sisson
Upsalquitch, W. O.		Restigouche N B	George Crosswell
Uptergrove	Mara	Ontario, N. R. O	Thomas Byrne

NAME OF POST OFFICE.	TOWNSHIP OR PARISH.	ELECTORAL COUNTY OR DIVISION.	NAME OF POSTMASTER.
Urbania, W. O.	Maitland	Hants **N S**	Alexander Cameron
Urquharts, W. O.		Kings **N B**	Nathaniel Urquhart
Usher, W. O.		Antigonishe **N S**	Richard Carroll
Utica	Reach	Ontario, N. R. **O**	Jacob Dafoe
Utopia	Essa	Simcoe, S. R. **O**	Thomas Dawson
Utterson	Stephenson	Muskoka **O**	Erastus Hanes
Uttoxeter	Plympton	Lambton **O**	S. Shepherd
**Uxbridge*	Uxbridge	Ontario, N. R. **O**	George Wheeler
Vachell	Georgina	York, N. R. **O**	Robert McClellan
Vallancourt	Dionne	L'Islet **Q**	W. F. Vaillancourt
Valcartier	Valcartier	Quebec **Q**	Charles S. Wolff
Valcourt	South Ely	Shefford **Q**	F. X. David
Vale Colliery, W. O.		Pictou **N S**	Charles McKinnon
Valentia	Mariposa	Victoria, S. R. **O**	Wm. Hobbs
Valetta	Tilbury, East	Kent **O**	J. Richardson
Vallentyne	Brock	Ontario, N. R. **O**	Samuel Brethour
Valletort	Aylmer	Beauce **Q**	Louis Paradis, jun.
**Valleyfield*	Beauharnois	Beauharnois **Q**	Marc C. Despocas
Valleyfield	Number 59	King's **P E I**	Alexander McLeod
Valmont	Notre Dame de Mont Carmel	Champlain **Q**	Pierre Bédard
Vanatter	Garafraxa	Wellington, C. R. **O**	J. C. Reid
Vanbrugh	Sebastopol	Renfrew, S. R. **O**	C. F. Holterman
Vandecar	Oxford, East	Oxford, S. R. **O**	W. J. Davis
Vandeleur	Artemesia	Grey, E. R **O**	
**Vankleek Hill*	Hawkesbury, West	Prescott **O**	Duncan McDonnell
Vanneck	London	Midd[illegible]	[illegible]

NAME OF POST OFFICE.	TOWNSHIP OR PARISH.	ELECTORAL COUNTY OR DIVISION.	NAME OF POSTMASTER.
Vanvlack	Flos	Simcoe, N. R. **O**	John Vanvlack
Van Winkle		Cariboo **B C**	Julius L. Lindhard
Varennes	Varennes	Verchères **Q**	Joseph T. L. Archambeault
Varna	Stanley	Huron, S. R. **O**	Josiah B. Secord
Varney	Normanby	Grey, S. R. **O**	Francis Eden
Vasey	Tay	Simcoe, N. R. **O**	Benjamin Mackie
Vauban	Armand	Temiscouata **Q**	Alexis Morin
Vaudreuil	Vaudreuil	Vaudreuil **Q**	Dieudonné Brulé
Vaughan's, W. O.		Hants **N S**	Joseph Vaughan
Veighton	Cumberland	Russell **O**	James Lowrie
Vellore	Vaughan	York, W. R. **O**	John MacDonald
Venice	St. George	Missisquoi **Q**	Thomas Hunter
Vennachar	Abinger	Addington **O**	William Hames
Venesta	Low	Ottawa **O**	John Macauley
Ventnor	Edwardsburg	Grenville, S. R. **O**	John McAulay
Ventry	Proton	Grey, E. R **O**	Carby Johnson
Verchères	Verchères	Verchères **Q**	Treffié Lussier
Verdun	Huron	Bruce, S. R. **O**	J. Colling
Vereker	Colchester	Essex **O**	Tancred Caya
Vernal, W. O.		Antigonishe **N S**	Angus Power
Vernon	Osgoode	Russell **O**	Duncan McDonald
Vernon Mines, W. O.		King's **N S**	John R. Ilsley
Vernon River	Number 49	Queen's **P E I**	George O'Neill
Vornon River Bridge	Number 50	Queen's **P E I**	George Forbes
Vernonville	Haldimand	Northumberland, W. R. **O**	John G. Boyd
Verona	Portland	Addington **O**	Alexander Grant
Versailles	St. Grégoire	Iberville **Q**	Isidore Marcoux
Verschoyle	Dereham	Oxford, S. R. **O**	George Chambers
Vesta	Brant	Bruce, S. R. **O**	Robert Cannon
Vicars	Havelock	Huntingdon **Q**	James Wilson
Victoria		Victoria **B C**	Henry Wootton
Victoria, W. O.		Carleton **N B**	George R. Boyer
Victoria, W. O.		Cumberland **N S**	J. M. Henny

NAME OF POST OFFICE.	TOWNSHIP OR PARISH.	ELECTORAL COUNTY OR DIVISION.	NAME OF POSTMASTER.
Victoria Cross	Number 51..............	King's ....P E I	A. R. McQueen........
Victoria Corners.	Reach	Ontario, N. R.............O	Andrew St. John ....
Victoria Harbor, W.O	....	King's......................N S	John Brown ....
Victoria Harbor........	Tay	Simcoe, N. R. ....O	John Kean.... ....
Victoria Mines, W O...	....	Cape Breton ....N S	....
Victoria Road Station	Carden	Victoria, N. R. ....O	Michael Heapy.........
Victoria Square	Markham	York, E. R............. ....O	Robert P. Hopper......
* *Vienna*	Bayham	Elgin, E. R. ....O	Samuel Brasher... ....
Viger	Viger	Témiscouata ....Q	Virginie Gagne.........
Viger Mines	Chester	Arthabaska .... Q	Guillaume Lamothe...
Vigo	Flos	Simcoe, N. R. .... O	Dennis Gallagher .....
* *Village des Aulnaies*..	St. Roch des Aulnaies..	L'Islet.... ....Q	A. Dupuis ....
Village Richelieu......	St. Mathias..............	Rouville ....Q	N. D. D. Bessette......
Villanova	Townsend	Norfolk, N. R......... .....O	George Lemon..........
Villette	Hereford	Compton....................Q	Farrell McConney .....
Villiers	Otonabee	Peterborough..... ....O	W. Brotherston, sen...
Vincennes	St. Luc	Champlain ....Q	P. Lacourcière ....
Vine	Innisfil	Simcoe, S. R................O	James Goodfellow .....
Vinoy	Suffolk	Ottawa .. ..Q	Joseph Leduc...........
Vinton..................	Litchfield..	Pontiac .... Q	William Gilchrist .....
Violet	Ernestown	Lennox ....O	W. A. Rockwell.........
Virgil	Niagara	Niagara ....O	James S. Clement. ....
Virginia	Georgina	York, N. R. ....O	John Doyle ....
* *Vittoria*.........	Charlotteville	Norfolk, S. R. ....O	George D. McCall......
Vivian	Witchurch	York, N. R. .... O	Robert McCormick ...
Vogler's Cove, W. O...	....	Lunenburg ....N S	J. H. R. Fayle ....
Vroomanton	Brock	Ontario, N. R. ....O	John Tesky..............
Vyner	Sarnia........	Lambton.....................O	John Gates..... ....

NAME OF POST OFFICE.	TOWNSHIP OR PARISH.	ELECTORAL COUNTY OR DIVISION.	NAME OF POSTMASTER.
Waasis Station, W. O.		Sunbury N B	George Grass
Wabashene	Tay	Simcoe, N. R. O	T. W. Buck
Wagram	Arthur	Wellington, N. R. O	James Craig
Wakefield	Wakefield	Ottawa Q	James McLaren
Waldemar	Amaranth	Wellington, N. R. O	David Jenkins
Wales	Osnabruck	Stormont O	William Baker
* *Walkerton*	Brant	Bruce, S. R. O	Malcolm McLean
Walkerville	Sandwich, East	Essex O	Henry McAfee
Wallace	Wallace	Perth, N. R. O	James Taggart
Wallace		Cumberland N S	B. S. Seaman
Wallace Bridge, W. O.		Cumberland N S	Richard J. Scott
* *Wallaceburg*	Chatham	Kent O	Lionel H. Johnson
Wallace Ridge, W. O.		Cumberland N S	John McNiel
a Wallace River, W. O.		Cumberland N S	Lemuel Bigney
Wallacetown	Dunwich	Elgin, W. R. O	A. E. S. K. Barclay
Wallbridge	Sidney	Hastings, W. R. O	F. B. Prior
Wallenstein	Wellesley	Waterloo, N. R. O	Henry Powell
Walmer	East Zorra	Oxford, N. R. O	
Walsh	Charlotteville	Norfolk, S. R. O	D. W. McCall
Walter's Falls	Holland	Grey, N. R O	Thomas P. Walker
Waltham	Waltham	Pontiac Q	John Landon
Walton	Mckillop	Huron, C. R. O	Robert Pattison
Walton		Hants N S	J. W. Stephens
Wanstead	Plympton	Lambton O	Maurice McVicar
Warburton	Lansdown	Leeds, S. R. O	J. H. Keating
Warden	Shefford	Shefford Q	
Ward's Creek Road, W. O.		King's N B	A. Stapleford
* *Wardsville*	Mosa	Middlesex, W. R. O	W. D. Hammond
Wareham	Osprey	Grey, E. R. O	George Wright
Warkworth	Percy	Northumberland, E. R. O	Israel Humphries
Warminster	Medonte	Simcoe, N. R. O	W. George Deacon
Warner	Caistor	Monck O	Jonas R. Mellick
Warren, W. O.	...	Cumberland N S	C. S. Chapman
W[illegible]	D[illegible]	[illegible]borough, E. R. O	Thomas Choat

NAME OF POST OFFICE.	TOWNSHIP OR PARISH.	ELECTORAL COUNTY OR DIVISION.	NAME OF POSTMASTER.
Wartburg	Ellice	Perth, N. R. O	E. Frommhagen
Warwick, East	St. Medard	Arthabaska Q	Louis Triganne
Warwick, West	Warwick	Lambton O	John H. Morris
Washago	Orillia	Simcoe, N. R. O	Abial Marshall
Washburn	Pittsburgh	Frontenac O	John McGillivray
Washington	Blenheim	Oxford, N. R. O	William Dunn
Waterborough, W. O.		Queen's N B	C. H. Fanjoy
* *Waterdown*	Flamboro', East	Wentworth, N. R. O	James B. Thompson
* *Waterford*	Townsend	Norfolk, N. R. O	David Wilson
* *Waterloo, East*	Shefford	Shefford Q	Gardner Stevens
* *Waterloo, West*	Waterloo, North	Waterloo, N. R. O	C. Kumpf
Waterside, W. O.		Albert N B	George Coonan
Waterville	Compton	Compton Q	L. W. Wyman
Waterville, W. O.		Carleton N B	Charles J. Laskey
a Waterville		King's N S	J. P. Pineo
Watford	Warwick	Lambton O	Murdo McLeay
Watson's Corners	Dalhousie	Lanark, N. R. O	John Munro
Watson Settlement, W. O.		Carleton N B	John Watson
Waubamik	McDougal	Muskoka O	Robert Reid
Waubuno	Moore	Lambton O	Thomas Moore
Waugh's River, W.O.		Colchester N S	J. Murphy
Waupoos	Marysburg	Prince Edward O	James Kerr
Waverley	Tay	Simcoe, N. R. O	John Bannister
Waverley		Halifax N S	John Lingley
Waweig, W. O.		Charlotte N B	
Way's Mills	Barnston	Stanstead Q	E. S. Southmayd
Weaver Settlement, W. O.		Digby N S	Michael Weaver

NAME OF POST OFFICE.	TOWNSHIP OR PARISH.	ELECTORAL COUNTY OR DIVISION.	NAME OF POSTMASTER.
* *Wellesley*	Wellesley	Waterloo, N. R. **O**	John Zoeger
Wellington	Number 16	Prince **P E I**	Patrick Ayers
Wellington	Hillier	Prince Edward **O**	Donald Campbell
Wellington, W. O		Albert **N B**	William Beatty
* *Wellington, Square*	Nelson	Halton **O**	Walter S. Bastedo
Wellington, W. O		Yarmouth **N S**	Jacob Landers
Wellman's Corners	Rawdon	Hastings, N. R **O**	David N. Ostrander
Welsford		Queen's **N B**	
Wendover	Plantagenet, N	Prescott **O**	William Lamb.
*a*Wentworth, W. O		Cumberland **N S**	David Purdy
West Arichat, W. O		Richmond **N S**	Gilbert Paon
West Arran	Saugeen	Bruce, N. R **O**	Miss A. Patterson
West Bay		Inverness **N S**	James McDonald
West Bolton	Bolton	Brome **Q**	Martin Duboyce
Westbourne	Portage la Prairie	Marquette **M**	Peter Garrioch
West Branch, East River of Pictou, W. O		Pictou **N S**	William Dunbar
West Branch Nicholas River, W. O		Kent **N B**	T. Curran
West Branch River John, W. O		Pictou **N S**	Mrs. J. McKay
West Branch, River Philip, W. O		Colchester **N S**	R. F. Black
West Brome	Brome	Brome **Q**	Luther Scott
West Brook	Kingston	Frontenac **O**	Andrew Bridge
West Brook, W. O		Cumberland **N S**	Henry Jeffers
West Broughton	Broughton	Beauce **Q**	Cyrille Vallée
Westbury	Westbury	Compton **Q**	Allan Lothrop
West Cape	Number 7	Prince **P E I**	A. McWilliams
West Chester, W. O		Cumberland **N S**	Mrs. Mary J Purdy
West Chester Lake, W. O		Cumberland **N S**	Mrs. N. Pequignot
Westcock, W. O		Westmoreland **N B**	James E. Evans
West Ditton	Ditton	Compton **O**	Pierre Gendreau
West Dublin, W. O		Lunenburg **N S**	R. B. Currie
Western Covehead	Number 33	Queen's **P E I**	J. K. Beariste

NAME OF POST OFFICE.	TOWNSHIP OR PARISH.	ELECTORAL COUNTY OR DIVISION.	NAME OF POSTMASTER.
Western Road	Number 6	Prince ... P E I	J. McNaught
West Essa	Essa	Simcoe, S. R. ... O	David Henderson
* *West Farnham*	Farnham	Missisquoi ... Q	E. Donahue
Westfield	Wawanosh, East	Huron, N. R. ... O	Mrs. Helps
Westfield, W. O.		King's ... N B	N. H. Deveber
West Flamboro	Flamboro', W.	Wentworth, N. R. ... O	J. B. Irving
West Glassville, W. O.		Carleton ... N B	J. R. Roland
West Gore, W. O.		Hants ... N S	M. Wallace
West Huntingdon	Huntingdon	Hastings, N. R. ... O	James Gay
West Huntley	Huntley	Carleton ... O	Edward Horan
West Lake	Hallowell	Prince Edward ... O	Henry Lambert
West Lorne	Aldborough	Elgin, W. R. ... O	Duncan McKillop
West Lynne	St. Agathe	Provencher ... M	F. F. Bradley
West McGillivray	McGillivray	Middlesex, N. R. ... O	[illegible]
West Magdala	Southwold	Elgin, W. R. ... O	Donald Turner
Westmeath	Westmeath	Renfrew, N. R. ... O	Alexander Fraser
West Merigonish, W. O.		Pictou ... N S	James McDonald
West Montrose	Woolwich	Waterloo, N. R. ... O	Noah Bowman
Westmoreland Point		Westmoreland ... N B	Thos. E. Oulton
West Newdy Quoddy, W. O.		Halifax ... N S	Michael O'Leary
* *Weston*	York	York, W. R. ... O	Robert Johnston
West Osgoode	Osgoode	Russell ... O	Hugh Cleland
Westover	Beverley	Wentworth, N. R. ... O	B. McIntosh
Westport	North Crosby	Leeds, S. R. ... O	John H. Whelan
Westport		Digby ... N S	Benjamin H. Ruggles
West Point	Number 8	Prince ... P E I	Angus [illegible]
West Potton	Potton	Brome ... Q	[illegible]

NAME OF POST OFFICE.	TOWNSHIP OR PARISH.	ELECTORAL COUNTY OR DIVISION.	NAME OF POSTMASTER.
West Side of Middle River, W. O.		Victoria N S	Hector Campbell
Westville		Pictou N S	Duncan Balfour
* *West Winchester*	Winchester	Dundas O	William [illegible]
Westwood	Asphodel	Peterborough, E. R. O	Cristopher Lancaster
Wexford	Scarboro'	York, E. R. O	J. T. McBeath
Weymouth		Digby N S	Cereno D. Jones
Weymouth Bridge		Digby N S	Jasper Journeay
Whalen	Biddulph	Middlesex, N. R. O	J. H. Milson
Wheatland	Wickham	Drummond Q	Edward McCabe
Wheatley	Mersea	Essex O	George Middleton
Wheatley River	Number 24	Queen's P E I	James Power
Wheaton Settlement, W. O		Westmoreland N B	John M. Killam
Whim Road Cross	Number 59	King's P E I	John Martin
* *Whitby*	Whitby	Ontario, S. R. O	R. F. Lauder
White	Darling	Lanark, N. R. O	George W. Beaton
Whitehead, W. O		Guysborough N S	James N. Feltmate
Whitehurst	Elizabethtown	Brockville O	James E. [illegible]
White Lake	McNab	Renfrew, S. R. O	Alexander Stirling
White Point, W. O		Victoria N S	J. Challoner
White Rock Mills, W. O		King's N S	Augustus Freeman
White Rose	Whitchurch	York, N. R. O	Jared Lloyd
White's Cove		Queen's N B	S. V. White
White's Point, W. O.		Queen's N B	Thomas Carmichael
Whitevale	Pickering	Ontario, S. R. O	Donald McPhee
Whitfield	Mulmur	Simcoe, S. R O	P. D. Henry
Whitney W. O.		Northumberland N B	James Russell
[illegible] W. O		Charlotte N B	Merrill Whittier
Whittington	Amaranth	Wellington, N. R. O	R. Bo[illegible]field
Whitton	Whitton	Compton Q	Donald Beaton
Whycocomagh		Inverness N S	Peter McDonald
Whycocomagh Rear, W. O		Inverness N S	Hugh McDonald
[illegible]	Amabel	Bruce, N. R. O	B. B. Miller

NAME OF POST OFFICE.	TOWNSHIP OR PARISH.	ELECTORAL COUNTY OR DIVISION.	NAME OF POSTMASTER.
Wick	Brock	Ontario, N. R. **O**	Charles McLean
*a*Wickham, West	Wickham	Drummond **Q**	M. Leonard
Wickham, W. O.		Queen's **N B**	G. N. Golding
Wicklow	Haldimand	Northumberland, W. R. **O**	Caleb Southon
Wicklow		Carleton **N B**	Thomas H. Estey
Wickwire Station, W. O.		Halifax **N S**	Samuel Key
Widder	Bosanquet	Lambton **O**	Adam Duffus
Widder Station	Bosanquet	Lambton **O**	Thomas Kirkpatrick
Wilfrid	Brock	Ontario, N. R. **O**	John Chambers
Wilkesport	Sombra	Bothwell **O**	William Kinball
Willetsholme	Pittsburgh	Frontenac **O**	Josiah Abrams
Williamsdale, W. O.		Cumberland **N S**	Andrew Taylor
Williamsford Station	Holland	Grey, N. R. **O**	Alfred Williams
Williamstown	Charlottenburg	Glengarry **O**	Albert McGillis
Williamstown, W. O.		Carleton **N B**	Thomas Lindsay
Williscroft	Elderslie	Bruce, N. R. **O**	George Williscroft
Willowdale	York	York, W. R. **O**	Jacob Rumner
Willowgrove	Oneida	Haldimand **O**	Hugh Stewart
Willowgrove, W. O.		St. John **N B**	William Francis
Wilmot		Annapolis **N S**	E. Cumminger
Wilmot Valley	No. 19	Prince **P E I**	D. Dickieson
Wilmur	Loughborough	Addington **O**	Robert Mavety
Wilson s Beach, W. O.		Charlotte **N B**	Mrs. Susan Brown
Wilton	Ernestown	Lennox **O**	Sydney Warner
Wilton Grove	Westminster	Middlesex, E. R. **O**	Thomas Hogg
Winchelsea	Usborne	Huron, S. R. **O**	John Smith
Winchester	Winchester	Dundas **O**	C. T. Casselman
Winchester Springs	Williamsburg	Dundas **O**	James Greer
Windermere	Watt	Muskoka **O**	Thomas Aitkin
Windham Centre	Windham	Norfolk, N. R. **O**	John Lindabury
Windham Hill, W. O.		Cumberland **N S**	John Bragg
b Winding Ledges, W. O.		Victoria **N B**	S. C. Hudon
* *Windsor*	Sandwich, East	Essex **O**	Alex. H. Wagner

NAME OF POST OFFICE.	TOWNSHIP OR PARISH.	ELECTORAL COUNTY OR DIVISION.	NAME OF POSTMASTER.
Windsor, W. O		Carleton N B	William H. Britton
Windsor		Hants N S	Peter S. Burnham
Windsor Junction, W. O.		Halifax N S	Williams Rennells
Windsor Mills	Windsor	Richmond Q	J. A. E. McCabe
Wine Harbor, W. O.		Guysboro' N S	John Gillis
Winfield	Peel	Wellington, C. R. O	Thomas Cornish
Winger	Wainfleet	Monck O	George W. Moore
Wingham	Turnberry	Huron, N. R. O	Peter Fisher
Winona	Saltfleet	Wentworth, S. R. O	Joseph Carpenter
Winterbourne	Woolwich	Waterloo, N. R. O	P. S. Kilborne
Winthrop	McKillop	Huron, C. R. O	Alex. Murchie
Wisbeach	Warwick	Lambton O	Joanna Bowes
Woburn	Scarborough	York, E. R. O	J. R. Thomson
Wolf Island	Wolfe Island	Frontenac O	Edward Baker
Wolfstown	Wolfstown	Wolfe Q	Norbert Roy
Wolfville		King's N S	George V. Band
Wolseley	Keppel	Grey, N. R. O	Andrew Johnson
Wolverstown	Blenheim	Oxford, N. R. O	Thomas Dawson
* *Woodbridge*	Vaughan	York, W. R. O	C. H. Dunning
Woodburn	Binbrook	Wentworth, S. R. O	William McEvoy
Woodford	Sydenham	Grey, N. R. O	John Thompson
Woodham	Blanchard	Perth, S. R. O	Jonathan Shier
Woodhill	Toronto Gore	Peel O	Thomas Ward
Woodlands	Osnabruck	Stormont O	R. H. Stewart
Wood Island	Number 62	Queen's P E I	John Kennedy
Wood Point, W. O.		Westmoreland N B	S. Outhouse
Woodside	Halifax	Megantic Q	Thomas Wood
Woodslee	Maidstone	Essex O	
* *Woodstock*	Blandford	Oxford, N. R. O	Alex. McCleneghan
Woodstock		Carleton N B	John C. Winslow
Woodstock Road Station, W. O.		Carleton N B	John Shiels
* *Woodville*	Eldon	Victoria, N. R. O	John C. Gilchrist
Woodville, W. O.		Hants N S	Shubael Parker

NAME OF POST OFFICE.	TOWNSHIP OR PARISH.	ELECTORAL COUNTY OR DIVISION.		NAME OF POSTMASTER.
Wooler	Murray	Northumberland, E. R.	O	Lorenzo F. Gould
Wotton	Wotton	Wolfe	Q	Benjamin Milette
Wreck Cove, W. O.		Victoria	N S	John Morrison
Wright	Wright	Ottawa	Q	Joshua Ellard
* *Wroxeter*	Howick	Huron, N. R.	O	George A. Powell
Wyandot	Maryboro'	Wellington, N. R.	O	Mrs. Margaret Bond
Wyebridge	Tiny	Simcoe, N. R.	O	Daniel McGregor
* *Wyoming*	Plympton	Lambton	O	John Anderson
Yale		Yale	B C	Benj. Douglas
Yamachiche	Machiche	St. Maurice	Q	Arthur Lacerte
Yamaska	Yamaska	Yamaska	Q	Maxime Reaupré
Yarker	Camden, East	Addington	O	J. A. Shibley
Yarm	Clarendon	Pontiac	Q	Robert McJanet
Yarmouth		Yarmouth	N S	A. J. Hood
Yarmouth Centre	Yarmouth	Elgin, E. R.	O	William Mann
Yatton	Peel	Wellington, C. R.	O	John Rafferty
Yelverton	Manvers	Durham, E. R.	O	James A. Curry
Yeovil	Egremont	Grey, S. R.	O	Joseph Bunston
Yoho, W. O.		York	N B	Robert McLaughlin
* *York*	Seneca	Haldimand +	O	Hy. A. Duggan
York Mills	York	York, E. R.	O	William Hogg
York River	Faraday	Hastings, N. R.	O	J. C. George
* *Yorkville*	York	York, E. R.	O	James Dobson

NAME OF POST OFFICE.	TOWNSHIP OR PARISH.	ELECTORAL COUNTY. OR DIVISION.	NAME OF POSTMASTER.
Young's Point	Smith	Peterborough, W. R. O	Patrick Young
Youngsville	W. Zorra	Oxford, N. R. O	Edward Young
Zealand	Oso	Addington O	Joseph Davis
Zephyr	Scott	Ontario, N. R. O	Manuel N. Dafoe
Zetland	Turnbury	Huron, N. R. O	L. J. Brace
Zimmerman	Nelson	Halton O	Robert Miller
Ziska	Monck	Muskoka O	W. H. Spencer
Zurich	Hay	Huron, S. R. O	Robert Brown

LIST OF POST OFFICES closed and not subsequently reopened, between the 1st July, 1873, and the 1st July, 1874.

NAME OF OFFICE.	ELECTORAL DISTRICT.	DATE OF CLOSING.
Ashburnham	Peterborough, E. R. ... O	1 March, 1874.
Becher	Bothwell ... O	1 May, 1874.
Charrington	Compton ... Q	1 May, 1874.
Edgecombe	Perth, N. R. ... O	1 July, 1874.
Frogmore	Peel ... O	1 May, 1874.
Glen James (late Lochiel)	Glengarry ... O	1 July, 1874.
Grouse Creek	Cariboo ... B C	1 May, 1874.
Harlowe	Frontenac ... O	1 June, 1874.
Kinglake	Norfolk, S. R. ... O	1 July, 1874.
Kingsford	Hastings, E. R. ... O	1 August, 1873.
Lower Ward of St. Margaret's Bay, W. O.	Halifax ... N S	1 April, 1874.
Marsh Settlement of McLellan's Mountain, W. O.	Pictou ... N S	1 October, 1873.
Neguac, W. O.	Northumberland ... N B	1 November 1873.
Pomona	Grey, S. R. ... O	1 December, 1873.
Richby	Compton ... Q	1 May, 1874.
River Debert, W. O.	Colchester ... N S	1 March, 1874.
Stisted	Norfolk ... O	1 July, 1874.

List of Changes in the Names of Post Offices between the 1st July, 1873, and the 1st July, 1874, inclusive.

LATE NAME OF OFFICE.	ELECTORAL DISTRICT.		NEW NAME OF OFFICE.
Allendale	Simcoe, S. R.	O	Allandale.
Baker's Creek, W. O.	Victoria	N B	St. Hilaire, W. O.
Drew's Mills	Stanstead	Q	Dixville.
Dryden	Perth, N. R.	O	Palmerston.
Etobicoke	York, N. R.	O	Lambton Mills.
Galena (late Galway)	Victoria, N. R.	O	Silver Lake.
Galway	Victoria, N. R	O	To Galena.
Gorvan Settlement, W. O	Kent	N B	Pine Ridge, W. O.
Glen Stuart	Norfolk, S. R	O	Glenshee.
Greensville	Wentworth, N. R.	O	Bullock's Corners.
Hullsville	Haldimand	O	Garnet.
Kent's Island, W. O	Halifax	N S	Pleasant Point, W. O.
Lakevale, W. O.	Antigonishe	N S	Morristown, W. O.
Lapum	Frontenac	O	Perth Road.
Leonard's Hill	Drummond	Q	Wickham, West.
Lochiel	Glengarry	O	Glen James.
Mary Lake	Muskoka	O	Port Sydney.
Normanton	Bruce, N. R	O	Port Elgin.
Pineo Village	King's	N S	Waterville.
Point Abino	Welland	O	Ridgeway.
Point du Chene	Provencher	M	St. Annes.
Ripley	Bruce, S. R.	O	Dingwall.
Robert's Island, W. O	Yarmouth	N S	Glenwood.
Rochester	Essex	O	Belle River.
Sandfield	Glengarry	O	Glen Sandfield.
Sierra	Glengarry	O	Glenroy.
Speedie	Grey, N. R.	O	Annan.
St. Christophe	Arthabaska	Q	Arthabaskaville.
Thurlow	Hastings, E. R	O	Phillipston.
Wallace River, W. O	Cumberland	N S	Wentworth, W. O.
Washademoak, W. O.	Queen's	N B	McAlpin, W. O.
Waterville, W. O.	King's	N S	Millville, W. O.
		N B	Winding Ledges, W. O

POST OFFICES IN CANADA,

ON THE 1st JULY, 1874,

ARRANGED ACCORDING TO THE

PROVINCES AND ELECTORAL DISTRICTS.

POST OFFICES

IN THE

PROVINCE OF ONTARIO

ARRANGED ACCORDING TO

ELECTORAL DISTRICTS AND TOWNSHIPS.

ADDINGTON.

Abinger.

Vennachar.

Anglesea.

Cloyne.

Ashby.

—

Barrie.

Hardinge.

Bedford.

Fermoy,
Glendower,
Tichborne.

Camden, East.

Camden, East,
Centreville,
Colebrook,
Croydon,
Desmond,
Enterprise,
Hinch,
Moscow,
Napanee Mills,
Newburgh,
Overton,
Yarker.

Canonto, South.

—

Clarendon.

Ardoch,
Buchshot.

Denbigh.

Denbigh.

Effingham.

Hinchinbrooke.

Deniston,
Parham.

Kaladar.

Flinton,
Glastonbury,
Kaladar.

Kennebec.

Arden.

Loughboro'.

Desert Lake,
Loughboro',
Perth Road,
Railton,
Spaffordton,
Wilmur.

Miller.

Gemley.

Olden.

Long Lake,
Mountain Grove.

Oso.

Deerdock,
Zealand.

Palmerston.

Ompah.

Portland.

Bellrock,
Harrowsmith,
Hartington,
Murvale,
Petworth.
Verona.

Sheffield.

Clareview,
Erinsville,
Tamworth.

Post Offices in the Province of Ontario, arranged according to Electoral Districts and Townships.—Continued.

ALGOMA.

ASSIGINACK.
Manitowaning.

FISHER.
Batchewana.

HOWLAND.
Little Current.

KORAH.
Sault Ste. Marie.

TEKERMAGH.
Michael's Bay.

NEEBING.
Fort William.

PARKE.
Pointe au Pins.

The following Post Offices are in the unsurveyed portion of Algoma :—

Bruce Mines,
Collin's Inlet,
Garden River,
Killarney,
Michipicoten River,
Red Rocks,
Silver Islet,
Spanish River,
Thunder Bay,
Ullin.

BOTHWELL.

CAMDEN.
Dawn Mills,
**Dresden,*
Thamesville.

DAWN.
Rutherford.

EUPHEMIA.
Florence,
Shetland,
Sutherland's Corners.

HOWARD.
Botany,
**Morpeth,*
Ridgetown,
Selton.

ORFORD.
Clachan,
Clearville,
Duart,
Highgate.

SOMBRA
Baby's Point,
Becher,
Port Lambton.
Sombra,
Wilkesport.

ZONE.
**Bothwell*

BRANT, NORTH RIDING.

BRANTFORD, EAST.
Cainsville,
Langford.

DUMPHRIES, SOUTH.
Glen Morris,
Harrisburg.

DUMPHRIES, SOUTH.—*Continued.*
**Paris.*
Paris Station,
Rosebank,
St. George.

ONONDAGA.
Onondaga,
Tuscarora.

Post Offices in the Province of Ontario, arranged according to Electoral Districts and Townships.—Continued.

BRANT, SOUTH RIDING.

Brantford, West.

*Brantford,
Burtch,
Falkland,
Mohawk,
Mount Vernon,
Newport.

Burford.

Burford,
Cathcart,
Fairfield Plain,
Harley,

Burford—*Continued.*

New Durham.

Oakland.

Oakland,
Scotland.

Tuscarora.

Ohsweken.

BROCKVILLE, TOWN.

Elizabethtown.

Addison,
*Brockville,
Fairfield, East.
Greenbush,

Elizabethtown.—*Continued.*

*Lyn,
New Dublin,
Whitehurst.

BRUCE, NORTH RIDING.

Albermarle.

Cape Croker,
Colpoy's Bay,
Mar.

Amabel.

Allenford,
Park Head,
Skipness,
Wiarton.

Arran.

Arkwright,
Burgoyne,
Elsinore,
Invermay,
Tara.

Bruce.

Glammis,
Gresham,
Inverhuron,
North Bruce,
Underwood.

Bury.

—

Eastnor.

—

Elderslie.

Carnegie,
Chesley,
Dobbington,
*Paisley,
Scone,
Williscroft.

Lindsay.

—

Saugeen.

Dumblane,
Port Elgin,
*Saugeen,
West Arran.

BRUCE, SOUTH RIDING.

Brant.

Dunkeld,
Ellengowan,
Elmwood,
Malcolm,
Maple Hill,
Outram,
Vesta,
*Walkerton.

Carrick.

Ambleside,
Carlsruhe,
Formosa,
Mildmay.

Culross.

Cheviot,
*Teeswater.

Post Offices in the Province of Ontario, arranged according to Electoral Districts and Townships.—Continued.

BRUCE, SOUTH RIDING.—*Concluded.*

Greenock.

Chepstow,
Greenock,
Lovat,
Pinkerton,
Riversdale.

Huron.

Dingwall,
Lisburn,
Lurgan,
Pine River,
Verdun.

Kincardine.

Armow,
Bervie,
**Kincardine*,
Lorne,
Tiverton.

Kinloss.

Holyrood,
Kinloss,
Kinlough,
Langside,
**Lucknow.*

CARDWELL.

Adjala.

Arlington,
Athlone,
Ballycroy,
Connor,
Fintona,
Hockley,
Keenansville,
Loretto,
Sheldon.

Albion.

**Albion,*
Coventry,
Hunsdon,
Lockton.
Macville,
Mono Mills,
Mount Hurst,
Mount Wolfe,
Palgrave.

Caledon.

Alton,
Belfountain,
Caldwell,
Caledon,
Caledon, East,
Cataract,
Rockside,
Sleswick,
Sligo.

Mono.

Camilla,
Elba,
Elder,
Lorraine,
Mono Centre,
Primrose,
Relessey.

CARLETON.

Fitzroy.

Antrim,
Diamond,
Fitzroy Harbor,
Kinburn,
Marathon,
Panmure,
Mohr's Corners.

Goulbourn.

Ashton,
Dwyer Hill,
Hazledean,
Munster,
**Richmond, West,*
Stittsville.

Gower, North.

Carsonby,
Kars,
Manotic,
North Gower.

Huntley.

Clandeboye,
Carp,
Elm,
Huntley.

Huntley.—*Continued.*

Powell,
West Huntley.

March.

March,
South March.

Marlborough.

Malakoff.

Nepean.

Bell's Corners,
Fallowfield,
Merivale,
Rochesterville,
Skeads Mills.

Torbolton.

Dunrobin,

Post Offices in the Province of Ontario, arranged according to Electoral Districts and Townships.—Continued.

CORNWALL, TOWN.

Cornwall.

**Cornwall,*
Harrison's Corners,
**Mill Roches,*
Northfield,
St. Andrew's, West.

DUNDAS.

Matilda.

Brinston's Corner,
Dixon's Corners,
Dundela,
Glen Stewart,
**Iroquois,*
New Ross.

Mountain.

Inkerman,
North Mountain,
Lockville,
Smirleville,
South Mountain.

Williamsburg.

Bouck's Hill,
Dunbar,
East Williamsburg,
Grantley,
Hoasic,
**Morrisburgh,*
North Williamsburg.

Winchester.

Cass Bridge,
Connaught,
Morewood,
North Winchester,
Ormond,
**West Winchester,*
Winchester,
Winchester Springs.

DURHAM, EAST RIDING.

Cavan.

Bailieboro',
Cavan,
Ida,
**Mill Brook,*
Mount Pleasant.

Hope.

Canton,
Elizabethville,
Garden Hill,
Osaca,
Perrytown.

Hope. *Continued.*

**Port Hope,*
Welcome.

Manvers.

Ballyduff,
Bethany,
Brunswick,
Burton,
Drum,
Fleetwood,
Franklin,
Glamorgan,
Janetville,
Lifford,
Lotus,
Yelverton.

DURHAM, WEST RIDING.

Cartwright.

Cadmus,
Cæsarea,
Cartwright.

Clarke.

Clarke,
Kendal,
Kirby,
Leskard.

Clarke.—*Continued.*

**Newcastle,*
**Orono,*
Port Granby.

Darlington.

**Bowmanville,*
Enfield,
Enniskillen,
Hampton,
Haydon,
Solina,
Tyrone.

Post Offices in the Province of Ontario, arranged according to Electoral Districts and Townships.—Continued.

ELGIN, EAST RIDING.

BAYHAM.

Bayham,
Calton,
Corinth,
Eden,
Port Burwell,
Straffordville,
Vienna.

DORCHESTER, SOUTH.

Lyons,
Springfield.

MALAHIDE.

Aylmer, West,
Copenhagen.

MALAHIDE.—*Continued.*

Grovesend,
Kingsmill,
Luton,
Mount Salem,
Port Bruce.

YARMOUTH.

Dexter,
Mapleton,
New Sarum,
Orwell,
Port Stanley,
St. Thomas, West,
Killerby,
Sparta,
Union,
Yarmouth Centre.

ELGIN, WEST RIDING.

ALDBORO'.

Aldboro',
Crinan,
Eagle,
Rodney,
West Lorne.

DUNWICH.

Iona,
Largie,

DUNWICH.—*Continued.*

Tyrconnell,
Wallacetown.

SOUTHWOLD.

Cowal,
Fingal,
Frome,
Talbotville, Royal,
West Magdala.

ESSEX.

ANDERDON.

Anderdon.

COLCHESTER.

Colchester,
Harrow,
Essex, Centre,
Gesto,
Oxley,
Vereker.

GOSFIELD.

Kingsville,
North Ridge,
Olinda,
Ruthven.

MAIDSTONE.

Pa
Woodslee.

MALDEN.

Amhersburg.

MERSEA.

Blytheswood,
Leamington,
Wheatly.

ROCHESTER.

Belle River,
Ruscom River.

SANDWICH, EAST.

Maidstone,
Ryegate,
Walkerville,
Windsor.

SANDWICH, WEST.

Canard River,
Sandwich.

TILBURY, WEST.

Comber,
Stoney Point.
Trudell.

Post Offices in the Province of Ontario, arranged according to Electoral Districts and Townships.—Continued.

FRONTENAC.

GARDEN ISLAND.

Garden Island.

HOWE ISLAND.

Howe Island.

KINGSTON.

Cataraqui,
Collin's Bay,
Elginburg,
Glenburnie,
Glenvale,
Kingston Station,
Kepler,
Kingston Mills,
Portsmouth,
Sharpton,
West Brooke.

PITTSBURG.

Ballantyne Station,
Birmingham.
Brewer's Mills,
Pittsferry,
Washburn.
Willetsholme,

STORRINGTON.

Battersea,
Inverary,
Latimer,
Lake Opinicon,
Sunbury.

WOLFE ISLAND.

Wolfe Island.

GLENGARRY.

CHARLOTTENBURG.

Camerontown,
Cashion's Glen,
Glenroy,
Glen Donald,
Glen Gordon,
Glen Walter,
Martintown,
Munroe's Mills,
St. Raphael, West,
Summerstown,
Williamstown.

KENYON.

Athol,
Dunvegan,
Greenfield,
Laggan,
Loch Garry,
Notfield,
Skye.

LANCASTER.

Curry Hill,
Dalhousie Mills,
Glennevis.
Glen Norman,
Lancaster,
North Lancaster,
Riviére Raisin.

LOCHIEL.

**Alexandria*,
Dalkeith,
Glen Sandfield,
Kirkhill,
Lochiel,
Lochinvar,
South La Graisse.

ST. REGIS.

GRENVILLE, SOUTH RIDING.

AUGUSTA.

Algonquin,
Centre Augusta,
Charleville,
Maitland,
Maynard,
North Augusta,
**Prescott*,
Roebuck,

EDWARDSBURG.

Edwardsburg,
Pittston,
Shanly,
Spencerville,
Ventnor.

GREY, EAST RIDING.

ARTEMESIA.

Eugenia.
Flesherton,
Inistioge.
Priceville,
Vandeleur.

COLLINGWOOD.

**Clarksburg*,
Craigleith,
Gibraltar,
Ravenna,
Thornbury.

EUPHRASIA.

Blantyre,
Duncan,
Epping,
Heathcote,
Kimberley.

MELANCTHON.

Dundalk,
Horning's Mills,
Shelburne,
Shrigley.

OSPREY.

Feversham,
McIntyre,
Maxwell,
Rob Roy,
Wareham.

PROTON.

Cedarville,
Dundalk Station,
Ronaldsay,
Ventry.

ST. VINCENT.

Bayview,
Cape Rich,
**Meaford*,
Morley,

Post Offices in the Province of Ontario, arranged according to Electoral Districts and Townships.—Continued.

GREY, NORTH RIDING.

Derby.

Alvanley,
Ashley,
Jackson,
Keady,
Kilsyth.

Holland.

Arnott,
Berkeley,
Chatsworth,
Massie,
Sullivan,
Water's Falls,
Williamsford Station.

Keppel.

Clavering,
Cruickshank,
Hepworth,
Kemble,
North Keppel,
Oxenden,
Wolseley.

Sarawak.

Sarawak.

Sullivan.

Desboro',
Marmion,
Peabody.

Sydenham.

Annan,
Daywood,
Hoath Head,
Johnson,
Leith,
**Owen Sound*,
Woodford,
Sydenham Mills.

GREY, SOUTH RIDING.

Bentinck.

Allan Park,
Coverley,
Crawford,
Hanover.

Egremont.

Dromore,
Egremont,
Holstein,
Orchard,
Yeovil.

Glenelg.

**Durham*,
Glascott,
Latona,
Markdale,
Traverston.

Normanby.

Ayton,
Nenagh,
Neustadt,
Varney.

HALDIMAND.

Cayuga, North.

Canfield,
**Cayuga*.

Cayuga, South.

Bingham Road,
De Cewsville,
South Cayuga.

Oneida.

Dufferin,
Mount Healey,
Oneida,
Willowgrove.

Post Offices in the Province of Ontario, arranged according to Electoral Districts and Townships.—Continued.

HALDIMAND.—*Continued.*

RAINHAM.

Balmoral,
Fisherville,
Rainham,
Rainham, Centre.

SENECA.

Indiana,
North Seneca,
**Seneca*,
Tyneside,
**York*.

WALPOLE.

Cheapside,
Erie,
Garnet,
Hagersville,
Jarvis,
Nanticoke,
Selkirk,
Springvale.

HALTON.

ESQUESING.

Acton,
Ashgrove,
Esquesing,
**Georgetown*,
Glen Williams,
Hornby,
Limehouse,
Norval,
Speyside.

NASSAGIWEYA.

Campbellville,
Knatchbull,
Moffatt,
Nassagiweya.

NELSON.

Appleby,
Cumminsville,
Kilbride,
Lowville,
Nelson,
Port Nelson,
**Wellington Square*,
Zimmerman.

TRAFALGAR.

Boyne,
Bronte,
Drumquin,
**Milton West*,
**Oakville*,
Omagh,
Palermo,
Sheridan,
Trafalgar.

HAMILTON, CITY.

**Hamilton*.

HASTINGS, EAST RIDING.

HUNGERFORD.

Bogart,
Chapman,
Lime Lake,
Marlbank,
Moneymore,
Stoco,
Thomasburg,
Tweed.

THURLOW.

Cannifton,
Foxboro'
Halloway,
Hilda,

THURLOW.—*Continued.*

Plainfield,
Philipston,
Roslin.

TYENDINAGA.

Albert,
Blessington,
Lonsdale,
Marysville,
Melrose,
Mill Point,
Myrehall,
Read,
Shannonville.

Post Offices in the Province of Ontario, arranged according to Electoral Districts and Townships.—Continued.

HASTINGS, NORTH RIDING.

AIREY.

—

BANGOR.

Purdy.

CARLOW.

Boulter.

CASHEL.

—

DUNGANNON.

Bronson,
L'Amable,
Umfraville,

ELZIVER.

**Bridgewater*,
Queensborough.

FARADAY.

York River.

GRIMSTHORPE.

—

HERSCHEL.

—

HUNTINGDON.

Ivanhoe,
West Huntingdon,
Moira.

LAKE.

—

LIMERICK.

St. Ola.

LYELL.

—

M'CLURE.

—

MADOC.

Bannockburn,
Cooper,
Eldorado,
**Madoc*,
Rimington.

MARMORA.

Malone,
Marmora,
Shanick.

MAYO.

—

MONTEAGLE.

Greenview,
Maynooth,
Monteagle Valley.

MURCHISON.

—

RAWDON.

Brinkworth,
Harold,
Spring Brook,
**Stirling*,
Wellman's Corners.

SABINE.

—

TUDOR.

Glanmire,
Millbridge.

WICKLOW.

—

WOOLLASTON

Thanet.

HASTINGS, WEST RIDING.

SIDNEY.

**Belleville*,
Frankford.

SIDNEY.—*Continued.*

**Trenton*,
Sidney Crossing,
Wallbridge.

HURON, CENTRE RIDING.

COLBORNE.

Benmillier,
Carlow,
**Goderich*,
Nile.

GREY.

Brussels,
Ethel,
Grey,
Stowe.

HULLETT.

HULLETT.—*Continued.*

Constance,
Londesborough.

McKILLOP.

Walton,
Winthrop.

TUCKERSMITH.

Brucefield.
Kippen,

Post Offices in the Province of Ontario, arranged according to Electoral Districts and Townships.—Continued.

HURON, NORTH RIDING.

Ashfield.

Amberley,
Belfast,
Kingsbridge,
Kintail,
Port Albert.

Howick.

Fordwich,
Gorrie,
Lakelet,
Newbridge,
**Wroxeter.*

Morris.

Belgrave,
Busfield.

Morris.—*Continued.*

Bluevale,
Blyth,
Morrisbank,
Sunshine.

Turnberry.

Belmore,
**Wingham,*
Zetland.

Wawanosh, East and West.

Auburn,
**Dungannon,*
Fordyce,
Marnoch,
St. Helen's,
Ulster,
Westfield.

HURON, SOUTH RIDING.

Goderich.

**Clinton,*
Holmesville,
Porter's Hill.

Hay.

Berne,
Dashwood,
Hay,
Hill's Green,
Johnson's Mills,
Screpta,
Zurich.

Stanley.

**Bayfield,*
Drysdale,
Varna.

Stephen.

Brewster,
Crediton,
Centralia,
**Exeter,*
Harpley,
Offa.

Usborne.

Elimville,
Farquhar,
Kirkton,
Lumley,
Rodgerville,
Winchelsea.

KENT.

Chatham.

Darrell,
Keith,
Kent Bridge,
Louisville,
Oungah,
**Wallaceburg.*

Dover, East and West.

Mitchell's Bay,
Dover, South.

Harwich.

Bentley,
Buckhorn,
Charing Cross,
Fa[illegible]
Harwich,
**Rondeau,*
Rondeau Harbor.

Raleigh.

Buxton,
**Chatham,*
Dealton,
Merlin.

Romney.

Old Montrose,
Romney.

Tilbury, East.

Edgeworth,
Tilbury, East,
Valetta.

74

Post Offices in the Province of Ontario, arranged according to Electoral Districts and Townships.—Continued.

KINGSTON, CITY.

**Kingston.*

LAMBTON.

Bosanquet.

Grand Bend,
Jura,
Port Franks,
Ravenswood,
Widder,
Widder Station.

Brooke.

Alvinston,
Aughrim.

Enniskillen.

Copleston,
**Oil Springs,*
Oil City,
Ossian,
Petrolea.

Moore.

Birkhall,
Colinville,
Corunna,
Courtright,
Logierait,
Moore,
Waubuno.

Plympton.

Aberarder,
Camlachie.
Erroll,
Forest,
Hillsborough,
Kertch,
Mandamin,
Matlock,
Uttoxeter,
Vyner,
Wanstead,
Wyoming.

Sarnia.

Oban,
Perch Station,
Point Edward,
**Sarnia.*

Warwick.

**Arkona,*
Warwick,
Watford,
Wisbeach.

LANARK, NORTH RIDING.

Dalhousie.

McDonald's Corners,
Poland,
Watson's Corners.

Darling.

Tatlock,
White.

Lanark.

Galbraith,
Hopetown,
**Lanark,*
Middleville,
Rosetta.

Lavant.

Lavant.

Packenham.

Cedar Hill,
**Pakenham.*

Ramsay.

**Almonte,*
Appleton,
Bennie's Corners,
Blakeney,
Clayton,
Huntersville.

Sherbrooke, North.

Elpin.

LANARK, SOUTH RIDING.

Post Offices in the Province of Ontario, arranged according to Electoral Districts and Townships.—Continued.

LANARK, SOUTH RIDING—*Continued.*

BURGESS, NORTH.

Allan Mills,
Hamlet.

DRUMMOND.

Balderson,
Ferguson's Falls,
Innisville,
**Perth*,
Tennyson.

ELMSLEY, NORTH.

Port Elmsley.
**Smith's Falls.*

MONTAGUE.

Montague.

SHERBROOKE, SOUTH.

Bolingbroke,
Maberley,
Rokeby.

LEEDS AND GRENVILLE, NORTH RIDING.

ELMSLEY, SOUTH.

Lombardy.

GOWER, SOUTH.

Heckston,
South Gower.

KITLEY.

Frankville,
Newbliss,
Toledo.

OXFORD.

Bishop's Mills,
Burritt's Rapids,
**Kemptville*,
Oxford Mills,
Oxford Station.

WOLFORD.

Easton's Corners,
Jasper,
Kilmarnock,
Merrickville,

LEEDS, SOUTH RIDING.

BASTARD.

Chantry,
Delta,
Forfar,
Harlem,
Newboyne,
Philipsville,
Plum Hollow,
Portland.

BURGESS.

Cramworth.

CROSBY, NORTH.

**Newborough*,
Westport.

CROSBY, SOUTH.

Elgin,
Morton.

ESCOTT, FRONT AND REAR.

Charlestown,
Escott,
Rockport.

LANSDOWN, FRONT AND REAR.

Lansdown,
Lyndhurst,
Soperton,
Warburton.

LEEDS, FRONT AND REAR.

**Gananoque*,
Marble Rock,
Seeley's Bay,
South Lake.

YONGE, FRONT AND REAR.

Caintown,
Dickins,
Farmersville,
Mallorytown,
Sherwood Spring.

Post Offices in the Province of Ontario, arranged according to Electoral Districts and Townships.—Continued.

LENNOX.

ADOLPHUSTOWN.

Adolphustown,
Gosport.

AMHERST ISLAND.

Emerald,
Stella.

ERNESTOWN.

Bath,
Mill Haven,
Morvan,
**Odessa*,
Ernestown Station,
Switzerville,
Violet,
Wilton.

FREDERICKSBURG, NORTH AND SOUTH.

Conway,
Gretna,
Hamburg,
Parma,
Sandhurst,
Sillsville.

RICHMOND.

Forest Mills,
Leinster,
**Napanee*,
Roblin,
Selby.

LINCOLN.

CLINTON.

**Beamsville*,
Campden.
Tintern,

GRANTHAM.

Homer,
Merritton,
**Port Dalhousie*,
**St. Catharine's, West*.

GRIMSBY.

Fulton,
**Grimsby*,
**Smithville*.

LOUTH.

**Jordan*.

LONDON, CITY.

Lilly's Corners,
**London*.
Petersville, (sub.)

MIDDLESEX, EAST RIDING.

DORCHESTER, NORTH.

Avon,
Derwent,
Crumlin,
Dorchester Station,
Gladstone,
Harrietsville,
Mossley,
Nilestown.
Putnam.

LONDON.

Arva,
Ballymote,
Birr,
Bryanston,
Denfield,
Devizes,
Elginfield,
Hyde Park Corner,
Ilderton,
Masonville.

LONDON.—*Continued*.

**Muir*,
Telfer,
Union Hill,
Vanneck.

NISSOURI, WEST.

Evelyn,
St. Ives.
Thorndale.

WESTMINSTER.

Belmont,
Byron,
Glanworth,
Lambeth,
St. James' Park, (sub.)
Tempo'.
Wilton Grove.

Post Offices in the Province of Ontario, arranged according to Electoral Districts and Townships.—Continued.

MIDDLESEX, NORTH RIDING.

Adelaide.

Adelaide,
Crathie,
Kerrwood,
Keyser,
Napperton.

Biddulph.

Granton,
**Lucan*,
Whalen.

Lobo.

Amiens,
Coldstream,
Duncrief,
Fernhill,
Komoka,
Lobo.

McGillivray.

Adare,
Brinsley,
Corbett,
Lieury,
McGillivray,
Moray,
West McGillivray.

Williams.

Ailsa Craig,
Bornish,
Falkirk,
Nairn,
Springbank.

Williams, West.

Park Hill,
Sable,
Sylvan.

MIDDLESEX, WEST RIDING.

Caradoc.

Longwood Station,
**Mount Brydges*,
Muncey,
**Strathroy*.

Delaware.

Calder,
Delaware.

Ekfrid.

Appin,
Glencoe,
Longwood,
Mayfair.

Metcalfe.

Cairngorm,
Kilmartin,
Napier.

Mosa.

Cashmere,
Knapdale,
**Newbury*,
Strathburn,
**Wardsville*.

MONCK.

Caistor.

Abingdon,
Attercliffe,
Caistorville,
Warner.

Canboro'.

Canboro'.

Dunn.

Byng.

Gainsboro'.

Bismark,
Candasville,
Elcho,
Rosedene,
St. Ann's,
Welland Port.

Moulton.

**Dunville*,
Lowbanks.

Pelham.

Effingham,
Fenwick,
**Fonthill*,
North Pelham,
Pelham Union,
Ridgeville.

Sherbrooke.

Port Maitland
Stromness.

Wainfleet.

Marshville.
Winger.

Post Offices in the Province of Ontario, arranged according to Electoral Districts and Townships.—Continued.

MUSKOKA.

AUMICK LAKE TERRITORY.

—

BLAIR.

—

BROWN.

—

BRUNEL.

Seely.

CARDWELL.

—

CARLING.

—

CHAFFEY.

Huntsville,
Meliesu,
Ravenscliffe.

CHAPMAN.

Magnetawan.

CHRISTIE.

—

CONGER.

—

COWPER.

—

CROFT.

—

DRAPER.

Muskoka Falls,
Uffington.

FERGUSON.

Waubamik.

FERRIE.

—

FOLEY.

Falding.

HAGARMAN.

Newcombe.

HUMPHREY.

Ashdown,
Rosseau,
Trout Lake,
Turtle Lake.

LOUNT.

—

McDOUGALL.

Parry Sound.

McKELLAR.

Hurdville.
McKellar,

McKENZIE.

McLEAN.

McMURRICH

—

MACAULEY.

**Bracebridge*,
Falkenburg,
Stoneleigh.

MAGANETAWAN.

—

MATCHITT.

—

MEDORA.

Bala,
Port Carling.

MONCK.

Bardsville,
Point Kaye,
Ziska.

MONTEITH.

Segeun Falls.

MORRISON.

Severn Bridge.

MOWAT.

—

MUSKOKA.

Alport,
Gravenhurst.

OAKLEY.

—

PARRY ISLAND.

—

PARRY SOUND.

—

RYDE.

—

RYERSON.

—

SPENCE.

Spence.

STEPHENSON.

Allensville,
Port Sydney,
Utterson.

STISTED.

Aspdin.

WALLBRIDGE.

Byng Inlet.

WATT.

Beatrice,
Raymond,
Ufford,
Ullswater,
Windermere.

WILSON.

WOOD.

Post Offices in the Province of Ontario, arranged according to Electoral Districts and Townships.—Continued.

NIAGARA TOWN.

Niagara.

* *Niagara*, Queenston, St. David's, Virgil.

NIPISSING DISTRICT.

Deux Rivières, Mattawa, Nippissingan.

NORFOLK, NORTH RIDING.

Middleton.

Acacia, Courtland, *Delhi*, Gravelotte, Guysborough, Ronson, South Middleton.

Townsend.

Bealton, Bloomsburg, Boston, Hartford, Renton, Rockford, Round Plains, Townsend Centre.

Townsend.—*Continued.*

Tyrrell, Villa Nova, **Waterford.*

Windham.

Atherton, Bookton, Brandy Creek, Kelvin, Lynnville, Ranelagh, **Simcoe*, Teeterville, Windham, Centre.

NORFOLK, SOUTH RIDING.

Charlotteville.

Forestville, Glenshee, *Lynedoch*, Normandale, Silver Hill, **Vittoria*, Walsh.

Houghton.

Clear Creek, Glen Meyer, Houghton.

Walsingham.

Langton, Marston, Pleasant Hill, **Port Rowan*, Port Royal, *St. Williams*, Spring Arbour.

Woodhouse.

Port Dover, *Port Ryerse.*

NORTHUMBERLAND, EAST RIDING.

Brighton.

**Brighton*, Codrington, Hilton, Newcomb Mills, Ongly, Smithfield.

Cramahe.

Castleton, * *Colborne*, Dundonald, Morganston.

Murray.

Murray, Rosa.

Murray.—*Continued.*

Stockdale, Wooler.

Percy.

Dartford, Norham, *Warkworth.*

Seymour.

Burn-brae, **Campbellford*, Menie, Meyersburg, Rylstone, Tilton, Trent Bridge.

Post Offices in the Province of Ontario, arranged according to Electoral Districts and Townships.—Continued.

NORTHUMBERLAND, WEST RIDING.

Alnwick.

Alderville,
Roseneath.

Haldimand.

Bomanton,
Burnley,
Centreton,
Eddystone,
Fenella,
Grafton.

Haldimand.—*Continued.*

Vernonville,
Wicklow.

Hamilton.

**Baltimore,*
Bewdley,
**Cobourg,*
Coldsprings,
Gore's Landing,
Harwood.

ONTARIO, NORTH RIDING.

Brock.

**Cannington,*
Derryville,
Layton,
Pinedale,
Sunderland,
Valentyne,
Vroomanton,
Wick,
Wilfrid.

Mara.

Atherly,
Brechin,
Rathburn,
Uptergrove.

Rama.

Fawkham,
Rama,
Sebright.

Reach.

Epsom,
Greenbank,
**Manchester,*
Marsh Hill,
Port Perry,
**Prince Albert,*
Saintfield,
Seagrave.

Reach.—*Continued.*

Shirley,
Utica,
Victoria Corners.

Scott.

Ashworth,
Athens,
Leaskdale,
Sandford,
Udora,
Zephyr.

Scugog.

Scugog.

Thorah.

**Beaverton,*
Gamebridge.

Uxbridge.

Glasgow,
Goodwood,
Glen Major,
Siloam,
** Uxbridge.*

ONTARIO, SOUTH RIDING.

Pickering.

Altona,
Atha,
Audley,
Balsam,
Brougham,
Cherrywood,
Claremont,
Dunbarton,
Green River,
Greenwood,
Kinsale,
Pickering,
Port Union,
Rouge Hill,
Whitevale.

Whitby, East and West.

Ashburn,
**Brooklin,*
Cedar Dale,
Columbus,
Foley,
Myrtle,
**Oshawa,*
Raglan,
Taunton,
** Whitby.*

OTTAWA CITY.

Post Offices in the Province of Ontario, arranged according to Electoral Districts and Townships.—Continued.

OXFORD, NORTH RIDING.

BLANDFORD.

Ratho,
**Woodstock.*

BLENHEIM.

**Bright,*
Canning,
Chesterfield,
Drumbo,
Goble's Corners,
Plattsville,
**Princeton,*
Richwood,
Washington,
Wolverton.

NISSOURI, EAST.

Kintore,
'Lakeside.

NISSOURI, EAST.- *Continued.*

Medina,
Nissouri,
Thamesford.

ZORRA, EAST.

Braemar,
Cassel,
Innerkip,
South Zorra,
Strathallen,
Walmer.

ZORRA, WEST.

Bennington,
Brooksdale,
**Embro,*
Harrington, West,
Maplewood,
Youngsville.

OXFORD, SOUTH RIDING.

DEREHAM.

Brownsville,
Culloden,
Mount Elgin,
Salford,
**Tilsonburg,*
Verschoyle.

NORWICH, NORTH.

Burgessville,
Holbrook,
Newark,
**Norwich.*

NORWICH, SOUTH.

Hawtrey,
**Otterville,*
Springford.

OXFORD, EAST.

Eastwood,
Oxford Centre,
Vandecar.

OXFORD, NORTH.

**Ingersoll.*

OXFORD, WEST.

**Beachville,*
Sweaburg.

PEEL.

CHINGUACOUSY.

**Alloa,*
Brampton,
Campbell's Cross,
Cheltenham,
Claude,
Edmonton,
Huttonsville,
Kilmanagh,
Mayfield,
Mono Road Station,
Salmonville,
Sandhill,
Stanley's Mills.

TORONTO.

Britannia,
Churchville.

TORONTO.—*Continued.*

Credit,
Derry, West,
Dixie,
Elmbank,
Malton,
Meadowvale,
Mount Charles,
Port Credit,
Richview,
**Streetsville,*
Summerville,

TORONTO GORE.

Castlemore,
Coleraine,
Grahamsville,
Gribbin.
Tullamore,
Tormore,
Woodhill.

Post Offices in the Province of Ontario, arranged according to Electoral Districts and Townships.—Continued.

PERTH, NORTH RIDING.

Easthope, North.

Hampstead, Lisbon, Nithburg, **Stratford*, Topping.

Ellice.

Brunner, Gad's Hill, Kinkora, Sebringville, Wartburg.

Elma.

Donegal, Hammond, Monkton, Newry, Trowbridge.

Logan.

Bornholm, Brodhagen.

Mornington.

Burns, Carthage, *Millbank*, *Milverton*, Morningdale Mills, Musselburg, Poole.

Wallace.

Gowanstown, **Listowel*, Molesworth, Palmerston, Shipley, Trecastle, Wallace.

PERTH, SOUTH RIDING.

Blanshard.

Anderson, Fish Creek, **St. Mary's*, *Woodham.*

Downie.

Avonbank, Avonton, Conroy, Fairview.

Easthope, South.

Harmony, *Shakespeare*, *Tavistock.*

Fullarton.

Carlingford, Fullarton, **Mitchell*, Motherwell, Russeldale.

Hibbert.

Carronbrook, Cromarty, Staffa.

PETERBORO', EAST RIDING.

Anstruther.

Apsley.

Asphodel.

**Hastings* **Norwood*, Westwood.

Belmont.

**Blairton*, Havelock, Round Lake.

Bruton.

—

Burleigh.

Burleigh, Haultain.

Cardiff.

Cheddar, Paudash.

Post Offices in the Province of Ontario, arranged according to Electoral Districts and Townships.—Continued.

PETERBORO', EAST RIDING.—*Continued.*

CAVENDISH.

—

CHANDOS.

Chandos.

CLYDE.

—

DOURO.

North Douro, South Douro.

DUDLEY.

—

DUMMER.

South Dummer,
Stony Lake,
Warsaw.

DYSART.

**Haliburton.*

EYRE.

—

GALWAY.

—

GLAMORGAN.

Gooderham.

GUILFORD.

Eagle Lake.

HARBURN.

—

HARCOURT.

—

HARVEY.

Hall's Bridge, Lakehurst.

HAVELOCK.

—

LAWRENCE.

—

LIVINGSTON

—

MCCLINTOCH.

—

METHUEN.

—

MINDEN.

Ingoldsby, Peterson.

MONMOUTH.

—

NIGHTINGALE.

—

OTONABEE.

Graystock,
Hiawatha,
Indian River,
**Keene,*
Lang,
Villiers.

PAPINEAU.

—

SHERBURNE.

—

SNOWDON.

Devil's Creek,
Minden.

STANHOPE.

Carnarvon.

PETERBORO', WEST RIDING.

ENNISMORE.

Ennismore.

MONAGHAN, NORTH.

**Peterborough,* Springville.

MONAGHAN, SOUTH.

Bensfort, South Monaghan.

SMITH.

Bridgenorth,
Selwyn,
Young's Point.

Post Offices in the Province of Ontario, arranged according to Electoral Districts and Townships.—Continued.

PRESCOTT.

Alfred.

Alfred.

Caledonia.

Caledonia Springs, Fenaghvale.

Hawkesbury, East.

Chute au Blondeau, East Hawkesbury, Little Rideau, Macbeth, St. Eugène, **Vankleek Hill.*

Hawkesbury, West.

**Hawkesbury.*

Longueuil.

Henry, **L'Orignal.*

Plantagenet, North.

Curran, **Plantagenet,* Treadwell, Wendover.

Plantagenet, South.

Fournier, Kerry, Pendleton, Riceville.

PRINCE EDWARD.

Ameliasburg.

Albury, Ameliasburg, *Consecon,* Mountain View, Rednersville.

Athol.

Cherry Valley, Point Petre.

Hallowell.

Allisonville, Bloomfield, **Picton,* West Lake.

Hillier.

Hillier, Melville, Rosehall, Wellington.

Marysburg.

Bongard's Corners, Cardwell, Cressy, *Milford,* Point Traverse, Prinyer, South Bay, Waupoos.

Sophiasburg.

Crofton, Demorestville, Gilbert's Mills, Green Point, *Northport.*

RENFREW, NORTH RIDING.

Post Offices in the Province of Ontario, arranged according to Electoral Districts and Townships.—Continued.

RENFREW, NORTH RIDING.—*Continued.*

PEMBROKE.

**Pembroke.*

PETAWAWA.

Petawawa.

ROLPH.

Point Alexander.

ROSS.

Cobden,
Forester's Falls,
Ross.

STAFFORD.

Stafford.

WESTMEATH.

Beachburg,
Gower Point,
Perretton,
Westmeath.

WILBERFORCE.

Lake Doré,
Rankin.

WYLIE.

—

RENFREW, SOUTH RIDING.

ADMASTON.

Admaston,
Shamrock.

BAGOT.

Bagot,
Calabogie.

BLITHFIELD.

High Falls.

BROUGHAM.

Dacre,
Mount St. Patrick.

BRUDENELL.

Brudenell,
**Rockingham.*

BURNS.

—

GRATTAN.

Eganville.

GRIFFITH.

Griffith.

HAGARTY.

—

HORTON.

Castleford,
Harcourt,
Renfrew.

JONES.

Bark Lake.

LYNEDOCH.

—

McNAB.

**Arnprior,*
Braeside,
Burnstown,
Sand Point,
Stewartville,
White Lake.

MATAWATCHAN.

Matawatchan.

RADCLIFFE.

Combermere,
Hopefield.

RAGLAN.

Palmer Rapids.

RICHARDS.

—

SEBASTOPOL.

Clontarf,
Foymount,
Vanbrugh.

SHERWOOD.

—

Post Offices in the Province of Ontario, arranged according to Electoral Districts and Townships.—Continued.

RUSSELL.

Cambridge.

Bentonville,
Casselman,
Grant.

Clarence.

Clarence,
Clarence Creek,
Rockland.

Cumberland.

Bear Brook,
Cumberland,
Cumberland Mills,
Navan,
Veighton.

Gloucester.

Billings' Bridge,
Eastman's Springs,
Hawthorne,
**New Edinburgh,*
Orleans,
Ramsay's Corners,
Rock Village.

Osgoode.

Kenmore,
Osgoode,
South Gloucester,
Vernon,
West Osgoode.

Russell.

Embrun,
Russell.

SIMCOE, NORTH RIDING.

Balaklava.

—

Flos.

Allenwood,
Apto,
Elmvale,
Fergusonvale,
Phelpston,
Vanvlack,
Vigo.

Matchedash.

—

Medonte.

**Coldwater,*
Coulson,
Craighurst,
Creighton,
Hillsdale,
Medonte,
Mount St. Louis,
Warminster.

Nottawasaga.

Avening,
**Collingwood,*
**Creemore,*
Dunedin,
Duntroon,
Glen Huron,
Maple Valley,
Nottawa,
Singhampton,
**Stayner.*

Orillia.

Ardtrea,
Couchiching,
Marchmont,
Orillia,
Washago.

Oro.

East Oro,
Edgar,
Hawkstone,
Jarrat's Corners,
Nevis,
Price's Corner,
Rugby,
Shanty Bay,
Steele.

Robinson.

—

Sunnidale.

Brentwood,
New Lowell,
Sunnidale.

Tay.

Midland,
Port Severn, (sub),
Vasey,
Victoria Harbor,
Wabashene,
Waverley.

Tiny.

Gibson,
Lafontaine,
**Penetanguishene,*
Wyebridge.

Vespra.

**Barrie,*
Dalston,
Grenfell,
Midhurst,
Minesing.

Post Offices in the Province of Ontario, arranged according to Electoral Districts and Townships.—Continued.

SIMCOE, SOUTH RIDING.

Essa.

**Angus,*
Egbert,
Elm Grove,
Ivy,
Nicolston,
Utopia,
West Essa.

Gwillimbury, West.

**Bondhead,*
**Bradford,*
Deerhurst,
Gilford.

Innisfil.

Allandale,
Bell Ewart,
Bramley,
Cherry Creek,
Churchill,
Craigvale,
Fennells,
Innisfil,
Lefroy,
Lennox,
Painswick,
Stroud,
Thornton,
Vine.

Mulmur.

Banda,
Black Bank,
Honeywood,
Lavender,
Mansfield,
Mulmur,
Perm,
Randwick,
**Rosemont,*
Stanton,
Whitfield.

Tecumseth.

Alliston,
Clover Hill,
**Cookstown,*
Newton Robinson,
Penville,
Tecumseth,
Thompsonville,
Tottenham,
Tuam.

Tosorontio.

Airlie,
Everett,
Glencairn.

STORMONT.

Finch.

Berwick,
Crysler,
South Finch.

Osnabruck.

Aultsville,
Dickinson's Landing,
Farran's Point,
Gallingertown,

Osnabruck.—*Continued.*

Lunenburg,
Newington.
Osnabruck Centre,
Wales.
Woodlands.

Roxborough.

Avonmore,
Gravel Hill,
Monckland,
Moose Creek.

TORONTO CITY, CENTRE, EAST AND WEST.

**Toronto.*

VICTORIA, NORTH RIDING.

Anson.

—

Bexley.

Aros,
Bexley.

Carden.

Carden,
Dalrymple,
Victoria Road Station.

Post Offices in the Province of Ontario, arranged according to Electoral Districts and Townships.—Continued.

VICTORIA, NORTH RIDING.—*Continued.*

Dalton.

Dartmoor,
Uphill.

Digby.

—

Eldon.

Argyle,
Bolsover,
Hartley,
**Kirkfield,*
Lorneville,
**Woodville.*

Fenelon.

Cambray,
Cameron,
**Fenelon Falls,*
Glenarm,
Islay,
Rosedale.

Franklin.

—

Hindon.

—

Laxton.

Head Lake,
Norland,
Oak Hill.

Longford.

—

Lutterworth.

—

Ridout.

—

Somerville.

Burnt River,
Bury's Green,
Kinmount,
Shedden,
Silver Lake.

VICTORIA, SOUTH RIDING.

Emily.

Downeyville,
Frank Hill,
**Omemee.*

Mariposa.

Little Britain,
Manilla,
Oakwood,
Port Hoover,
Sonya,
Valentia.

Ops.

**Lindsay,*
Mount Horeb,
Reaboro.

Verulam.

**Bobcaygeon,*
Dunsford.

Post Offices in the Province of Ontario, arranged according to Electoral Districts and Townships.—Continued.

WATERLOO, NORTH RIDING.

WATERLOO, NORTH.

**Berlin*,
Bloomingdale,
Breslau,
Bridgeport,
Erbsville,
Freiburg,
Kossuth,
**Waterloo*.

WELLESLEY.

Bamberg,
Crosshill,
Dorking,
Hawkesville.

WELLESLEY.—*Continued.*

Linwood,
St. Clements,
Wallenstein,
**Wellesley*.

WOOLWICH.

Conestogo,
Elmira,
Flora,
Heidelberg,
**St. Jacob's*,
West Montrose,
Winterbourne.

WATERLOO, SOUTH RIDING.

DUMFRIES, NORTH.

**Ayr*,
Branchton,
**Galt*,
Roseville.

WATERLOO, SOUTH.

Blair,
Doon.

WATERLOO, SOUTH.—*Continued.*

Freeport,
**Hespeler*,
New Aberdeen,
**Preston*.

WILMOT.

Baden,
Haysville,
Mannheim,
New Dundee,
**New Hamburg*,
Petersburg,
Philipsburg, West,
St. Agatha.

WELLAND.

BERTIE.

**Fort Erie*,
Mulgrave,
Ridgeway,
Stevensville.

CROWLAND.

Crowland,
**Welland*.

HUMBERSTONE.

Humberstone,
Netherby,
**Port Colborne*,
Sherkston.

STAMFORD.

**Chippawa*,
**Clifton*,
Clifton House (sub.),
**Drummondville, West*,
Montrose,
Stamford.

THOROLD.

Allanburg,
**Port Robinson*,
St. John's, West,
**Thorold*.

WILLOUGHBY.

Black Creek.

Post Offices in the Province of Ontario, arranged according to Electoral Districts and Townships.—Continued.

WELLINGTON, CENTRE RIDING.

Garafraxa, East and West.

Craigsholme,
**Garafraxa,*
Hereward,
Metz,
Marsville,
**Orangeville,*
Reading,
Vanatter.

Nichol.

Barnett,
Cumnock,
**Fergus,*
Salem.

Peel.

Alma,
Bosworth,
Creek Bank,
Drayton,
**Glenallan,*
Goldstone,
Macton,
Parker,
Stirton,
Winfield,
Yatton.

Pilkington.

**Elora,*
Pentland,
Ponsonby.

WELLINGTON, NORTH RIDING.

Amaranth.

Amaranth Station,
Bowling Green,
Farmington,
Laurel,
Waldemar,
Whittington.

Arthur.

**Arthur,*
Conn,
Kenilworth,
**Mount Forest,*
Petherton,
Riverstown,
Wagram.

Luther.

Colbeck,
Damascus,
Egerton,
Luther,

Luther.—*Continued.*

Monck.
Peepabun,
Tarbert.

Maryboro'.

Hollen,
Huston,
Lebanon,
Moorefield,
Rothesay,
Wyandott.

Minto.

Clifford,
Cotswold,
Drew,
**Harriston,*
Smithurst,
Teviotdale.

WELLINGTON, SOUTH RIDING.

Eramosa.

Eden Mills,
Eramosa,
Everton,
Oustic,
Rockwood,
Shiloh,
Speedside.

Erin.

Ballinafad,
Brisbane,
Coningsby,
**Erin,*
Hillsburgh,
Mimosa,
Ospringe.

Guelph.

Gourock,
**Guelph,*
Marden.

Puslinch.

Aberfoyle,
Arkell,
Crieff,
Killean,
Morriston,
Puslinch.

Post Offices in the Province of Ontario, arranged according to Electoral Districts and Townships.—Continued.

WENTWORTH, NORTH RIDING.

BEVERLEY.

Clyde,
Copetown,
Kirkwall,
Lynden,
Rockton,
Sheffield,
Troy,
Westover.

FLAMBORO', EAST.

Aldershot,
Carlisle.

FLAMBORO', EAST.—*Continued.*

Mountsberg,
**Waterdown.*

FLAMBORO', WEST.

Bullock's Corners,
**Dundas,*
Freelton,
Greensville,
Hayesland,
Mill Grove,
Strabane,
West Flamboro'.

WENTWORTH, SOUTH RIDING.

ANCASTER.

Alberton,
Ancaster,
Carluke,
Jerseyville,
Renforth,

BARTON.

Bartonville,
Hannon,
Ryckman's Corners.

BINBROOK.

Binbrook,
Black Heath.

BINBROOK.—*Continued.*

Sinclairville,
Woodburn.

GLANFORD.

Glanford,
North Glanford,
Renton Station.

SALTFLEET.

Elfrida,
Mount Albion,
Stony Creek,
Tapleytown,
Tweedside,
Winona.

YORK, EAST RIDING.

MARKHAM.

Almira,
Belford,
Boxgrove,
Buttonville,
Cashel,
Cedar Grove,
Dollar,
Gormley,
Hagerman's Corners,
Headford,
Langstaff (sub.),
**Markham,*
Milliken,
Milnesville,
Mongolia,
Unionville,
Victoria Square.

SCARBORO'.

Agincourt,
Armadale.

SCARBORO'.—*Continued.*

Danforth,
Ellesmere,
Highland Creek,
Malvern,
Scarboro' Junction,
**Scarboro',*
Wexford,
Woburn.

YORK, EAST.

Davisville,
Don,
Doncaster,
Eglinton,
Lansing,
Leslie,
Norway,
York Mills,
Yorkville.

YORK, NORTH RIDING.

Post Offices in the Province of Ontario, arranged according to Electoral Districts and Townships.—Concluded.

YORK, NORTH RIDING.—*Continued.*

Gwillimbury, North.

Belhaven,
Keswick,
Ravenshoe,
Roache's Point.

King.

Eversly,
Kettleby,
King,
King Creek,
Laskay,
Linton,

King.—*Continued.*

Lloydtown,
Nobleton.
Schomburg,
Temperanceville.

Whitchurch.

**Aurora*,
Ballantrae,
Bethesda,
Bloomington,
Lemonville,
**New Market*,
Oak Ridges,
Pine Orchard,
Ringwood,
**Stouffville*,
Vivian,
White Rose.

YORK, WEST RIDING.

Etobicoke.

Highfield,
Humber,
Islington,
Mimico,
Thistletown.

Vaughan.

Carrville,
Concord,
Edgely,
Elder's Mills,
Klineburg,
Maple,
Patterson,
Pinegrove,
Purpleville,
**Richmond Hill.*

Vaughan.—*Continued.*

Teston,
**Thornhill*,
Vellore,
Woodbridge.

York, West.

Brockton,
Davenport,
Downsview,
L'Amaroux,
Lambton Mills,
Newton Brook,
Seaton,
**Weston*,
Will owdale.

POST OFFICES

IN THE

PROVINCE OF QUEBEC,

ARRANGED ACCORDING TO ELECTORAL DISTRICTS.

ARGENTEUIL.

Arundel, Avoca, Britonville, Brownsburg, Cambria, *Carillon,*	Chatboro, Cushing, Dalesville, Dunany, Edina, Geneva,	Genoa, *Grenville,* Harrington, East, Lachute, Lakefield,	Mille Isles, **St. Andrew's, East,* Shrewsbury, Stonefield, St. Philippe d'Argenteuil

BAGOT.

**Actonvale,* Britannia Mills, St. Dominique,	St. Ephrem d'Upton, Ste. Hélène de Bagot, *St. Hugues,*	St. Liboire, St. Pie, Ste. Rosalie,	St. Simon de Yamaska, St. Théodore.

BEAUCE.

Broughton, East Broughton, Grandes Coudées, Jersey, River Chaudière, Kennebec, Line,	La Beauce, Lambton, Marlow, River Gilbert, St. Elzéar,	St. Ephrem de Tring, St. Evariste de Forsyth, St. François, St. Frédéric, St. George,	St. Honoré, St. Joseph, St. Victor de Tring, Valletort, West Broughton.

BEAUHARNOIS.

**Beauharnois,* Landreville,	Melocheville, St. Etienne de Beauharnois	St. Louis de Gonzague, St. Stanislas de Kostka,	St. Timothée, **Valleyfield.*

BELLECHASSE.

Armagh, Beaumont, [illegible]	St. Charles, River Boyer, St. Gervais, [illegible]	St. Magloire, St. Michel,	St. Raphael, East, St. Vallier.

Post Offices in the Province of Quebec, arranged according to Electoral Districts.—Continued.

BERTHIER.

**Berthier (en haut)*, Isle Dupas, Lanoraie,	Lavaltrie, St. Barthélemi, St. Cuthbert,	St. Damien de Brandon, St. Gabriel de Brandon, St. Michel des Saints,	St. Norbert, St. Zenon.

BONAVENTURE.

Assametquagan Avignon, Bonaventure (sub), Bonaventure River, Broadlands, Caplin,	*Carleton*, Cross Point, Dee Side, Escuminac (sub), Fleurant, Lanse aux Gascons,	Maria, *Matapédia*, New Carlisle, New Richmond, Nouvelle (sub),	*Paspebiac*, Port Daniel, Runnymede, Shigawake, Shoolbred.

BROME.

Abercorn, *Adamsville*, Bolton, Centre, Bolton Forest, *Brigham*, Brome, Bromemere,	*Dillonton*, East Bolton, East Farnham, Emerson, Farnham, Centre, Fulford, Glen Sutton,	Herbert, Iron Hill, **Knowlton*, Knowlton Landing. *Mansonville—Potton*, North Sutton,	St. Etienne de Bolton, South Bolton, **Sutton*, West Bolton, West Brome, West Potton.

CHAMBLY.

Boucherville, Chambly Basin,	**Chambly Canton*, *Longueuil*,	St. Bazil le Grand, St. Bruno,	St. Hubert, St. Lambert, Montreal.

CHAMPLAIN.

Batiscan, Batiscan Bridge, Cap. Magdeleine, Champlain,	Ste. Anne de la Pèrade, Ste. Flore, St. Maurice,	St. Narcisse, St. Prosper, St. Stanislas,	St. Tite, Valmont, Vincennes.

CHARLEVOIX.

Cap à l'Aigle (sub), Clairvaux (sub), Isle aux Coudres (sub), La Petite Rivière St. François (sub),	Les Eboulemens, **Murray Bay*, Pointe à Pic, Port au Persil,	Ste. Agnes, St. Fidèle, St. Irénée,	**St. Paul's Bay*, Settrington, St. Urbain.

Post Offices in the Province of Quebec, arranged according to Electoral Districts.—Continued.

CHATEAUGUAY.

Allan's Corners,
Aubrey,
Chateauguay,
Chateauguay Basin,
Howick,
North Georgetown,
Norton Creek,
Ormstown,
Russeltown,
St. Jean Crysostôme,
St. Martine,
Ste. Philomène,
St. Urbain,
Stockwell.

CHICOUTIMI AND SAGUENAY.

Chicoutimi.

Bagotville,
Chambord,
Chicoutimi,
Grande Baie,
Jonquières,
Labarre,
L'Anse au Foin,
L'Anse St. Jean,
Laterrière,
Metabechouan,
Roberval,
St. Cyriac,
Tremblay,
St. Prime.

Saguenay.

Bersimis,
Esquimaux Point,
Les Escoumains,
Les Petites Bergeronnes,
Magpie,
Mille Vaches,
Mingan,
Moisic,
Natashquan,
Pointe au Bouleau,
Sault au Cochon,
Sheldrake,
Tadousac.

COMPTON.

Birchton,
Brookbury,
Bulwer,
Canterbury,
**Compton,*
Cookshire,
East Clifton,
East Hereford,
Eaton,
Glidden,
Gould,
Hereford,
Island Brook,
Johnville,
Lake Megantic,
Learned Plain,
Linda,
Maple Leaf,
Martinville,
Moe's River,
Paquette,
Perryboro',
Piopolis,
Richby,
Robinson,
St. Edwige,
St. Malo,
St. Romaine,
Sawyerville,
Scottstown,
Stornoway,
Vilette,
Waterville,
Westbury,
West Ditton,
Whitton.

DORCHESTER.

Cranbourne,
Frampton,
Hemison,
Lake Etchemin,
Langevin,
St. Anselme,
St. Bernard,
Ste. Claire,
St. Edouard de Frampton,
Ste. Hénédine,
St. Isidore,
St. Malachie,
Ste. Marguerite,
Standon.

DRUMMOMD AND ARTHABASKA.

Drummond.

Danby,
Drummondville, East,
French Village,
Kingsey,
Kingsey Falls,
Kirkdale,
L'Avenir,
Ruisseau des Chênes,
St Bonaventure
St. Germain de Grantham,
St. Guillaume d'Upton,
South Durham,
Sydenham Place,
Trenholm,
Ulverton,
Wheatland,
Wickham, West.

Arthabaska.

Arthabaskaville,
Arthabaska Station,
Blandford,
Bulstrode,
Chester,
Domaine de Gentilly,
East Arthabaska,
East Chester,
Maddington,
St. Albert,
Ste. Clothilde,
St. Patrick's Hill,
Stanfold,
Trout Brook,
Viger Mines,
Warwick, East. 12

Post Offices in the Province of Quebec, arranged according to Electoral Districts.—Continued.

GASPÉ.

Barachois de Malbay,
Cap Chat,
Cap des Rosiers,
Cape Cove,
Chlorydormes,
Douglastown,
Etang du Nord (sub),
Fox River,
Gaspé Basin,
Grand Entry,
Grande Grêve,
Grande Vallée,
Grande Pabos,
Grand River,
House Harbor (sub),
Magdalen Islands,
Mont Louis,
Newport,
Newport Point,
Peninsula, Gaspé,
Percé,
Point St. Peter,
Rivière la Madeleine,
Ste. Anne des Monts,
Sandy Beach.

HOCHELAGA.

Cote des Neiges,
Cote St. Paul,
Hochelaga,
Long Point,
Mile End,
Pointe aux Trémbles,
Rivière des Prairies,
St. Agnes de Dundee,
St. Jean Baptiste de Montreal,
Sault au Recollet,
Tannery West.

HUNTINGDON.

Anderson's Corners,
Athelstan,
Barrington,
Cazaville,
Corbin,
Covey Hill,
Dewittville,
Dundee,
Dundee, Centre,
Franklin, Centre,
Hallerton,
Helena,
Hemmingford,
Herdman's Corners,
Huntingdon,
Kelso,
La Guerre,
Maritana,
Port Lewis,
Powerscourt,
Rockburn,
Ste. Agnèse de Dundee,
St. Anicet,
St. Regis,
Starnesboro',
Trout River,
Vicars.

IBERVILLE,

Henryville,
Mount Johnson,
St. Alexandre,
St. Athanase,
Ste. Brigide,
St. Sebastian,
Sabrevois,
Versailles.

JACQUES CARTIER.

Isle Bizard,
**Lachine*,
Pointe Claire,
**Point St. Charles*,
Ste. Anne Bout de L'Isle,
Ste. Geneviève,
St. Laurent.

JOLIETTE.

Daillebout,
De Ramsay,
**Joliette*,
Kildare,
Radstock,
St. Alphonse,
Ste. Beatrix,
St. Côme,
Ste. Elizabeth,
Ste. Emelie de l'Energie,
St. Félix de Valois,
St. Jean de Matha,
St. Paul d'Industrie,
St. Thomas, East,

Post Offices in the Province of Quebec, arranged according to Electoral Districts.—Continued.

KAMOURASKA.

Coteaux Rivière Ouelle, *Kamouraska,* Mount Carmel, Rivière Ouelle, St. Alexandre,	St. André, *Ste. Anne la Pocatière,* St. Denis de la Bouteillerie,	Ste. Hélène, St. Onézime, St. Pacômé,	St. Paschal, St. Philippe de Néry.

LAPRAIRIE.

Caughnawaga, **Laprairie,*	St. Constant, St. Isidore,	St. Jacques le Mineur,	St. Philippe.

L'ASSOMPTION.

Charlemagne, Lachenaie, **L'Assomption.*	L'Epiphanie, Mascouche, Mascouche Rapids,	Repentigny, St. Lin, St. Paul l'Hermite,	St. Roch l'Achigan, St. Sulpice.

LAVAL.

Bord à Plouffe, St. Dorothee,	St. François de Sales, St. Martin,	Ste. Rose,	St. Vincent de Paul.

LEVIS.

Baillargeon, Bienville, Chaudiere Mills, Chaudiere Station,	Craig's Road Station, Indian Cove, *Lauzon,* **Levis,*	New Liverpool, St. Henri, St. Henri Station, St. Jean Chryostôme,	St. Lambert, St. Nicholas, **South Quebec,*

L'ISLET.

Garneau, Isle aux Grues, Lac Noir, Lamartine,	L'Anse à Giles, L'Islet, St. Aubert, St. Cyrille,	St. Jean, Port Joli, Ste. Louise, St. Roch des Aulnaies,	Trois Saumons, Vaillancourt, *Village des Anlnaies.*

LOTBINIÈRE.

Post Offices in the Province of Quebec, arranged according to Electoral Districts.—Continued.

MASKINONGÉ.

Hunterstown, Maskinongé, Pont de Maskinongé,	*River du Loup (en haut),* St. Didace,	St. Justin, St. Léon,	St. Paulin, Ste. Ursule.

MEGANTIC.

Adderley, Bécancour Station, Bute, Clapham, East Magdala, Glenloyd, Glen Murray, Harvey Hill Mines,	**Inverness,* Irvine, Kinnear's Mills, Larochelle, **Leeds,* Leeds Village, Lemesurier,	Lower Ireland, Lyster Station, Lyster, Maple Grove, Millfield, New Ireland, Redesdale,	*St. Ferdinand,* Ste. Julie de Somerset, St. Pierre Baptiste, Ste. Sophie, *Somerset,* Thiers, Woodside.

MISSISQUOI.

Abbott's Corners, Aird, *Bedford,* Clarenceville, *Cowansville,* *Durham,* East Dunham, Farnboro', Farndon,	**Frelighsburg,* Haseville, Malmaison, Miranda, Moore's Station, Mystic, North Pinnacle, North Stanbridge, Noyan,	Nutt's Corners, Pearceton, *Philipsburg East,* Pigeon Hill, *Pike River,* Riceburg, St. Armand, Centre, St. Armand Station, St. Charles de Stanbridge,	Stanbridge Ridge, Stanbridge, East, Stanbridge Station, Stanbury, *Sweetsburg,* Upper Bedford, Venice, **West Farnham.*

MONTCALM.

Beaulac, Chantelle, Kilkenny, Montcalm,	Mount Loyal, Rawdon, St. Alexis,	St. Esprit, St. HippolytedeKilkenny St. Jacques,	Ste. Julienne, St. Liguori, St. Théodore de Chertsey.

MONTMAGNY.

Berthier *(en bas),* Cap St. Ignace,	**Montmagny,* St. François,	St. Paul du Buton,	St. Pierre.

MONTMORENCY.

Anges Gardien, Beaulieu, Château Richer, Laval,	Ste. Anne de Beaupré, Ste. Famille St. Féréol *(sub.),*	St. François d'Orléans, St. Jean d'Orléans, St. Joachin,	St. Laurent d'Orléans, St Pierre d'Orléans, St. Tite des Caps.

Post Offices in the Province of Quebec, arranged according to Electoral Districts.—Continued.

MONTREAL, CITY, CENTRE, EAST AND WEST.

**Montreal.*

NAPIERVILLE.

La Pigeonnière, *Napierville,*	St. Edouard,	*St. Rémi,*	Sherrington.

NICOLET.

Aston Station, *Bécancour,* Gentilly, *Nicolet,*	Ste. Angele de Laval, Ste. Brigitte des Saults, St. Célestin, Ste. Gertrude,	St. Grégoire, St. Leonard, Ste. Monique,	St. Perpetue, St. Pierre les Becquets, St. Wenceslas.

OTTAWA.

Angers, Aubigny, **Aylmer, East,* Aylwin, Bassin du Liévre, Blanche, **Buckingham,* Cantley, Cascades, **Chelsea,*	Eardley, East Templeton, Heyworth, **Hull,* Ironside, Kazubazua, Kirk's Ferry, Lochaber Bay, Low, Lucerne,	Masham Mills, Mayo, Montebello, North Nation Mills, North Wakefield, Papineauville, Pelissier, Perkins, River Desert, Rupert,	St. André Avellin, Sevigné, Six Portages, Templeton, **Thurso,* Upper Wakefield, Venosta, Vinoy, Wakefield, Wright.

PONTIAC.

Allumette Island, Bristol, *Bryson,* Calumette Island, Chichester, Chippewa, Clarendon Centre,	Clarendon Front (sub), Collfield, Danford Lake, Dunraven, Fort Coulonge, Fort William, Kippewa,	Lake Temiscamingue, North Bristol, North Onslow, **Onslow,* Otter Lake, **Portage du Fort,* Rapides des Joachims,	Rowanton, Sheenboro', Thornby, Thorne Centre, Vinton, Waltham, Yarm.

PORTNEUF.

Post Offices in the Province of Ontario, arranged according to Electoral Districts.—Continued.

QUEBEC CITY, CENTRE, EAST AND WEST.

Hedleyville,	**Quebec*,	*St. Roch de Québec.*	*St. Sauveur de Québec.*

QUEBEC COUNTY.

Ancienne Lorette, Ancienne Lorette (sub.), Beauport, Bergerville,	Cap Rouge, Charlesbourg, Lake Beauport, Lorette,	Montmorency Falls, St. Foy, Sillery Cove,	Spencer Cove, Stoneham, Valcartier.

RICHELIEU.

St. Aimé, St. Marcel,	St. Ours, St. Robert,	St. Roch de Richelieu, Ste. Victoire,	**Sorel.*

RICHMOND AND WOLFE.

Richmond.		Wolfe.	
Brompton, *Brompton Falls*, Castlebar, *Danville*, Denison's Mills, Fontenoy, Kingsbury, **Melbourne*,	Melbourne Ridge, North Stoke, **Richmond, East*, Richmond Station, St. George de Windsor, Stoke, Centre, Stoketon, Windsor Mills,	Dudswell, Garthby, Lake Aylmer, Lake Weedon, Marbleton, North Ham, St. Camille,	St. Fortunat, Sanborn, South Ham, Weedon, Wolfstown, Wotton.

RIMOUSKI.

Bic, Causapscal, Cedar Hall, Dalibaire, Father Point,	Macnider, *Matane*, *Métes*, Neigette, Petit Métis,	**Rimouski*, St. Anaclet, St. Fabien, Ste. Félicité, Ste. Flavie,	Ste. Luce, St. Mathieu, St. Moïse, St. Octave, St. Simon de Rimouski. Tiessierville.

ROUVILLE.

Post Offices in the Province of Quebec, arranged according to Electoral Districts.—Continued.

ST. HYACINTHE.

La Présentation, St. Barnabé, River Yamaska,	St. Charles, River Richelieu, St. Damase,	St Denis, River Richelieu, **St. Hyacinthe*,	St. Jude, Soixante.

ST. JOHN'S.

Belle Alodie, Grand Ligne, Henrysburg,	L'Acadie, *Lacolle*, Roxham,	St. Bernard (sud), **St. John's, East*, St. Luc,	St. Valentin, Stottville.

ST. MAURICE.

Mont Elie, Pointe du Lac, St. Barnabé,	St. Elie, St. Etienne des Grés,	St. Maurice Forges, St. Sévère,	Shawenegan, *Yamachiche*.

SHEFFORD.

Bethel, Boscobel, Clarina, Egypte, Frost Village, Granboro', **Granby*,	Lawrenceville, Mawcook, Milton, East, North Stukely, Rochelle, *Roxton Falls*, Roxton Pond,	St. Joachim de Shefford, St. Valérien, Savage's Mills, Shefford Mountain, South Ely, South Granby,	South Roxton, South Stukely, Valcourt, Warden, **Waterloo*, West Shefford.

SHERBROOKE TOWN.

Ascot Corner, Capelton,	Huntingville, **Lennoxville*,	Milby, Rock Forest,	**Sherbrooke*.

SOULANGES.

Cedars, Coteau du Lac, *Coteau Landing*,	Coteau Station, Mountjoy, Pont Chateau.	River Beaudette, St. Clet, St. Dominique des Cedres,	*St. Polycarpe*, St. Zotique.

STANSTEAD.

Post Offices in the Province of Quebec, arranged according to Electoral Districts.—Continued.

TEMISCOUATA.

Armand, Bégon, *Cacouna,* Détour du Lac, Green River,	Isle Verte, Notre Dame du Portage, **River du Loup (en bas),* River Trois Pistoles, St. Antonin,	St. Arsène, St Eloi, St. Francois Xavier de Viger, Ste Françoise,	Ste. Modeste, Trois Pistoles, Vauban, Viger.

TERREBONNE.

Beresford, Lac Masson, Montmorin, New Glasgow,	Ste. Adèle, Ste. Anne des Plaines, St. Janvier,	*St. Jérome,* St. Sauveur, Ste. Sophie de Lacorne,	*Ste. Therèse de Blainville,* Shawbridge. **Terrebonne.*

THREE RIVERS, CITY.

**Three Rivers.*

TWO MOUNTAINS.

Belle Rivière, Oka, St. Augustin, St. Benoit,	St. Canute, St. Columbin, *St. Eustache,* St. Hermas,	St. Joseph du Lac, St. Monique de Deux Montagnes,	Ste. Placide, *Ste. Scholastique.*

VAUDREUIL

Como, Hudson, Isle Perrot,	Mongenais, Mount Oscar, Peveril,	Point Fortune, Rigaud, Ste. Justine de Newton,	Ste. Marthe, Vaudreuil.

VERCHÈRES.

Belœil Station, Belœil Village,	Contrecœur, St. Antoine,	Ste. Julie, St. Marc,	Varennes, Verchéres.

YAMASKA.

Chatillon, La Baie, Pierreville,	Pierreville Mills, Rivière aux Vaches,	*River David,* St. François du Lac,	St. Zéphirin, Yamaska.

POST OFFICES AND WAY OFFICES

IN THE

PROVINCE OF NOVA SCOTIA,

ARRANGED ACCORDING TO ELECTORAL DISTRICTS.

ANNAPOLIS.

Annapolis
Belleisle, W.O.
Bridgetown
Chute's Cove, W.O.
Clementsport
Clementsvale, W.O.
Deep Brook, W. O.
Granville Centre, W.O.
Granville Ferry
Lawrencetown
Lequille, W.O.
Lower Granville, W.O.
Maitland, W.O.
Margaretsville, W.O.
Marshall's Cove, W.O.
Melvern Square, W.O.
Middleton
Milford, W.O.
Saw Mill Creek, W.O.
Mount Hanly, W.O.
New Albany, W.O.
Nicholl's Corner, W.O.
Nicteau Falls, W.O.
Paradise Lane, W.O.
Parker's Cove, W.O.
Port George, W.O.
Round Hill, W.O.
Spa Springs, W.O.
Springfield, W.O.
Stoddart's, W.O.
Stronach Mountain, W.O.
Torbrook, W.O.
Tupperville, W.O.
Webber's W.O.
Wilmot.

ANTIGONISHE.

Antigonishe Harbour W.O.
Addington Forks, W.O.
Antigonishe
Arisaig, W.O.
Back Lands, W.O.
Barrio's Beach, W.O.
Bayfield, W.O.
Big Tracadie, W.O.
Black River, W.O.
Briley's Brook, W.O.
Caledonia Mills, W.O.
Cape George
Cape George, North side, W.O.
Cross Roads, Ohio, W.O.
Big Mountain, W.O.
Fraser's Grant, W.O.
Glen, W.O.
Glen, Alpine, W O
Glen Road, W.O.
Goshen, W.O.
Harbor au Bouche, W.O.
Harbor Road, W.O.
Head of South River Lake, W.O.
Keppoch, W.O.
Lakevale, W.O.
Little River, W.O.
Little Tracadie, W.O.
Livingston's Cove, W.O.
Lochaber, W.O.
Lowe Settlement South River, W.O.
Malignant Cove, W.O.
Marshy Hope, W.O.
Marydale, W.O.
Maryvale, W.O.
Middle Settlement of South River, W.O.
Morristown, W.O.
Ohio, W.O.
Point of Cape, W.O.
Pomquet Chapel, W.O.
Pomquet Forks, W.O.
St. Andrews
Tracadie
Upper Settlement of South River, W.O.
Usher, W.O.
Vernal, W.O.
West side of Lochaber, W.O.

CAPE BRETON.

Albert Bridge, W.O.
Beaver Cove, W.O.
Benacadie, W.O.
Big Lorraine, W.O.
Big Pond, W.O.
Black Brook, W.O.
Boisdale Chapel, W.O.
Bridgeport, W.O.
Cariboo Cove, W.O.
Catalone, W.O.
Christmas Island, W.O.
Cow Bay
East Bay, W.O.
East Bay, North side, [W.O.
Enon, W.O.
Eskasoni, W.O.
False Bay Beach, W.O.
Frenchvale, W.O.
Gabarus, W.O.
Gardiner Mines, W.O.
Georgis River, W.O.
Gillies Lake, W.O.
Grand Mira, North
Grand Mira, South
Hillside, W.O.
Irish Cove, W.O.
Leitches Creek
Lewis Bay, W.O.
Lingan
Little Bras d'Or
Little Glace Bay,
Little Lorraine, W.O.
Lorway Mines, W.O.
Louisburg, W.O.
McAdam's Lake, W.O.
Mainadieu, W.O.
Marion Bridge, W.O.
Mira Gut, W.O.
North Sydney
North West Arm, W.O.
Port Caledonia, W.O.
Reserve Mines, W.O.
Salmon River, W.O.
Shunacadie, W.O.
South Bar of Sydney River, W.O.
Sydney Forkes, W.O.
Sydney
Sydney Mines
Victoria Mines, W.O.

Post Offices and Way Offices in the Province of Nova Scotia, arranged according to Electoral Districts.—Continued.

COLCHESTER.

Acadia Mines
Bass River, W.O.
Brookfield
Central Onslow, W.O.
Chigonaise River, W.O.
Cook's Brook, W.O.
Dickson's Store, W.O.
Earltown, W.O.
Eastville, W.O.
Economy
Five Islands
Folly Lake, W.O.
Folly Mountain, W.O.
Folly River, W.O.
Forbes, W.O.
Gold Fields, W.O.
Goshen, W.O.
Great Village,
Green's Creek, W.O.
Halfway Brook, W.O.
Hardwood Lands, W.O.
Head of Tatamagouche, W.O.
Kempt Town, W.O.
Londonderry
Londonderry Station
Lower Stewiacke
Mast Town, W.O.
Middle Stewiacke
New Annan, W.O.
Newton Mills, W.O.
North River, W.O.
North River Bridge, W.O.
North Section of Earltown, W.O.
Old Barns, W.O.
Onslow, W.O.
Point Bruley, W.O.
Portapique, W.O.
Portapique Mountain, W.O.
Princeport, W.O.
Riversdale, W.O.
St. Andrew's, W.O.
Shubenacadie
South Branch, W.O.
Stewiacke Cross Roads,
Tatamagouche
Tatamagouche Mountain, W.O.
Teviotdale Station, W.O.
Truro
Upper Economy, W.O.
Upper Stewiacke
Waugh's River, W.O.
West Branch, River Philip, W.O.

CUMBERLAND.

Advocate Harbor
Amherst
Amherst Hill, W.O.
Amherst Point, W.O.
Apple River, W.O.
Athol, W.O.
Barronsfield, W.O.
Black Rock, W.O.
Brookville, W. O.
Brown's Brook, W.O.
Cannonville, W.O.
Claremont, W.O.
Eel Creek, W.O.
Fenwick, W.O.
Fox Harbor, W.O.
Fox River, W.O.
Goose River
Greenville Station
Greenville, W.O.
Gulf Shore, W.O.
Halfway River, W
Hastings, W.O.
Head of Amherst, W O.
Head of Wallace Bay, W.O.
Head of Wallace Bay, North Side, W.O.
Henderson Settlement, W.O.
Hornsey, W.O.
Joggin Mines, W.O
Kirk Hill, W.O.
Kolbeck, W.O.
Lakelands, W.O.
Lake Road, W.O.
Lawrence Factory, W.O
Leicester, W.O.
Little River, W.O.
Lower Cove, W.O.
Maccan, W.O.
Maccan Mountain, W.O.
Malagash, W.O.
Middleboro' W.O.
Minudie, W.O.
Mount Pleasant, W.O.
Nappan, W.O.
North Shore, W.O.
Oxford
Parrsborough
Parrsborough Shore, W. O.
Partridge Island, W.O.
Port Greville, W.O.
Port Philip, W.O.
Pugwash
Pugwash River, W.O.
River Hébert, W.O.
River Philip
Rockly, W.O.
Rockwell Settlement, W.O.
Roslin, W.O.
Salem, W.O.
Section 7, W.O.
Shinemicas Bridge
Shulie, W.O.
Six Mile Road, W.O.
Southampton, W.O.
Spencer's Island, W.O.
Spring Hill, W.O.
Springhill Mines, W.O.
Street's Ridge, W.O.
Thompson's Mills
Three Sisters, W.O.
Tidnish, W.O.
Victoria, W.O.
Wallace
Wallace Bridge, W.O.
Wallace Ridge, W.O.
Wallace River, W.O.
Warren, W.O.
Wentworth, W.O.
Westbrook, W.O.
West Chester, W.O.
West Chester Lake, W. O.
Williamsdale, W.O.
Windham Hill, W.O.

DIGBY.

Bear River, (West Side)
Beaver River, W.O.
Beaver River Corner
Belliveaus Cove, W.O.
Cedar Lake, W.O.
Clare, W.O.
Digby
Gilbert Cove, W.O.
Gross Coques
Havelock, W.O.
Head of St. Mary's Bay, W.O.
Little River, W.O.
Long Island
Marshall's Town, W.O.
Metaghan, W.O.
Metaghan River, W.O.
New Tusket, W.O.
North Range Corner, W.O.
Petite Passage, W.O.
Pleasant Valley, W.O.
Port Acadie, W.O.
Rossway, W.O.
St. Mary's Bay
Salmon River, W.O.
Sandy Cove
Saulnierville, W.O.
Smith's Cove, W.O.
South Range, W.O.
Speitche's Cove, W.O.
Trout Cove, W.O.
Weaver Settlement, W.O.
Westport
Weymouth
Weymouth Bridge

GUYSBOROUGH.

Caledonia, St. Mary's, W.O
Canso
Charlo's Cove, W.O.
Cole Harbor, W.O.
Cross Roads (Country Harbor)
Cross Roads, Middle Melford, W.O.
Crow Harbor, W.O.
East River, St. Mary's, W.O.
Erinville, W.O.
Forristalls, W.O.
Giant's Lake, W.O.
Glenelg
Goldenville

Post Offices and Way Offices in the Province of Nova Scotia, arranged according to Electoral Districts and Townships.—Continued.

GUYSBOROUGH.—*Continued*.

Grosvenor, W.O.
Guysborough
Guysborough Intervale, W.O.
Half Island Cove, W.O.
Indian Harbour, W.O.
Isaac's Harbour, W.O.
Isaac's Harbour, (East Side) W.O.
Larry's River, W.O.
Liscomb, W.O.
Manchester, W.O.
Maria Joseph, W.O.
Melrose
Milford Haven Bridge, W.O.
New Harbour, W.O.
New Town, W.O.
Oyster Ponds, W.O.
Pirate Harbour
Port Felix, W.O.
Port Mulgrave
Ragged Head, W.O.
Roman's Valley, W.O.
Salmon River, W.O.
Salmon River, Lake Settlement, W.O.
Sand Point, W.O.
Sherbrooke
Smithfield, W.O.
Sonora, W.O.
Steep Creek, W.O.
Still Water, W.O.
Stormont, W.O.
Torbay, W.O.
Upper Cross Roads, St. Mary's, W.O.
White Head, W.O.
White Harbour, W.O.

HALIFAX CITY AND HALIFAX COUNTY.

Antrim, W.O.
Beaver Bank, W.O.
Bedford Basin, W.O.
Black Point, W.O.
Brookvale
Cambridge, W.O.
Carroll's Corners, W.O.
Chezzetcook, W.O.
Clam Harbour, W.O.
Dartmouth
Dean, W.O.
Dover, West, W.O
East Jeddore, W.O.
East Side of Chezzetcook, W.O.
Ecum Secum, W.O.
English Corner, W.O.
Fletcher's Station, W.O.
Gay's River, W.O.
Gay's River Road, W.O.
Hackett's Cove, W.O.
Halifax
Harrigan Cove, W.O.
Head of St. Margaret's Bay, W.O.
Head of St. Margaret's Bay, Middle District, W.O.
Hubbard's Cove
Indian Harbour, W.O.
Ingram River, W.O.
Jeddore, W.O.
Ketch Harbour, W.O.
Lawrencetown, W.O.
Little River, (Middle Musquodoboit)
Lower Prospect, W.O.
Lower Ward, St. Margaret's Bay, W.O.
Lower Ship Harbour, W. O.
Meagher's Grant, W.O.
Middle Musquodoboit
Montague Gold Mines, W.O.
Moser's River, W.O.
Musquodoboit Harbour, W.O.
Necum Tench, W.O.
New Caledonia, W.O.
Newcomb Corner
Oakfield, W.O.
Oldham, W.O.
Peggy's Cove, W.O.
Pleasant Point, W.O.
Porter's Lake, W.O.
Portuguese Cove, W.O.
Preston Road, W.O.
Prospect, W.O.
Richmond Terminus, W. O.
St. Margaret's Bay
Salmon Hole, W.O.
Salmon River, W.O.
Sambro, W.O.
Sandy Beaches, W.O.
Sheet Harbour
Ship Harbour, W.O.
South-East Passage, W.O.
Spry Bay, W.O.
Tangier
Terence Bay, W.O.
Trafalgar, W.O.
Upper Caledonia, W.O.
Upper Musquodoboit
Waverley
West Newdy Quoddy, W.O.
Wickwire Station
Windsor Junction, W.O.

HANTS.

Burnt Coat, W.O.
Cheverie, W.O.
Cogmagun River, W.O.
Densmores, W.O.
Densmores Mills, W.O.
Ellershausen, W.O.
Elmsdale
Enfield
Falmouth, W.O.
Falmouth (Windsor Bridge, W.O.)
Five Mile River, W.O.
Gore, W.O.
Hantsport
Highfield, W.O.
Indian Road, W.O.
Kennetcook, W.O.
Kennetcook Corner, W. O.
Lower Selmah, W.O.
Maitland
Millers Creek, W.O.
Moose Brook, W.O.
Mortonville, W.O.
Mosherville, W.O.
Mount Denison, W.O.
Mount Uniacke
Newport
Newport Corner, W.O.
Newport Landing
Newport Station
Nine Mile River, W.O.
Noel, W.O.
Noel Shore, W.O.
North Salem, W.O.
Rawdon, W O
Renfrew
St. Croix, W O
Scotch Village, W O
Selmah, W O
South Rawdon, W O
Summerville, W O
Tenecape, W O
Three Mile Plains, W O
Upper Kennetcook, W O
Upper Newport, W O
Upper Rawdon, W O
Urbania, W O
Vaughans, W O
Walton
West Gore, W O
Windsor
Woodville, W O

INVERNESS.

Big Brook, W O
Big Harbour, W O
Big Intervale, Grand Nar- W O
Blue's Mill, W O
Boom, W O
Broad Cove Chapel, W O
Broad Cove, Marsh, W O
Cape Mabou, W O
Cheticamp, W O
...imney Corner, W O
Cross Roads, Lake Ainslie, W O
Cross Roads, St. George's Channel, W O

Post Offices and Way Offices in the Province of Nova Scotia, arranged according to Electoral Districts.—Continued.

INVERNESS.—*Continued.*

Eastern Harbor, W O
Emerald, W O
Glenedale, W O
Grand Etang, W O
Hay's River, W O
Hillsborough, C B., W O
Judique, W O
Kewstoke, W O
Lake Ainslie, W O
Lake Ainslie (East side) W O
Lake Ainslie (South side) W O
Lake Law, W O
Little Judique, W O
Little Narrows, W O
Long Point, W O
Low Point, W O
Mabou
Mabou Coal Mines, W O
Mabou Harbor, W O
Malagawatch, W O
Marble Mountain, W O
Margaree, W O
Margaree, (Forks)
Middle Section of North-East Margaree, W O
Middle Settlement of River Inhabitants, W O
Mull River, W O
New Bridge, W O
North-East Branch, Margaree, W O
North Side of Basin, River Dennis, W O
Pleasant Bay, W O
Port Hastings
Port Hawkesbury
Port Hood
Port Hood Island, W O
Queensville, W O
Rear Judique, W O
River Dennis, W O
River Dennis Road, W O
Shea's River, W O
Sight Point, W O
Sky Glen, W O
South Side of Basin, (River Dennis), W O
South side of Whycocomagh Bay, W O
South side of West Margaree, W O
South-West Mabou, W O
Upper Margaree, W O
Upper Settlement of River Dennis, W O
West Bay
Whycocomagh
Whycocomagh Rear

KING'S.

Avonport, W O
Avonport Station, W O
Aylesford
Baxter's Harbor, W O
Beech Hill, W O
Berwick
Berwick Station, W O
Bill Town, W O
Buckley's, W O
Burlington, W O
Cambridge Station, W O
Canaan, W O
Canaan Road, W O
Canada Creek, W O
Canard
Canning
Centreville, W O
Chipman's Brook, W O
Chipman's Corners, W O
Church Street, W O
Cold Brook Station, W O
Condon Settlement, W O
Cornwallis, East
Dalhousie, East, W O
Dempsey's Corner, W O
Factory Dale, W O
Gaspereaux, W O
Hall's Harbor, W O
Harborville, W O
Harmony, W O
Horton Landing, W O
Jackson Road, W O
Kentville
Kingston Village, W O
Kinsman's Corner, W O
Lake George, W O
Lakeville, W O
Lockhartville, W O
Long Point, W O
Lower Horton
Lower Pereaux, W O
Medford, W O
Middle Pereaux, W O
Millville, W O
Morden, W O
Morristown, W O
Nerepis Station, W O
New Minas, W O
New Ross Road, W O
Niely Road
North Mountain, W O
Ogilvie, W O
Palmer's Road, W O
Port Williams
Port Williams Station
Rhodes, W O
Ross' Corner, W O
Scott's Bay, W O
Sheffield Mills
Somerset, W O
Steam Mills Village, W O
Upper Dyke Village, W O
Upper Pereaux, W O
Vernon Mines, W O
Victoria Harbor, W O
Waterville, W O
White Rock Mills
Wolfville

LUNENBURG.

Blandford, W O
Bridgewater
Broad Cove, W O
Chelsea, W O
Chesley's Corners, W O
Chester
Chester Basin, W O
Conquerall Bank, W O
Dalhousie Road, W O
Dublin Shore, W O
Duncan, W O
Forties Settlement
Foster's, W O
Getson's Point, W O
Gold River, W O
Hebb's Cross, W O
Indian Point, W O
Kingsbury, W O
La Have Cross Roads, W O
La Have River, W O
Laugill's, W O
Lantz, W O
Lower La Have, W O
Lunenburg
Mahone Bay
Marriott's Cove, W O
Martin's River, W O
Middle La Have Ferry, W O
Mill Cove, W O
Morton's Corner, W O
Mossman's Grant, W O
New Canada, W O
New Cornwall, W O
New Germany, W O
New Ross
Northfield, W O
North-West Cove, W O
Petite Reviére Bridge, W O
Tancook Islands, W O
Upper Branch, W O
Upper La Have, W O
Vogler's Cove, W O
West Dublin, W O

PICTOU.

Alma, W O
Avondale, W O
Bailey's Brook, W O
Barney's River, W O
Big Island, W O
Blanchard's Road, W O
Blue Mountain, W O
Bridgeville, W O
Brookville, W O
Cape John, W O
Churchville, W O
Concord, W O
Dalhousie Settlement,
McLellan's Mountain, W O
Poplar Hill, W O
West Merigonishe, W O

Post Offices and Way Offices in the Province of Nova Scotia, arranged according to Electoral Districts.—Continued.

PICTOU.—*Continued.*

Durham
East River, St. Mary's, W O
East side of West Branch East River of Pictou, W O
Elmsville, W O
Fraser's Mills, W O
French River, W O
Garden of Eden, W O
Glengary Station
Glenshee, W O
Green Hill, W O
Hopewell, W O
Knoydart, W O
Lime Rock, W O
Little Harbor, W O
Loganville, W O
Lower Barney's River, W O
McLellan's Brook, W O
McLellan's Mountain, W O
Marsh Settlement, (McLellan's Mountain), W O
Merigonish, W O
Middle River, W O
Mill Brook, W O
Millsville, W O
Mount Thom, W O
New Gairloch, W O
New Glasgow
New Lairg, W O
Pictou
Piedmont Valley, W O
Plainfield, W O
Ponds, W O
Poplar Hill, W O
River John
Rocklin, W O
Roger's Hill, W O
St. Paul's, W O
Six Mile Brook, W O
South McLellan's Mountain, W O
Springville, W O
Stellarton
Sumerville, W O
Sutherland's Mills, W O
Sutherland's River, W O
Toney River, W O
Upper Settlement of Barney's River, W O
Upper Settlement of West River, W O
Vale Colliery, W O
West Merigonishe, W O
West Branch, East River, of Pictou, W O
West Branch, River John, W O
West River
West River Station
Westville

QUEEN'S.

Brookfield, W O
Brooklyn, W O
Caledonia Corner
East Port Medway, W O
Greenfield, W O
Hunts Point, W O
Kempt, W O
Liverpool
Middlefield, W O
Mill Village
Milton
North Brookfield, W O
Pleasant River, W O
Port Matoon, W O
Port Medway.

RICHMOND.

Arichat
Cariboo Cove, W O
Discoose, W O
Fourche, W O
Framboise, W O
Grand Anse, W O
Grandigue Ferry, W O
Grand River, W O
Kempt Road, W O
L'Ardoise, W O
Lennox Ferry, W O
Loch Lomond, W O
Lochside, W O
Lower L'Ardoise, W O
Lower River Inhabitants, W O
McPherson's Ferry, W.O.
Petite de Grat, W O
Port Richmond, W.O.
Port Royal, W.O.
Rear of Black River, W O
Rear Lands' Sporting Mountain, W.O.
Red Islands, W.O.
River Bourgeois, W.O.
Soldiers Cove, W.O.
St. Esprit, W.O.
St. George's Channel, W.O.
St. Peter's
West Arichot, W O.

SHELBURNE.

Barrington
Barrington Passage, W.O.
Bear Point, W.O.
Big Port le Bear, W.O.
Cape Negro, W.O.
Cape Sable Island, W.O.
Clarke's Harbour. W.O.
Clyde River, W.O.
Crowell
Doctor's Cove, W.O.
East side of Ragged Island, W.O.
Gunning Cove, W.O.
Head of Jordan River, W.O.
Jordan Bay, W.O.
Lewis Head, W.O.
Littlewood, W.O.
Locke Port
Lower Wood Harbor, W.O.
Middle Clyde River, W.O.
Middle Ohio, W.O.
North-east Harbor, W.O.
Oak Park, W.O.
Port Clyde, W.O.
Port Jolly, W.O.
Port la Tour, W. O.
Pubnico Beach, W.O.
Ragged Island, W.O.
Roseway, W.O.
Sable River, W.O.
Sandy Point, W.O.
Shag Harbor, W.O.
Shelburne
Upper Wood Harbor, W.O.
Upper Clyde River, W.O.

VICTORIA.

Baddeck
Baddeck Bay
B[illegible]
Bay St. Lawrence, W O
Big Bank, W O
[illegible]
Big Intervale, Margaree, W O
[illegible]oularderie
Cape North
Englishtown
Forks, Baddeck, W O.

Post Offices and Way Offices in the Province of Nova Scotia, arranged according to Electoral Districts.—Concluded.

VICTORIA.—*Continued.*

Bucklaw, W O
Groves Point, W O
Hunter's Mountain, W O
Indian Brook, W O
Ingonish, W O
Kempt Head, W O
Lower Settlement, Middle River, W O
McAulays, W O
McKay's Point, W O
Middle River, W O
Munro's, W O
New Campbelton
Niel's Harbor, W O
North River Bridge, W O
North Shore, W O
Point Clear, W O
St. Ann's, W O
St. Patrick's Channel, W O
South Bay, W O
South Cove, W O
South Gut of St. Ann's, W O
South side of Little Narrows, W O
South side of Boulardarie, W O
Sugar Loaf, W O.
Upper Settlement of Baddeck River, W O
Upper Settlement of Middle River, W O
Upper Washabuck, W O
West side of Middle River, W O
White's Point, W O
Wreck Cove, W O

YARMOUTH.

Argyle, W O
Carlton, W O
Central Chebogue, W O
Chebogue, W O
Deerfield, W O
East side of Pubnico Harbor, W O
Eel Lake, W O
Eel Brook, W O
Glenwood
Hebron
Kemptville, W O
Kempt Bridge, W O
Lake George, W O
Lower East Pubnico, W O
Lower West Pubnico, W O
Maitland, W O
Plymouth, W O
Pubnico Harbor, W O
Rockville
Sand Beach, W O
Short Beach, W O
South Ohio, W O
Tusket
Tusket Wedge, W O
Tusket Forks, W O
Yarmouth
Wellington, W O

POST OFFICES AND WAY OFFICES

IN THE

PROVINCE OF NEW BRUNSWICK.

ARRANGED ACCORDING TO ELECTORAL DISTRICTS.

ALBERT.

Alma
Albert Mines, W O
Beaver Brook, W O
Berryton, W O
Bridgedale, W O
Caledonia Settlement, W. O.
Cap de Moselle Creek, W O
Centreville, W O
Church Hill, W O
Coverdale, W O
Curryville, W O
Dawson Settlement, W O
Edgett's Landing, W O
Elgin
Germantown, W O
Goshen, W O
Gowland Mountain, W O
Harvey
Hastings, W O
Hebron, W O
Hillsborough
Hillside
Hopewell, W O
Hopewell Cape
Hopewell Corner
Hopewell Hill, W O
Irving Settlement, W O
Little Ridge, W O
Little River (Coverdale), W O
Little River (Elgin), W O
Little Rocher, W O
Little Shemogue, W O
Lower Cape, W O
Lower Coverdale, W O
Lower Turtle Creek, W O
Mapleton, W O
Middle Coverdale, W O
New Horton, W O
New Ireland, W O
New Ireland Road, W O
Pleasant Vale, W O
Point Wolfe, W O
Prosser Brook, W O
River Side, W O
Rosevale, W O
Roxburgh, W O
Salem, W O
Stoney Creek, W O
Upper New Horton, W O.
Waterside, W O
Wellington, W O

CARLETON.

Avondale, W O
Bairdsville, W O
Bath
Belleville, W O
Benton, W O
Bloomfield, W O
Boundary Presqu' isle, W O.
Carlow, W O
Centreville, W O
Charlestown, W O
Coldstream, W O
Debeck Station, W O
East Glassville, W O
Farley's Mills, W O
Farmerston, W O
Farryville, W O
Florenceville
Florenceville, East, W O
Foreston, W O
Glassville, W O
Good Corner, W O
Gordonsville, W O
Greenfield, W O
Hartland
Holmsville, W O
Jacksontown, W O
Jacksonville, W O
Johnville, W O
Kirkland, W O
Knowlesville, W O
Knoxford, W O
Lakeville, W O
Lindsay, W O
Long Settlement, W O
Lower Brighton, W O
Lower Wakefield, W O
Lower Woodstock, W O
McKenzie Corner, W O
Middle Simonds, W O
Monument Settlement, W O
Newburgh, W O
Northampton, W O
Peel, W O
Richmond Corner
River de Chute, W O
Shiktehawke, W O
Somerville, W O
Tracey's Mills, W O
Turtle Creek, W O
Union Corner, W O
Upper Kent, W O
Upper Peel, W O
Upper Wicklow, W O
Upper Woodstock, W O
Victoria, W O
Waterville, W O
Watson Settlement, W O
West Glassville, W O
Wicklow
Williamstown, W O
Windsor, W O
Woodstock
Woodstock Road Station, W O

Post Offices and Way Offices in the Province of New Brunswick, arranged according to Electoral Districts.—Continued.

CHARLOTTE.

- Back Bay, W.O.
- Baillie, W.O.
- Basswood Ridge, W.O.
- Bayside, W.O.
- Beaver Harbor, W.O.
- Bocabec. W.O,
- Campo Bello.
- Clarendon, W.O,
- Dumbarton, R.R. Station, W.O.
- Fairhaven, W.O.
- Grand Harbor, W.O.
- Grand Manan.
- Indian Island, W.O.
- Lawrence Station, W.O.
- Ledge, W.O.
- *Lepreaux.*
- L'Etete, W.O.
- Little Lepreaux, W.O.
- Little Ridge, W.O.
- Lord's Cove, W.O.
- Lynnfield, W.O.
- Mace's Bay.
- Mascarene, W. O.
- Milltown.
- Moore's Mills, W.O.
- New River, W.O.
- Oak Bay, W.O.
- Oak Hill, W.O.
- Pennfield, W.O.
- Pennfield Ridge, W.O.
- Pleasant Ridge, W.O.
- Pomery Ridge, W.O.
- Rolling Dam, W.O.
- Scotch Ridge, W.O.
- *St. Andrews.*
- *St. George.*
- St. Patrick, W.O.
- *St. Stephen.*
- Second Falls, W.O.
- Tower Hill, W.O.
- Upper Mills.
- Waweig, W.O.
- Whittier's Ridge, W.O.
- Wilson's Beech, W.O.

GLOUCESTER.

- Alexander's Point, W.O.
- *Bathurst.*
- Bathurst Village, W.O.
- Belledune, W.O.
- Belledune River, W.O.
- *Caraquet.*
- Clifton, W.O.
- Grand Anse, W.O.
- Janeville, W.O.
- Little Shippigan, W.O.
- Lower Pockmouche, W.O
- Madisco, W.O.
- New Bandon, W.O.
- Pockmouche, W.O.
- Pockshaw, W.O.
- Poplar Grove, W.O.
- Salmon Beach, W.O.
- Shippigan.
- Tracadie, W.O.
- Upper Caraquet, W.O.

KENT.

- Aldouane, W.O.
- Bass River, W.O.
- Bourgeois, W.O.
- *Bactouche.*
- Chockfish, W.O.
- Coal Branch, W.O.
- Coate's Mills, W.O.
- Cocaigne.
- Cocaigne River, W.O.
- Doherty's Mills, W.O.
- Gailey, W.O.
- Grandigue, W.O.
- Gueguen, W.O.
- *Kingston.*
- *Kouchibouguac.*
- Lake Settlement, W.O.
- McLaughlan Road, W.O.
- McLeod's Mills, W.O.
- Mill Creek, W.O.
- Moulie's River, W.O.
- Palmerston, W.O.
- Pine Ridge, W.O.
- Point Sapin, W.O.
- *Richibucto.*
- Richibucto Village, W.O.
- St. Anthony, W.O.
- St. Mary's, W.O.
- St. Paul's, W.O.
- Scovil's Mills, W.O.
- South Branch of St. Nicholas River, W.O.
- Upper Buctouche, W.O.
- Welford, W.O.
- West Branch, Nicholas River, W O.

KING'S.

- Anagance.
- *Apohaque.*
- Barnesville.
- Belleisle Bay, W.O.
- Belleisle Creek, W.O.
- Bloomfield, W.O.
- Butternut Ridge.
- Campbell Settlement W.O.
- Carsonville, W.O.
- Case Settlement, W.O.
- Central Norton, W.O.
- Clifton.
- Collina, W.O.
- Cornhill, W.O.
- Cromwell, W.O.
- Donegal, W.O.
- East Scotch Settlement, W.O.
- Fenwick, W.O.
- French Village.
- Grand Bay.
- Greenwich Hill, W.O.
- Hammond River.
- Hammond Vale.
- Hampton, W.O.
- Hanford Brook, W.O.
- Head of Millstream, W.O.
- Hillsdale.
- Kars, W.O.
- *Kingston.*
- Lakefield, W.O.
- Londonderry, W.O.
- Long Point, W.O.
- Long Reach, W.O.
- Markkamville, W.O.
- Mechanic's Settlement, W.O.
- Midland, W.O.
- Millstream, W.O.
- Mouth of Nerepis.
- Mount Pleasant, W.O.
- Nerepis Station, W.O.
- Newtown, W.O.
- Norton, W.O.
- Norton Station.
- Oak Point, W.O.
- *Ossekeag.*
- Pearsons, W O
- *Penobsquis.*
- Perry Settlement, W.O.
- Poodiac, W.O.
- Ratter's Corner, W.O.
- Rockville, W.O.
- Round Hill, W.O.
- Rothsay.
- Salt Springs, W.O.
- Seeley's Mills, W.O.
- Shepody Road, W.O.
- Smith Creek, W.O.
- Smith Town.
- South Branch, W.O.
- Sprague's Point, W.O.
- *Springfield.*
- Sussex Corner, W.O.
- Sussex Portage, W.O.
- *Sussex Vale.*
- Tenant's Cove, W.O.
- Thorne Brooke, W.O.
- Titusville.
- Upham.
- Upper Greenwich, W.O.
- Urquhart's, W.O.
- Ward's Creek Road, W.O
- Westfield, W.O.

Post Offices and Way Offices in the Province of New Brunswick, arranged according to Electoral Districts.—Continued.

NORTHUMBERLAND.

Barnaby River, W.O.
Bartibog, W.O.
Bay du Vin, W.O.
Bay du Vin Mills, W.O
Black Brook, W.O.
Black River, W.O.
Black River Bridge, W.O.
Blackville, W.O.
Blissfield, W.O.
Boiestown.
Burnt Church, W.O.
Cains River, W.O.
Chatham.
Church Point, W.O.
Derby, W.O.
Doaktown, W.O.
Douglastown, W.O.
Dumphy, W.O.
Escuminac, W.O.
Hardwick, W. O.
Little Branch, W.O.
Lower Newcastle, W.O.
Ludlow, W.O.
Lyttleton, W.O.
Newcastle.
North Esk Boom, W.O.
North West Bridge, WO.
Oak Point, W.O.
Portage River, W.O.
Red Bank, W O
Renou's Bridge, W.O.
Renou's River, W.O.
South Nelson, W.O.
Stymast Settlement, W O
Tabucintac, W.O.
Upper Bay du Vin, W.O.
Upper Neguac, W.O.
Whitney, W.O.

QUEEN'S.

Akerly, W.O.
Armstrong's Corner, W.O.
Belyea's Cove, W.O.
Big Cove, W.O.
Brigg's Corner, W.O.
Brookvale. W O.
Cambridge, W.O.
Canaan Rapids, W.O.
Central Cambridge, W.O.
Chipman.
Clones, W.O.
Coal Mines, W.O.
Cody's, W.O.
Cole's Island.
Cumberland Bay, W.O.
Cumberland Point, W.O.
Douglas Harbor, W.O.
English Settlement, W. O.
Enniskillen Station, W. O.
Ferris, W.O
Fork's, W.O.
Gagetown.
Gaspereaux, W.O.
Gaspereaux Station.
Hampstead.
Henderson Settlement, W O.
Hibernia, W.O.
Jemseg, W.O.
Jenkins, W.O.
Johnson, W.O.
Lakeview, W O
Long Creek, W.O.
McAlpine, W.O.
McDonald's Corner, W. O.
McDonald's Point, W.O.
Mill Brook, W O
Mill Cove, W.O.
Mouth of Jemseg, W.O.
Narrows.
New Canaan, W.O.
Newcastle Bridge, W.O.
Newcastle Creek, W O
New Jerusalem, W O
Oakham, W O
Olinville, W O
Otnabog, W O
Petersville, W O
Petersville Church, W O
Scotch Town, W O
Starkeys, W O
Summer Hill. W O
Sypher's Cove, W O
The Range, W O
Thorne Town, W O
Upper Gagetown
Upper Gaspereaux, W O
Upper Hampstead, W O
Waterborough, W O
Welsford
White's Point, W O
Wickham, W O
Young's Cove, W O

RESTIGOUCHE.

Archibald Settlement, W O
Armstrong's Brook, W O
Black Land, W O
Black Point, W O
Breadalbane, W O
Campbelltown
Dalhousie.
Doyle Settlement, W O
Dundee, W O
Eel River, W O
Flatlands
Head of Tide, W O
Heron Island, W O
Maple Green, W O
New Mills
Point la Nim, W O
River Charlo, W O
River Louison, W O
Shannonvale, W O
Upsalquitch, W O

ST. JOHN CITY, AND ST. JOHN CITY AND COUNTY.

Black River
Carleton
Chance Harbor, W O
Clinch's Mills
Dipper Harbor, W O
Fairfield
Fairville
Gardner's Creek
Golden Grove
Goose Creek, W O
Indian Town
Loch Lomond
Milledgeville
Mispec, W O
Musquash
Pisarinco
Prince of Wales
Quaco Road
St John's
St Martin's
St Martin's, W O
Salmon River, W O
Shanklin
South Bay
Spruce Lake
Ten Mile Creek
Upper Loch Lomond, W O
West Quaco
Willow Grove

SUNBURY.

Blissville
Burton, W O
Central Blissville, W O
Fredericton Junction
French Lake, W O
Geary, W O
Juvenile Settlement, W O
Lakeville Corner, W O
Lincoln, W O
Lintons, W O
Little River. W O
Northfield, W O
Oromocto
Patterson Settlement, W O
Rusagornis, W O
Rusagornis Station, W O
Sheffield
Sheffield Academy
Tracey Station, W O
Upper Maugerville, W O
Upper Sheffield
Waasis Station, W O

Post Offices and Way Offices in the Province of New Brunswick, arranged according to Electoral Districts.—Concluded.

VICTORIA.

Andover.
Aroostook, W.O.
Arthurst, W.O.
Caron Brook, W.O.
Edmundston.
Foster's Cove, W.O.
Grand Falls.
Grand Falls Portage, W.O.
Grand River, W.O.
Green River, W.O.
Hellerup, W.O.
Kincardine, W.O.
Middle St. Francis, W.O.
Perth, W.O.
Riley Brook, W.O.
St. Leonard's, W.O.
St. Hilaire, W.O.
Silverstream, W.O.
Three Brooks, W.O.
Undine, W.O.
Upper St. Basil.
Upper St. Francis, W.O.
Winding Ledges, W.O.

WESTMORELAND.

Anderson, W.O.
Au Lac, W.O.
Baie Verte.
Baie Verte Road, W O
Barachois, W O
Bayfield, W O
Belliveaus Village, W O
Botsford Portage, W O
Boudreau Village, W O
Boundary Creek, W O
Cape Spear, W O
Centre Village, W O
Chapman, W O
Cherry Vale, W O
Dorchester
Dover, W O
Dungiven, W O
Dupey's Corner, W O
Emigrant Road, W O
Emigrant Settlement, W O
Fox Creek, W O
Fredericton Road, W O
Great Shemogue
Hard Ledge, W O
Harewood, W O
Intervale, W O
Irishtown, W O
Johnson's Mills, W O
Jolicure, W O
Kay Settlement, W O
Kent's, W O
Lewis Mountain, W O
Lewisville, W O
Lutz Mountain, W O
McDougall Settlement, W O
Memramcook
Midgic, W O
Moncton
Moncton Road, W O
Mount Whatley, W O
Murray's Corner, W O
North Joggins, W O
North Lake, W O
North River
North River Platform W O
Petitcodiac
Point du Chêne, W O
Pollett River, W O
Port Elgin
Painsec, W O
Read, W O
Rockland
Rockport, W O
St Joseph, W O
Sackville
Salisbury
Scotch Settlement, W O
Shediac
Shediac Bridge, W O
Shediac Road, W O
Smith's, W O
South Rockland
Spence, W O
Steeves Mountain, W O
Steeves Settlement, W O
Taylor Village, W O
Tedish, W O
Tidnish Bridge, W O
Upper Cape, W O
Upper Sackville, W O
Westcock, W O
Westmoreland Point
Wheaton Settlement, W O
Wood Point, W O

YORK.

Bear Island, W O
Birdton, W O
Blayney Ridge, W O
Campbell Settlement, W O
Canterbury
Canterbury Station
Central Kingsclear, W O
Cork Station, W O
Douglas, W O
Dumfries, W O
Forest City, W O
Fredericton
Hamtown, W O
Hanwell, W O
Harvey Station
Keswick Ridge, W O
Kingsclear, W O
Kingsley, W O
Lake George, W O
Lower Canterbury, W O
Lower French Village, W O
Lower Haynesville, W O
Lower Line, Queensbury, W O
Lower Prince William, W O
Lower Queensbury, W O
Lower Southampton, W O
McAdam Junction, W O
Mactaquack, W O
Magaguadavic, W O
Magundy, W O
Manners Sutton, W O
Marysville, W O
Middle Southampton, W O
Millville, W O
Mouth of Keswick, W O
Nackawick, W O
Nashwaak, W O
Nashwaak Station, W O
Nashwaaksis, W O
Nashwaak Village, W O
New Maryland, W O
North Lake, W O
Norton Dale, W O
Pemberton Ridge, W O
Poquiock, W O
Prince William, W O
Royal Road, W O
St. Croix, W O
St. Mary's Ferry, W O
Southampton, W O
Springfield, W O
Stanley, W O
Tay Mills, W O
Tay Settlement, W O
Temperance Vale, W O
Tweedside, W O
Upper Caverhill, W O
Upper Haynesville, W O
Upper Keswick, W O
Upper Keswick Ridge, W O
Upper Magaguadavic, W O
Upper Queensbury, W O
Upper Southampton, W O
Yoho, W O

POST OFFICES

IN THE

PROVINCE OF MANITOBA,

ARRANGED ACCORDING TO ELECTORAL DISTRICTS.

LISGAR.

Cook s Creek Eagle's Nest Lower Fort Garry	Mapleton Middle Church Park Creek	Rockwood St Andrew's St Peter's	Scanterbury Springfield

MARQUETTE.

Baie St Paul Burnside High Bluff	Oak Point Palestine Pigeon Lake	Poplar Point Portage la Prairie St Laurent	St François Xavier Westbourne

PROVENCHER.

Point a Grouette St Anne's	St Norbert St Vital	Scratching River West Lynne	—

SELKIRK.

POST OFFICES

IN THE

PROVINCE OF BRITISH COLUMBIA.

ARRANGED ACCORDING TO ELECTORAL DISTRICTS.

CARIBOO.

Antler Creek Barkerville Canoe Creek Clinton	Dog Creek Dunkeld Harvey Creek Keithly Creek	Lac La Hache Lilloet Omineca 150 Mile House	Quesnelle Quesnelle Forks Soda Creek Van Winkle

NEW WESTMINSTER.

Burrard's Inlet Granville	Langley Moodyville	New Westminster	Sumas

VANCOUVER.

Chemainus Comox	Cowichan Maple Bay	Nanaimo Somenos	Sooke

VICTORIA.

Esquimalt	Victoria	—	—

YALE.

Ashcroft Cache Creek Duck and Pringle's	Hope Kamloops Kootenay (sub)	Lytton Nicola Lake	Spence's Bridge Yale

POST OFFICES

IN THE

PROVINCE OF PRINCE EDWARD ISLAND,

ARRANGED ACCORDING TO ELECTORAL DISTRICTS.

PRINCE.

Albany
Alberton
Augustine Cove
Barrett's Cross
Bedeque
Big Brook
Bloomfield
Brae
Burlington
Cape Traverse
Cape Wolfe
Carleton
Darnley
Egmont Bay
Fifteen Point
Freetown
Hamilton
Higgin's Road
Indian River
Inverness
Kildare
Little Tignish
Lower Freetown
Lot No. 1
Do 4
Do 6
Do 8
Do 10
Do 11
Do 12
Lot No. 14
Do 16
Do 30
Margate
Middleton
Miminegash
Miscouche
Montrose
Mount Pleasant
Muddy Creek
Newton
North Bedeque
North Tryon
O'Leary's Road
Pork Hill
Princetown
St Eleanors
Searletown
Skinner's Pond
Somerset
South-West, Lot 16
Summerside
Tignish
Traveller's Rest
Tryon
Tyne Valley
Wellington
West Cape
Western Road
West Point
Wilmot Valley

Post Offices in the Province of Prince Edward Island, arranged according to Electoral Districts.—Continued.

QUEEN'S.

Belfast	Hazel Grove	Pisquid	
Belle Creek	Hope River	Pisquid Road	
Bonshaw	Johnston's River	Point Prim	
Brackley Point	Kelly's Cross	Pownal	
Brackley Point Road	Kinross	Princetown Road	
Caledonia	Little York	Rona	
Cavendish	Long Creek	Rose Valley	
Cavendish Road	Long River	Rustico	
Charlottetown	Lot 35	St. Ann's	
Cherry Valley	" 67	Selkirk Road	
Cornwall	Mermaid Farm	Scotchfort	
Covehead	Monaghan	Southport	
Covehead Road	Montague Cross	South Wiltshire	
Crapaud	Mount Stewart	Springfield	
Darlington	Murray Harbor Road	Stanley Bridge	
De Sable	New Glasgow	Suffolk Road	
Emy Vale	New Haven	Tracadie Cross	
Flat River	New London	Vernon River	
Fort Augustus	New Wiltshire	Vernon River Bridge	
French River	Nine Mile Creek	Victoria	
French Village	North River	Western Covehead	
Graham's Road	North Rustico	Wheatley River	
Grand Tracadie	Orwell	Wood Islands	
Granville	Orwell Cove		
Hartsville	Park Corner		

KING'S.

Bay Fortune	Marie Bridge		
Big Marsh	Montague Bridge		
Bothwell	Morell		
Brooklin	Morell Rear		
Bull Creek	Murray Harbor, North		
Cable Head	Do do South		
Cardigan Bridge	Murray River		
Cardigan Road	New Perth		
Cherry Grove	North Lake		
De Gros Marsh	Peter's Road		
Dundas	Red Point		
East Point	Rollo Bay		
Fairfield	Rollo Bay Cross		
Farmington	St Andrews		
Gaspereaux	St Margaret's		
Georgetown	St Mary's Road		
Goose River	Souris, East		
Head St Peter's Bay	Souris, West		
Little Harbor	Sturgeon		
Little Sands	Summerville		
Lower Montague	Valleyfield		
Lot 45	Victoria Cross		
" 56	Whim Road		

POSTAL DIVISIONS

UNDER THE CHARGE OF

THE SEVERAL INSPECTORS.

THE FOLLOWING ARE THE ELECTORAL DISTRICTS IN THE SEVERAL POSTAL DIVISIONS.

CHIEF INSPECTOR'S DIVISION.

The Provinces of

Manitoba.	North West Territories.	Prince Edward Island.

NOVA SCOTIA INSPECTOR'S DIVISION.

Annapolis	Digby	Kings.	Richmond
Antigonishe	Guysboro'	Lunenburg	Shelburne
Cape Breton	Halifax	Pictou	Victoria
Colchester	Hants	Queen's	Yarmouth
Cumberland	Inverness		

NEW BRUNSWICK DIVISION.

Albert	Kent	Restigouche	Victoria
Carleton	King's	St. John (city & county)	Westmoreland
Charlotte	Northumberland	St. John (city)	York
Gloucester	Queen's	Sunbury	

QUEBEC DIVISION (Province of Quebec.)

Arthabaska	Dorchester	Lotbinière	Quebec (city)
Beauce	Drummond, township of Kingsey only	Megantic	Richmond, townships of Cleveland and Shipton only
Bellechasse	Gaspé	Montmagny	Rimouski
Bonaventure	Kamouraska	Montmorency	Temiscouata
Champlain	Levis	Nicolet	Wolfe
Charlevoix	L'Islet	Portneuf	
Chicoutimi & Saguenay		Quebec	

Postal Divisions under the charge of the several Inspectors.—Continued.

MONTREAL DIVISION.—(Province of Quebec.)

Argenteuil. Bagot. Beauharnois. Berthier. Brome. Chambly. Chateauguay. Compton. Drummond, except Township of Kingsey. Hochelaga.	Huntingdon. Iberville. Jacques Cartier. Joliette. Laprairie. L'Assomption. Laval. Maskinongé. Missisquoi. Montcalm.	Montreal (city). Napierville. Richelieu. Richmond, except Township of Cleveland and Shipton. Rouville. St. Hyacinthe. St. John's. St. Maurice.	Shefford. Sherbrooke (town). Soulanges. Stanstead. Terrebonne. Three Rivers (city). Two Mountains. Vaudreuil. Verchères. Yamaska.

OTTAWA DIVISION.

Carleton (Ont.) Nipissing District (Ont.)	Ottawa City (Ont.) Ottawa County (Quebec.)	Pontiac (Quebec.) Renfrew, N.R. (Ont.)	Renfrew, S.R. (Ont.) Russell (Ont.)

KINGSTON DIVISION.—(Province of Ontario.)

Addington. Brockville (town) Cornwall (town) Dundas Frontenac Glengarry	Grenville, S R Hastings, N R Hastings, E R Hastings, W R Kingston (city) Lanark, N R	Lanark, S R Leeds, S R Leeds & Grenville, N R Lennox Northumberland, N R Northumberland, W R	Peterboro' E R Peterboro' W R Prescott Prince Edward Stormont

TORONTO DIVISION.—(Province of Ontario.)

Algoma Bruce, N R Bruce, S R Cardwell Durham, E R Durham, W R Grey, E R	Grey, N R Grey, S R Halton Muskoka Ontario, N R Ontario, S R Peel	Simcoe, N R Simcoe S. R Toronto (city) Victoria, N R Victoria, S R Waterloo, N R Waterloo, S R	Wellington, N R Wellington, S R Wellington, C R York, E R York, W R York, N R

LONDON DIVISION.—(Province of Ontario.)

Bothwell Brant, N R Brant, S R Elgin, E R Elgin, W R Essex Haldimand Hamilton (city)	Huron, C R Huron, N R Huron, S R Kent Lambton Lincoln London (city)	Middlesex, N R Middlesex, E R Middlesex, W R Monck Niagara Norfolk, N R Norfolk, S R	Oxford, N R Oxford, S R Perth, N R Perth, S R Welland Wentworth, N. R Wentworth, S R

BRITISH COLUMBIA DIVISION.

LIST

OF

POSTMASTERS IN CANADA.

Abbott, Adam, Hazledean ....O
Abbott, Ephraim W., Lennoxville .... .Q
Abbott, Luther, Massawippi ....Q
Abbott, Robert, Port Royal ....O
Abel, David, Port Dover ....O
Abrams, Josias, Willetsholme ... .O
Abrey, G. B., Little Current .... O
Acteson, Joseph, L'Anse aux Gascons ....Q
Adam, Thomas, Lindsay.......................................O
Adams, A., Rokeby ....O
Adams, George, Adamsville............ ....Q
Adams, Isaac, Tracey's Mills, W. O....................N B
Adams, Melvin, Broadlands................... .... Q
Adams, Nehemiah N., Oak Park, W. O. ....N S
Adams, Wm., Southampton, W. O.............. ....N S
Addison, Henry, Brompton ....Q
Addshead, Mary, St. Charles ....M
Akerly, B. H., Akerly, W. R......... ....N B
Akin, Wm. S., Edwardsburgh ....O
Airth, Wm., Horning's Mills............ ....O
Aitkin, Thomas, Windermere ....O
Alain, Vital, Upper Neguac, W. O........................N B
Alderson, W. M., Nanticoke .. ..O
Alexander, F., Alexander's Point, W. O...........N B
Alexander, R. L., Newry........ ....O
Alguire, Mrs. Lydia, Plum Hollow ....O
Allan, Alexander, Riverstown..................... ....O
Allan, D., Rylstone...... ....O
Allan, W., Allan's Mills ....O
Allan, Isaac H., Black Creek.................................O
Allan, John, Mono Mills ....O
Allan, Alex. D., Marlbank.................... ....O
Allan, George, Glenallan ....O
Allchim, Samuel, Canning.. O
Allen, James, Bandon... ....O
Allen, J. B., Malton...... ....O
Allen, Thomas, Cooper ....O
Allen, Thomas, Lovat ....O
Al[redacted]nstrong, Henry, Inistioge........................ ......O

Allin, Thomas, Derryville .... O
Allison, A. C., Dunbar ... .O
Allison, J. W., Newport Landing ....N S
Allison, Thaddeus, Neily Road.............................N S
Ambrose, Mrs. M., Princeport, W. O........ ....N S
Amy, John, Portage du Fort......... ....Q
Anderson, Alex., Bræmar............................. .... O
Anderson, George, Marysville .. ..O
Anderson, James, Anderson's Corners.....................Q
Anderson, Jesse, Cross Roads, Middle Medford, W. O. ....N S
Anderson, John, Cumnock...... ....O
Anderson, John, Wyoming . ...O
Anderson, Joseph, Springvale ....O
Anderson, J. R., Kendal................... .... O
Anderson, Thomas, Keppewee ....Q
Anderson, James, Craithie........... ....O
Angers, Elie, Murray Bay ....Q
Anglin, Robert, Brewer's Mills ....O
Anglin, W. J., Battersea ....
Anthony, Thomas, Ogilvie, W. O...... ....N S
Applebe, John S., Ballinafad..................................... O
Applebe, James, Trafalgar..................... ....O
Applebee, Mark, Latona...O
Appleford, Wm., Mapleton................ ....O
April, George, Green River ....Q
Arbo, John H., Blissfield, W. O ....N B
Arcand, Miss F. A. A., St. Joseph.............................Q
Archambeault, J. T. L., Varennes......... .... Q
Archibald, Ebenezer, Old Barns, W. O....... ....N S
Archibald, Levi, Alma, W. O.....................................N S
Archibald, J. W., Smithfield, W. O..........................N S
Archibald, Mathew, Glenelg ....N S
Archibald, R., Archibald Settlement, W. O.......N B
Argue, J. S, Stittsville........ ....O
Armour, Thomas, Dunville.. ....O
Armstrong, Foster, Point Alexander..........................O
Armstrong, F. P., East Port Medway, W. O. ......N S

List of Postmasters in Canada—Continued.

Armstrong, Samuel, McKellar .... O
Armstrong, Simon, Belgrave.......................................O
Armstrong, William, Falmouth, Windsor Bridge, W. O..... ....N S
Arnold, George, Bell's Corners ... .O
Arseneaux, T., Egmont Bay........... ....P E I
Arseneaux. Stephen T., Little Tignish..........P E I
Arthurs, John, Napier.................................. ....O
Ash, Cyrus, Centreville..O
Ashdown, F. W., Spence.......................... ....O
Ashdown, James, Ashdown ....O
Ashton, Robert, Columbus...... ....O
Askew, Thomas G., Chemainus ....B C
Aspdin, James, Aspdin ....O
Asselin, Eusèbe, Joliette.......................... ....Q
Atkinson, John, Glanford ....O
Aubé, Joseph, Poplar Grove, W. O......... ....N B
Aubé Marcel, St. Gervais ....Q
Aubry, P. G., Aubigny ....Q
Auclair, Rev. E., St. Prime ....Q
Audette, Antoine, North Stukeley..........................Q
Auger, Louis A., Mount Johnson..... ....Q
Auld, D., Freetown.. .. ..P E I
Ault, J. R., Aultsville ....O
Avard, William, Great Shemogue, W. O. ....N B
Ayer, C., Ayer's Flat ....Q
Ayers, Patrick, Wellington ....P E I
Aylward, James H., Queensville ....O
Aylsworth, James, Tamworth........... .... O

Babcock, Edward, Johnston's Mills, W. O.........N B
Babin, Eustache, Painsec, W. O.............. ..... N B
Bachaud, J. C., St. Liboire..... ....Q
Bachelder, D., Rougemont . ...Q
Bacon, Sarah D., St. Pierre, Montmagny ....Q
Bagnall, R. P., Springfield ....P E I
Bagnall, R., Hazel Grove .... .P E I
Bagrie, John, Brooksdale ....O
Bailey, Luke E., Central Blissville, W. O..........N B
Bailey, James, Shanick ....O
Bailey, George, Shrigley........ ....O
Bailey, Nicholas, Sandy Beach ....Q
Bailey Alexander, Church Hill, W. O. ....N B
Bailey, G. D., Newcastle Creek, W. O. ....N B
Bailey, W. W., Island Brook ....Q
Bailey, William, Dartford ....O

Baker, William, Barronsfield, W. O. ....N S
Baldwin, Henry, Ouskay......................................O
Baldwin, R. C., Dixville............ ....Q
Balfour, Duncan, Westville ....N S
Ball, James, Rugby ....O
Ball, G. H., North-west Arm, W. O. ....N S
Ball, Wright, South Roxton .. ..Q
Ballam, W. G., Arichat ....N S
Ballantyne, Mrs. E., L'Islet ....Q
Ballard, Cyprus, Middleboro', W. O....................N S
Balmain, Abner, Douglas Harbor, W. O ....N B
Balmer, R., Oakville ....O
Bambrich, P., Cardigan Road ....P E I
Bangs, John, Mattawa ....O
Banks, John H., Torbrook, W. O. ....N S
Banning, O., jun., Clayton ....O
Bannister, John, Waverley............... ....O
Banting, Thomas M., Clover Hill........ ....O
Baptie, Alexander, Ida ....O
Barbeau, Albert, Isle Bizard ....Q
Barberie, Mrs. O. A., Apohaqui ....N B
Barber, Thomas, Folly Lake, W. O................. N S
Barclay, A. E. S. K., Wallacetown ....O
Barclay, Patrick, Petrolea . ...O
Bard, Charles, Bardsville ....O
Barfoot, S., Chatham ....O
Baribeau, Louis A., Rivière du Loup (en haut)..... Q
Barker, Whitehead, Sheffield Academy ....N B
Barker, J. W., Waterville, W. O. ....N B
Barker, Mrs. Vasey, Montague Gold Mines, W.O...N S
Barker, David, Picton............... ....O
Barker, John, Dundonald ....O
Barker, James J., Markham ....O
Barlow, Alexander, Quesnel ....B C
Barnes, Vereton, North Pinnacle ....Q
Barr, Peter, Devil's Creek ....O
Barr, Seth, Putnam ....O
Barron, John, Newcomb Corner, W. O. ....N S
Barry, A. A., Rock Island ....Q
Barry, John C., Les Escoumains ....Q
Barteaux, C. W., Somerset, W. O. ....N S
Bartlett, G., Little Ridge, W. O. ....N B
Bartlett, R. T., Monteagle Valley......................... O
Bartlett, G., Bethel ....Q
Bartley, George, Kennebec Line ....Q
Bastedo, Walter S., Wellington Square ....O

List of Postmasters in Canada—Continued.

Bearman, Thomas, Scone .... O
Beaton, Donald, Whitton .... Q
Beaton, Angus, Little Judique, W. O. .... N S
Beaton, G. W., White .... O
Beaton, Alex., East Point .... P E I
Beaton, Donald, Mabou Coal Mines, W. O. .... N S
Beattie, William, Melbourne .... Q
Beattie, Porter, Stanbury .... Q
Beattie, George, French Village .... N B
Beattie, John, Highgate .... O
Beatty, Johnstone, Elizabethville .... O
Beatty, William H., Stanton .... O
Beatty, William, Wellington, W. O. .... N B
Beauchemin, A. O. T., Roxton Falls .... Q
Beaudette, Joseph S., St. Patrick's Hill .... Q
Beaudoin, Louis, East Broughton .... Q
Beaupré, Maxime, Yamaska .... Q
Beaulieu, Napoleon, St. Francoise .... Q
Beaulieu, J. B., Cacouna .... Q
Beaumont, John, Curryville, W. O. .... N B
Beaumont, William, Maple Bay .... B C
Beck, Jacob, Baden .... O
Beck, J. H., Medina .... O
Becker, A. A., Hilton .... O
Beckman, J., Ellershausen, W. O. .... N S
Beckwith, N., Mill Creek, W. O. .... N B
Beckwith, A., Upper Dyke Village, W. O. .... N S
Bédard Pierre, Valmont .... Q
Bédard, Charles, St. Remi .... Q
Bédard, L., St. Flavien .... Q
Bedard, Elzear, Levis .... Q
Beeman, David H., Prosser Brook, W. O. .... N B
Beer, Hy., Southport .... P E I
Begg, Mrs. Sarah, Innerkip .... O
Bégin, Oliver, St. Ephrem de Tring .... Q
Bégin, Joseph, Lake Etchemin .... Q
Bègin, Louis C., Kamouraska .... Q
Bélanger, J. O., Maskinongé .... Q
Bélanger, Celestin, Chlorydormes .... Q
Bélanger, E., St. Romaine .... Q
Bélanger, F., St. Vallier .... Q
Bélanger, Louis, Rivière des Prairies .... Q
Belcourt, J. L., La Baie .... Q
Belfour, John, Bath .... O
Belfry, Jacob, Carden .... O
Belisle, Jos., Montmorin .... Q
Bell, John M., Atha .... O
Bell, George, Caledon .... O
Bell, P. W., Michipicoton River .... O
Bell, Archibald, Nairn .... O
Bell, G. L., East Oro .... O
Bell, Gilbert, Nine Mile Creek .... P E I
Bell, Thomas, Sligo .... O
Bell, T. W., Fish Creek .... O
Bell, James. Whitehurst .... O
Belleau, E. S., St. Michel .... Q
Belleau, John, Rivière Ouelle .... Q
Belleveau, Pacifique, St. Paul's, W. O. .... N B
Belleveaux, Urbain, Belleveaux Cove .... N S
Belmore, D., Dipper Harbor, W. O. .... N B
Belyea, G. N., Belyea's Cove, W. O. .... N B
Bender, James, Long Lake .... O
Benner, Jacob, West Montrose .... O
Bennett, William, Masham Mills .... Q
Bennett, Wm., North Mountain, W. O. .... N S
Bennett, Edmund, Castile .... O
Benson, Albert, Stromness .... O
Bent, Calvin, Port Elgin .... N B
Bent, James, Short Beach, W. O. .... N S
Bent, John C., Armstrong's Brook, W. O. .... N B
Bent, Clara W., Digby .... N S
Bent, W. W., Maugerville .... N B
Bentley, David, Marmora .... O
Benton, John, Bentonville .... O
Bergeron, D. Blanford .... Q
Bergeron, Jacques, Metabechouan .... Q
Bermingham, W., South Lake .... O
Bernard, George, Rivière Bois Clair .... Q
Bernard, J., Cap Sante .... Q
Bernard, John, Brechin .... O
Berney, W. H., Mill Grove .... O
Bernier, Antoine, St. Simon de Rimouski .... Q
Berry, Solomon, Turtle Creek. W. O. .... N B
Berry, Edward, Berryton, W. O. .... N B
Berry, J., St. Martin's, W. O. .... N B
Berry, W. H., March .... O
Berteaux, Charles, Nictaux Falls, W. O. .... N S
Bertrand, Paul, St. Mathias .... Q
Bertrand, Louis A., Isle Verte .... Q
Berwick, Edward, Shelburne .... O
Besancon, Henry, Gorrie .... O
Besner, J. B., Pont Chateau .... Q
Bessette, N. D. D., Village Richelieu .... Q
Best, F. A., Corinth .... O
Best, Leonard, Beaver Harbor, W. O. .... N B
Best, Abraham, Mount Pleasant .... O
Best, Joseph, Eldorado .... O
Bethune, Roderick, Loch Lomond, W. O. .... N S
Beveridge, Wm. B., Andover .... N B
Bhérour, Archille, St. Fidèle .... Q
Bigelow, W. H., Spencer Island, W. O. .... N S
Bigney, Lemuel, Wallace River, W. O .... N S
Bilodeau, F. X., Bailargeon .... Q
Bilodeau, Jean, St. Elzear .... Q
Bilodeau, Job, Chambord .... Q
Bingham, Wesley, Orillia .... O
Bingham, R., Athens .... O
Bingham, C. W., Crysler .... O
Bingham, David, Lotus .... O
Bird, Robert, Birdton, W. O. .... N B
Birks, Charles, Maynard .... O
Birmingham, Mrs. E., Birmingham .... O
Be——on, F. X. A., St. Cuthbert .... Q

List of Postmasters in Canada—Continued.

Bishop, James, Perth, W. O.... N B
Bishop, Asa W., Bishop's Mills.... O
Bishop, J. B., Marbleton.... Q
Bishop, Wm. E., Irving's Settlement, W. O.... N B
Bisson, Philip, Magpie.... Q
Bissett, George, River Bourgeois, W. O.... N S
Bistodeau, G. E., St. Maurice.... Q
Black, Andrew, Greensville.... O
Black, E., Salem, W. O.... N S
Black, J. C., Claremont, W. O.... N S
Black, James, jun., Bramley.... O
Black, R. F., West Branch, River Philip, W. O.. N S
Black, Robert, Craigvale.... O
Black, D., Marysville.... O
Black, Charles E., Sunya.... O
Blackburn, Robert, Lucerne.... Q
Blackburn, Samuel, Lower Prospect, W. O.... N S
Blackhall, J. G. C., Caraquet.... N B
Blackwood, Robert, Martintown.... O
Blackwood, Charles W., Thunder Bay.... O
Bluin, J., St. Eduuard.... Q
Blair, Henry, North River Bridge, W. O.... N S
Blair, Wm., Ardtrea.... Q
Blair, James, Hallerton.... Q
Blais, Alexis, St. Aubert.... Q
Blais, Patrick, North Ham.... Q
Blais, Narcisse, Point aux Trembles.... Q
Blais, Prùdent, Beaulieu.... Q
Blaisdell, Mrs. E. D., Bolton Centre.... Q
Blake, Robert, Black Brook, W. O.... N B
Blake, Mrs. C., Sydenham Place.... Q
Blakeny, Wm., Jeddore, W. O.... N S
Blanchard, Daniel, Greenbush.... O
Blanchard, J. B., Forest City, W. O.... N B
Blaney, Henry, Millville, W. O.... N B
Bliss, W., New Annan, W. O.... N S
Bloomburg, Isaac, Elphin.... O
Blue, Malcolm, Blue's Mills, W. O.... N S
Blyth, C. McD., Marden.... O
Boadway, George, Bexley.... O
Boardman, Luther, Crowland.... O
Bogart, Gilbert, Napanee.... O
Bogart, A., Bogart.... O
Boggs, B. B., Joggin Mines, W. O.... N S
Boileau, Godfroi, St. Genevieve.... Q
Boisonneau, E., Newbois.... Q
Boisvert, Anèsime, Angeline.... Q
Bolduc, Theodule, Roberval.... Q
Bond, Edwin, Sheffield.... O
Bond, Mrs. M., Wyandot.... O
Bongard, J. D., Bongard's Corners.... O
Bonneville, Caroline, La Beauce.... Q
Bonthron, James, Rogerville.... O
Boon, Stephen, Tay Mills, W. O.... N B
Booth, Mrs. M. J., Prospect, W. O.... N S
Booth, Thomas, Chester.... Q
Borden, Levi, Pugwash....
Borden, T. W., Canning.... N S
Boright, Curtis S., Sweetsburg.... Q
Bothwell, Wm., Grovesend.... O
Bouchard, J. M., Pointe à Pic.... Q
Boucher, H., Bégon.... Q
Boucher, Et., St. Apollinaire.... Q
Boucher, Pierre, St. Honore.... Q
Boudrot, Alex., Boudreau Village, W. O.... N B
Boudrot, Benj., Bario's Beach, W. O.... N S
Boudrot, Stephen, Port Felix.... N S
Boulliane, R., Les Petites Bergeronnes.... Q
Boulonger, L., St. Agathe.... Q
Boul t, E. C., St. François Montmagny.... Q
Bourchier, J. R., Georgina.... O
Bourgeault, F. S., St. Anicet.... Q
Bourgeois, John, Bourgeois, W. O.... N B
Bourget, Charles, Lauzon.... Q
Bourke, Thomas, Albert Bridge, W. O.... N S
Bourier, Alexis, St. Barnabé.... Q
Bourassa, F., Dover, South.... O
Bourque, A., St. Clet.... Q
Bourque, Damase V., Etang du Nord (sub).... Q
Boutalier, Miss M., Port Caledonia, W. O.... N S
Bow, Wm., West Winchester.... O
Bowden, Wm., Second Falls, W. O.... N B
Bowen, James, Mill Point.... O
Bowers, Jesse, Upper Clyde River.... N S
Bowes, Joanna, Wisbeach.... O
Bowley, Wm., Marée Bridge.... P E I
Bowerman, James, Pine Orchard.... O
Bowman, John, Almira.... O
Bowman, Noah, West Montrose.... O
Bowron, John, Barkerville.... B C
Bowsfield, R., Whittington.... O
Boyart, A., Boyart.... O
Boyd, John, Johnville, W. O.... N B
Boyd, John, Lytton.... B C
Boyer, George R., Victoria.... N B
Boyer, Wm. P., Somerville, W. O.... N B
Boyle, James, Chance Harbor, W. O.... N S
Boyle, John, Caledonia Mills, W. O.... N S
Boyd, Byron, Jura.... O
Boyd, J. G., Vernonville.... O
Boyle, Daniel, Grèbbin.... O
Brace, L. J., Zetland.... O
Bradford, Charles A., Chatboro'.... Q
Bradley, M., Eddystone.... O
Bradley, Joseph A., Lansdown.... O
Bradley, Richard, Airlie.... O
Bradshaw, W. C., Everett.... O
Brady, Bridget, Mount St. Patrick.... O
Bragg, John, Windham Hill, W. O.... N S
Branan, J. W., Alvinston.... O
Brannen, John B., Kenmore.... O
Branscomb, A., sen., Cumberland Bay, W. O.... N B
Brash, Richard, New Richmond.... Q

List of Postmasters in Canada—Continued.

Brassard, Amable J., Napierville..........Q
Brassard, Xavier, Jonquières..........Q
Breau, Urbain, Richibucto Village, W. O..........N B
Breadner, Joshua, Athelstan..........Q
Breckenridge, Robert, Heyworth..........Q
Breeze, Wm., Forest Mills..........O
Brehaut, C. T., Murray Harbor, South..........P E I
Brennan, Peter Golden Grove..........N B
Brenan, Eneas, Graham's Road..........P E I
Bresnahan, J., Damascus..........O
Brethour, Samuel, Valentyne..........O
Brewster, W. R., Beaver Brook, W. O..........N B
Briard, Edward, Cheticamp, W. O..........N S
Bridge, Andrew, Westbrook..........O
Brien, A. A. L., St. Alexandre..........Q
Brien, Alfred, St. Simon de Yamaska..........Q
Brière, François, Lake Weedon..........Q
Briggs, James, Pearceton..........Q
Briggs, Thomas, Hepworth..........O
Brigham, E. O., Brigham..........Q
Brigham, Robert, Rondeau Harbor..........O
Brillon, J. B., Belœil Village..........Q
Brine, J. S., St. Margaret's Bay..........N S
Brisbin, Alexander, Covey Hill..........Q
Brittain, Wm. H., Windsor, W. O..........N S
Brittain, Stephen, Lower Wakefield, W. O..........N B
Brittain, Joseph, Enniskillen Station, W. O..........N B
Britton, D. F., Gananoque..........O
Bristow, Edward, Shibley..........O
Broad, John, Little Britain..........O
Broad, Isaac, Holmesville, W. O..........N B
Broad, Wm., Hayden..........O
Brochu, M., St. Lambert..........Q
Brodie, J. L., Charing Cross..........O
Brodhagen, Chas., Brodhagen..........O
Brooks, Asa D., Southampton, W. O..........N B
Brooks, Caleb, Low..........Q
Brotherston, W., sen., Villiers..........O
Brouillette, Alexis, Mont St. Hilaire..........Q
Brousseau, Julien, Laprairie..........Q
Brown, J., Sillery Cove..........Q
Brown, Samuel, Pownall..........P E I
Brown, W. H., Baysville..........O
Brown, Mrs. S., Wilson's Beach, W. O..........N B
Brown, Dr. Charles, Cowansville..........Q
Brown, William S., Red Bank, W. O..........N B
Brown, George, Shakespeare..........O
Brown, A. N., St. John's, West..........O
Brown, John, Rutherford..........O
Brown, James, Newport Corner, W. O..........N S
Brown, James, Coal Mines, W. O..........N B
Brown, Robert, Bass River, W. O..........N B
Brown, James, sen., Motherwell..........O
Brown, John, Monkland..........O
Brown, David F., Moe's River..........Q
Brown, James, Nithburg..........O
Brown, James, Melancthon..........O
Brown, James E., Lakelands, W. O..........N S
Brown, Alexander, Aldershot..........O
Brown, James Ross, Angus..........O
Brown, Francis, Clifford..........O
Brown, Nicholas J., Marble Mountain, W. O..........N S
Brown, Philip, Lower Pereau, W. O..........N S
Brown, William, Chesterfield..........O
Brown, Charles A., Chester..........N S
Brown, Francis, Cairngorm..........O
Brown, George, Hereward..........O
Brown, Geo., Head of Wallace Bay, W.O..........N S
Brown, H. V., Eskasoni, W. O..........N S
Brown, William G., Indian Town..........N B
Brown, John, Victoria Harbor, W. O..........N S
Brown, J. L., Harvey Hill Mines..........Q
Brown, Hiram, Brown's Brook, W. O..........N S
Brown, James W., Lower Queensbury, W. O..........N B
Brown, E. J., Gresham..........O
Brown, George, Phillipsville..........O
Brown, Robert, Zurich..........O
Browne, J. A., New Dublin..........O
Browning, Archibald, Lavant..........O
Brownlee, James, Ellengowan..........O
Bruce, R., Ragged Head, W. O..........N S
Brunelle, Uldoric, St. Etienne..........Q
Brunelle, L., Gentilly..........Q
Brunner, Jacob, Brunner..........O
Brunning, A. H., St. Croix, W. O..........N B
Bryce, William, Muir..........O
Bryden, Walter, Landreville..........Q
Bryson, Thomas, Allan's Corners..........Q
Bryson, James, Cameron..........O
Bryson, Thomas, Fort Coulonge..........Q
Buchan, John, Fullarton..........O
Buchanan, William, Sullivan..........O
Buchanan, James, Copleston..........O
Bucke, T. W., Wabashene..........O
Bucke, Richard, Harold..........O
Buckley, Thomas, Buckley's, W. O..........N S
Buckley, David, Isaac's Harbor, W.O. (E. Side) N S
Buckwell, William S., Onondaga..........O
Budd, George, North Rustico..........P E I
Bullock, Increase, Georgeville..........Q
Bundy, George, Houghton..........O
Bunn, George, Ullswater..........O
Bunnell, Alfred M., Lute's Mountain, W. O..........N B
Bunston, Joseph, Yeovil..........O
Bunston, Thomas, Petherton..........O
Bunton, Robert, Walmer..........O
Burchell, Geo., Bridgeport, W. O..........N S
Burdett, Robert, Griersville..........O
Burdett, Richard, Dundee..........P E I
Bureau, Rev. J. A., Ste. Agnes..........Q
Burgar, G. H., Welland..........O
Burge, J., Dalston..........O

List of Postmasters in Canada—Continued.

Burgess, E. W., Burgessville....O
Burgess, John, Cheverie, W. O....N S
Burgess, Joseph L., Drumbo....O
Burgess, Robert M., Richview....O
Burk, Eustache, Fox Creek, W. O....N B
Burk, D. F., Segeun Falls....O
Burke, J. W., Ingonish, W. O....N S
Burke, J. G., Brougham....O
Burnham, Peter, Windsor....N S
Burns, John, Evelyn....O
Burns, George, Lower Freetown....P E I
Burpee, C. J., Sheffield....N B
Burpee, M. E. A., Burton, W. O....N B
Burpee, Isaac C., Upper Gaspereaux....N B
Burpee, Stephen G., Florenceville....N B
Burrell, C., Stanley's Mills....O
Burrill, William, Rirkdale....O
Burrows, William, Prospect....O
Burt, John W., Coningsby....O
Burton, Israel, Belford....O
Buttemer, R., Salmon Beech....N B
Butler, James, St. Edward de Frampton (sub)....Q
Butler, R. P., Oakwood....O
Butler, W. H., Richmond, West....O
Butler, John, Colinville....O
Butterfield, J. A., Norwood....O
Byrne, Thomas, Uptergrove....O
Byron, Anthony, Stoke Centre....Q
Byron, Luke, Campo Bello....N B

Cabana, Ant., St. Rosalie....Q
Cahill, John, Calumet Island....Q
Cahill, Michael, Jersey River, Chaudiere....Q
Caie, Robert C., Janeville, W. O....N B
Cairns, Thomas, Perth....O
Cairns, John, Prince of Wales....N B
Cairns, George, Dillonton....Q
Cairns, Robert, Bulwer....Q
Cairns, H. A., East Clifton....Q
Calder, James, Carluke....O
Caldwell, Mathew, New Carlisle....Q
Caldwell, Sharman, Gaspereaux, W. O....N S
Caldwell, Samuel, Auburn....O
Caldwell, J. A., Gaspereaux....N S
Calhoun, Joseph, Uphill....O
Calkin, G. E., Kentville....N S

Cameron, Isabella, Black River Bridge, W. O....N B
Cameron, A. S., Daywood....O
Cameron, Hugh, Kempt Road, W. O....N S
Cameron, Andrew, Camerontown....O
Cameron, J. A., Blanche....Q
Cameron, Duncan, Cayuga....O
Cameron, Donald, Underwood....O
Cameron, John, Big Island, W. O....N S
Cameron, J. A., Batchewana....O
Cameron, J. A., Bridgeville, W. O....N S
Cammidge, Henry, Clavering....O
Campbell, Archibald, Hartley....O
Campbell, Archibald, Lochaber Bay....Q
Campbell, Archibald J., Liverpool....N S
Campbell, Donald, Margaree Forks....N S
Campbell, Charles C., New Campbelton....N S
Campbell, Donald B., Harrington East....Q
Campbell, Geo., East River, St. Mary's, W. O....N S
Campbell, G. F., St. Andrews....N B
Campbell, Malcolm, Mildmay....O
Campbell, William, Calder....O
Campbell, A. T., Holyrood....O
Campbell, Hector, West Side of Middle River, W. O....N S
Campbell, James, Cash Creek....B C
Campbell, John, Escuminac (sub.)....Q
Campbell, Donald, Wellington....O
Campbell, D. K., Campbell Settlement, W. O....N B
Campbell, M., Lucknow....O
Campbell, D., Mount Pleasant....P E I
Campbell, D., Lot 16....P E I
Campbell, D., Glenshee, W. O....N S
Canniff, Jonas, jun., Canniffton....O
Cannon, Robert, Vesta....O
Cannon, M., New Horton, W. O....N B
Cannon, Abraham, Point Traverse....O
Cantwell, William, Franklin Centre....Q
Carbonneau, Moise, St. Leonard....Q
Cardwell, Henry, Chatsworth....O
Cardwell, William, Drew....O
Carey, John, Baie Verte....N B
Carland, John, Pubnico Harbor, W, O....N S
Carle, John R., Scotch Town, W. O....N B
Carman, L. D., Musquash....N B
Carmichael, Dougald, English Settlement, W. O....N B
Carmichael, Thomas C, White's Point, W. O....N B

List of Postmasters in Canada—Continued.

Carrigan, B., Emigrant Settlement, W. O..........N B
Carroll, Richard, Usher, W. O.....................N S
Carrol, Dennis, Lot 4..............................P E I
Carrol, R. M., Tignish ....P E I
Carscallen, J. A., Glastonbury......................O
Carson, Mrs. Sarah, Newbridge ....O
Carson, S W., Cressy ....O
Carson, B, B., Port Lewis ....Q
Carson, William. Roger's Hill ....N S
Carswell, Thomas M., Gower Point ....O
Carter, A. H., Bondhead.............................O
Carter, L. G., Port Colborne ....O
Cartier, S., Ste. Aimé ....Q
Cartier, Narcise, St. Antoine, River Richelieu ......Q
Carvell, J. S., Lakeville, W. O. ....N B
Carvell, Richard, Temperance Vale, W. O. ....N B
Case, George, Case Settlement, W. O...............N B
Case, W. Mitchell, Midland, W. O..................N B
Casement, Robert, North Douro ....O
Cashion, Caroline, Cashion's Glen ....O
Cass, Joseph, jr., Cass Bridge ....O
Casselman, C. T., Winchester........................O
Casselman, Martin, Casselman ....O
Cassidy, William, Loretto ....O
Cassidy, J. W., Point Bruley, W. O................N S
Cattanach, Donald, Laggan ....O
Cattanach, P., Sombra...............................O
Cattellier, Hubert St. George, Beauce ....Q
Catton, John, Burford...............................O
Cavanah, Thomas, Creighton..........................O
Cavers, Peter A., Homer.............................O
Caya, Tancred, Vereker ....O
Cazeau, Joseph, Montmorency Falls ....Q
Chaffey, J. B. W., Indian Island, W. O............N B
Chaisson, L., Rollo Bay Cross ....P E I
Challoner, J., White Point, W. O. ....N S
Chalmers, John, Belledune, W. O. ....N B
Chamberlin, Otis, Mont Elie ....Q
Chambers, John, Wilfred.............................Q
Chambers, John, Shrewsbury..........................Q
Chambers, George, Verschoyle ....O
Champagne, J. Bte., St. Severin de Beaurivage.......Q
Champoux, Leon, St. Gertrude ....Q
Champoux, George, Lake Aylmer.......................Q
Chandonnais, E., St. Jean des Chaillons.............Q
Channell, James T., Bolton Forest ....Q
Chant, Samuel, Chantry..............................O
Chantler, James G., Newton Robinson ....O
Chapedelaine, L. St. Ours ....Q
Chapeleau, Edouard, St. Paschal ....Q
Chapman, Alexander, Chapman ....O
Chapman, Bowden, Chapman, W. O....................N B
Chapman, G. H., Hastings, W. O. ....N S
Chapman, George W., River Gilbert...................Q
Chapman, John, North Augusta ....O
Chapman, John, Frankfort............................O
Chapman, Dixon, Mount Whatley, W. O. ....N B
Chapman, Michael, Goodwood ....O
Chapman, Robert A., South Rockland ....N B
Chapmon, C. S., Warren, W. O. ....N S
Charbonneau, V., Beresford ....Q
Charbonneau, C. T., L'Acadie ....Q
Charland, Joseph, Lavaltrie ....Q
Charlebois, A. W.. Rigaud ....Q
Charlton, S., Milford, W. O. ....N S
Charlton, William, Lynedoch.........................O
Charters, S. C., Memdomcook ....N B
Chase, Albert, Port Williams......................N S
Chase, Arthur G., Upper Sackville, W. O...........N B
Chase, Reuben, Lakeville, W. O. ....N S
Chaurette, Cyprien, Oka ....Q
Chenier, Felix, Baie St. Paul ....M
Chenier, Hercule, Sevigné ....Q
Chesley, Nelson, Chesley's Corners, W. O..........N S
Chittendon, Andrew, Cainsville ....O
Childerhose, Robert, Stafford.......................O
Chillas, Miss Margaret, Nicolet.....................Q
Chipman, Samuel, Chipman's Corners, W. O..........N S
Chipman, Mrs. A., Amherst ....N S
Chisholm, Alexander, St. Ann's ....M
Chisholm, Archibald, St. Andrews ....N S
Chisholm, John, Antigonishe Harbor, W. O ....N S
Chisholm, Mrs. M., Pomquet Forks, W. O............N S
Chisholm, R., Sutherland's Mills, W. O............N S
Chisholm, Colin, Marydale, W. O...................N S
Chisholme, Wm., Dalhousie Mills.....................O
Choat, Thomas, Warsaw...............................O
Chouinard, Elié, Garneau............................Q
Christie, Joseph, Ryegate...........................O
Christie, Alex. R., Port Severn (sub.)..............O
Christie, John H., Little Bras d'Or...............N S
Christie, John G., Apple Grove......................O
Christie, James B., Trenton ....O
Christie, Thomas, Campbellville ....O
Church, W. S., Bersimis.............................Q
Church, Mrs. Ann, Brockton ....O
Church, Richard, Cataract ....O
Clairoux, P. E., St. Hermas ....Q
Clapperton, John, Nicola Lake ....B C
Clark, Robert, Canterbury...........................Q
Clark, Wm., Shanly..................................O
Clark, Benjamin, Camden, East.......................O
Clark, Wm. H., Nackawick, W. O....................N B
Clark, Wm., Oak Park, W. O........................N S
Clarke, Peter, Montague.............................O
Clark, Bibins, Cloyne ....O
Clark, Norman, Tichborne ....O
Clark, Adam, Farnham Centre ....Q
Clark, E., Newcomb Mills ....O
Clark, H., North Bedeque ....P E I
Clark, Jesse, Springfield, W. O...................N B
Clark, N. J., Farquhar ....O

List of Postmasters in Canada—Continued.

Clarke, Robert, Downsview .... O
Clarke, P. T., Coxheath, W. O........ N S
Clark, Pulaski, Byng Inlet........ O
Clay, Wm., Norval .... O
Clays, Geo., jun., Bedford........ Q
Clayton, W. R., Carlow .... O
Cleland, Hugh, West Osgoode .... O
Cleland, James, North Mountain .... O
Clemens, Joseph, Silver Lake .... O
Clement, James S., Virgil .... O
Clement, Ovide A., St. Paul's Bay .... Q
Clement, A. D., Brantford .... O
Cleminger, John, Banda .... O
Clendinning, R., Dungannon........ O
Cleveland, Isaac, Sandy Beaches, W. O........ N S
Clifford, A., Mount Albert .... O
Clifford, Henry A., Muskoka Falls .... O
Clinch, Charles F., Clinch's Mills........ N B
Clough, Daniel, Lennox Ferry, W. O........ N S
Cloutier, C. P., St. Victoire .... Q
Cloutier, J. B., St. Cyrille .... Q
Cloutier, Mdme. A., Detour du Lac........ Q
Cloutier, Polycarpe, Lamartine........ Q
Clow, Elias, South Granby .... Q
Coates, Thomas H., Smith Creek, W. O........ N B
Coates, Thomas, Coates' Mills, W. O........ N B
Coatsworth, Caleb, Romney .... O
Coburn, Thos., Upper Keswick Ridge. W. O...N B
Coburn, M. H., Little River (Sun), W. O........ N B
Cochran, B. W., Halifax .... N S
Cochran, J. T., Scotch Village, W. O........ N S
Cochran, J. F., Newport........ N S
Cochran, Charles, New Durham........ O
Cockburn, J. P., Gravenhurst .... O
Cockerline, Wm., Henrysburg .... Q
Code, G. Trowbridge .... O
Code, Thomas, Innisville........ O
Codys, Charles F., Codys, W. O........ N B
Coglan, Isaac J., Kepler .... O
Cohan, Charles, Hebron........ N S
Cohoon, Freeman, Port Medway .... N S
Colbeck, Wm., Colbeck .... O
Colclough, J. R., Bic........ Q
Colcleugh, F. W., Carlisle .... O
Cole, Allen, Milby .... Q
Cole, John, Cole's Island........ N B
Cole, Thomas, North Nation Mills .... Q
Coleman, T., Heart's Mills, W. O .... N B
Coleman, Wm., Seeley's Bay........ O
Colgan, John, Cranbourne .... Q
Coleman, H. N., Cookstown .... O
Coleman, Wm., Cedar Dale .... O
Colhoun, John C., Hopewell Corner, W. O........ N B
Collet, Charles A., St. Henri .... Q
Collette, Joseph, Ste. Julie........ Q
Collerette, Zephirin, Grand Etang, W. O........ N S
Colliout, P., Hillside, W. O........ N B
Colling, J., Verdun .... O
Colliver, Thomas, Cherry Valley .... O
Colpitts, R. Alder., Pleasant Vale, W. O........ N B
Colpitts, W. A., Mapleton, W. O........ N B
Culver, W. S., Garnet .... O
Comeau, Justien, Metaghan River, W. O........ N S
Comeau, A. F., Clare, W. O........ N S
Comeau, Louis, Point du Lac .... Q
Commeault, J. D., River David .... Q
Commins, A. B., Centre Augusta .... O
Compton, H., Brooklyn........ P E I
Condon, Lewis, Locke Port, W. O........ N S
Connor, Charles, Poland........ O
Conn, C., Elder........ O
Conn, R. W., Conn .... O
Conn, James, Ashton .... O
Connacher, H., Black Point, W. O........ N B
Cook, G. W., 150 Mile House .... B C
Cook, Charles, Six Mile Road, W. O........ N S
Cook, James, Belle Creek .... P E I
Cook, Wm., Black Land, W. O........ N B
Cook, James, Milford .... O
Cook, James R., Mount Albion .... O
Cook, Wm., Carrville .... O
Cook, Asa A., Bassin du Liévre........ Q
Coonan, George, Waterside, W. O........ N B
Cooper, Francis, South Barnston .... Q
Cooper, Samuel, Keyser .... O
Cooper, H. N., Round Lake .... O
Copeland, W. L., St. Catharine's, West .... O
Copp, John, jun., Baie Verte Road, W. O........ N B
Copp, Timothy, Centre Village, W. O........ N B
Copping, E., Montcalm .... Q
Coppinger, Thomas, Hanover .... O
Corbett, Edmund, Harmony .... O
Corbett, Andrew, Clones, W. O........ N B
Corbett, R. A., Perrytown .... O
Corbett, Edmund, Harbor au Bouche, W. O........ N S
Corbett, George, Gold Fields, W. O........ N S
Corbett, R., Grenville........ P E I
Corbin, John, Cornwall .... P E I
Cormeck, Joseph, Moor's Mills, W. O........ N B
Cormier, Joseph G., Doherty Mills, W. O........ N B
Cormier, S., Upper Caraquet, W. O .... N B
Cornell, B., Rockton .... O
Cornell, F. W., Sunshine .... O
Cornish, Thomas, Winfield........ O
Cornock, William, Erin .... O
Cornwall, Charles, Rockport .... O
Cornwall, H. P., Ashcroft .... B C
Correll, Mrs. Phœbe A., Stamford........ O
Corrigan, A., Inkerman .... O
Corrigan, Wm., Stoneham .... Q
Coryell, Abram O., Seagrave .... O
Cossar, Mrs. James, Dufferin........ O
Costello, John, Brudenell........ O
Costin, R. M., Alberton .... P E I

List of Postmasters in Canada—Continued.

Coté, George, St. Giles .... Q
Coté, Marcel, Tremblay .... Q
Coté, Cléophe, Les Eboulemons .... Q
Coté, Edward, Rivière aux vaches .... Q
Cotter, James W., Appleby .... O
Cottle, N. B., Jemseg, W. O .... N B
Cotton, Robert, Port Credit .... O
Coughlin, John, Soixante .... Q
Coughlin, M., Meyersburg .... O
Coulson, James, Coulson .... O
Coulter, John, Long Point, W. O .... N B
Counter, Henry, Spaffordton .... O
Courtemanche, F., St. Edwige .... Q
Cousins, Arch., Long River .... P E I
Coutu, O. H., St. Francois du Lac .... Q
Coutu, C. H., St. Elie .... Q
Couture, O., St. Anaclet .... Q
Couture, Eusèbe, Buckland .... Q
Couture, George, Beaumont .... Q
Couture, Wilbrod, St. Paul du Buton .... Q
Coverly, Silas, Latimer .... O
Covert, Henry, Crofton .... O
Covey, Charles, Indian Harboor, W. O .... N S
Cowan, James, Ronson .... O
Cowan, David, Rossway, W. O .... N S
Cowan, W. C., Scratching River .... M
Cowie, John W., Balderson .... O
Cowie, Robert, Springbank .... O
Cowie, Thomas, Hannon .... O
Cown, L., St. Dominique des Cédres .... Q
Cox, John, Upper Stewiacke, W. O .... N B
Cox, C. B., South Branch, W. O .... N S
Cox, Wm., Norten Dale, W. O .... N B
Craig, James, Wagram .... O
Craig, Murdoch, Craigsholme .... O
Craig, Thomas, Craighurst .... O
Craig, Leslie M., Pleasant Valley, W. O .... N S
Craig, George, East side of Ragged Island .... N S
Craig, Mrs. James, Eel River, W. O .... N B
Crandal, Joseph, Moncton .... N B
Craven, Cranswick, Port Huron .... O
Crawford, John, Brockville .... O
Crawford, John, Gravel Hill .... O
Creed, George, South Rawdon, W. O .... N S
Creelman, F., Stewiacke Cross Roads, W. O .... N S
Creelman, James, Newton Mills, W. O .... N S
Creelman, William, Lower Selmah, W. O .... N S
Crepeau, Guillaume, St. Camille .... Q
Crepeau, Max., St. Félix de Valois .... Q
Cridland, Edwin, Marston .... O
Crocker, James, Elimville .... O
Croft, William, Middleville .... O
Crombie, E. R., Brandy Creek .... O
Cronan, Mrs. M. A., La Have River, W. O .... N S
Crooks, W., Peggy's Cove, W. O .... N S
Crosby, John, Boynton .... P E I
Crosby, Moses, Gordonsville, W. O .... N B
Crosby, Charles, Lake George, W. O .... N S
Crosby, Richard, Deerfield, W. O .... N S
Crosby, William, South Ohio, W. O .... N S
Cross, Thomas, South Zorra .... O
Cross, Henry, jun., Maple Grove .... Q
Crossfield, O., Abbotsford .... Q
Crossley, John, Bennie's Corners .... O
Crosswell, George, Upsalquitch, W. O. .... N B
Crothers, Thomas, Upper Gagetown .... N B
Crowdis, J. G., Middle Section of N. E. Margaree, W. O. .... N S
Crowe, R. S., Londonderry .... N S
Crowell, Israel, Crowell .... N S
Crowell, R. H., Barrington .... N S
Crowell, William, Highfield, W. O .... N S
Crowther, James, Attercliffe .... O
Crozier, S., Topping .... O
Cruickshank, James, Cruickshank .... O
Crumb, Benoni, Tintern .... O
Cryan, William James, Fafard .... Q
Cuddahee, Timothy, Rathburn .... O
Cummer, W. W., Newton Brook .... O
Cumming, John, Fergusonvale .... O
Cumming, George, Rosemont .... O
Cumming, George, Garden Island .... O
Cumminger, E., Wilmot .... N S
Cumminger, Jesse, Goldenville .... N S
Cummings, Charles, Milford .... N B
Cummins, S., Carlow, W. O .... N B
Cumner, Jacob, Willowdale .... O
Cunningham, Charlotte, Canso .... N S
Cunningham, E. J., Guysbcrough .... N S
Cunningham, James, Gourock .... O
Cunningham, W., Cape Sable Island, W. O .... N S
Curran, M., Pisquid Road .... P E I
Curran, Patrick, Milltown .... N B
Curran, T., West Branch Nicholas River, W. O .... N B
Currelly, John, Hay .... O
Currie, Hugh, Camilla .... O
Currie, Thomas, New Ross .... O
Currie, R. B., West Dublin, W. O. .... N S
Curry, John, Farmington .... O
Curry, Frederick G., Horton Landing, W. O .... N S
Curry, J. A., Yelverton .... O
Curtis, Robert, Mongolia .... O
Curtis, Edward, Oak Ridges .... O
Cushing, James B., Cushing .... Q
Cusson, Gilbert, St. François de Sales .... Q
Cutting, Horace, Coaticook .... Q
Cyr, François S., Maria .... Q

Dafoe, Jacob, Utica .... O
Dafoe, Manual, Zephyr .... O
Dagenais, J., St. Hippolyte de Kilkenny .... Q
Dagget, E., Grand Manan .... N B

Demouchelle, P., Bel River .... **O**
D'Entremont, M., Lower West Pubnico, W. O. .... **N S**
Denaut, W. H., Delta .... **O**
Denison, Joseph R., Denison's Mills .... **Q**
Dennis, Dennis L., Tuscorora .... **O**
Dennison, B., Marysville, W. O. .... **N B**
Densmore, R. T., Densmore's Mill, W. O. .... **N S**
Densmore, Mrs. L., Kennetcook Corner, W. O. .... **N S**
Dépot, J., Egypte .... **Q**
Dereek, S. B., Miranda .... **Q**
Derenzy, Edward, Sand Point .... **O**
Derham, P. H., Tuam .... **O**
Derick, T. B, Noyan .... **Q**
Derome, I. J. L , St Jean, Chrysostôme, Chateauguay .... **Q**
Deruchie, D. J., Glen Walter .... **O**
Desaulniers, Joseph, Shawonegan .... **Q**
Desaultel, S., Augustin, Rochelle .... **Q**
Des Brisay, Mrs. A. C., Madisco .... **N B**
Deschéne, François, St. Philip de Nery .... **Q**
Dechénes, Jean, St. Cyriac .... **Q**
Deselet, Olivier, Ste. Angéle de Laval .... **Q**
Deséve, A., Tannery, West .... **Q**
Desjardins, H., Stony Point .... **O**
Desparais dit Champagne, Antoine, Charlemagne .... **Q**
Desforgés, Clovis, Newport .... **Q**
Despocas, Marc C., Valleyfield .... **Q**
Després, E. L. R. C., St. Hyacinthe .... **Q**
Desroches, David, St. Janvier .... **Q**
Desroches, Ulrick B., St. Ligouri .... **Q**
Deveber, N. H., Westfield, W. O .... **N B**
Devitt, Isaac, Flora .... **O**
Devine, Solomon, Petewawa .... **O**
Dewar, David, North Keppel .... **O**
Déziel, L. I., Daillebout .... **Q**
Dibb, Mitchell, Derwent .... **O**
Dick, James, Maple Valley .... **O**
Dick, George, sen., L'Etete, W. O .... **N B**
Dick, R. W., Springfield .... **M**
Dickens, William, Upper Bay du Vin, W. O .... **N B**
Dickenson, Edward, North Glanford .... **O**
Dickey, Mrs. Agnes, Bass River, W. O .... **N S**
Dickey, John, Middle Stewiacke, W. O .... **N S**
Dickie, Clement B., Cornwallis, East, W. O .... **N S**
Dickie, E. M., Upper Hampstead, W. O .... **N B**
Dickie, John, Muddy Creek .... **P E I**
Dickieson, D., Wilmot Valley .... **P E I**
Dickinson, J. G., Allenwood .... **O**
Dickinson, Samuel, Coldstream, W. O .... **N B**
Dickinson, G. L., Manotick .... **O**
Dickson, Hugh, Central Onslow, W. O .... **N S**
Dickson, John, Paudash .... **O**
Dickson, Samuel, Seaforth .... **O**
Dickson, William, Henry .... **O**
Dickson, A., Goderich .... **O**
Dickson, Robert, Peepabun. .... **O**

List of Postmasters in Canada—Continued.

Dieudonné, D. Brulé, Vaudreuil ..... Q
Digdon, John, Half-Island Cove, W. O ..... N S
Dillabough, Isaac, Lockville ..... O
Dillon, D., Calabogie ..... O
Dillon, Mrs. T. H., High Falls ..... O
Dillman, Daniel, Meagher's Grant, W. O ..... N S
Dimock, J. H., Moser's River, W. O ..... N S
Dimock, J. G., Ingram River, W. O ..... N S
Dinnigan, William, Norton Creek ..... Q
Dinnin, William, Lumley ..... O
Dion, Adhimar, Rimouski ..... Q
Dionne, Paschal, St. Denis de la Bouteillerie ..... Q
Dionne, Joseph, Ste. Anne la Pocatiére ..... Q
Dionne, Cyprian, St. Anthony, W. O ..... N B
Disher, Ralph, Ridgway ..... O
Dissette, George, Price's Corner ..... O
Ditchburn, William, Rosseau ..... O
Ditz, Adam, Dorking ..... O
Dixon, Mary C., Middleton, W. O ..... N B
Dixon, Joseph, Sackville ..... N B
Dixon, John, Paudash ..... O
Doan, Charles, Aurora ..... O
Doane, Mrs. Mary, Gunning Cove, W. O ..... N S
Dobie, J. B., Bruce Mines ..... O
Dobbin, James, Dobbington ..... O
Dobson, Wm., Head of Tatamagouche Bay, W.O. N S
Dobson, James, Yorkville ..... O
Dodd, George, Primrose ..... O
Dodds, George, Tullamore ..... O
Dodge, Enoch, jun., Bridgetown ..... N S
Dodge, William W., Hammond River ..... N B
Dogherty, John, Selkirk Road ..... P E I
Doherty, John, Uffington ..... O
Doherty, Michael, Poquiock, W. O ..... N B
Donahue, E., West Farnham ..... Q
Donald, Alexander, Burnbrae ..... O
Donaldson, Robert, Reading ..... O
Donaldson, W., Mount Healy ..... O
Donaldson, Henry F., Enfield ..... N S
Donavan, Thomas, South Bay, W. O ..... N S
Donelly, James, Albany ..... P E I
Donkin, F. A., Athol ..... N S
Dorais, Onesime, St. Stanislas de Kostka ..... Q
Doran, William, Doran ..... O
Dorron, John, Shippigan ..... N B
Douglas, A., Middle St. Francis, W. O ..... N B
Douglas, Thomas, Cambray ..... O
Douglas, Alexander, Norham ..... O
Douglas, B., Yale ..... B C
Douglas, Mary, Manilla ..... O
Douglas, James, Londonderry, W. O ..... N B
Dow, J. L., Lower Brighton, W. O ..... N B
Downie, John, Jordan Bay, W. O ..... N S
Dowsley, John, Prescott ..... O
Dowsley, Joseph L., Escott ..... O
Doyle, John, Bornish ..... O
Doyle, James, Park Corner ..... P E I
Doyle, John, Virginia ..... O
Doyle, L., Farmington ..... P E I
Doyle, William, Back Lands, W. O ..... N S
Doyle, J. W., Guysborough ..... O
Drain, Edward, Head St. Peter's Bay ..... P E I
Drake, P. Edward, Bell Ewart ..... O
Dreany, Robert, Crumlin ..... O
Drolet, Pierre A., St. Pierre d'Orleans ..... Q
Drope, R., Harwood ..... O
Drouillard, Louis, Canard River ..... O
Dryden, Robert, Eramosa ..... O
Drysdale, John, Tatamagouche Mountain, W.O. N S
Drysdale, Robert, Drysdale ..... O
Duaine, J. B. L., St. Barnabé, St Maurice ..... Q
Duboyce, Martin, West Bolton ..... Q
Dubuque, Joseph, St. Boniface ..... M
Duck, James, Duck and Pringle ..... B C
Duck, W. W., Suffolk Road ..... P E I
Ducket, Rodger, Côteau Station ..... Q
Duff, Alexander, Stewartville ..... O
Duffus, Adam, Widder ..... O
Dufour, Rev. E., St. Lazare ..... Q
Dufresne, George, Ancienne, Lorette (sub) ..... Q
Dugal, Adelme, M.D., St. Anne, Bout de l'Isle ..... Q
Duggan, Henry A., York ..... O
Duguay, Nestor, St. Zephirin ..... Q
Duignan, Thomas, Nenagh ..... O
Dukeshire, W. H., Maitland, W. O ..... N S
Dumaresque, Miss H., Tracadie ..... N B
Dumouchelle, P., Rochester ..... O
Dumphy, Edward, Douglas, W. O ..... N B
Dumphy, George, Dumphy, W. O ..... N B
Dunbar, William, West Branch, East River of Picou, W. O ..... N S
Dunbar, Alexander, Elmsdale ..... N S
Duncan, George, Melrose ..... O
Duncan, James, Thamesville ..... O
Duncan, Daniel, Duncan, W. O ..... N S
Duncan, George, St. Malachie ..... Q
Dunham, Henry, Ompah ..... O
Dunham, C. F., Kaladar ..... O
Dunn, William, Washington ..... O
Dunning, Levi E., East Templeton ..... Q
Dunlop, R. S., Mandamin ..... O
Dunlop, W. M., Sable River, W. O ..... N S
Duong, Constant, Pomquet Chapel, W. O. ..... N S
Duplessis, J. O., Sorel ..... Q
Duplesea, D. S., Tracey Station ..... N B
Dupré, Oliver, St. Robert ..... Q
Duprey, Jeremiah, Ruscom River ..... O
Dupuis, A., Village des Aulnaies ..... Q
Dupuis, Hugh, Orleans ..... O
Dupuis, Calixte, St. Herménégilde ..... Q
Durnan, Mrs. S. A., Rosebank ..... O
Dutch, George, Heron's Island, W. O ..... N B

List of Postmasters in Canada—Continued.

Duvernay, Pierre, St. Marc ....Q
Dyer, Richard, St. Patrick, W. O.................N B
Dyer, G. C., Sutton ....Q
Dyer, James, Garden Hill ....O

Eakin, George, Unionville ....O
Eakins, John A., Sparta ....O
Easson, William, Kintore............................O
East, C., St. Augustin, Portneuf....................Q
Eastabrook, H. A., Swan Creek, W. O............N B
Eastabrooks, Joel F., Brigg's Corner, W. O......N B
Easter, G., New Wiltshire........................P E I
Easterbrook, Elias, Nassagiweya ....O
Eastey, Charles W., Royal Road, W O............N B
Eastland, H., Apsley..................................O
Eastman, Benjamin, Carsonby ....O
Eastman, D. H., Eastman's Springs ....O
Easton, H. S., Easton's Corners....................O
Eastwood, Anthony, Lloydtown ....O
Easton, C., Canada Creek, W. O ....N S
Eaton, Geo. W., Palmer's Road, W. O. ....N S
Eby, Elias, Bridgeport ....O
Echlin, D. C., Buxton.................................O
Ecrement, J. F., St. Jacques........................Q
Ecrement, Joseph A., St Damien de Brandon ......Q
Eden, Francis, Varney ....O
Edgar, John, Newbliss ....O
Edgar, John, Three Brooks, W. O.................N B
Edgett, Hiram, River Side, W. O. ....N B
Edgett, Ward, Edgett's Landing, W. O. ....N B
Edmonds, N., Summerville ....P E I
Edmonstone, James, Grant............................O
Edwards, George, Thurso ....Q
Edward, James, Barrie ....O
Edwards, John, Hemmingford ....Q
Edwards, T. S., Lobo ....O
Edwards, W. P., Rankin ....O
Edwards, William C., Rockland ....O
Edwards, William, Maritana..........................Q
Edwards, W. H., Bosworth ....O
Egan, Denis, Powell ....O
Egan, Francis L., Kingsbridge.......................O
Egan, D., Mount Stewart ....P E I
Ehler, John, Crow Harbor, W. O. ....N S
Eisenheur, Jos., Chester Basin, W. O.............N S
Elderkin, Mrs. Jane, Port Greville, W. O.........N S
Ellis, George, Melocheville............................Q
Ellis, James R., Eastville, W. O....................N S
Ells, Watson, Sheffield Mills, W. O................N S
Elmsley, R., Baddeck ....N S
Elmslie, James, Barnett ....O
Elsworth, James, Fisherville ....O
Emerson, N. P., Emerson ....Q
Emery, George, Marble Rock.........................O
Emo, Thomas, Ivanhoe ....O
Engel, John, Poole ....O
England, Philo, Fulford ....Q
Eplett, Samuel D., Coldwater ....O
Erb, John L., Erbsville ....O
Ermatinger, F. E., St. Thomas, West ....O
Ernst, Christian, New Hamburg ....O
Ernst Louis, Point Edward ....O
Ernst, John, Petersburg ....O
Erskine, William, Bocabec, W. O. ....N B
Esnouf, Charles, Grand Grève ....Q
Estabrook, C. L., St. Mary's Ferry, W. O. ....N B
Estey, Charles W., Royal Road, W. O. ....N B
Estey, W. E., Farmerston, W. O....................N B
Esty, Thomas H., Wicklow, W. O. ....N B
Esty, James, Glen Sutton ....Q
Ethier, Daniel, St. Joseph, W. O. ....N B
Evans, Miss E. M., Rock Village ....O
Evans, George, Albion................................O
Evans, Zerah, Dudswell ....Q
Evans, J. E., Westcock, W. O......................N B
Everett, Edward, St. Mary's Bay ....N S
Ewart, Thomas, Carnegie ....O

Fafard, Pierre, St. Hélène de Bagot.................Q
Fair, Thomas, Clinton.................................O
Fairburn, J. B., Bowmanville ....O
Fairweather, A., Springfield.........................N B
Falconbridge, S., Aberfoyle ....O
Fanjoy, C. H., Waterborough, W. O................N B
Faragher, Mrs. E. P., Hillsdale ....O
Fares, Joshua, Netherby..............................O
Farnsworth, Thomas, Morden, W. O. ....N S
Farquharson, J., Mermaid Farm ....P E I
Farquharson, William, Fordyce......................O
Farran, John R., Farran's Point ....O
Farrel, Patrick, Upper Wakefield....................Q
Farrell, Charles, Indiana ....O

List of Postmasters in Canada—Continued.

Ferguson, John, jun., Bathurst Village, W. O......N B
Ferguson, Isaac G., Rosehall......O
Ferguson, Malcolm, Cariboo Cove, W. O......N S
Ferguson, Duncan, Douglas......O
Ferguson, D., Kilean......O
Ferguson, Robert, Stowe......O
Ferris, James M., Campbellford......O
Fettmate, James, White Head, W. O......N S
Fiddes, Alexander, Corbin......Q
Fieldhouse, H., Rosa......O
Filiatreault, Gilbert, St. John Baptiste de Montreal......Q
Fillmore, William, Germantown, W. O......N B
Fillmore, G. A., Lower Turtle Creek, W. O......N B
Finlay, Ephraim, Head of Amherst, W. O......N S
Finlayson, Edward, Merigonish, W. O......N S
Finley, Isaac, Scugog......O
Fish, Robert Y., Linwood......O
Fisher, William, Halfway Brook, W. O......N S
Fisher, C., St. Davids......O
Fisher, M. A., Athol......O
Fisher, Lewis, New Maryland......N B
Fisher, Peter, Wingham......O
Fitzgerald, J., Greenview......O
Fitzgerald, M. Frampton......Q
Fitzgerald, William, Maynooth......O
Flanagan, Mrs. Anne, Spencer Cove......Q
Flannigan, M., Lake Settlement, W. O......N B
Fleming, John, Berkeley......O
Fleming, A. G., Craigleith......O
Fletcher, John L., Nashwaak Village, W. O......N B
Fletcher, George, Alliston......O
Fletcher, Thomas, Shanty Bay......O
Fletcher, William, Carrillon......Q
Flewelling, J. L., Oak Point, W. O.......N B
Flewelling, G. H., Clifton, W. O......N B
Flewelling, John, Hampton, W. O......N B
Flint, George, jun., Greenbank......O
Flood, H., Sweaburg......O
Floyd, J. A., Fairfield......N B
Flynn, Edward, Conroy......O
Foisy, Louis, Arthabaska Station......Q
Foley, B. H., Buctouche......N B
Foley, J. D. Pookshaw, W. O.......N B
Follis, George, Ashley......O
Folmsbee, John, Canboro'......O
Fontaine, Siméon, Weedon......Q
Foot, W. G., Point-aux-Pins......O
Forbes, George, Vernon River Bridge......P E I
Forbes, John, North Sydney......N S
Forbes, John, Forbes, W. O.......N S
Forbes, Peter, Dickenson Landing......O
Ford, H. W., Bouck's Hill......O
Ford, George, Pentland......O
Ford, C. R., Colborne......O
Forman, Robert, Acadia Mines......N S
Forest, John M., Tangier......N S
Forester, Oliver, Forester's Falls......O
Forrest, Richard, Fairview......O
Forrestall, John, Forrestall's, W. O......N S
Forshner, G. H. D., Head of Wallace Bay, W. O. N S
Forshner, J. S., Greenville Station......N S
Forsyth, Hezekiah C., Princeton......O
Forsyth, Enoch A., Fort William Station......N S
Forsyth, Elijah, Fairfield Plain......O
Fortier, A., Ste. Scholastique......Q
Fortier, Pierre, St. Anselme......Q
Fortin, F., St. Pierre d'Orleans......Q
Fortune, James, Lake Law, W. O......N S
Foss, Samuel J., Sherbrooke......Q
Foster, Edward H., Salmon River, W. O.......N S
Foster, H. M., Chute's Cove, W. O......N S
Foster, G. K., Richmond, East......Q
Foster, George N., Kingsley, W. O......N B
Foster, William, North Lake......N B
Foster, James P., Marshall's Cove, W. O......N S
Foster, Henry, Foster's, W. O......N S
Foster, Samuel, Kingston......N B
Fougère, Jos., Larry's River, W. O......N S
Fournier, Marie, St. Jean Port Joli......Q
Fournier, Joseph, Métbot's Mills......Q
Fournier, Louis, Grand Valée......Q
Fournier, P. C. Auguste, St. Raphael, East......Q
Fournier, Joseph, Ste. Flavie......Q
Fournier, Jacques, Majenta......Q
Fowler, Joseph, Dalrymple......O
Fowlds, H. M., Hastings......O
Fowler, James, Salmon Creek, W. O......N B
Fowler, Miss Jane, Lifford......O
Fowler, W. E., Steeve's Settlement, W. O......N B
Fowler, W., Hammondvale......N B
Fowlie, Mrs. Micha. Brookvale, W. O......N B
Fox, Alex. J., Sand Point, W. O......N S
Fox, G. W., Overton......O
Fox, John C., Olinda......O
Foy, Peter, Tramore......O
Foy, John, Foymount......O
Frame, H. M., Glen Huron......O
Frame, Archibald, Selmah, W. O......N S
Frame, M., Gay's River......N S
Francis, Wm., Willowgrove......N B
Francis, John G., Owen Sound......O
Frayney, Robert, Dalhousie Road, W. O......N S
Franks, Thomas, Frank Hill......O
Fraser, Alex., Toney River, W. O......N S
Fraser, Alex., Westmeath......O
Fraser, Donald, McLellan's Mountain, W. O......N S
Fraser, J. A., Big Bras d'Or, W. O......N S
Fraser, Robert, Rocklin, W. O......N S
Fraser, Jas., South Bar of Sydney River, W. O..N S
Fraser, James, Kildonan......M
Fraser, John, Densmores, W. O......N S
Fraser, John, Harrington Cove, W. O......N S

List of Postmasters in Canada—Continued.

Fraser, Jessie McG., Head of St. Margaret's Bay (Middle District), W. O....N S
Fraser, Wm., West McGillivray....O
Fraser, John, Lancaster....O
Fraser, D., Matapedia....Q
Fraser, James, Maple Green, W. O....N B
Fraser, Chas., Cross Roads, Lake Ainslie, W. O...N S
Fraser, Wm., New Glasgow....N S
Fraser, George M., North Brookfield, W. O....N S
Fraser, John, Crosspoint....Q
Fraser, Donald, Dumblane....O
Fraser, Alexander, McLennan's Brook, W. O....N S
Fraser, James, Loch Garry....O
Fraser, David, Grandigue Ferry, W. O....N S
Fraser, A. D., Hamburg....O
Fraser, John, Glengarry Station....N S
Fraser, R., Fontenoy....Q
Fraser, John, Fraser's Grant, W. O....N S
Fraser, Simon, Lochinvar....O
Fraser, Thomas A., Pugwash River, W. O.... N S
Fraser, Archibald, Alma, W. O....N S
Fraser, David, Ecum Secum, W. O....N S
Fraser, John, Eel Creek, W. O....N S
Fraser, J. T., St. Eleanor's....P E I
Fraser, W., Goshen, W. O....N S
Fréchette, Louis J., St. Ferdinand....Q
Fréchette, Nazaire, Craigs Road Station....Q
Fréchette, Thomas, Cedar Hall....Q
Freeman, Mrs. N., Greenfield, W. O....N S
Freeman, B. C., Deniston....O
Freeman, Jos. M., Pleasant River, W. O....N S
Freeman, Samuel E., Nappan, W. O....N S
Freeman, Augustus, White Rock Mills, W. O....N S
Freeman, E. P. Kempt, W. O....N S
Freney, John, Perkins....Q
Freeze, Hiram, Doaktown, W. O....N B
Freid, Noah, Dashwood....O
Frigon, Joseph, St. Prosper....Q
Frizzle, Robert, Shaw's River, W. O....N S
Frommhagen, E., Wartburg....O
Frost, P. W., Little River, W. O....N S
Fry, Isaac, South Cayuga....O
Fry, Henry, Hunsdon....O
Fuchor, John, North Seneca....O
Fugere, Narcisse, Batiscan Bridge....Q
Fullerton, G. D., Halfway River, W. O....N S
Fullerton, Edward D., Cannonville....N S
Fuller, J. A., New Minus, W. O....N S
Fulmer, W. A., Economy....N S
Fulton, Thomas, Knoxford, W. O....N B
Fulton, James, Langton....O
Fulton, Lewis, Teviotdale Station....N S
Furse, James, New Glasgow....Q

Gaboury, J. E., St. Cesaire....Q
Gage, W. J., Bartonville....O
Gagné, Virginie, Viger....Q
Gagnier, Frs. X., Neigette....Q
Gagnon, H., Upper St. Basil....N B
Gagnon, C., L'Avenir....Q
Gagné, Rev. J., Natashquan....Q
Gagnon, Rev. H., St. Catherines....Q
Gagnon, George, St. Rochdes Aulnaies....Q
Gairdner, James, Bayfield....O
Galbraith, William, Boyne....O
Galbraith, T., Pisarinco....N B
Gallant, Joseph, Rustico....P E I
Gallagher, Dennis, Vigo....Q
Gallagher, Ann, Salmon River, W. O....N S
Gallagher, Paul, Perm....O
Gallang, Thomas, Barachois, W. O....N B
Gallant, Athanase, Shediac Bridge, W. O....N B
Galloway, James, Harrisburg....O
Galloway, Alex. D., Bensfort....O
Gamsby, J. W., Huntingville....Q
Gannan, Patrick, Lake La Hache....B C
Gairner, Wm., Minden....O
Garden, J. R., Nashwaak Station, W. O....N B
Gardiner, John, Dartmoor....O
Gardiner, David, Hibernia, W. O....N B
Gardner, Alex., Armow....O
Gardner, Simeon, Tusket Forks, W. O....N S
Gardner, Joseph, Britannia....O
Gareau, Philip, Curran....O
Garrault, Thomas, St. Lin....Q
Garriocke, Peter, Westbourne....M
Garrison, W. A., Upper Sheffield....N B
Gates, John, Vyner....O
Gates, Emerson, Millville, W. O....N S
Gatien, E. H., Ste. Marie de Monnoir....Q
Gaudet, Venant, St. Come....Q
Gaudette, Dr. G., St. Annedes Plains....Q
Gaudry, Charles A., Rivière du Loup (en bas)....Q
Gauld, John D., River John....N S
Gauthier, dit Landerville, A., St. Pie....Q
Gauthier, Philias, St. Eustache....Q
Gauvin, Louis C., St. Charles de Stanbridge....Q
Gavaza, Thomas A., Annapolis....N S
Gay, G., West Huntingdon....O
Gavin, M. Bloomfield....P E I
Gebbie, Thomas, Howick....Q
Geer, M., Herbert....Q
Gehan, Jeremiah, Streetsbridge, W. O....N S
Gélinas, C., St. Clothilde....Q
Gendreau, Pierre, West Ditton....Q
Genereux, Esdras, St. Alphonse....Q
Genest, F. E., St. Marguerite....Q
Genoir, William, Big Tracadie, W. O....N S
Genong, F. D., Sprague's Point....N B
George, J. C., York River....O
George, James, Huttonsville....O
Germain, C., jun., St. Vincent de Paul....Q

List of Postmasters in Canada—Continued.

Germain, Elzéar, St. Didace.................................Q
Germain, George, Gosport...................................O
German, G. R., Pringer.......................................O
Gerard, R., Head of Tide, W. O..........................N B
Getchell, John J., Lynnfield, W. O.......................N B
Ghent, D. A., Priceville.......................................O
Giasson, G. F., L'Anse à Giles..............................Q
Gibb, W., W., Langley..B C
Gibbon, James, Collins, W. O...............................N B
Gibbons, John, Goldstone.....................................O
Gibson, Robert, Glenvale......................................O
Gibson, George, Tilton...O
Gibson, Wm., Gibson..O
Giddens, Daniel, Portapique Mountain, W. O.....N S
Gifford, Henry C., Silver Hill................................O
Gilbault, Joseph, St. Paul d'Industrie.....................Q
Gilbert, William, Mansfield...................................O
Gilbert, John D., Gilbert's Mills.............................O
Gilchrist, James, Keady..O
Gilchrist, John C., Woodville..................................O
Gilchrist, Wm., Pontiac...Q
Gill, H. W., Ufford..O
Gillard, J. Grafton..O
Gillespie, Alexander, Creemore...............................O
Gillespie, Alexander, Sunnidale...............................O
Gillespie, George, Round Plains..............................O
Gillespie, George M., Glenarm.................................O
Gillespie, Charles, Milton, East...............................Q
Gilley, Walter, Oak Bay, W. O...............................N B
Gillies, Collin, Margaree, W. O..............................N S
Gillies, Donald, Grand Mira South, W. O...............N S
Gillies, John, Braeside..O
Gillies, Donald, Soldier's Cove, W. O....................N S
Gilliott, Wm., Churchstreet, W. O..........................N S
Gillis, Niel, Point Clear, W. O..............................N S
Gillis, John, Wine Harbor, W. O............................N S
Gillis, Wm., Arisaig, W. O...................................N S
Gillis, Donald, Lewis Bay, W. O............................N S
Gillis, Donald, Big Intervale (Grand Narrows), W. O..........N S
Gilman, Francis, Parker's Creek..............................M
Gingras, François X., St. Casimir..........................Q
Gingrich, Moses, Roseville.....................................O
Girard, Rev. M. L'Anse, St. Jean............................Q
Girardin, R. A., Grande Ligne................................Q
Girouard, Joseph, St. Urbain..................................Q
Giroux, Nazaire, Clarine..O

Goble, Frederick, Harrow......................................O
Goble, J. G., Goble's Corners.................................O
Godard, Daniel, South Branch (Kent)...................N B
Godfrey, E. L., Mountain Grove..............................O
Goehringer, Joseph, Bingham Road.........................O
Golding, G. N., Wickham, W. O...........................N B
Gonthro, Belloni, French Vale, W. O.....................N S
Good, Archibald, Good Corner, W. O.....................N B
Goodenow, Lafayette, Georgetown...........................O
Gooderham, A. L., Pine Grove...............................O
Gooderham, C. H., Meadowvale..............................O
Goodeve, Chas. F., Allan Park................................O
Goodfellow, A., Springville....................................O
Goodfellow, James, Vine..O
Goodhue, Samuel, Barnston....................................Q
Goodhue, James, Arthabaskaville............................Q
Gordanier, J. L. P., Morven...................................O
Gordon, John, St. Helens.......................................O
Gordon, David, Osnea..O
Gordon, James, Genoa..Q
Gordon, Thomas, Longwood....................................O
Gordon, H., Port Perry..O
Gordon, Thomas, Elm Grove...................................O
Gorman Patrick, Shamrock......................................O
Gorman, George, Metaghan, W. O........................N S
Gormely, Patrick, Morrisburgh...............................O
Gormley, P., Johnston's River............................P E I
Gormley, J., St Mary's Road...............................P E I
Gormly, Patrick, Morrisburg...................................O
Gormley, James, Gormley.......................................O
Gorvell, Wm. O., Spanish River.............................O
Gorvett, W., Miliken..O
Gosselin, François, jun., St. Victor de Tring.............Q
Gosselin, M., St. Jean Crysostôme, Lévis.................Q
Gosselin, Jean Baptiste, St. Laurant d'Orleans..........Q
Gosselin, Joseph, St. Irénée....................................Q
Gould, Lorenzo T., Wooler.....................................O
Gould, Edward N., Plainfield..................................O
Goulding, T. B., Bryanston.....................................O
Goulet, L. G. E., St. Jean Baptiste de Rouville.........Q
Goulet, E., St. Hilaire Village.................................Q
Goulette, William, Belœil Station............................Q
Graham, W. M., Bethany..O
Graham, Andrew K., Five Islands.........................N S
Graham, Robert, Enterprise.....................................O
Graham, W. S., West River Station......................N S
Graham, Hugh, Rouge Hill.....................................O

List of Postmasters in Canada—Continued.

Grandy, John, Berne .... O
Grandy, Robert, Omemee .... O
Grant, Alexander, Verona .... O
Grant, Alexander, Frazer's Mills, W. O .... N B
Grant, James, Coverley .... O
Grant, A. W., Shulie, W. O .... N S
Grant, James A., St. Stephen .... N B
Grant, William, Parrsborough Shore, W. O .... N S
Grant, William, Kintail .... O
Grant, William, Mabou .... N S
Grant, John R., Brussels .... O
Grant, James, Hardwood Lands, W. O .... N S
Grant, Angus, Port Hawkesbury .... N S
Grant, Jonas, Playfair .... O
Grant, James, Granton .... O
Grant, Peter, Springville, W. O .... N S
Grass George, Waasis Station, W. O .... N B
Grassie, John, Fulton .... O
Graveline, David U., Castlebar .... Q
Graves, W. H., Springfield .... O
Gray, Wm., Fleurant (sub) .... Q
Gray, A. S., Ponds, W. O .... N S
Gray, J. C., Foreston, W. O .... N B
Gray, M. S., Laurel .... O
Graydon, Robert, Streetsville .... O
Graystock, Mark, Graystock .... O
Green, Joseph, Davenport .... O
Green, P. F., Charleston .... O
Green, Caleb, Fairhaven, W. O .... N B
Green, George, H. H., Port Nelson .... O
Green, Joshua, Spring Brook .... O
Green, H. C., Summerville .... P E I
Greenshields, James, Nevis .... O
Greensides, Edward, Monkton .... O
Greenway, Wlliam, Centralia .... O
Greenwood, William, Port Clyde, W. O .... N S
Greenwood, A. R., North East Harbor, W. O .... N S
Greer, James, Winchester Springs .... O
Gregor, Lewis, Crieff .... Q
Grenier, David, Garthby, ... Q
Grier, James, Iroquois .... O
Griffin, J. S, Preston Road, W. O. .... N S
Griffith, David, Parma .... O
Griffith, John, Parham .... O
Grimm, C., Springfield, W. O. .... N S
Grindley, W. H., Blackville, W. O. .... N B
Grono, Elias, Hackett's Cove, W. O. .... N S
Gropp, Henry, Brunner .... N
Grosvenor, C. E., Canterbury .... N B
Grosvenor, George, Lower Southampton, W. O .... N B
Grouchey, David, Discoose, W. O. .... N B
Grout, James C., Solina .... O
Grundy, William, Greenock .... O
Gueguen, Magloire, Gueguen, W. O. .... N B
Guerin, Seraphin, Port au Persil .... Q
Guilbert, Mrs. H., Britannia Mills .... O
Guild, Julius, Bentley .... O
Guimond, Baptiste, Silver Stream, W. O. .... N B
Gunn, Donald, Lower Fort Garry .... M
Gunn, Donald, Cross Roads, Country Harbor .... N S
Gunn, John, Hopewell, W. O. .... N S
Guthrie, Peter, Tatlock .... N S

Hackett, John, Hockley .... O
Hackett, Alexander, Colchester .... O
Hackett, John, Chambly Canton .... Q
Hacking, W. H., Listowell .... O
Hackwell, William, Boscobel .... Q
Haddock, James, McAdam Junction, W. O .... N B
Hadley, G. B., Port Mulgrave .... N S
Hagan, James, Templeton .... Q
Hagar, Elijah, Roseway, W. O .... N S
Hager, Charles, Hagersville .... O
Hagerman, L., Moray .... O
Hagyard, E. T., Campbell's Cross .... O
Haines, E. J., Marshall's Town, W. O .... N S
Hales, Richard, Forfar .... O
Hall, C. H. J., Broughton .... Q
Hall, Asa, Stoketon .... Q
Hall, Edward, Darrell .... O
Hall, Henry, Binbrook .... O
Hall, J. H., Brooklyn, W. O. .... N S
Hall, W., Sheet Harbor, W. O .... N S
Hall, Daniel B., Linda .... Q
Hall, George, Clyde .... O
Hall, W. J., Keene .... O
Hall, William, Skipness .... O
Hallamore, S. E., New Cornwall, W. O. .... N S
Halley, James L., Ponsonby .... O
Hally, Wilson, Rockville, W. O .... N S
Halloway, John, Crosshill .... O
Hallisay, Daniel, Beaver Bank, W. O. .... N S
Hamel, J., St. Croix .... Q
Hamelin, D., St. Narcisse .... Q
Hamelin, A. Damase, Deschambault .... Q
Hamelin, F. X. T., Portneuf .... Q
Hames, William, Vennachar .... O
Hamilton, James, Singhampton .... O
Hamilton, Samuel, St. Luc .... Q
Hamilton, W. B., Collingwood .... O
Hamilton, James, Carlingford .... O
Hamilton, James, Staffa .... O
Hamilton, George, Britonville .... Q
Hamilton, S. W., Kemptville, W. O. .... N S
Hamm, David, Grand Bay .... N B
Hammond, W. D., Warkisville .... O
Hammond, James, jun., Hammond .... O
Hammond, J. A., Kingsclear, W. O. .... N B
Hammond, Ross, Locke Port .... N S
Hamon, Philip, Newport Point .... Q
Hancock, L. S., Ridgetown .... O
Handron, Henry, Handford Brook, W. O .... N B

List of Postmasters in Canada—Continued.

Hanes, Erastus, Utterson .... **O**
Hanes, James F., Huntsville .... **O**
Hanley, J. C., Reed .... **O**
Hanna, Hugh, Brookvale, W. O. .... **N S**
Hannegar, Jacob, Upper Kennetcook, W. O. .... **N S**
Hannington, W. J. M., Pointe du Chêne, W. O. .... **N B**
Hannington, W., Smith's, W. O. .... **N B**
Hanrahan, Thomas, South Douro .... **O**
Hanson, Robert V., Mace's Bay .... **N B**
Hardwicke, V. F., Bear River (West side) .... **N S**
Hardy, J. N., Dorchester Station .... **O**
Hardy, N., Champlain .... **Q**
Hardy, William, Lot 6 .... **P E I**
Hargrave, Joseph, Eglington .... **O**
Harmon, Charles A., Peel, W. O. .... **N B**
Harnett, John, Kingston .... **N B**
Harrington, H. H., Tracadie .... **N S**
Harris, Richardson, Saw Mill Creek, W. O. .... **N S**
Harris, Mrs. Elizabeth, Myrehall .... **O**
Harris, C. S., Courtland .... **O**
Harris, S. G., Tapleyton .... **O**
Harris, Samuel, Cowichan .... **B C**
Harris, T. R., Aylesford .... **N S**
Harris, John L., Albert Mines, W. O. .... **N B**
Harris, Samuel, Tyrconnell .... **O**
Harrison, J. H., Rockville, W. O. .... **N B**
Harrison, Isabella, Drum .... **O**
Harrison, John, Kinloss .... **O**
Harrison, Richard, Glammis .... **O**
Harrison, Thomas, Thorndale .... **O**
Harrison, Charles, Kingston Mills .... **O**
Harron, Alexander, Debec Station, W. O. .... **N B**
Hartley, Jonathan, Pirate Harbor .... **N S**
Hart, Thomas N., Chatillon .... **Q**
Hartt, William, Derby, W. O. .... **N B**
Harvey, William, Elmvale .... **O**
Harvey, Henry, Granville .... **B C**
Hase, Thomas, Haseville .... **Q**
Hassard, George, Tyneside .... **O**
Hatfield, J. A., Brookville, W. O. .... **N S**
Hatfield, J. L., Fox River, W. O. .... **N S**
Hattee, John, New Caledonia, W. O. .... **N S**
Hawbolt, Elisha, Marie Joseph, W. O. .... **N S**
Hawkins, W. J. Lowville .... **O**
Hawkin, Thomas, Schoona .... **B C**
Hawley, H. A., Aird .... **Q**
Hawthorne, A., Upper Kent, W. O. .... **N B**
Hay, Shackleton, Ailsa Craig .... **O**
Hayes, John, Norton, W. O. .... **N B**
Hayes, Michoel, Hayesland .... **O**
Hayes, William, Lot 12 .... **P E I**
Hayes, Michael, Renois River, W. O. .... **N B**
Hayley, Wilson, Rockville, W. O. .... **N S**
Hayter, Thomas N., Harpley .... **O**
Hayward, Robert, Kenilworth .... **O**

Healey, Maurice, Harewood, W. O. .... **N B**
Heapy, Michael, Victoria Road Station .... **O**
Heard, William, Kemble .... **O**
Heath, Samuel, Tyrrell .... **O**
Heath, William, Clarendon Front, (sub) .... **Q**
Hébert, Antoine, St. Martine .... **Q**
Hébert, C., Labarre .... **Q**
Hébert, J. T., Larochelle .... **Q**
Hébert, F. J., Dupey's Corner, W. O. .... **N B**
Heckman, Isaac, La Have Cross Roads, W. O. .... **N S**
Heffernan, Jane, Carroll's Corners, W. O. .... **N S**
Helps, Mrs., Westfield .... **O**
Heming, C. H., Sydenham Mills .... **O**
Hemlow, James, Liscombe, W. O. .... **N S**
Hemphill, James, Ferryville, W. O. .... **N B**
Hendershot, A., Jerseyville .... **O**
Henderson, David, West Essa .... **O**
Henderson, J. M., Henderson Settlement, W. O. .... **N S**
Henderson, Wm., Henderson Settlement, W. O. .... **N B**
Henderson, Hy., Springford .... **O**
Henderson, John, Lime Lake .... **O**
Hendry, Charles, Conestogo .... **O**
Hendry, James, Porter's Hill .... **O**
Hendry, W., Brookfield, W. O. .... **N S**
Henley, W. B., Kolbeck, W. O. .... **N S**
Henesey, Wm., Chepstow .... **O**
Heney, Henry, Danford Lake .... **Q**
Henningar, John, Chester Grant, W. O. .... **N S**
Henry, S. L., Upper Musquodoboit .... **N S**
Henry, P. D., Whitfield .... **O**
Henry, James, Magundy, W. O. .... **N S**
Henry, William, Higgins' Road .... **P E I**
Herkins, Wm., Lewis Head, W. O. .... **N S**
Heron, Agnes, Dollar .... **O**
Heron, R., Bennington .... **O**
Herron, E. L. H., Sebright .... **O**
Héroux, Moise, Mekinac .... **Q**
Herring, Noah, Belfountain .... **O**
Hewitt, J., Spring Hill, W. O. .... **N S**
Hewitt, Miss J., Roslin .... **O**
Hewson, Jas. R., Earnestown Station .... **O**
Hewton, John, Bourg Lewis .... **Q**
Heyrock, Henry, Johnson's Mills .... **O**
Hicks, W. W., Mitchell .... **O**
Hicks, John, Killerby .... **O**
Hicks, Mariner, Midgic, W. O. .... **N B**
Hicks, Ira, McLaughlan Road, W. O. .... **N B**
Higgins, W. H., North River, W. O. .... **N S**
Higginson, James G., Hawkesbury .... **O**
Hilborn, T. L., Ullin .... **O**
Hillaker, George, Mount Salem .... **O**
Hill, Wm., Sandurst .... **O**
Hill, Robert, Ballantrae .... **O**
Hill, William, Welcome .... **O**
Hill, Alexander, Cross Roads, Saint George's Channel, W. O. .... **N S**
Hill, Joseph, Thornby .... **Q**

List of Postmasters in Canada—Continued.

Hill, H. P., Antigonishe............N S
Hill, Thomas L., Hillsborough............O
Hill, W. D., Hillside, W. O............N S
Hiltz, Samuel, Lawrencetown, W. O............N S
Hiltz, J. A., Fortee's Settlement, W. O............N S
Hinch, William, Hinch............O
Hines, Byron, East side of Pubnico Harbor, W. O. N S
Hingley, A. S., Kemptown, W. O............N S
Hingley, R. J., Riversdale, W. O............N S
Hirst, James, Freelton............O
Hislop, John, Marmion............O
Hitchen, John, Emerald............O
Hoath, R., Hoath Head............O
Hoare, John S., Adelaide............O
Hobbs, Wm., Valentia............O
Hodge, George N., Birchton............Q
Hodges, Hiram, Newcastle............O
Hodgkinson, Philip, Aylmer, West............O
Hodgson, John, Como............Q
Hodgson, J. T., Edmundston............N B
Hogan, M. J., Assametquagan............Q
Hogarth, Henry, Danforth............O
Hogg, William, York Mills............O
Hogg, John, Don............O
Hogg, Thomas, Wilton Grove............O
Holbert, John, Reaboro............O
Holbrooke, J., Helena............Q
Holbrook, ——, East Hereford............Q
Holden, Wm., Petite Rivière Bridge, W. O............N S
Holden, Hiram, Shannonville............O
Holden, Thomas, Head of Jordan River, W. O...N S
Holden, William, Rob-Roy............O
Holesworth, F. H., Lower Stowiacke............N S
Holland, Edward, Fairfield............P E I
Holmden, Thomas S., Pine Ridge, W. O............N B
Holmes, Andrew, Oxford Station............O
Holmes, D. C., Welland Port............O
Holterman, C. F., Vanburgh............O
Honsberger, Isaac, Rainham............O
Hood, A. T., Yarmouth............N S
Hooker, G. A., Geneva............Q
Hooper, Albert B., Fourche, W. O............N S
Hope, Robert, Newburgh............O
Hope, Charles, Abbott's Corners............Q
Hopgood, J. G., Park Hill............P E I
Hopkins, James P., Holloway............O
House, James W., Lineboro'............Q
Houston, Thomas, Camlachie............O
Houston, James, Hawkstone............O
How, William, sen., Hillsburgh............O
Howard, John T., Esquimalt............B C
Howard, Thomas, St. Ives............O
Howard, E., Arthurette, W. O............N B
Howard, M., Cape Wolfe............P E I
Howe, John, St. John............N B
Howes, Richard, Glendower............O
Howey, William, Massey............Q
Howland, F. A., Lambton Mills............O
Hoyt, Alfred, Lequille, W. O............N S
Hoyt, John Y., McKenzie's Corner, W. O............N B
Hoyt, Hezekiah, Blissville............N B
Hubbard, B. F., Stanstead............Q
Hubley, James, Black Point, W. O............N S
Hudgens, A. P., Lake George, W. O............N S
Hudon, Alexander, St. Pacome............Q
Hudon, dit Beaulieu, St. Elizabeth............Q
Hudon, S. C., Winding Ledges, W. O............N B
Huff, Lewis, Keith............O
Huff, J. W., Lebanon............O
Huggard, John, Painswick............O
Hughes, W. C., Sandhill............O
Hughes, G. P., Keenansville............O
Hughes, M., Collfield............Q
Hughes, Alexander, Kay Settlement, W. O............N B
Hughes, David, Millbrook, W. O............N B
Hughes, Hugh, Heckston............O
Humphrey, A., Rodney............O
Humphries, Hiram, McDonald's Corner, W. O..N B
Humphries, Israel. Warkworth............O
Humphries, John, Sussex Corner, W. O............N B
Hungerford, L. N., Mawcook............Q
Hunter, Thomas, Venice............Q
Hunter, Walter, Clarksburg............O
Hunter, George, Glenburnie............O
Hunter, James, Egerton............O
Hunter, John, Hunterville............O
Huntingdon, J., Salmon River, W. O............N S
Hurd, J. W., Hurdville............O
Hurlburt, Reuben, Myrtle............O
Hurly, Thomas, jun., Sanborn............Q
Hussey, J. B., Mount St. Louis............O
Huston, James, Stanford............O

List of Postmasters in Canada—Continued.

Imrie, Mrs. Mary, Spencerville........O
Ingles, Joseph, Strathnairn........O
Ingles, George, jun., Maple Hill........O
Innis, James, jun., Dundee, W. O........N B
Innis, Wm., Hunt's Point, W. O........N S
Irish, Levi, Little River, W. O........N B
Irons, John, Tower Hill, W. O........N B
Ironside, A. McGregor, Manitowaning........O
Ironside, John, Grand Bend........O
Irvine, William, Elder's Mills........O
Irvine, William, Desmond........O
Irving, J. B., West Flamboro'........O
Irving, Andrew, St. Lambert, Montreal........Q
Irving, James, Kerrwood........O
Irwin, John, Perch Station........O
Ivison, Robert, Oxley........O

Jack, James, Lorne........O
Jackson, Anthony, Eden Mills........O
Jackson, James, Kerby........O
Jackson, James H., Severn Bridge........O
Jackson, George E., Egmondville........O
Jacobie, E. R., Ardoch........O
Jaffray, Wm., Berlin........O
Jakes, Samuel, Merrickville........O
James, Edwin, Bridgewater........O
James, J. W., Laurencetown........N S
Jameson, Robert, B., Fenelon Falls........O
Jamieson, Geo. C., Cole Harbor, W. O........N S
Jardine, R., Renous Bridge, W. O........N B
Jardine, Ferguson, Newington........O
Jarmain, J. P., Matlock........O
Jarratt, Charles, Jarratt's Corners........O
Jarvis, Paul, Ravenswood........O
Jarvis, William, Peterson........O
Jean, George M., Petit de Grat, W. O........N S
Jeffers, Henry, Westbrook, W. O........N S
Jeffrey, Peter, Golden Lake........O
Jenkins, Joel, Jenkins, W. O........N B
Jenkins, David, Waldemar........O
Jenkins, John, Epping........O
Jenks, John W., Parrsborough........N S
Jerway, Samuel, Upper Buctouche, W. O........N B
Jess, Daniel, Scott's Bay........N S
Jewell, George, Big Lorraine, W. O........N S
Jewett, J. L., Lakeville Corner, W. O........N B
Jewitt, S. C., Lower Wakefield, W. O........N B
Jiggens, Sarah, Leeds........Q
Jimerson, Ira., South Ely........Q
Jobin, G., St. Bazile........Q
Jobin, Marie S., Isle Perrot........Q
Johns, Alonzo C., Fairfield East........O
Johnson, David W., Powers Court........Q
Johnson, Caleb, Melville........O
Johnson, Lionel H., Wallaceburg........O
Johnson, Carby, Ventry........O
Johnson, H. A., Dalhousie........N B
Johnson, T. Stewart, Tweedside........O
Johnson, Daniel, Cumbermere........O
Johnson, George, Pefferlaw........O
Johnson, C., L'Orignal........O
Johnson, T. W., Ballymote........O
Johnson, Augustus, Tracadie Cross........P E I
Johnson, Andrew, Wolseley........O
Johnson, William, Peter's Road........P E I
Johnston, S., Clapham........Q
Johnston, Joseph, Pelham Union........O
Johnston, Robert, Weston........O
Johnston, Richard, Palmerston........O
Johnston, Richard, Thistletown........O
Johnston, B. H., Port Carling........O
Johnston, Samuel, Newcastle........N B
Johnston, William, Aberader........O
Johnston, William, Lower Montague........P E I
Johnston, Joseph, Elsenore........O
Johnston, John, Huntley........O
Johnston, David, Temperanceville........O
Johnstone, Adam, Linton's, W. O........N B
Johnstone, William, Johnstone........O
Jollimore, J. W., Mill Cove, W. O........N S
Joncas, P. S., Berthier (*en bas*)........Q
Jones, Cereno D., Weymouth........N S
Jones, Maxon, Bloomington........O
Jones, C. H., Bromemere........Q
Jones, Joseph, Thompson's Mills........N S
Jones, J. M., Stanbridge, East........Q
Jones, Merritt, Mount Pleasant, W. O........N B
Jones, Charles, jun., Oxford Mills........O
Jones, Charles K., Bronte........O
Jones, Thomas, Sabrevois........Q
Jones, D. A., Tecumseth........O
Jones, John, Sunderland........O
Jones, Alva G., Stony Creek........O
Jones, Peter, Cranworth........O
Jones, Richard, Albert........O
Jordan, J. A., Upper Cross Roads, St. Mary's, W. O........N S
Jordan, M., Leinster........O
Jordan, Patrick, Connaught........O
Jordine, Ferguson, Newington........O
Journeay, Jasper, Weymouth Bridge........N S
Judd, Agnes, Stirling........O
Judge, John, Mono Road Station........O
Junker, Frederick, Gad's Hill........O
Jury, Thomas, Napperton........O
Jutras, Joseph, East Chester........Q
Jutras, H., Somerset........Q

Kain, John, South Nelson, W. O........N B
Kaiser, Anthony, Ste. Agathe........Q
Kaulback, R. A., Middle Musquodoboit........N S
Kavanagh, Michael, Craighton........O

List of Postmasters in Canada—Continued.

Kavanagh, D., Umfraville	O
Kavanagh, J. J., Gaspé Basin	Q
Kastner, John, Sebringville	O
Kay, W. F., Otterville	O
Kaye, Charles, Point Kaye	O
Kean, John, Victoria Harbor	O
Kearns, James, Glen Tay	O
Keating, James, Oil Springs	O
Keating, J. A., Warburton	O
Kedy, H., Chelsea, W. O.	N S
Keefer, Edwin, Thorold	O
Keith, R. F., Keat's	O
Keith, J. S., Point St. Charles	Q
Keith, Lewis, New Canaan, W. O	N B
Keith, C. I., Butternut Ridge, W. O	N B
Keith, George, Keithley Creek	B C
Keller, Charles, Kossuth	O
Kelley, George, Lambeth	O
Kelly, John, Spruce Lake	N B
Kelly, Edward, Baby's Point	O
Kelly, John, Roxborough, W. O	N B
Kelly, Edward, Holmesville	O
Kelly, W. R., Sheridan	O
Kelly, Mrs. M., Coleraine	O
Kelly, Hon. F., Fort Augustus	P E I
Kelso, John, Bute	O
Kemp, Thomas, Chandos	O
Kempton, E., Milton	N S
Kendrick, A. W., Campbellton	N B
Kendrick, A. W., Compton	Q
Kennedy, Peter, Notfield	O
Kennedy, Alexander, Cathcart	O
Kennedy, Patrick, Bagot	Q
Kennedy, John, Dixie	O
Kennedy, Joseph, Louisburg, W. O	N S
Kennedy, James, Monument Settlement, W. O.	N B
Kennedy, William, Hartington	O
Kennedy, Simon, Hagerman's Corners	O
Kennedy, Kendall, Glamorgan	O
Kennedy, John, Wood Islands	P E I
Kenny, Charles, Erinville, W. O	N S
Kenny, S. C., Kazubazua	Q
Kenny, H., Doctor's Cove, W. O	N S
Kent, Hugh, Hiawatha	O
Keough, John, Laval	Q
Kerr, John, New Bandon, W. O	N B
Kerr, Samuel, Antrim, W. O	N S
Kerr, Archibald, Nouvelle	Q
Kerr, James, Summer Hill, W. O	N B
Kerr, David, Caplin	Q
Kerr, John, New Bandon, W. O	N B
Kerr, James, Waupoos	O
Key, Samuel, Wickwire Station, W. O	N S
Key, William, New Aberdeen	O
Keys, Robert, Bornholm	O
Kickham, Thomas, Souris, West	P E I
Kidd, George J., Carronbrook	O
Kidd, Thomas, Arlington	O
Kidd, Thomas A., Burritt's Rapids	O
Kincaid, William, Harlow	O
Kimball, Warren, Leamington	O
Kier, Archibald R., Somenos	B C
Kierstead, George, Alma	N B
Kilbank, Wm., Codrington	O
Kilborne, P. S., Winterbourne	O
Killam, J. M., Wheaton Settlement, W. O.	N B
Killam, Hiram, Little River (Elgin) W. O.	N B
Killam, Wm., Lower East Pubnico, W. O.	N S
Killam, James, Sleswick	O
Killon, Andrew S., St. Martin's	N B
Killoan, M., Belledune River, W. O	N B
Kimball, Warren, Leamington	O
Kimball, Wm., Wilkesport	O
Kimball, Albert, Knowlton	Q
Kimpton, R. A., Roxton Pond	Q
Kincaid, Wm., Harlem	O
King, Charles H., Cheltenham	O
King, George G., Chipman, W. O	N B
King, John, Lyster	Q
King, George, Port Philip, W. O	N S
King, Oliver, Tidnish, W. O	N S
King, Samuel A., Pinkerton	O
King, Wm., Bristol	Q
King, George, Lockhartville, W. O	N B
King, John, East Scotch Settlement, W. O	N B
Kingsmill, Wm., Guelph	O
Kingston, John, Hanwell, W. O	N B
Kingston, C. H., Fredericton Junction	N B
Kinnear, James, Kinnear's Mills	Q
Kinny, Thomas, Oungah	O
Kinsman, Benjamin, Kinsman's Corners	N S
Kinsman, Danson, Fonthill	O
Kipp, Joseph B., Otnabog, W O	N B
Kirby, D., New Harbor, W O	N S
Kirk, John, Kirk's Ferry	Q
Kirk, George, Hard Ledge, W. O	N B
Kirkpatrick, Andrew, Shubenacadie	N S
Kirkpatrick, B., Quaco Road	N B
Kirkpatrick, Samuel, Aldboro	O
Kirkpatrick, Thomas, Widder Station	O
Kirkpatrick, F., Lunenburg	O
Kirkwood, D., Rockside	O
Kitchen, Harriet L., St. Williams	O
Kitchen, L. W., Bloomsburg	O
Kittson, Miss Zoe Berthier (*en haut*)	Q
Knack, A., Upper Branch, W. O	N S
Knaut, Lewis, Mahone Bay	N S
Knechtel, Jacob, Carlsruhe	O
Knight, Alfred, Petworth	O
Knight, Wm., Smith's Mills	Q
Knight, J. E., New River, W. O.	N
Knight, Richard, Bowmanton	O

List of Postmastess in Canada—Continued.

Knowlton, Luke H., South Stukely ... Q
Knox, G. W., Upper Caverhill, W. O ... N B
Korry, John, Bolingbroke ... O
Krassler, John, Heidelburgh ... O
Kumpf, C., Waterloo ... O
Kyle, Joseph S., North Winchester ... O
Kyte, David, Richwood ... O

Labrèque, Dr. Louis, Lambton ... Q
Labrosse, Simon, St. Eugène ... Q
Lacerte, Miss, Point à Grouette ... M
Lacerte, Arthur, Yamachiche ... Q
Lachaine, dit Jolicœur, B. G., Isle aux Grues ... Q
Lacosse, Napoleon, Ironside ... Q
Lacourcière, A. Jos., St. Stanislas ... Q
Lacourcière, P., Vincennes ... Q
Lacourcière, D. Batiscan ... Q
Ladell, Henry G., Port Sydney ... O
Ladd, C. J., Delaware ... O
Laflèche, T., Domaine de Gentilly ... Q
Lafleur, Odile, Ste. Adèle ... Q
Lafond, Olivier, St. Paulin ... Q
Lafond, F., Henryville ... Q
Lafontaine, Emory, St. Hugues ... Q
Lainesse, Prudent, St. Albert ... Q
Laing, G. Bayham ... O
Laird, Richard, Shetland ... O
Laird, J. B., Tryon ... P E I
Lajeunesse, C. C., Lac Masson ... Q
Lake, W., Purdy ... O
Lake, Benjamin, Ranelagh ... O
Lalonde, E. H., St. Marthe ... Q
Lalonde, R. J., Ste. Justine de Newton ... Q
Lalonde, Camille, Mountjoy ... Q
Lalonde, Joseph, Embrun ... O
Lalumière, Eusèbe, St. Bazile le Grand ... Q
Lamarche, J. O., Mascouche ... Q
Lamarche, Z. O. H., St. Valentin ... Q
Lamb, Archibald, Amaranth Station ... O
Lamb, Wm., Wendover ... O
Lamb, Thomas, St. Andrews, East ... Q
Lambert dit Champagne, Jean, Grand Coudées ... Q
Lambert, Henry, West Lake ... O
Lambert, Isaac, Dealtown ... O
Lambert, Franklin, Lord's Cove, W. O ... N B
Lambkin, Simen, Riceburg ... Q
Lammon, Andrew, Oakham, W. O ... N B
Lamontagne, O. A., Dalibaire ... Q
Lamorandière, F., Cape Croker ... O
Lamorandiere, P. R. de, Killarney ... O
Lamothe, Guillaume, Viger Mines ... Q
Lamoureux, Antoine, Pointe aux Trembles ... Q
Lamoureux, Luc, St. Sébastien ... Q
Lamoureux, Olivier, Contrecœur ... Q
Lamphier, Peter, Grahamsville ... O
Lamy, Adolphe, St. Sévère ... Q

Lance, Richard, Beatrice ... O
Landon, John, Waltham ... Q
Landon, Horace, Chichester ... Q
Landers, Jacob, Wellington, W. O ... N S
Landry, Honoré, Palmerston, W. O ... N B
Lane, Samuel, Denbigh ... O
Lane, Reuben, Mossley ... O
Lang, Robert, Chateauguay Basin ... Q
Langlois, Charles F. Y., Piopolis ... Q
Langevin, F. T., St. Isidore, Laprairie ... Q
Langford, John, Kent Bridge ... O
Langstaff, John, Langstaff (sub) ... O
Langstaff, D. J. Lower Canterbury, W. O ... N B
Lantz, Harvey, Lantz, W. O ... N S
Lapalme, Tréflé, St. Dominique ... Q
La Pinotière, W. H., Elora ... O
Lapointe, C. F., Ste. Flavie ... Q
Lapointe, Leandre, Mount Oscar ... Q
Lapointe, Jos. Robin, Mile End ... Q
Laporte, Rev. P. A., Ste. Emelie de l'Energie ... Q
Lappin, Miss Sarah Jane, Strathallan ... O
Largie, Edward, Fletcher's Station ... N S
Larivière, Thomas, Pont Rouge ... Q
Larouche, E., Clairvaux (sub) ... Q
Larracey, John, Irish Town, W. O ... NB
Larue, Edmund, St. Antoine, Lotbinière ... Q
Larue, Miss H. C., Cap St. Ignace ... Q
Lasalle, F. X., St. Jean de Matha ... Q
Laskay, C. J., Waterville, W. O ... N B
Latour, dit Forget, Joseph, St. Thomas, East ... Q
Latour, Edmond, Côte St. Paul ... Q
Latshaw, Christopher, Glen Morris ... O
Laugill, J. S., Laugill's, W. O ... N S
Laurie, Francis, Oakfield, W. O ... N S
Laurier, J. O., Lachenaie ... Q
Lavett, Agnes, Adare ... O
Lavoie, R., Mount Carmel ... Q
Lawler, D., Salmon River, W. O ... N S
Lawless, Lawrence, London ... O
Lawlor, Wm., Burnley ... O
Lawlor, J. B., Alfred ... O
Lawrence, Albert, Roebuck ... Q
Lawrence, George, Honeywood ... O
Lawrence, Erastus, Lawrenceville ... Q
Lawrence, W., Eastern Harbor, W. O ... N S
Lawrence, Chas., Lawrence Factory, W. O ... N S
Lawder, R. H., Whitby ... O
Lawson, D., Cove Head ... P E I
Lawson, Robert, Little York ... P E I
Lawson, James, Farley's Mills, W. O. ... N B
Laymen, Robert S., Fintona ... O
Layton, D. L., Meaford ... O
Leake, James R., Morton ... O
Leamy, John, Fallowfield ... O
Leemans, Wm., Little River, Coverdale, W. O ... N B
Leard, A. C., Victoria ... P E I
Learn, P., sen., Mulgrave ... O

List of Postmasters in Canada—Continued.

ıarned, E., Learned Plain ....Q
ıary, Bridget, Ledge, W. O. ....N S
ıask, George, Leaskdale ....O
ıavitt, John, Bloomfield, W. O....N B
ıavitt, W. H., Frankville....O
ı Baron, B., North Hatley ....Q
ı Baron, J. B., Hatley ....Q
ı Bel, J. B., St. Félicité ....Q
ıbel, Paschal, Armand ....Q
ı Blanc, J. E., St. Charles, River Richelieu....Q
ı Blanc, M., Tusket Wedge, W. O. ....N S
ı Blanc, F., L'Epiphanie ....Q
ı Blanc, J. M. A., Port Royal, W. O. ....N S
ı Blanc, Olivier, St. Mary's, W. O. ....N B
ı Blanc, Sylvain, Cocagne River, W. O....N B
ı Blanc, Stephen, River Beaudette ....Q
ıbourveau, Moses, Eaton....Q
ıcavallier, J. J., St. Laurent, Montreal....Q
ıclair, Charles, North Lancaster....O
eclerc, Francis, Lyster Station ....Q
ederman, Charles, Mannheim ....O
educ, Joseph, Vincy ....Q
ee, Thomas, Saugeen....O
ee, Horatio, Tabucintac, W. O. ....N B
ee, Frederick F., Mallorytown ....O
ee, Edward, Marshville ....O
ee, Robert, Connor ....O
ee, Thomas H., Mar ....O
ee, Frenière, A. J., Pont de Maskinongé....Q
ee, Andrew, Dempsey's Corner, W. O....N S
ee, Francis E., Trent Bridge ....O
efebvre, Joachim, Aubrey ....Q
efebvre, L. J., Lachine....Q
egendre, L. G. A., St. Frederick....Q
egère, Fidèle, Grandigue, W. O. ....N B
e Gresly, Francis, Grand Aunce, W. O. ....N B
e Hane, Thomas, S., Ennismore....O
eith, Smith, Kingsey Falls ....Q
ellis Jacob, Salmon Hole, W. O....N S
emaire, Ernest, St. Benoit ....Q
emay, Joseph, St. Norbert ....M
emay, V., Bord à Plouffe....Q
emay, M., Lotbinière....Q
emay, Hubert, St. Jude....Q
emieux, Antoine, Chaudiere Mills ....Q
emieux, Joseph, Mont Louis ....Q
emire dit Marsolait G., Ste. Béatrix....Q
emmer, Jacob, Fisherville....Q
emon, George, Villanova....O
emon, James, Morley....O
ent, J. M., Tusket....N S
eonard, M., Wickham, West....Q
éonard, Adelard E., Ste. Rose....Q
eonard, Damase, St. Moniquedesdeux Montagnes...Q
eonard, Thomas, Petersville Church, W. O....N B
épine, Marcel, St. Théodore....Q

Le Roy, W. G., Bryson ....Q
Le Roy, Mrs. Nancy, Shedden ....O
Leslie, Henry, Spry Bay, W O. ....N B
Leslie, Guy, Orangeville ....O
Leslie, William, Puslinch....O
Leslie, W. D., Rupert ....Q
Leslie, George, jun., Leslie ....O
Leslie, Robert, Kemptville....O
Leslie, W. T., Port Matoon, W. O. ....N S
Leslie, Joseph, Toronto ....O
Lespérance, P., Longueuil ....Q
Lesperance, Auguste, St. Timothee ....Q
Lessard, Eugène, St. Ephrem de Tring ....Q
Lessard, Jean, St. Sylvester, East....Q
Lester, George, Harvey Station ....N B
Letts, John, Dunraven....Q
Lévêque, Ulric, Ste. Sophie de Lacorne ....Q
Lévêque, Théophile, St. Mathieu ....Q
Lévêque, E., St. Alexandre....Q
Lévesque, E., Bagotville ....Q
Lewelleyn, William, Gaspereaux....P E I
Lewis, Coleman, Addison ....O
Lewis, George, Fort Erie....O
Lewis, Gains, Lake Road, W. O. ....N S
Lightbody, Andrew, Garafraxa....O
Lilley, Charles, Lilley's Corners....O
Lillie, Joshua, Lyn ....O
Lindabury, John, Windham Centre ....O
Lindard, Julius L., Van Winkle....B C
Linden, H., Charlo's Cove, W. O. ....N S
Lindermann, P. J., Eagle ....O
Lindsay, Alexander, Lindsay, W. O. ....N B
Lindsay, Thomas, Williamstown, W. O....N B
Lindsay, Thomas, Chignonaise River, W. O....N S
Lindsay, James, Kars ....O
Lindsay, W. S., Woodslee....O
Lingley, John, Waverley....O
Linton, John, Humber....O
Lipset, John, Charlestown, W. O....N B
Little, Peter, Moffatt ....O
Little, Thomas, Omagh ....O
Little, J., Head of Mill Stream, W. O. ....N B
Little, J., Aylwin ....Q
Littlewood, A., Littlewood, W. O. ....N S
Livingston, Donald, Upper Settlement of West River, W. O. ....N S
Livingston, John, Livingston's Cove, W. O. ....N S
Livingston, John, Silver Islet ....O
Livingstone, H., Black Brook, W. O. ....N S
Lloyd, Jared, White Rose ....O
Lloyd, Benjamin, King ....O
Lock, Charles, Brinston's Corners....O
Lock, William, McDonald's Corners ....O
Lockhart, D., Leicester, W. O. ....N S
Lockhart, John, Donegal, W. O. ....N B
Lockhart, James, Clarke ....O

List of Postmasters in Canada—Continued.

Lockwood, Thomas C., Brighton .... O
Lodge, W. B., Maccan Mountain, W. O. .... N S
Logan, Dougal, Loganville, W. O. .... N S
Logue, Charles, River Desert.............................. Q
Lohr, Daniel, Phillipsburg, West .... O
Loisel, Phillippe De N., Paspebiac......................... Q
Long, Wesley, Maxwell .... O
Longheed, Samuel, Molesworth................................ O
Longley, George C., Maitland .... N S
Lontin, J. O., St. Constant.................................. Q
Loranger, L. L. J., St. Sauveur............................ Q
Lord, Joseph, Leclercville .... Q
Lord, Donald M., Newbridge, W. O. .... N S
Losie, Joseph, Collins Bay.................................. O
Loth, John, jun., Cassel .... O
Lothrop, Allan, Westbury .... Q
Lothrop, F. H., North Stoke .... Q
Loucy, Thomas, Grand Pabos .... Q
Lough, William, jun., Cumberland Mills.................. O
Loughran, B., Orwell .... P E I
Loughrey, Owen, Beaurivage................................. Q
Loughrey, W., Petersville, West (sub)..................... O
Loughrin, James, Speedside .... O
Loucks, H. L., Hull... Q
Lounsbury, James, Lewis Mountain, W. O. .... N B
Love, Hugh, sen., Hill's Green............................ O
Love, Margaret, Basswood Ridge, W. O. .... N B
Lovely, John, Florenceville, East .... N B
Lovitt, G. H., Gros Coques, W. O. .... N S
Lowden, R. H., Knoydart .... N S
Lowrie, James, Veighton..................................... O
Lowry, William, jun., Reedsdale .... Q
Luby, Thomas, Radstock .... O
Lucas, James, Cocagne .... N B
Lumley, W. G., Glencoe .... O
Lundy, George B., Balmoral .... O
Lupien, L., St. Ursule .... Q
Lussier, Trefflé, Verchères .... Q
Luttis, David, Indian Harbor, W. O. .... N S
Lyman, H., Scotland .... O
Lyman, Horace, Granby....................................... Q
Lynch, John, Green River, W. O. .... N B
Lynch, Walter, Brome .... Q
Lynch, John, Allumette Island .... Q
Lynn, James, Bushfield .... O
Lynn, Joseph, Linton... O
Lyon, R. A., Michael's Bay.................................... O
Lyon, W. D., Milton West..................................... O
Lyttle, James, Newboyne....................................... O
Lyttle, Oliver, Barrington...................................... Q

McAdam, John, Briley's Brook, W. O................ N S
McAfee, Andrew, Seeley's Mills, W. O............. N B
McAfee, Henry, Walkerville.................................. O
McAlister, Donald, New Mills .... N B
McAlister, D., Comber.. O
McAlpine, Nevin, McAlpine, W. O. .... N B
McAlmon, Joseph, Hopewell Hill, W. O .... N B
McArdle, Joseph, Ronaldsay.................................. O
McArthur, John, Amions....................................... O
McArthur, Crosbie, Beauharnois .... Q
McArthur, Peter, Dalesville.................................. Q
McAskell, Neil, Cape North .... N S
McAskill, Hugh, Little Narrows, W. O. .... N S
McAulay, T. H., Centreton.................................... O
McAulay, John, Ventnor....................................... O
McAulay, Angus, False Bay Beach, W. O. .... N S
McAulay, M., South Side Basin of River Denis, W. O. .... N S
McAulay, James, Bull Creek.......................... P E I
McAulay, Joseph, Cherry Grove .... P E I
McAulay, Norman, McAulay's, W. O. .... N S
McBain, Thomas, New Town .... N S
McBean, Archibald, Macbeth................................ O
McBeath, J. T., Wexford...................................... O
McBrady, Daniel, Audley .... O
McBrane, Archibald, Missouri .... O
McBrayne, C., Botany .... O
McBride, John, Sunbury....................................... O
McBurney, R., Erie... O
McCabe, J. A. E., Windsor Mills........................... Q
McCabe, Edward, Wheatland................................. Q
McCaffery, John, Box Grove................................. O
McCalder, D., De Sable................................ P E I
McCall, D. W., Walsh.. O
McCall, George D., Victoria................................. O
McCall, Donald, Forestville.................................. O
McCallum, John, Avoca.. Q
McCann, William, Oak Hill, W. O. .... N B
McCardle, P., Emyvale .... P E I
McCarthy, Joseph, Lower River Inhabitants, W. O. .... N S
McCarty, N. C., Thamesford................................. O
McCaughrin, D., Trecastle.................................... O
McCaul, John, Durham .... N S
McCleneghan, Alexander, Woodstock .... O
McColl, Duncan, jun., Clachan.............................. O
McColl, John, St. Joseph du Lac........................... O
McConnell, W., Condon Settlement, W. O.......... N S
McConney, Farrell, Villette .... Q
McConnisky, John, Pubnico Beach, W. O. .... N S
McContrey, R. G., New Glasgow.................... P E I
McCool, James, Fort William................................ Q
McCoppen, James, Port Robinson .... O
McCordick, Robert, Roach's Point .... O
McCormack, Samuel, Saulmerville, W. O. .... N S
McCormack, William, Marsville............................ O
McCormack, James, St. Margaret's .... P E I
McCormick, J. D., St. Alban .... Q
McCormick, Robert, Vivian .... O
McCormick, J. M., Macton .... O
McCready, John E., Avondale, W. O. .... N B
McCready, Charles F., Rothsay .... N B

List of Postmasters in Canada—Continued.

McCready, Samuel, Norton Station................N B
McCracken, Mrs. E., Perretton........................O
McCrindle, James, Lurgan ....O
McCully, William, Truro ....N S
McCurdy, John, Kirkton......................................O
McCutcheon, John, Clarendon Settlement.........N B
McCutcheon, J., Chilliwack ....B C
McCutcheon, Hugh, Leeds Village ....Q
McCutcheon, James, Sonora, W. O......................N S
McDermid, D., Pine River ....O
McDermitt, Alexander, Portage River, W. O.....N B
McDonald, Charles, Baddeck Bay, W. O..........N S
McDonald, Mrs. C., French River, W. O..........N S
McDonald, Murdoch, Groves Point, W. O.........N S
McDonald, John, La Guerre..................................Q
McDonald, J., Lake Megantic ....Q
McDonald, Alex., Leitch's Creek, W. O............N S
McDonald, Mrs. Mary, Lime Rock, W. O ....N S
McDonald, John, Hunter's Mountain, W. O.......N S
McDonald, Daniel, Little Glace Bay ....N S
McDonald, Donald, Mabou Harbor, W. O.........N S
McDonald, Robert, Malagash, W. O..................N S
McDonald, L., Malagawatch, W. O....................N S
McDonald, Angus, Caledonia, St. Mary's, W. O..N S
McDonald, James, West Bay..............................N S
McDonald, Peter, Whycocomah...........................N S
McDonald, Robert, Avondale, W. O....................N S
McDonald, Duncan, Vernon ....O
McDonald, William, Blue Mountain, W. O.......N S
McDonald, James H., Sherbrooke......................N S
McDonald, A., Sable...O
McDonald, Donald, North Shore, W. O.............N S
McDonald, John, Ohio, W. O.............................N S
McDonald, John, Niel's Harbor, W. O...............N S
McDonald, Donald, Middle Settlement, River Inhabitants, W. O..N S
McDonald, James, Piedmont Valley, W. O........N S
McDonald, Colin, Black River, W. O.................N S
McDonald, Michael, Upper Settlement of River Dennis, W. O...N S
McDonald, Angus, Upper Washabuck, W.O.....N S
McDonald, J. R., Clontarf ....O
McDonald, John R., Cobden.....................................O
McDonald, Robert, Cape George.......................N S
McDonald, Donald, Cape George (North Side) W. O..N S
McDonald, Chas., Lake Ainslie (East side).......N S
McDonald, James, Brookville, W. O..................N S
McDonald, Michael, Irish Cove, W. O...............N S
McDonald, D., Elmsville, W. O.........................N S
McDonald, James, West Merigonishe................N S
McDonald, Angus, Lake Vale, W. O..................N S
McDonald, Angus, Port Hood ....N S
McDonald, A. S., South Cove, W. O..................N S
McDonald, Alexander, Keppoch, W. O.............N S
McDonald, Allen, Cherry Vale, W. O.................N B
McDonald, A. A., Charlottetown....................P E I
McDonald, A., Scotchfort ....P E I
McDonald, Charles, South Branch of St. Nicholas River, W. O...N B
McDonald, Duncan, Englishtown.....................N S
McDonald, D., Big Marsh.................................P E I
McDonald, F., Inverness ....P E I
McDonald, Hugh, Whycocomagh Rear, W. O....N S
McDonald, Thomas, Milford Haven Bridge, W.O..N S
McDonald, M., Lot 67.......................................P E I
McDonald, H., Rose Valley ....P E I
McDonald, H., Lot 45 ....P E I
McDonald, G., Moulinette..O
McDonald, John, Burleigh ....O
McDonald, M., Goose River.............................P E I
McDonald, R. A., Gillies Lake, W. O.................N S
McDonald, R., Pesquid......................................P E I
McDonald, Stephen, Grand Tracadie...............P E I
McDonald, William, Glen Donald ....O
McDonnell, Allan, South West Mabou, W. O.....N S
McDonnell, Duncan, Vankleek Hill.........................O
McDonnell, Duncan, Long Point, W. O..............N S
McDonnell, Hugh, Judique, W. O......................N S
McDonnell, Mrs. Mary, St. Raphael, West............O
McDonnell, George, Cornwall.................................O
McDonnell, J. R., Brompton Falls...........................Q
McDonnell, James, Middle Settlement of South River, W. O..N S
McDonnell, Robert, Clearview ....O
McDougal, Rod., Hay's River, W. O...................N B
McDougald, Alexander, Greenfield ....O
McDougall, D., Lockside, W. O..........................N S
McDougall, Col., McDougall Settlement, W.O...N B
McDougall, James, Marshy Hope, W. O............N S
McDougall, W., Brewster...O
McDougall, Niel, Scotch Settlement, W. O........N B
McDougall, Peter, Blakeney ....O
McDougall, Donald, Grand Mira North, W. O.....N S
McDougal, R., Rollo Bay...................................P E I
McEachan, D., Sight Point, W. O.......................N S
McEachern, John, South side of Wycocomah Bay, W. O. ....N S
McEachern, Archibald, Moulie's River, W. O......N B
McEachern, Alex., Boom, W. O.........................N S
McElman, Charles M., Folly River, W. O...........N S
McElroy, Henry, Concord ....O
McEvoy, William, Woodburn ....O
McEwan, George, Salt Springs ....N B
McEwan, M., Chockfish, W. O. ....N B
McEwen, E., Franktown...O
McFadden, M., New Ireland Road W. O............N B
McFarland, Henry, Campbell Settlement, W.O...N B
McFarland, W. J., Markdale.....................................O
McFarlane, Peter, Nashwaaksis, W. O...............N B
McFarlane, Robert, Rosetta ....O
McFarlane, James, Conquerall Bank, W. O.......N S

List of Postmasters in Canada—Continued.

McFarlane, Daniel, Haliburton ... O
McGarry, Owen, New Ross Road, W. O. ... N S
McGauvran, James, Treadwell ... O
McGibbon, Alex., Brownsburg ... Q
McGibbon, William, Point Wolf, W. O. ... N B
McGie, D. B., Esquimaux Point ... Q
McGill, J., Rusagornis Station, W. O. ... N B
McGill, James, Burton ... O
McGillis, Angus D., Harrison Corners ... O
McGillis, Albert, Williamstown ... O
McGillivray, John, Washburn ... O
McGillavray, C., Glen Road, W. O. ... N S
McGillivray, Archibald, Morristown, W.O. ... N S
McGillivray, Hugh, Harbor Road, W. O. ... N S
McGillivray, Hugh, East Bay, W. O. ... N S
McGilleroy, John, Summerville ... N S
McGinnis, Donald, Schomberg ... O
McGowen, W., Little Lepreaux, W. O. ... N B
McGregor, Mrs. D., Garden of Eden, W. O. ... N S
McGregor, Daniel, Wyebridge ... O
McGregor, David, South Gower ... O
McGregor, John, Matawatchan ... O
McGregor, D., Tennyson ... O
McHarry, H., Orleans ... O
McHenny, J., Victoria, W. O. ... N S
McInnis, Charles, Aros ... O
McInnis, N., Tiverton ... O
McInnis, Hugh, Point of Cape, W. O. ... N S
McInnis, Angus, Lake Ainslie, W. O ... N S
McInnis, J., Souris, East ... P E I
McInnis, J., Darlington ... P E I
McInnis, P. D., Dingwall ... O
McInnis, Stephen, Shunacadie, W. O. ... N S
McIntosh, D., Grenfell ... O
McIntosh, D., Westover ... O
McIntosh, P. N., Bookton ... O
McIntosh, Angus, Bay St. Lawrence, W. O. ... N S
McIntosh, D., Coldsprings ... O
McIntyre, D., New London ... P E I
McIntyre, A., Pleasant Bay, W. O. ... N S
McIntyre, C., French Village ... P E I
McIntyre, John, Cable Head ... P E I
McIntyre, Nichol, Bervie ... O
McIntyre, A., River Dennis, W. O. ... N S
McIntyre, W. H., Rockliffe (sub) ... O
McIntyre, D., Crinan ... O
McIntyre, Michael, Boisdale Chapel, W. O. ... N S
McIsaac, Donald, Mull River, W. O. ... N S
McIsaac, D., McAdam's Lake, W. O. ... N S
McJanet, Robert, Yarm ... Q
McKay, George W., Middle Southampton, W.O. ... N B
McKay, George, Mount Thom, W. O. ... N S
McKay, A., Morewood ... O
McKay, James, St. James ... M
McKay, John, Millsville, W. O. ... N S
McKay, D., Big Harbor, W. O. ... N S

McKay, Robert, Guysborough Intervale, W.O. ... N S
McKay, Cornelius, Rosedene ... O
McKay, John, Six Mile Brook, W. O. ... N S
McKay, Anna M., Ancaster ... O
McKay, Mrs. J., West Branch, River John, W.O ... N S
McKay, John, Upper Settlement of Barney's River, W. O. ... N S
McKay, L., Speitches Cove, W. O. ... N S
McKay, Donald, Saintfield ... O
McKay, John, Argyle ... O
McKay, John, Cape Spear, W. O. ... N B
McKay, W. J., Earltown, W. O. ... N S
McKay, D. E., South Side West Margaree, W.O. ... N S
McKay, G. D., Middle Clyde River, W. O. ... N S
McKay, James, Middle Ohio, W. O. ... N S
McKay, H. E., Princetown ... P E I
McKay, G. W., Cavendish Road ... P E I
McKay, Jane, French River ... P E I
McKay, H., Chimney Corner, W. O. ... N S
McKechnie, R., Sharpton ... O
McKeen, J. G., Port Hastings ... N S
McKeen, George, Getson's Point, W. O. ... N S
McKeggie, James H., Stayner ... O
McKellar, D., Kilmartin ... O
McKellar, John, Avonton ... O
McKendrick, M., Kincardine ... O
McKenney, Cyrus B., Pemberton Ridge, W.O. ... N B
McKenney, Thomas, Thornbury ... O
McKenzie, George, Laterriere ... Q
McKenzie, William, Gowland Mountain, W.O. ... N B
McKenzie, N. D., Holstein ... O
McKenzie, Alex., Red Islands, W. O. ... N S
McKenzie, M., St. Ann's, W. O. ... N S
McKenzie, A. M., Terrebonne ... Q
McKenzie, Angus, Appin ... O
McKenzie, James, Union ... O
McKenzie, Thomas, Millfield ... Q
McKenzie, David, Neripis Station, W. O. ... N B
McKenzie, John, North River Bridge, W.O. ... N S
McKenzie, K., Kempt Head, W. O. ... N S
McKenzie, William L., Algonquin ... O
McKenzie, John, Sarawak ... O
McKenzie, J. R., Skye ... O
McKenzie, R., South side of Boulardorie, W.O. ... N S
McKenzie, Archibald, Flatlands ... N B
McKenzie, H., Stellerton ... N S
McKenzie, William, St. George's Channel, W.O. ... N S
McKenzie, F., Birkhall ... O
McKenzie, Archibald, Durham ... O
McKenzie, Eliza, Augustine Cove ... P E I
McKenzie, Donald, Lower Settlement of South River, W. O. ... N S
McKenzie, R. K., Flat River ... P E I
McKeown, James W., Sutherland's Corners ... O
McKeune, J., Aughrim ... O
McKiel, Albert, Greenwich Hill, W. O. ... N B

List of Postmasters in Canada—Continued.

McKillican, William, Moose Creek .... O
McKillop, A., Cotswold ....O
McKillop, Duncan, West Lorne ....O
McKim, Robert, South Middleton .... O
McKim, William, Parker ....O
McKinlay, Robert, Clandeboye................................O
McKinly, Samuel, Onslow, W. O..........................N S
McKinney, Richard, Newburgh, W. O.............. N B
McKinnon, John, Glenedale, W. O.......................N S
McKinnon, John, Lake Ainslie, South side, W.O....N S
McKinnon, John, Cadmus ....O
McKinnon, John, Inverness ....Q
McKinnon, Duncan, North Shore, W. O. ....N S
McKinnon, D. B., Blyth..O
McKinnon, Donald, Rockly, W. O.......................N S
McKinnon, Charles, Vale Colliery, W. O. ....N S
McKinnon, William, Long Creek ....P E I
McKinnon, J. P., East Bay, North Side, W. O...N S
McKnight, F. H., Burnt Church, W. O ....N B
McLachlin, H. F., Palmer Rapids .... O
McLaren, J. H., Lower Argyle, W. O.................N S
McLaren, Alex., Osceola...O
McLaren, James, Wakefield.....................................Q
McLaren, Donald, Cape Rich....................................O
McLaren, Donald, Chezzetcook, W. O.................N S
McLaren, Mrs. Mary, Ross ....O
McLatchey, E., Lower Horton ....N S
McLaughlan, Duncan, Calton .... O
McLaughlin, A. A., Norland ....O
McLaughlin, C., Apto.. O
McLaughlin, Angus, Benacadie, W. O..................N S
McLaughlin, Robert, Yoho, W. O........................N B
McLauren, P., Riceville...O
McLean, Donald, Malignant Cove, W. O...........N S
McLean, Donald, Big Bank, W. O........................N S
McLean, M., McKay's Point, W. O......................N S
McLean, W. H., Eardley...Q
McLean, Allan, Grand Anse, W. O.......................N S
McLean, Alexander Henry, Kimberley.....................O
McLean, Richard, Mount Uniacke.......................N S
McLean, Hector, Knapdale ....O
McLean, James, Escuminac, W. O.......................N B
McLean, A., Cheviot ....O
McLean, Malcolm, Walkerton...................................O
McLean, Mrs. C. A., Toledo ....O
McLean, Donald, Scarboro'.......................................O
McLean, Allan, Tyne Valley ....P E I
McLean, Alex., South West, Lot 16 ....P E I
McLean, H., De Gros Marsh ....P E I
McLean, Charles, Wick ....O
McLean, John, Folly Mountain ....N S
McLean, John, Brae..P E I
McLearn, Joseph, Five Mile River, W. O. ....N S
McLeay, Murdo, Watford ....O
McLees, Robert, Soda Creek ....B C
McLeish, Robert, Branchton......................................O
McLellan, Alex., Broad Cove Chapel, W. O.......N S
McLellan, A. W., Great Village...........................N S
McLellan, Miss Margaret, Port Rowan.....................O
McLellan, W., Elliott..O
McLellan, A. W., Great Village...........................N S
McLellan, A., Cherry Valley...............................P E I
McLellan, J., Indian River..................................P E I
McLellan, Robert, Vachell..O
McLellan, Michael, Big Pond, W. O...................N S
McLelland, John, Parry Sound ....O
McLennan, John, Upper Settlement of Middle River, W. O...N S
McLennan, Donald, Indian Brook, W. O............N S
McLennan, A. S., Fournier..O
McLennan, John, Upper Margaree, W. O.......... N S
McLennan, A. B., Glen Gordon..................................O
McLeod, Charles L., Middle River, W. O...........N S
McLeod, Robert G., Mount Charles...........................O
McLeod, Robert, New Larig, W. O.....................N S
McLeod, Malcolm, Bucklaw, M. O.......................N S
McLeod, Wm., Kirkhill..O
McLeod, Donald, Broad Cove (Marsh), W. O.....N S
McLeod, George, Middle River, W. O.................N S
McLeod, John, Carsonville, W. O.......................N B
McLeod, Hugh, Cape John, W. O........................N S
McLeod, George, Portsmouth ....O
McLeod, Wm., Round Hill, W. O........................N B
McLeod, George, McLeod's Mills, W. O.............N B
McLeod, Isaac, Broad Cove (Intervale) W. O.....N S
McLeod, D. W., Enniskillen ....O
McLeod, Malcolm, Big Brook, W. O...................N S
McLeod, C. F., Belleisle Creek, W. O.................N B
McLeod, Malcolm, Big Intervale (Margaree,) W. O ....N S
McLeod, Donald, Newbridge, W. O.....................N S
McLeod, Alex., Curry Hill..O
McLeod, Alex., Valley Field...............................P E I
McLeod, H., Lot 35..P E I
McLeod, M., Hartsville ....P E I
McMannis, John, South Bolton ....Q
McManus, Mark, Chesley ....O
McMaster, Angus, Low Point, W. O..................N S
McMasters, D. J., Queensville, W. O. .... N S
McMillan, D., Glen, W. O..................................N S
McMillan, John, Breadalbane, W. O..................N B
McMillan, John, Harrietsville.................................. O
McMillan, Patrick, Grand Falls ....N B
McMillan, Duncan G., South Finch...........................O
McMillan, Alex., Stanley Bridge .... P E I
McMillan, Donald, Upper Settlement of Baddeck River, W. O...N S
McMillan, Allan, jun., Isaac's Harbor ....N S
McMillan, William, Kirkwall ....O
McMillan, John, Avonbank..O
McMillan, Duncan, Rear Judique, W. O............N S
McMillan, H., New Haven..................................P E I

List of Postmasters in Canada—Continued.

McMillan, John, Kingston Station ....O
McMillan, Thomas, Little River, Middle Musquodoboit, W. O....................N S
McMillan, W. D., Glen Normon....................O
McMillan, Zachariah, Osgoode ....O
McMillen, John, Hornby ....O
McMillen, Miles, Boiestown....................N B
McMonagle, H., Sussex Vale ....N B
McMurchy, M., Tarbert ....O
McMurray, L., Gladstone ....O
McNab, J., McM., Claremont....................O
McNair, Alex., Grey ....O
McNaught, J., Western Road ....P E I
McNaughton, John, St. Patrick's Channel, W. O..N S
McNaughton, R., Black River, W. O....................N B
McNeil, Hector, Marion Bridge, W. O. ....N S
McNeil, J. S., Grand Narrows, W. O. ....N S
McNeil, John, Giant's Lake, W. O....................N S
McNeil, Malcolm, Hillsborough, C. B., W. O......N S
McNeil, Hugh, Head of South River Lake, W. O..N S
McNeil, Charles, North Range Corner, W. O......N S
McNichol, Allen, Allensville ....O
McNiel, Michael, L'Ardoise, W. O....................N S
McNiel, Malcolm, North Side of Basin, River Dennis, W. O....................N S
McNiel, Moses, Rosedale ....O
McNeil, A. M., Cavendish ....P E I
McNeill, Stephen, Beaver Cove, W. O.....................N S
McPhail, Alex., Pictou....................N S
McPhail, Hugh, Cartwright ....O
McPhail, Neil, Grand Entry ....Q
McPhedrain, Archd., Kertch ....O
McPhee, Donald, Whitevale ....O
McPhee, Peter, Indian Road, W. O....................N S
McPherson, James, Rama ....O
McPherson, Alexander, River Charlo, W. O......N B
McPherson, Allan, Largie ....O
McPherson, Charles, Oronocto....................N B
McPherson, James, Rivière Raisin ....O
McPherson, G. S., Ossian....................O
McPherson, John, New Gairloch, W. O ....N S
McPherson, John, Cross Roads, Ohio, W. O......N S
McPherson, Robert, Speyside ....O
McPherson, John, Prince Albert ....O
McPherson, John, Murray Harbour Road ......P E I
McQuaid, J. C., Hastings, W. O....................N B
MQuaid, P., Kelly's Cross ....P E I
McQuain, Alexander, Kewstoke....................N S
McQuarrie, A., Cape Mabou, W. O....................N S
McQuarrie, C., George's River, W. O....................N S
McQueen, Mrs. M. A., North Pelham ....O
McQueen, James, Fergus ....O
McQueen, A. R., Victoria Cross....................P E I
McQueen, Wm., Rona....................P E I
McRae, Mrs., Glen Sandfield....................O
McRae, Hugh, Strathburn....................O
McRae, Donald, Burnstown....................O
McRae, Duncan, Bolsover ....O
McRae, Finlay, Lower Settlement, Middle River, W. O....................N S
McRae, Hector, Crawford....................O
McRae, William, Duncan....................O
McRae, C. J., Glenroy ....O
McRae, Alex., Baddeck Bridge, W. O....................N S
McRae, Malcolm, Garden River....................O
McVane, David, Bothwell ....P E I
McVey, John, Dungiven, W. O....................N B
McVicar, Miss C., Fort William ....O
McVicar, Morris, Wanstead....................O
McWilliams, Albert, Harold ....O
McWilliams, A., West Cape....................P E I
McWilliams, A. B., Harley ....O
Macaulay, John, Venosta ....Q
Macdonald, D. D., Bailey's Brook, W. O....................N S
Macdonald, John, Vellore ....O
Macdonald, D. A., Alexandria ....O
Macdonald, Norman, Addington Forks, W. O....N S
Macdougall, John, Fort Garry ....O
Macfadden, Urian, Edgecombe....................O
Machell, John, St. Sylvester....................Q
Mack, I. N., Mill's Village ....N S
Mackay, William, Renfrew ....O
Mackay, Levi, Kinsale ....O
Mackelcan, G. J., Brisbane ....O
Mackereth, John, St. Canute....................Q
Mackey, Heli, Northfield, W. O. ....N S
Mackie, Benjamin, Vasey ....O
Mackintosh, Henry B., Strathroy....................O
Mackinnon, J., Christmas Island....................N S
Macklem, J. S., Chippewa ....O
Maclure, David, Murray Harbor, North....................P E I
MacNider, John, Petit Métis....................Q
Maconchy, Thomas, Gilford ....O
Maconchy, Robert, Bradford....................O
Macrea, George, St. Sylvester, East....................Q
Macready, A., Harriston....................O
Macy, J. F., Corbett....................O
Maddon, Hugh, Loughborough....................O
Mader, Jeremiah, New Canada, W. O. ....N S
Magoon, Aaron, Magoon's Point ....Q
Maguire, John, Steep Creek, W. O....................N S
Maguire, William, Franklin ....O
Magwood, Robert, Bowling Green ....O
Maher, Philip, Richmond Station....................Q
Mahew, Robert, Renforth ....O
Main, William, Canterbury Station....................N B
Main, William, Cherry Creek....................O
Mair, Charles, Portage la Prairie....................M
Major, Charles, jun., Monte Bello ....Q
Major, Edward, Glen Major ....O
Major, J. G., South March....................O
Maher, Thomas, Pockmouche, W. O....................N B

List of Postmasters in Canada—Continued.

Malcolm, John, jun., Cariboo Cove, W. O. ....N S
Mallet, H. S., Gilbert Cove ....N S
Mallet, N., Chateauguay ....Q
Malloch, E., Hunterstown ....Q
Malone, Timothy, Petersville, W. O. ....N B
Maneely, Michael, East Hawkesbury ....O
Manamin, R., Ratter's Corner, W. O. ....N B
Mann, William, Yarmouth Centre ....O
Manning, Johnson, Hebb's Cross, W. O ....N S
Mansfield, George, Cashmere ....O
Manson, David A., Mansonville Potton ....Q
Manuel, C., Upper Haynezville, W. O. ....N B
Marceau, Rev. E. H. L., St. Tite des Caps ....Q
Marchand, Edouard, St. Jerome ....Q
Marchment, Edwin, Rivière Trois Pistoles ....Q
March, David, Port Granby ....O
Marcotte, Joseph U., Ste. Anne de la Pérade ....Q
Marcoux, Isidore, Versailles ....Q
Marcoux, T., Cedars ....Q
Margeson, T. A., Margaretsville, W. O. ....N S
Marion, Joseph, St. Paul l'Hermite ....Q
Markham, Alfred, Markhamville, W. O ....N B
Marks, Robert, Brucefield ....O
Marlow, W. F., Gesto ....O
Marquis, P. C., St. André ....Q
Marsh, Jacob, Coldstream ....N B
Marsh, A., Consecon ....O
Marshall, James, Trout River ....Q
Marshall, W., Huntingdon ....Q
Marshall, Obiah, Washago ....O
Marshall, Edward, Gallingertown ....O
Martel, Anthony, Cow Bay ....N S
Martell, Susanna, Mira Gut, W. O ....N S
Martell, Michael, Bloomingdale ....O
Martin, Robert, Sydney ....N S
Martin, James, Belleville, W. O. ....N B
Martin, E. D., Warden ....Q
Martin, N. C., Upper Bedford ....Q
Martin, Octave, Avignon ....Q
Martin, Elie, St. Arsene ....Q
Martin, John, Whim Road Cross ....P E I
Martin, Patrick, St. Leonard's, W. O. ....N S
Martindale, Noble, Stanbridge Ridge ....Q
Martineau, J. E., St. Alphonse ....Q
Martyn, William, Enfield ....O
Martyn, William, Shirley ....O
Mason, Robert, Masonville ....O
Mason, Mary, Donegal ....O
Mason, George, Beaulac ....Q
Mason, Charles, Beachville ....O
Mason, Thomas, Johnston, W. O. ....N B
Masters, William, Upper Rawdon, W. O. ....N S
Masterson, Lackey, St. Andrew's, West ....O
Mastin, I. B., Lavender ....O
Mather, James, Menie ....O
Mather, John, Otter Lake ....Q
Matheson, Hugh, Inverhuron ....O
Matheson, George, Tavistock ....O
Matheson, D., Embro ....O
Matheson, J., St. Esprit, W. O. ....N S
Matheson, James, Lower L'Ardoise, W. O. ....N S
Matheson, John, South side of Little Narrows, W. O. ....N S
Matheson, W. H., Upper Woods Harbor, W. O. ....N S
Matthews, E. J., Flinton ....O
Matthews, J., Acton ....O
Matthie, Joseph, Galbraith ....O
Matthiou, J. B., St Urbain ....Q
Maudsley, Henry, Moorefield ....O
Mavety, Robert, Wilmur ....O
Maxwell, W. A., Head Lake ....O
May, Nelson, Pine Orchard ....O
May, James, Dundalk ....O
Mayberry, Richard, Maberly ....O
Mayrand, Z., St. Phillippe ....Q
Meacham, J. H., Belleville ....O
Meagher, Joseph, Carleton ....Q
Meecham, Eli, Elginburg ....O
Meek, Agnes, Alton ....O
Meen, Frederick, Greenwood ....O
Meikle, G. L., Lachute ....Q
Melançon, M., Port Acadie, W. O. ....N S
Melick, Jonas R., Warner ....O
Mellis, Robert, Kippen ....O
Mellon, Samuel H., Sillsville ....O
Mellow, W. J., Gretna ....O
Mellville, Andrew, Nottawa ....O
Menhennick, John, Putnam ....O
Mercier, H., St. Guillaume d'Upton ....Q
Mercier, Joseph, Ste. Hénédine ....O
Merritt, John, Pelham Union ....O
Messier, Ambrose, Belle Alodie ....Q
Mesner, F. X., Formosa ....O
Messer, John, Bluevale ....O
Metcalfe, Alfred, Roseneath ....O
Meunier, C., Starnesboro' ....Q
Meunier, François, Canrobert ....Q
Meyer, George E., Glenmeyer ....O
Merseroll, Nicholas, Point Sapin, W. O. ....N B
Michaud, B., Ste. Hélène ....Q
Michaud, Peter, St. Hilaire, W. O. ....N B
Michaud, Maximilian, Burrard's Inlet ....B C
Michaud, Miss Adée, Notre Dame du Portage ....Q
Michener, Isaac, Lowbanks ....O
Middlemas, George, Caledonia Corner ....N S
Middleton, George, Wheatley ....O
Middleton, J. J., Dundalk Station ....O
Mignault, Joseph E., St. Dennis, River Richelieu ....Q
Milburn, John, Peabody ....O
Milette, Benjamin, Wotton ....Q
Millar, James, Magnetawan ....O
Millar, Miss C. M., Drummondville, East ....Q

List of Postmasters in Canada—Continued.

Miller, B. B., Wiarton....O
Miller, Robert, Zimmerman....O
Miller, M. G., Teviotdale....O
Miller, James, Ulverton....Q
Miller, James, St. Luce....Q
Miller, John P., Carleton, W. O....N S
Miller, William, Peninsula, Gaspé....Q
Miller, H. J., Corunna....O
Miller, Hiram, Miller's Creek, W. O....N S
Miller, Caleb, Mount Hanley, W. O....N S
Miller, Jonathan, Benmiller....O
Miller, John, Blytheswood....O
Miller, David W., Sumas....B C
Miller, Peter, Switzerville....O
Miller, George, Cook's Creek....M
Miller, W. A., Forestville....O
Miller, John, Abingdon....O
Millett, Benjamin, Marriott's Cove, W. O....N S
Millett, Alexis, La Présentation....Q
Millett, Edouard, St. George de Windsor....Q
Milligan, D. S., Moodyville....B C
Milligan, Joshua, Massie....O
Millin, Arthur, Newcombe....O
Milloy, Colin, Newport....O
Mills, Stephen, Lewisville, W. O....N B
Mills, Wm. B., Arden....O
Mills, George E., Tedish, W. O....N B
Mills, George, Armstrong's Corner, W. O....N B
Mills, John, Lorraine....O
Mills, Horatio, Old Montrose....O
Mills, William, Muir....O
Milne, Alexander, Langford....O
Milne, Thomas, Copetown....O
Milne, John, Agincourt....O
Milner, Thomas, Parker's Cove, W. O....N S
Milson, J. H., Whalen....O
Milward, Thomas F., Stormont, W. O....N S
Miscampbell, Andrew, Allendale....O
Mitchell, Mrs. M., Cook's Brook, W. O....N S
Mitchell, Arthur, Fordwich....O
Mitchell, James, Nactaquack, W. O....N B
Mitchell, John, Metz....O
Mitchell, David, Marie Joseph, W. O....N S
Mitchel, John, Riley Brook, W. O....N B
Mitchell, James, Shiloh....O
Miville, Narcisse, Ste. Modeste....Q
Moffatt, Alexander, Pembroke....O
Moffatt, Henry, Pendleton....O
Moffitt, Charles, Kinmount....O
Mohr, Charles, Mohr's Corners....O
Moncion, L., Angers....Q
Monkhouse, Joseph, Altona....O
Monkman, John, Eagles Nest....M
Montgomery, J. W., Keswick....O
Montmigney, M., St. Evereste de Forsyth....Q
Montminy, T., St. Charles, River Boyer....Q
Moon, Robert J., Medonte....O
Mooney, Andrew, Little Harbor....P E I
Moore, G. W., Winger....O
Moore, Gilbert, Norwich....O
Moore, P. C., Moore's Station....Q
Moore, Alex., Mechanics' Settlement, W. O....N B
Moore, John, Shinemacas Bridge....N S
Moore, J. S., Upper Economy, W. O....N S
Moore, Mathias, Falkenburg....O
Moore, Alfred, Carnarvon....O
Moore, Thomas, Waubuno....O
Moore, James, Belfast....P E I
Moore, Simon, Burnt River....O
Moorehouse, Mrs. M. J., Trout Cove, W. O....N S
Mordon, W. J., Bullock's Corners....O
Morden, W. H., North Port....O
Morgan, William, Pleasant Hill....O
Morgan, Ira., Ormond....O
Moriarty, James, Kinkora....O
Morin, B., St Isidore, Dorchester....Q
Morin, P., Bienville....Q
Morin, Dolphin, Chantelle....Q
Morin, Alexis, Vauban....Q
Morin, M., Ste. Moise....Q
Morris, John H., Warwick....O
Morris, David, Ste. Thérèse de Blainville....Q
Morris, J. K., Rondeau....O
Morris, R., Avening....O
Morris, Nathan B., Advocate Harbor....N S
Morris, Bernard, Summerville....O
Morrisey, E., Orwell Cove....P E I
Morrison, D. J., South Gut of St. Ann's, W. O....N S
Morrison, R. R., Gaberouse....N S
Morrison, R., Everton....O
Morrison, Thomas, Lorneville....O
Morrison, D., Carleton....P E I
Morrison, R., Hawkesville....O
Morrison, John, Wreck Cove, W. O....N S
Morrison, R. G., St. Peter's....N S
Morrison, John, Rear of Black River, W. O....N S
Morrison, Alexander, Peveril....Q
Morrison, R. B., Moriston....O
Morrison, John, Moore....O
Morison, Alice M., Upper Mills....N B
Morrison, John, River Denis Road, W. O....N S
Morrison, George, Poplar Hill, W. O....N S
Morrow, James, Fleetwood....O
Morrow, John, Dacre....O
Morrow, Joseph, Ratho....O
Morrow, Wm., North Lake....P E I
Morse, John G., Sandy Cove....N S
Morton, E., Middlefield, W. O....N S
Morton, James, Morton's Corner, W. O....N S
Morton, William, St. Ola....O
Moss, James, Indian Point, W O....N S
Mosher, Daniel, St. Croix, W. O....N S

List of Postmasters in Canada—Continued.

Moss, James, Port Maitland ...O
Mossman, Edward, Kinsbury, W. O ...N S
Mott, Isaac, Blessington ...O
Mott, Amos, Central Cambridge, W. O ...N B
Mowat, Andrew, St. Andrew's ...M
Mowat, John, Deeside ...Q
Mowbray, John, Ulster ...O
Moxon, Thomas, Rawdon, W. O ...N S
Moyer, Moses, Breslaw ...O
Moyer, H. W., Campden ...O
Mulkins, Henry, Simcoe ...O
Mullan, P. J., Sheenboro' ...Q
Mullett, F., Bronson ...O
Mulrine, Chas., Emigrant Road, W. O ...N B
Mulvihill, Rev. J., St. Laurent ...M
Munn, D., Little Sands ...P E I
Munro, Alexander, Lanark ...O
Munro, John, Watson's Corners ...O
Munro, William, West River ...N S
Munro, A., Boulardorie ...N S
Munro, William, Kilmaurs ...O
Munro, John C., Grantley ...O
Munro, M., Munro's Mills, W. O ...N S
Munroe, N., Epsom ...O
Munsie, William, Nobleton ...O
Munsie, James, Caledon East ...O
Murchie, Alexander, Winthrop ...O
Murchie, John, Doyle Settlement, W. O ...N B
Murchie, J. E., Benton, W. O. ...N B
Murchison, Hector, Grand River, W. O ...N S
Murchison, M. N., Point Prim ...P E I
Murdoch, Mrs. Christy A., Cain's River, W. O ...N B
Muir, Michael, Sooke ...B C
Murphy, John, Mulmur ...O
Murphy, Patrick, Stoco ...O
Murphy, William, Sarnia ...O
Murphy, J., Waugh's River, W. O ...N S
Murphy, Patrick, Caldwell ...O
Murphy, Thomas, Chipman's Brook, W. O ...N S
Murphy, Michael, St. Ann's ...P E I
Murphy, J. T., Newton ...P E I
Murphy, Felix, Hope River ...P E I
Murray, William G., Arnott ...O
Murray, John, Esquesing ...O
Murray, John, Glen Murray ...Q
Murray, William, Ste. Brigide ...Q
Murray, John G., Port Richmond, W. O ...N S
Murray, Joseph, Murray's Corner, W. O ...N B
Murray, Robert, St. Helen's ...O
Murray, John, Spence's Bridge ...B C
Mussells, William, Webber's, W. O ...N S
Musson, Thomas, Islington ...O
Mustard, John, Ashworth ...O
Mutchmore, J. T., Oneida ...O
Muttart, J. L., Cape Traverse ...P E I
Myers, E. B., Lynnville ...O

Nagle, G. J., Rock Forest ...Q
Naise, J. M., Mouth of Nerepis ...N B
Nation, J. C., Morpeth ...O
Naubert, Fernandez, St. Philipe d'Argenteuil ...Q
Nauffs, John, Pleasant Point, W. O ...N S
Nash, William, L'Amaroux ...O
Neckerson, James A., Lower Ward, Ste. Marguerite's Bay, W. O ...N S
Needham, J., Bay Fortune ...P E I
Neelands, Abraham, Invermay ...O
Neff, John R., Troy ...O
Neiley, John C., Cambridge Station, W. O ...N S
Neilans, Thomas, Harlock ...O
Nelles, H. E., Grimsby ...O
Nelson, N., North Salem, W. O ...N S
Nelson, G. W., Dickson's Store, W. O ...N S
Nelson, John, Trafalgar, W. O ...N S
Nelson, John, Ludlow, W. O ...N B
Nethercott, John, Eden ...O
Newcomb, J. S., Upper Perreaux, W. O ...N S
Newcomb, J. B., Avonport Station ...N S
Newell, John, Black Bank ...O
Newman, W. J., Morganston ...O
Newsome, George, Kilmarnock ...O
Newton, John, Limehouse ...O
Nichol, Alexander, Jackson Road, W. O ...N S
Nichol, Peter M., St. Mary's ...O
Nichols, S. J., Berwick Station, W. O ...N S
Nicholls, D., Nicholl's Corner, W. O ...N S
Nicholls, Wm., New Germany, W. O ...N S
Nicholson, Donald, Barney's River, W. O ...N S
Nicholson, A., Concord, W. O ...N S
Nicholson, John, Kirkland, W. O ...N B
Nicklin, J., Morningdale Mills ...O
Nickerson, James, Clarke's Harbor, W. O ...N S
Nickerson, E., Wood Harbor, W. O ...N S
Nickerson, S. W., Shag Harbor, W. O ...N S
Nicol, John, Nicolston ...O
Nispel, Conrad, Preston ...O
Niven, Rev. Hugh, Herdman's Corner's ...Q
Noble, John, Park Hill ...O
Noble, Colin, Stornoway ...Q
Noble, Robert, Hardwicke, W. O ...N B
Noonan, Daniel, North-West Cove, W. O ...N S
Norman, R. M., Mill Bridge ...O
Normandin, Louis, Boucherville ...Q
Normansell, James, Kootenay ...B C
Northey, Richard, Selwyn ...O
Northmore, Joseph, Cataraqui ...O
Norton, William, Lot 56 ...P E I
Nowlan, John G., Havelock, W. O ...N S
Noxen, Richard, Hillier ...O
Nugent, Miss D., Grand Baie ...Q
Nugent, Mrs C., West Quaco ...N B
Nutt, David, Nutt's Corners ...Q
Nye, D. T. R., Philipsburg, East ...Q

List of Postmasters in Canada—Continued.

Oaks, Albert, New Albany, W. O....N S
O'Brien, E. R., St. George....N B
O'Brien, F. X., Repentigny....Q
O'Brien, Osmond, Noel, W. O....N S
O'Brien, Margaret, Beauport....Q
O'Brien, Mrs. Mary, Lower Ship Harbor, W. O..N S
O'Connor, H. B. C., Riversdale....O
O'Connor, John, Lot 14....P E I
Odell, W. H., Belmont....O
O'Donell, R., Ferris, W O....N B
O'Donnell, John, North Onslow....Q
Odonnell, Thomas, Lakeview, W. O....N S
O'Flynn, W. H., Madoc....O
Ogden, C. K., Three Rivers....Q
O'Heir, M., St. Gabriel de Brandon....Q
O'Keif, Cornelius, Okanagon....B C
O'Leary, Michael, West Newdy Quoddy....N S
Oldmixon, Edmund, East Side of Chizzetcook, W. O....N S
Oliver, A., Rockburn....Q
Oliver, Edward, Ashburn....O
Oliver, John, Dewitville....Q
Olivier, Louis, Black River Station....Q
Olmstead, Albert D., Aroostook, W. O....N B
O'Loane, L. T., Stratford....O
O'Meara, James, Lombardy....O
O'Meara, M., Navan....O
O'Niel, Samuel, Grosvenor, W. O....N S
O'Neill, Michael, Downerville....O
O'Neill, Thomas, Salmon River (Lake Settlement) W. O....N S
O'Neill, George, Vernon River....P E I
Oehlenschlager, J., Chaudière Station....Q
Omon, Miss M., St. Alexis....Q
Orchard, John G., Orchard....O
Ord, George, Ilderton....O
Orman, George, Porter's Lake, W. O....N S
Orr, Allen, Seaton....O
Orr, James, Morrisbank....O
Orr, James E., Lynden....O
Osborne, Sydney, Renten....O
Osbornes, J. B., Beamsville....O
Osgood, W. A., St. John's, East....Q
Ostrom, Henry, Moira....O
O'Sullivan, Cornelius, Meyersburg....O
Ouellet, L., St. Onésime....Q
Oulton, Thomas E., Westmoreland Point....N B
Oulton, Thomas, Little Shemogue, W. O....N B
Ostrander, D. A., Wellman's Corners....O
Outhouse, S., Wood Point, W. O....N B
Outhouse, Charles, Pelete Passage, W. O....N S
Owen, G. F., Cardigan Bridge....P E I
Owen, Jenkins, Fernhill....O
Owens, Wm., Stonefield....Q
Oxner, Joseph, Lower La Have, W. O....N S

Packwood, George, Point St. Peter....Q
Page, W. E., Métis....Q
Page, Francis, Omineca....B C
Pagé, Pierre, Les Ecureuils....Q
Painchaud, F., Hochelaga....Q
Paisley, James, Ravenswood....O
Palmer, Benjamin, Hilda....O
Palmer, John, Morristown, W. O....N S
Palmer, F. L., Jacksontown, W. O....N B
Palmer, Ira, Balsam....O
Palmer, Hanford, Anagance....N B
Paon, Gilbert, West Arichat, W. O....N S
Paquette, J. B., St. Roch de Richelieu....Q
Paquette, Louis, St. Augustin, Two Mountains....Q
Paquette, F., Paquette....Q
Paquet, Edward D., House Harbor (sub)....Q
Paradis, Louis, jun., Valetort....Q
Paradis, C., Ruisseau des Chénes....Q
Paré, A. P., St. Bruno....Q
Paré, Mrs. E., St. Germain de Grantham....Q
Paré, Adolphe, Ste. Anne de Beaupré....Q
Parent, David C., Upper Queensbury, W. O....N B
Parent, Hermyle, Tessierville....Q
Parent, J. C., Fox River....Q
Parent, Isaiah, Bear Island, W. O....N B
Parent, Mrs. L., Kerry....O
Pargerit, Felix, Malmaison....Q
Parish, Arza, Farmersville....O
Park, Ernest G., Amherstburgh....O
Parker, John S., Ten Mile Creek....N B
Parker, Benjamin, Glasgow....O
Parker, Robert, Kilbride....O
Parker, J. M., Borwick....N S
Parker, Nelson, Dexter....O
Parker, John, Dunbarton....O
Parker, Shutnel, Woodville, W. O....N S
Parker, D. P., Harbourville, W. O....N S
Parkhill, Wm., Randwick....O
Parnall, Wm., Merritton....O
Parry, H. H., Copleston....O
Parsons, John, Crediton....O
Passmore, Robert, Rockwood....O
Paton, P., New Lowell....O
Pattenoude, M., Stockwell....Q
Patterson, W. C., Patterson....O
Patterson, Thomas B., Smithurst....O
Patterson, H., Steam Mill Village, W. O....N S
Patterson, David, Goose River....N S
Patterson, Jane, Admaston....O
Patterson, Ira H., Au Lac, W. O....N B
Patterson, James C., Blantyre....O
Patterson, Miss L. A., West Arran....O
Patterson, G. H., Drumquin....O
Patterson, William, Rochesterville....O
Pattison, Ambrose, Canfield....O
Pattison, Robert, Walton....O

List of Postmasters in Canada—Continued.

Payne, Manuel, Port Stanley .... O
Paxton, Robert, Kinlough .... O
Peaker, Mrs. H., Cooksville .... O
Pearson, W. W., Pearson's W. O. .... N S
Peck, James H., Albury .... O
Peebles, Matthew, Strabane .... O
Peers, John, Mapleton .... M
Pelissier, P. N. E., Pelissier .... Q
Pelletier, T. P., Trois Pistoles .... Q
Pelletier, J. B., Lac Noir .... Q
Pelletier, O., St. Roch l'Achigan .... Q
Pelletier, Theodore, Caron Brook, W. O. .... N B
Pellow, U. T., Kintail .... O
Pennock, Philemon, Elgin .... O
Pennock, John C., Castleton .... O
Pepin, dit Lachance, Emilion, St. François d'Orleans .... Q
Pequignol, Mrs. Nancy, West Chester Lake, W.O. N S
Percy, John, Bangor .... O
Pernette, C. R., Middle La Have Ferry, W. O. ... N S
Perré, J., Ste. Anne des Monts .... Q
Perrin, John D., Bailieboro' .... O
Perrin, William, Mount Vernon .... O
Perrott, Nathaniel, Shannonvale, W.O. .... N B
Perry, Calvin, Perryboro' .... Q
Perry, Robert E., Bracebridge .... O
Peterman, S. W. Purpleville .... O
Petit, P. H., St. Damase .... Q
Petitclerc, Mrs. C., Bergeville .... Q
Petrey, W. B., Russell .... O
Petty, Charles, Cherry Wood .... O
Phair, A. S., Fredericton .... N B
Phelan, M. J., St. Columbin .... Q
Phelan, James, Morell Rear .... P E I
Phelps, Joshua A., Mystic .... Q
Phelps, Linius W., Dickens .... O
Philips, Levi, Alma .... O
Phillips, E. D. W. R., Bath .... N B
Phillips, Robert, Canaan Rapids, W. O .... N B
Phillips, George, Phillipston .... O
Phillips, Edwin, Shiktehawk Bridge .... N S
Phillipps, Thomas, St. Piérre les Becquets .... Q
Phillipps, Mrs. Grace, River Philip .... N S
Phillips, Oran, Burns .... O
Phillips, William, Belfast .... O
Philpott, Edward, Foxboro' .... O
Phipps, G. W., Kelvin .... O
Pickering, William, Branchton .... O
Pierce, W. J., Malakoff .... O
Pierson, John, Milverton .... O
Pilcher, Thomas, Port Burwell .... O
Pim, Mrs., Sault Ste. Marie .... O
Pineo, J. P., Waterville .... N S
Pinkney, W. R., Sand Beach, W. O. .... N S
Piper, Charles, sen., Stoneleigh .... O
Pipes, W. C., Hopewell Corner .... N B
Pipes, Jonathan, Amherst Point, W. O. .... N S
Pitt, H., Pierreville .... Q
Pitt, William, son., Pittson .... O
Piuze, J. A., Mille Vaches .... Q
Plamondon, Edouard, St. Raymond .... Q
Plamondon, Anselme, St. Marcel .... Q
Planch, William G., Maple Leaf .... Q
Plant, William, Stanley, W. O. .... N B
Plante, Pierre, St. Bernard .... Q
Playfair, Elisha, Buckshot .... O
Plews, Simon, Salmonville .... O
Plinguet, Rev. V., Isle Dupas .... Q
Plummer, R. H., New Perth .... P E I
Poaps, Jacob J., Osnabruck Centre .... O
Pointer, James E., Churchville .... O
Poirier, Joseph O., St. Jacques le Mineur .... Q
Poirier, J. A., St. Grégoire .... Q
Pollock, Solomon, Mille Isles .... Q
Pollock, Samuel, Nile .... O
Pomeroy, William, Pomeroy Ridge, W. O. .... N B
Poole, Ambrose, Cedar Lake, W. O. .... N S
Poor, Mark, Central Kingsclear, W. O. .... N B
Pope, Charles E., Clinton .... B C
Pope, Lemuel, Robinson .... Q
Porte, William, Lucan .... O
Porter, Richard C., New Ireland .... Q
Porter, Henry, Cold Brook Station, W. O. .... N S
Porter, Leon, Eel Lake, W. O. .... N S
Porter, J. B., River de Chute, W. O. .... N B
Porterfield, P., Marnoch .... O
Pothier, François, French Village .... Q
Potter, E. W., Smith's Cove, W. O. .... N S
Potts, Edward, McIntyre .... O
Potvin, P., L'Anse au Foin .... Q
Polin, Hilaire, St. François, Beauce .... Q
Poulin, Louis, St. Etienne de Boulton .... Q
Powell, Henry, Wallenstein .... O
Powell, George A., Wroxeter .... O
Powley, Charles, Marchmont .... O
Power, James, Wheatley River .... P E I
Power, Angus, Vernal, W. O. .... N S
Pratt, Mrs. Rebecca, Skead's Mills .... O
Pratt, John, New Ross .... N S
Pratt, James C., Second Falls, W. O. .... N B
Prefontain, Fulgence, South Durham .... Q
Premont, Joseph, Ste. Famille .... Q
Prentice, John, Alberton .... O
Prentiss, H. B., Chelsea .... Q
Prescott, Jesse, Pennfield, W. O. .... N B
Prescott, John, Goose Creek, W. O. .... N B
Pretty, Hezekiah, Bethesda .... O
Price, W. W., Petiocodiac .... N B
Pridham, Edward, Grenville .... Q
Prieur, Anicet B., Coteau Landing .... Q
Prieur, O. F., St. Zotique .... Q
Prior, F. B., Wallbridge .... O

List of Postmasters in Canada—Continued.

Pritchard, A., North Wakefield ....**Q**
Proctor, J. W., New Edinburgh .... **O**
Proctor, John, Leskard ....**O**
Prosser, Daniel, Belhaven ....**O**
Prudhomme, Alex., Cantley .... **Q**
Pruneau, J. Bte., Quebec .. ..**Q**
Publicover, Mrs. Eliza, Blandford, W. O. ....**N S**
Pugsley, Daniel, Amherst Hill, W. O. ....**N S**
Pugsley, Michael, River Hébert, W. O. ....**N S**
Pugsley, William, Cheapside...................................**O**
Purdy, Allan G., Greenville, W. O.....................**N S**
Purdy, C., Deep Brook, W. O. ....**N S**
Purdy, Joseph Lawrence, Little River, W. O..... **N S**
Purdy, David, Wentworth, W. O.........................**N S**
Purdy, Mrs. Mary J., West Chester, W. O.........**N S**
Purdy, R. McLean, Eugenia ....**O**
Purdy, William, Pomona ....**O**
Purkiss, Josiah, Thornhill ....**O**
Purney, John, Sandy Point, W. O. ....**N S**
Purves, Robert, jun., Tatamagouche ....**N S**
Purves, ——, Kossuth..... ....**O**

Quance, Robert, Gravelotte ....**O**
Quarry, John G., Offa...**O**
Quealy, John, Eganville..**O**
Queen, Felix, St. Antonin ....**Q**
Queenville, O., Cazaville.......................................**Q**
Quibell, John, Holt ....**O**
Quigley, Edmund, Beech Hill, W. O. ... .**N S**
Quintin, dit Duboise A., Action Vaie ....**Q**
Quirk, Dennis, Glascott ....**O**

Raby, H. N., St. André Avellin ....**Q**
Racette, Jos., Ste. Julienne .. ..**Q**
Racey, Thomas, Mohawk ....**O**
Radford, Joseph, Tadousac . ...**Q**
Raiche, S. G. A., Clarence Creek ....**O**
Rafferty, John, Yatton ....**O**
Ramsay, A., Lot 8 ....**P E I**
Ramsey, Robert, Ramsey's Corners........... ....**O**
Rand, George V., Wolfville ....**N S**
Randall, E. W., Bayfield, W. O. ....**N S**
Rankin, D., Sutherland's River, W. O. .. .. **N S**
Rankin, Matthew, Falding....... ....**O**
Ranson, Robert, Deux Rivieres... ....**Q**
Raworth, Alfred, Upper Cape, W. O............. **N B**
Ray, Andrew, Upper Magaguadavic, W. O...... **N B**
Ray, John, Glanmire ....**O**
Ray, Robert R., Factory Dale, W. O....................**N S**
Raymond, S. P., Beaver River, W. O..................**N S**
Raymond, C. W., Mitchell's Bay ....**O**
Raymond, Wm. S., Beaver River Corner...........**N S**
Raymond, David N., Middle Simonds, W. O....**N B**
Raymond, George, Kouchibouguac.....................**N B**
Raymond, Silas, Central Norton, W. O...... .....**N B**
R[illegible]

Read, Eliphalet, Read, W. O..................................**N B**
Read, James, De Ramsey......... ....**Q**
Read, J. G., North Joggins, W. O......................**N B**
Read, Charles, Baie Vérte .... **N B**
Reading, Joseph, Cromarty.... ....**O**
Reardon, P., Pockshaw, W. O...............................**N B**
Redman, Edward, Lower Ireland............ .... **Q**
Redner, James, Rednersville. ....**O**
Redpath, Geo., Effingham ....**O**
Redy, Benjamin, Gold River, W. O.......................**N S**
Reece, John R., Danby....... .... **Q**
Reed, Nathaniel, Mimosa.. ....**O**
Reed, William, Knatchbull .... **O**
Reed, James R., Carleton ....**N B**
Reed, James, Caledonia Settlement, W. O.........**N B**
Reeve, George, Hornsey, W. O..... ... .**N S**
Reeve, Arthur, Atherley.. **O**
Reeve, Thomas H., Oxendon .... **O**
Regnier, P., St. Athanase ....**Q**
Reid, Donald, Harrington, West ....**O**
Reid, J. C., Vanatter..... .. ..**O**
Reid, James, Tweed..... ....**O**
Reid, Robert, Waubaumik...**O**
Reid, Thomas M., Moose Brook, W. O..............**N S**
Reid, G. B., Port George, W. O ....**N S**
Reid, Minor, Upper New Horton, W. O...........**N B**
Reid, Thomas, Cascades ....**Q**
Reid, W. A., Avonport, W. O......... ... .**N S**
Reid, A., North Tryon.. ....**P E I**
Reinhardt, John, Elmwood ....**O**
Remey, A., Tempo ....**O**
Rennells, Wm., Windsor Junction, W. O....... ...**N S**
Renner, J. D., Bealton ....**O**
Renshaw, J., Blair......... ....**O**
Renton, Mrs. Ann, Renton.... ....**O**
Reyner, John, Coventry............................. ......**O**
Reynolds, Wm., Sarepta..**O**
Reynolds, Wm., Mount Horeb ....**O**
Reynolds, W. K., Lepreaux ....**O**
Rhodes, Wm., Rhodes, W. O ....**N S**
Richard, Lewis, Belliveaux Village, W. O... ......**N B**
Richard, Aimé, Fifteen Point............................**P E I**
Richard, N., St. Octave..**Q**
Richard, Peter, Big Brook...............................**P E I**
Richardson, John, Little Rocher.........................**N B**
Richardson, George, Malone ....**O**
Richardson, Henry, Trudel....... ....**O**
Richardson, J., Valetta...... ....**O**
Richardson, Thomas, Big Port le Bear, W. O.....**N B**
Richardson, Samuel H., South Mountain.............**O**
Richardson, W., Patillo..**O**
Rickaby, Seth, Glenarm...**O**
Ricker, R., Knowlesville......................... ....**N B**
Rider, H. M, Fitch Bay.......... ....**Q**
Rigby, Miss Henrietta F., Sydney Mines..........**N S**
Rigby, Clara, Mainadieu, W. O ....**N S**

List of Postmasters in Canada—Continued.

Ring, James, Panmure .... O
Riordon, John, Lower Woodstock, W. O........ N B
Risteen, George, Lower French Village, W. O... N B
Ritchie, Frederick, Hamilton .... O
Ritchie, John, South Quebec........ Q
Rivard, F. X. A., St. Léon........ Q
Rivard, Miss M. E., Bécancour........ Q
Rivet, Narcisse, St. Brigitte de Saults........ Q
Roach, W., Grand Falls, Portage, W. O........ N B
Roach, Robert Maccan, W. O........ N S
Robb, James, Stoney Lake........ O
Roberge, Louis, Ste. Julie de Somerset........ Q
Roberge, Damase, New Liverpool........ Q
Robert, Raymond, Sherrington .... Q
Robert, François, St. Hubert........ Q
Robert, Flavien, La Pigeonnière .... Q
Roberts, William, Middleton........ P E I
Robertson, Arch., Fox Harbor, W. O........ N S
Robertson, John, Thomasburg .... O
Robertson, L., Port Jolly, W. O........ N S
Robertson, S., Hollen .... O
Robertson, Daniel, Loch Lomond .... N B
Robertson, Charles, Belle Rivière........ Q
Robertson, Wm., Lanark .... O
Robertson, A., Bonshaw........ P E I
Robertson, D., Red Point .... P E I
Robbins, Ansell, Chebogue, W. O........ N S
Robicheau, P., Lower Pocmouche, W. O........ N B
Robinson, W. S., Baillie, W. O........ N B
Robinson, James, Selton........ O
Robinson, E. A., Goshen, W. O........ N B
Robinson, Thomas, Newbury........ O
Robinson, R. D., Elgin........ N B
Robinson, John, Rockwood .... M
Robinson, Wm., Tecterville .... O
Robitaille, Louis, Ancienne, Lorette .... Q
Roblin, Owen, Ameliasburgh........ O
Roblin, Philip, Green Point........ O
Robson, John W., Vanneck........ O
Roch, N., St. Norbert .... Q
Roche, Edmund, Iona........ O
Rockingham, Joseph, Glenloyd........ Q
Rockwell, Aaron, Rockwell Settlement, W. O..... N S
Rodd, W. S., Brackley Point Road........ P E I
Roddick, John, Lyndhurst........ O
Roddy, James, Farran's Point........ O
Rodell, Alexander, Comox........ B C
Rodgerson, James, Shédiac Road, W. O........ N B
Roe, Frederick A., Woodbridge .... O
Roe, William, New Market .... O
Rogers, George, Lakefield .... Q
Rogers, H. C., Peterborough........ O
Rogers, James, Lower Coverdale, W. O........ N B
Rogers, Patrick, Romans Valley, W. O........ N S
Rogers, Thomas, Cedarville........ O
Rogers, Joseph C., Fermoy........ O
Rombach, Ferdinand, Freiburg .... O
Ronald, J. R., West Glassville, W. O .... N B
Roop, James P., Clementsport........ N S
Root, L., Pittsferry .... O
Rorke, Thomas J., Heathcote .... O
Ross, Alexander, Turtle Lake........ O
Ross, Benjamin, Innisfil .... Q
Ross, Alexander Gould........ Q
Ross, D. E., Ross' Corner, W. O........ N S
Ross, Seth W., Farndon .... Q
Ross, James G., Maryvale, W. O........ N S
Ross, James, Leith........ O
Ross, Thomas, Little Rideau........ O
Ross, Rev. D., Dundee Centre........ Q
Ross, M. G., Mill Brook, W. O........ N S
Ross, John, North-East Branch Margaree, W. O. N S
Ross, W., Dalhousie Settlement, W. O........ N S
Ross, Donald, Blanchard Road, W. O........ N S
Ross, H. S., Spring Hill Mines, W. O........ N S
Ross, Wm., North Section of Earltown, W. O..... N S
Ross, Arnold, North Bruce........ O
Ross, D., Kinross........ P E I
Rosser, B. H., Denfield........ O
Rothwell, A. T., Dwyer Hill .... O
Rouleau, Pierre D., Father Point........ Q
Rouse, Oliver C., Boston........ O
Rousseau, Godfroi, St. Monique........ Q
Rousseau, Onésime, St. Perpetue .... Q
Rousseau, Mdme. L. B., Chateau Richer........ Q
Routledge, Wm., Gardiner Mines, W. O........ N S
Rowe, R., Brookbury........ Q
Rowe, Peter, Murray........ O
Rowell, Elijah, Frelighsburg........ Q
Roy, Norbert, Wolfstown........ Q
Roy, Alex., Maitland .... N S
Roy, Mrs. Mary, Port Elgin........ O
Roy, dit Lauzon, Vital, St. Fabien .... Q
Roy, Moyse, St. Malo .... Q
Roy, C., Armagh .... Q
Roy, M. E., Settrington .... Q
Roy, Telesphore, Cap Chat........ Q
Roy, F. Y., St. George de Windsor........ Q
Royal, Jacques, St. Sulpice........ Q
Royer, L. V., St. Claire .... Q
Rudolf, Josiah, Upper La Have, W. O........ N S
Rudolph, Mrs. A. M., Lunenburgh. .... N S
Ruggles, B. H., Westport........ N B
Runnions, B. G., Northfield........ O
Rupert, J. P., Maple........ O
Rusco, J. M., Centreville, W. O........ N S
Rusk, Robert, Stockdale........ O
Russell, James, Duntroon .... O
Russell, James, Whitney, W. O........ N B
Russell, Wm., jun., Douglastown, W. O........ N B
Russell, Archibald, Baltimore........ O
Rutherford, John, Tweedside, W. O........ N B

List of Postmasters in Canada—Continued.

Rutherford, William, Millbank........................ O
Ruthven, Hugh, Ruthven........................ O
Ryan, J. S. Middle Coverdale, W. O........................ N B
Ryan, John, St. Andrews........................ P E I
Ryder, Mrs. S., Argyle, W. O........................ N S
Ryerse, Wm. H., Port Ryerse........................ O

Sabeans, Charleton, New Tusket, W. O........................ N S
Sadler, Robert, Byron........................ O
Sager, Noah, Pigeon Hill........................ Q
Salois, O., St. Bonaventure........................ Q
Salt, Daniel, Stottville........................ Q
Salter, W. M., Church Point, W. O........................ N B
Samson, T., Indian Cove........................ Q
Sanders, William, Exeter........................ O
Sanderson, Joseph, Stirton........................ O
Sanderson, Thomas, Kilmanagh........................ O
Sandford, Richard, Clementsville, W. O........................ N S
Sandford, Mrs. S., Summerville, W. O........................ N S
Sandford, T. S., Kennetcook, W. O........................ N S
Sargent, Alex., East Bolton........................ Q
Saucier, J. L., St. Sauveur de Québec........................ Q
Saucier, F., Macnider........................ Q
Saunders, T. W., Prince William, W. O........................ N B
Saunders, James, Paisley........................ O
Saunders, Robert, Murray River........................ P E I
Sauriol, Léon, St. Martin........................ Q
Savage, A. H., Savage's Mill........................ Q
Savage, George, Burnhamthorpe........................ O
Savard, Joseph, Cap a l'Aigle (sub)........................ Q
Savard, O., Point au Bouleau........................ Q
Saxby, Wm., Shefford Mountain........................ Q
Scarrow, William, Arva........................ O
Schnell, John, Cedar Grove........................ O
Scholefield, William S., Sawyerville........................ Q
Schmietendorf, J. T., Thompsonville........................ O
Schneider, John, Hampstead........................ O
Schneider, Charles, Carthage........................ O
Schooley, E. F., New Durham........................ O
Schooley, Louisa, Arkona........................ O
Schooley, Nelson, Oxford Centre........................ Q
Schooley, E. F., Newark........................ O
Schwedfeger, Lewis, Hoasic........................ O
Scidmore, R. P., Acacia........................ O
Scott, Benjamin, Mingan........................ Q
Scott, Hiram, North Gower........................ O
Scott, Robert, Onstic........................ O
Scott, James, Point Petre........................ O
Scott, George, Mimico........................ O
Scott, John, Stony Creek, W. O........................ N B
Scott, John, Thornton........................ O
Scott, Richard, Wallacebridge, W. O........................ N S
Scott, Mrs., Caistorville........................ O
Scott, Morris, St. Nicholas........................ Q
Scott, John, Seneca........................ O
Scott, Alexander, Forest........................ O

Scott, Luther, West Brome........................ Q
Scovil, S. S., Portland........................ O
Scribner, Elias, Mouth of Jemseg, W. O........................ N B
Seaman, Guilbert, Minadie, W. O........................ N S
Seaman, Amos, Lower Cove, W. O........................ N S
Seaman, A. J., Clifton, W. O........................ N B
Seaman, B. S., Wallace........................ N S
Sears, Mrs. M., Lochaber, W. O........................ N B
Seaton, Benjamin, Abercorn........................ Q
Secord, John, jun., Long Creek........................ N B
Secord, Josiah B., Varna........................ O
Secord, George, St. Ann's........................ M
Seely, Obadiah, Seely........................ O
Segeworth, William, Monck........................ O
Selby, Benjamin, Stanbridge Station........................ Q
Seller, John, North River........................ P E I
Sellis, Jacob, Salmon Hole, W. O........................ N S
Sensabaugh, D. H., Elcho........................ O
Setter, John, Park's Creek........................ M
Sewell, J. H., Port Lambton........................ O
Shackleton, John, Colpoy's Bay........................ O
Shanklin, S. J., Shanklin........................ N B
Shannon, Thomas, Picton........................ O
Sharon, Thomas, Frome........................ O
Sharp, Mrs. C. M., Sharp's Bridge, W. O........................ N S
Sharp, William, Allenford........................ O
Sharp, George J., Lower Hayneville, W. O........................ N B
Sharp, James, Ravenscliffe........................ O
Shatford, Samuel, Head of St. Margaret's Bay, W. O........................ N S
Shaver, E. N., Avonmore........................ O
Shaver, R. C., Port Hoover........................ O
Shaw, James, jun., Smith's Falls........................ O
Shaw, S. H., Hartland........................ N B
Shaw, Mrs. J. E., Mount Denison, W. O........................ N S
Shaw, William, Shawbridge........................ Q
Shaw, James, Shawville........................ Q
Shaw, John, jun., Lake Doré........................ O
Shaw, Daniel, East side of West Branch, East River of Pictou, W. O........................ N S
Shaw, John, Eastwood........................ O
Shaw, John, Nipissingan........................ O
Shaw, James, Brackley Point........................ P E I
Shawnwhite, James W., Terence Bay, W. O........................ N S
Sheals, John, Woodstock Road Station, W. O........................ N B
Shearer, George, Musselburg........................ O
Shears, J., Clifton House (sub)........................ O
Sheffer, E., Oldham, W. O........................ N S
Shehan, Terence, Salmon River, W. O........................ N S
Sheldon, E. J., South Bay, W. O........................ N B
Shell, Alfred, Burgoyne........................ O
Shell, Colin, Cashel........................ O
Shepphard, John W., Normandale........................
Shepphard, Joseph, Lansing........................ O
Shepherd, S., Uttoxeter........................ O
Shibley, J. A., Yarker........................ O

List of Postmasters in Canada—Continued.

Shier, Jonathan, Woodham........ .... **O**
Shirreff, Wm. Alexander, Fitzroy Harbor............**O**
Shirley, William, North Bristol ....**Q**
Shoebottom, J. G., Devizes ....**O**
Shoff, D., McGillivary ....**O**
Short, Richard, sen., Lang..................................**O**
Short, Albert M., New Jerusalem, W. O ....**N B**
Shufelt, J. D., Iron Hill......................................**Q**
Shuttleworth, Thomas, Tormore.......... ....**O**
Sibley, Asel Benjamin, St. Andrews, W. O...... ..**N S**
Sicart, J., Mongenais ....**Q**
Sidey, John, Bewdley..**O**
Silcox, Grant, Corral...................................... ....**O**
Sill, Robert, Jarvis ....**O**
Sills, G. B., Conway.................................... ....**O**
Silverthorne, Mahlon, Alloa ....**O**
Silvester, G. H., Ringwood ....**O**
Simard, Isaie, St. Joachim....................................**Q**
Simmons, A., Lake Beauport............... ....**Q**
Simonson, James, Jacksonville, W. O....... .....**N B**
Simpson, William, Park Head......... ....**O**
Simpson, Isaac, Mount Pleasant, W. O....... .....**N S**
Sithes, W. F., Arkwright. ....**O**
Simpson, Alexander, Titusville.......... ....**N B**
Simpson, Edward, Gagetown............ ....**N B**
Simpson, Alex., Black Heath ....**O**
Simpson, Archibald, Anderson, W. O..............**N B**
Simpson, James, Sherwood Spring.......................**O**
Sims, Wilson G., Plymouth, W. O............... ...**N S**
Sinclair, Donald, Goshen, W. O...........................**N S**
Sinclair, Edward, North West Bridge, W. O. ....**N B**
Sirois, Joseph O., Grand River..............................**Q**
Sisson, William H., Upper Woodstock, W. O.....**N B**
Skelly, Michael, Rawdon ....**Q**
Slaght, Israel, Townsend Centre.........................**O**
Slee, Thomas, Doon...**O**
Slipp, Edward W., Hampstead........... ....**N B**
Sloan, Thomas, Kilsyth ....**O**
Sloan, W. H., South Bay......................... ...**O**
Sloane, H., Churchill...**O**
Small, Janet, Arthur...**O**
Small, Peter, Ballycroy..**O**
Smallman, Wm., O'Leary's Road ....**P E I**
Smart, Robert W., Port Hope...............................**O**
Smart, James H., Kingsville..................................**O**
Smart, John, Plattsville ....**O**
Smart, Andrew, Culloden ....**O**
Smeath, George, Midhurst ....**O**
Smiley, Wm., Mount Loyal....... ....**Q**
Smith, Alexander, Lieury........................ ....**O**
Smith, Alfred, Lilloet ....**B C**
Smith, William, Rothsay ....**O**
Smith, Robert, Ayton ....**O**
Smith, John, New Sarem.................... ......**O**
Smith, John, Winchelsea....................... ....**O**
Smith, Mrs. N., Elm ....**O**
Smith, J. H., Green River ....**O**
Smith, Richard, Ingoldsby................ ....**O**
Smith, Charles, Johnville................................ ......**Q**
Smith, Wm., Kirkhill, W. O........ .... **N S**
Smith, D. A., McDonald's Point, W. O..... .....**N B**
Smith, Nathan, Hampton, W. O........... ....**N B**
Smith, T. H., Sky Glen, W. O.......................**N S**
Smith, S. D., Smithfield ....**O**
Smith, David, Smith Town ... .**N B**
Smith, James, McPherson's Ferry, W O..... ......**N S**
Smith, James M., Long Reach, W. O.............. **N B**
Smith, Josiah, Mortonville, W. O.................. **N S**
Smith, George, Desboro'....... ....**O**
Smith, Josiah, Cape Negro, W. O.....................**N S**
Smith, David, Bear Point, W. O........... ....**N B**
Smith, G. C., Avon..... ....**O**
Smith, William, Billing's Bridge ....**O**
Smith, William, Fallbrook............. ....**O**
Smith, John, Edgar...**O**
Smith, Thomas, Egremont............ ....**O**
Smith, Mrs. Mary, Big Mountain, W. O..... ......**N S**
Smith, James, Tilbury, East ....**O**
Smith, James E., Upper Keswick, W. O...........**N B**
Smith, Henry S., Oxford, W. O ....**N S**
Smith, David, Outram...... ... .**O**
Smith, John, East Glassville, W. O ....**N B**
Smith, E., Sambro', W. O................... ....**N S**
Smith, Charles, Elba............... ....**O**
Smith, Thomas, Dublin Shore, W. O...............**N S**
Smith, Henry, Plantagenet..................................**O**
Smith, C. A., Thorne Centre..................................**Q**
Smith, Samuel, Dunany ....**O**
Smith, Peter, St. Armand Station.. ....**Q**
Smith, Walton, Onslow..**Q**
Smith, Wm., Necum Tench, W. O...................**N S**
Smith, George, Milton, West...... ....**O**
Smith, T. G., Mount Forest...................... .. .. **O**
Smith, Mrs. Joshua, Port Hood Island, W. O...**N S**
Smith, David, Oshawa ....**O**
Smith, Abner, Rusagornis..................................**N B**
Smith, David, Coverdale, W. O........................**N B**
Smith, B., Demorestville......................................**O**
Smith, William, Cumberland Point, W O..........**N B**
Smith, Jesse, Edgeley ....**O**
Smith, George, Young's Cove, W. O..................**N B**
Smith, John S., Anderdon......................................**O**
Smith, John, Indian River ....**O**
Smith, Mrs. Mary M., Glenshee ....**O**
Smith, W. C., Gowanstown ....**O**
Smuck, R. W., Staffordville...................................**O**
Smyth, Robert, Ashgrove ....**O**
Smyth, Wm. J., East Magdala ....**Q**
Smyth, James, sen., Hebron, W. O...................**N B**
Snell, Robert, The Range, W. O........................**N B**
Snider, John F., Salford.......................................**O**
Snook, John M., Desert Lake................................**O**

List of Postmasters in Canada—Continued.

... . **O**
. ... **O**
lliamsburg......... **O**
. O......... **N B**
.... **Q**
ille......... **O**
.... **O**
.... **Q**
.... **O**
lls......... **Q**
.... **O**
.... **O**
ve, W. O......... **N B**
e......... **O**
.... **O**
ner......... **O**
s Joachims......... **Q**
.... **O**
n Road......... **P E I**
Station......... **N S**
.... **O**
.... **O**
W. O......... **N S**
e......... **N S**
nsville......... **O**
.... **O**
.... **O**
nent, W. O......... **N B**
.... **Q**
.... **O**
V. O......... **N S**
yal......... **Q**
ner......... **Q**
.... **O**
.... **O**
.... **O**
oucester......... **O**
.... **O**
k Road, W. O......... **N B**
t......... **O**
.... **O**
V. O......... **N B**
ge, W. O......... **N S**
well Cape......... **N B**
.... **O**
.... **O**
W. O......... **N S**
dge, W. O......... **N B**
.... **N S**
ie, W. O......... **N S**
n......... **O**
irk......... **O**
.... **O**
. ... **N B**
V. O......... **N B**

Stevens, John, Rose Vale, W. O. .... **N B**
Stevens, J. M., Harvey .... **N B**
Stevens, Simon, Trenholm......... **Q**
Stevens, William, Bedford Basin, W. O......... **N S**
Stevens, Gardner, Waterloo, East......... **Q**
Stevens, James, Mount Elgin .... **O**
Stevens, George C., Mast Town, W. O. .... **N S**
Stevens, J. C., Trout Brook .... **Q**
Steeves, R. E., Hillsborough .... **N B**
Steeves, Millidge, Bridgedale, W. O......... **N B**
Sterratt, Melessa, Dalhousie, East, W. O. .... **N S**
Stewart, Peter, Point la Nim, W. O......... **N B**
Stewart, Samuel F., Harrowsmith......... **O**
Stewart, James, Little Harbor, W. O. .... **N S**
Stewart, James, Melrose......... **N S**
Stewart Alexander, West side of Lochaber, W. O.... **N S**
Stewart, Hugh, Willowgrove .... **O**
Stewart, Donald, River Louison, W. O......... **N B**
Stewart, R. H., Woodlands......... **O**
Stewart, Charles, Clarenceville......... **Q**
Stewart, Robert, Black River .... **N B**
Stewart, David, Roslin, W. O. .... **N S**
Stewart, Angus, West Point......... **P E I**
Stewart, Charles, Hamilton .... **P E I**
Stewart, James, Hall's Bridge .... **O**
Stewart, William, Glen Stewart......... **O**
Still, Mrs. Mary, Raglan .... **O**
Stirling, Alexander, White Lake .... **O**
Stirton, H. A., Sault au Cochon .... **Q**
St. Laurent, A. Amable, St. Flavie .... **Q**
Stockdale, Peter Milligan, Stockdale .... **O**
Stockwell, J. W., Danville......... **Q**
Stoddart, John, Stoddarts, W. O......... **N S**
Stoddart, Thos., Clam Harbor, W. O......... **N S**
Stocks, John J., Sharon......... **O**
Stokes, William, King Creek......... **O**
Stone, A. M., North Stanbridge .... **Q**
Stone, Giles, Haultain......... **O**
Stone, John, Maquapit Lake, W. O. .... **N B**
Stonehouse, George, Armadale .... **O**
Stoneness, James, Perth Road .... **O**
Stoutenburg, Martin, Ravenna......... **O**
Strachan, Kenneth, Framboise, W. O......... **N S**
Strange, Edwin L., Causapscal .... **Q**
Stratford, John E., Hubbard's Cove, W. O. .... **N S**
Striker, Jonathan, Bloomfield .... **O**
Stripp, F. H., Buckhorn .... **O**
Stroh, John, St. Clements .... **O**
Stronach, George, Stronach Mountain......... **N S**
Strong, J. B., Somerset .... **P E I**
Strong, Samuel, Moisic .... **Q**
Strum, Joseph, Martin's River, W. O......... **N S**
Struthers, R. C., Louisville .... **N S**
Struthers, P., Carleton Place......... **O**
Stuart, James, Epping......... **O**
.rt, William, Cambria .... **Q**

List of Postmasters in Canada—Continued.

Stymast, John, Stymast Settlement, W. O.........N B
Styres, James, Oshweken ....O
Suffern, Anthony, Raymond ....O
Sullivan, Patrick, Merlin ....O
Sullivan, J. O., Fredericton Road, W. O. ....N B
Sullivan, Daniel, Malcolm ....O
Sullivan, T., Portuguese Cove, W. O.............N S
Sullivan, John, Corinth ....O
Surtees, George, Beachburg ....O
Sutherland, D., Orwell ....O
Sutherland, A., Plainfield, W. O. ....N S
Sutherland, A. W., East River, St. Mary's, W.O....N S
Sweet, S., North Sutton ....Q
Sweet, J. L., Newport Station ....N S
Sweet, Stubbard, Billtown, W. O. ....N S
Sweetman, Patrick, Port Daniel ....Q
Sweetman, J. McD., High Bluff ....M
Switzer, H. M., Palermo ....O
Sweazie, Hamilton, Elfrida ....O
Sykes, William, Cobourg ....O
Symon, William, Ospringe ....O
Symons, Joseph, Little Tracadie, W. O...........N S
Syphers, Jacob, Syphers' Cove, W. O. ....N B
St. Amour, Cyriac, St. Francois de Sales ....Q
St. Antoine, Louis, St. Justin ....Q
St. Denis, Ernest A., Point Fortune ....Q
St. Germain, F. H., Maddington ....Q
St. John, Andrew, Victoria Corners ....O
St. Julien, Clothilde, Papineauville ....Q
St. Louis, C., Sandwich ....O
St. Pierre, Richard, Becancour Station ....Q
St. Pierre, Damase, St. Fortunat ....Q

Taggart, James, Wallace ....O
Tait, David, Poplar Point ....M
Tait, George, West Shefford ....Q
Tait, W. M., Mille Roches ....O
Tait, John R., L'Amable ....O
Tait, James, Duart ....O
Tait, Valantine B., New Wéstminster ....B C
Tait, John, Park's Creek ....M
Talbot, Robert, Cannington ....O
Tarlington, John, Lakehurst ....O
Tanguay, Pierre, St. Magloire ....Q
Tapp, Thomas, Barachois de Malbay ....Q

Taylor, J., North River, W. O. ....N B
Taylor, A. L., Pike River ....Q
Taylor, Edward, Sandford ....O
Taylor, John, St. Polycarpe ....Q
Taylor, Emerson, Credit ....O
Taylor, Alexander, Dromore ....O
Taylor, John F., Adderly ....Q
Taylor, John, Bothwell ....O
Taylor, W. H., Alport ....O
Taylor, Charles, Taylor Village, W. O. ....N B
Taylor, George, Burtch ....O
Taylor, ——, Kincardine, W. O. ....N B
Taylor, Jonas, Rockland ....N B
Taylor, George, sen., Scarboro' Junction ....O
Teakles, William, Sussex Portage, W. O. ....N B
Teefy, Matthew, Richmond Hill ....O
Teel, Alkanah, Broad Cove, Lunenburg, W.O.......N S
Teeple, S. W., Kingsmill ....O
Tennant, W., jun., Caintown ....O
Terriff, Peter, Belmore ....O
Terry, D., Hartman ....O
Teskey, John, Vroomanton ....O
Teskey, Albert, Appleton ....O
Teskey, Daniel, Lisburn ....O
Têtu, Nazaire, Rivière Trois-Pistoles ....Q
Theriault, Jacques, St. Eloi ....Q
Thérien, Ferdinand, St. Wenceslas ....Q
Thibaudeau, F. X., Grondines ....Q
Thibeault, J. B., St. Francois Xavier ....M
Thirkell, Joseph, Ingersoll ....O
Thivierge, Dominique, Cap Rouge ....Q
Thom, Archibald, Egbert ....O
Thomas, B., Hartford ....O
Thomas, Charles, Cogmagun River, W. O...........N S
Thomas, Edward, St. Peters ....M
Thompson, Thomas, Port Bruce ....O
Thompson, Daniel, Gore, W. O. ....N S
Thompson, John, Humberston ....O
Thompson, Evan, Nine-Mile River, W. O...........N S
Thompson, James B., Waterdown ....O
Thompson, Thomas, Howe Island ....O
Thompson, R., Smithville ....O
Thompson, William, St. Paul's, W. O. ....N S
Thompson, John, Moneymore ....O
Thompson, George, Darnley ....P E I

List of Postmasters in Canada—Continued.

Thomson, Joseph, Marlow .... Q
Thomson, Robert, Cumminsville .... O
Thomson, T., Buttonville .... O
Thomson, James M., Byng .... O
Thomson, R. R., Shelburne .... N S
Thomson, John, Woodford .... O
Thomson, James, English Corner, W. O .... N S
Thomson, William, Arundel .... Q
Thorne, Butler, Thorne Town, W. O .... N B
Thornton, J. M., Dundas .... O
Thornton, R. A., Sturgeon .... P E I
Thorp, Sidney R., Hall's Harbour .... N S
Thouin, Damase, Kilkenny .... Q
Throop, Rufus S., Charleville .... O
Thurber, S. B., Irvine .... Q
Tibbits, R. W. S., Wellerup, W. O .... N B
Tilley, William, Olinville, W. O .... N B
Tilley, Leveret S., Lake George, W. O .... N B
Tillson, E. D., Tilsonburg .... O
Tilly, William, Cape Cove .... Q
Tilton, C. F., Fairville .... N B
Tingley, S. W., Dorchester .... N B
Tinline, James, Eversley .... O
Timmerman, P. S., Odessa .... O
Titemore, Abram, St. Armand Centre .... O
Titus, Benjamin, Allisonville .... O
Tobey, John, Tara .... O
Tobin, John J., Milledgeville .... N B
Tobin, Richard, Upper St. Francis, W. O .... N B
Tobin, M. A., Berwick .... O
Tobin, Charles, Sydney Forks, W. O .... N S
Todd, Henry, Narrows .... N B
Tom, John C., Welcome .... O
Tomalty, William, Edina .... Q
Tomkins, W. B., Upper Peel, W. O .... N B
Tompkins, Thomas, Emerald, W. O .... N S
Tompkins, Aaron, Northampton, W. O .... N B
Tomlinson, W., Tay Settlement, W. O .... N B
Tomlinson, William, Marsh Hill .... O
Toupin, C., Cap Magdeleine .... Q
Touzel, P., Sheldrake .... Q
Townsend, J., Traveller's Rest .... P E I
Toyne, John, Oakland .... O
Tracy, S. W., Granboro .... Q
Trafton, John, Foster's Cove, W. O .... N B
Trainer, Patrick, Lot 30 .... P E I
Troop, W. B., Granville Centre, W. O .... N S
Troop, W. H., Paradise Lane, W. O .... N S
Troop, Alfred, Granville Ferry .... N S
Trott, Thomas, Gaspereaux Station .... N B
Trottier, A. G., St. Ubalde .... Q
Trottier, Jane, Shoolbred .... Q
Trudeau, Félix M., St. Zènon .... Q
Trudeau, Joseph G., St. Bernard (Sud) .... Q
Trudel, P. O., St. Tite .... Q
Trueman, John, Elmbank .... O
Trueman, H., Searletown .... P E I
Trumm, W. H., Bismarck .... O
Tubby, Samuel, Fingal .... O
Tubman, Thomas, Munster .... O
Tuck, J. F., Knowlton Landing .... Q
Tucker, Joseph L., Orono .... O
Tucker, R., Allenburg .... O
Tuplin Reuben, Margate .... P E I
Tupling, Christopher, Alvanley .... O
Tupper, J. H., Lower Line, Queensbury, W. O .... N B
Tupper, R. La T., Bobcaygeon .... O
Turcot, Joseph, North Georgetown .... Q
Turcotte, F. X., St. Jean d'Orléans .... Q
Turcotte, Cyrille, Russelltown .... Q
Turnbull, John, Glanworth .... O
Turner, Donald, West Magdala .... O
Turner, Edward T., Penville .... O
Turner, S. E., Tottenham .... O
Tuttle, J. E., Dundela .... O
Tuzo, J. E., Pearcé .... Q
Tuzo, John D., Magdalen Islands .... Q
Tyre, Robert, St. Regis .... Q
Tyrell, L. R., Luton .... O
Tyrrell, Thos. B., Cookshire .... Q

Umphrey, J., Big Cove, W. O .... N B
Upper, Jacob, Rockford .... O
Urquhart, William, Dunvegan .... O
Urquhart, Nathaniel, Urquaharts, W. O .... N B
Urquhart, Wm., Rear Lands, Sporting Mountain W. O .... N S

Vachon, Edward, Riviere la Madeleine .... Q
Vachon, Léandre, St. Louis de Gonzague .... Q
Vail, Solomon, Magaguadavic, W. O .... N B

List of Postmasters in Canada—Continued.

Vanvlack, John, Vanvlack .... O
Van Vliet, T., Lacolle........ Q
Vassal, Henry, Pierreville Mills........ Q
Vatour, Jean C., Richibucto........ N B
Vaughan, Joseph, Vaughan's, W. O........ N S
Veit, S. A., Douglastown .... Q
Venton, Anderson, Mill Haven........ O
Vigneault, O., Kildare .... Q
Vigneau, Joseph, St. Sylvester, East........ Q
Vincent dit Maheux, F., St. Flore .... Q
Vincent, J. G., Lorette........ Q
Vincent, William, Lot 10 .... P E I
Violette, F., Grand River, W. O .... N B
Vipond, Albert, Hudson. .... Q
Voady, Thomas, jun., Chatham........ N B

Waddell, James, Edgeworth........ O
Waddell, Robert, South Monaghan........ O
Wagner, Alex. H., Windsor........ O
Wagstaff, William E., North Ridge........ O
Wait, Whitney, Bayview .... O
Wait, Helen, Bathurst........ N B
Wakem, Thomas, Greenfield, W. O........ N B
Waldo, Samuel, Teeswater........ O
Wales, Robert A., East Durham........ Q
Walford, W. M., Locksley........ O
Walker, Edward, Bellrock........ O
Walker, Christopher, Duncrief .... O
Walker, Charles, Coal Branch, W. O .... N B
Walker, David, Cavan........ O
Walker, James, Caledonia........ P E I
Walker, R., jun., Diamond........ O
Walker, D. J., Inverary .... O
Walker, Samuel, Deerhurst .... O
Walker, Thomas, Parkhurst........ Q
Wall, Robert, Bartibog, W. O........ N B
Wallace, Hugh, Londesborough .... O
Wallace, M., West Gore, W. O........ N S
Wallace, Joseph, Shepody Road, W. O........ N B
Wallace. John, Mount Hurst .... O
Wallace, William, Gardner's Creek, W. O........ N B
Wallace, Thomas, Roxham .... Q
Wallace, W. J., Canaan........ N S
Wallace, William, Lockton .... O
Wallace, Joseph, Smirleville........ O
Walsh, Mrs. Mary, Railton .... O
Walsh, Patrick, Erinsville .... O
Walsh, R. N., Ormstown .... Q
Walter, F., Bamberg .... O
Walter, Thomas P., Walter's Falls........ O
Walton, Jacob, Kettleby........ O
Walton, Henry, Upper Greenwich .... N B
Wanless, James, Wanstead .... O
Wannacott, G. D., Copenhagen........ O
Wannemake, N. P., Hillsdale........ N B
Ward Rufus, Rockport .... N B

Ward, Thomas, Woodhill........ O
Ward, W. A., Dawn Mills........ O
Wardell, Isaac S., Fawkham........ O
Warner, Sydney, Wilton .... O
Warner, S. B., St. Ephrem d'Upton........ Q
Warner, Charles, Colebrook........ O
Warnock, John, Castleford........ O
Warrell, T., Barnesville .... N B
Warren, Joseph, Harper........ O
Warren, Robert, Niagara .... O
Warren, John, Deerdock........ O
Wartman, David, Selby........ O
Wason, Isaac, Partridge Island, W. O .... N S
Wasson, John, Lower Prince William, W. O........ N B
Watson, Alex. L., Undine, W. O........ N B
Watson, C. P., Dresden .... O
Watson, J. S. J., Rockingham........ O
Watson, John, Watson Settlement, W. O........ N B
Watson, A. R., Forks Baddeck, W. O........ N S
Watson, Henry, Clearville .... O
Watson, Wm., Arkell........ O
Watson, J. J., Adolphustown........ O
Watson, Arch., Glenwood, W.O........ N S
Watt, William, West Lynne .... M
Waugh, William, Gulf Shore, W. O .... N S
Waugh, James, R. L., Nilestown .... O
Way, W. H., Mountain View........ O
Way, Charles, Gooderham .... O
Weaver, Michael, Weaver, W. O........ N S
Webb, James, Stroud........ O
Webber, William, Torbay, W. O........ N S
Webber, David, East Jeddore, W. O........ N S
Webster, M., Sheldon .... O
Webster, Marion, South McLellan's Mountain. W. O........ N S
Webster, Thomas, Newborough .... O
Webster, P. B., Jasper .... O
Weir, Allan, Churchville, W. O........ N S
Weldon, R. B. C., Boundary Creek, W. O .... N B
Wellard, William, Taunton .... O
Wells, William, Rickman's Corners .... O
Wells, Leonard, Farnboro' .... Q
Welch, John T., Tyrone. .... O
Welton, Jonathan, Northfield, W. O........ N B
Wensley, Charles, Eagle Lake........ O
West, David, Rowanton .... Q
West, William, Medford, W. O........ N S
West, Elijah C., Middle Pereaux, W. O........ N S
Westervelt, James, Claude........ O
Wetmore, Susannah, Cromwell, W. O........ N B
Whalan, Peter, Cap des Rosiers .... Q
Wheelock, John, Kingston Village, W. O........ N S
Wheeler, George, Uxbridge .... O
Wheeler, Mrs. Barbara, Runnymede .... O
Wheeler, Edward, Stouffville........ Q
Whelan, John H., Westport .... O

List of Postmasters in Canada—Continued.

Whelan, John, Cove Head Road..........P E I
Wheldon, A. R., Shediac..........N B
White, Oliver Longwood Station..........N B
White, W. H., Springfield..........N B
White, William H., Cambridge, W. O..........N B
White, Thomas, Klineburg..........O
White, John, jun., Hopetown..........O
White, S. V., White's Cove..........N B
White, Nelson, Patterson's Settlement, W. O....N B
White, Humphrey, Anderson..........O
White, W. L., Lemonville..........O
White, L. M., Scovil's Mills, W. O..........N B
White, Isaac, South Range, W. O..........N S
Whitehead, Thomas, Dunkeld..........O
Whitehead, W., Dumfries, W. O..........N B
Whitfield, A. M., Holbrook..........O
Whitfield, Joseph, Bridgewater..........N S
Whiting, R. E., Muncey..........O
Whiting, George, Erroll..........O
Whitman, James M., Manchester, W. O..........N S
Whitney, Mrs. Eliza, Pickering..........O
Whitesides, James, Delhi..........O
Whittaker, J., S., North Williamsburg..........O
Widderfield, Samuel, Siloam..........O
Widman, John L., St. Jacob's..........O
Widman, Richard, Lonsdale..........O
Wightman, Wm., Georgetown..........P E I
Wilde, Thomas E., Havelock..........O
Wilkie, James, Amberley..........O
Wilkie, George, Sugar Loaf, W. O..........N S
Wilkin, John, Lemesurier..........Q
Wiley, Joseph, Fenwick, W. O..........N B
Wilkinson, Thomas, Renton Station..........O
Will, Charles, Pinedale..........O
Willet, W. F., Tupperville, W. O..........N S
Wilton, Samuel, New Sarum..........O
Williams, Charles, Glen Williams..........O
Williams, Allen, Brinkworth..........O
Williams, Mrs. L., South East Passage, W. O.....N S
Williams, John, Frost Village..........Q
Williams, Ira, Croydon..........O
Williams, Alfred, Williamsford Station..........O
Williams, Alex., Holland Landing..........O
Williamson, J. C., Ballyduff..........O
Williamson, George, Kingsbury..........Q
Williamson, Thomas, Foley..........O
Williger, James, Blackrock, W. O..........N S
Williscroft, George, Williscroft..........O
Williston, Alexander, Baie du Vin, W. O..........N B
Wilson, G. C., Atherton..........O
Wilson, George, Teston..........O
Wilson, Amos, Steeve's Mountain, W. O..........N B
Wilson, Robert, Relessey..........O
Wilson, Seth, Macville..........O
Wilson, W. H., Bannockburn..........O
Wilson, William, Cumberland..........O
Wilson, Mary, Little Shippigan, W. O..........N B
Wilson, Thomas, Clarence..........O
Wilson, James, Vicars..........Q
Wilson, David, Waterford..........O
Wilson, John, Antrim..........O
Wilson, John, Mono Centre..........O
Wilson, John, Canfield..........O
Wilson, James, Buckingham..........Q
Wilson, James, sen., Boulter..........O
Wilson, John, Cap de Moselle Creek, W. O..........N B
Wilson, John, Russeldale..........O
Wilson, Edward, Sinclairville..........O
Winger, Peter, Elmira..........O
Winkler, D., Neustadt..........O
Winslow, John C., Woodstock..........N B
Winyard, Robert J., Selkirk..........O
Wirth, John, Hope..........B C
Wissler, John R., Salem..........O
Wolfe, John, jun., Mount Wolfe..........O
Wolf, James, Falmouth, W. O..........N S
Wolff, Charles S., Valcartier..........Q
Wood, Thomas, Woodside..........Q
Wood, Richard, Port Dalhousie..........O
Wood, W. S., De Cewsville..........O
Woodbury, E., Courtright..........O
Woodruff, W. F., Drummondville, West..........O
Wood, William, Dixon's Corners..........O
Woodbury, Egbert S., Spa Springs, W. O..........N S
Woodruff, W. W., Clifton..........O
Woods, F., Welsford..........N B
Woods, J. R., Aylmer, East..........Q
Woodward, Richard, Melbourne Ridge..........Q
Woodworth, R. W., Central Chebogue, W. O.....N S
Woodworth, William, Centreville, W. O..........N B
Wooster, Turner, Grand Harbor, W. O..........N B
Wootton, Henry, Victoria..........B C
Worden, James G., Tennant's Cove, W. O..........N B
Worden, William, Kars, W. O..........N B
Workman, Aaron, Hereford..........Q
Wormesley, Charles, Nanaimo..........B C
Worrell, Thomas, Barnesville, W. O..........N B
Worth, William, Crapaud..........P E I
Wortley, W. C., Drayton..........O
Wright, George, Wareham..........O
Wright, George, Stella..........O
Wright, H. M., Napanee Mills..........O
Wright, G. R., Jackson..........O
Wright, James, Hopewell, W. O..........N B
Wright, David A., Thornbrook, W. O..........N B
Wright, Major, Bedeque..........P E I
Wry, Rufus C., Jolicure, W. O..........N B
Wurtele, C. E., Windsor Mills..........Q
Wycott, William, Dog Creek..........B C
Wylie, James H., jun., Almonte..........O
Wylie, Robert, Ayr..........O
Wylie, Robert, Palgrave..........O
Wyman, L. W., Waterville..........Q

List of Postmasters in Canada—Continued.

Wynn, James, Queenston .... O

Yeo, Thomas, South Wiltshire.................. P E I
Yeomans, R. P., Newcastle Bridge, W. O. ......N B
Young, James, Nashwaak, W. O. .... N B
Young, Myles, Lakelet .... O
Young, William, Head of St. Mary's Bay, W.O.....N S
Young, Joseph, Birr...O
Young, Patrick, Young's Point..............................O
Young, John A., Florence ....O
Young, James, Doncaster ....O
Young, Andrew, Shigawake ....Q
Young, David, Stanhope..Q
Young, John B., Pennfield Ridge, W. O. ....N B
Younghusband, Henry, Dunrobin ....O
Youngs, Edward, Youngsville ....O

Zavitz, H. B., Sherkston ....O
Zerxa, Mrs. Margaret, Mouth of Keswick, W.O...N S
Zimmerman, H., Rainham Centre .... O
Zinkann, John, Lisbon ....O
Zinger, William, Ambleside ....O
Zoeger, John, Wellesley. ....O

TABLES

OF

RATES OF POSTAGE

IN CANADA.

TABLES

OF

RATES OF POSTAGE

IN CANADA,

AND ALSO BETWEEN

CANADA AND THE UNITED KINGDOM, BRITISH COLONIES, AND FOREIGN COUNTRIES.

TABLE No. 1.

RATES OF POSTAGE on letters within the Dominion of Canada, (including the Provinces of Ontario, Quebec, New Brunswick, Nova Scotia, Manitoba, British Columbia, and Prince Edward Island.)

	POSTED PREPAID.	POSTED UNPAID.
On a letter weighing not more than ½ an oz.	3 Cents.	5 Cents.
On a letter weighing more than ½ an oz., but not more than 1 oz.	6 "	10 "
On a letter weighing more than 1 oz., but not more than 1½ oz.	9 "	15 "
On a letter weighing more than 1½ oz., but not more than 2 oz.	12 "	20 "
On a letter weighing more than 2 oz., but not more than 2½ oz.	15 "	25 "

and so on, 3 cents or 5 cents (according as the letter is paid or unpaid), being charged for every additional ½ oz., or fraction of a ½ oz.

Letters addressed as above which are only partially prepaid, are to be rated as if *wholly* unpaid, credit being given, however, for the amount prepaid thereon. Thus, if a letter weighing more than ½ an oz., but less than 1 oz., and liable to two rates (equal to 10 cents) is prepaid only 3 cents, it is subject to a further charge of 7 cents.

Postage to French Colonies of St. Pierre and Miquelon, same as above, subject to an additional charge on delivery.

The charge on local or drop letters is one cent for each letter, which must be prepaid by stamp. Unpaid drop letters should be put under cover to the Postmaster General by first mail after receipt.

The charge for the Registration of a letter is 2 cents, to be prepaid by stamp.

CANADA AND NEWFOUNDLAND.

Letters for Newfoundland are charged at the rate of 6 cents per half ounce, and must in all cases be *prepaid*.

The Registration fee to Newfoundland is the same as to places within the Dominion, viz., 2 cents.

CANADA AND THE UNITED STATES.

	POSTED PREPAID.	POSTED UNPAID.
On a letter weighing not more than ½ an ounce	6 Cents.	10 Cents.
On a letter weighing more than ½ an oz., but not more than 1 oz.	12 "	20 "
On a letter weighing more than 1 oz., but not more than 1½ oz.	18 "	30 "
On a letter weighing more than 1½ oz., but not more than 2 oz.	24 "	40 "
On a letter weighing more than 2 oz., but not more than 2½ oz.	30 "	50 "

and so on, 6 cents or 10 cents (according as the letter is paid or unpaid) being charged for every additional ½ oz., or fraction of a ½ oz.

Letters addressed as above which are only partially prepaid, are to be rated as if *wholly* unpaid.

TABLE No. 2.

BRITISH AND FOREIGN POSTAGE TABLE.

[*VIA ENGLAND.*]

BLE shewing the amount of Postage, to be collected in the Dominion of Canada, upon Letters, Newspapers, and Book Packets, forwarded by Canadian Mail Steamers, to the United Kingdom, and through the United Kingdom to the undermentioned Colonies and Foreign Countries.

ı. 1.—In all cases the postage must be prepaid. Letters for the United Kingdom, if posted unpaid, or insufficiently prepaid, will be forwarded,—but they will be charged on delivery with the amount of deficient postage, and a fine of threepence sterling each letter.

2.—Letters may be registered to all places, except those the names of which are followed by the letters *n r*, indicating that no registration can be effected.

3.—The Registration Fee on letters addressed to the United Kingdom is 8 cents each. In all other cases the Registration Fee is 16 cents from Canada to the place of destination, except to Egypt (Alexandria and Suez excepted) the registration fees to which are 30 cents each letter, and to places marked *a*, in which cases a registration fee of 8 cents each letter, and in addition, double the ordinary rates of postage, as given in this table, must be collected. (See note at foot of Table marked A.)

4.—No Book Packet addressed to Portugal, Madeira, the Azores, or Cape de Verds, must exceed 1 lb. in weight; to Russia and Poland no such packet must exceed 8 oz. A Packet of Patterns for Germany or Belgium, or any Country, *via* Belgium, must not exceed 8 oz. A Book Packet for Greece must not exceed 3 lbs. in weight nor must it exceed 2 feet in length by 1 foot in width or depth.

5.—Upon Letters, and Book Packets, forwarded through the United States, the following additional rates must be collected, viz., 2 cents per ½ oz. on Letters, and 2 cents per 4 oz. on Book Packets.

6.—An additional postage of 6 cents per half ounce must be collected on Letters, 2 cents each on Newspapers, and 6 cents per 4 ounces on Book Packets and Patterns for places marked thus * when addressed to be sent *via* Brindisi.

7.—On Book Packets for the United Kingdom, not exceeding one ounce in weight, the postage is 2 cents. On Book Packets, weighing more than one ounce, the progressive rates of postage will be found in the table below.

COUNTRIES, &c.	For a Letter.					For each Newspaper.	For Book Packets and Patterns.					
	Not exceeding ¼ oz.	Above ¼ oz. and not exceeding ½ oz.	Above ½ oz. and not exceeding ¾ oz.	For every additional ¼ oz.	For every additional ½ oz.		Not exceeding 2 oz.	2 ozs. to 4 ozs.	4 ozs. to 8 ozs.	8 ozs. to 12 ozs.	12 ozs. to 1 lb.	For every additional 4 ozs.
	$ cts.	$ cts.	$ cts.	$ cts.	$ cts.		$ cts.	$ cts.	$ cts.	$ cts.	$ cts.	$ cts.
en	0 22	0 22	0 44	—	0 22	6 cents.	0 10	0 12	0 24	0 36	0 48	0 12
ca, West Coast of (*n r*)	0 16	0 16	0 32	—	0 16	4 cents.	0 08	0 10	0 20	0 30	0 40	0 10
ɩandria { *via* Brindisi	0 20	0 20	0 40	—	0 20	6 cents.	0 14	0 16	0 30	0 46	0 60	0 16
ɩandria { *via* Southampton	0 16	0 16	0 32	—	0 16	4 cents.	0 08	0 10	0 20	0 30	0 40	0 10
geria	0 10	0 16	0 26	0 06	0 04	Book Rate.	0 06	0 12	0 24	0 36	0 48	0 12
ension (*n r*)	0 28	0 28	0 56	—	0 28	4 cents.	0 08	0 10	0 20	0 30	0 40	0 10
stralia, South	0 16	0 16	0 32		0 16	6 cents.	0 10	0 12	0 24	0 36	0 48	0 12
stralia, Western	0 16	0 16	0 32	—	0 16	6 cents.	0 10	0 12	0 24	0 36	0 48	0 12

:tria	0 10	0 10	0 20	—	0 10	Book rate.	0 08	0 16	0 32	0 48	0 64	0 16
:res	0 16	0 28	0 44	0 12	0 04	do	0 06	0 12	0 24	0 36	0 48	*see mem* 4
len	0 10	0 10	0 20	—	0 10	do	0 08	0 16	0 32	0 48	0 64	0 16
:aria	0 10	0 10	0 20	—	0 10	do	0 08	0 16	0 32	0 48	0 64	0 16
gium	0 10	0 10	0 20	—	0 10	do	0 06	0 12	0 24	0 36	0 48	0 12
rout	0 24	0 24	0 48		0 24	12 cents.	0 14	0 16	0 32	0 48	0 64	0 16
ivia (*n r*)	0 40	0 40	0 80	—	0 40	6 cents.	0 10	0 12	0 24	0 36	0 48	0 12
rneo (*n r*)	0 28	0 28	0 56	—	0 28	6 cents.	0 10	0 12	0 24	0 36	0 48	0 12
urbon	0 24	0 24	0 48	—	0 24	8 cents.	0 14	0 16	0 32	0 48	0 64	0 16
zil (*n r*)	0 28	0 28	0 56	-	0 28	4 cents.	0 08	0 10	0 20	0 30	0 40	0 10
men	0 10	0 10	0 20	—	0 10	Book rate.	0 08	0 16	0 32	0 48	0 64	0 16
nswick	0 10	0 10	0 20	—	0 10	do	0 08	0 16	0 32	0 48	0 64	0 16
nos Ayres (*n r*)	0 28	0 28	0 56	—	0 28	4 cents.	0 08	0 10	0 20	0 30	0 40	0 10
ary Islands	0 16	0 28	0 44	0 12	0 04	Book rate.	0 08	0 16	0 32	0 48	0 64	0 16
e de Verds	0 16	0 16	0 32	—	0 16	do	0 06	0 12	0 24	0 36	0 48	*see mem* 4
e of Good Hope	0 28	0 28	0 56	—	0 28	4 cents.	0 08	0 10	0 20	0 30	0 40	0 10
ylon	0 22	0 22	0 44	—	0 22	6 cents.	0 10	0 12	0 24	0 36	0 48	0 12
li (*n r*)	0 40	0 40	0 80	—	0 40	6 cents.	0 10	0 12	0 24	0 36	0 48	0 12
ina—(except Hong Kong)—(*n r*)	0 28	0 28	0 56	—	0 28	6 cents.	0 10	0 12	0 24	0 36	0 48	0 12
stantinople	0 12	0 12	0 24	—	0 12	Book rate.	0 08	0 16	0 32	0 48	0 64	0 16
ta Rica (*n r*)	0 28	0 28	0 56	—	0 28	4 cents.	0 08	0 10	0 20	0 30	0 40	0 10
a (*n r*)	0 28	0 28	0 56		0 28	4 cents.	0 08	0 10	0 20	0 30	0 40	0 10
rdanelles	0 16	0 28	0 44	0 12	0 04	Book rate.	0 06	0 12	0 24	0 36	0 48	0 12
mark	0 10	0 10	0 20	—	0 10	do	0 08	0 16	0 32	0 48	0 64	0 16
cuador (*n r*)	0 40	0 40	0 80	—	0 40	6 cents.	0 10	0 12	0 24	0 36	0 48	0 12
Egypt—Alexandria and Suez *via* Brindisi	0 24	0 24	0 48		0 24	8 cents.	0 14	0 16	0 32	0 48	0 64	0 16
Egypt—Cairo and all places except above, *via* Southampton	0 20	0 20	0 40	—	0 20	6 cents.	0 10	0 12	0 24	0 36	0 48	0 12
England	0 06	0 06	0 12	—	0 06	2 cents.	0 04	0 06	0 12	0 18	0 24	0 06
Falkland Islands	0 16	0 16	0 32	—	0 16	4 cents.	0 08	0 10	0 20	0 30	0 40	0 10
Fernando Po (*n r*)	0 16	0 16	0 32	—	0 16	4 cents.	0 08	0 10	0 20	0 30	0 40	0 10
France	0 10	0 16	0 26	0 06	0 04	Book rate.	0 04	0 08	0 16	0 24	0 32	0 08
Frankfort	0 10	0 10	0 20	—	0 10	do	0 08	0 16	0 32	0 48	0 64	0 16
Galatz	0 16	0 28	0 44	0 12	0 04	do	0 06	0 12	0 24	0 36	0 48	0 12
Galliopoli (*n r*)	0 16	0 28	0 44	0 12	0 04	do	0 06	0 12	0 24	0 36	0 48	0 12
Gambia	0 16	0 16	0 32	—	0 16	4 cents.	0 08	0 10	0 20	0 30	0 40	0 10
Gibraltar	0 16	0 16	0 32	—	0 16	4 cents.	0 08	0 10	0 20	0 30	0 40	0 10
Gold Coast	0 16	0 16	0 32	—	0 16	4 cents.	0 08	0 10	0 20	0 30	0 40	0 10
Greece	0 20	0 20	0 40	—	0 20	Book rate.	0 08	0 16	0 32	0 48	0 64	0 16
Grey Town (*n r*)	0 28	0 28	0 56	—	0 28	4 cents.	0 08	0 10	0 20	0 30	0 40	0 10
Guatemala (*n r*)	0 28	0 28	0 56	—	0 28	4 cents.	0 08	0 10	0 20	0 30	0 40	0 10
Hamburg	0 10	0 10	0 20	—	0 10	Book rate.	0 08	0 16	0 32	0 48	0 64	0 16
Hanover	0 10	0 10	0 20		0 10	do	0 08	0 16	0 32	0 48	0 64	0 16
Hayti (*n r*)	0 28	0 28	0 56	—	0 28	4 cents.	0 08	0 10	0 20	0 30	0 40	0 10
Hesse	0 10	0 10	0 20	—	0 10	Book rate.	0 08	0 16	0 32	0 48	0 64	0 16
Hesse Homburg	0 10	0 10	0 20	—	0 10	do	0 08	0 16	0 32	0 48	0 64	0 16
Holland	0 10	0 10	0 20	—	0 10	do	0 06	0 12	0 24	0 36	0 48	0 12
Hong Kong	0 28	0 28	0 56	—	0 28	6 cents.	0 10	0 12	0 24	0 36	0 48	0 10
India	0 22	0 22	0 44	—	0 22	6 cents.	0 10	0 12	0 24	0 36	0 48	0 12
Ionian Islands	0 20	0 28	0 40	—	0 20	Book rate.	0 08	0 16	0 32	0 48	0 64	0 16

BRITISH AND FOREIGN POSTAGE TABLE.—*Continued.*

COUNTRIES, &c.	For a Letter. Not exceeding ¼ oz.	Above ¼ oz. and not exceeding ½ oz.	Above ½ oz. and not exceeding ¾ oz.	For every additional ¼ oz.	For every additional ½ oz	For each Newspaper.	For Book Packets and Patterns. Not exceeding 2 ozs.	2 ozs. to 4 ozs.	4 ozs. to 8 ozs.	8 ozs. to 12 ozs.	12 ozs. to 1 lb.	For every additional 4 ozs.
	$ cts.	$ cts.	$ cts.	$ cts.	$ cts.		$ cts.	$ cts.	$ cts.	$ cts.	$ cts.	$ cts.
and	0 06	0 06	0 12	—	0 06	2 cents.	0 04	0 06	0 12	0 18	0 24	0 06
y	0 14	0 14	0 28	—	0 14	Book rate.	0 08	0 16	0 32	0 48	0 64	0 16
buan	0 28	0 28	0 56	—	0 28	6 cents.	0 10	0 12	0 24	0 36	0 48	0 12
naca	0 16	0 16	0 32	—	0 16	Book rate.	0 08	0 16	0 32	0 48	0 64	0 16
menburg	0 10	0 10	0 20	—	0 10	do	0 08	0 16	0 32	0 48	0 64	0 16
eria	0 16	0 16	0 32	—	0 16	4 cents.	0 08	0 10	0 20	0 30	0 40	0 10
pe Detmold	0 10	0 10	0 20	—	0 10	Book rate.	0 08	0 16	0 32	0 48	0 64	0 16
ec	0 10	0 10	0 20	—	0 10	do	0 08	0 16	0 32	0 48	0 64	0 16
eira	0 16	0 16	0 32	-	0 16	do	0 06	0 12	0 24	0 36	0 48	see mem 4
a	0 16	0 16	0 32	—	0 16	4 cents.	0 08	0 10	0 20	0 30	0 40	0 10
ritius	0 24	0 24	0 48	—	0 24	8 cents.	0 14	0 16	0 32	0 48	0 64	0 16
klenburg	0 10	0 10	0 20	—	0 10	Book rate.	0 08	0 16	0 32	0 48	0 64	0 16
ico (*n r*)	0 28	0 28	0 56	—	0 28	4 cents.	0 08	0 10	0 20	0 30	0 40	0 10
lavia	0 14	0 14	0 28	—	0 14	Book rate.	0 08	0 16	0 32	0 48	0 64	0 16
te Video (*n r*)	0 28	0 28	0 56	—	0 28	4 cents.	0 08	0 10	0 20	0 30	0 40	0 10
elene (*n r*)	0 16	0 28	0 44	0 12	0 04	Book rate.	0 06	0 12	0 24	0 36	0 48	0 12
au, Duchy of	0 10	0 10	0 20		0 10	do	0 08	0 16	0 32	0 48	0 64	0 16
l	0 28	0 28	0 56	—	0 28	4 cents.	0 08	0 10	0 20	0 30	0 40	0 10
Granada (*n r*)	0 28	0 28	0 56	—	0 28	4 cents.	0 08	0 10	0 20	0 30	0 40	0 10
w South Wales	0 16	0 16	0 32	—	0 16	6 cents.	0 10	0 12	0 24	0 36	0 48	0 12
w Zealand	0 16	0 16	0 32	—	0 16	6 cents.	0 10	0 12	0 24	0 36	0 48	0 12
vay	0 14	0 14	0 28	—	0 14	Book rate.	0 08	0 16	0 32	0 48	0 64	0 16
nburg	0 10	0 10	0 20	—	0 10	do	0 08	0 16	0 32	0 48	0 64	0 16
hang	0 28	0 28	0 56	—	0 28	6 cents.	0 10	0 12	0 24	0 36	0 48	0 12
(*n r*)	0 40	0 40	0 80	—	0 40	6 cents.	0 10	0 12	0 24	0 36	0 48	0 12
nd	0 16	0 16	0 32	—	0 16	Book rate.	0 08	0 16	0 32	*See mem 4*		
o Rico (*n r*)	0 28	0 28	0 56	—	0 28	4 cents.	0 08	0 10	0 20	0 30	0 40	0 10
ugal	0 16	0 28	0 44	0 12	0 04	Book rate.	0 06	0 12	0 24	0 36	0 48	see mem 4
sia	0 10	0 10	0 20	—	0 10	do	0 08	0 16	0 32	0 48	0 64	0 16
eensland	0 16	0 16	0 32	—	0 16	6 cents.	0 10	0 12	0 24	0 36	0 48	0 12
nion	0 24	0 24	0 48	—	0 24	8 cents.	0 14	0 16	0 32	0 48	0 64	0 16
ss	0 10	0 10	0 20	—	0 10	Book rate.	0 08	0 16	0 32	0 48	0 64	0 16
odes	0 16	0 28	0 44	0 12	0 04	do	0 06	0 12	0 24	0 36	0 48	0 12
sia	0 14	0 14	0 28	—	0 14	do	0 08	0 16	0 32	*See mem 4*		
Helena	0 28	0 28	0 56	—	0 28	4 cents.	0 08	0 10	0 20	0 30	0 40	0 10

nica	0 16	0 28	0 44	0 12	0 04	Book rate.	0 06	0 12	0 24	0 36	0 48	0 12
soun	0 16	0 28	0 44	0 12	0 04	do	0 06	0 12	0 24	0 36	0 48	0 12
Altenburg												
Coburg Gotha												
Meiningen												
Weimar	0 10	0 10	0 20	—	0 10	Book rate.	0 08	0 16	0 32	0 48	0 64	0 16
ıy												
ımburg Lippe												
ırtzburg Rudolstadt												
ırtzburg Sonderhausen												
ınd	0 06	0 06	0 12	—	0 06	2 cents.	0 04	0 06	0 12	0 18	0 24	0 06
ri	0 16	0 16	0 32	—	0 16	Book rate.	0 08	0 16	0 32	0 48	0 64	0 16
	0 16	0 16	0 32	—	0 16	do	0 08	0 16	0 32	0 48	0 64	0 16
, Leone	0 16	0 16	0 32	—	0 16	4 cents.	0 08	0 10	0 20	0 30	0 40	0 10
apore	0 28	0 28	0 56	—	0 28	6 cents.	0 10	0 12	0 24	0 36	0 48	0 12
rna	0 16	0 28	0 44	0 12	0 04	Book rate.	0 06	0 12	0 24	0 36	0 48	0 12
	0 20	0 20	0 40	—	0 20	do	0 08	0 16	0 32	0 48	0 64	0 16
via Brindisi	0 20	0 20	0 40	—	0 20	6 cents.	0 14	0 16	0 30	0 46	0 60	0 16
via Southampton	0 16	0 16	0 32	—	0 16	4 cents.	0 08	0 10	0 20	0 30	0 40	0 10
am	0 28	0 28	0 56	—	0 28	4 cents.	0 08	0 10	0 20	0 30	0 40	0 10
en	0 14	0 14	0 28	—	0 14	Book rate.	0 08	0 16	0 32	0 48	0 64	0 16
erland, *via* Belgium	0 10	0 10	0 20	—	0 10	do	0 08	0 16	0 32	0 48	0 64	0 16
zerland, *via* France	0 14	0 24	0 38	0 10	0 04	do	0 06	0 12	0 24	0 36	0 48	0 12
(*n r*)	0 16	0 28	0 44	0 12	0 04	do	0 06	0 12	0 24	0 36	0 48	0 12
ıania	0 16	0 16	0 32	—	0 16	6 cents.	0 10	0 12	0 24	0 36	0 48	0 12
me	0 16	0 16	0 32	—	0 16	Book rate.	0 08	0 16	0 32	0 48	0 64	0 16
dos						do	0 08	0 16	0 32	0 48	0 64	0 16
bizond	0 16	0 28	0 44	0 12	0 04	do	0 06	0 12	0 24	0 36	0 48	0 12
tcha	0 16	0 28	0 44	0 12	0 04	do	0 06	0 12	0 24	0 36	0 48	0 12
ıis	0 16	0 28	0 44	0 12	0 04	do	0 06	0 12	0 24	0 36	0 48	0 12
ına	0 16	0 28	0 44	0 12	0 04	do	0 06	0 12	0 24	0 36	0 48	0 12
zuela (*n r*)	0 28	0 28	0 56	—	0 28	4 cents.	0 08	0 10	0 20	0 30	0 40	0 10
toria	0 16	0 16	0 32	—	0 16	6 cents.	0 10	0 12	0 24	0 36	0 48	0 12
achia	0 14	0 14	0 28	—	0 14	Book rate.	0 08	0 16	0 32	0 48	0 64	0 16
Indies, British	0 28	0 28	0 56	—	0 28	4 cents.	0 08	0 10	0 20	0 30	0 40	0 10
Indies, Foreign (*n r*) except places specified	0 28	0 28	0 56	—	0 28	4 cents.	0 08	0 10	0 20	0 30	0 40	0 10
temburg	0 10	0 10	0 20	—	0 10	Book rate.	0 08	0 16	0 32	0 48	0 64	0 16

A.

REGISTERED LETTERS.

TABLE shewing the Postage, including Registration Fee, to be collected on Registered Letters sent from Canada to the undermentioned Countries.

COUNTRIES.	Not exceeding ¼ oz.	Over ¼ and not exceeding ½ oz.	Over ½ and not exceeding ¾ oz.	Over ¾ and not exceeding 1 oz.	Over 1 and not exceeding 1¼ oz.	Over 1¼ and not exceeding 1½ oz.
	$ cts.	$ cts.	$ cts.	$ cts.	$ cts.	$ cts.
Belgium	0 26	0 26	0 36	0 36	0 46	0 46
France	0 2	0 40	0 60	0 72	0 92	1 04
Hamburg	0 26	0 26	0 36	0 36	0 46	0 46
India	0 38	0 38	0 60	0 60	0 82	0 82
Italy	0 30	0 30	0 44	0 44	0 58	0 58
Norway	0 32	0 32	0 48	0 48	0 64	0 64
Prussia	0 26	0 26	0 36	0 36	0 46	0 46

TABLE No. 3.

RATES OF POSTAGE.

From Canada to the United Kingdom, British Colonies, and Foreign Countries by Cunard or other Steamers, sailing from New York or Boston, for England.

On Letters.—If addressed to the United Kingdom, 8 cents per ½ oz. If addressed to British Colonies, or Foreign Countries, add to the rates, in Table No. 1, 2 cents per ½ oz.

Newspapers.—Addressed to the United Kingdom must be prepaid at the ordinary commuted rate, or *two cents* each paper, if *transient.* Newspapers addressed to British Colonies and Foreign Countries are not forwarded by the above Steamers.

On Book Packets and Packets of Patterns and Samples addressed to the United Kingdom, 8 cents per 4 ounces (see Table of Rates, page 263), which must be prepaid. Book Packets, and Packets of Patterns and Samples addressed to British Colonies and Foreign Countries are not forwarded by the above Steamers.

The Registration Fees are the same as by Canadian Steamers in Table No. 2.

Letters, &c., intended for despatch by the Packets sailing from New York or Boston should be specially so addressed.

TABLE No. 4.

RATES of Postage to Bermuda and West Indies, by British Mail Packet, sailing from Halifax to Bermuda and St. Thomas, monthly.

COUNTRY.	Letters.	For each Newspaper.	On Printed matter.
Bermuda	6 cents per ½ oz.	2 cents	6 cents per 4 oz. weight
West Indies, British and Foreign	12 cents "	"	" "
British Guiana	12 cents "	"	" "

TABLE No. 5.

SHEWING the Rates of Postage to be collected in Canada on Letters, Newspapers, Pamphlets, Magazines, Printed Matter and Books sent by way of the United States to the undermentioned Colonies and Foreign Countries.

COUNTRIES, &c.	Letters per ½ oz.	News-papers, each.	Other Printed Matter.	Registra-tion Fees.
	cts.	cts.	cts.	cts.
Argentine Republic (Buenos Ayres)	21	6	12 per 4 oz.	....
Aspinwall (Colon)—Registered Letters	21	....	....	10
do Unregistered Letters	13	4	3 per 2 oz.	....
Australia (ex New South Wales and New Zealand)	10	4	3 per 2 oz.	....
Bahamas	3	4	3 per 2 oz.	....
(B) Belize, British Honduras	21	6	12 per 4 oz.	10
Bermuda	10	4	3 per 2 oz.	....
Bolivia	25	6	12 per 4 oz.	10
*Brazil	18	3	2 per 2 oz.	12
Chili	25	6	12 per 4 oz.	10
(A) China (ex Hong Kong and dependent ports)	10	4	3 per 2 oz.	10
Costa Rica	13	4	3 per 2 oz.	....
Cuba	10	4	3 per 2 oz.	....
(B) East Indies (British and Straits Settlements)	13	4	10 per 4 oz.	....
Ecuador	23	4	6 per 4 oz.	....
Fiji Islands	10	4	3 per 2 oz.	....
(B) Guatemala	13	4	3 per 2 oz.	....
(C) Hawaiian Kingdom, Sandwich Islands	9	2	6 per 4 oz.	....
Honduras (not British)	13	4	3 per 2 oz,	....
B Hong Kong and dependent ports	13	4	....	....
Jamaica	10	4	3 per 2 oz.	10
A) Japan	10	4	3 per 2 oz.	10
*Mexico	13	4	2 per 2 oz.	....
New South Wales	15	4	6 per 4 oz.	12
New Zealand	15	4	6 per 4 oz.	12
Nicaragua	13	4	3 per 2 oz.	....
Panama	13	4	3 per 2 oz.	10
Peru	25	6	12 per 4 oz.	10
(B) San Salvador	13	4	3 per 2 oz.	....
St. Domingo	10	4	3 per 2 oz.	....
U. S. of Columbia, ex Panama and Aspinwall (Colon)	21	6	12 per 4 oz.	10
(B) Venezuela	13	4	3 per 2 oz.	10
West Indies (Danish)	13	4	3 per 2 oz.	....
(B) do not otherwise specified, including British Guiana	21	6	12 per 4 oz.	10

(A) Letters can be registered to Shanghae, in China, and to Yokohama, in Japan, by San Francisco, but to no other place in either country.

(B) Printed Prices Current and Mercantile Circulars can, where this letter is prefixed, be forwarded as Newspapers.

(C) The postage to be collected on Newspapers for the Sandwich Islands is two cents for each paper, and an additional charge of one cent for each two ounces weight or fraction thereof, thus, on a single paper weighing three ounces, collect four cents.

* Where an asterisk is prefixed, an additional charge of one cent per two ounces weight on Newspapers, and one cent per ounce on printed matter, must be collected.

Registration can be effected on correspondence for those places only to which the fee is given.

TABLE

RATES of Postage on all matter transmissible by Post—not of the character and the

NOTE.—The Postage upon all matter included in

DESCRIPTION OF MATTER.	Between any place in Canada and to Newfoundland.	To Great Britain, Mail Steam Packets sailing from Quebec or Portland and Halifax.
Books	1 cent per 2 oz.	Canadian Pkt. Book Post...(*a*)
Cartes de visite	do	do do
Circulars—Printed	1 cent each when sent singly, or one cent per 2 oz.	do do
Handbills	1 cent per 2 oz.	do do
Lithographed Letters and Circulars	1 cent each when sent singly, or 1 cent per 2 oz.	do do
Newspapers, Canadian	Once a week, 5 cts. per quarter* Twice " 10 " Thrice " 15 " Daily " 30 "	At commuted rate, if prepaid from office of publication, or at 2 cents each.
Newspapers, transient	2 cents each	2 cents each
Pamphlets and occasional Publications	1 cent per 2 oz.	Canadian Pkt. Book Post ...(*a*)
"*Parcel Post*" *Packages*	Parcels cannot be sent by Post beyond the Dominion of Canada. For rates, see margin(*d*)	
Patterns of Merchandize for sale	1 cent per 2 oz.	Canadian Pkt. Book Post ...(*a*)
Periodicals	1 cent per 4 ozs., whether package contains one or more Nos. Weighing less than 1 oz. ½ cent each if sent separately	2 cents each No. if published in Canada; Canadian Pkt. Book Post, if foreign
†*Photographs in Cases*	Parcel post	Canadian Pkt. Book Post... (*a*)
" on card, *see Cartes de Visite*		
" Albums	do	do do
Prices Current	1 cent per 2 oz.	2 cents each, or in bulk at Canadian Packet Book Post...(*a*)
Book and Newspaper Manuscript, Printers' Proof, Maps, &c.	do	Canadian Pkt. Book Post ...(*a*)
Printed Matter—of the same character as Circulars, Handbills, &c.	do	do do
Samples of Merchandize—See Patterns.		
School Returns—Half-yearly	do	do do
School Returns—by School Trustees to Superintendent, even although filled up in writing	1 cent each or 1 cent per 2 oz...	do do
Seeds, &c.,—samples of (including Cuttings, Bulbs, Roots, Scions, or Grafts)	1 cent per 2 oz.	do do
Parliamentary Papers *Petitions* and Addresses to Provincial Legislatures, Votes and Proceedings, and other papers, printed by order of said Legislatures	See P. O. Act and regulations for conditions of transmission.	do do

No. 6.

of a Letter — within Canada, to Newfoundland, Great Britain, France, United States,

this table should be prepaid by Postage Stamps.

To Great Britain by Cunard and other Steamers sailing from New York or Boston.	To France by Mail Steam Packets sailing from Quebec, &c.	To United States.
CunardPktBookPost(b)	French Book Post(c)	1 ct. per 2 oz., subject on delivery to U.S. postage
do do	do	do
do do	do	do
do do	do	do
do do	do	do
As by Canadian Str.....	do	At commuted rate, if prepaid from office of publication, or at 2 cents each.
2 cents each	do	At 2cts. each.
CunardPktBookPost(b)	do	1 ct. per 2 oz., subject on delivery to U. S. postage.
....	....	....
CunardPktBookPost(b)	French Book Post (c)	Cannot be sent... ....
do do	do	1 ct. per 2 oz., subject on delivery to U. S. postage.
do do	do	do ....
do do	do	do
4 cents each	do	do
CunardPktBookPost(b)	do	do
do do	do	do
do do	do	do
do do	do	do
do do	do	do
do do	do	do

(*a*)—CANADIAN PACKET BOOK POST.

Not exceeding 1 oz.	2 cents.
1 to 2 oz.	4 "
2 to 4 oz.	6 "
4 to 8 oz.	12 "
8 to 12 oz.	18 "
12 ozs. to 1 lb.	24 "

and so on.

(*b*)—CUNARD PACKET BOOK POST.

Not exceeding 1 oz.	4 cents.
1 to 2 oz.	6 "
2 to 4 oz.	8 "
4 to 8 oz.	16 "
8 to 12 oz.	24 "
12 oz. to 1 lb.	32 "

and so on.

(*c*)—FRENCH BOOK POST.

Not exceeding 2 oz.	4 cents.
2 to 4 oz.	8 "
4 to 8 oz.	16 "
8 to 12 oz.	24 "
12 oz. to 1 lb.	32 "

and so on.

A Book Packet may contain any number of separate books, publications, works of literature and art, maps or prints, photographs, daguereotypes, when not on glass, or in frames containing glass; any quantity of paper, vellum, or parchment (to the exclusion of letters); and the books, maps, papers, &c., may be either written, printed, or plain, or any mixture of the three; and may be either British, colonial or foreign.

Book Packages must be open at *both ends or both sides.*

(*d*)—PARCEL POST.

Not exceeding ½ lb.	12½ cents.
½ lb. to 1 lb.	25 "
1 lb. to 1½ lb.	37½ "
1½ lbs. to 2 lbs	50 "
2 lbs. to 2½ lbs.	62½ "
2½ lbs. to 3 lbs.	75 "
3 lbs. to 3½ lbs.	87½ "
3½ lbs. to 4 lbs...	$1.00.

Registration Fee 5 cents.

Parcels can only be sent by Post to places in Canada, and may contain books, daguereotypes, photographs, printers' proof and copy, military returns, states and rolls containing written figures and signatures, returns, deeds, legal papers, and all transmissions of a like character, not being strictly letters ....

REGISTRATION.

No letter, book, newspaper, parcel or packet of any kind whatever, can in future be received for registration unless both postage and registration fee are fully prepaid; prepayment should, if possible, be by postage

www.ingramcontent.com/pod-product-compliance
Lightning Source LLC
Chambersburg PA
CBHW051156300426
44116CB00006B/332
9783742862518